Communications in Computer and Information Science 682

Commenced Publication in 2007
Founding and Former Series Editors:
Alfredo Cuzzocrea, Dominik Ślęzak, and Xiaokang Yang

Editorial Board

More information about this series at http://www.springer.com/series/7899

Maoguo Gong · Linqiang Pan
Tao Song · Gexiang Zhang (Eds.)

Bio-inspired Computing – Theories and Applications

11th International Conference, BIC-TA 2016
Xi'an, China, October 28–30, 2016
Revised Selected Papers, Part II

 Springer

Editors

Maoguo Gong
Xidian University
Xi'an
China

Linqiang Pan
Huazhong University of Science
 and Technology
Wuhan
China

Tao Song
China University of Petroleum
Qingdao
China

and

Faculty of Engineering, Computing
 and Science
Swinburne University of Technology
 Sarawak Campus
Kuching
Malaysia

Gexiang Zhang
Southwest Jiaotong University
Chengdu
China

ISSN 1865-0929   ISSN 1865-0937 (electronic)
Communications in Computer and Information Science
ISBN 978-981-10-3613-2   ISBN 978-981-10-3614-9 (eBook)
DOI 10.1007/978-981-10-3614-9

Library of Congress Control Number: 2016962020

Printed on acid-free paper

This Springer imprint is published by Springer Nature
The registered company is Springer Nature Singapore Pte Ltd.
The registered company address is: 152 Beach Road, #21-01/04 Gateway East, Singapore 189721, Singapore

Preface

Bio-inspired computing is a field of study that abstracts computing ideas (data structures, operations with data, ways to control operations, computing models, etc.) from living phenomena or biological systems such as evolution, cells, tissues, neural networks, immune system, and ant colonies. Bio-Inspired Computing: Theories and Applications (BIC-TA) is a series of conferences that aims to bring together researchers working in the main areas of natural computing inspired from biology, for presenting their recent results, exchanging ideas, and cooperating in a friendly framework. The conference has four main topics: evolutionary computing, neural computing, DNA computing, and membrane computing.

Since 2006, the conference has taken place at Wuhan (2006), Zhengzhou (2007), Adelaide (2008), Beijing (2009), Liverpool and Changsha (2010), Penang (2011), Gwalior (2012), Anhui (2013), Wuhan (2014), and Anhui (2015). Following the success of previous editions, the 11th International Conference on Bio-Inspired Computing: Theories and Applications (BIC-TA 2016) was organized by Xidian University, during October 28–30, 2016.

BIC-TA 2016 attracted a wide spectrum of interesting research papers on various aspects of bio-inspired computing with a diverse range of theories and applications. We received 343 submissions, of which 115 papers were selected for two volumes of *Communications in Computer and Information Science*.

We gratefully thank Xidian University, Huazhong University of Science and Technology, and Northwestern Polytechnical University for extensive assistance in organizing the conference. We also thank Dr. Jiao Shi and all other volunteers, whose efforts ensured the smooth running of the conference.

The editors warmly thank the Program Committee members for their prompt and efficient support in reviewing the papers, and the authors of the submitted papers for their interesting papers.

Special thanks are due to Springer for their skilled cooperation in the timely production of these volumes.

October 2016

Maoguo Gong
Linqiang Pan
Tao Song
Gexiang Zhang

Organization

Steering Committee

Guangzhao Cui	Zhengzhou University of Light Industry, China
Kalyanmoy Deb	Indian Institute of Technology Kanpur, India
Miki Hirabayashi	National Institute of Information and Communications Technology (NICT), Japan
Joshua Knowles	University of Manchester, UK
Thom LaBean	North Carolina State University, USA
Jiuyong Li	University of South Australia, Australia
Kenli Li	University of Hunan, China
Giancarlo Mauri	Università di Milano-Bicocca, Italy
Yongli Mi	Hong Kong University of Science and Technology, Hong Kong, SAR China
Atulya K. Nagar	Liverpool Hope University, UK
Linqiang Pan	Huazhong University of Science and Technology, China
Gheorghe Păun	Romanian Academy, Bucharest, Romania
Mario J. Pérez-Jiménez	University of Seville, Spain
K.G. Subramanian	Universiti Sains Malaysia, Malaysia
Robinson Thamburaj	Madras Christian College, India
Jin Xu	Peking University, China
Hao Yan	Arizona State University, USA

Program Committee

Rosni Abdullah, Malaysia
Muhammad Abulaish, Saudi Arabia
Chang Wook Ahn, South Korea
Adel Al-Jumaily, Australia
Bahareh Asadi, Iran
Li He, USA
Eduard Babulak, European Commission, Community Research and Development Information
Mehdi Bahrami, Iran
Soumya Banerjee, India
Jagdish Chand Bansal, India
Debnath Bhattacharyya, India
Monowar H. Bhuyan, India
Kavita Burse, India

Michael Chen, China
Tsung-Che Chiang, Taiwan, China
Sung-Bae Cho, South Korea
Kadian Davis, Jamaica
Sumithra Devi K.A., India
Ciprian Dobre, Romania
Amit Dutta, India
Carlos Fernandez-Llatas, Spain
Pierluigi Frisco, UK
Maoguo Gong, China (Chair)
Shan He, UK
Jer Lang Hong, Malaysia
Tzung-Pei Hong, Taiwan, China
Wei-Chiang Hong, Taiwan, China
Mo Hongwei, China

Sriman Narayana Iyengar, India
Antonio J. Jara, Spain
Sunil Kumar Jha, India
Guoli Ji, China
Mohamed Rawidean Mohd Kassim,
   Malaysia
M. Ayoub Khan, India
Razib Hayat Khan, Norway
Joanna Kolodziej, Poland
Ashwani Kush, India
Shyam Lal, India
Kenli Li, China
Chun-Wei Lin, China
Wenjian Luo, China
Mario J. Pérez-Jiménez, Spain
Vittorio Maniezzo, Italy
Francesco Marcelloni, Italy
Hasimah Mohamed, Malaysia
Chilukuri K. Mohan, USA
Abdulqader Mohsen, Malaysia
Holger Morgenstern, Germany
Andres Muñoz, Spain
G.R.S. Murthy, India
Akila Muthuramalingam, India
Atulya Nagar, UK
Asoke Nath, India
Linqiang Pan, China (Chair)
Mrutyunjaya Panda, India
Manjaree Pandit, India
Gheorghe Păun, Romania
Andrei Păun, USA
Yoseba Penya, Spain
Ninan Sajeeth Philip, India
Hugo Proença, Portugal

Balwinder Raj, India
Balasubramanian Raman, India
Nur' Aini Abdul Rashid, Malaysia
Mehul Raval, India
Rawya Rizk, Egypt
Thamburaj Robinson, India
Samrat Sabat, India
S.M. Sameer, India
Rajesh Sanghvi, India
Aradhana Saxena, India
Sonia Schulenburg, UK
G. Shivaprasad, India
K.K. Shukla, India
Madhusudan Singh, South Korea
Pramod Kumar Singh, India
Ravindra Singh, India
Sanjeev Singh, India
Satvir Singh, India
Don Sofge, USA
Tao Song, China
Kumbakonam Govindarajan
   Subramanian, Malaysia
Ponnuthurai Suganthan, Singapore
S.R. Thangiah, USA
Nikolaos Thomaidis, India
D.G. Thomas, India
Ravi Sankar Vadali, India
Ibrahim Venkat, Malaysia
Sudhir Warier, India
Ram Yadav, USA
Umi Kalsom Yusof, Malaysia
Sotirios Ziavras, USA
Pan Zheng, Malaysia

Sponsors

Xidian University
Huazhong University of Science and Technology
Northwestern Polytechnical University

Contents – Part II

Evolutionary Computing

Multi-objective Optimization

Pattern Recognition

Others

Contents – Part I

Neural Computing

Machine Learning

Evolutionary Computing

Kernel Evolutionary Algorithm for Clustering

Xiangming Jiang, Jingjing Ma, and Chao Lei[(✉)]

Key Laboratory of Intelligent Perception and Image Understanding
of Ministry of Education, Xidian University, Xi'an 710071, China
chiangshm@gmail.com

Abstract. In this paper, we propose a novel clustering algorithm named KECA based on kernel function and evolutionary optimization. As we know, Euclidean distance based similarity metrics can help clustering algorithms handle datasets with compact super-sphere distributions perfectly, but it is undesirable for the complex structural or irregular shaped datesets. Proper mapping function can map the data in original space to high-dimensional feature space, which exposes more features and sheds light on complex structural datasets. However, clustering in feature space is time-consuming and often suffers from curse of dimensionality. Fortunately, we can cluster the mapped data in feature space which performs nonlinearly in original space with the help of kernel function in our proposed KECA. What's more, evolutionary algorithm is used in KECA to avoid local optimal. Experimental results on artificial as well as UCI datasets show the effectiveness and robustness of the proposed KECA in compare with the genetic algorithm-based clustering and the K-means clustering.

Keywords: Kernel function · Evolutionary algorithm · Clustering · Similarity metric

1 Introduction

Cluster [4,13] is a kind of important tool for data analysis, which has been widely used in computer vision, data mining and pattern recognition. The goal of clustering analysis [9] is to find the best category under some evaluating criteria using only the metrics of similarities among samples without training. The Euclidean distance based similarity metrics are widely used in typical clustering algorithms and the gradient descent methods are usually used to optimize it's objective function. However, the Euclidean distance based similarity metric is undesirable for datasets with complex manifold and the gradient descent methods often get trapped in local minimum when confront nonlinear and multimodal evaluate function.

Kernel clustering is proposed as a new kind of clustering method in the field of clustering analysis [2,3]. These methods [6,8,10] first map the data from original space to high-dimensional feature space using nonlinear mapping. Then the differences (dissimilarity) among data are enlarged to a certain degree, which

© Springer Nature Singapore Pte Ltd. 2016
M. Gong et al. (Eds.): BIC-TA 2016, Part II, CCIS 682, pp. 3–9, 2016.
DOI: 10.1007/978-981-10-3614-9_1

promotes a better clustering results [12]. Therefore, we attempt to use the kernel-based similarity metric to replace Euclidean distance-based similarity metric in evolutionary clustering algorithms in this paper. The resultant method is called kernel evolutionary clustering algorithm, which is written as KECA for short.

The rest of this paper are organized as follows: In the second section, we analyze the drawbacks of Euclidean distance based similarity metrics, and introduce the favourable characters of kernel function. We describe the proposed KECA in detail in the third section. The experimental results are shown in the fourth section, in which we test KECA on the artificial as well as UCI datesets in compare with GAC and KM algorithms and analyze the robustness of these algorithms. Conclusions are drawn in the final section.

2   Existing Problems and Kernel Methods

From the example illustrated in Fig. 1, we expect that the sample 1 and sample 3 belong to the same category. But the Euclidean distance between sample 1 and sample 3 is higher than that between sample 1 and sample 2. Therefore, the sample 1 and sample 2 are more likely to be clustered into the same category according to the similarity metrics based on Euclidean distance, which is inconsistent with the fact. As a conclusion, the similarity metrics based on Euclidean distance will discount the performance of clustering algorithms on the complex structural datasets. Therefore, we propose a kernel mapping method which is more suitable for clustering problems in the next subsection [13].

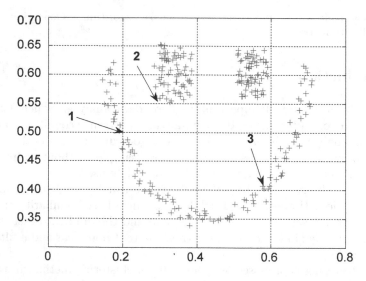

Fig. 1. Illustration of shortcomings of the pure Euclidean distance-based clustering

In kernel methods, mapping functions are designed to map the nonstructured data from original space into high-dimensional space, in which the mapped data shall be structured, separable and desirable (see Fig. 2 for illustration). Readers can refer to [11] for more details about kernel functions.

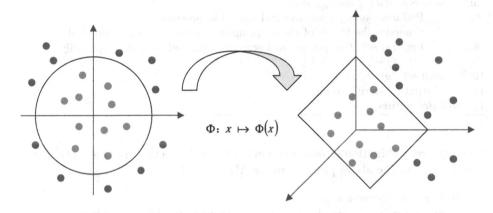

Fig. 2. Illustration of samples mapped from original space to feature space

3 Kernel Evolutionary Clustering Algorithm

3.1 Kernel Function Used in KECA

Assuming that input sample set $X = \{x_1, x_2, \cdots x_N\}, x_n \in \mathbb{R}^d$ has been mapped into feature space as $\tilde{X} = (\Phi(x_1), \Phi(x_2), \cdots \Phi(x_N))$. In our KECA, we use

$$
\begin{aligned}
d_H(x_i, x_j) &= \sqrt{\|\Phi(x_i) - \Phi(x_j)\|^2} \\
&= \sqrt{\Phi(x_i) \cdot \Phi(x_i) - 2\Phi(x_i) \cdot \Phi(x_j) + \Phi(x_j) \cdot \Phi(x_j)}
\end{aligned}
\tag{1}
$$

as a similarity metric for clustering. By denoting $K(x_i, x_i) = \Phi(x_i) \cdot \Phi(x_i)$, the expression (1) becomes

$$
d_H(x_i, x_j) = \sqrt{K(x_i, x_i) - 2K(x_i, x_j) + K(x_j, x_j)}
\tag{2}
$$

In this paper, we simply use expression (2) with the Gaussian kernel function to measure the clustering similarity. Finally, the KECA algorithm is given in 1.

3.2 Evolutionary Strategies of KECA

Evolutionary algorithm (EA) is a generic population-based metaheuristic algorithm which imitates the evolution of the species. The concept "evolution" is implemented with a series of biological mechanisms, namely, reproduction

---

Algorithm 1. The kernel evolutionary clustering algorithm (KECA)

1: **procedure** KECA(k)   ▷ $2 \leq k \leq N$, N is the size of sample set
2:    Initialize the clustering centers, and set $gen(it) \leftarrow 0$
3:    Compute the distances of every sample to the centers of categories using (2)
4:    Compute the fitness of the initial population
5:    **while** $gen(it) < max_{gen}$ **do**
6:        Perform cloning, crossover and mutation processes
7:        Compute the fitness of the offspring in temporary population pool
8:        Perform selection process and store selected individuals temporarily
9:        $gen(it) \leftarrow gen(it) + 1$
10:   **end while**
11:   Output clustering results
12: **end procedure**

(cloning), recombination (crossover), mutation, and selection. In this section, we mainly explain the above procedures for Algorithm 1.

(1) Individual representation

Every individual is encoded by a real integer array, which records the indexes of K categories. For a clustering problem of K categories, the length of a chromosome (an array) is K, the first gene (the first element of array) records the index of first category, the second one records the index of second category, and so on [7].

(2) Fitness function

The point $x_i, (i = 1, 2, \cdots, n)$ in data set can be classified into the jth category $C_j \in C$, $j \in \{1, 2, \cdots, K\}$ if

$$j = \arg \min_{j=1,2,\cdots,K} (D(x_i, u_j)) \qquad (3)$$

where u_j represents the clustering center of C_j, the expression 3 can be regarded as a classifier. After the classification, the fitness of individual C is computed as

$$Dev(C) = \sum_{C_k \in C} \sum_{i \in C_k} D(i, \mu_k) \qquad (4)$$

where C represents the code (genotype) of an individual, μ_k is the clustering center of category C_k, $D(i, \mu_k), (i \in C_k)$ represents the shortest distance from the ith data of category C_k to its center μ_k.

(3) Recombination and Mutation

Because the code for an individual is real-valued and discrete in our proposed encoding method, we use uniform crossover operator and single-point mutation in our proposed algorithm. With a randomly generated mask code array whose elements are either 0 or 1, the elements of an offspring are selected from either the parent A or B accordingly.

4   Experimental Study

In this part, we apply KECA to cluster some representative data sets including some artificial data sets and UCI data sets[1] [1], and compare its performance with Genetic algorithm-based clustering technique (GAC) and K-means clustering algorithm (KM).

In order to quantize the performance of the KECA and two comparison methods, we intuitively construct a metrics for clustering accuracy which is the ratio of the number of correct clustered data and the size of data sets. Clustering accuracy is a positive number in $[0, 1]$, and the bigger the value of clustering accuracy of an algorithm is, the better performance it has. We also adopt the robustness analysis method used in [5] to compare the robustness of the three algorithms on the thirteen datasets. In order to make the comparison intuitively, we normalize the clustering accuracy of three algorithms for each data set as follows

$$a_k = \frac{R_k}{\max\limits_i R_i}, \ i = 1, 2, 3 \tag{5}$$

where R_k represents the clustering accuracy of the k-th algorithm.

The parameters settings for experiments are as follows, the stopping threshold for all these three algorithms are set as 100 iterations or 10^{-4} relative tolerance, the crossover and mutation probability for KECA and GAC are set identically as $P_c = 1$ and $P_m = 1/(k * size(Datas, 2))$ respectively, the size of population is set as 20. For each data set, we run these algorithms for 30 times, and the average results are shown in Table 1.

Table 1. Clustering accuracy and robustness of three algorithms on thirteen datsets

Date set	(Accuracy, Robustness)		
	KECA	GAC	KM
Square1	(0.9870, 0.9975)	(0.9895, 1)	(0.9820, 0.9924)
Square2	(0.9346, 1)	(0.9345, 0.9999)	(0.9270, 0.9919)
Long1	(1,1)	(0.5631, 0.5631)	(0.5140, 0.5140)
Spiral	(0.9000, 1)	(0.5956, 0.6618)	(0.5940, 0.6600)
Line-blobes	(1, 1)	(0.7366, 0.7366)	(0.7444, 0.7444)
Sticks	(1, 1)	(0.7336, 0.7336)	(0.7188, 0.7188)
Iris	(0.9000, 1)	(0.9000, 1)	(0.8867, 0.9852)
Wine	(0.8138, 1)	(0.7022, 0.8629)	(0.7022, 0.8629)
Zoo	(0.8369, 1)	(0.7921, 0.9464)	(0.7007, 0.833)
Balance	(0.6448, 1)	(0.5504, 0.8535)	(0.5072, 0.7866)
Australian	(0.6507, 1)	(0.5551, 0.8530)	(0.5522, 0.8436)
Pimaindians	(0.6741, 1)	(0.5260, 0.7802)	(0.5482, 0.8132)
German	(0.7000, 1)	(0.5930, 0.8471)	(0.5970, 0.8528)

---

[1] http://archive.ics.uci.edu/ml/.

From Table 1, we can see that KECA achieves the most accurate clustering results than the other two algorithms for twelve of thirteen datsets except for Square1. Even for the Square1 datset, the KECA achieves the comparable clustering accuracy to the other algorithms. Due to the representative characters of these datasets, we conclude that our proposed KECA is more applicable to complex structural problems than GAC and KM algorithms.

5   Concluding Remarks

In this paper, we propose an evolutionary clustering algorithm based on kernel function. In this algorithm, the data in original space are firstly mapped into a feature space where the mapped data are separable and structural. Then we can cluster the mapped data in feature space nonlinearly in the original space. What's more, the evolutionary algorithm is designed to search the optimal clustering centers in the KECA. The results of comparison tests on thirteen benchmark datasets show the effectiveness and robustness of our proposed KECA.

Acknowledgments. This work was supported by the National Natural Science Foundation of China (Grant no. 61422209), the National Program for Support of Top-notch Young Professionals of China and the Specialized Research Fund for the Doctoral Program of Higher Education (Grant no. 20130203110011).

References

1. Blake, C., Merz, C.: UCI repository of machine learning databases, Department of Information and Computer Sciences, University of California, Irvine, USA (1998)
2. Chen, H., Zhang, Y., Gutman, I.: A kernel-based clustering method for gene selection with gene expression data. J. Biomed. Inform. **62**, 12–20 (2016)
3. Ding, Y., Fu, X.: Kernel-based fuzzy c-means clustering algorithm based on genetic algorithm. Neurocomputing **188**, 233–238 (2015)
4. Dubes, R., Jain, A.K.: Clustering techniques: the user's dilemma. Pattern Recogn. **8**(4), 247–260 (1976)
5. Geng, X., Zhan, D.C., Zhou, Z.H.: Supervised nonlinear dimensionality reduction for visualization and classification. IEEE Trans. Syst. Man Cybern. Part B (Cybern.) **35**(6), 1098–1107 (2005)
6. Girolami, M.: Mercer kernel-based clustering in feature space. IEEE Trans. Neural Netw. **13**(3), 780–784 (2002)
7. Gong, M., Jiao, L., Wang, L., Bo, L.: Density-sensitive evolutionary clustering. In: Zhou, Z.-H., Li, H., Yang, Q. (eds.) PAKDD 2007. LNCS (LNAI), vol. 4426, pp. 507–514. Springer, Heidelberg (2007). doi:10.1007/978-3-540-71701-0_52
8. Kim, D.W., Lee, K.Y., Lee, D., Lee, K.H.: A kernel-based subtractive clustering method. Pattern Recogn. Lett. **26**(7), 879–891 (2005)
9. Maulik, U., Bandyopadhyay, S.: Genetic algorithm-based clustering technique. Pattern Recogn. **33**(9), 1455–1465 (2000)
10. Müller, K.R., Mika, S., Rätsch, G., Tsuda, K., Schölkopf, B.: An introduction to kernel-based learning algorithms. IEEE Trans. Neural Netw. **12**(2), 181–201 (2001)

11. Saunders, C., Stitson, M.O., Weston, J., Bottou, L., Schölkopf, B., Smola, A.J.: Support vector machine reference manual, Royal Holloway University, London, Technical report CSD-TR-98-03 (1998)
12. Wang, C.D., Lai, J.H.: Nonlinear clustering: methods and applications. In: Celebi, M.E., Aydin, K. (eds.) Unsupervised Learning Algorithms, pp. 253–302. Springer International Publishing, Heidelberg (2016)
13. Xu, R., Wunsch, D.: Survey of clustering algorithms. IEEE Trans. Neural Netw. **16**(3), 645–678 (2005)

A Multi-parent Crossover Based Genetic Algorithm for Bi-Objective Unconstrained Binary Quadratic Programming Problem

Chao Huo[1], Rongqiang Zeng[1,2(✉)], Yang Wang[3], and Mingsheng Shang[4]

[1] School of Computer Science and Engineering, University of Electronic Science and Technology of China, Chengdu 610054, Sichuan, People's Republic of China
chaohuo0811@gmail.com
[2] School of Mathematics, Southwest Jiaotong University, Chengdu 610031, Sichuan, People's Republic of China
zrq@home.swjtu.edu.cn
[3] School of Management, Northwestern Polytechnical University, Xi'an 710072, Shanxi, People's Republic of China
sparkle.wy@gmail.com
[4] Chongqing Institute of Green and Intelligent Technology, Chinese Academy of Sciences, Chongqing 400714, People's Republic of China
msshang@cigit.ac.cn

Abstract. In this paper, we present a multi-parent crossover based genetic algorithm for the bi-objective unconstrained binary quadratic programming problem, by integrating the multi-parent crossover within the framework of hypervolume-based multi-objective optimization algorithm. The proposed algorithm employs a multi-parent crossover operator to generate the offspring solutions, which are used to further improve the quality of Pareto approximation set. Experimental results on 10 benchmark instances demonstrate the efficacy of our proposed algorithm compared with the original multi-objective optimization algorithms.

Keywords: Multi-objective optimization · Hypervolume contribution · Genetic algorithm · Multi-parent crossover · Unconstrained binary quadratic programming problem

1 Introduction

The Unconstrained Binary Quadratic Programming (UBQP) problem is one of the most studied NP-hard problem with its various practical applications. The multi-objective UBQP problem can be mathematically formulated as follows [15]:

$$f_k(x) = x'Q^k x = \sum_{i=1}^{n} \sum_{j=1}^{n} q_{ij}^k x_i x_j \tag{1}$$

where $f_k(x)$ ($k \in \{1, \ldots, m\}$) is the kth objective and to be maximized, $Q^k = (q_{ij}^k)$ is an $n \times n$ matrix of constants and x is an n-vector of binary (zero-one) variables, i.e., $x_i \in \{0, 1\}$ ($i = 1, \ldots, n$).

© Springer Nature Singapore Pte Ltd. 2016
M. Gong et al. (Eds.): BIC-TA 2016, Part II, CCIS 682, pp. 10–19, 2016.
DOI: 10.1007/978-981-10-3614-9_2

The formulation of UBQP is notable for its ability to represent a wide range of important combinatorial optimization problems, including traffic management [9], financial analysis [20], molecular conformation [25], cellular radio channel allocation [26], and so on. The literature reports a large number of heuristic and metaheuristic algorithms to deal with the UBQP problem [14], which include scatter search [2], directed local search [7], simulated annealing [1,13], evolutionary algorithms [6,17,22], tabu search [10,23,24], etc.

Moreover, Liefooghe et al. [15] first extended the single UBQP problem into the multi-objective case and proposed a hybrid metaheuristic algorithm to solve the multi-objective UBQP problem. In [16], they further proposed three versions of multi-objective local search algorithms with different search strategies to solve the bi-objective UBQP problem.

In the current paper, we study a multi-parent crossover based genetic algorithm for the bi-objective UBQP problem, which integrates a multi-parent crossover within the framework of hypervolume-based multi-objective optimization algorithm. The proposed algorithm consists of two main procedures: hypervolume contribution selection procedure and genetic algorithm with multi-parent crossover. The hypervolume contribution selection procedure iteratively improves the Pareto approximation set until it can not be improved any more. Then, the multi-parent crossover is used to further improve the entire quality of the Pareto approximation set.

The remaining part of the paper is organized as follows. In the next section, we introduce the basic notations and definitions of multi-objective optimization. In Sect. 3, we briefly review the previous work related to the uniform crossover and the multi-parent crossover. Afterwards, we describe our proposed multi-objective genetic algorithm with multi-parent crossover in Sect. 4. Section 5 is dedicated to the computational results and concluding remarks are given in the last section.

2   Multi-objective Optimization

In this section, we present the basic notations and definitions of multi-objective optimization. Let X denote the search space of the optimization problem under consideration and Z the corresponding objective space. Without loss of generality, we assume that $Z = \Re^n$ and that all n objectives are to be maximized. Each $x \in X$ is assigned exactly one objective vector $z \in Z$ on the basis of a vector function $f : X \to Z$ with $z = f(x)$, and the mapping f defines the evaluation of a solution $x \in X$ [8].

Actually, we are often interested in those solutions that are Pareto optimal with respect to f. The relation $x_1 \succ x_2$ means that the solution x_1 is *preferable* to x_2. The dominance relation between two solutions x_1 and x_2 is often defined as follows [8]:

Definition 1 (Pareto Dominance). A decision vector x_1 is said to dominate another decision vector x_2 (written as $x_1 \succ x_2$), if $f_i(x_1) \geq f_i(x_2)$ for all $i \in \{1, \ldots, n\}$ and $f_j(x_1) > f_j(x_2)$ for at least one $j \in \{1, \ldots, n\}$.

Definition 2 (Pareto Optimal Solution). $x \in X$ is said to be Pareto optimal if and only if there does not exist another solution $x' \in X$ such that $x' \succ x$.

Definition 3 (Pareto Optimal Set). S is said to be a Pareto optimal set if and only if S is composed of all the Pareto optimal solutions.

Definition 4 (Non-dominated Solution). $x \in S$ ($S \subset X$) is said to be non-dominated if and only if there does not exist another solution $x' \in S$ such that $x' \succ x$.

Definition 5 (Non-dominated Set). S is said to be a non-dominated set if and only if any two solutions $x_1 \in S$ and $x_2 \in S$ such that $x_1 \nsucc x_2$ and $x_2 \nsucc x_1$.

In fact, there does not exist the total order relation among all the solutions in multi-objective optimization. Thus, the aim is to generate the Pareto optimal set, which keeps the best compromise among all the objectives.

Nevertheless, in most cases, it is impossible to generate the Pareto optimal set in a reasonable time. Therefore, we are interested in finding a non-dominated set which is as close to the Pareto optimal set as possible, and the overall goal is often to identify a good Pareto approximation set.

3 Related Work

The uniform crossover and its variants are usually integrated into the hybrid metaheuristics as an important part for further improvement, which are widely used to solve many combinatorial optimization problems, such as quadratic assignment problem [5], gate assignment problem [12], single-objective UBQP problem [14]. In this section, we briefly review the literature on solving the UBQP problem with the uniform crossover and the multi-parent crossover.

Merz and Freisleben [21] proposed a hybrid genetic algorithm, which incorporates a simple local search into the traditional genetic algorithm. A variant of uniform crossover is used to generate offspring solutions based on Hamming distance from the parents. Computational results on the UBQP problem show that the proposed algorithm is sufficient to find best known results for the problem instances with less than 200 variables, but not very effective on the problem instances with large size.

Lodi et al. [17] presented an effective evolutionary method for solving the UBQP problem. In this algorithm, a uniform crossover operator is used to produce the offspring solutions, where the variables with common values in parental solutions are temporarily fixed in the current round of local search. Computational results on the problem instances with up to 500 variables show the attractiveness and the effectiveness of the proposed method, especially on the small problem instances.

Lü et al. [18] proposed a hybrid metaheuristic approach for solving the UBQP problem, which incorporates a tabu search procedure into the framework of evolutionary algorithms. In this algorithm, a uniform crossover operator and a diversification-guided combination operator are used to generate offspring solutions in order to further enforce the search capacity of the proposed algorithm. The extensive computational studies on problem instances with up to 7000 variables reveal that their proposed algorithm is very competitive.

Wang et al. [27] integrated four multi-parent crossover operators (called MSX, Diagonal, U-Scan and OB-Scan) within the memetic algorithm framework for dealing with unconstrained binary quadratic programming problem. Their proposed algorithms apply these crossover operators to further improve the results generated by the tabu search procedure. The experimental results and the analysis on the behavior of the algorithm provide the evidences and the insights as to key role of the crossover operators.

4 Multi-parent Crossover Based Genetic Algorithm

The Multi-Parent Crossover based Genetic Algorithm (MPCGA) is proposed to solve the bi-objective UBQP problem, which consists of two main procedures: hypervolume contribution selection and genetic algorithm with the multi-parent crossover. The general architecture of the MPCGA algorithm is described in Algorithm 1.

Algorithm 1. Multi-Parent Crossover based Genetic Algorithm

    Input: N (Population size)
    Output: A: (Pareto approximation set)
    Step 1: $P \leftarrow N$ randomly generated individuals
    Step 2: $A \leftarrow \Phi$
    Step 3: Calculate a fitness value for each individual $x \in P$ with HC indicator
    Step 4:
    while Running time is not reached **do**
      repeat
        1) Hypervolume Contribution Selection: $x \in P$
      until all neighbors of $x \in P$ are explored
        2) $A \leftarrow$ Non-dominated solutions of $A \bigcup P$
        3) Genetic Algorithm: $z \in A$
    end while
    Step 5: Return A

In MPCGA, all the individuals in an initial population are randomly generated, i.e., each variable of an individual is randomly assigned a value 0 and 1 (Step 1). Then, each individual is calculated a fitness value by the Hypervolume Contribution (HC) indicator defined in [4] (Step 3) and optimized by the hypervolume contribution selection procedure. Afterwards, we employ the multi-parent crossover operator proposed in [19] to produce the offsprings, in order to further improve the quality of Pareto approximation set.

4.1   Hypervolume Contribution Selection

After the fitness assignment for each individual, we apply the Hypervolume Contribution Selection (HCS) procedure [4] presented in Algorithm 2 to the initial population, in order to generate a set of efficient individuals.

Algorithm 2. Hypervolume Contribution Selection (HCS)

Steps:
   1) $x^* \leftarrow$ one randomly chosen unexplored neighbors of x
   2) $P \leftarrow P \bigcup x^*$
   3) calculate x^* fitness: $HC(x^*, P)$
   4) update all $z \in P$ fitness values
   5) $\omega \leftarrow$ the worst individual in P
   6) $P \leftarrow P \backslash \{\omega\}$
   7) update all $z \in P$ fitness values
   8) if $\omega \neq x^*$, Progress $\leftarrow$ True

In the HCS procedure, an individual x^*, which is one of the unexplored neighbors of x in the population P, is assigned to a fitness value by the HC indicator. If x^* is dominated, the fitness values of all the individuals in P remain unchanged. If x^* is non-dominated, we need to update the fitness values of non-dominated neighbors of x^*.

Actually, the neighborhood of UBQP is usually defined by the simple one-flip move, which flips the value 0 (or 1) of the kth variable of each solution $x \in P$ to 1 (or 0) to obtain a new individual x^* as the neighbor of x [11]. Then, we calculate the objective function values of this new neighbor with the fast incremental neighborhood evaluation formula [19] below:

$$\Delta_i = (1 - 2x_i)(q_{ii} + \sum_{j \in N, j \neq i, x_j = 1} q_{ij}) \tag{2}$$

Afterwards, the individual ω with the worst fitness value is deleted from the population P. If ω is dominated, the fitness values of the other individuals remain unchanged. If ω is non-dominated, the fitness values of the non-dominated neighbors of ω need to be updated. The HCS procedure will repeat until the termination criterion is satisfied.

4.2   Genetic Algorithm

The main idea of uniform crossover is to assign values to the variables of offspring that represent assignments made in common by both parents, and to randomly assign values to remaining variables of the offspring solution [18]. Based on this idea, a multi-parent crossover operator called MSX is proposed to solve the UBQP problem [19]. In this work, we employ the MSX crossover operator to

---

Algorithm 3. Genetic Algorithm (GA)

Steps:

1) randomly select a subset of individuals E from A

2) $z \leftarrow$ MSX_Crossover_Operator(E)

3) $A \leftarrow$ HCS(z)

---

improve the Pareto approximation set A generated by the HCS procedure. The exact steps are presented in Algorithm 3.

In our algorithm, we randomly select a set E ($|E| = s$) of non-dominated individuals from the Pareto approximation set A. Let $E = \{x^{(1)}, x^{(2)}, \ldots, x^{(s)}\}$, where $x^{(i)} = \{x_1^{(i)}, x_2^{(i)}, \ldots, x_n^{(i)}\}$ and the individuals in E are ordered in terms of their fitness values, i.e., $x^{(1)}$ is the best individual in E and $x^{(s)}$ is the worst individual in E. As suggested in [19], we set s to be a random number between 4 and 8. Then, the MSX crossover operator is defined below [27]:

MSX Crossover Operator: we define a weight $w(i)$ for the individual $x^{(i)}$ and a strength value $Strength(j)$ for variables x_j as: $w(i) = 1/\sum sum(i) = 1/\sum_{j=1}^{n} x_j^{(i)}$ and $Strength(j) = \sum_{i=1}^{s} w(i)x_j^{(i)}$.

The value $Strength(j)$ gives a relative indication of the tendency of the individuals in E to favor $x_j = 1$ or $x_j = 0$. Furthermore, we take an advantage of the $sum(i)$ values over E to get a value for the number of x_j components that should be 1 in an average individual, denoted by $Avg = \sum_{i=1}^{s} sum(i)/s$ [19]. Then, the variables with the first Avg largest $Strength$ values receive assignment 1 and other variables receive assignment 0. Afterwards, a new offspring is generated and inserted into the Pareto approximation set A with the HC indicator for further improvement.

5 Experiments

In order to evaluate the efficiency of our proposed algorithm, we carry out the experiments on 10 benchmark instances of bi-objective UBQP problem, which are generated by the tools provided in [15]. The MPCGA algorithm is programmed in C++ and compiled using Dev-C++ 5.0 compiler on a PC running Windows 7 with Core 2.50 GHz CPU and 4 GB RAM.

5.1 Parameters Settings

The MPCGA algorithm requires to set a few parameters, we mainly discuss two important ones: the running time and the population size. The exact information about the instances and the parameter settings is presented in Table 1.

Table 1. Parameter settings used for bi-objective UBQP instances: instance dimension (D), population size (P) and running time (T).

	Dimension (D)	Population (P)	Time (T)
bubqp_1000_01	1000	10	100″
bubqp_1000_02	1000	10	100″
bubqp_2000_01	2000	20	200″
bubqp_2000_02	2000	20	200″
bubqp_3000_01	3000	30	300″
bubqp_3000_02	3000	30	300″
bubqp_4000_01	4000	40	400″
bubqp_4000_02	4000	40	400″
bubqp_5000_01	5000	50	500″
bubqp_5000_02	5000	50	500″

5.2 Performance Assessment Protocol

In this paper, we evaluate the efficiency of multi-objective optimization algorithms using a test procedure that has been undertaken with the performance assessment package provided by Zitzler et al.[1]. The quality assessment protocol works as follows: we first create a set of 20 runs with different initial populations for each algorithm and each benchmark instance. Afterwards, we calculate the reference set PO^* in order to determine the quality of k different sets $A_0 \ldots A_{k-1}$ of non-dominated solutions. Furthermore, we define a reference point $z = [w_1, w_2]$, where w_1 and w_2 represent the worst values for each objective function in $A_0 \cup \cdots \cup A_{k-1}$. Then, the evaluation of a set A_i of solutions can be determined by finding the hypervolume difference between A_i and PO^* [28], and this hypervolume difference has to be as close as possible to zero.

5.3 Computational Results

In this subsection, we present the computational results obtained by our proposed MPCGA algorithm, the indicator-based multi-objective local search algorithm (IBMOLS) proposed in [3] and the hypervolume-based multi-objective local search algorithm (HBMOLS) proposed in [4].

The computational results are summarized in Table 2. Each line in this table contains a value both **in bold** and **in grey box**, which is the best result obtained on the considered instance. The values both **in italic** and **in bold** mean that the corresponding algorithms are **not** statistically outperformed by the algorithm which obtains the best result (with a confidence level greater than 95%).

---

[1] http://www.tik.ee.ethz.ch/pisa/assessment.html.

Table 2. The computational results on bi-objective UBQP problem obtained by the algorithms: IBMOLS, HBMOLS and MPCGA

Instance	Algorithm		
	IBMOLS	HBMOLS	MPCGA
bubqp_1000_01	0.175422	*0.102101*	**0.100887**
bubqp_1000_02	0.125044	0.093831	**0.091997**
bubqp_2000_01	0.102348	0.100722	**0.094091**
bubqp_2000_02	0.122507	0.094502	**0.093091**
bubqp_3000_01	0.103768	0.102531	**0.066613**
bubqp_3000_02	0.105664	*0.093186*	**0.093022**
bubqp_4000_01	0.120652	*0.104065*	**0.103641**
bubqp_4000_02	0.931491	0.930591	**0.901945**
bubqp_5000_01	0.944998	0.959954	**0.287479**
bubqp_5000_02	0.115645	*0.101692*	**0.101490**

From Table 2, we can observe that all the best results are obtained by MPCGA, and the most significant result is achieved on the instance bubqp_5000_01, where the average hypervolume difference value obtained by MPCGA is much smaller than the values obtained by IBMOLS and HBMOLS.

However, the values on the instances (bubqp_1000_01, bubqp_3000_02, bubqp_4000_01 and bubqp_5000_02) obtained by HBMOLS are not statistically outperformed by MPCGA. Actually, the new offsprings generated by the MSX crossover operator evidently improve the entire quality of Pareto approximation set, which makes the MPCGA algorithm have a chance to search the high-quality individuals in the objective space. Thus, MPCGA has a better performance on all the instances.

6 Conclusion

In this paper, integrating the multi-parent crossover within the hypervolume-based multi-objective optimization algorithm to further improve the overall quality of Pareto approximation set, the MPCGA is proposed to deal with the bi-objective unconstrained binary quadratic programming problem. The computational results of MPCGA on 10 benchmark instances have shown the feasibility of the improvements and the effectiveness of MPCGA for the bi-objective UBQP problem.

Acknowledgments. The work in this paper was supported by the Fundamental Research Funds for the Central Universities (Grant No. A0920502051614-24), supported by the Research Foundation for International Young Scientists of China (Grant No. 61450110443), supported by the Scientific Research Foundation for the Returned Overseas Chinese Scholars (Grant No. 2015S03007) and supported by National Natural Science Foundation of China (Grant No. 61370150 and 71501157).

References

1. Alkhamis, T.M., Hasan, M., Ahmed, M.A.: Simulated annealing for the unconstrained binary quadratic pseudo-boolean function. Eur. J. Oper. Res. **108**, 641–652 (1998)
2. Amini, M., Alidaee, B., Kochenberger, G.: A scatter search approach to unconstrained quadratic binary programs. New Methods Optim. **108**, 317–330 (1999)
3. Basseur, M., Liefooghe, A., Le, K., Burke, E.: The efficiency of indicator-based local search for multi-objective combinatorial optimisation problems. J. Heuristics **18**(2), 263–296 (2012)
4. Basseur, M., Zeng, R.-Q., Hao, J.-K.: Hypervolume-based multi-objective local search. Neural Comput. Appl. **21**(8), 1917–1929 (2012)
5. Benlic, U., Hao, J.-K.: Memetic search for the quadratic assignment problem. Expert Syst. Appl. **42**, 584–595 (2015)
6. Borgulya, I.: An evolutionary algorithm for the binary quadratic problems. Adv. Soft Comput. **2**, 3–16 (2005)
7. Boros, E., Hammer, P.L., Tavarse, G.: Local search heuristics for quadratic unconstrained binary optimization (QUBO). J. Heuristics **13**, 99–132 (2007)
8. Coello, C.A., Lamont, G.B., Van Veldhuizen, D.A.: Evolutionary Algorithms for Solving Multi-objective Problems (Genetic and Evolutionary Computation). Springer-Verlag New York Inc., Secaucus (2007)
9. Gallo, G., Hammer, P., Simeone, B.: Quadratic knapsack problems. Math. Program. **12**, 132–149 (1980)
10. Glover, F., Kochenberger, G., Alidaee, B.: Adaptive memory tabu search for binary quadratic programs. Manag. Sci. **44**, 336–345 (1998)
11. Hoos, H., Stützle, T.: Stochastic Local Search Foundations and Applications. Morgan Kaufmann, San Francisco (2004)
12. Hu, X.-B., Paolo, E.D.: An efficient genetic algorithm with uniform crossover for the multi-objective airport gate assignment problem. Multi-Objective Memetic Algorithm **171**, 71–89 (2009)
13. Katayama, K., Narihisa, H.: Performance of simulated annealing-based heuristic for the unconstrained binary quadratic programming problem. Eur. J. Oper. Res. **134**, 103–119 (2001)
14. Kochenberger, G., Hao, J.-K., Glover, F., Lewis, M., Lü, Z., Wang, H., Wang, Y.: The unconstrained binary quadratic programming problem: a survey. J. Comb. Optim. **28**, 58–81 (2014)
15. Liefooghe, A., Verel, S., Hao, J.-K.: A hybrid metaheuristic for multiobjective unconstrained binary quadratic programming. Appl. Soft Comput. **16**, 10–19 (2014)
16. Liefooghe, A., Verel, S., Paquete, L., Hao, J.-K.: Experiments on local search for bi-objective unconstrained binary quadratic programming. In: Gaspar-Cunha, A., Henggeler Antunes, C., Coello, C.C. (eds.) EMO 2015. LNCS, vol. 9018, pp. 171–186. Springer, Heidelberg (2015). doi:10.1007/978-3-319-15934-8_12
17. Lodi, A., Allemand, K., Liebling, T.M.: An evolutionary heuristic for quadratic 0–1 programming. Eur. J. Oper. Res. **119**(3), 662–670 (1999)

18. Lü, Z., Glover, F., Hao, J.-K.: A hybrid metaheuristic approach to solving the UBQP problem. Eur. J. Oper. Res. **207**, 1254–1262 (2010)
19. Lü, Z., Hao, J.-K., Glover, F.: A study of memetic search with multi-parent combination for UBQP. In: Cowling, P., Merz, P. (eds.) EvoCOP 2010. LNCS, vol. 6022, pp. 154–165. Springer, Heidelberg (2010). doi:10.1007/978-3-642-12139-5_14
20. McBride, R.D., Yormark, J.S.: An implicit enumeration algorithm for quadratic integer programming. Manag. Sci. **26**, 282–296 (1980)
21. Merz, P., Freisleben, B.: Genetic algorithms for binary quadratic programming. In: Proceedings of The 1st Genetic and Evolutionary Computation Conference (GECCO 1999), pp. 417–424, Orlando, Florida, USA (1999)
22. Merz, P., Katayama, K.: Memetic algorithms for the unconstrained binary quadratic programming problem. BioSystems **78**, 99–118 (2004)
23. Palubeckis, G.: Multistart tabu search strategies for the unconstrained binary quadratic optimization problem. Ann. Oper. Res. **131**, 259–282 (2004)
24. Palubeckis, G.: Iterated tabu search for the unconstrained binary quadratic optimization problem. Informatica **17**(2), 279–296 (2006)
25. Rosen, J.B., Phillips, A.T.: A quadratic assignment formulation of the molecular conformation problem. J. Glob. Optim. **4**, 229–241 (1994)
26. Sutter, A., Chardaire, P.: A decomposition method for quadratic zero-zero programming. Manag. Sci. **41**(4), 704–712 (1994)
27. Wang, Y., Lü, Z., Hao, J.-K.: A study of multi-parent crossover operators in a memetic algorithm. In: Schaefer, R., Cotta, C., Kołodziej, J., Rudolph, G. (eds.) PPSN 2010. LNCS, vol. 6238, pp. 556–565. Springer, Heidelberg (2010). doi:10.1007/978-3-642-15844-5_56
28. Zitzler, E., Thiele, L.: Multiobjective evolutionary algorithms: a comparative case study and the strength pareto approach. Evol. Comput. **3**, 257–271 (1999)

Unsupervised Image Segmentation Based on Watershed and Kernel Evolutionary Clustering Algorithm

Chao Lei$^{(\boxtimes)}$, Jingjing Ma, and Xiangming Jiang

Key Laboratory of Intelligent Perception and Image Understanding of Ministry of Education, Xidian University, Xi'an 710071, China
`leichao139636@163.com`

Abstract. In this study, a novel image segmentation algorithm based on watershed and kernel evolutionary clustering algorithm (WKECA) is proposed. An improved watershed algorithm, marker driven watershed transform, is used to segment image into many small regions and the image features of every region are extracted. By using kernel functions, the image features in the original space are mapped to a high-dimensional feature space, in which we can perform clustering efficiently on the unsupervised segmentation task. The proposed algorithm can be used to cope with different types of images, such as natural image, texture image and remote sensing image. The experimental results show that WKECA is competent for segmenting most of the testing images with high quality.

Keywords: Evolutionary algorithm · Clustering · Image segmentation · Watershed algorithm · Kernel function

1 Introduction

Image segmentation [1–3] is an important step of image processing and analytical application, whose purpose is to divide an image into several regions with some kinds of uniform consistency. To extract objects or interesting regions from complex scene and locate the edges of regions as accurately as possible, many algorithms are purposed. Currently, these segmentation algorithms can be classified into two categories, including edge-based methods and region-based methods [4]. The essence of edge-based methods is to extract the edge of interesting regions of segment objects, such as Snake algorithm [5] and Level Set algorithm [6]. Snake algorithm has strict requirements for the initial contour selection, and Level Set algorithm extends 2-dimensional plane to 3-dimensional surface, whose complexity is very high. Therefore, these two methods cannot achieve ideal segmentation results on weak edge detection. The essence of region-based methods is to connect the regions with some similar characters together, and then construct the segmentation regions. About region-based methods, watershed algorithm [7] is most typical. Watershed algorithm has several advantages, such as light computational burden and high precision segmentation, so it has been widely used in

© Springer Nature Singapore Pte Ltd. 2016
M. Gong et al. (Eds.): BIC-TA 2016, Part II, CCIS 682, pp. 20–34, 2016.
DOI: 10.1007/978-981-10-3614-9_3

the field of image segmentation. However, traditional watershed algorithm has two serious disadvantages. One is particularly sensitive to noise, and the other is over-segmentation. Watershed and multi-scale method are often used to relieve over-segmentation. It is easy to make the contour fuzzy and shift when the scale is large for multi-scale method. Based on the above analysis, we propose an image segmentation method by combining watershed with kernel evolutionary clustering algorithm (WKECA). The advantages of WKECA is overcoming the noise and over-segmentation. Therefore, the segmentation results are satisfactory, which can reflect the relation of image data much better, and get good results in image segmentation.

This paper propose a method that combines watershed algorithm with clustering algorithm. An novel kernel evolutionary clustering algorithm which is different from traditional clustering algorithms is adopted to improve the performances of traditional ones. Its main idea is to apply a median filter on the image, which can filter noises and won't reduce the edge strength of image; image morphological gradient is computed after de-noising, after that the watershed transformation according to the morphological gradient is taken; then the region texture feature is made which is obtained by discrete wavelet transformation as input samples of clustering; the image characteristics in the original space are mapped to the high-dimensional feature space by using kernel mapping, where to take clustering; finally, using clustering method to merge region, our algorithm obtains the segmentation results.

The rest of the paper is organized as follows: In Sect. 2, the principle, characteristics, mathematical description and improvement of watershed algorithm are introduced. In Sect. 3, the kernel evolutionary clustering algorithm is proposed. In Sect. 4, the method of image segmentation by combining watershed and kernel evolutionary clustering algorithm is depicted in detail. Section 5 shows experiment results and analysis, in which WKECA is applied to natural images, texture images and SAR images segmentation. Finally, the concluding remarks are presented.

2   Watershed Algorithm

The common methods of image segmentation are threshold method, edge detection method, region growing method, clustering method and watershed transformation based on mathematical morphology. Watershed transformation based on mathematical morphology [8] is a classical and effective segmentation method. The watershed transformation [9–11] always gets closed, continuous and single-pixel wide contour of objects, and it has the advantages of accurate location, high precision segmentation, and easy for parallel processing. So it arouses great attention and widespread concern, and becomes a hot spot of image segmentation.

2.1 Principle and Characteristics of Watershed Algorithm

The idea of watershed transformation comes from geomorphology and it regards the image as topology landform in geomorphology. The gray value of each pixel in the image represents its altitude, and every region has its local minimum. Every local minimum and its affect region is called catchment basin, and the edges of catchment basins become watershed. There are two kinds of description of watershed transformation [12]. One is the raindrop method, namely, because of gravity, when the raindrops drop from different terrain surface, they have to drop down along the steepest path and decline to the minimum point. The set of the points together to same local minimum point becomes a connected region called catchment basin, and the edge of neighbor catchment basin is watershed. The other one is simulation water immersion method that is a kind of method applying bottom-up iterations to generate regions. A small hole is made at every local minimum point, and immerse the terrain model of image into the land vertically. Making the water immerse into every hole uniformly and slowly, then the water rises continuously. When different minimum regions of water increase to converge gradually, a dam is built to prevent water eventually converging. When the water gets to the highest point of the terrain, the overflow procession ends. Surrounded by the dams that are corresponding watershed lines, every minimum region is becoming to a catchment basin. No matter using which methods, the main goal is to find the watershed. Figure 1 is the illustration of watershed algorithm.

Watershed transformation is a kind of useful image segmentation method in mathematical morphology algorithm, which takes advantages of contrast features (gradient) and neighborhood space relation (side affective area) fully [13,14]. The reason for arousing attention of researcher is that watershed algorithm can get closed, continuous and single-pixel wide contour of objects with accurate location. But traditional watershed algorithm has two serious disadvantages that is particularly sensitive to noises and over-segmentation of image. In this paper, we propose a kind of image segmentation method combining watershed and kernel evolutionary clustering algorithm. We first use the watershed method to get the contour of region, and then use kernel evolutionary clustering algorithm

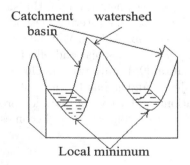

Fig. 1. Illustration of watershed algorithm.

to merge categories among regions. Our algorithm uses kernel cluster to eliminate over-segmentation, which retains the advantages of watershed algorithm and works more effective than traditional clustering algorithms [12].

2.2 Mathematical Description of Watershed Algorithm

According to the theory of watershed algorithm above, set $M_1, M_2, \cdots, M_r$ as the minimum regions of the image waiting for segmentation (gradient image). $C(M_i)$ is the related basin, min and max are the minimum and maximum of gradient respectively. Assuming that the overflow procession increases by single gray value and n is the increasing value of the overflow (the deep of the overflow at the nth step). $T[n]$ is the set subjected to $f(x) < n$ and $f(x)$ is gray value of gradient image. For a given basin, at the nth step, it is possible to appear overflow in different degrees, or maybe not. Assuming that at the nth step, minimum region M_i appears overflow, and set $C_n(M_i)$ as minimum region M_i's part of the related basin. Namely, when the deep of overflow is n, the plane in $C(M_i)$ constructs the region. Obviously, $C_n(M_i)$ is binary image, which can be expressed as:

$$C_n(M_i) = C(M_i) \cap T[n]. \qquad (1)$$

If the gray value of minimum region M_i is n, then at the $(n+1)$th step, the overflow part of basin is same as M_i totally, that is $C_{n+1}(M_i) = M_i$. Set $C[n]$ as the union of the overflow part at the nth step, and $C[\max + 1]$ is the union of all the basins. When the algorithm initializes, set $C[\max + 1] = T[\min + 1]$.

The definition of overflow is recursive. Assuming that at the nth step, it has constructed $C[n-1]$. Based on (1), $C[n]$ is a subset of $T[n]$. And because $C[n-1]$ is a subset of $C[n]$, $C[n-1]$ is a subset of $T[n]$. D is a set of $T[n]$'s connected components, but for each component $d \in C[n]$, there are 3 kinds of possibilities:

(1) $d \cap C[n-1]$ is empty;
(2) $d \cap C[n-1]$ is not empty, has one connected component of $C[n-1]$;
(3) $d \cap C[n-1]$ is not empty, has more than one connected components of $C[n-1]$.

When the increasing overflow arrives to a new minimum region, the situation (1) would happen. As for the situation (1), d locates in some minimum region and must have some basins $C_{n-1}(M_i)$ to construct $C[n-1]$. So it has to make a dam to prevent the overflow from overflowing in a single catchment basin.

2.3 Marker Driven Watershed Transformation

Watershed algorithm borrows the concept of geomorphology, and the essence is a kind of region growing algorithm. The difference is that it begins to grow from local minimum of the image. It takes the gradient of the image as input and the output is continuous contour. However, due to the dark noises and texture details, there are many pseudo-minima which generate corresponding pseudo-catchment basin. So every pseudo-minimum and the true minimums are regarded as an independent region through watershed algorithm to be divided into small regions, which leads to over-segmentation and makes the results meaningless finally.

In most cases, it always adopts pre-processing and post-processing to overcome over-segmentation. Pre-processing, one of the most commonly method of overcoming over-segmentation, is to add some markers [13,16,25] to guide segmentation that the segmentation regions of unmarked minimums will be merged into the regions of marked minimums. In fact, it is researcher who decide the number of segmentation regions.

Among the recent pre-processing methods, the inside and outside marker driven watershed algorithm in [25] is widely used. The basic idea is that using marker can revise the gradient image and make local minimum regions just locate in the places of markers. As a result, when delete other local minimum regions it relieves the problem of over-segmentation.

A marker belongs to the connected components of an image. The typical selecting markers has two steps that is pre-processing and defining a set that all the markers subject to it. As a result of some small scale of regions, a lot of these minimums are details that are not related to each other. Assuming that the inside markers are defined as follows: the regions are surrounded by points with high altitude; the points in the region construct a connected component; all the points belong to this connected component have same gray value. After smoothing process of the image, the one which satisfies these above definitions is inside marker. Using watershed algorithm for the image after smoothing process, these inside markers are limited to the local minimums required, and get the watershed lines that are outside markers. It is worth noting that the points along watershed lines are good candidate points for the background, because they pass the highest point among the adjacent markers.

The steps of this marker driven watershed transformation [16] are shown below:

(1) compute the gradient image of the image waiting for segmentation,
(2) select inside markers: the course of selecting inside markers is find the local minimums which the range of gray value is in a continuous gray area and the gray value is lesser than the value near this area,
(3) select outside markers: the outside markers are the watershed transformation of inside markers,
(4) gradient revision: use (2) and (3), and apply mandatory minimum technology to revise the gradient that make sure the local minimum regions just appear in the places of markers,
(5) watershed transforms the revised gradient images and texture segmentation images are obtained finally.

3   Kernel Evolutionary Clustering Algorithm

3.1   Kernel Method

Minky and Papert pointed that the limited abilities of linear learning in 20th century 60s [15]. In application, complex applications need richer expression of the hypothesis space than linear functions. Kernel method [17–19] expression supplies another way for solution, namely, mapping the data to the high-dimensional feature space to increase the computation ability of linear learning machine, and the expression in dual space of linear learning makes this step as implicit procession become possible. In the problems of learning, training samples not appear independently, and always appear with paired samples that product by inner. Through selection, we use suitable kernel functions to replace the inner product, which can map the training data to the high-dimensional feature space implicitly. Another advantage of kernel method is that the learning algorithm and theory can be separated in some degree, which makes the hard solved problem in the original space become obvious in the feature space, as Fig. 2 shows.

For the complex distributed data, we introduce the learning method based on kernel. Through the kernel, we map the samples into the high-dimensional feature space, and then cluster in the feature space. As for the samples is mapped by kernel functions, it can be clustered easliy.

Assuming that sample set in input space $X = \{x_1, x_2, \cdots x_N\}, x_n \in R^d$, and it is mapped to some feature space H to get $\Phi(x_1), \Phi(x_2), \cdots \Phi(x_N)$ by nonlinear mapping Φ. So the inner product in the input space can be expressed in Mercer kernel [21] as follows:

$$K(x_i, x_j) = (\Phi(x_i)\Phi(x_j)). \tag{2}$$

All the samples make up a kernel function matrix $K_{i,j} = K(x_i, x_j)$. Supporting vector machine uses Mercer kernel to build a linear decision function in feature space, and it corresponds to a nonlinear function on the input space. The basic idea of kernel clustering is using Mercer kernel to map the input samples into the feature space, which makes the samples has better clustering.

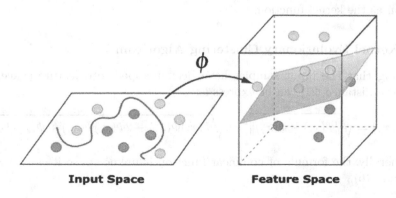

Fig. 2. Samples mapped from input space to feature space

Table 1. Kernel functions

Polynomial Kernel	$K(x_i, x_j) = (x_i{}^T x_j + \gamma)^\delta$
Gaussian Kernel	$K(x_i, x_j) = \exp(-\|x_i - x_j\|^2 / 2\sigma^2)$
Sigmoid Kernel	$K(x_i, x_j) = \tanh(\gamma(x_i{}^T x_j) + \theta)$

In fact, every function satisfying Mercer condition that can be a Mercer kernel decomposed to inner product in the feature space. Mercer condition can be described as follows, for every square integrable function $g(x)$, it satisfies:

$$\iint_{L_2 \otimes L_2} K(x, y) g(x) g(y) dx dy \geqslant 0. \tag{3}$$

Then it is easy to find the feature function and feature value of kernel function K, its kernel function is defined as:

$$K(x, y) = \sum_{i=1}^{N_H} \lambda_i \Phi_i(x) \Phi_i(y). \tag{4}$$

In the high dimension of feature space, the nonlinear functions can be wrote as,

$$\Phi(x) = (\sqrt{\lambda_1} \Phi_1(x), \sqrt{\lambda_2} \Phi_2(x), \cdots \sqrt{\lambda_{N_H}} \Phi_{N_H}(x))^T. \tag{5}$$

It is easy to get (2) by (4) and (5). Table 1 shows some conventional kernel functions used widely. More kernel functions are shown in [15]. Currently, the selection of the kernel function is still inconclusive that in the supervised learning model. Although kernel function can be selected by cross validation, the time complexity is high. However, in the non-supervised learning model, it is selected by experiences. It is worth mentioning that Gaussian Kernel function [24] is the most widely used kernel function and in the formula that $\sigma \neq 0 \in R$. The feature space of Gaussian Kernel function is infinite dimensional, so limited samples is linearly separable in this feature space. This paper chooses Gaussian Kernel function as the kernel function.

3.2   Kernel Evolutionary Clustering Algorithm

Assuming that the input samples have been mapped into feature space, the Euclidean distance [21] can be express as

$$d_H(x_i, x_j) = \sqrt{\|\Phi(x_i) - \Phi(x_j)\|^2} = \sqrt{\Phi(x_i)\Phi(x_i) - 2\Phi(x_i)\Phi(x_j) + \Phi(x_j)\Phi(x_j)}. \tag{6}$$

Generally, the formula of nonlinear function is unknown, so it can be wrote as (2) and (6).

$$d_H(x_i, x_j) = \sqrt{K(x_i, x_i) - 2K(x_i, x_j) + K(x_j, x_j)}. \tag{7}$$

This paper chooses (7) as measure function of clustering similarity.

The explicit steps of kernel evolutionary clustering algorithm are shown below:

Step (1). Determine the number of cluster categories k, $2 \leq k \leq N$, and initialize $gen\,(it) \leftarrow 0$.

Step (2). Construct mapping of kernel function:

$$K_{ii} = K(x_i, x_i);$$

$$K_{ij} = K(x_i, x_j);$$

$$K_{jj} = K(x_j, x_j).$$

Step (3). Compute the distances of every sample to the centers of categories according to (7), namely $d_H(x_i, x_j)$.

Step (4). Compute the individual fitness of the initial population.

Step (5). If $gen\,(it) > gen_{\max}$, then stop, otherwise go on.

Step (6). Take evolutionary operators.

Step (7). Compute the fitness of the offspring in temporary population pool.

Step (8). Apply selection operator, make the best individual of current generation come into the temporary population.

Step (9). Go to the next generation and set $gen\,(it) \leftarrow gen\,(it) + 1$ that replace the current generation with the temporary population, then go to Step 5.

4   Algorithm of WKECA

Watershed algorithm is sensitive to noise [20] and it leads to over-segmentation which can not express the meaningful regions of the image, so it has to merge the segmentation results. For digital images, the changed gray among pixels is nonlinear and the average gray of every region is also nonlinear. Kernel evolutionary clustering uses Mercer kernel to take nonlinear mapping, which can identify the nonlinear characters of changed average gray well and cluster more correctly.

WKECA algorithm is proposed based on marker driven watershed image segmentation algorithm [23] and combines with kernel clustering algorithm. The method has two strategies: First, in order to get better segmentation effect, some post-processions are used for the image segmentation; Second, the single pixel wide, connected, and accurate contour is obtained by using watershed algorithm that takes a coarse segmentation. However, a problem of watershed algorithm is that the performance of segmentation influenced by the noise and quantization error seriously and there will be many small segmentation regions appearing in the region which should be surrounded by the large edge. So inside marker driven watershed segmentation based on median filter is used to solve this problem.

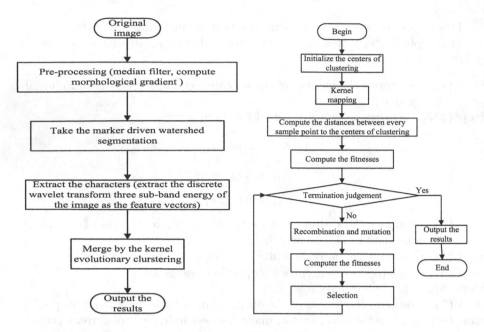

Fig. 3. Flow chart of WKECA

Fig. 4. Flow chart of kernel evolutionary merge

The flow chart of WKECA is shown in Fig. 3, and the flow chart of kernel evolutionary clustering is shown in Fig. 4.

The steps of WKECA algorithm are shown below:

Step (1). Take the median filtering to filter the noise and compute the morphological gradient of the image after median filtering.

Step (2). Extract the inside and outside markers of the image and use the markers to revise the gradient image (use mandatory minimum technology to revise the gradient, and make local minimum regions just locate in the places of markers), then take the watershed algorithm to coarse segmentation.

Step (3). Extract the three sub-band energy of discrete wavelet transformation for the image and set the wavelet feature median of every block as the feature of this block in the coarse segmentation image.

Step (4). Set the features of the blocks as samples of input and initialize the number of cluster categories and population.

Step (5). Construct kernel function mapping,

$$K_{ii} = K(x_i, x_i);$$

$$K_{ij} = K(x_i, x_j);$$

$$K_{jj} = K(x_j, x_j).$$

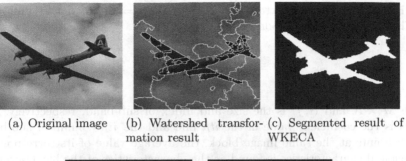

(a) Original image (b) Watershed transfor- (c) Segmented result of
mation result WKECA

(d) Segmented result of (e) Segmented result of
WGAC WKM

Fig. 5. The experimental results of nature image 1

Step (6). Compute the distances between each sample and center of clustering according to (7).

Step (7). Compute the fitness of each individual, and take clustering by evolutionary algorithm.

Step (8). If $gen(it) > max\_gen$, then stop, otherwise go on.

Step (9). Take the course of cloning, recombination and mutation.

Step (10). Compute the fitness of the offspring in the temporary population pool.

Step (11). Apply selection of optimal, take the best individual of current generation into the population.

Step (12). Go to the next generation that replace the current generation with the population, then go to Step 7.

Step (13). If $gen(it) > max\_gen$, then stop, output the optimal clustering result, which is the final segmentation result.

In this paper, the image has been taken initial segmentation by watershed method before the kernel evolutionary clustering, which is equivalent to already have a defined initial segmentation result. The number of samples be decreased significantly, at the same time, the algorithm further merges by kernel evolutionary clustering.

Here the three sub-band energies are chosen to implement discrete wavelet transformation for the image as the feature vector $\{f_1, f_2, \cdots, f_t\}$, in which t is the dimension of feature vector. In this example, $t = 10$ but not be limited to 10. The energy in this sub-bond is:

$$f = \frac{1}{MN} \sum_{i=1}^{M} \sum_{j=1}^{N} |x(i,j)|, \tag{8}$$

where $M \times N$ and (i, j) is the size and index of sub-band, respectively. And $x(i, j)$ is the coefficient value in the ith line and the jth column of sub-band. For all points at the same image block, the average value of its corresponding dimensional characteristics is found as the characteristics of the block after the coarse segmentation.

5   Experiments

5.1   Results on the Nature Image

The basic content of image segmentation has been stated in the former part. WKECA method is made up of 3 parts: watershed transformation, character extraction and merging of regions based on clustering. In this image segmentation algorithm, the sub-band energy of discrete wavelet transformation (DWT) is used and image gray values as features. The sub-band energy of DWT vectors has ten features, and image gray values have one feature.

In order to validate the effectiveness of this method, the segmentation for the nature image, texture image and SAR image have been implemented respectively. In the experiments, the parameters of WKECA and watershed genetic algorithm of clustering (WGAC) are set as Table 2. Based on parameter sensitivity tests that the parameter of Gaussian Kernel function has little effect on the experimental results, so the maximum number of iterations of WKM is set 100 and stopped threshold is set 10^{-4}.

In the first experiment, nature image 1 is shown as Fig. 5(a), it is made up of plane and sky and the size is 256×256. Figure 5(b)–(e) show the results of watershed transformation, WKECA, WGAG and WKM. We analyze the result of our algorithm that it is better than WGAC and WKM. From the figures, it can be seen that the result of WKECA is more smooth and with higher regional

Table 2. The experimental parameters

Parameters	Meaning	Values
it	The number of iterations	100
Nm	Size of population	20
Pc	The probability of crossover	1
Pm	The probability of mutation	0.06
Np	Mating pool size	100

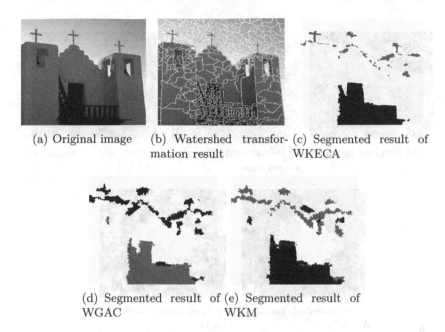

(a) Original image   (b) Watershed transfor- (c) Segmented result of
                      mation result   WKECA

(d) Segmented result of (e) Segmented result of
WGAC   WKM

Fig. 6. The experimental results of nature image 2

consistency compared with WGAC and WKM. And the worse effects of last two algorithms indicate that WKECA has effectiveness and feasibility.

Nature image 2 is shown as Fig. 6(a), and the size is 320×320. It is expected to divide into 3 categories that is architecture, sky and wood. Figure 6(b)–(e) show the results of watershed transformation, WKECA, WGAG and WKM and the result of our algorithm is better than WGAC and WKM. From the figures, it can be seen that the three algorithms can not distinguish the 3 categories completely, but comparatively speaking, WKECA obtains a much better performance and the contour is more clear.

5.2 Results on the Texture Image

Texture image is shown as Fig. 7(a) that size is 256×256. Figure 7(b)–(e) show that the results of watershed transformation, WKECA, WGAC and WKM, respectively. From the figures, the result of WKECA has unsmooth edge, but it is divided into 2 categories precisely. The results of WGAG has the situation of misclassification, and the problem of WKM is sensitive with initializes.

5.3 Results on the SAR Image

Finally, the third experiment is intended to assess the performance of WKECA in SAR image. The SAR image is shown in Fig. 8(a), and it is expected to divide into 2 categories which is ridge and valley. Unlike the previous dataset, SAR

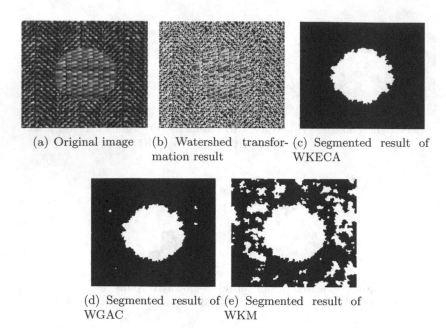

(a) Original image   (b) Watershed transfor- (c) Segmented result of
                      mation result   WKECA

(d) Segmented result of (e) Segmented result of
WGAC   WKM

Fig. 7. The experimental results of texture image

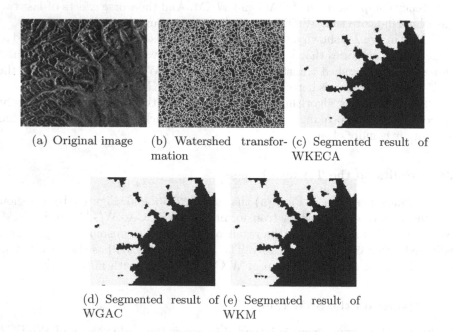

(a) Original image   (b) Watershed transfor- (c) Segmented result of
                      mation   WKECA

(d) Segmented result of (e) Segmented result of
WGAC   WKM

Fig. 8. The experimental results of SAR image

images often involve more details and the texture information of SAR is astatic. Figure 8(b)–(e) show the results of segmentation. As the figures shown that the result of WKECA is more smooth and higher regional consistency than WGAC and WKM.

6 Conclusion

Image segmentation is one of important tasks in computer vision and image analysis. This paper has pointed out the shortcomings of watershed algorithm and kernel evolutionary clustering algorithm, and has proposed an image segmentation method by combining watershed and kernel evolutionary clustering algorithm. WKECA not only solves the shortcomings of watershed transformation, but also uses the information of DWT sub-band energy and the image gray value in kernel evolutionary clustering algorithm. The new method has retained the advantages of the two algorithms, which enhances the completeness of segmentation regions. The experiments has proved that WKECA has better effects on segmentation of nature images, texture images and SAR images.

References

1. Shi, J., Malik, J.: Normalized cuts and image segmentation. IEEE Trans. Pattern Anal. Mach. Intell. **22**(8), 888–905 (2000)
2. Unnikrishnan, R., Pantofaru, C., Hebert, M.: Toward objective evaluation of image segmentation algorithms. IEEE Trans. Pattern Anal. Mach. Intell. **29**(6), 929–944 (2007)
3. Lee, D.S., Yeom, S., Son, J.Y., Kim, S.H.: Automatic image segmentation for concealed object detection using the expectation-maximization algorithm. Opt. Express **18**(10), 10659–10667 (2010)
4. Sijbers, J., Scheunders, P., Verhoye, M., van der Linden, A., van Dyck, D., Raman, E.: Watershed-based segmentation of 3D MR data for volume quantization. Magn. Reson. Imaging **15**(6), 679–688 (1997)
5. Kass, M., Witkin, A., Terzopoulos, D.: Snakes: active contour models. Int. J. Comput. Vis. **1**(4), 321–331 (1988)
6. Osher, S., Sethian, J.A.: Fronts propagating with curvature-dependent speed: algorithms based on Hamilton-Jacobi formulations. J. Comput. Phys. **79**(1), 12–49 (1988)
7. Vincent, L., Soille, P.: Watersheds in digital spaces: an efficient algorithm based on immersion simulations. IEEE Trans. Pattern Anal. Mach. Intell. **13**(6), 583–598 (1991)
8. Serra, J.: Image Analysis and Mathematical Morphology. Academic Press, Orlando (1982)
9. Osma-Ruiz, V., Godino-Llorente, J.I., Senz-Lechn, N., Gmez-Vilda, P.: An improved watershed algorithm based on efficient computation of shortest paths. Pattern Recogn. **40**(3), 1078–1090 (2007)
10. Levner, I., Zhang, H.: Classification-driven watershed segmentation. IEEE Trans. Image Process. **16**(5), 1437–1445 (2007). A Publication of the IEEE Signal Processing Society

11. Cousty, J., Bertrand, G., Najman, L., Couprie, M.: Watershed cuts: minimum spanning forests and the drop of water principle. IEEE Trans. Pattern Anal. Mach. Intell. **31**(8), 1362–1374 (2008)
12. Wang, Z.Y.: The application of the watershed transformation in medical image segmentation. Comput. Knowl. Technol. (2009)
13. Meyer, F., Beucher, S.: Morphological segmentation. J. Vis. Commun. Image Represent. **1**(1), 21–46 (1990)
14. Smet, P.D., Vleeschauwer, D.D.: Performance and scalability of a highly optimized rainfalling watershed algorithm. In: CISST 1998: Proceedings of the International Conference on Imaging Science, Systems and Technology, pp. 266–273 (1998)
15. Saunders, C., Stitson, M.O., Weston, J., Holloway, R., Bottou, L., Scholkopf, B., et al.: Support vector machine - reference manual. J. Chongqing Univ. Arts Sci. **26**(5), 107–118 (1998)
16. Salembier, P., Pardas, M.: Hierarchical morphological segmentation for image sequence coding. IEEE Trans. Image Process. **3**(5), 639–651 (1994)
17. Linton, O., Nielsen, J.P.: A kernel method of estimating structured non-parametric regression based on marginal integration. Biometrika **82**(1), 93–100 (1995)
18. Takeda, H., Farsiu, S., Milanfar, P.: Deblurring using regularized locally adaptive kernel regression. IEEE Trans. Image Process. **17**(4), 550–563 (2008). A Publication of the IEEE Signal Processing Society
19. Mishra, A., Wong, A., Bizheva, K., Clausi, D.A.: Intra-retinal layer segmentation in optical coherence tomography images. Opt. Express **17**(26), 23719–23728 (2009)
20. Bora, D.J., Gupta, A.K.: A new efficient color image segmentation approach based on combination of histogram equalization with watershed algorithm. Int. J. Comput. Eng. **4**(6), 156–167 (2016)
21. Handl, J., Knowles, J.: An evolutionary approach to multiobjective clustering. IEEE Trans. Evol. Comput. **11**(1), 56–76 (2007)
22. Hruschka, E.R., Campello, R., Freitas, A.A., de Carvalho, A.: A survey of evolutionary algorithms for clustering. IEEE Trans. Syst. Man Cybern. Part C **39**(2), 133–155 (2009)
23. Liu, W.: A marker-based watershed algorithm using fractional calculus for unmanned aerial vehicle image segmentation. J. Inf. Comput. Sci. **12**(14), 5327–5338 (2015)
24. Kim, D.W., Lee, K.Y., Lee, D., Lee, K.H.: Evaluation of the performance of clustering algorithms in kernel-induced feature space. Pattern Recogn. **38**(4), 607–611 (2005)
25. Soille, P.: Morphological Image Analysis: Principles and Applications. Springer Science & Business Media, Heidelberg (2013). **4**(5), 94–103

Classification Based on Fireworks Algorithm

Yu Xue[✉], Binping Zhao, and Tinghuai Ma

School of Computer and Software, Nanjing University of Information
Science and Technology, Nanjing 210044, People's Republic of China
{xueyu,thma}@nuist.edu.cn, binpingzhao@126.com

Abstract. Data classification has attracted many researchers' attention. Many evolutionary algorithms (EAs) were employed to take advantage of their global search ability. In supervised classification research issues, EAs were only used to improve the performance of classifiers either by optimizing the parameters or structure of the classifiers, or by pre-processing the inputs of the classifiers. Although genetic programming or evolutionary based decision tree approaches are proposed for classification, the development of these approaches is limited by their special structure. In this paper, we propose a new mathematical optimization model for the supervised classification problem and use fireworks algorithm (FWA) to do classification directly without modification. In the new optimization model, a linear equations set is constructed based on training set, and we propose an objective function which can be optimized by FWA. Four different data sets have been employed in the experiments, and 70% samples are used as train sets while the rest are used as test sets. The results show that the label of test sets can be identified accurately by our new methods. This paper also shows that the optimization model can be used for classification and employing EA to solve this optimization model is feasible.

Keywords: Data classification · Evolutionary classification algorithm · Evolutionary algorithm · Evolutionary learning · Fireworks algorithm (FWA)

1 Introduction

Data classification has been researched for several decades and this problem can be classified into two categories, i.e. unsupervised classification and supervised classification.

Unsupervised classification problem is usually called clustering problem. Supervised classification methods, such as support vector machine (SVM) [1], artificial neural network (ANN) [2], and k-nearest neighbor (KNN) [3], have become a hot research direction. However, the existing methods are deterministic algorithm in some extend. They are also easy to fall into local optimum. Although genetic programming or evolutionary based decision tree approaches are proposed for classification, the development of these approaches is limited

© Springer Nature Singapore Pte Ltd. 2016
M. Gong et al. (Eds.): BIC-TA 2016, Part II, CCIS 682, pp. 35–40, 2016.
DOI: 10.1007/978-981-10-3614-9_4

by their special structure. At present, the situation in the classification research field is different from that in clustering research field. EAs have been only used to improve the classification accuracy either by optimizing the parameters or structure of classifiers, or by pre-processing the inputs of classifiers [4–6].

In this paper, we choose EAs to solve the classification problem from another direction in order that any existing excellent EA can be used to do classification directly and easily almost without modification. First, we proposed a new optimization classification model for the classification problem. Through this optimization model or framework, classification problem can be solved by EAs. Second, we introduced fireworks algorithm (FWA) [7] into supervised classification problem. Furthermore, four different data sets from UCI were employed in the experiments. The purpose of this paper is to investigate the feasibility to solve classification problems by EA through the new optimization model, and investigate the performance of EA when it is employed to solve classification problem.

2 Fireworks Algorithm

FWA, inspired by observing fireworks explosion, was proposed for global optimization of complex functions. The explosion process of a firework can be viewed as a search in the local space around a specific point where the firework is set off through the sparks generated in the explosion. The framework of the FWA is described in Algorithm 1.

Algorithm 1. Framework of the FWA

Randomly select n locations for fireworks;
While stop criteria = false do
    Set off n fireworks respectively at the n locations;
    for each firework x_i do
        Calculate the number of sparks that the firework yields: $\hat{s}_i$;
        Obtain locations of $\hat{s}_i$ sparks of the firework x_i;
    end for
    for k=1: $\hat{m}$ do
        Randomly select a firework x_j;
        Generate a specific spark for the firework with Gaussian explosion;
    end for
    Select the best location and keep it for next explosion generation;
    Randomly select n-1 locations from the two types of sparks and the current fireworks according to the probability;
end while

When considering the minimization problem, for a real function $f(x) \in R$ and $x \in [x_{\min}, x_{\max}]$, a continuous variable with the domain R^d, the global minimum point x^* satisfies condition $f(x^*) \leq f(x)$ in the case of $\forall x \in [x_{\min}, x_{\max}]$. The bounds of search space are $x_{\min}$ and $x_{\max}$.

The number of sparks generated by each firework x_i is defined as follows.

$$s_i = m \cdot \frac{y_{\max} - f(x_i) + \xi}{\sum\limits_{i=1}^{n} (y_{\max} - f(x_i)) + \xi} \qquad (1)$$

where m is a parameter controlling the total number of sparks generated by the n fireworks, $y_{\max} = \max(f(x_i))\,(i = 1, 2, \ldots, n)$ is the maximum value of the objective function among the n fireworks, and ξ denotes the smallest constant in the computer. There is a limit to the number of sparks generated by fireworks.

$$\hat{s}_i = \begin{cases} round\,(a \cdot m) & \text{if } s_i < am \\ round\,(b \cdot m) & \text{if } s_i > bm, a < b < 1 \\ round\,(s_i) & otherwise \end{cases} \qquad (2)$$

where a and b are constant.

Amplitude of explosion for each firework is defined as follows.

$$A_i = \hat{A} \cdot \frac{f(x_i) - y_{\min} + \xi}{\sum\limits_{i=1}^{n} (f(x_i) - y_{\min}) + \xi} \qquad (3)$$

where $\hat{A}$ denotes the maximum explosion amplitude, $y_{\min} = \min(f(x_i))\,(i = 1, 2, \ldots, n)$ is the minimum value of the objective function among the n fireworks. The effects of explosion from random z directions are considered as follows.

$$z = round\,(d \cdot rand\,(0, 1)) \qquad (4)$$

where d is the dimensionality of the location x. $\hat{m}$ sparks of this type are generated in each explosion generation. The general distance between a location x_i and other locations is defined as follows.

$$L(x_i) = \sum_{j \in K} d(x_i, x_j) = \sum_{j \in K} \|x_i - x_j\| \qquad (5)$$

where K is the set of all current locations of both fireworks and sparks, and $\|x_i - x_j\|$ is the Euclidean distance between x_i and x_j. The selection probability of a location x_i is defined as follows.

$$p(x_i) = \frac{L(x_i)}{\sum\limits_{j \in K} L(x_j)} \qquad (6)$$

3 Classification Method Based on EA

Given a data set $D = \{x_1, x_2, ..., x_m\}$ and a training set $T = \{(x_1, y_1), \cdots, (x_m, y_m)\}$, where (x_i, y_i) is the ith example, $x_i = x_{i1}, x_{i2}, ..., x_{id} \in X = R^d$ is the ith sample, $y_i \in Y = \{1, 2, \cdots, l\}\,(i = 1, 2, \cdots, m)$ is the label of the ith

sample. The task of classification problem is to learn a model $f(x) : X \to Y$ from the training set T.

The examples of training data can be written as

$$
\begin{bmatrix}
x_{11}, & x_{12}, & \dots, & x_{1d}, & y_1 \\
x_{21}, & x_{22}, & \dots, & x_{2d}, & y_2 \\
\dots, & \dots, & \dots, & \dots, & \dots \\
x_{m1}, & x_{m2}, & \dots, & x_{md}, & y_m
\end{bmatrix}
\tag{7}
$$

First, we introduce a weight vector $W = (w_1, w_2, ..., w_d)$, and let

$$
\begin{cases}
w_1 x_{11} + w_2 x_{12} + \dots + w_d x_{1d} = y_1 \\
w_1 x_{21} + w_2 x_{22} + \dots + w_d x_{2d} = y_2 \\
\dots + \dots + \dots + \dots = \dots \\
w_1 x_{m1} + w_2 x_{m2} + \dots + w_d x_{md} = y_m
\end{cases}
\tag{8}
$$

However, there is no necessarily exact solution for these linear equations. Fortunately, it is a classification problem in fact, so it is not necessary to find the exact solution. For a classification problem, it is enough to find an approximate solution of the following equations:

$$
\begin{cases}
w_1 x_{11} + w_2 x_{12} + \dots + w_d x_{1d} \approx y_1 \\
w_1 x_{21} + w_2 x_{22} + \dots + w_d x_{2d} \approx y_2 \\
\dots + \dots + \dots + \dots \approx \dots \\
w_1 x_{m1} + w_2 x_{m2} + \dots + w_d x_{md} \approx y_m
\end{cases}
\tag{9}
$$

Obviously, EAs can be employed to solve this kind of problems. The objective function can be defined as follows:

$$
\min(f(W) = \sqrt{\sum_{i=1}^{m} \sum_{j=1}^{d} (w_j \cdot x_{ij} - y_i)^2})
\tag{10}
$$

In fact, this model is feasible when the following equations are satisfied. Because we can predict label of x_i belongs to y_i when $y_i + \delta \leq w_1 x_{i1} + w_2 x_{i2} + \dots + w_d x_{id} < y_i + \delta$.

$$
\begin{cases}
y_1 + \delta \leq w_1 x_{11} + w_2 x_{12} + \dots + w_d x_{1d} < y_1 + \delta \\
y_2 + \delta \leq w_1 x_{21} + w_2 x_{22} + \dots + w_d x_{2d} < y_2 + \delta \\
\dots \leq + \dots + \dots + \dots < \dots \\
y_m + \delta \leq w_1 x_{m1} + w_2 x_{m2} + \dots + w_d x_{md} < y_m + \delta
\end{cases}
\tag{11}
$$

There are a lot of methods to ensure lower boundary and upper boundary of $w_i, i = 1, 2, ..., d$. In this paper, we estimate the lower boundary and upper boundary by following equations:

$$
\pm \sigma \frac{\sum_{i=1}^{N} y_i}{\sum_{i=1}^{N} \sum_{j=1}^{d} x_{ij}}
\tag{12}
$$

4   Experiments and Comparisons

4.1   Data Sets Used in Classification

Four data sets from the Machine learning repository [8] are employed in this paper. The information of all the data sets is summarized in Table 1.

Table 1. Description of data

Dataset	Number of features	Number of classes	Number of examples
Iris	4	3	150
Thyroid	5	3	215
Musk1	166	2	476
Biodegradation	41	2	1055

4.2   Parameter Settings for FWA

For the FWA, run time is set to 26, number of fitness evaluations is set to 500000. The other settings of FWA are: $n = 8, m = 64, a = 0.04, b = 0.8, \hat{A} = 2$, and $\hat{m} = 8$, which is applied in all the comparison experiments.

After W is found, we calculate classification accuracy for each class and the whole data set. For each example (x_i, y_i), if $-0.5 \leq (W^T \cdot x_i - y_i) < +0.5$, then we deem the class of (x_i, y_i) is correct. In the experiment, we chose 70% samples of each data to constitute training sets, and the rest were used for test data sets.

4.3   Experimental Results and Analysis

The results of the experiment are listed as Tables 2 and 3.

We can see from Tables 2 and 3 that the performance of the data sets (iris, thyroid, musk1, and biodegradation) is excellent as high value of classification accuracy. The minimum mean value of classification accuracy is 74.7% on biodegradation data set and the classification accuracy on iris can reach up to 100% at maximum. Besides, all the values of std are lower than 0.2 and the amplitude of the experimental results is small.

"min" and "max" mean the minimum and maximum value of classification accuracy, "mean" and "std" denote the average and standard deviation of the corresponding classification accuracy obtained in 26 runs.

Table 2. Classification accuracy on iris and thyroid data set

Classification accuracy	Iris				Thyroid			
	Min	Max	Mean	Std	Min	Max	Mean	Std
Test data	91.111%	100%	95.38%	0.14714	68.75%	85.94%	78.43%	0.18621

Table 3. Classification accuracy on musk1 and biodegradation data set

Classification accuracy	Musk1				Biodegradation			
	Min	Max	Mean	Std	Min	Max	Mean	Std
Test data	65.034%	80.42%	72.24%	0.18336	69.304%	80.38%	74.7%	0.14317

5 Conclusion

Data classification is a classical problem in machine learning or data mining research field. Many researchers have proposed excellent methods to solve classification problems and they all have been proved with good performance. We proposed a new optimization classification model and can be solved by any EA easily and directly. We chose FWA to search for global optimal solution on four different data sets. The results show that the label of test sets can be identified accurately by our new methods. On the whole, the optimization model which be used for classification and the performance of EA on classification problems is feasible and promising. Our next work is to improve the optimization model and the FWA. More different data sets will be employed in the experiments and the number of fitness evaluations, the structure of optimal classification model will be also taken into account.

References

1. Cortes, C., Vapnik, V.: Support-vector networks. Mach. Learn. **20**, 273–297 (1995)
2. Hopfield, J.J.: Neural networks and physical systems with emergent collective computational abilities. Proc. Natl. Acad. Sci. **79**, 2554–2558 (1982)
3. Goin, J.E.: Classification bias of the k-nearest neighbor algorithm. IEEE Trans. Pattern Anal. Mach. Intell. **6**, 379 (1984)
4. Chen, Z.Y., Kuo, R.J., Hu, T.L., Herrera, F.: An integrated hybrid algorithm based on nature inspired evolutionary for radial basis function neural network learning. Int. J. Artif. Intell. Tools **25**, 25 (2016)
5. Oong, T.H., Isa, N.A.M.: Adaptive evolutionary artificial neural networks for pattern classification. IEEE Trans. Neural Netw. **22**, 1823–1836 (2011)
6. Qasem, S.N., Shamsuddin, S.M., Hashim, S.Z.M., et al.: Memetic multiobjective particle swarm optimization-based radial basis function network for classification problems. Inf. Sci. **239**, 165–190 (2013)
7. Tan, Y., Zhu, Y.: Fireworks algorithm for optimization. In: Tan, Y., Shi, Y., Tan, K.C. (eds.) ICSI 2010. LNCS, vol. 6145, pp. 355–364. Springer, Heidelberg (2010). doi:10.1007/978-3-642-13495-1_44
8. Frank, A., Asuncion, A.: UCI Machine Learning Repository (2010)

Overlapping Community Detection in Network: A Fuzzy Evaluation Approach

Wei Zhao, Yangzhi Guo$^{(\boxtimes)}$, Chao Lei, and Jianan Yan

School of Computer Science and Technology, Xidian University, Xi'an 710071, China
ywzhao@mail.xidian.edu.cn, guoyzj@gmail.com

Abstract. A community is typically viewed as a group of nodes, and most connections in the community generally happen between interior nodes. Community in network also overlap as a person may belong to more than one social group. Therefore, detecting overlapping partition of a network is necessary for the realistic social analysis. In this paper, We develop a fuzzy evaluation using the membership degree of each node belonging to every community, and present a fuzzy evaluation based memetic algorithm for overlapping community detection in network. Our proposed algorithm is a synergy of genetic algorithm with a variant of fuzzy K-means strategy as the local search procedure. Experiments in real-world networks show that our method has an excellent performance in identifying overlapping structures.

Keywords: Overlapping community detection · Fuzzy evaluation · Memetic algorithm · Fuzzy K-means

1 Introduction

Many systems in real world can be represented as various complex networks, and have received remarkable attentions in recent years. Most researches have demonstrated that network has complex internal connection and various structure characteristics, e.g., small-world, scale-free and community structure. Community structure is considered to be a significant property of real-world social network, and numerous methods have been developed for efficient community detection. The Modularity proposed by Girvan and Newman [1] can quantitatively describe the community structure, which has been widely used. Many optimization algorithms have been proposed to optimize Modularity, including the greedy algorithm [2], simulated annealing [3], extremal optimization [4], etc. However, some researchers found that this function has the resolution limitation [5], which cannot obtain reasonable result when there are small communities in the large-scale network. For this reason, Li et al. proposed a quality function called modularity density [6], which includes a tunable parameter to explore the network at different resolutions.

However, in many real networks, the communities are not isolated but overlap and intersect with each other, which means that some nodes may belong

© Springer Nature Singapore Pte Ltd. 2016
M. Gong et al. (Eds.): BIC-TA 2016, Part II, CCIS 682, pp. 41–46, 2016.
DOI: 10.1007/978-981-10-3614-9_5

to no less than one community. For instance, in social network, a person may usually simultaneously associate with serval social groups like school, family and colleagues; and this is also happens in biological networks, where a cell might have multiple functions. Therefore, the research of overlapping community is indeed significant in real-world networks. There is growing interest in overlapping community detection and many algorithms have been proposed, e.g., GCE [7], CPMw [8] and CONGA [9]. Most methods have trouble scaling to large networks, and the lack of reliable accurate networks partitions makes evaluations of detect overlapping communities surprisingly difficult.

In this paper, we propose an effective metric based on the fuzzy theory, named Fuzzy evaluation (M), and the metric can find these nodes locating in the overlapping communities using membership degree of each node belonging to every community. Due to the good performance of the evolutionary algorithms (EAs), EA has been successfully used to detect the communities in many complex networks [10,11]. We design a memetic algorithm (FMD) and a variant of fuzzy K-means strategy as the local search procedure. Experiments on real-world networks, the results demonstrate that our algorithm shows effectiveness of overlapping community detection.

The rest of this paper is organized as follows. Section 2 introduces the Fuzzy evaluation function and describe the algorithm in detail, while experiments are given in Sect. 3. Finally, conclusions of this method are given in Sect. 4.

2   Relate Work

2.1   Fuzzy Evaluation

To solve the problems existing in the overlapping communities, in this paper, we proposed a Fuzzy evaluation M. The membership degree of each node belonging to each community is defined as:

$$\mu_{i,k} = \frac{|L(v_i, V_k)|}{|L(v_i, \bar{v}_i)|} \tag{1}$$

where v_i is the ith node in the network, V_k is the kth partition of the network. Then the membership degree of v_i to V_k is the ratio of the number of the edges that v_i connected with V_k between the other connected nodes. Thus, membership degree matrix can be presented as:

$$U = \begin{bmatrix} \mu_{1,1} & \mu_{2.1} & \cdots & \mu_{n,1} \\ \vdots & \vdots & \ddots & \vdots \\ \mu_{m,1} & \mu_{m,2} & \cdots & \mu_{m,n} \end{bmatrix} \tag{2}$$

which represents the membership degree matrix, and $\mu_{m,n}$ denotes of n nodes in m communities. Therefore, a Fuzzy evaluation metric is proposed as follow.

$$M_\lambda = \sum_{i=1}^{k} \frac{\lambda\mu_{k,i} - (1 - \lambda)(1 - \mu_{k,i})}{|V_k|} \tag{3}$$

where $\mu_{k,i}$ denotes the membership degree, of which node v_i belongs to community V_k. It is worth mentioning that the network could effectively avoid dividing all nodes into a community by ratio V_k. Optimizing $\mu_{k,i}$ will divide a network into many small communities while optimizing $-(1, \mu_{(k,i)})$ will divides a network into large communities. Where λ is an tunable parameter, and proper λ can detect the true partitions of the network community.

2.2   The Proposed Algorithm

In this section, we will give a detailed description of the proposed algorithm and local search procedure. The objective is Fuzzy evaluation M defined in Eq. 3, and it is taken as the fitness function. First, the framework of FMD is given, and then further explanations of the algorithm are introduced.

Algorithm 1. The framework of FMD

Input:
> G_{max}: Maximum number of generations
> N_m: The size of mating pool
> N_p: The population size
> N_t: The tournament size
> P_c: The crossover probability
> P_m: The mutation probability

1: $P \leftarrow$ Population Initialization
2: **while** Termination criterion are not satisfied(G_{max}) **do**
3:     $P_{parent} \leftarrow$ Selection Operation(P, N_p, N_m)
4:     $P_{child_1} \leftarrow$ Genetic operators(P_{parent}, P_c, P_m)
5:     $P_{child_2} \leftarrow$ Local Search(P_{child_1})
6:     $P \leftarrow$ Tournament Selection(P, R_{child_2})
7: **end while**

Output:
> Convert the fittest chromosome in P into a overlapping community solution.

The local search procedure used in our method is a variant of fuzzy K-means strategy, which is shown in Algorithm 2. K-means is simple and effective, and works as follows: (1) randomly select k objects as the center of the initial cluster, which represents a cluster; (2) calculate the distance from each vertex to each cluster and assign it to the nearest cluster; (3) repeat until the iteration is exhausted.

As shown in Algorithm 2, MDM() function aims to calculate the membership degree matrix in the input population, K-means() function is used to the find the maximum membership degree of the vertex i in each community by using K-means strategy, and Fit() function is responsible for evaluating the fitness of a solution.

Algorithm 2. Local search procedure

Input:P_{child_1}
Output:P_{child_2}
1: **for** each chromosome of population **do**
2:    $P \leftarrow$ MDM(chromosome)
3:    $X_{current} \leftarrow$ K-means(P)
4:    $X_{next} \leftarrow X_{current}$
5: **end for**
6: **if** Fit(P_{next}) > Fit(P_{child_1}) **then**
7:    $P_{child_2} = P_{next}$
8: **end if**

---

3   Experiments

In this section, we apply our algorithm to the real-world networks whose real clusters are known to investigate the performance of FMD. We test the overlapping community detection of Zachary's karate club networks (karate) [12], and λ are 0.2, 0.5 and 0.8 respectively. The partition of each node for $\lambda = 0.5$ in karate is shown in Table 1.

Table 1. The membership degree of each node

Vertex(i)	1	2	3	4	5	6	7	8	9	10	11	12	13	14	15	16	17	18	19	20
μ_{1i}	0.31	0.11	0.1	0.17	1	1	1	0.25	0.2	0	1	1	0.5	0.2	0	0	1	0.5	0	0.33
μ_{2i}	0.44	0.56	0.3	0.7	0	0	0	0.25	0	0	0	0	0.5	0.2	0	0	0	0.5	0	0.33
μ_{3i}	0.25	0.33	0.6	0.33	0	0	0	0.25	0.8	1	0	0	0	0.4	1	1	0	0	1	0.33

Vertex(i)	21	22	23	24	25	26	27	28	29	30	31	32	33	34
μ_{1i}	0	0.5	0	0	0	0	0	0	0	0	0	0.17	0	0
μ_{2i}	0	0.5	0	0	0	0	0	0	0	0	0.25	0	0	0.05
μ_{3i}	1	0	1	1	1	0	0	0	0	0	0.75	0.83	1	0.95

In the membership degree matrix, those nodes (the value of which is not 1) are within the overlapping community, e.g., nodes 1, 2, 3, 4, 8, 9, 13, 14, 18 and 20. Similarly, the size of the value can be used to denote the overlapping level, e.g., node 8 has greater overlapping level than node 9. Therefore, the problem of overlapping community detection can be solved by algorithm FMD.

Figure 1 displays the overlapping community corresponding to I_{max} on this network for different value of λ. In the inside of the dotted line is the overlapping partitions. As we can see from the figure, for $\lambda = 0.2$, the whole network is grouped into two overlapping communities, which containing one overlapping

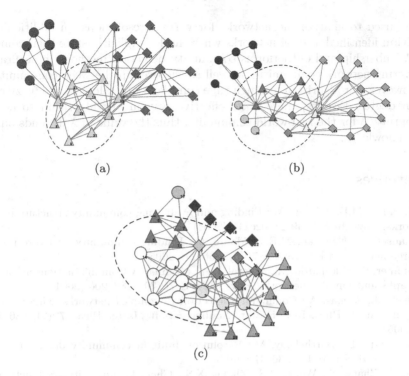

(a)   (b)

(c)

Fig. 1. Overlapping partitions on kareta network for (a) $\lambda = 0.2$, (b) $\lambda = 0.5$, (c) $\lambda = 0.8$

partition as well as is the closest to the true partition, of which the corresponding NMI (Normalize Mutual Information) [13] is 0.83717; for $\lambda = 0.5$, the network is grouped into three overlapping communities, which contains four overlapping partitions and the corresponding NMI is 0.73292; for $\lambda = 0.8$, the network is grouped into four overlapping communities, which contains five overlapping partitions and the corresponding NMI is 0.68726. For λ is larger, more small overlapping communities will be found. The experiments show that by tuning the parameter λ, we could explore the network at different resolutions. In general, the larger the λ value is, the smaller the overlapping communities FMD tends to find.

4   Conclusions

In this paper, we developed a novel community detection method that accurately discovers the overlapping community structure of real-world networks. Our algorithm is a synergy of a memetic algorithm with a variant of K-means strategy as the local search procedure. Experimental results demonstrate that, compared to conventional modularity and modularity density, Fuzzy evaluation has more significant superiority and practicability. By tuning parameter λ, our algorithm can be used to analyze the networks for various resolutions. In addition, our algorithm identified a set of networks where nodes explicitly state their community membership and outperforms community detection methods in accurately discovering network communities as well as the overlaps between communities.

However, our algorithm has high time complexity to calculate the fuzzy evaluation degree. Besides, there is no effective way in our algorithm to choose appropriate λ for the real-world community, thus the value of λ depends on the priori knowledge.

References

1. Newman, M.E., Girvan, M.: Finding and evaluating community structure in networks. Phys. Rev. E **69**(2), 026113 (2004)
2. Clauset, A., Newman, M.E.J., Moore, C.: Finding community structure in very large networks. Phys. Rev. E **70**(6), 066111 (2005)
3. Guimer, R., Salespardo, M., Amaral, L.A.: Modularity from fluctuations in random graphs and complex networks. Phys. Rev. E **70**(70), 188–206 (2004)
4. Duch, J., Arenas, A.: Community detection in complex networks using extremal optimization. Phys. Rev. E Stat. Nonlinear Soft Matter Phys. **72**(2), 986–1023 (2005)
5. Fortunato, S., Barthelemy, M.: Resolution limit in community detection. Proc. Natl. Acad. Sci. **104**(1), 36–41 (2007)
6. Li, Z., Zhang, S., Wang, R.S., Zhang, X.S., Chen, L.: Quantitative function for community detection. Phys. Rev. E **77**(3), 036109 (2008)
7. Lee, C., Reid, F., McDaid, A., Hurley, N.: Detecting highly overlapping community structure by greedy clique expansion. arXiv preprint arXiv:1002.1827 (2010)
8. Farkas, I., Ábel, D., Palla, G., Vicsek, T.: Weighted network modules. New J. Phys. **9**(6), 180 (2007)
9. Gregory, S.: An algorithm to find overlapping community structure in networks. In: Kok, J.N., Koronacki, J., Lopez de Mantaras, R., Matwin, S., Mladenič, D., Skowron, A. (eds.) PKDD 2007. LNCS (LNAI), vol. 4702, pp. 91–102. Springer, Heidelberg (2007). doi:10.1007/978-3-540-74976-9_12
10. Gong, M., Fu, B., Jiao, L., Du, H.: Memetic algorithm for community detection in networks. Phys. Rev. E Stat. Nonlinear Soft Matter Phys. **84**(2), 4146–4152 (2011)
11. Gong, M., Cai, Q., Li, Y., Ma, J.: An improved memetic algorithm for community detection in complex networks. In: IEEE Congress on Evolutionary Computation, pp. 1–8. IEEE (2012)
12. Tibly, G., Kertsz, J.: On the equivalence of the label propagation method of community detection and a Potts model approach. Phys. A Stat. Mech. Appl. **387**(19–20), 4982–4984 (2008)
13. Buzna, L., Lozano, S., Dazguilera, A.: Synchronization in symmetric bipolar population networks. Phys. Rev. E Stat. Nonlinear Soft Matter Phys. **80**(6), 869–875 (2009)

Multifactorial Brain Storm Optimization Algorithm

Xiaolong Zheng[1], Yu Lei[1], Maoguo Gong[2(✉)], and Zedong Tang[2]

[1] School of Electronics and Information, Northwest Polytechnical University,
ADD:127 West Youyi Road, Xi'an 710072, Shaanxi, China
`xlzheng@mail.nwpu.edu.cn`, `leiy@nwpu.edu.cn`
[2] Key Laboratory of Intelligent Perception and Image Understanding,
Xidian University, Xi'an, China
`gong@ieee.org`, `omegatangzd@gmail.com`

Abstract. Multifactorial optimization (MFO) is an optimization problem proposed in recent years to solve the multiple problems simultaneously. In this article we will introduce brain storm optimization (BSO) algorithm into MFO, and name this new methodology as multi-factorial brain storm optimization algorithm (MFBSA). In addition, we propose a new strategy of applying clustering technique into multitasking. The clustering process gathers the tasks who have similar information into a class, promoting the solving process of these tasks. The individuals in MFBSA have different cultural and biological characteristics, and their interaction in the evolutionary process format the ways of the exchange and sharing of information between multiple tasks.

Keywords: Evolutionary multitasking · Multifactorial optimization · Brain storm optimization

1 Introduction

Since the birth of swarm intelligence algorithms, many scientific and engineering problems in real-life have been solved. The main reason, I think, is that this type of algorithm is very suitable for all kinds of maximum or minimum problems in real life. In this article, we will focus on another novel optimization problems, multitasking [5] optimization problems (MFO), in the aim of proposing an efficient algorithm to solve such problems.

The main feature of MFO [5] is the coexistence of multiple different search spaces, the spaces corresponding to different tasks. In MFO, the tasks with different cultural backgrounds [4] commonly affect each individual in the population. The first multifactorial optimization algorithm (MFEA) is first proposed by several scholars from Nanyang Technological University [5]. Based on genetic algorithm framework, MFEA introduces multifactorial inheritance model [6] into MFO. This algorithm solves the two major problems in MFO, individual allocation strategy and presentation of culture. The use of multifactorial inheritance models enhances the exchanges and cooperation between different cultures,

© Springer Nature Singapore Pte Ltd. 2016
M. Gong et al. (Eds.): BIC-TA 2016, Part II, CCIS 682, pp. 47–53, 2016.
DOI: 10.1007/978-981-10-3614-9_6

which greatly improves the global searching ability of the genetic algorithm and achieves a considerable accelerating rate on the convergence speed.

Multifactorial optimization tries to optimize several issues who have different optima and solution space. Suppose we now have a multitasking optimization problem containing k independent minimization problems. The searching spaces $X_1, X_2, \ldots, X_k$ of these k questions are encoded into a unified $[0, 1]$ space as mentioned before. So the purpose of MFO is to find the k solutions:

$$\{x_1, \ldots, x_i, \ldots, x_k\} = \arg\min\{f_1(x_1), \ldots, f_i(x_i), \ldots, f_k(x_k)\}, i = 1, \ldots, k. \quad (1)$$

The optima set can be expressed as:

$$S^* = (x_1{}^*, x_2{}^*, \ldots, x_k{}^*), x_i{}^* \in X_i \text{ and } \forall x \in X_i, f_i(x_i{}^*) < f_i(x), i = 1, \ldots, k. \quad (2)$$

where X_i is the d_i-dimensional search space of T_i.

In this article, we propose a novel multifactorial brain storm algorithm (MFBSA) for MFO. In MFBSA, we use clustering technique to cluster similar solution into a class, and find the relationship between tasks and each class through the best individual of each task. Then, each class will mainly solve the tasks with which have a relationship, and assist in solving other tasks not related. Each individual in the population carries the information to solve its related task. To cluster these individuals into different group is actually a cluster of tasks who have similar characteristics. Clustering them into one group can help speed up the solving process.

Algorithm 1. Basic Structure of MFBSO

1: Randomly generate initial population P.
2: Evaluate all solutions on every task. Record the function value of each individual and the optima on each task.
3: **while** (stopping conditions are not satisfied) **do**
4:     Cluster P into n classes. The optima of all tasks are used as the initial cluster centres.
5:     Find out the class that each task belongs to using its optima. For each class containing k tasks, execute the following procedure.
6:     **for** $i = 1$ to k **do**
7:         Calculate the individuals' probability of producing offspring in class i.
8:         Generate $k \times \frac{size\ of\ P}{num\ of\ tasks}$ new solutions.
9:         Assess the new solutions. Record the function value of each individual and the optima for each task.
10:    **end for**
11:    Combine all new solutions generated by each class into the new population P.
12: **end while**

---

2   Multifactorial Brain Storm Optimization Algorithm

MFBSA simulates the process of human society to solve a set of problems simultaneously. And it is the first attempt to extend a variant BSO [8] to solve multitasking problems in aid of the transmission of both biological [3,7] and cultural information [2].

The procedure of MFBSA is as show in the Algorithm 1. We do not generate new individuals based on each task but based on each class. This is because gathering similar individuals into a class and gathering similar tasks into a class are substantially equivalent. We generate offspring based on each class, just like the similar tasks produce their next generations together. Also, because the similarities of the tasks in the different classes are very low, the exchange of information between the different classes can be reduced, which thus avoids the phenomenon of mutual inhibition between these tasks.

3   Experiments

3.1   Test Problems

In order to fully verify the performance of MFBSA on solution quality and convergence rate, we select the following continuous objective functions, including five unimodal benchmark functions and four multimodal functions. These functions and their properties are descripted in paper [1]. Here we list these functions and their labels in Table 1.

Table 1. Function lists

Label	Unimodal functions	Label	Multimodal functions
F1	Sphere function	F6	Ackley function
F2	Schwefel function	F7	Griewank function
F3	Rosenbrock function	F8	Rastrigin function
F4	Perm function	F9	Weierstrass function
F5	Levy function		

3.2   Definitions of Related Terms

We measure the number of function calls (NFCs) corresponding to each function. A small NFCs means a faster convergence rate. Because function values of the optima in all test functions are 0, we set VTR (value to reach) as a threshold to determine whether the algorithm successfully find the accurate enough optima.

We define the success rate (SR) as the ratio of the number of times reached VTR and the total number of trials.

$$SR = \frac{\text{number of times reached VTR}}{\text{total number of trials}} \tag{3}$$

Because there are k functions in a MFO problem set, it's reasonable to calculate the average number of function calls (ANFCs) and the average success rate (ASR). The specific formula of ANFCs and ASR are as follows:

$$ANFCs = \frac{1}{K} \sum_{i=1}^{K} NFCs_i \tag{4}$$

$$ASR = \frac{1}{K} \sum_{i=1}^{K} SR_i \tag{5}$$

3.3 Experiment 1: Problem-Sets with the Same Dimensionalities but Separated Optima

In any set of tasks for this experiment, the optima of the two tasks are different. Herein, we set the offset O of task 1 to 0.1, and keep the offset O of task 2 as 0. The dimensions of each task is 30. The final results of the experiment as listed in Table 2, which are the average values of 30 times.

Experimental results in Table 2 show that, MFBSA has a higher average success rate of 0.94 than MFEA of 0.78. We then look at the average number of function calls. MFBSA achieves a faster convergence rate in 25/27 experiments than MFEA in ANFCs. This experiment shows that the individuals of the population can share information more efficiently in our model, accelerating the solving speed of each task in MFO.

3.4 Experiment 2: Three Tasks of the Same Dimension and the Separated Optima

In the dual-task problems, we have tested the performance of the algorithm under several different factors. We will only test the performance of MFBSA in three different tasks with various optima. The problem set is listed in Table 3. In the set, the optima of the tasks are different. And their optima are showed in encoded format as follow. The dimensionality of all tasks is 30 in the following experiments. We run MFBSA and MFEA on the problem set1 in Table 3 30 times.

The optima's distribution of the two algorithms on set 1 can be seen in Fig. 1. In the figure, MFBSA get a more stable solution than MFEA on the two tasks T1 and T3. On the task T2, MFEA is performed relatively well.

Table 2. Problem-sets with the same dimensionalities but separated optima

Task1		Task2		MFBSA		MFEA	
Dim	O	Dim	O	ANFCs	ASR	ANFCs	ASR
30	0.1	30	0				
F1		F1		**19,902**	1	31,150	1
		F2		**276,640**	1	538,340	1
		F3		**404,190**	1	679,850	1
		F4		**902,400**	1	1,216,300	1
		F5		**6,780,400**	1	8,235,100	1
		F6		**1,190,800**	1	1,760,200	1
		F7		**121,320**	1	2,052,300	1
		F8		**5,403,200**	0.98	12,269,000	0.65
		F9		**16,333,000**	0.50	16,872,000	0.50
F5		F1		**1,414,400**	1	1,762,100	1
		F2		**6,533,200**	1	7,680,600	1
		F3		**4,336,000**	1	6,105,600	1
		F4		**4,191,300**	1	4,638,500	1
		F5		**8,941,900**	1	16,018,000	1
		F6		**3,067,700**	1	5,033,700	1
		F7		**4,084,700**	1	5,436,000	1
		F8		**12,469,086**	1	24,549,000	0.63
		F9		29,662,000	0.50	**29,550,000**	0.50
F7		F1		**4,743,100**	0.98	11,738,000	0.60
		F2		**28,787,000**	0.98	49,388,000	0.63
		F3		**15,315,000**	1	37,667,015	0.57
		F4		**17,763,000**	0.98	23,162,000	0.58
		F5		**23,304,000**	1	39,739,000	0.65
		F6		**12,132,000**	0.98	27,940,000	0.58
		F7		**19,791,000**	0.98	34,158,000	0.57
		F8		**12,466,000**	0.95	21,491,000	0.23
		F9		29,662,000	0.50	**29,550,000**	0.50
Ave				-	**0.94**	-	0.78

Table 3. Problem-sets with 3 tasks.

Problem set	Task		
	Objective label	Optimal objective value	Optima in unified space
Set 1	Griewank	0	[0.3, 0.3, ..., 0.3]
	Ackley	0	[0.5, 0.5, ..., 0.5]
	Rastrigin	0	[0.7, 0.5, ..., 0.7]

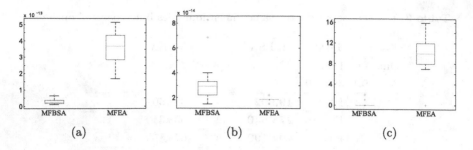

Fig. 1. Box plots of the distribution of optimal obtained by MFEA and MFBSA on the 3 objectives in set 1 by (a) Task 1, (b) Task 2 and (c) Task 3.

4   Conclusion

In this paper, a novel multifactorial optimization algorithm has been proposed for multitasking optimization. The proposed MFBSA employs a unique way of cooperation to make the individuals share information. By the use of clustering technology, the objects that individuals cooperate to in the MFO environment has undergone tremendous changes compared to MFEA. Later in the article we conduct a series of experiments to test the algorithm in terms of the convergence rate, the success rate and robustness. As what we can see in the above experimental analysis, MFBSA generally performes well on the convergence rate. In other respects, MFBSA's performance is not bad too, which in totally is similar to MFEA. However there are still many problems to be solved in MFBSA. Especially when problems become complicated, the stability problem of optima is gradually revealed. In future studies, we need to consider how to apply MFBSA into cross domain issues in addition to solve the stability problem.

Acknowledgments. This work was supported by the National Natural Science Foundation of China (Grant No. 61603299)

References

1. Ali, M.M., Khompatraporn, C., Zabinsky, Z.B.: A numerical evaluation of several stochastic algorithms on selected continuous global optimization test problems. J. Glob. Optim. **31**(4), 635–672 (2005)
2. Chen, X., Ong, Y.S., Lim, M.H., Tan, K.C.: A multi-facet survey on memetic computation. IEEE Trans. Evol. Comput. **15**(5), 591–607 (2011)
3. Cloninger, C.R., Rice, J., Reich, T.: Multifactorial inheritance with cultural transmission and assortative mating. II. A general model of combined polygenic and cultural inheritance. Am. J. Hum. Genet. **31**(2), 176–198 (1979)
4. Dawkin, R.: The Selfish Gene. Oxford University Press, London (1976)
5. Gupta, A., Ong, Y.S., Feng, L.: Multifactorial evolution: toward evolutionary multitasking. IEEE Trans. Evol. Comput. **20**(3), 343–357 (2016)

6. Li, Y.L., Zhan, Z.H., Gong, Y.J., Chen, W.N., Zhang, J., Li, Y.: Differential evolution with an evolution path: a DEEP evolutionary algorithm. IEEE Trans. Cybern. **45**(9), 1798–1810 (2015)
7. Mills, R., Jansen, T., Watson, R.A.: Transforming evolutionary search into higher-level evolutionary search by capturing problem structure. IEEE Trans. Evol. Comput. **18**(5), 628–642 (2014)
8. Shi, Y.: Brain storm optimization algorithm. In: Tan, Y., Shi, Y., Chai, Y., Wang, G. (eds.) ICSI 2011. LNCS, vol. 6728, pp. 303–309. Springer, Heidelberg (2011). doi:10.1007/978-3-642-21515-5_36

An Improved Heuristic Algorithm for UCAV Path Planning

Kun Zhang[1]([✉]), Peipei Liu[1], Weiren Kong[1], Yu Lei[1], Jie Zou[2], and Min Liu[2]

[1] School of Electronics and Information, Northwestern Polytechnical University,
Xi'an, Shaanxi 710072, China
kunnpu@gmail.com
[2] Science and Technology on Electro-Optic Control Laboratory,
Luoyang, Henan 471009, China

Abstract. It is more important in study of unmanned combat aerial vehicle (UCAV) path planning in military and civil field. This paper presents a new mathematical model and an improved heuristic algorithm based on Sparse A* Search (SAS) for UCAV path planning problem. In this paper, flight constrained conditions will be considered to meet the flight restrictions and task demands. With three simulations, the impacts of the model on the algorithms will be investigated, and the effectiveness and the advantages of the models and algorithms will be validated.

Keywords: Unmanned combat aerial vehicle · Path planning · Heuristic algorithm · Sparse A* Search

1 Introduction

Nowadays, unmanned combat aerial vehicle (UCAV) path planning has long been a challenging area for researchers in military and civil field. Currently, the represented techniques of UCAV path planning include PSO [1,12], dynamic programming method [2], the A* algorithm [9], ant colony algorithm [3], genetic algorithm [4,11], and so on [5–8]. Reference [9] adopted sparse A* algorithm, but angle heuristic function is not taken into consideration; Reference [10,11] proposed the algorithms with large amount of calculation. To address these problems, an improved heuristic algorithm is studied and corresponding simulation is given in this paper.

2 Related Works

2.1 Basic Mathematical Model

The planning space is divided into two-dimensional grids or three-dimensional grids, the nodes are acquired and built into a network graph, as shown in Fig. 1.

© Springer Nature Singapore Pte Ltd. 2016
M. Gong et al. (Eds.): BIC-TA 2016, Part II, CCIS 682, pp. 54–59, 2016.
DOI: 10.1007/978-981-10-3614-9_7

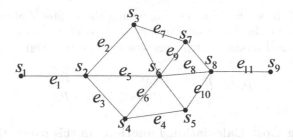

Fig. 1. Network graph

Supposing the nodes of network graph form a set $S = \{s_1, s_2, s_3, ...s_m\}$. Define a set that includes all paths from the starting point to the ending point as $E = \{e_1, e_2, e_3, ...e_n\}$. Let s_i and s_j be two adjacent nodes on the path, the cost value of the connecting line between two nodes can be expressed by u_{ij}, the path planning problems are defined as follows

$$\begin{cases} \min f(e_k) = \sum_{(s_i, s_j) \in \varepsilon_k} u_{ij} \\ s.t. e_k \in E, s_i \in S, s_j \in S \end{cases} \tag{1}$$

Compared with reference [9], our new mathematical model takes more constraints into account.

Models of Threats

Threat Model of Radar. Supposing the flying height is h, the horizontal distance from aircraft to radar is R, radar maximal horizontal range is R_{max}, radar performance coefficient is k. Threat model of radar can be represented as follows:

$$P_R = \begin{cases} \frac{R_{max}^4}{R^4 + R_{max}^4} & R \leqslant R_{max} \\ 0 & R > R_{max} \end{cases} \tag{2}$$

Threat Model for SAM. Supposing R_m is the horizontal distance. R_{Mmax} is the maximum attack radius. Threat model of missile can be presented as follows:

$$P_R = \begin{cases} \frac{R_{Mmax}}{R_m + R_{Mmax}} & R_m \leqslant R_{Mmax} \\ 0 & R > R_{Mmax} \end{cases} \tag{3}$$

Threat Model of Terrain. Supposing the horizontal cross-section of the peak is a circumference at the flight height, and the radius of circumference is R_d. R_{AT} is the horizontal distance from aircraft to the central of the peak. Threat model of peaks can be presented as follows:

$$P_T = \begin{cases} 0 & R_{AT} > 10\,km + R_d \\ 1 & R_{AT} \leqslant 2\,km + R_d \\ \frac{1}{R_{AT}} & 2\,km + R_d < R_{AT} < 100\,km + R_d \end{cases} \tag{4}$$

Threat Model of Atrocious Weather. Supposing the radius of atrocious weather is R_c and horizontal distance from aircraft to the center of atrocious weather is R_{AW}. Mathematical model of atrocious weather can be given as follows:

$$P_W = \begin{cases} 0 & R_{AW} > 5\,km + R_c \\ \frac{1}{R_{AW}} & R_{AW} \leqslant 5\,km + R_c \end{cases} \tag{5}$$

Path Planning Cost Calculation Function. In this paper, the cost calculation function can be given as:

$$J = \sum_{i=1}^{n} (w_s l_i + w_t f_{TAi}) \tag{6}$$
$$J_i = (w_s l_i + w_t f_{TAi})$$

where J is the total cost of the route, J_i is the ith route cost, l_i is the ith route leg length, f_{TAi} is the ith threat index of route, w_s, w_t are the weight coefficients of distance factors and threat factors and $w_s + w_t = 1$.

3 Path Planning Methods Based on Sparse A* Searching Algorithm

3.1 Extensible Rules of Nodes

The medial axis of the fan shaped region is the direction of the current nodes. The fan-shaped region is divided into m equal parts, the cost of knot vector whose distance between each sub-part and the current nodes is calculated. Before inserting the nodes with the minimum cost into OPEN table, make a judgment:

$$DL(x) + SL(x) \leqslant d_{max} \tag{7}$$

where $DL(x)$ is the distance between the start point and the end point, $SL(x)$ is the line between current node to the target point, d_{max} is a multiple of straight-line distance which is between the starting point to the destination point.

3.2 Trajectory Cost Function

The cost function of heuristic search can be represented as $f(x) = g(x) + h(x)$. $g(x)$ can be calculated by the formula (6), here we discuss $h(x)$. The Manhattan distance can be given as follow:

$$h_1(x) = |x - x_m| + |y - y_m| \tag{8}$$

where (x, y) is the coordinate of the current nodes, (x_m, y_m) is the coordinate of the target nodes. In this paper, the cost function [1] can be expressed as follow:

$$h_2(x) = w_d h_1(x) + w_\theta h(\theta) \tag{9}$$
$$h_\theta = \sqrt{\Delta\theta^2} \tag{10}$$

where $h_1(x)$ is distance heuristic function; $h(\theta)$ is angle heuristic function, θ be maximum turning angle w_d and w_θ are the weight coefficients of distance heuristic and angle heuristic and $w_d + w_\theta = 1$. $\Delta\theta = \theta_x - \theta_m$, θ_x is the direction of the line which connects current nodes and target nodes, θ_m is the predetermined target approaching angle. Suppose $\theta_x \in (-\pi, +\pi]$, $\theta_m \in (-\pi, +\pi]$, $\Delta\theta \in (-2\pi, +2\pi]$, $\Delta\theta$ is regulated as follow:

$$\Delta\theta = \begin{cases} -(2\pi - \Delta\theta) & \pi < \Delta\theta \leqslant 2\pi \\ \Delta\theta + 2\pi & -2\pi < \Delta\theta \leqslant -\pi \end{cases} \tag{11}$$

Let radius be $a * d$, d be the simulation step size, a be range coefficient, $f(x)$ can be expressed as follow:

$$f(x) = \begin{cases} J(x) + h_1(x) & DL(x) > a * d \\ J(x) + h_2(x) & DL(x) \leqslant a * d \end{cases} \tag{12}$$

where $DL(X)$ is the distance between current nodes and target nodes, $J(X)$ is the actual cost value.

3.3   Trajectory Smooth Straighten Processing

The first method is as follows. Set start points as current points, traverse other nodes. If the connection line of current node and a certain visiting node encounters threat, go back to the previous node, set it as current node, delete all nodes between current node and last current node, update information of current notes, and reiterate traverse backward the beginning with this current node until reaching the target node. Otherwise it continues to traverse and repeat above steps; Another method is as follows, let A be current node, B be father node of current node, C be ancestral node, their cost value are f_a, f_b, f_c. The route cost from A to C is $\Delta f_3 = f_a - f_c$, the route cost from A to B is $\Delta f_1 = f_a - f_b$, the route cost from B to C is $\Delta f_2 = f_b - f_c$. If $\Delta f_3 < \Delta f_1 + \Delta f_2$, set ancestral node of current node as its father node and adjust its cost value.

4   Experimental Study

Define the range of path planning as $500\,km \times 500\,km$, d as $5\,km$. Define $w_s = 0.5$, $w_t = 0.5$. Define $w_d = 0.5$ and $w_\theta = 0.5$. The maximum route distance constraint is 1.5 times of the straight distance between the start point and target point. Let a be 5, maximum turning angle be 60, m be 3.

(1) Supposing the coordinate of start point is $(100, 100)$, the coordinate of target point is $(500, 450)$, target approaching angle is 120. The result is presented in Fig. 2. (2) The coordinate of start point and end point are the same as the first settings, target approaching angle is 80, the result is shown as Fig. 3. The result which considers the first method of trajectory smooth straighten processing can be shown as Fig. 4. (3) Supposing the coordinate of start point is $(100, 100)$, the coordinate of target point is $(300, 300)$, target approaching angle is 80. The result which considers the first method of trajectory smooth straighten processing can be shown as Fig. 5.

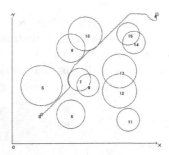

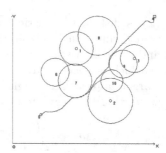

Fig. 2. The first result

Fig. 3. The second result

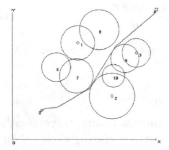

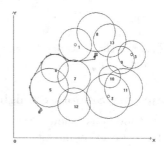

Fig. 4. The third result

Fig. 5. The fourth result

5   Conclusion

This paper presents an improved heuristic algorithm which is an improved version of SAS algorithm for UCAV path planning. Compared with reference [9], our algorithm considers not only traditional constraints of path planning but also various flight constrained conditions, such as angle information, track smooth straighten processing and so on. The simulation results show that angle information and trajectory smooth straighten processing are advisable, effective and feasible. And the running efficiency is much better. Besides, Some simulations have shown that our proposed new model and algorithm can meet the flight restrictions and task demands of UCAV path planning.

Acknowledgments. This research was financially supported by National Natural Science Foundation of China (No. 61401363), the Science and Technology on Avionics Integration Laboratory and Aeronautical Science Foundation (20155153034), the Fundamental Research Funds for the Central Universities (3102016AXXX005, 3102015BJJGZ009).

References

1. Wen, Y.E.: Application of improved particle swarm optimization algorithm in UCAV path planning. Comput. Eng. **34**, 178–180 (2008)
2. Huang, G.R., Zhang, J., Liu, H.: Route planning for unmanned aerial vehicles based on adaptive mutation particle swarm optimization. Electron. Opt. Control **16**, 19–37 (2009)
3. Feng, Q.Y., Dan, J., Liu, B.: A multi-pipe path planning by modified ant colony optimization. Comput. Aided Draft. Des. Manuf. **21**, 2–5 (2011)
4. Qu, Y., Liu, Y.C., Yi, P.: A genetic algorithm based approach to pipe routing design. Comput. Chem. Eng. **20**, 9–13 (2010)
5. Liu, J.F., Li, G., Geng, H.T.: A new heuristic algorithm for the circular packing problem with equilibrium constraints. Sci. China Inf. Sci. **54**, 1572–1584 (2011)
6. Yu, Z., Jing, C., Lin, C.S.: Hybrid hierarchical trajectory planning for a fixed-wing UCAV performing air-to-surface multi-target attack. J. Syst. Eng. Electron. **23**, 536–552 (2012)
7. Wang, G., Guo, L., Duan, H., Wang, H.: A hybrid meta-heuristic DE/CS algorithm for UCAV path planning. J. Inf. Comput. Sci. **9**, 4811–4818 (2012)
8. Yuan, J., Yang, F., Zhang, G.Y., Liang, Y.: A navigation method and its simulation for UAV formation flight. Comput. Simul. **28**, 64–67 (2011)
9. Chen, S., Liu, C.W., Huang, Z.P., Cai, G.S.: Global path planning for AUV based on sparse A* search algorithm. Torpedo Technol. **20**, 271–275 (2012)
10. Wang, G., Guo, L., Duan, H., Wang, H.: Path planning for uninhabited combat aerial vehicle using hybrid meta-heuristic DE/BBO algorithm. Adv. Sci. **4**, 550–564 (2012)
11. Wang, Z.C., Wang, J., Jin, X.: Reach on multi-path routing based on genetic algorithm. Comput. Eng. **37**, 197–199 (2011)
12. Zhang, Y., Wu, L., Wang, S.: UCAV path planning by fitness-scaling adaptive chaotic particle swarm optimization. Math. Probl. Eng. **2013**, 147–170 (2013)

An Efficient Benchmark Generator for Dynamic Optimization Problems

Changhe Li[(✉)]

Hubei Key Laboratory of Intelligent Geo-Information Processing,
China University of Geosciences, Wuhan 430074, China
changhe.lw@gmail.com

Abstract. A number of benchmark generators have been proposed for dynamic single objective optimization problems. The moving peaks benchmark and the GDBG benchmark are widely used to test the performance of an evolutionary algorithm. The two benchmarks construct a fitness landscape with a number of peaks that can change heights, widths, and locations. The two benchmarks are simple and easy to understand. However, they exist two major issues: (1) the time complexity is high for evaluating a solution and (2) peaks may become invisible when changes occur. To address the two issues, this paper proposes an efficient generator with enriched features. The generator applies the k-d tree to partition the search space and sets a simple unimodal function in each sub-space. The properties of the proposed benchmark are discussed and verified by a set of evolutionary algorithms.

Keywords: Dynamic optimization problem · Generator

1 Introduction

In recent years, there has been a growing interest in developing evolutionary algorithms in dynamic environments. To comprehensively evaluate the performance of an evolutionary algorithm (EA), an important task is to develop a good benchmark generator. Over the years, a number of benchmark generators for dynamic optimization problems (DOPs) have been proposed. Generally speaking, these benchmark generators can be classified to the following three classes in terms of the way to construct problems. Note that, this paper focuses on only dynamic continuous unconstrained single objective optimization problems.

The first class of generators switch the environment between several stationary problems or several states of a problem. Early generators normally belong to this class. A generator based on two static landscapes A and B was proposed in [7]. Changes can occur in three ways: (1) linear translation of peaks in landscape A; (2) only the global optimum randomly moves in landscape A; (3) switching landscapes between A and B. In [15], the environment oscillates among a set of fixed landscapes.

Like the first class of generators, the second class of generators also consist of a number of basic functions. However, the environment normally takes the form

© Springer Nature Singapore Pte Ltd. 2016
M. Gong et al. (Eds.): BIC-TA 2016, Part II, CCIS 682, pp. 60–72, 2016.
DOI: 10.1007/978-981-10-3614-9_8

$f(\mathbf{x}) = max\{g_i(\mathbf{x})\}, i = 1, \ldots, N$ to construct the fitness landscape and it does not switch among the basic functions. The environmental changes are caused by the changes of every $g(\mathbf{x})$. Many generators fall into this class. The moving peaks benchmark (MPB) [15] is one of the widely used generators. The MPB consist of a number of peaks. Each peak is constructed by a simple unimodal function which can change in height, width, and location. The DF1 generator [15] and the rotation dynamic benchmark generator (RDBG) [10] use a similar way to construct the fitness landscape. The DF1 generator uses the logistic function to change the height, width and location of a peak, while the RDBG rotates the fitness landscape to generate changes. A new generator based on the framework of the DF1 was proposed in [20], where the basic function used to construct a peak in DF1 was replaced by two traditional functions in [20]. A fitness landscape consists of a number Gaussain peaks was introduced in [8] where a peak changes in its center, amplitude, and width. A challenging dynamic landscape was proposed in [10], called composition dynamic benchmark generator (CDBG), where a set of composition functions are shifted in the fitness landscape. The CDBG introduces several change types, e.g., small step changes, large step changes, random changes, chaotic changes, recurrent changes and noisy environments.

The third class of generators divide the search space into subspaces and set simple unimodal functions in each subspace. A disjoint generator was proposed in [21], where each dimension of the search space is evenly divided into w segments. The total number of subspaces is w^D (D denotes the number of dimensions). In each subspace, a peak function is defined where its global optimum is at the center of the subspace.

The first and the third classes of generators lack of the ability of manipulating a single peak. In the literature of EAs for DOPs, the second class of generators are mostly used for experimental studies. This class of generators are flexible and easy to manipulate the characteristics of a change for every peak. However, it has two disadvantages. Firstly, to evaluation a solution $\mathbf{x}$, we need to compute the objective value of $\mathbf{x}$ for each basic function ($g(\mathbf{x})$) in $O(D)$ and then find out the maximum value as the fitness value of $\mathbf{x}$. Therefore, the time complexity of evaluating a solution is at least $O(ND)$. Secondly, a peak may become invisible when a change occurs, and hence the total number of peaks will be less than the predefined value.

Besides the way of the construction of the fitness landscape, researchers have also been interested in developing characteristics of changes to simulate real-world applications, such as the predictability–whether changes are predictable in a regular pattern, time-linkage–whether future changes depend on the current/previous solutions found by optimizers [4,17], detectability–whether changes are detectable, severity– determines the magnitude of a change, and change factors (objective functions, the number of dimensions, constraints, domain of the search space, and function parameters).

A good benchmark generator should have the following characteristics [16]: (1) Flexibility, the generator should be configurable regarding different aspects, e.g., the number of peaks, change severity, and change features, etc.; (2) Simplicity and efficiency, the generator should be simple to implement, analyze, and computationally efficient; (3) The generator should be able to resemble real-world problems to some extent. Most real-world problems are very hard and complex, with nonlinearities and discontinuities [14].

Based on the above considerations, this paper aims to propose a novel generator, which is able to (1) address the two issues mentioned above of the current mainly used generators and (2) provide enriched characteristics of changes. To achieve the aims, this paper uses the idea of space partition and chooses a peak function for every sub-space from a predefined function set. A new benchmark generator, called Free Peaks (FPs), is proposed. The k-d tree [1] is used to partition the solution space. Each peak in a sub-space can be freely manipulated regarding its height, peak location, shape, and basin of attraction. A set of characteristics of changes are also introduced in this paper.

The rest of this paper is organized as follows. Section 2 introduce the construction of the FPs in detail, including the partition process of the k-d tree, a set of basic peak functions, and the setup of subspaces. Section 3 gives the construction of different types of changes. Section 4 presents the results of the experimental studies. Finally, conclusions are given in Sect. 5.

2   Free Peaks

The section introduces the basic elements of the free peaks (FPs) benchmark generator. Without loss of generality, maximization optimization problems are assumed in this paper. Before the introduction of the generator, we need to prepare a set of simple shape functions.

2.1   One Peak Function

In this paper, eight simple symmetrical unimodal functions are defined as follows:

$$s_1(\mathbf{x}) = h - d(\mathbf{x}), \tag{1a}$$

$$s_2(\mathbf{x}) = h \cdot \exp(-d(\mathbf{x})), \tag{1b}$$

$$s_3(\mathbf{x}) = h - \sqrt{h \cdot d(\mathbf{x})}, \tag{1c}$$

$$s_4(\mathbf{x}) = h/(1 + d(\mathbf{x})), \tag{1d}$$

$$s_5(\mathbf{x}) = h - d^2(\mathbf{x})/h, \tag{1e}$$

$$s_6(\mathbf{x}) = h - \exp\left(2\sqrt{d(\mathbf{x})/\sqrt{D}}\right) + 1, \tag{1f}$$

$$s_7(\mathbf{x}) = \begin{cases} h * \cos(\pi \cdot d(\mathbf{x})/r) & d(\mathbf{x}) \le r \\ -h - d(\mathbf{x}) + r & d(\mathbf{x}) > r \end{cases}, \tag{1g}$$

$$s_8(\mathbf{x}) = \begin{cases} \frac{h*(\cos(m\pi \cdot d(\mathbf{x})(1-1/r)) - \eta m d(\mathbf{x})/r)}{\sqrt{d(\mathbf{x})+1}} & d(\mathbf{x}) \le r \\ -h(\eta(m-1)+1)/\sqrt{r+1} & d(\mathbf{x}) > r \end{cases} \tag{1h}$$

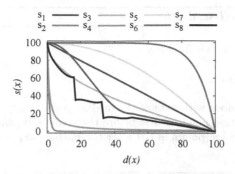

Fig. 1. Shapes of the eight functions with $D = 1$, where $h = 100, r = 50, \eta = 5.5$, and $m = 3$ (objective values of all functions are standardized within $[0, 100]$.

where $d(\mathbf{x}) = \sqrt{\sum_i^D (x_i - X_i)^2}$ is the *Euclidean* distance from $\mathbf{x}$ to the peak, which is located at a user-defined location $\mathbf{X}^{s_v}$ with a height of $h > 0$ ($v = 1, \ldots, 8$), r is a parameter of value in $[0, \sqrt{\sum_i^D (u_i^{s_v} - l_i^{s_v})^2}]$ ($u_i^{s_v} = 100, l_i^{s_v} = -100$), and m and η determine the number of segments and the gap between two neighbor segments of s_8, respectively. The default values of $\mathbf{X}^{s_v}=0$, $h = 100, r = 50, m = 3$ and $\eta = 5.5$ are used in this paper.

Figure 1 shows the shapes of the eight functions. Among these functions, s_1 is a linear function, s_2-s_4 are convex functions, s_5 and s_6 are concave functions, s_7 is partially convex, partially concave, and partially linear and s_8 is a disconnected function. Each function has a single peak located at X and is monotonic from the peak.

2.2 Partition the Search Space

The k-d tree [1] is a binary tree where each node is a k-dimensional point. Every non-leaf node can be thought of as implicitly generating a splitting hyperplane that divides the space into two parts. Points to the left of this hyperplane are represented by the left subtree of that node and points to the right of the hyperplane are represented by the right subtree. Every leaf node denotes a sub-space

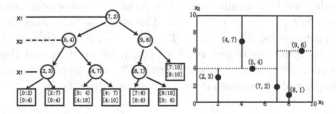

Fig. 2. An example of the k-d tree for the division of a 2-D space with ranges ($[0:10]$, $[0:10]$) by a set of six points.

Algorithm 1. kdtree(*list, depth*)

1: axis ← *depth%D*;
2: Select the median by axis from *list*
3: **if** ‖*list*‖=1 **then**   ▷ A leaf node
4:      Create a sub-space;
5: **else**
6:      Create a node *node* with data of the median point;
7:      *node*.left ← kdtree(points in *list* before the median, *depth*+1);
8:      *node*.right← kdtree(points in *list* after the median, *depth*+1);
9:      **return** *node*;
10: **end if**

Algorithm 2. inquire(**x**, *node,depth*)

1: i ← *depth%D*;
2: **if** *node* is a leaf node **then** return the sub-space; **end if**
3: **if** $x_i < node_i$ **then**
4:      inquire(**x**, *node.left,depth*+1);
5: **else**
6:      inquire(**x**, *node.right,depth*+1);
7: **end if**

---

of the solution space. Fig. 2 shows a k-d tree (Fig. 2-left) for the decomposition of a 2-D solution space (Fig. 2-right) with six points.

To construct a balanced tree, the canonical method [1] is used, where a median point is selected with the cutting axis. Algorithms 1 and 2 present the space partition process and the inquiry of a sub-space, respectively. In this paper, the solution space is divided by default into N subspaces with random sizes

2.3   Setup of the Sub-space

A function $f(x)$ constructed based on the FPs can be defined by

$$f(\mathbf{x}) = \begin{cases} f^{b_1}(\mathbf{x}), \mathbf{x} \in [\mathbf{l}^{b_1}, \mathbf{u}^{b_1}] \\ f^{b_2}(\mathbf{x}), \mathbf{x} \in [\mathbf{l}^{b_2}, \mathbf{u}^{b_2}] \\ \dots\dots\dots\dots\dots \\ f^{b_N}(\mathbf{x}), \mathbf{x} \in [\mathbf{l}^{b_N}, \mathbf{u}^{b_N}] \end{cases} \tag{2}$$

where each subspace b_k contains a basic function f^{b_k} associated with a shape function $s_v(k = 1, 2, \dots N, v = 1, 2, \dots, 8)$. The whole search space of $f([\mathbf{l}, \mathbf{u}])$ is divided into N subspaces: $[\mathbf{l}^{b_1}, \mathbf{u}^{b_1}], \dots, [\mathbf{l}^{b_N}, \mathbf{u}^{b_N}]$, i.e., $[\mathbf{l}, \mathbf{u}] = \{[\mathbf{l}^{b_k}, \mathbf{u}^{b_k}], \dots\}, k = 1, 2, \dots N$. To compute the objective of $\mathbf{x}$ ($f(\mathbf{x})$), we need to find the subspace b_k where $\mathbf{x}$ is (i.e., $\mathbf{l}^{b_k} \leq \mathbf{x} < \mathbf{u}^{b_k}$) by Algorithm 2, then map $\mathbf{x}$ to a solution $\mathbf{x}^{s_v}$ in the search space of s_v associated with f^{b_k} in subspace b_k by

$$map(x_i) = x_i^{s_v} = l_i^{s_v} + (u_i^{s_v} - l_i^{s_v})\frac{x_i - l_i^{b_k}}{u_i^{b_k} - l_i^{b_k}}, i = 1, 2, \dots D, \tag{3}$$

where the mapping is linear from a solution in the subspace b_k of $\mathbf{f}([\mathbf{l}^{b_k}, \mathbf{u}^{b_k}])$ to a solution in the search space of s_v ($[\mathbf{l}^{s_v}, \mathbf{u}^{s_v}]$). Eventually, we set the objective $f(\mathbf{x})$ by

$$f(\mathbf{x}) = f^{b_k}(\mathbf{x}) = s_v(\mathbf{x}^{s_v}). \tag{4}$$

2.4 Time Complexity

According to the above description of the FPs, to evaluate a solution $\mathbf{x}$ we need to perform the following three steps of procedures: (1) find out the sub-space (b_k) where $\mathbf{x}$ is; (2) map $\mathbf{x}$ to a location ($\mathbf{x}^{s_v}$) in the search space of f^{b_k}; (3) compute the objective of ($\mathbf{x}^{s_v}$) by one of the eight shape functions. Identifying a solution in which sub-space has a time complexity of $O(log(N))$ by Algorithm 2. Both the second and the third steps run in $O(D)$. Therefore, the total time complexity of evaluating a solution in the FPs is $O(log(N)) + 2O(D)$.

3 Constructing Dynamic Optimization Problems

This section introduces two types of changes: physical changes and non-physical changes. Physical changes are changes, which can be observed, including changes in peak location, peak shape, peak height, the size of the basin of attraction, and the number of peaks. Non-physical changes are characteristics of physical changes, including detectability, predictability, time-linkage, and noise. The physical changes are listed as follows.

3.1 The Change in a Peak's Location Within the Peak's Basin

To change a peak's location ($\mathbf{X}^{b_k}(t)$) within its basin b_k at time t, we change its mapping location $\mathbf{X}^{s_v}(t)$ (see Eq. (3)) in the search space of the associated component function s_v by

$$\mathbf{X}^{s_v}(t+1) = (\mathbf{X}^{s_v}(t) - \mathbf{X}^{s_v}(t-1))\lambda + \nu(1-\lambda)\mathrm{N}(0, \sigma^{s_v}), \tag{5}$$

where ν is a normalized vector with a random direction; $\mathrm{N}(0, \sigma^{s_v})$ returns a random number of the normal distribution with mean 0 and variance σ^{s_v} (the shift severity with a default value of (1); $\lambda \in [0, 1]$ is a parameter to determine the correlation between the direction of the current movement and the previous movement. $\lambda = 1$ indicates the direction of a peak's movement is predictable, and $\lambda = 0$ indicates the movement of a peak is completely in a random direction. The ith dimension of $\mathbf{X}^{s_v}(t)$ will be re-mapped to a valid location if it moves out of the range of the component function as follows:

$$X_i^{s_v} = \begin{cases} l_i^{s_v} + (u_i^{s_v} - l_i^{s_v})\frac{(l_i^{s_v} - X_i^{s_v})}{(u_i^{s_v} - X_i^{s_v})} & X_i^{s_v} < l_i^{s_v}, \\ l_i^{s_v} + \frac{(u_i^{s_v} - l_i^{s_v})^2}{(X_i^{s_v} - l_i^{s_v})} & X_i^{s_v} > u_i^{s_v} \end{cases} \tag{6}$$

3.2   The Change in the Size of a Peak's Basin of Attraction

To vary the size of the basin of attraction of a peak, we just need to change the value of the cutting hyper-plane constructed with the dimension c of a division point $\mathbf{dp}$ (point $\mathbf{dp}$ should be a parent node of a leaf node in the kd-tree, e.g., node (2,3) in Fig. 2) as follows.

$$dp_c = dp_c + \mathrm{R}(-\sigma_c, \sigma_c)(b^u_{k+1,c} - b^l_{k,c}), \tag{7}$$

where $\sigma_c = 0.01$ is the severity, $b^l_{k,c}$ and $b^u_{k+1,c}$ are the upper boundary and lower boundary of two neighbour subspaces b_k and b_{k+1}, respectively, which are generated by cutting the cth dimension of the hyper-rectangle for the generation of sub-spaces b_k and b_{k+1}; Note that, two neighbour subspaces will change if we change the value of a cutting dimension.

3.3   The Change in a Peak's Height

The height of a peak at time t is changed as follows:

$$H_i(t+1) = \begin{cases} H_i(t) - \delta_{h_i} & H_i(t+1) < H_{min} || H_i(t+1) > H_{max}, \\ H_i(t) + \delta_{h_i} & Otherwise, \end{cases} \tag{8}$$

where $\delta_{h_i} = \mathrm{N}(0, \sigma_{h_i})$, σ_{h_i} is the height severity of peak p_i, σ_{h_i} is set to a random value in $[0,7]$; H_{min} and H_{max} are the minimum and maximum heights, which are set to 0 and 100, respectively, in this paper.

3.4   The Change in the Number of Peaks

The number of peaks follows a recurrent change as follows:

$$N(t+1) = \begin{cases} \sigma_N(N(0) + t)\%T + N_{min} & (N(0) + t)\%T = 0, \\ \sigma_N(T - (N(0) + t)\%T) + N_{min} & Otherwise, \end{cases} \tag{9}$$

where $N(t)$ is the number of peaks at time t ($N(0)$ is the initial number of peaks); $\sigma_N = 2$ is a change step; $T = 25$ is the time period; $N_{min} = 1$ is the minimum number of peaks. If the number of peaks increases, σ_N random division points are added to the division set; Otherwise, σ_N points are randomly removed from the division set.

In addition to the predictable change in a peak's location and the recurrent change in the number of peaks, three other non-physical features are introduced: a time-linkage change, a partial change, and noisy environments. In the time-linkage change, a peak changes only when it is found by an optimizer. For the partial change, a part of peaks change when an environmental change occurs. In the noisy environment, noise is added to a solution when it is to be evaluated by

$$x_i = x_i + \sigma_{noi} BR_{b_k} \mathrm{N}(0, 1), \tag{10}$$

where $i = 1, \ldots, D$, $b_k = inquire(\mathbf{x})$, $\sigma_{noi} = 0.01$ is the noise severity; BR_{b_k} is the basin ratio of the subspace b_k where $\mathbf{x}$ is located.

Table 2 summarizes the feature comparison between FPs and other four popular benchmarks. From the table, the FPs provides many more features than the other four benchmarks.

Table 1. Default settings for the FPs, where u means that the problem changes every u objective evaluations, a peak is found if the distances in objective space and decision space are less than ϵ_o and ϵ_s, respectively.

Parameter	Value	Parameter	Value
Number of peaks (N)	10	Number of dimensions (D)	5
Change frequency (u)	5000	Correlation coefficient (λ)	0
Basin change	No	Ratio of changing peaks (r_c)	1.0
Time-linkage change	No	Noisy environments	No
Height severity(σ_h)	[0,7]	Basin severity (σ_c)	0.01
Height range	(0,100]	Domain range	[−100, 100]
Initial peak shape	Random	Initial peak height	100
Initial peak location	Sub-space center	Number of steps (σ_N)	2
Shift severity (σ^{sv})	1.0	Noise severity (σ_{noi})	0.01
Objective threshold (ϵ_o)	0.01	Distance threshold (ϵ_s)	0.1

Table 2. Feature comparison with peer benchmarks

Physical change/ Non-physical change	MPB [5]	DF1 [15]	RDBG [10]	CDBG [10]	FPs
Peak location	✓	✓	✓	✓	✓
Peak height	✓	✓	✓	✓	✓
Peak width	✓	✓	✓	✓	✓
Movement within the basin	×	×	×	×	✓
Manageable basin size	×	×	×	×	✓
Number of peaks	×	×	✓	×	✓
Recurrent	×	×	✓	✓	✓
Partial	×	×	✓	×	✓
Time-linkage	×	×	×	×	✓
Noise	×	×	✓	×	✓
Predictable	✓	×	×	×	✓

4 Experimental Studies

In this section, two groups of experiments are carried out. The first group of experiments aim to investigate the performance of the FPs and the second group of experiments aim to compare the performance of a set of existing EAs on the FPs.

4.1 Comparison of Computing Efficiency

In this subsection, an experiment is carried out to compare the performance of the FPs with two peer benchmark generators (the MPB [5] and the rotation DBG [10]) in terms of two different aspects. The first comparison is the computational efficiency. Figure 3 shows the time cost on evaluating one million random points for the three benchmarks in different scenarios. The left graph of Fig. 3 shows the comparison on problems with different numbers of peaks with 100 dimensions and the right graph shows the comparison on problems with different numbers of dimensions with 1,000 peaks. From the results, it can be seen that the time spent with the FPs is significantly smaller than the other two benchmarks. In both cases, the time spent with the FPs is almost constant as the number of dimensions/peaks increases in comparison with the time spent with the other two benchmarks.

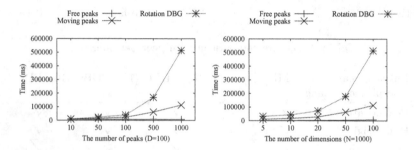

Fig. 3. Time cost of three benchmarks for evaluating one million random points in different scenarios.

The second comparison is the number of invisible peaks. Table 3 shows the average number of invisible peaks for the three benchmarks over 1,000 changes. From the results, the issue of the rotation DBG is more serious than the MPB in all test cases. Moreover, the number of invisible peaks will increase as the number of peaks increases for the MPB and the rotation DBG. This is because, in the two peer benchmarks a peak can be hidden by a higher peak with a broader basin of attraction. This issue does not exist in the FPs as each peak takes a different subspace.

4.2 The Performance of Existing Algorithms

In this subsection, 11 peer algorithms are selected. They are mQSO [3], SAMO [2], SPSO [18], AMSO [12], CPSO [22], CPSOR [11], FTMPSO [24], DynDE [13], DynPopDE [19], mNAFSA [23], and AMP/PSO [9]. For parameters of all the peer algorithms, default values suggested in their proposals are used. Note that, the parameter settings for these algorithms may be not the optimal values. The stopping criterion is 100 changes. All the results are averaged over

Table 3. The number of invisible peaks of three benchmarks with $D = 5$

Problem	The number of peaks (N)				
	10	50	100	500	1000
Free peaks	0	0	0	0	0
Moving peaks [15]	0	0.04	0.124	4.77	18.85
Rotation DBG [10]	0.12	4.12	10.23	90.22	217.24

30 independent runs of an algorithm on each problem. The offline error (E_O) [6] and the best-before-change error (E_{BBC}) are used. The offline error used in this paper is the average of the best error found every two objective evaluations and the best-before-change error is the average of the best error achieved at the fitness evaluation just before a change occurs.

A two-tailed t-test with $58°$ of freedom at a 0.05 level of significance was conducted for each pair of algorithms on E_O and E_{BBC}. The t-test results are given with the letters "w", "l", or "t", which denote that the performance of an algorithm is significantly better than, significantly worse than, or statistically equivalent to its peer algorithms, respectively.

Tables 4, 5 and 6 show the comparison between the chosen algorithms on the FPs with different numbers of peaks, different changing ratios, and the time-linkage feature, respectively. From the results, it can be seen that different features have very different impacts on the performance of a particular algorithm. For example, the partial change feature cause difficulties for algorithms

Table 4. Performance comparison on the FPs with different number of peaks, where the default settings in Table 1 are used.

N		AMP/PSO	SAMO	DynPopDE	SPSO	mQSO	CPSOR	CPSO	FTMPSO	DynDE	AMSO	mNAFSA
10	E_O	**2.62±0.1**	3.11±0.081	7.75±1.7	13.2±3.5	2.7±0.075	4.14±0.25	7.53±0.3	3.97±0.13	3.23±0.049	3.36±0.7	10.2±0.97
	w,t,l	10,0,0	7,1,2	2,1,7	0,0,10	9,0,1	4,0,6	2,1,7	5,0,5	6,1,3	6,2,2	1,0,9
	E_{BBC}	**0.426±0.12**	1.64±0.12	6.25±1.4	12.2±3.7	1.22±0.11	2.39±0.25	6.26±0.28	2.96±0.088	2.22±0.079	1.95±0.91	7.48±0.87
	w,t,l	10,0,0	7,1,2	2,1,7	0,0,10	9,0,1	5,0,5	2,1,7	4,0,6	6,1,3	6,2,2	1,0,9
20	E_O	**3.04±0.16**	3.16±0.11	6.93±1.8	11.8±2.2	3.56±0.81	4.46±0.75	7.37±0.35	3.96±0.082	3.44±0.6	3.88±0.79	9.1±0.82
	w,t,l	10,0,0	9,0,1	2,1,7	0,0,10	6,2,2	4,0,6	2,1,7	5,1,4	7,1,2	5,2,3	1,0,9
	E_{BBC}	**1.2±0.19**	2.08±0.13	5.64±1.6	11.3±2.4	2.2±0.75	2.85±0.71	6.3±0.36	3.08±0.06	2.59±0.55	2.8±0.92	6.99±0.8
	w,t,l	10,0,0	8,1,1	3,0,7	0,0,10	8,1,1	4,3,3	2,0,8	4,2,4	5,2,3	4,3,3	1,0,9
30	E_O	**2.08±0.065**	2.24±0.08	5.36±1.3	9.9±2.3	3.23±0.77	3.65±0.68	5.23±0.2	2.69±0.084	3.73±0.88	2.57±0.5	8±0.65
	w,t,l	10,0,0	9,0,1	2,1,7	0,0,10	6,0,4	4,1,5	2,1,7	7,1,2	4,1,5	7,1,2	1,0,9
	E_{BBC}	**1.17±0.069**	1.65±0.077	4.24±1.2	9.24±2.7	2.28±0.69	2.51±0.66	4.36±0.21	2.03±0.053	3.08±0.84	1.92±0.51	5.83±0.51
	w,t,l	10,0,0	9,0,1	2,1,7	0,0,10	5,2,3	5,1,4	2,1,7	6,2,2	4,0,6	7,1,2	1,0,9
50	E_O	**2.73±0.15**	2.8±0.11	4.7±1.2	9.91±1.7	4.16±0.9	4.86±1.2	5.84±0.24	3.42±0.2	5.72±1.3	3.12±0.4	6.49±0.37
	w,t,l	9,1,0	9,1,0	4,2,4	0,0,10	5,1,4	4,1,5	2,1,7	7,0,3	2,1,7	8,0,2	1,0,9
	E_{BBC}	**1.7±0.13**	2.1±0.1	3.83±0.97	9.64±1.8	3±0.77	3.52±1.1	4.99±0.23	2.67±0.16	4.88±1.2	2.33±0.39	4.82±0.3
	w,t,l	10,0,0	9,0,1	4,1,5	0,0,10	6,0,4	4,1,5	1,1,8	7,0,3	1,2,7	8,0,2	2,1,7
100	E_O	**2.5±0.16**	3±0.25	4.87±1.3	12.5±1.8	9.59±2.2	5.99±1.8	6.14±0.17	4.17±0.5	9.89±2.7	2.96±0.36	7.33±0.67
	w,t,l	10,0,0	8,1,1	6,0,4	0,0,10	1,1,8	4,1,5	4,1,5	7,0,3	1,1,8	8,1,1	3,0,7
	E_{BBC}	**1.66±0.16**	2.26±0.24	3.97±1.1	12.3±1.8	8.41±2.2	4.73±1.7	5.26±0.17	2.79±0.34	9.2±2.6	2.18±0.31	5.51±0.59
	w,t,l	10,0,0	8,1,1	6,0,4	0,0,10	1,1,8	4,1,5	4,1,5	7,0,3	1,1,8	8,1,1	3,0,7
200	E_O	**1.94±0.16**	2.21±0.22	3.92±2.8	10.3±1.8	8.3±2.2	7.12±1.9	4.56±0.19	3.2±0.3	8.63±2	2.39±0.45	5.9±0.53
	w,t,l	10,0,0	8,1,1	5,2,3	0,0,10	1,1,8	3,0,7	5,1,4	6,1,3	1,1,8	8,1,1	4,0,6
	E_{BBC}	**1.32±0.14**	1.6±0.21	3.14±2.5	10.2±1.8	7±2.1	5.82±1.8	3.87±0.2	2.06±0.22	7.9±2	1.83±0.4	4.21±0.51
	w,t,l	10,0,0	9,0,1	5,1,4	0,0,10	1,1,8	3,0,7	5,1,4	7,0,3	1,1,8	8,0,2	4,0,6
	w-l	119	87	-23	-120	6	-15	-43	31	-29	60	-73

Table 5. Performance comparison on the FPs with different ratios of the number of changing peaks, where the default settings in Table 1 are used.

r_c		AMP/PSO	SAMO	DynPopDE	SPSO	mQSO	CPSOR	CPSO	FTMPSO	DynDE	AMSO	mNAFSA
0.1	E_O	1.52±0.15	0.496±0.087	11.7±2.5	16.5±5.8	**0.398±0.3**	2.12±0.25	28.9±5	1.22±0.12	0.872±0.047	1.97±3.8	5.9±1.7
	w,t,l	5,1,4	9,1,0	2,0,8	1,0,9	9,1,0	4,1,5	0,0,10	6,1,3	7,1,2	4,4,2	3,0,7
	E_{BBC}	**0.00983±0.022**	0.161±0.094	9.84±2.1	16.4±5.8	0.163±0.3	1.11±0.25	28.7±5.1	0.872±0.12	0.479±0.051	1.5±3.9	4.99±1.6
	w,t,l	10,0,0	7,2,1	2,0,8	1,0,9	7,2,1	4,1,5	0,0,10	5,1,4	6,1,3	4,5,1	3,0,7
0.3	E_O	1.68±0.13	1.25±0.097	10.9±1.5	11.8±5.1	**0.99±0.048**	2.86±0.18	21.7±1.9	2.58±0.16	1.83±0.044	2.19±0.77	6.65±1.1
	w,t,l	8,0,2	9,0,1	1,1,8	1,1,8	10,0,0	4,0,6	0,0,10	5,0,5	7,0,3	6,0,4	3,0,7
	E_{BBC}	**0.126±0.077**	0.622±0.12	9.05±1.3	11.5±5.1	0.448±0.054	1.79±0.19	21.2±1.9	1.96±0.12	1.24±0.054	1.46±0.85	5.39±1.1
	w,t,l	10,0,0	8,0,2	2,0,8	1,0,9	9,0,1	5,0,5	0,0,10	4,0,6	6,1,3	6,1,3	3,0,7
0.5	E_O	2.23±0.24	1.86±0.16	7.9±0.85	9.24±1.6	**1.57±0.094**	3.48±0.27	15.5±1.3	3.59±0.077	2.61±0.054	3.13±0.93	8.71±0.86
	w,t,l	8,0,2	9,0,1	3,0,7	1,1,8	10,0,0	5,1,4	0,0,10	4,0,6	7,0,3	5,1,4	1,1,8
	E_{BBC}	**0.482±0.2**	1.09±0.19	6.32±0.81	8.5±1.7	0.786±0.1	2.39±0.29	14.8±1.3	2.83±0.076	1.97±0.068	2.3±0.99	6.93±0.79
	w,t,l	10,0,0	8,0,2	3,0,7	1,0,9	9,0,1	5,1,4	0,0,10	4,0,6	6,1,3	5,2,3	2,0,8
0.7	E_O	2.12±0.083	2.41±0.13	8.89±1.3	12.1±1.9	**1.96±0.15**	3.59±0.17	11.5±0.7	3.79±0.08	2.73±0.059	2.91±0.74	8.68±0.96
	w,t,l	9,0,1	8,0,2	2,1,7	0,1,9	10,0,0	5,0,5	0,1,9	4,0,6	6,1,3	6,1,3	2,1,7
	E_{BBC}	**0.287±0.1**	1.3±0.15	7.34±1.4	11±2	0.918±0.15	2.26±0.19	10.5±0.75	2.75±0.097	1.94±0.065	1.82±0.78	6.74±0.87
	w,t,l	10,0,0	8,0,2	2,0,8	0,1,9	9,0,1	5,0,5	0,1,9	4,0,6	6,1,3	6,1,3	3,0,7
0.9	E_O	2.57±0.11	2.73±0.11	7.82±2.1	13.8±2.4	**2.31±0.079**	3.64±0.19	9.24±0.65	3.84±0.15	2.98±0.053	3.54±1.4	11.1±1.1
	w,t,l	9,0,1	8,0,2	3,0,7	0,0,10	10,0,0	5,1,4	2,0,8	4,1,5	7,0,3	4,2,4	1,0,9
	E_{BBC}	**0.465±0.11**	1.55±0.12	6.46±1.9	13.4±2.5	1.09±0.11	2.21±0.22	8.13±0.67	2.79±0.063	2.17±0.078	2.42±1.4	8.63±0.99
	w,t,l	10,0,0	8,0,2	3,0,7	0,0,10	9,0,1	5,2,3	2,0,8	4,1,5	5,2,3	4,3,3	1,0,9
1	E_O	**2.62±0.1**	3.11±0.081	7.75±1.7	13.2±3.5	2.7±0.075	4.14±0.25	7.53±0.3	3.97±0.13	3.23±0.049	3.36±0.7	10.2±0.97
	w,t,l	10,0,0	7,1,2	2,1,7	0,0,10	9,0,1	4,0,6	2,1,7	5,0,5	6,1,3	6,2,2	1,0,9
	E_{BBC}	**0.426±0.12**	1.64±0.12	6.25±1.4	12.2±3.7	1.22±0.11	2.39±0.25	6.26±0.28	2.96±0.088	2.22±0.079	1.95±0.91	7.48±0.87
	w,t,l	10,0,0	7,1,2	2,1,7	0,0,10	9,0,1	5,0,5	2,1,7	4,0,6	6,1,3	6,2,2	1,0,9
w-l		99	77	-62	-104	103	-1	-100	-10	40	28	-70

Table 6. Performance comparison on the FPs with the time-linkage on different numbers of peaks, where the default settings in Table 1 are used except the time-linkage feature.

N		AMP/PSO	SAMO	DynPopDE	SPSO	mQSO	CPSOR	CPSO	FTMPSO	DynDE	AMSO	mNAFSA
10	E_O	**2.17±0.41**	8.38±5.8	18.2±9.9	4.16±3.4	2.9±0.73	4.65±1.4	26.6±14	4.81±0.86	3.22±0.57	4.21±2.2	2.77±3.6
	w,t,l	9,1,0	1,0,9	3,5,2	7,2,1	3,3,4		0,0,10	3,3,4	6,3,1	3,4,3	5,5,0
	E_{BBC}	**0.246±0.23**	6.38±5.7	17±9.9	3.73±3.3	1.35±0.62	2.93±1.3	26.5±14	3.7±0.71	2.27±0.39	2.73±2.3	1.93±3.7
	w,t,l	10,0,0	2,0,8	1,0,9	3,4,3	8,1,1	4,3,3	0,0,10	3,1,6	6,2,2	4,4,2	4,5,1
20	E_O	**3.01±1.3**	6.89±4.3	28.4±19	3.1±4.1	11±3.6	5.52±3.1	42.7±17	10.1±2.9	9.23±3.5	5.25±2.7	4.48±1.3
	w,t,l	9,1,0	5,2,3	1,0,9	8,2,0	2,2,6	5,3,2	0,0,10	2,2,6	2,2,6	5,3,2	6,3,1
	E_{BBC}	**1.24±1.3**	5.69±4.1	26.5±9.7	2.89±3.9	9.64±3.6	4.01±3	42.7±17	9.16±2.8	8.55±3.4	4.06±2.6	3.25±1.3
	w,t,l	10,0,0	5,2,3	1,0,9	6,3,1	2,2,6	5,4,1	0,0,10	2,2,6	2,2,6	5,4,1	6,3,1
30	E_O	**1.74±0.45**	4.68±2.3	13.3±11	5.45±3	3.32±2.2	3.95±2	6.6±7	4.1±2	2.14±1.4	3.68±1.8	6.07±3.8
	w,t,l	9,1,0	1,6,3	0,0,10	1,3,6	5,3,2	3,5,2	1,5,4	3,5,2	9,1,0	4,4,2	1,3,6
	E_{BBC}	**0.514±0.32**	3.84±2.2	11.7±10	5.12±2.7	2.38±2.1	2.91±1.9	6.59±7	3.64±1.9	1.75±1.4	2.86±1.6	5.56±3.6
	w,t,l	10,0,0	4,3,3	0,0,10	1,2,7	6,3,1	4,4,2	1,2,7	4,3,3	8,1,1	4,4,2	1,2,7
50	E_O	**2.39±0.74**	3.59±1.4	13.8±7	6.28±4	4.34±1.6	3.94±1.3	25.4±22	5.02±1.2	3.16±1	3.55±1.3	6.8±2.4
	w,t,l	10,0,0	5,4,1	1,0,9	2,2,6	4,3,3	5,3,2	0,0,10	3,2,5	7,2,1	6,3,1	2,1,7
	E_{BBC}	**1.06±0.71**	3.06±1.3	11.6±6.1	6.12±3.8	3.47±1.6	2.88±1.2	25.4±22	4.67±1.2	2.72±0.97	2.87±1.3	6.22±2.5
	w,t,l	10,0,0	5,4,1	1,0,9	2,2,6	5,3,2	5,4,1	0,0,10	3,1,6	6,3,1	5,4,1	2,1,7
100	E_O	**2.27±0.77**	2.38±0.99	13.8±3.2	7.02±2.8	5.61±2.3	3.53±1.3	17.3±14	5.55±1.7	6.21±3	3.5±1.6	6.28±2.3
	w,t,l	9,1,0	9,1,0	0,1,9	2,2,6	3,3,4	7,1,2	0,1,9	3,3,4	2,4,4	7,1,2	2,4,4
	E_{BBC}	**0.948±0.81**	1.87±0.95	11.2±2.8	6.9±2.7	4.85±2.2	2.64±1.3	17.3±14	5.35±1.7	5.84±3	2.84±1.6	5.56±2.3
	w,t,l	10,0,0	9,0,1	1,0,9	2,1,7	3,3,4	7,1,2	0,0,10	3,3,4	2,4,4	7,1,2	3,3,4
200	E_O	3.29±0.91	**2.81±0.82**	9.29±1.9	4.39±2.3	7.55±1.7	6.78±1.8	24.4±19	6.14±1.2	6.78±1.6	3.38±1.1	2.98±1.1
	w,t,l	7,2,1	9,1,0	1,0,9	6,0,4	2,2,6	2,3,5	0,0,10	3,2,5	2,3,5	7,2,1	7,3,0
	E_{BBC}	2.44±1	**2.37±0.79**	6.18±1.5	4.27±2.3	6.86±1.7	6.03±1.7	24.4±19	6.01±1.2	6.42±1.6	2.84±1.1	2.4±1.1
	w,t,l	7,3,0	7,3,0	1,4,5	6,0,4	1,3,6	1,4,5	0,0,10	2,3,5	1,4,5	7,3,0	7,3,0
w-l		109	32	-97	-10	6	20	-108	-22	17	45	8

(e.g., CPSO) that need the detection of changes. In this case, changes are hard to be detected as only a part of the fitness landscape is allowed to change. The detection will fail by monitoring the changes of the fitness of a set of solutions if these solutions are in unchange areas. As a result, mechanisms for handling changes will be not triggered. Therefore, the performance of this type of algorithm is poor in this case. The time-linkage feature is hard for most algorithms, where their performance gets worse when this feature is enabled. For all the algorithms, AMP/PSO, which was recently proposed, performs best in terms of both performance metrics in most test cases Table 5.

5 Conclusions

This paper proposes a efficient benchmark generator, named free peaks, for constructing dynamic optimization problems. The framework is simple, feature enriched, and computing efficient. The properties and difficulties are analytical without the assistance of the visualization of the fitness landscape. The approach uses the building-blocks approach to construct a problem, therefore users can construct a problem with desired features. Users can replace the component functions used in this paper with their own functions. To test an algorithm's performance on a problem with a certain feature, users just need to switch on or off that particular feature instead of switching to another problem with a quite different structure.

Acknowledgments. This work was supported by the National Natural Science Foundation of China under Grant 61673355.

References

1. Bentley, J.L.: Multidimensional binary search trees used for associative searching. Commun. ACM **18**(9), 509–517 (1975)
2. Blackwell, T.: Particle swarm optimization in dynamic environments. In: Yang, S., Ong, Y.-S., Jin, Y. (eds.) Evol. Comput. Dynamic Uncertain Environ. Studies in Computational Intelligence, vol. 51, pp. 29–49. Spinger, Heidelberg (2007). doi:10.1007/978-3-540-49774-5_2
3. Blackwell, T., Branke, J.: Multiswarms, exclusion, and anti-convergence in dynamic environments. IEEE Trans. Evol. Comput. **10**(4), 459–472 (2006)
4. Bosman, P.A.N.: Learning, anticipation and time-deception in evolutionary online dynamic optimization. In: Proceedings of 2005 Genetic and Evolutionary Computation Conference, pp. 39–47. ACM (2005)
5. Branke, J.: Memory enhanced evolutionary algorithms for changing optimization problems. In: Proceedings of 1999 IEEE Congress on Evolationary Computation, vol. 3, pp. 1875–1882 (1999)
6. Song, T., Liu, X., Zhao, Y., Zhang, X.: Spiking neural P systems with white hole neurons. IEEE Trans. Nanobiosci. (2016). doi:10.1109/TNB.2016.2598879
7. Cobb, H.G., Grefenstette, J.J.: Genetic algorithms for tracking changing environments. In: 5th International Conference on Genetic Algorithms, pp. 523–530 (1993)
8. Grefenstette, J.J.: Evolvability in dynamic fitness landscapes: a genetic algorithm approach. In: Proceedings of 1999 IEEE Congress on Evolutionary Computation, vol. 3, p. 2038 (1999)
9. Li, C., Nguyen, T.T., Yang, M., Mavrovouniotis, M., Yang, S.: An adaptive multi-population framework for locating and tracking multiple optima. IEEE Trans. Evol. Comput. **99**, 1 (2015)

10. Li, C., Yang, S.: A generalized approach to construct benchmark problems for dynamic optimization. In: 7th International Conference on Simulated Evolution and Learning, pp. 391–400 (2008)
11. Li, C., Yang, S.: A general framework of multipopulation methods with clustering in undetectable dynamic environments. IEEE Trans. Evol. Comput. **16**(4), 556–577 (2012)
12. Li, C., Yang, S., Yang, M.: An adaptive multi-swarm optimizer for dynamic optimization problems. Evol. Comput. **22**(4), 559–594 (2014)
13. Mendes, R., Mohais, A.S.: DynDE: a differential evolution for dynamic optimization problems. In: Proceedings of 2005 IEEE Congress on Evolationary Computation, pp. 2808–2815 (2005)
14. Michalewicz, Z.: The emperor is naked: evolutionary algorithms for real-world applications. ACM Ubiquity **2012**, 1–13 (2012)
15. Morrison, R.W., De Jon, K.A.: A test problem generator for non-stationary environments. In: Proceedings of 1999 IEEE Congress on Evolationary Computation, pp. 2047–2053 (1999)
16. Nguyen, T.T., Yang, S., Branke, J.: Evolutionary dynamic optimization: a survey of the state of the art. Swarm Evol. Comput. **6**, 1–24 (2012)
17. Nguyen, T.T., Yao, X.: Dynamic time-linkage problems revisited. In: Giacobini, M., et al. (eds.) EvoWorkshops 2009. LNCS, vol. 5484, pp. 735–744. Springer, Heidelberg (2009). doi:10.1007/978-3-642-01129-0_83
18. Parrott, D., Li, X.: Locating and tracking multiple dynamic optima by a particle swarm model using speciation. IEEE Trans. Evol. Comput. **10**(4), 440–458 (2006)
19. du Plessis, M.C., Engelbrecht, A.P.: Differential evolution for dynamic environments with unknown numbers of optima. J. Glob. Optim. **55**, 1–27 (2012)
20. Tfaili, W., Siarry, P.: Fitting of an ant colony approach to dynamic optimization through a new set of test functions. Int. J. Comput. Intell. Res. **3**, 203–216 (2007)
21. Trojanowski, K., Michalewicz, Z.: Searching for optima in non-stationary environments. In: Proceedings of 1999 IEEE Congress on Evolutionary Computation, vol. 3, p. 1850 (1999)
22. Song, T., Pan, Z., Dennis, M.W., Wang, X.: Design of logic gates using spiking neural P systems with homogeneous neurons and astrocytes-like control. Inf. Sci. **372**, 380–391 (2016)
23. Yazdani, D., Nasiri, B., Sepas-Moghaddam, A., Meybodi, M., Akbarzadeh-Totonchi, M.: mNAFSA: a novel approach for optimization in dynamic environments with global changes. Swarm Evol. Comput. **18**, 38–53 (2014)
24. Yazdani, D., Nasiri, B., Sepas-Moghaddam, A., Meybodi, M.R.: A novel multi-swarm algorithm for optimization in dynamic environments based on particle swarm optimization. Appl. Soft Comput. **13**(4), 2144–2158 (2013)

Ensemble of Different Parameter Adaptation Techniques in Differential Evolution

Liang Wang and Wenyin Gong[✉]

School of Computer Science, China University of Geosciences, Wuhan 430074,
People's Republic of China
wygong@cug.edu.cn

Abstract. Differential evolution has been proved to be one of the most powerful evolutionary algorithms for the numerical optimization. However, the performance of differential evolution is significantly influenced by its parameter settings. To remedy this limitation, different parameter adaptation techniques are proposed in the literature. Generally, different parameter adaptation techniques have different rationales and may be suitable to different problems. Based on this consideration, in this paper, we attempt to develop the ensemble of different parameter adaptation techniques to enhance the performance of differential evolution. In our proposed method, different parameter adaptation techniques are combined together to adjust the parameters of different solutions in the population. As an illustration, two parameter adaptation techniques proposed in the literature are used in our proposed method. To verify the performance of our proposal, the functions proposed in CEC 2005 are chosen as the test suite. Experimental results indicate that, on the whole, our proposed method is able to provide better results than the single parameter adaptation based differential evolution variants with respect to the non-parametric statistical tests.

1 Introduction

In the field of evolutionary computation, different evolutionary algorithms (EAs) have been developed over the last few decades, such as genetic algorithms, evolution strategies, evolutionary programming, genetic programming [1]. As one of most powerful EAs, differential evolution (DE), proposed by Storn and Price, is very simple and highly efficient for the numerical optimization problems [2]. The main advantages of DE are its simple structure, ease of use, fast convergence speed, etc. Due to these merits, DE has obtained successful applications in diverse fields [3].

In DE, there are three parameters, *i.e.*, population size (μ), crossover rate (Cr), and scaling factor (F), which need to be set properly by the user. However, for a problem at hand, the parameter settings of DE are difficult. More importantly, the performance of DE is significantly influenced by different parameter settings [4]. In EAs, the parameter adaptive control technique is a possible way to remedy the fine-tuning task of parameters [5,6]. Therefore, in the DE literature, different parameter adaptation techniques are developed to enhance its

© Springer Nature Singapore Pte Ltd. 2016
M. Gong et al. (Eds.): BIC-TA 2016, Part II, CCIS 682, pp. 73–79, 2016.
DOI: 10.1007/978-981-10-3614-9_9

performance, such as jDE [7], SaDE [8], JADE [9], SHADE [10]. Based on the classification of the parameter control techniques in [5], jDE is a self-adaptive control method, while SaDE, JADE, and SHADE belong to the adaptive control methods.

Generally, different parameter control techniques have different features and may be suitable to different problems. In order to solve a wider range of problems, in this paper, the ensemble of different parameter adaptation techniques is proposed, where different parameter control techniques are combined together to adaptively adjust the parameters of different solutions in the population for the problem at hand. As an illustration, two parameter adaptation techniques proposed in jDE [7] and SHADE [10] are used in our proposed framework. The reasons to select the two techniques are two-fold: (i) these two techniques are two different types of parameter control techniques as classified in [5]; and (ii) both of them obtained very promising performance among different DE variants [7,10]. The proposed method is referred to as EADE, *i.e.*, Ensemble of Adaptive DE. To investigate the performance of our proposed EADE, the benchmark functions presented in CEC 2005 are chosen as the test suite [11]. EADE is compared with jDE and SHADE. Experimental results indicate that EADE yields on the whole better results than jDE and SHADE based on the non-parametric statistical test.

2   Our Approach: EADE

In this section, we first present the framework of ensemble of different parameter adaptation techniques. Then, the EADE algorithm is proposed as an illustration, where the parameter adaptation techniques presented in jDE [7] and SHADE [10] are combined together.

2.1   The Framework

Suppose that we have n parameter adaptation techniques (PATs), then, the population $\mathcal{P}$ with μ solutions will be divided into n sub-populations, $\mathcal{P}_1, \cdots, \mathcal{P}_n$, satisfying $\mathcal{P}_1 \cup \cdots \cup \mathcal{P}_n = \mathcal{P}$ and $\mathcal{P}_1 \cap \cdots \cap \mathcal{P}_n = \phi$. Note that the number of solutions in each sub-population may be different, and the mutation strategy can also be different in each sub-population. The framework is plotted in Fig. 1.

Figure 1 indicates that each sub-population has its own PAT to adaptively adjust the parameters of Cr and F for each solution. Although each sub-population has its own PAT, they do not evolve independently: when generating the offspring, the parents (such as $\mathbf{x}_{r1}, \mathbf{x}_{r2}$, and $\mathbf{x}_{r3}$ in "DE/rand/1/bin") in the mutation are chosen from the whole parent population $\mathcal{P}$ as originally used in DE. The main advantage is that it can promote the information sharing for each sub-population. After the offspring population $\mathcal{O}$ is generated, the selection process is performed as originally used in DE. Note that, in the selection process,

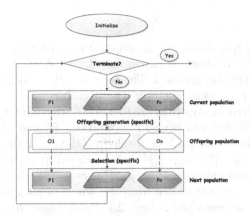

Fig. 1. Framework of ensemble of different parameter adaptation techniques in DE.

the successful parameters need to be saved like JADE [9] and SHADE [10]. In this work, for each PAT the storage of successful parameters is independent, *i.e.*, the successful parameters of each PAT are not influenced mutually.

From above analysis, we can see that the proposed framework still maintains the simple structure of DE. The framework is flexible, different PATs and different mutation strategies can be combined together.

Algorithm 1. The pseudo-code of EADE

1: Generate the initial population
2: Evaluate the fitness for each individual
3: **while** the halting criterion is not satisfied **do**
4:     Divide the population into two sub-populations $\mathcal{P}_1$ and $\mathcal{P}_2$
5:     **for** $i = 1$ to $|\mathcal{P}_1|$ **do**
6:         Adaptively update the parameters Cr_i and F_i for each solution using the PAT proposed in jDE [7]
7:         Generate the trial vector $\mathbf{u}_i$ using "DE/rand/1/bin" strategy as originally used in jDE [7]
8:     **end for**
9:     **for** $i = |\mathcal{P}_1| + 1$ to μ **do**
10:         Adaptively update the parameters Cr_i and F_i for each solution using the PAT proposed in SHADE [10]
11:         Generate the trial vector $\mathbf{u}_i$ using "DE/current-to-$p$best/1/bin" strategy as originally used in SHADE [10]
12:     **end for**
13:     **for** $i = 1$ to $|\mathcal{P}_1|$ **do**
14:         Evaluate the offspring $\mathbf{u}_i$
15:         **if** $f(\mathbf{u}_i)$ is better than **or** equal to $f(\mathbf{x}_i)$ **then**
16:             Replace $\mathbf{x}_i$ with $\mathbf{u}_i$
17:         **end if**
18:     **end for**
19:     **for** $i = |\mathcal{P}_1| + 1$ to μ **do**
20:         Evaluate the offspring $\mathbf{u}_i$
21:         **if** $f(\mathbf{u}_i)$ is better than **or** equal to $f(\mathbf{x}_i)$ **then**
22:             Replace $\mathbf{x}_i$ with $\mathbf{u}_i$
23:             Store the successful parameters for SHADE
24:         **end if**
25:     **end for**
26:     Update the parameters as used in SHADE [10]
27: **end while**

2.2 EADE

Based on the above framework, as an illustration, the ensemble adaptive DE (referred to as EADE, in short) is implemented. In EADE, two PATs proposed in jDE [7] and SHADE [10] are used. The reason is that both jDE and SHADE have obtained very promising results in the literature [7,10,12][1]. The pseudo-code of EADE is given in Algorithm 1. In EADE, the parent population $\mathcal{P}$ at each generation is divided into two sub-populations $\mathcal{P}_1$ and $\mathcal{P}_2$. The number of solutions in each sub-population is controlled by the population ratio $\delta \in (0,1)$, i.e., $|\mathcal{P}_1| = \lfloor \delta \times \mu \rfloor$, and $|\mathcal{P}_2| = \mu - |\mathcal{P}_1|$. In each sub-population, the solutions use their own PAT and mutation strategy. However, the selection of parents to generate the trial vectors are chosen from the whole population to promote the information sharing as mentioned in Sect. 2.1. From Algorithm 1, we can observe that EADE is very similar to jDE and SHADE, however, in EADE both PATs proposed in jDE and SHADE are used. In this way, it can borrow the two merits in both jDE and SHADE as verified in the following experimental results.

3 Experimental Results and Analysis

3.1 Benchmark Functions

To verify the performance of our proposed EADE, 25 benchmark functions presented in CEC 2005 are chosen as the test suite [11]. These functions have been widely used in the literature [10,13,14]. They can be classified into four categories, i.e., unimodal functions (F1–F5), basic multimodal functions (F6–F12), expanded multimodal functions (F13–F14), and hybrid composition multimodal functions (F15–F25). In this work, $D = 30$ is used for all functions.

3.2 Parameter Settings

For all experiments, we use the following parameters for EADE unless a change is mentioned.

– Dimension of each function: $D = 30$;
– Population size: $\mu = 100$;
– Population ratio: $\delta = 0.1$;
– For all functions: $Max\_NFEs = D \times 10,000$.

Note that all other parameters involved in the parameter adaptation techniques in jDE and SHADE are kept the same as originally used in jDE [7] and SHADE [10].

Moreover, in our experiments, each function is optimized over 25 independent runs as suggested in [11]. To avoid any initialization bias, we also use the same set of initial random populations to evaluate different algorithms.

---

[1] Due to the tight space limitation, jDE and SHADE are not described in this paper. More details can be found in the corresponding references in [7,10], respectively.

3.3   Compared with jDE and SHADE

In this subsection, EADE is compared with jDE and SHADE, because EADE adopts the parameter adaptation techniques proposed in these two algorithms. To make a fair comparison, the parameter settings of jDE and SHADE are set to be the same as used in [7,10], respectively.

Table 1. Comparison on the errors among EADE, jDE, and SHADE in all functions. All results are averaged over 25 runs. In the last row, the average rankings of different algorithms are obtained by the Friedman test according to the mean values of all functions.

Prob.	EADE		jDE		SHADE	
	Mean	Std	Mean	Std	Mean	Std
F1	0.00E+00	0.00E+00	0.00E+00	0.00E+00	0.00E+00	0.00E+00
F2	9.62E-29	9.74E-29	1.26E-05	1.65E-05	**8.46E-29**	8.39E-29
F3	8.46E+03	5.66E+03	1.91E+05	9.38E+04	**7.47E+03**	5.38E+03
F4	**1.07E-15**	2.41E-15	3.97E-01	7.10E-01	1.04E-14	3.70E-14
F5	1.28E-05	3.84E-05	1.03E+03	4.01E+02	**4.38E-07**	1.67E-06
F6	**1.01E-26**	2.02E-26	2.71E+01	2.69E+01	1.59E-01	7.81E-01
F7	**8.37E-03**	6.57E-03	1.31E-02	1.03E-02	1.02E-02	7.70E-03
F8	**2.08E+01**	1.94E-01	2.09E+01	5.36E-02	**2.08E+01**	1.44E-01
F9	0.00E+00	0.00E+00	0.00E+00	0.00E+00	0.00E+00	0.00E+00
F10	2.17E+01	4.17E+00	5.89E+01	1.02E+01	**2.09E+01**	4.62E+00
F11	**2.61E+01**	1.95E+00	2.80E+01	1.48E+00	2.64E+01	1.67E+00
F12	**1.11E+03**	1.60E+03	1.11E+04	8.55E+03	2.36E+03	3.50E+03
F13	**1.16E+00**	8.18E-02	1.66E+00	1.50E-01	**1.16E+00**	1.00E-01
F14	1.25E+01	2.72E-01	1.30E+01	1.55E-01	**1.24E+01**	2.92E-01
F15	3.28E+02	8.26E+01	**3.27E+02**	1.15E+02	3.44E+02	7.53E+01
F16	**6.81E+01**	7.34E+01	7.60E+01	8.41E+00	8.36E+01	9.82E+01
F17	**9.26E+01**	7.01E+01	1.33E+02	1.36E+01	1.28E+02	1.09E+02
F18	**9.04E+02**	9.97E-01	9.07E+02	1.83E+00	9.05E+02	1.29E+00
F19	**9.04E+02**	1.04E+00	9.07E+02	1.77E+00	9.05E+02	1.17E+00
F20	9.05E+02	1.40E+00	9.06E+02	1.89E+00	**9.05E+02**	1.15E+00
F21	5.00E+02	1.14E-13	5.00E+02	1.14E-13	5.00E+02	1.14E-13
F22	**8.63E+02**	1.78E+01	9.08E+02	6.11E+00	8.68E+02	1.80E+01
F23	5.50E+02	7.89E+01	**5.34E+02**	9.80E-05	**5.34E+02**	1.55E-04
F24	2.00E+02	5.91E-13	2.00E+02	0.00E+00	2.00E+02	0.00E+00
F25	**2.09E+02**	1.31E-01	2.10E+02	3.65E-01	**2.09E+02**	1.06E-01
Ranking	**1.56**		2.66		1.78	

The detailed results are reported in Table 1, where the best results are high-lighted in **boldface**. In the last row of Table 1, the average rankings of different algorithms are obtained by the Friedman test[2] according to the mean values of all functions. It can be seen that in 14 out of 25 functions EADE is able to get the best mean values. SHADE obtains the best mean values in 10 functions, whereas jDE only provides the best mean values in 2 functions. By carefully looking at the results in Table 1, we observe that SHADE provides better results in unimodal functions, while EADE gets better results in multimodal functions. The reason might be that in EADE the parameter adaptation technique in jDE is combined with "DE/rand/1/bin" strategy, which is less greedy; in this way, EADE enhances the performance in multimodal functions. In addition, according to the averaging rankings by the Friedman test, EADE obtains the best ranking, followed by SHADE and jDE. The p-value computed by Iman and Daveport test is $4.88E - 05$, which indicates that the results of EADE, jDE, and SHADE are significantly different.

Based on the above results and analysis, we can conclude that ensemble of different parameter adaptation techniques might be useful to enhance the performance of DE variants with single parameter adaptation technique. Ensemble of different parameter adaptation techniques can borrow each of the advantages of different parameter adaptation techniques, and hence, makes the algorithm solve a wider range of problems.

4   Conclusions and Future Work

DE is a simple yet powerful EA when solving the numerical optimization problems. Parameter adaptation is an efficient way to improve the performance of DE. In this paper, we do not propose new parameter adaptation techniques, but present the ensemble of different parameter adaptation techniques. In our approach, different parameter adaptation techniques presented in the literature are cooperated together to evolve the population. As an example, we implement the EADE algorithm, where two parameter adaptation techniques presented in jDE [7] and SHADE [10] are used. Experimental results verified our expectation that EADE improves the performance of jDE and SHADE.

References

1. Bäck, T., Hammel, U., Schwefel, H.P.: Evolutionary computation: comments on the history and current state. IEEE Trans. Evol. Comput. **1**(1), 3–17 (1997)
2. Storn, R., Price, K.: Differential evolution-a simple and efficient heuristic for global optimization over continuous spaces. J. Global Optim. **11**(4), 341–359 (1997)
3. Das, S., Suganthan, P.N.: Differential evolution: a survey of the state-of-the-art. IEEE Trans. Evol. Comput. **15**(1), 4–31 (2011)

---

[2] Note that, in this work, the non-parametric statistical tests are calculated by the KEEL software [15], which is available online at http://www.keel.es/.

4. Gämperle, R., Müler, S., Koumoutsakos, P.: A parameter study for differential evolution. In: Proceedings of the WSEAS International Conference Advances in Intelligent Systems, Fuzzy Systems, Evolutionary Computation, pp. 293–298 (2002)
5. Eiben, Á.E., Hinterding, R., Michalewicz, Z.: Parameter control in evolutionary algorithms. IEEE Trans. Evol. Comput. **3**(2), 124–141 (1999)
6. Karafotias, G., Hoogendoorn, M., Eiben, A.E.: Parameter control in evolutionary algorithms: trends and challenges. IEEE Trans. Evol. Comput. **19**(2), 167–187 (2015)
7. Brest, J., Greiner, S., Bošković, B., Mernik, M., Žumer, V.: Self-adapting control parameters in differential evolution: a comparative study on numerical benchmark problems. IEEE Trans. Evol. Comput. **10**(6), 646–657 (2006)
8. Qin, A.K., Huang, V.L., Suganthan, P.N.: Differential evolution algorithm with strategy adaptation for global numerical optimization. IEEE Trans. Evol. Comput. **13**(2), 398–417 (2009)
9. Zhang, J., Sanderson, A.C.: JADE: adaptive differential evolution with optional external archive. IEEE Trans. Evol. Comput. **13**(5), 945–958 (2009)
10. Tanabe, R., Fukunaga, A.: Success-history based parameter adaptation for differential evolution. In: 2013 IEEE Congress on Evolutionary Computation (CEC), pp. 71–78 (2013)
11. Suganthan, P.N., Hansen, N., Liang, J.J., Deb, K., Chen, Y.P., Auger, A., Tiwari, S.: Problem definitions and evaluation criteria for the CEC_2005 special session on real-parameter optimization (2005)
12. Brest, J., Zumer, V., Maucec, M.: Self-adaptive differential evolution algorithm in constrained real-parameter optimization. In: IEEE Congress on Evolutionary Computation, pp. 215–222 (2006)
13. Wang, Y., Cai, Z., Zhang, Q.: Differential evolution with composite trial vector generation strategies and control parameters. IEEE Trans. Evol. Comput. **15**(1), 55–66 (2011)
14. Gong, W., Cai, Z.: Differential evolution with ranking-based mutation operators. IEEE Trans. Cybern. **43**(6), 2066–2081 (2013)
15. Alcalá-Fdez, J., Sánchez, L., García, S.: KEEL: a software tool to assess evolutionary algorithms to data mining problems. Soft Comput. **13**, 307–318 (2015)

Research on Multimodal Optimization Algorithm for the Contamination Source Identification of City Water Distribution Networks

Xuesong Yan, Jing Zhao, and Chengyu Hu[✉]

School of Computer Science, China University of Geosciences,
Wuhan 430074, Hubei, China
huchengyu@cug.edu.cn

Abstract. In recent years, drinking water contamination happens from time to time and causes severe damage to social stability and safety. Setting the sensor in the town water distribution networks can dramatically decrease the occurrence of contamination events by real-time monitoring on water quality. However, how to make a reverse localization on contamination source by the detection information of water quality sensor is a challenging issue. The difficulty is that the limited sensor amounts, large-scale nodes in town distribution networks and changing water demands from users lead to the uncertainty of the optimal problem. In this paper, we mainly study the uncertainty issue of the Contamination Source Identification(CSI) problem. In the previous studies, simulation-optimization model has been utilized for the conversion from CSI problem to the unimodal function optimization problem in many documents. But it is a multimodal function optimization problem in essence and the number of its solution has non-uniqueness. This paper uses dynamic niching genetic algorithm and can calculate multiple contamination sources through one operation, which provides the possibility for screening the true contamination source. Furthermore, this paper has a try and verifies the validity after the threshold formulation as well as the effectiveness of algorithm.

Keywords: Contamination source determination · Niching methods · Genetic algorithm · Multimodal function optimization

1 Introduction

In recent years, China's water faces contamination emergency frequently. It makes great economic losses and bad social influence for our country and vicious attacks to water distribution networks. To prevent major disasters and losses from water contamination events, it is necessary to configure real-time monitoring system on drinking water safety in the town water distribution networks. In this system, it can achieve real-time monitoring by configuring water quality

© Springer Nature Singapore Pte Ltd. 2016
M. Gong et al. (Eds.): BIC-TA 2016, Part II, CCIS 682, pp. 80–85, 2016.
DOI: 10.1007/978-981-10-3614-9_10

sensors in the key nodes or water sources. However, when the contamination event happens, challenge remains in predicting information, such as contaminant location, injection time, injection duration and injection quality and so on by the collected information from water quality sensor.

Many scholars tried to transform CSI problem to optimization problem by using simulation-optimization model, then optimized and got the optimal solution by utilizing evolutionary algorithms [1–3]. The model is better in the aspect of solving accuracy and robustness, but most of current studies ignore the uniqueness of solution about CSI problem. From the qualitative perspective [4], the amounts of water quality sensor is limited, while water distribution networks nodes with huge scale are potential contaminant sources. In addition, mixing and timeliness of contamination source injection are considered. Therefore, the amount of contamination source tends to be no less than one.

This paper firstly discusses the essential characteristics of CSI problem and builds a model for it; then uses niching genetic algorithm to solve the CSI problem. Divide niching by thresholds after the formulation, search for multimodal and verify the effectiveness of proposed algorithm by simulation.

2   Contamination Source Identification Problem Model

The simulation-optimization model transforms CSI problem to optimization problem and then optimizes solution by evolutionary computation. From the view of optimization, when the minimum variance between cumulative simulated concentration and actual cumulative detectable concentration of contamination event in the sensor is 0 or less than one certain threshold value, so it is considered that the injecting node of this contamination event is the real contamination source. On the basis of previous studies [5], this paper formulizes the threshold value, and describes the contamination source optimization problem as follows:

$$\min_{M,n,t_I} \quad f = \sum_{j=1}^{N_s} \sum_{t=1}^{T_s} (c_j(t) - c_j^*(t))^2 \tag{1}$$

$$\text{S.T.} \quad M = m_1, m_2, \ldots, m_k, \qquad\qquad m_i \geq 0$$
$$n \in \{1, N\}$$
$$t_I \leq T_s$$

$$\varepsilon = \sqrt{\sum_{j=1}^{N_s} \sum_{t=1}^{T_s} (c_j^*(t))^2}. \tag{2}$$

Where, N is node sum of pipe network. N_s represents the number of sensors, and T_s is simulated cycle. M is vector of contaminant injection, n is pipe network node serial number of contamination source injection. t_I is the starting time of injecting contaminant. $c_j(t)$ represents the contaminant concentration of sensor j in time t. And it is the function of (M, n, t_I). Furthermore, $c_j^*(t)$ is the contaminant concentration of sensor j for actual detection in time t. The threshold value is shown in the formula 2. The objective of optimization is that the variance is the minimum by solving.

3 Solving Contamination Source Identification Problem Based on Niching Genetic Algorithm

Multimodal function optimization problem is generally solved by the evolutionary computation method, and common evolution techniques include niching technique [6], differential evolution technique [7] and optimization technique based on species evolution [8]. This paper mainly adopts sharing mechanism of niching fitness value, adjusts fitness value of each individual in groups by sharing function, and maintains the population diversity. The algorithm framework is shown in Fig. 1.

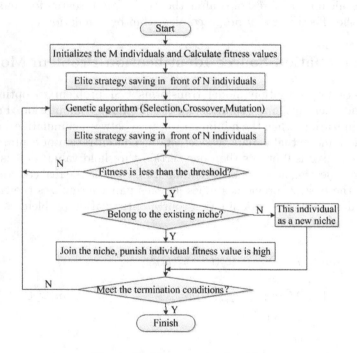

Fig. 1. Niching genetic algorithm

In the population, each individual represents one contamination event, and individual includes four variables (Location, injection time, Duration and injection mass). The former three variables are integer variables which use integer coding, while the fourth variable is a real vector which uses real coding. In this paper, it can be divided into one niching for the individuals with same location but different mass, injection time and duration. Therefore, each niching can output one optimal solution to satisfy fitness threshold value and make punishment for fitness values which are not the optimal solution in the niching.

4   Experimental Simulation and Analysis

4.1   Parameters Setting of Water Distribution Networks and Algorithm

One is standard testing network [9] which includes 129 nodes, 2 reservoirs, 2 pools, 170 pipelines, 2 water pumps and 8 valves. Assuming that two water quality sensors of testing network are put into the nodes 10 and 83 respectively, the real contamination source is located in the node 44, as shown in Fig. 2. Starting time of injection is 1:00. Duration is 2 h. Time step of pattern is 30 min, and contaminant injection qualities are $\{100\,mg/L, 60\,mg/L, 80\,mg/L, 60\,mg/L\}$. Then, Crossover probability is 0.95. Mutation probability is 0.7. Retaining the former 10 individual by elitist strategy. Population size is 100. Punishment coefficient is 1.5.

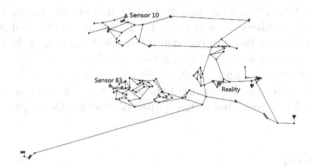

Fig. 2. The sensor and real contamination source locations in testing network

4.2   Experiment: Result Analysis

In this paper, assuming that the actual contamination source is single. Before the formulation of threshold value, the threshold value has been set depending on empirical value through the experiment. But there are different corresponding threshold values with different contamination events. Therefore, in order to make algorithm have adaptivity, the threshold values should be normalized.

To verify the rationality of threshold value formulation and the solving feasibility by algorithm, this section sets the threshold value as 5 in accordance with empirical value to make experiment, and the calculated threshold value is 4.5 according to formula (2).

Through the above niching genetic algorithm, it can be found out 11 solutions whose fitness values are less than 5. Then its solutions are injected as contamination events, and the detected contaminant concentration figure by corresponding

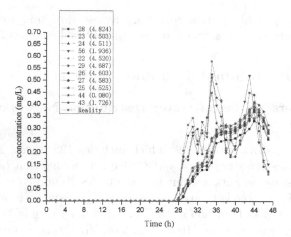

Fig. 3. Experimental results of testing network when the threshold value is 5

sensor 83 is shown in Fig. 3 (the brackets behind the labels of location are fitness values). In this figure, there are mainly two trends about curves. One kind of curve whose fitness values are less than 4.5 is similar to the real result, while there has vast difference between real detection information and the curve trends whose fitness values are greater than 4.5 but less than 5.

By means of experimental result figures of testing network, it illustrates that the designed formula to calculate threshold value is reasonable and niching genetic algorithm presented in this paper is effective for solving multimodal problem.

5   Conclusion

Contamination source determination problem is an interdisciplinary problem in the fields of environmental sciences and computing science. This paper uses simulation-optimization model for the conversion from contamination source determination problem to the unimodal function optimization problem, and quantitatively illustrates that the contamination source determination problem is a multimodal function optimization problem in essence. To solve this problem, this paper adopts dynamic niching genetic algorithm that multiple optimal solutions can be found in one operation. Through simulation experiments, the rationality and feasibility of formulaic threshold value have been studied. And the algorithm has been applied to network in order to verify the effectiveness of algorithm.

In the study of contamination source determination problem, when town network nodes exceeds 1000 and water demands of users make real-time changes, this problem can be abstracted as a dynamic, large-scale and multimodal function optimization problem. Therefore, the methods to solve dynamic multimodal large-scale optimization problem need to be further proposed and are the subsequent research work of this paper.

Acknowledgments. This research was supported in part by the NSF of China (Grant No. 61402425, 61272470, 61305087, 61440060, 41404076 and 61673354), the Provincial Natural Science Foundation of Hubei(No.2015CFA065)the Foundation of Hubei Key Laboratory of Intelligent Geo-Information Processing (China University of Geosciences (Wuhan)).

References

1. Guan, J., Aral, M.M., Maslia, M.L., Grayman, W.M.: Identification of contaminant sources in water distribution systems using simulation-optimization method: case study. J. Water Resour. Plann. Manag. **132**(4), 252–262 (2006)
2. Liu, L., Ranjithan, S.R., Mahinthakumar, G.: Contamination source identification in water distribution systems using an adaptive dynamic optimization procedure. J. Water Resour. Plann. Manag. **137**, 183–192 (2010)
3. Yan, X., Zhao, J., Hu, C., et al.: Contaminant source identification in water distribution network based on hybrid encoding. J. Comput. Methods Sci. Eng. **16**(2), 379–390 (2016)
4. Hu, C.: A Map Reduce based Parallel Niche Genetic Algorithm for contaminant source identification in water distribution network. Ad Hoc Netw. **35**, 116–126 (2015)
5. Zechman, E.M., Ranjithan, S.R.: Evolutionary computation-based methods for characterizing contaminant sources in a water distribution system. J. Water Resour. Plann. Manag. **135**(5), 334–343 (2009)
6. Qu, B.Y., Liang, J.J., Suganthan, P.N.: Niching particle swarm optimization with local search for multi-modal optimization. Inf. Sci. **197**, 131–143 (2012)
7. Das, S., Suganthan, P.N.: Differential evolution: a survey of the state-of-the-art. IEEE Trans. Evol. Comput. **15**(1), 4–31 (2008)
8. Parrott, D., Li, X.: Locating and tracking multiple dynamic optima by a particle swarm model using speciation. IEEE Trans. Evol. Comput. **10**(4), 440–458 (2006)
9. Ostfeld, A.: The battle of the water sensor networks (BWSN): a design challenge for engineers and algorithms. J. Water Resour. Plann. Manag. **134**(6), 556–568 (2008)

Visual Tracking by Sequential Cellular Quantum-Behaved Particle Swarm Optimization Algorithm

Junyi Hu, Wei Fang$^{(\boxtimes)}$, and Wangtong Ding

School of IoT Engineering, Jiangnan University, Wuxi, Jiangsu, China
fangwei@jiangnan.edu.cn

Abstract. Visual tracking is a very important application in the field of computer vision. The tracking process can be formulated as a dynamic optimization problem, which can be solved by particle swarm optimization (PSO) algorithms. PSO algorithm with particle filter (PF) has been actively used in visual tracking. In this paper, we propose an improved resampling cellular quantum-behaved PSO (RScQPSO) algorithm, which is a probabilistic variant of PSO, and combine the PF to solve the tracking problem. The cQPSO algorithm can better keep the population diversity and balance the global and local search than PSO algorithm. For better tracking performance, we further improve the tracking algorithm by improving the particle initialization approach in cQPSO, resampling technique in PF as well as using the Gaussian mixture model in fitness assessment. Experimental results demonstrate that the proposed tracking algorithm is more effective and accurate, especially for the cases that the object has an arbitrary motion or undergoes large appearance changes, than the compared algorithms.

Keywords: Visual tracking · Quantum-behaved particle swarm optimization · Particle filter

1   Introduction

Visual tracking has been a core issue in many applications, such as monitor, visual-based control, human-machine interface, intelligent transportation and augmented reality, etc. Robust target tracking algorithm needs to undergo a more stringent test of complex conditions (such as sudden movement, fast-moving, shape variation, and occlusion, etc.). Particle Filter (PF) [1,2] is an effective target tracking technology. Compared with traditional filtering method, PF has unique advantages in dealing with the parameter estimation and filtering problem of non-Gaussian and nonlinear time-varying system. In PF, when the importance weight variance increasing over the time, the weight only concentrates on a small number of particles so that the particle collector cannot express the true posterior probability distribution, which is termed as the 'degradation of particles'. Resampling method [3] can inhibit the degradation of particles, but it

© Springer Nature Singapore Pte Ltd. 2016
M. Gong et al. (Eds.): BIC-TA 2016, Part II, CCIS 682, pp. 86–94, 2016.
DOI: 10.1007/978-981-10-3614-9_11

may cause the loss of particle diversity. Particle Swarm Optimization (PSO) is a new optimization algorithm proposed in recent years, which is inspired by the social behavior of bird flocking [4]. PSO algorithm has been used with PF for visual tracking problems in order to improve the diversity of particles and the stability of particle filter. In [5], a target tracking method based on PSO-PF is proposed to solve the problem of particle diversity recession. However the precision of this PSO-PF target tracking algorithm still depends on the accuracy of PSO. Similarly, In [6], another method called PPF can also deal with the particle diversity recession to some extent with the help of PSO. However, the standard PSO algorithm has some shortcomings, such as low precision, easily getting into local optimum and slow convergence. A lot of PSO variants have been proposed to address the shortcomings. Quantum-behaved particle swarm optimization (QPSO) algorithm is one of the PSO variants and is proposed based on the trajectory analysis of particles in PSO [7] and the quantum potential well model [8,9]. QPSO algorithm has been used for solving many optimization problems with satisfying performance [10]. In [11], a decentralized form of QPSO (cQPSO) is proposed by using the cellular structured population. In cQPSO algorithm, the local attractor in the sub-population is also modified in order to accelerate the diffusion of the best solution. The cQPSO algorithm can better keep the population diversity and balance the global and local search than QPSO algorithm. In this paper, we propose the tracking algorithm based on the cQPSO and combining the resampling section of PF. For better tracking performance, we further improve the tracking algorithm by improving the particle initialization approach in cQPSO, resampling technique in PF as well as using the Gaussian mixture model in fitness assessment.

The rest of this paper is organized as follows. Section 2 introduces related work on particle filter and QPSO algorithm. In Sect. 3, the improved tracking algorithm, which is called improved resampling cQPSO(RScQPSO), is proposed. Experimental results are given in Sect. 4. Section 5 concludes this paper.

2   Related Work

2.1   Particle Filter

Particle filter is commonly used in solving Bayesian probability, and it is a technique to estimate target motion state from data with noise. The main idea of PF is generating a random sample called particles in the state space, combing the observation of each moment to adjust the weight and position of each particle. Through continuous searching, decision-making and resampling, particle filter replace integral calculation with sample mean as estimation value of system state. This algorithm only requires simple iteration, and can be applied to predicting and smoothing problems. It can also handle non-Gaussian noise, and allow the use of non-linear system equations. Particle filter is flexible and easy to be implemented. Therefore it is widely used in target tracking. Specific processes of particle filter includes initialization, sampling, state transition, and systematic observation.

2.2 Cellular QPSO (cQPSO) Algorithm

The particle's position $X_{i,j}$ of QPSO algorithm updates according to the following equations:

$$X_{i,j}(t+1) = p_{i,j}(t) \pm \alpha \cdot |C_j - X_{i,j}(t)| \cdot \ln\left(\frac{1}{u_{i,j}(t)}\right) \tag{1}$$

$$p_{i,j}(t) = \varphi_{i,j}(t) \cdot P_{i,j}(t) + (1 - \varphi_{i,j}(t)) \cdot G_{i,j}(t) \tag{2}$$

$$C_j(t) = \frac{1}{M}\left(\sum_{i=1}^{M} P_{i,1}(t), \sum_{i=1}^{M} P_{i,2}(t), \cdots, \sum_{i=1}^{M} P_{i,N}(t)\right) \tag{3}$$

where $p_{i,j}(t)$ is the local attractor position, $P_{i,j}(t)$ is the personal best position of the ith particle at the tth iteration, $G_{i,j}(t)$ is the global best position of the population, $\varphi_{i,j}(t)$ is a random number being in the range of [0, 1], M and N represent the population size and problem dimension respectively.

We expanded the QPSO algorithm to cQPSO algorithm by modifying the neighborhood structure according to the cellular automata (CA) [11]. In cQPSO algorithm, the particles distributed in the two dimensional toroidal mesh and they can only interact with the neighbors. Six kinds of neighborhood structure have been studied in cQPSO as shown in Fig. 1.

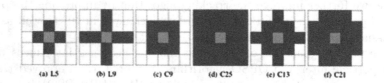

(a) L5   (b) L9   (c) C9   (d) C25   (e) C13   (f) C21

Fig. 1. Six kinds of neighborhood structure

In this paper, we use the C9 structure in cQPSO and then the average position equation $C_j(t)$ is changed to

$$lmbest_j(t) = \frac{1}{9}\left(\sum_{i=1}^{9} P_{i,1}(t), \sum_{i=1}^{9} P_{i,2}(t), \cdots, \sum_{i=1}^{9} P_{i,N}(t)\right) \tag{4}$$

Therefore the particle in cQPSO updates according to the following equation

$$X_{i,j}(t+1) = lbest_{i,j}(t) \pm \alpha \cdot |lmbest_j(t) - X_{i,j}(t)| \cdot \ln\left(\frac{1}{u_{i,j}(t)}\right) \tag{5}$$

where $lbest_{i,j}(t)$ is best $P_{i,j}$ position of the particles in the C9 neighborhood.

3   Improved Sequential cQPSO Algorithm for Target Tracking

For better tracking the object with higher accuracy, we improve the tracking algorithm which is based on the sequential cQPSO algorithm in this section. There are four improvements on the proposed sequential cQPSO algorithm, including the improvement on the particle initialization for cQPSO, resampling technique learnt from PF as well as the application of Gaussian mixture model.

3.1   The Improvement on the Particle Initialization

Since the video sequence is continuous, we can model the target movement according to previous motion results. The particles are distributed within the scope where the target is most likely to appear in the next frame. Let the successfully searching target position of the present frame and the previous frame be $g(t)$ and $g(t-1)$, the $v_{pre}(t+1)$ can be predicted by the following formula:

$$v_{pre}(t+1) = g(t) - g(t-1) \qquad (6)$$

We should preset a v_{min}, when $v_{pre}(t+1) < v_{min}$, $v_{pre}(t+1) = v_{min}$. Next, use the following Gaussian distribution $x_{i,0}(t+1) \sim N(g(t), \Sigma)$ or motion model $x_{i,0}(t+1) = Ax_{i,0}(t) + Bw_{i,0}(t)$ to make particles evenly distributed around the current target. Σ is a covariance matrix of Gaussian distribution in which the diagonal elements is the $v_{pre}(t+1)$. A generally take 1, and B is aforementioned $v_{pre} \cdot k_v$ (k_v is a predefined constant). $w_{i,0}(t)$ is a random number in $[-1, 1]$.

3.2   The Improvement on the State Representation of Particles

The particles state of the proposed target tracking algorithm is represented by $par_i = (X, S, \theta)$. $X = (x, y)$ represents the corresponding position of the particles in images to be tracked, $S = (sx, sy)$ represents scaling ratio between the images corresponding to particles and the original image of the target, θ is the deflection angle of the image. Under the initial state, the location of corresponding pixels can be obtained by the following transformation and the tracking result is shown in Fig. 2.

$$(x, y) = X + T \times \begin{vmatrix} sx & 0 \\ 0 & sy \end{vmatrix} \times \begin{vmatrix} \cos(\theta) & sin(\theta) \\ -\sin(\theta) & \cos(\theta) \end{vmatrix} \qquad (7)$$

Fig. 2. Affine result

3.3   The Improvement on MOG Appearance Mode

The model used in the proposed algorithm is the MOG (mixture of Gaussian) model, which is used to evaluate the fitness value of particles. Similar to [12,13], three components, which are S, W, F, exist in the appearance model. The S component describes temporarily stable images, the W component characterizes the two-frame variations, and the F component is a fixed template of target which is used to prevent the model from drifting away. Based on this appearance model, we can calculate individual's fitness value according to the following equation,

$$f(x(t)) = p(o(t)|x(t)) = \Pi_{j=1}^{d} \left\{ \Sigma_{l=s,w,f} \pi_{l,j}(t) N(o_j(t); \mu_{l,j}(t), \sigma_{l,j}^2(t)) \right\} \quad (8)$$

where $\{\pi_{l,j}(t), \mu_{l,j}(t), \sigma_{l,j}^2(t), l = s, w, f\}$ respectively represent mixture probabilities, mixture centers and mixture variances of these three components, $o_j(t)$ is the candidate region corresponding to state of particle $x(t)$ and d is the number of pixels inside $o_j(t)$. $N(\cdot)$ is a Gaussian density defined as follows,

$$N(x; \mu, \sigma^2) = (2\pi\sigma^2)^{-1/2} exp\{-\frac{(x - \mu)^2}{2\sigma^2}\} \quad (9)$$

More importantly, we use a forgetting factor to avoid keeping all the data from the previous frame. This makes the model parameters be more dependent on recent observations. An online EM algorithm is used as follows:

E-step:

The ownership probability of each component is computed as:

$$m_{l,j}(t) \propto \pi_{l,j}(t) N(o_j(t); \mu_{l,j}(t), \sigma_{l,j}^2(t)) \quad (10)$$

which fulfills $\Sigma_{l=s,w,f} m_{l,j}(t) = 1$

The mixing probability of each component is computed as:

$$\pi_{l,j}(t+1) = \partial m_{l,j}(t) + (1 - \partial)\pi_{l,j}(t); l = s, w, f \quad (11)$$

And the first- and second-moment images are evaluated as (14)

$$M_{k,j}(t+1) = \partial o_j^k(t) m_{s,j}(t) + (1 - \partial)M_{k,j}(t); k = 1, 2 \quad (12)$$

where $\partial = 1 - e^{-1/\tau}$ acts as a forgotten factor, and τ is predefined.

M-step:

The mixture centers and the variances are estimated in the M-step:

$$\mu_{s,j}(t+1) = \frac{M_{1,j}(t+1)}{\pi_{s,j}(t+1)}, \sigma_{s,j}^2(t+1) = \frac{M_{2,j}(t+1)}{\pi_{s,j}(t+1)} - \mu_{s,j}^2(t+1) \quad (13)$$

$$\mu_{w,j}(t+1) = o_j(t), \sigma_{w,j}^2(t+1) = k_{MOG}\sigma_{s,j}^2(t+1) \quad (14)$$

$$\mu_{f,j}(t+1) = \mu_{f,j}(1), \sigma_{f,j}^2(t+1) = k_{MOG}\sigma_{s,j}^2(t+1) \quad (15)$$

3.4   The Improvement on Resampling

When cQPSO iteration comes into the later period, the convergence speed becomes slower. We introduce the resampling step of the particle filter into the proposed algorithm. In that way, we can reduce the search region as well as improve the convergence speed and the solution accuracy. In the proposed algorithm, when the number of iterations is greater than IF (IF is predefined), after each iteration, generate a random number $u \sim U(0,1)$. If $u > p$ (p is predefined), resample as follows.

Firstly, calculate the weight of each particle (w_i) according to the distance between it and the global best of particles and normalize them. Let $C_i = C_{i-1} + w_i$. Then generate n random numbers $u_i \sim U(0,1) i \in [1,n]$. For each u_i, find the Minimal j that meet $C_j > u_i$. Finally, copy the j_{th} particle into the new particle population.

3.5   The Improved Sequential RscQPSO Based Tracking Algorithm

Above all, the process of the proposed algorithm is shown in Table 1.

Table 1. The process of the proposed algorithm

1. Load and display the original image, outline the target
2. Built the appearance models
3. Randomly initialize the particles $X_{i+1} = \left\{ x^{i,0} \right\}_{i=1}^{N}$
4. For k=0 to T do
For i=1 to N do
5.   Calculate particles' fitness by the SWF model according to Eq.(8)
6.   Update particles, personal best and global best
7.   If the particles are converged then Terminate the QPSO iteration
Else Resample
8.   end for
end for
9. Update the appearance models
10. Output

4   Experimental Results

The proposed tracking algorithm is implemented in Opencv/Matlab on a PC with AMD A4 CPU (1.9 Ghz) and 2.74 GB memory. For each sequence, the state of the target object is manually set in the first frame. Parameters set as follows (Table 2).

Table 2. Parameter setting

Parameter	p	M	v_{min}	k_{MOG}
Value	0.75	25	0.04* image length/width	3

4.1 Experiment 1

In this section, we conduct the comparison experiments between QPSO based tracking algorithm and the proposed algorithm. One video sequence named "Dog", contains a dog face moving to the left and right with appearance and scale variation. The other dataset is called "Boy" in which a boy moves quickly. All datasets mentioned are available at http://cvlab.hanyang.ac.kr/tracker_benchmark/seq/name.zip. "name" in the URL need to be replaced with the dataset names when you download them.

As shown in Fig. 3, QPSO based tracking algorithm also successfully finish this tracking task. However, the proposed algorithm tracks the target more accurately, which shows a better performance in search for the global optimum in a long tracking task. Compared to the "Dog", the "Boy" dataset are more difficult to be tracked. As can be seen from Fig. 4, when the tracking window of the QPSO based tracker fails to cover the object after the frame 251, the proposed algorithm still locks the target. The result shows that the improved RScQPSO is a relatively robust tracking algorithm.

In order to comprehensively evaluate the result of the two algorithm, we calculate the MSE (mean square error) between the estimated position and the labeled ground truth as well as the rate of successful tracking. Here only the successful frame is taken into consideration to calculate MSE. The comparison result is shown in Table 3. We can see from the tables that our tracker achieves very favorable performance in terms of both accuracy and successful rate.

frame 1 frame 368 frame 1000 frame 1200   frame 1 frame 368 frame 1000 frame 1200
    (a) QPSO based algorithm   (b) the proposed tracking algorithm

Fig. 3. Tracking performance of "Dog" sequence

4.2 Experiment 2

In order to further evaluate the performance of our algorithm, more dataset are used for testing. The first video "fish", shown in Fig. 5(a), contains a static object with camera motion, which means everything in the sequence is under illumination variation. Despite all this, our algorithm is able to track the target

Frame 1 Frame 85 Frame 173 Frame 251　　Frame 1 Frame 85 Frame 173 Frame 267
(a) QPSO based algorithm　　　　　　　(b) the proposed tracking algorithm

Fig. 4. Tracking performance of "Boy" sequence

Table 3. The tracking results of "Dog" and "Boy"

Tracking algorithm	MSE of position		Frame tracked	
	Dog	Boy	Dog	Boy
QPSO	5.951298	6.470549	1200/1200	251/267
Improved RScQPSO	4.837096	6.040748	1200/1200	267/267

(a) dataset: fish

(b) dataset: Jumping　　　　　　　　　　(c) dataset: seq_sb

Fig. 5. The more performance of our algorithm

correctly. The second dataset "Jumping" is a jumping person with a vaguely face. Results in Fig. 5(b), demonstrate that the proposed improved RScQPSO algorithm performs well even though the target undergo fast and abrupt motion. The last dataset, "seq_sb", describes a person undergoing large pose, appearance, and lighting changes, as well as partial occlusions. The result in Fig. 5(c) shows that our tracker finishes the task successfully.

5　Conclusion

In this paper, we proposed an improved tracking algorithm based on cQPSO and PF. The proposed tracking algorithm can deal with tracking tasks with objects undergoing various environments such as illumination, scale, appearance variation, partial occlusion, abrupt and fast motion. Compared with the color histogram, the MOG (mixture of Gaussian) based appearance model we use can make a better object description. From the experiment results, the improved

RScQPSO based tracker has a favorable performance compared with the QPSO based tracker both in terms of accuracy and efficiency.

Acknowledgement. This work was partially supported by the National Natural Science foundation of China (Grant Nos. 61673194, 61105128, 61170119, 61373055), the Natural Science Foundation of Jiangsu Province, China (Grant No. BK20131106), the Postdoctoral Science Foundation of China (Grant No. 2014M560390), the Fundamental Research Funds for the Central Universities, China (Grant No. JUSRP51410B), Six Talent Peaks Project of Jiangsu Province (Grant No. DZXX-025).

References

1. Kitagawa, G.: Monte Carlo filter and smoother for non-Gaussian nonlinear state space models. J. Comput. Graph. Stat. **1**(1), 1–25 (1996)
2. Isard, M., Blake, A.: CONDENSATION-conditional density propagation for visual tracking. Int. J. Comput. Vis. **29**(1), 5–28 (1998)
3. Liu, J.S., Chen, R., Logvinenko, T.: A theoretical framework for sequential importance sampling with resampling. In: Doucet, A., de Freitas, N., Gordon, N. (eds.) Sequential Monte Carlo Methods in Practice, pp. 225–246. Springer, New York (2001)
4. Kennedy, J., Eberhart, R.: Particle swarm optimization. In: IEEE International Conference on Neural Networks, Proceedings, vol. 4, pp. 1942–1948. IEEE (1995)
5. Zhang, L.: Application of Particle Filtering with Particle Swarm Optimization to Target Tracking. Lanzhou University of Technology (2010)
6. Zhang, C-q, Ge, L., Han, D.: Research on particle swarm particle filter algorithm based on target tracking. Comput. Simul. **31**(08), 392–396 (2014)
7. Clerc, M., Kennedy, J.: The particle swarm - explosion, stability, and convergence in a mul-tidimensional complex space. IEEE Trans. Evol. Comput. **6**(1), 58–73 (2010)
8. Sun, J., Fang, W., Wu, X., et al.: Quantum-behaved particle swarm optimization: analysis of individual particle behavior and parameter selection. Evol. Comput. **20**(3), 349–393 (2012)
9. Sun, J., Feng, B., Xu, W.: Particle swarm optimization with particles having quantum behavior. IEEE 2004 Congress on Evolutionary Computation, pp. 1571–1580 (2004)
10. Fang, W., Sun, J., Ding, Y., et al.: A review of quantum-behaved particle swarm optimization. IETE Techn. Rev. **27**(4), 336–348 (2010)
11. Fang, W., Sun, J., Chen, H., et al.: A decentralized quantum-inspired particle swarm optimization algorithm with cellular structured population. Inf. Sci. **330**, 19–48 (2016)
12. El-Maraghi, T.F.: Robust online appearance models for visual tracking. IEEE Trans. Pattern Anal. Mach. Intell. **25**(10), 1296–1311 (2003)
13. Sun, B., Wang, B., Shi, Y., et al.: Visual tracking using quantum-behaved particle swarm optimization. In: Control Conference. IEEE (2015)

An Improved Search Algorithm About Spam Firewall

Kangshun Li[1,2(✉)], Lu Xiong[1,2], and Zhichao Wen[2]

[1] Department of Computer Science,
Guangdong University of Science and Technology, Dongguan 523000, China
[2] College of Mathematics and Informatics, South China Agricultural University,
Guangzhou 510642, China
likangshun@sina.com

Abstract. Although most of the existing encryption system takes the privacy issues of storing data into consider, the reveal of user access pattern is inevitable during the e-mail filtering. Therefore, how to protect the private data in the process of spam filtering becomes one of the urgent problems to be solved. Combined with two filtering techniques which are based on keyword and blacklist respectively, this paper achieves the goal of sorting and filtering spams. Meanwhile, given the privacy issues in sorting and filtering the spams, the paper is based on an experimental project, the Pairing Based Cryptography, which is performed by Stanford University to achieve the e-mail encryption program. It adopts a searchable public key encryption in the process of sorting and filtering, which needs no decryption and can realize searching and matching operations. By this method, it fully protects the privacy and access patterns of the mail receiver from disclosing.

Keywords: Privacy-protection · Public-key-encryption searchable

1 Introduction

Contemporarily, with the advantages of simplicity, fastness, convenience and low-cost, e-mail has become the most widely used service of the Internet, changing the way of modern communication [1]. However, since the first spam e-mails' appearance in the mid-1980s, the growing proliferation of spam e-mail inevitably became a widespread concern and a variety of spam filtering technology came into being naturally [2,3]. But with the rapid development of network storage services, many enterprises and individuals use third-party servers to store large amount of mail data. Although the majority of existing encryption systems takes privacy issues of storing data into consider, yet in the process of e-mail filtering, there are more or less leakages of the user access mode. Therefore, how to protect the private data in the process of spam filtering becomes one of the urgent problems to be solved.

Spam Firewall privacy search is mainly to achieve two goals: spam filtering and protection of users' privacy [4,5]. First of all, the basic designed objective

© Springer Nature Singapore Pte Ltd. 2016
M. Gong et al. (Eds.): BIC-TA 2016, Part II, CCIS 682, pp. 95–100, 2016.
DOI: 10.1007/978-981-10-3614-9_12

is to realize message classification and filtering. In this project, the mail filters must be able to classify and filter the mails according to its content, so that the unexpected spam mails won't be received. Moreover, it is necessary to balance privacy concerns. In the process of sorting and filtering mail, it requires to achieve the searching and matching operation of the e-mail data without having to decrypt it in order to ensure the privacy and access mode of the mail recipient will not be let out.

2   Theoretical Foundation

2.1   Bilinear Diffe-Hellman Problem

BDH parameter generator is an important concept of bilinear Diffe-Hellman problem. Input a security parameter k in BDH parameter generator, and output the prime, description of and the admissible bilinear map. Footnotes Computing bilinear Diffe-Hellman (Computational Bilinear Diffe-Hellman, CBDH) can be defines as follow: Enter; Work out. Determination of bilinear Diffe-Hellman (Decisional Bilinear Diffe-Hellman, DBDH) can be defined as follow: input and, among them, a, b, c, k, g are random parameters; if and can be distinguished in polynomial time, then output the result YES; otherwise, output the result NO.

2.2   Public Key Encryption with Keyword Search

Public Key Encryption with keyword Search (PEKS) is a new type of cryptosystem, which allows us to go through a keyword search on the public key encrypted data. Thus not only does it protect the privacy and access mode of the receiver from leaking. Meanwhile, it also offers a way that we will be able to match and search operation quickly and effectively without decrypting the data.

A public non-interactive scheme, with Public Key Encryption with keyword Search, includes the following four probabilistic polynomial time algorithms:

(1) Initialization algorithm: Input a security parameter, draw a key pair (public key and private key).
(2) Public Key Encryption with keyword Search algorithm: Enter keyword, use the acquired public key to calculate the ciphertext of the keyword used for searching.
(3) Construction algorithm: Enter keyword, use the private to calculate the trapdoor of keyword.
(4) Keyword search algorithm: Enter a searchable encryption ciphertext S of keyword W and a trapdoor Tw of keyword W', if $W = W'$, then the output the result YES, otherwise draw the result NO.

3   Transformation Plan of Mail System

3.1   Generation of the Key

Generate type A pairing based on A type parameter, define three elements [12]. Its steps are as follows:

(1) Based on the pairing, construct cyclic group on elliptic curves.
(2) Initialize to the generator of group.
(3) is a random initialized parameter which meets.
(4) Calculate and draw.
(5) Output the public key, private key.

3.2 Mail Encryption of Sender

Set two elements and, a bilinear map, two hashing functions, and meets, meets. Encryption as follows:

(1) Obtain the public key.
(2) Gain mail metadata, read the sender's Username.
(3) Initialize t to a generator of group G2.
(4) r is a random initialized parameter which meets.
(5) Set as the input string of Hash1 (), work out the hash value Hash1 ().
(6) Calculate.
(7) Set t as the input string of Hash2 (), calculate the hash value Hash2 (t).
(8) Draw the encrypted result.

3.3 The Settings of the Mail Recipients' Trapdoor and Black and White Lists

The Structure of Trapdoor. Set an element Tw, a bilinear mapping e (), a hash function Hash1 (), Where Hash1 () meets.
Construction as follows:

(1) Get private key.
(2) Use the acquired the mail recipient for constructing trapdoor's keyword.
(3) Initialize Tw to a generator of group G1.
(4) Set W' as the input string of Hash1 (), calculate the hash value Hash1 ().
(5) Calculate.
(6) Output.

3.4 Sorting and Filtering the Mail Servers

Set three elements A, B, S, a bilinear map e (), a hash function Hash2 () and Hash2 () meets.
Mail sorting and filtering steps are as follows:

(1) Get the public key.
(2) Get the encryption result of mail sender username $PEKS(A_{pub}, W_{sender}) = [g^r, Hash2(t)]$, set A = gr, B = Hash2(t).
(3) Read the processed blacklist stored in the server Trapdoor() || Trapdoor() || Trapdoor() || ...... Trapdoor(). That is || || || ......||
(4) Calculate, and is the i-th encrypted username of blacklist.
(5) Set S as the input string of Hash2 (), calculate the hash value Hash2 (S).

(6) Match Hash2 (S) with B. If S = B, then the message sender is users in blacklist, so determine it as spam and filter it; if S ≠ B, the message sender is in the whitelist, therefore reserve the mail temporarily.

(7) Repeat step (4) (5) (6) until all the usernames in the blacklist have been matched.

(8) If the username does not exist in the blacklist, finally determined the message sender is in the whitelist, reserve the mail temporarily.

4 Security and Efficiency Analysis

4.1 Security Analysis

(1) Provide verifiable encryption. When merely knows the ciphertext data of the mail, the third-party server cannot know any of the information in plain text messages. In this article, the random number used in the generation of the key and encrypted key is unknown to the server. So when the keyword ciphertext is known only, the server cannot get any information about the keywords.

(2) Independent inquiry. In addition to search the matched results, the mail server cannot get any information about the plaintext message. In this article, we only use the received trapdoor, blacklists and the generated public key when the mail server is matching the ciphertext. There is no decryption during the searching and matching process, so the mail server cannot know anything about the plaintext message.

(3) The controlled query. Without the user's permission, the mail server and external attackers cannot search whether any message of the user contains certain keyword. In the article, the generated key is kept secret, servers and external attackers cannot know. When making a request for e-mail filtering, you need to enter the private key of the user. Therefore, we can ensure the server and external attacker cannot generate trapdoor and user blacklists keywords to retrieve whether the user's mail contains certain information.

(4) Supports implicit query. When the user sends filter conditions to the mail server, it can be achieved that any information of the filter conditions won't be leaked to the servers. In this paper, the mail server can only verify whether the sender of a message is in the blacklist or the e-mail contains the keyword during mail filtering. It is inaccessible to the filter conditions.

4.2 Efficiency Analysis

Analyze the efficiency of the design in its operating efficiency from the point of time. For example, in sending an e-mail, analysis the operational efficiency based on the filtering of blacklist and keywords.

The practical configurations in tests are as follows:

In the program, the main time consumed in encryption and matching process of operation of mapping pair e(), Hash functions and modular exponentiation, therefore we will focus on analyzing operational efficiency of these three operations. Suppose the message sender sends an e-mail with N keywords, and the current server has M names in the blacklist, the operation of various parts are shown in Tables 1 and 2.

Table 1. Operation of the mail sender

Running function	Blacklist-based filtering	The keyword-based filtering
The number of calculations of mapping e ()	1	$1 \times N$
The number of calculations of Hash function	2	$2 \times N$
The number of calculations of modular exponentiation	2	$2 \times N$

Table 2. Operation of the mail recipient

Running function	Blacklist-based filtering	The keyword-based filtering
The number of calculations of mapping e ()	0	0
The number of calculations of Hash function	M	1
The number of calculations of modular exponentiation	M	1

To facilitate the observation, assume that it has been run for 1000 times, and times required are:

The data above indicates that the time required in spam filtering is primarily related to the number of blacklist M and the number of keywords N and the running time is reasonable. It can be explained, the combination of searchable encryption scheme and spam filtering technology is feasible.

5 Conclusion

In this article, we make spam mail as an object, design a spam filters which protect the personal privacy of e-mail users, achieving a searchable encryption scheme. In order to ensure the user's privacy when searching, a new type of encryption system is introduced - Public-key Searchable Encryption Technology. Based on the characteristics of Public-key Searchable Encryption Technology, the article achieve the goal of filtering respectively by black and white list filtering and keyword matching filtering.

Acknowledgements. This work is supported by the National Natural Science Foundation of China with the Grant No. 61573157, the Fund of Natural Science Foundation of Guangdong Province of China with the Grant No. 2014A030313454.

This work was jointly supported by Natural Science Foundation of Guangdong Province of China (2015A030313408).

References

1. Cui, G., Xu, P., Lei, F.: Improved prototype scheme of PETKS and its expansion. Comput. Sci. **36**(3), 58–60 (2009)
2. Meng, X.: Analysis of privacy proetction of electornic mails. J. Northeast Agric. Univ. (Soc. Sci. Ed.) **1**, 37 (2009)
3. Yang, H., Sun, S., Li, H.: Research on bilinear Diffie-Hellman problem. J. Sichuan Univ. (Eng. Sci. Ed.) **1**(38), 137–141 (2006)
4. Baek, J., Safavi-Naini, R., Susilo, W.: Public key encryption with keyword search revisited. In: Gervasi, O., Murgante, B., Laganà, A., Taniar, D., Mun, Y., Gavrilova, M.L. (eds.) ICCSA 2008. LNCS, vol. 5072, pp. 1249–1259. Springer, Heidelberg (2008). doi:10.1007/978-3-540-69839-5_96
5. Boneh, D., Crescenzo, G., Ostrovsky, R., Persiano, G.: Public key encryption with keyword search. In: Cachin, C., Camenisch, J.L. (eds.) EUROCRYPT 2004. LNCS, vol. 3027, pp. 506–522. Springer, Heidelberg (2004). doi:10.1007/978-3-540-24676-3_30
6. Zhang, B., Wang, X.: Public key encryption schemes search with keyword. Comput. Eng. **36**(06), 155–157 (2010)
7. Dodis, Y., Katz, J., Xu, S., Yung, M.: Key-insulated public key cryptosystems. In: Knudsen, L.R. (ed.) EUROCRYPT 2002. LNCS, vol. 2332, pp. 65–82. Springer, Heidelberg (2002). doi:10.1007/3-540-46035-7_5
8. Boneh, D., Franklin, M.: Identity-based encryption from the Weil pairing. Siam J. Comput. **32**(3), 586–615 (2003)

Artificial Bee Colony Algorithm Based on Clustering Method and Its Application for Optimal Power Flow Problem

Liling Sun and Hanning Chen[✉]

Tianjin Polytechnic University, Tianjin 300387, China
sll198257@163.com, perfect_chn@hotmail.com

Abstract. In this paper, an improved multi-objective ABC algorithm based on k-means clustering, called CMOABC, is proposed. For keeping the population diversity, the multi-swarm technology based on k-means clustering is employed to decompose the population into many clusters. Due to each subcomponent evolving separately, after every specific iterations, the population will be re-clustered to facilitate information exchange among different clusters. CMOABC is applied to solve the real-world Optimal Power Flow (OPF) problem that considers the cost, loss, and emission impacts as the objective functions. The simulation results demonstrate that, compared to NSGA-II, MOPSO, and MOABC, the proposed CMOABC is superior for solving OPF problem, in terms of optimization accuracy.

Keywords: K-means clustering · Artificial bee colony algorithm (ABC) · Multi-objective optimization problems (MOPs) · Optimal power flow (OPF)

1 Introduction

Swarm intelligence (SI) is an innovative artificial intelligence technique for solving complex multi-objective optimization problems (MOPs), such as non-dominated sorting genetic algorithm II [1], multi-objective particle swarm optimization [2], multi-objective evolutionary algorithm based on Decomposition [3]. Artificial bee colony (ABC) algorithm is a powerful search technique that drew inspiration from the biological foraging behaviors observed in bee colony [4]. Many researchers have presented several existing multi-objective ABC algorithms [5]. However, these proposed algorithms still suffer from low convergence rate and lacking the diversity of swarm.

To conquer the weakness of initial MOABC, an improved multi-objective ABC algorithm based on k-means clustering, named CMOABC, is proposed. The population is partitioned into several sub-populations based on k-means clustering. Information communication between the sub-populations depends on re-clustering the population after each specific iterations. To further enhance the

© Springer Nature Singapore Pte Ltd. 2016
M. Gong et al. (Eds.): BIC-TA 2016, Part II, CCIS 682, pp. 101–106, 2016.
DOI: 10.1007/978-981-10-3614-9_13

population diversity, a number of individuals with worse performance re-generate in the re-clustering process.

Optimal Power Flow (OPF) is a classical multi-objective problem. Traditionally, the basic objective of OPF is to schedule the committed generating units to meet the system load demand at minimum operating cost while satisfying the various system equality and inequality constraints [6]. But the passage of clean air act amendments in 1990 forced the utilities to reduce the emission from fossil fuel fired thermal station [7–10]. Therefore, in addition to fuel cost, emission must also be considered as an objective. OPF problem is a non-linear, constrained optimization problem where many competing objectives are present. CMOABC is utilized to solve OPF problem. Compared with MOABC, MOPSO and NSGAII, CMOABC can accommodate considerable potential for solving OPF problem.

2   Optimal Power Flow Problem Formulation

2.1   Minimization of Total Fuel Cost

The fuel cost curves of the thermal generators are modeled as a quadratic cost curves and can be represented as follows:

$$f_{cost} = \sum_{i=1}^{N_g} f_i(a_i P_{Gi}{}^2 + b_i P_{Gi} + c_i) \tag{1}$$

where a_i, b_i and c_i are the the fuel cost coefficients of the ith generator, P_{Gi} is real power output of the ith generator.

2.2   Minimization of Total Power Losses

The power flow solution gives all bus voltage magnitudes and angles. Then, the total MW active ower loss in a transmission network can be described as follows:

$$f_{lost} = \sum_{k=1}^{N_l} g_k(V_i^2 + V_j^2 - 2V_i V_j \cos(\delta_i - \delta_j)) \tag{2}$$

where N_l is the number of transmission lines, V_i and V_j are the voltage magnitudes at the ith bus and jth bus, respectively; δ_i and δ_j are the voltage angles at the ith bus and the jth bus, respectively.

2.3   Total Emission Cost Minimization

In this paper, two important types of emission gasses, namely, sulpher oxides SOx and nitrogen oxides NOx, are taken as the pollutant gasses. Here, the total emission cost is defined as bellow:

$$f_{emission} = \sum_{i=1}^{N_g} (\alpha_i + \beta_i P_{Gi} + \gamma_i P_{Gi}{}^2) \tag{3}$$

where $f_{emission}$ is the total emission cost (ton/h) and α_i, β_i and γ_i are the emission coefficients of the ith unit.

$$|S_{Li}| \leq S_{Li,\max} \quad i = 1, \ldots, N_l \tag{4}$$

3 CMOABC Algorithm

The stochastically generated population is partitioned into n subpopulations based on the widely adopted k-means cluster method [8]. The number of clusters is determined by the predefined set $G = \{g_1, g_2, \ldots, g_m\}$, where $g_1 > g_2 > \ldots > g_m$. It may happen that two or more clusters come close to each other or get overlapped to a high degree. The distances between each two clusters are calculated as following equation:

$$Dis\_cluster = \left\| cluster_i^{center} - Nei\_cluster_i^{center} \right\| \tag{5}$$

where $Dis\_cluster$ is the distance between one cluster and its neighbor, $Nei\_cluster_i^{center}$ is the center of the ith cluster's neighbor. $cluster_i^{center}$ is the center of the ith cluster. If the distance is smaller than the specific distance DIS_m, one of the clusters will be removed and its non-domination solutions are store.

$$DIS_m = 0.2 * min\left(R_i, R_{i\_neighbor}\right) \tag{6}$$

where R_i is the radius of $cluster_i$ and $R_{i\_neighbor}$ is the radius of the neighbors of $cluster_i$.

In order to exchange information among individuals, the whole population is re-partitioned into g_{i+1} clusters based on k-means clustering after each TI iterations, where g_i and g_{i+1} are orderly chosen from the predefined set G. The individuals in a cluster may be distributed into different new clusters when the number of the clusters is changing. To balance the exploration and exploitation, TI is not a constant.

$$TI = \begin{cases} floor\left(0.03 * iter_{max}\right) & \text{if iter} \leq 0.5 * iter_{max} \\ floor\left(0.06 * iter_{max}\right) & \text{if iter} > 0.5 * iter_{max} \end{cases} \tag{7}$$

where $iter_{max}$ is the maximum iterations; $iter$ is the current iteration.

After each TI iterations, a certain number of individuals in each cluster should be regenerated according to this cluster's contribution to the external archive. For the jth cluster, the number of solutions updating to the external archive during each TI iterations is recorded in $Num\_Update(j)$. Then, according to its position in the sort of Num_Update, the number of individuals needed to regenerate in the jth cluster is calculated in Eq. (32). The individuals which will be removed in cluster j are determined by non-domination sort.

$$Num\_regenerate(j) = \frac{Sort\_Update(j)}{g_i} * \frac{Num\_ind(j)}{2} \tag{8}$$

where $Num\_ind(j)$ is the number of individuals in the jth cluster; $Sort\_Update(j)$ indicates the jth cluster's position in the sort of Num_Update; and g_i is the current number of clusters (Table 1).

Table 1. Pseudocode of CMOABC

//Step 1: Initialization
Generalize a population of *NP* individuals in the search region randomly;
Set the numbers of clusters *G*; Create the external archive *EA*; initial the current iteration *iter* = 1;
//Step 2: Loop
while stopping criteria are not satisfied **do**
　　Calculate *TI* according to Eq. (7)
　　Decide the number g_i of clusters according to *G*
　　Partition the whole population based on K-means clustering
　　For all cluster
　　　　Compute *Dis _ cluster* according to Eq. (5)
　　　　Decide whether some clusters need to be removed according to *DIS_m*
　　　　Select x_{up} individuals based on non-domination.
　　End for
　　For *iter*=1:*TI*
　　　　Update the individuals' position
　　　　Update the external archive and update *Num_Update*
　　　　iter = *iter*+1;
　　End for
　　Calculate the number of individuals in each cluster needing to be regenerated, according to Eq. (8)
　　Cenerate a certain number of the new individuals in every cluster;
End while

4   Multi-objective Optimal Power Flow Based on CMOABC

In order to validate the robustness of the proposed CMOABC method, a standard IEEE 30 bus system has been used as the test system. The system represents a portion of the American Electric Power System (in the Midwestern US).

The three objectives are optimized simultaneously by the four algorithms and the corresponding best solutions are given in Table 2. Figure 1 also shows the result values of three competing objectives. As shown in Fig. 13, compare to other three algorithms, the Pareto-optimal solutions obtained by the CMOABC are better distributed on the front with good diversity. Among other three algorithms, the Pareto-optimal solutions obtained by the standard MOABC are also well distributed, the diversification of them is not as well as the ones obtained by the proposed CMOABC.

Furthermore, from the Table 2, CMOABC is able to discover a well-distributed and diverse solution set for three-objective problem. However, other three algorithms cannot archive the true Pareto front for three-objective OPF problem. CMOABC obtains the best emission, cost, though the system loss obtained by CMOABC is 2.1601MW, which is a little more than 2.1598MW obtained by MOABC.

Table 2. The best compromise solutions for cost, emission and loss using different multi-objective algorithms

	CMOABC	MOABC	NSGAII	MOPSO
PG1	19.0732	18.9234	35.6214	22.0152
PG2	32.9875	27.9542	53.9065	15.1023
PG3	68.0549	70.8965	47.6936	90.0136
PG4	82.0132	85.9831	45.4762	84.2253
PG5	29.0385	27.0467	54.9945	7.2104
PG6	52.1248	53.0102	46.0154	65.3609
f1 fuel cost	612.0513	614.0154	622.5149	631.4003
f2 (emisson)	0.2120	0.2171	0.2225	0.2341
f3 (loss)	2.1601	2.1598	3.0301	2.8998

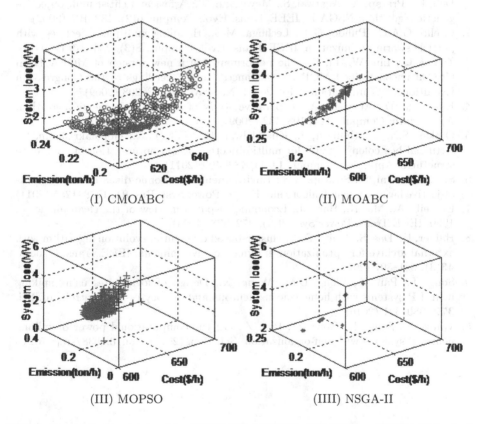

(I) CMOABC

(II) MOABC

(III) MOPSO

(IIII) NSGA-II

Fig. 1. Pareto fronts obtained by CMOABC, MOPSO, MOABC, and NSGA-II for fuel cost, emission and loss

5 Conclusions

An improved multi-objective ABC algorithm based on k-means cluster, called CMOABC, is proposed. CMOABC adopts k-means clustering method to partition the population into many clusters and the number of the clusters is changing to implement information exchange among the different clusters. CMOABC is used to handle multi-objective OPF problem, and 30-bus IEEE test system is adopted to test the proposed algorithm. By comparing the simulation results of CMOABC, MOABC, MOPSO and NSGAII, the proposed method is able to give well distributed Pareto optimal solutions than other three methods for OPF problem with different objectives.

References

1. Deb, K., Pratap, A., Agarwal, S., Meyarivan, T.: A fast and elitist multiobjective genetic algorithm: NSGA-II. IEEE Trans. Evol. Comput. **6**(2), 182–197 (2002)
2. Coello, C.A.C., Pulido, G.T., Lechuga, M.S.: Handling multiple objectives with particle swarm optimization. IEEE Trans. Evol. Comput. **8**(3), 256–279 (2004)
3. Zhang, Q., Liu, W., Li, H.: The performance of a new version of MOEA/D on CEC09 unconstrained MOP test instances. In: Proceedings of the Congress on Evolutionary Computation (CEC 2009), Norway, pp. 203–208 (2009)
4. Karaboga, D., Akay, B.: A comparative study of artificial bee colony algorithm. Appl. Math. Comput. **214**, 108–132 (2009)
5. Omkar, S.N., Senthilnath, J., Khandelwal, R., Naik, G.N., Gopalakrishnan, S.: Artificial bee colony (ABC) for multi-objective design optimization of composite structures. Appl. Soft Comput. **11**(1), 489–499 (2011)
6. Sivasubramani, S., Swarup, K.S.: Environmental/economic dispatch using multi-objective harmony search algorithm. Electr. Power Syst. Res. **81**, 1778–1785 (2011)
7. El-Keib, A., Ma, H., Hart, J.: Economic dispatch in view of the clean air act of 1990. IEEE Trans. Power Syst. **9**(2), 972–978 (1994)
8. Halder, U., Das, S., Maity, D.: A cluster-based differential evolution algorithm with external archive for optimization in dynamic environments. IEEE Trans. Cybern. **43**(3), 881–897 (2013)
9. Song, T., Pan, Z., Wong, D.M., Wang, X.: Design of logic gates using spiking neural P systems with homogeneous neurons and astrocytes-like control. Inf. Sci. **372**, 380–391 (2016)
10. Wang, X., Song, T., Gong, F., Pan, Z.: On the computational power of spiking neural P systems with self-organization. Sci. Rep. (2016). doi:10.1038/srep27624

Study on Hybrid Intelligent Algorithm with Solving Pre-stack AVO Elastic Parameter Inversion Problem

Qinghua Wu[1,2], Ying Hao[2], and Xuesong Yan[2(✉)]

[1] Faculty of Computer Science and Engineering, Wuhan Institute of Technology,
Wuhan 430205, Hubei, China
[2] School of Computer Science, China University of Geosciences,
Wuhan 430074, Hubei, China
yanxs@cug.edu.cn

Abstract. The process of pre-stack AVO(Amplitude Variation with Off-set) elastic parameter inversion is the process of optimization, which can be solved by using genetic algorithm. However, when solving the problem, the traditional genetic algorithm converges speedily and is easily trapped into the problems like local optimum, etc., which leads to unsatisfactory inversion effect. To solve the above problems, this paper introduces simulated annealing algorithm into genetic algorithm and improves the genetic algorithm in the aspects of population initialization, selection strategy and generic manipulation. A hybrid intelligent algorithm is proposed in this paper which is more suitable for solving pre-stack AVO elastic parameter inversion problem. The experimental results show that the proposed hybrid intelligent algorithm in this paper can fully exert the global searching capability of genetic algorithm and prevent the algorithm from being trapped into local optimum by using simulated annealing algorithm. The Gardner relation is utilized to initialize population in order to make initialization of density correspond to the practical terrain conditions better and obviously improve the inversion accuracy.

Keywords: Intelligent algorithm · Pre-stack AVO · Elastic parameter inversion · Simulated annealing

1 Introduction

At present, AVO (Amplitude Variation with Offset) technique [1] is the most common technique which applies pre-stack data to predict oil and gas. This technique can make full use of the information on seismic data and is extensively used for hydrocarbon detection. A lot of useful information on pre-stack data can be used for the prediction of underground oil and gas conditions [2], where P-wave velocity V_p, S-wave velocity V_s and density ρ are three key elastic parameters. These three elastic parameters from one side can reflect the saturation conditions of underground oil and gas [3]. The relation between P-wave velocity V_p and gas saturation is nonlinear, while the relation between density ρ and gas

© Springer Nature Singapore Pte Ltd. 2016
M. Gong et al. (Eds.): BIC-TA 2016, Part II, CCIS 682, pp. 107–113, 2016.
DOI: 10.1007/978-981-10-3614-9_14

saturation is linear. And S-wave velocity V_s can reflect some rock characters. Therefore, the information on these three elastic parameters are needed when judging the underground oil and gas saturation. The inversion of pre-stack AVO elastic parameter needs to construct a suitable objective function and optimize it, so generally the objective function is nonlinear. When linear and quasi-linear methods are used to solve this problem, due to the defects of these methods like strong dependency on initial model, etc., the wrong selection for initial model will cause unreliable inversion results; especially when solving nonlinear inversion problem with the properties of multiple parameters and extreme values, etc., these linear inversion methods meet the bottleneck.

In the mid-1980s, nonlinear global intelligent optimization inversion technique began to be paid attentions by specialists and scholars in the field of geophysics, and many new ideas and methods in other fields were continuously introduced into the field of geophysics [4–16]. In more than 30 years, a series of nonlinear global intelligent optimization inversion techniques has been extensively applied in all sorts of inversion problems and made many significant research achievements. Therefore, specialists and scholars tried to combine intelligent algorithms with other algorithms for realizing hybrid optimization inversion and improving inversion precision [17–20].

2 Pre-stack AVO Elastic Parameter Inversion Problem

Simulation-optimization method firstly transforms pre-stack AVO elastic parameter inversion problem into optimization problem, and then uses optimization algorithm to solve. From the angle of optimization, when the difference value between inversion seismic data generated by elastic parameter after optimization and actual seismic record data is 0 or less than some threshold, this elastic parameter is considered to meet the requirements. Optimization algorithm evaluates individuals according to the fitness function transformed by objective function, so the constructed objective function for inversion problem is the main factor of influencing pre-stack AVO elastic parameter inversion effect. In this paper, firstly use Aki&Rechard approximate equation [21] to calculate R_{pp}, which is reflection coefficient of reflected p-wave. Then make a convolution for R_{pp} and wavelet to gain and synthesize seismic recorded data. Let sampling number be n. Each sampling point needs different angles. And calculate $n * m$ seismic recorded data. Finally, make the difference between groups of seismic recorded data of each sampling point through optimization, square it, divide after accumulation and summation, then accumulate the data solved by n sampling points and divide n. Lastly square the final result. That is what we want to gain. According to derivations of the above equations, inversion object function can be established as follow:

$$f(x) = \sqrt{\sum_{i=1}^{n}\sum_{j=1}^{m}(s(\theta_{i,j}) - s'(\theta_{i,j}))^2/n * m}. \tag{1}$$

Wheres $s(\theta_{i,j})$ is forward seismic record and $s'(\theta_{i,j})$ is inversion seismic record.

3 Pre-stack AVO Elastic Parameter Inversion Based on Intelligent Algorithm

The flow chart for solving elastic parameter inversion problem by using intelligent optimization algorithm is shown in Fig. 1.

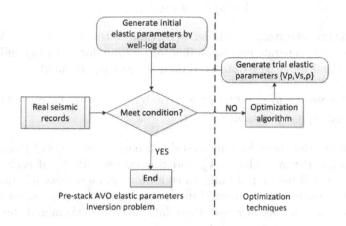

Fig. 1. Algorithm flow chart

3.1 Population Space and Initialization

Individuals in algorithm are composed by inversion parameters. For actual logging curve model, each sampling point can be seen as a layer, that is one dimension. Because what this paper studies is inversion of three parameters, the length of individual is triple of sampling point. Assuming there are n sampling points and the number of solving model parameters is 3*n, so the corresponding individual encoding mode is:

$$G_i = (V_{p1}, V_{s1}, \rho_1, \cdots, V_{pj}, V_{sj}, \rho_j, \cdots, V_{pn}, V_{sn}, \rho_n)$$

Let the number of population individuals be N, and each individual is represented by one-dimensional array. The array length is 3*n. Select individual initial value within the definitive experimental value range(bound function to restrain), later use genetic algorithm to optimize each parameter, finally output an optimal individual which is the optimal group of elastic parameter solutions. Bound range constraints are as follows:

$$0.8 \bullet V_{pwell} \leq V_p \leq 1.2 \bullet V_{pwell} \tag{2}$$
$$0.8 \bullet V_{swell} \leq V_s \leq 1.2 \bullet V_{swell}$$
$$0.9 \bullet \rho_{well} \leq \rho \leq 1.1 \bullet \rho_{well}$$

Although logging can provide the density ρ, P-wave velocity V_p and S-wave velocity V_s of rock, in practical application, people often make inversion by establishing the simple relations among three parameters. For different lithology, Gardner [21] utilized statistical method to establish the relation between rock density and P-wave velocity:

$$\log(\rho) = a \bullet \log(V_p) + b \qquad (3)$$

Through this relational expression, according to the data of ρ and V_p in logging curve model, generate corresponding logarithmic forms $\log(\rho)$ and $\log(V_p)$, and obtain a and b by these data according to least square method:

$$a = (n \times sum(x, y) - sum(x) \times sum(y))/(n \times sum(x^2) - sum(x)^2) \qquad (4)$$
$$b = sum(y)/n - a \times sum(x)/n$$

According to the above formulas, establish hard constraints of P-wave velocity and density. P-wave velocity V_p and S-wave velocity V_s of each group of sampling point still use bound range to constrain, while density ρ is determined by V_p which is determined by bound function and corresponding constraint equation. This formula can better reflect the relation between them and the obtained density value is closer to the real data.

3.2   Simulated Annealing Strategy

This paper adopts proportion cooling method for the simulated annealing operation. Annealing cooling function is $T_{k+1} = T_k * r$. Initial temperature is 10. The final temperature is 0.001 and annealing factor is $r = 0.05$. Select the optimal individual from new population after genetic operation, then generate a new individual at random and compare fitness values of them. If the fitness value of new individual is superior to that of optimal individual, substitute directly. If it is inferior to that of optimal individual, whether the new individual is accepted is judged by Metropolis acceptance criteria.

4   Experimental Simulation and Analysis

Logging curve data from dataset 1 is the one with 241 sampling points including P-wave velocity v_p, S-wave velocity v_s and density ρ. Each sampling point corresponds to 8 different angles: $[0°, 6°, 11°, 17°, 23°, 29°, 34°, 40°]$, and each dataset also uses these 8 angles. Aki&Rechard formula is used to conduct a forward logging curve theory modeling. Then the logging curve model is adopted to calculate reflection coefficient, which is made convolution with wavelet. Because it needs to utilize the relation between two groups of sampling points for generating seismic records, the data of seismic records include 240*8 data.

One twentieth of the sampling point data is selected and compared in terms of these three parameters. The results are as follows Table 1:

Table 1. Partial results of genetic algorithm and hybrid intelligent algorithm

	V_p			V_s			ρ		
	GA	GASA	well	GA	GASA	well	GA	GASA	well
1	2894.63	3529.83	3534.34	2049.81	1703.22	1818.18	2.1868	2.4876	2.4009
2	4094.86	3473.10	3512.97	1580.10	2024.67	1963.53	2.5650	2.4652	2.3532
3	3866.21	3548.09	3556.64	2129.88	1787.21	1898.77	2.6257	2.5099	2.4055
4	3323.15	3749.53	3745.83	2061.21	1948.49	1984.91	2.6095	2.6002	2.4647
5	4158.59	3744.54	3691.67	2145.51	1960.77	1867.41	2.5336	2.5179	2.5266
6	3200.91	3688.33	3720.09	2255.41	1884.47	1913.77	2.4124	2.5297	2.5125
7	3765.68	3662.99	3718.24	1510.21	1866.86	1887.69	2.6237	2.5088	2.5237
8	4387.15	3722.84	3741.65	2093.42	2109.54	1900.32	2.3203	2.5187	2.5571
9	3261.08	3654.89	3694.35	1570.61	1917.73	1863.21	2.4899	2.5292	2.5734
10	3744.94	3678.60	3671.08	1602.56	2149.43	1984.94	2.6550	2.5081	2.4276
11	3659.02	3768.45	3756.23	2305.18	2226.55	2046.00	2.2229	2.4951	2.4313
12	3515.94	3646.81	3651.18	1545.08	1944.24	1896.27	2.5401	2.5610	2.4609

It can be seen form the table that the effect on three elastic parameters of hybrid intelligent algorithm is better than that of genetic algorithm after optimization and approaches actual logging data. Through inversion trial, the experimental results of genetic algorithm and hybrid intelligent algorithm are compared. In the early stage of algorithm, hybrid intelligent algorithm has faster convergence speed and the value of objective function falls rapidly, while genetic algorithm has slower convergence speed. When algorithms enter into the middle and later periods, genetic algorithm is trapped in premature convergence and the value of objective function remains around 0.02. While hybrid intelligent algorithm still makes global searching and the overall effect is better than that of genetic algorithm. Besides, the value of objective function remains around 0.005 and the error decreases an order of magnitude.

5   Conclusion

This paper mainly proposes a hybrid intelligent algorithm which is more suitable for solving pre-stack AVO elastic parameter inversion problem. The inversion accuracy is improved by hybrid intelligent optimization inversion by means of combining intelligent algorithm with other algorithms. Simulated annealing algorithm is introduced into genetic algorithm and we improve population initialization, selection, crossover and mutation strategies. Meanwhile, we study the implementation process and steps of hybrid intelligent algorithm in the pre-stack AVO elastic parameter inversion. Through the inversion trail for actual logging curve model, the inversion results are evaluated. It can be known from the experimental results that the proposed hybrid intelligent algorithm has higher inversion efficiency than single genetic algorithm.

Acknowledgment. This paper is supported by Natural Science Foundation of China. (No. 61272470, 61305087, 61440060, 41404076, 61673354), the Provincial Natural Science Foundation of Hubei (No. 2015CFA065).

References

1. Neidell, N.S.: Amplitude variation with offset. Lead. Edge **5**(3), 47–51 (1986)
2. Li, S.: The Study and Application of AVO Seismic Parameter Inversion Method, China University of Petroleum (2009)
3. Chen, J.: Study of Three-term AVO Inversion Method, China University of Petroleum (2007)
4. Wang, J.: Lecture on nonlinear inverse methods in geophysics (1)-introduction to geophysical inverse problems. Chin. J. Eng. Geophys. **4**(1), 1–3 (2007)
5. Wang, J.: Lecture on nonlinear inverse methods in geophysics (2)-Monte Carlo method. Chin. J. Eng. Geophys. **4**(2), 81–85 (2007)
6. Shi, X., Wang, J.: Lecture on nonlinear inverse methods in geophysics (3)-simulated annealing method. Chin. J. Eng. Geophys. **4**(3), 165–174 (2007)
7. Shi, X., Wang, J.: Lecture on nonlinear inverse methods in geophysics (4)-genetic algorithm. Chin. J. Eng. Geophys. **5**(2), 129–140 (2008)
8. Wang, J.: Lecture on nonlinear inverse methods in geophysics (5)-the artificial neural network method. Chin. J. Eng. Geophys. **5**(3), 255–265 (2008)
9. Zhu, P., Wang, J.: Lecture on nonlinear inverse methods in geophysical data (6)-conjugate gradient method. Chin. J. Eng. Geophys. **5**(4), 381–386 (2008)
10. Wang, S., Liu, Y., Wang, J.: Lecture on nonlinear inverse methods in geophysical data (9)-ant colony optimization. Chin. J. Eng. Geophys. **2**, 131–136 (2009)
11. Yi, Y., Wang, J.: Lecture on nonlinear inverse methods in geophysical data (10)-particle swarm optimization inversion method. Chin. J. Eng. Geophys. **6**(4), 385–389 (2009)
12. Berg, E.: Simple convergent genetic algorithm for inversion of multiparameter data. In: SEG Annual Meeting. Society of Exploration Geophysicists (1990)
13. Mallick, S.: Model-based inversion of amplitude-variations-with-offset data using a genetic algorithm. Geophysics **60**(4), 939–954 (1995)
14. Misra, S., Sacchi, M.D.: Global optimization with model-space preconditioning: application to AVO inversion. Geophysics **73**(5), R71–R82 (2008)
15. Lu, P., Yang, C., Guo, A.: Modified simulated annealing algorithm and its applicationin pre-stack inversion of reservoir parameters. Prog. Geophys. **23**(1), 104–109 (2008)
16. Tongzhu, X.L., Li, Y.: Seismic scalar wave equation inversion based on an improved particle swarm optimization algorithm. Chin. J. Eng. Geophys. **54**(11), 2951–2959 (2011)
17. Stoffa, P.L., Sen, M.K., Chunduru, R., et al.: A combined genetic and linear inversion algorithm for seismic waveform inversion (1993)

18. Priezzhev, I., Shmaryan, L., Bejarano, G.: Nonlinear multitrace seismic inversion using neural network and genetic algorithm. In: EAGE Conference on Genetic Inversion Extended abstract, Saint Petersburg (2008)
19. Soupios, P., Akca, I., Mpogiatzis, P., et al.: Applications of hybrid genetic algorithms in seismic tomography. J. Appl. Geophys. **75**(3), 479–489 (2011)
20. Junyu, B., Zilong, X., Yunfei, X.: Nonlinear hybrid optimization algorithm for seismic impedance inversion. In: Hao, H., Beijing, L.A., et al. (eds.) International Geophysical Conference and Exposition, Beijing, China, 21–24 April 2014, pp. 541–544. Society of Exploration Geophysicists and Chinese Petroleum Society (2014)
21. Wang, L.: Study on intelligent optimization algorithm with application to pre-stack AVO nonlinear inversion, China University of Petroleum (2015)

A Hybrid Multi-objective Discrete Particle Swarm Optimization Algorithm for Cooperative Air Combat DWTA

Guang Peng[✉], Yangwang Fang, Shaohua Chen, Weishi Peng, and Dandan Yang

School of Aeronautics and Astronautics Engineering,
Air Force Engineering University, Xi'an 710038, Shaanxi, China
pg1445334307@163.com

Abstract. In this paper, a hybrid multi-objective discrete particle swarm optimization (HMODPSO) algorithm was proposed to solve cooperative air combat dynamic weapon target assignment (DWTA). First, based on the threshold of damage probability and time window constraints, a new cooperative air combat DWTA multi-objective optimization model is presented. Second, in order to tackle the DWTA problem, a mixed MODPSO and neighborhood search algorithm is proposed. Finally, a typical two-stage DWTA scenario is performed by HMODPSO and compared with other three state-of-the-art algorithms. Simulation results verify the effectiveness of the new model and the superiority of the proposed algorithm.

Keywords: Dynamic weapon target assignment · Multi-objective optimization · Discrete particle swarm optimization · Neighborhood search · Repairing operator · Cauchy mutation

1 Introduction

The weapon target assignment (WTA) is a typical NP-complete constrained combinatorial optimization problem [1], which can be classified into two categories: static WTA (SWTA) and dynamic WTA (DWTA) [2]. Most of the previous researches on WTA are focus on SWTA. However, DWTA has begun to gain more attention of researchers since it was put forward by Hosein and Athans in 1990 [2]. Cai et al. [3] provided a survey of the research on DWTA problem and introduced some basic concepts on DWTA. However, the WTA problem is a multi-objective optimization problem. Liu et al. proposed an improved MOPSO algorithm to solve the multi-objective programming model of static WTA in [4]. However, MOPSO easily falls into the local optimum. So this paper proposed a efficient HMODPSO algorithm to solve the DWTA multi-objective problem.

2 The Cooperative Air Combat Model for DWTA

Definition 1. Time window of target. The time window of target (t^T) is the exposure time of target which the weapon can attack efficiently.

© Springer Nature Singapore Pte Ltd. 2016
M. Gong et al. (Eds.): BIC-TA 2016, Part II, CCIS 682, pp. 114–119, 2016.
DOI: 10.1007/978-981-10-3614-9_15

Definition 2. Time window of algorithm. The time window of algorithm (t^A) is the running time for solving the DWTA.

2.1   The DWTA Multi-objective Optimization Model

Assuming in the cooperative air combat, there are F flights in blue formation, and each flight carries $M_f(f = 1, 2, \cdots, F)$ missiles, so the total number of weapons is $M = \sum_{f=1}^{F} M_f$. At a certain time, the formation detects N targets, which can be attacked by the weapons. p_{ij} is the damage probability that the i-th missile attacks j-th target. w_j is the threat value of target j.

In order to describe the DWTA problem, a decision matrix is introduced:

$$
X = \begin{bmatrix}
x_{11} & x_{12} & \cdots & x_{1N} \\
x_{21} & x_{22} & \cdots & x_{2N} \\
& & \vdots & \\
x_{M1} & x_{M2} & \cdots & x_{MN}
\end{bmatrix}
$$

where $x_{ij} = 1$ if weapon i is assigned to target j, and $x_{ij} = 0$ otherwise.

We define the maximum of the target damage efficiency and minimum of using weapon units as two objective functions. Hence, the formulation of the objective functions for stage t is constructed:

$$
\max f(t) = \sum_{j=1}^{N(t)} w_j(t) \left[1 - \prod_{i=1}^{M(t)} (1 - p_{ij}(t))^{x_{ij}(t)} \right] \tag{1}
$$

$$
\min g(t) = \sum_{j=1}^{N(t)} \sum_{i=1}^{M(t)} x_{ij}(t) \tag{2}
$$

where t is the stage index; $M(t)$, $N(t)$ is the number of existing weapons and targets at stage t, respectively; $p_{ij}(t)$ is the damage probability that the i-th missile attacks j-th target at stage t; $x_{ij}(t)$ is the decision variable at stage t.

The following three categories of constraints are incorporated in the model:

$$
P_j(t) \geq P_{dj}(t), \ \forall t \in \{1, 2, \cdots, S\}, \forall j \in \{1, 2, \cdots, N\} \tag{3}
$$

$$
\sum_{j=1}^{N(t)} x_{ij}(t) \leq 1, \ \forall t \in \{1, 2, \cdots, S\}, \forall i \in \{1, 2, \cdots, M\} \tag{4}
$$

$$
t_j^T(t) \geq t^A(t), \forall t \in \{1, 2, \cdots, S\}, \forall j \in (1, 2, \cdots, N) \tag{5}
$$

Constraint set (3) represents the threshold of damage probability of each target. Constraint set (4) reflects the capability of weapons attacking targets at the same time. Constraint set (5) is very important for DWTA model, which takes the time windows of target and algorithm into account.

3   HMODPSO Algorithm for DWTA

3.1   Particle Encoding

Decimal encoding for particles is adopted in this paper [4]. The length of the particle encoding (denoted by D) is the total number of weapons.

3.2   The Leader Particle Selecting

In PSO [5], each particle in the swarm corresponds to a potential solution of the optimization problem. For specific DWTA problem, the velocity and position of the particle are updated by the following equations, respectively:

$$V_{ij}(k+1) = wV_{ij}(k) + c_1r_1(P_{ij}(k) - X_{ij}(k)) + c_2r_2(G_j(k) - X_{ij}(k)) \qquad (6)$$

$$X_{ij}(k+1) = round(X_{ij}(k) + V_{ij}(k+1)) \qquad (7)$$

$$V_{ij}(k+1) \rightarrow \max(\min(V_{ij}(k+1), V_{\max}), V_{\min}) \qquad (8)$$

$$X_{ij}(k+1) = \max(\min(X_{ij}(k+1), X_{\max}), X_{\min}) \qquad (9)$$

where i represents the i-th particle of the swarm, j represents the j-th dimension in the search space, k is the number of current iteration, w is the inertia weight, c_1, c_2 are the acceleration coefficients, $r_1, r_2 \in [0, 1]$ are uniformly distributed random variables. $X_{\max}$ and $X_{\min}$ are the lower and upper boundaries of the position, respectively; $V_{\max}$ and $V_{\min}$ are the lower and upper boundaries of the velocity, respectively. $round()$ is said to be a integer operator. In MOPSO, selecting the global best position or the leader ($Gbest$) randomly from the external archive is a popular way [4]. However, the roulette method may damage evolution direction of the particles. Considering the weakness, a new method (square root distance, SRD) [6] of selecting the leader particle is applied.

3.3   Repairing Operator

Clearly, unfeasible solutions which don't satisfy the constraint set (3) may be generated for solving the DWTA. To cope with this issue, a repairing operator is introduced [7], which includes two parts: deleting the redundant allocation and supplementing the insufficient allocation.

3.4   Cauchy Mutation

In order to further maintain the diversity of particles, the Cauchy mutation is introduced into HMODPSO algorithm. The mutation is defined as:

$$X_{ij} = \begin{cases} X_{ij} + round((X_{\max} - X_{\min}) \times Cauchy(0,1)), & rand \leq p_b \\ X_{ij}, & rand > p_b \end{cases} \qquad (10)$$

$$Cauchy(0,1) = \tan((rand - 0.5) \times \pi) \qquad (11)$$

where p_b is the mutation rate, $rand$ is a random value uniformly distributed in $[0, 1]$, $Cauchy(0, 1)$ is a standard Cauchy-distributed random value. The adapting mutation rate is computed as:

$$P_b = 1 - \sqrt{\frac{t}{MaxIt}} \qquad (12)$$

3.5 Neighborhood Search

Neighborhood search (NS) algorithm begins with an initial solution, and searches the better solution in its neighborhood range [8]. This paper proposed three kinds of operations: NS-1, NS-2 and NS-3. The procedures are described as:

NS-1: Exchange two positions of the initial solution randomly to get a new solution. If the new solution is better than the initial solution, then replace it with the new solution; otherwise, remain the initial solution.

NS-2: Select the best solution from the neighborhood range of the initial solution; If the best solution is better than the initial solution, then replace it with the new solution; otherwise, remain the initial solution.

NS-3: Exchange two positions of the initial solution in sequence to get a new solution, if the new solution is better than the initial solution, replace it with the new solution, then serve the new solution as the initial solution and repeat the above operation; otherwise, remain the initial solution.

4 Simulations and Results

In the experimental scenario, consider $F = 5, M_f = 4(f = 1, 2, 3, 4, 5)$ and $N = 10$, so obtain $M = 20$. When $t = 1$, the time window of each target $t_j^T (j = 1, 2, \cdots, 10)$ is $[8.3, 11.4, 16.2, 13.8, 20.1, 25.4, 19.6, 13.5, 17.2, 22.8]$; and each target's threat coefficient $w_j (j = 1, 2, \cdots, 10)$ is$[0.6, 0.7, 0.3, 0.5, 0.6, 0.35, 0.65, 0.55, 0.4, 0.75]$. The damage probability threshold of each target can be set 0.9. The weapon's damage probability $p_{ij} (i = 1, 2, \cdots, 20, j = 1, 2, \cdots, 10)$ can be consulted from literature [7]. To verify the efficiency of HMODPSO algorithm, three different kinds of algorithms were proposed: HMODPSO-1 (adopt NS-1 operation), HMODPSO-2 (adopt NS-2 operation) and HMODPSO-3 (adopt NS-3 operation). At the same time, comparing the proposed algorithms with NSGA-II [9], MODPSO [10] and MODPSO-GSA [11] to show their potential competences. In the experiment, population size is 60, 100 iterations are carried out, the external archive size is chosen 30, the crossover probability of NSGA-II is 0.8, the mutation rate of NSGA-II is 0.1. All the simulations were performed under the same environment (Matlab) on Intel Core i5-4590 3.3 GHz CPU with 4 GB RAM.

For each algorithm, 30 independent runs were executed. The computational time of algorithm is represented by T. The average results of the Pareto optimal solutions attained by six algorithms are shown in Table 1.

Table 1. The average results of the Pareto optimal solutions

Pareto solutions	NSGA-II	MODPSO	MODPSO-GSA	HMODPSO-1	HMODPSO-2	HMODPSO-3
13	*	*	5.0500	5.0524	5.0524	5.0524
14	*	*	5.0779	5.0998	5.1052	5.1054
15	5.0551	5.0550	5.1516	5.1510	5.1536	5.1576
16	5.1220	5.0635	5.1971	5.1975	5.1976	5.1980
17	5.1346	5.1306	5.2380	5.2372	5.2382	5.2291
18	5.2158	5.2031	5.2682	5.2639	5.2680	5.2682
19	5.2375	5.2283	5.2894	5.2876	5.2899	5.2904
20	5.2637	5.2614	5.3038	5.3095	5.3135	5.3183
T/s	56.23	3.1364	6.8735	4.4328	8.7426	12.5279

Owing to the time window constraint of the DWTA model, the computational time of algorithm must satisfy requirements of the targets time window. From Table 1, NSGA-II, HMODPSO-2 and HMODPSO-3 algorithm don't meet the requirements. MODPSO has the fastest convergence speed, but it easily falls into the local optimum. Compared with MODPSO-GSA, HMODPSO-1 has better comprehensive performance. So in the $t = 1$ stage, the assignment ($f = 5.0524$, $g = 13$) which succeeded one time by HMODPSO-1 can be selected for the engagement.

Assume in the $t = 2$ stage, $M(2) = 7, N(2) = 4$. The damage probability threshold of each target can be set 0.9. The time window of each target $t_j^T(2)$ is [6.5, 8.1, 5.9, 0.2]; and each target's threat coefficient $w_j(2)$ is [0.6, 0.8, 0.5, 0.7]. The weapon's damage probability $P(2)$ is [0.65 0.74 0.85 0.81; 0.72 0.77 0.92 0.59; 0.86 0.63 0.71 0.78; 0.53 0.80 0.73 0.65; 0.90 0.62 0.79 0.74; 0.82 0.91 0.75 0.84; 0.56 0.65 0.73 0.94].

Since $t_4^T(2) = 0.2\,s$ is so small that it is difficult to satisfy the time window of the special target, a new priority selecting method is efficiently adopted to deal with several special targets whose time windows don't satisfy the time window constraint of the proposed algorithm. From the existing weapons at a certain stage, select the missile with the maximum damage probability to attack the special target, repeat this operation until the special target's joint damage probability satisfies the threshold. As seen from $P(2)$, the 7-th missile attacking the target can satisfy the threshold of damage probability. The assignment of the remaining targets can be solved by HMODPSO-1 algorithm.

The average results attained by HMODPSO-1 are shown in Table 2.

In the $t = 2$ stage, the assignment ($f = 1.7280$, $g = 3$) can be selected for the engagement. HMODPSO-1 can efficiently solve the DWTA until no targets or weapons left in the cooperative air combat.

Table 2. The average results of the Pareto optimal solutions

Pareto solutions	HMODPSO-1
3	1.7280
4	1.7856
5	1.8372
6	1.8712
T/s	1.1155

5   Conclusions

This paper proposed a HMODPSO algorithm to efficiently solve cooperative air combat DWTA problems. Future research will focus on optimizing DWTA instances under larger scales.

References

1. Lloyd, S.P., Witsenhausen, H.S.: Weapons allocation is NP-complete. In: IEEE Summer Simulation Conference, pp. 1054–1058. IEEE Press, Reno (1986)
2. Hosein, P.A., Athans, M.: Preferential defense strategies. Part II: the dynamic case. MIT Laboratory Information and Decision System, Cambridge, MA, Report LIPSP-2003 (1900)
3. Cai, H., Liu, J., Chen, Y., Wang, H.: Survey of the research on dynamic weapon-target assignment problem. J. Syst. Eng. Electron. **17**, 559–565 (2006)
4. Liu, X., Liu, Z., Hou, W.S., Xu, J.H.: Improved MOPSO algorithm for multi-objective programming model of weapon-target assignment. J. Syst. Eng. Electron. **35**, 326–330 (2013). (in Chinese)
5. Kennedy, J., Eberhart, R.: Particle swarm optimization. In: Proceedings of IEEE International Conference on Neural Networks, pp. 1942–1948. IEEE Press, Perth (1995)
6. Leung, M.F., Ng, S.C., Cheung, C.C., Lui, A.K.: A new strategy for finding good local guides in MOPSO. In: IEEE Congress on Evolutionary Computation, pp. 1900–1997. IEEE Press, Beijing (2014)
7. Yan, J., Li, X.M., Liu, L.J., Zhang, F.X.: Weapon-target assignment based on memetic optimization algorithm in beyond-visual-range cooperative air combat. J. Beijing Univ. Aeronaut. Astronaut. **40**, 1424–1429 (2014). (in Chinese)
8. Wang, Y.C., Shan, G.L., Tong, J.: Solving sensor-target assignment problem based on cooperative memetic PSO algorithm. J. Syst. Eng. Electron. **35**, 1000–1007 (2013). (in Chinese)
9. Deb, K., Pratap, A., Agarwal, S.: A fast and elitist multiobjective genetic algorithm: NSGA-II. J. IEEE Trans. Evol. Comput. **6**, 182–197 (2002)
10. Wang, X., Song, T., Gong, F., Zheng, P.: On the computational power of spiking neural P systems with self-organization. Sci. Rep. **6**, 27624 (2016). doi:10.1038/srep27624
11. Gu, J.J., Zhao, J.J., Yan, J., Chen, X.D.: Cooperative weapon-target assignment based on multi-objective discrete particle swarm optimization-gravitational search algorithm in air combat. J. Beijing Univ. Aeronaut. Astronaut. **41**, 252–258 (2015). (in Chinese)

A Novel Image Fusion Method Based on Shearlet and Particle Swarm Optimization

Qiguang Miao$^{(\boxtimes)}$, Ruyi Liu, Yiding Wang, and Jianfeng Song

The School of Computer Science and Technology, Xidian University, Xi'an, China
qgmiao@126.com

Abstract. Multi-focus image fusion aims to fuse a set of images with different focus objects into one image which contains more information than that of individual source image. Along with the development of multi-scale geometric analysis tools, shearlet has been widely applied into image processing. In order to obtain an image with every object in focus, we propose a novel image fusion method based on shearlet and particle swarm optimization. Shearlet is used to decompose the images. Particle swarm optimization is applied to optimize the weighted factors of fusion. Experimental results show that our method can acquire better fusion quality than other methods.

Keywords: Shearlet · Particle swarm optimization · Fitness function

1 Introduction

Multi-focus image fusion has been widely applied into many different fields. It can create new images that are more informative and suitable for both visual perception and further computer processing. Recently, multi-resolution analysis has become a widely adopted technique to perform image fusion, including the Laplacian pyramid [1], the gradient pyramid [2], and the wavelet [3,4]. However, it is difficult for these traditional fusion methods to get a satisfactory result.

As the development of multi-scale geometric analysis (MGA) tools, there exist many MGA tools, such as ridgelet, curvelet and contourlet, which provide higher directional sensitivity than wavelets. Shearlet [5,6], a new approach proposed in 2005, not only possesses all the above properties, but also is equipped with a rich mathematical structure similar to wavelet. Besides, compared with contourlet, the limitation of the number of directions has been successfully eliminated by shearlet. So it has been used to image fusion widely [7]. As a new optimal tool, intelligent optimization algorithms play a vital role in solving optimization problems [8,9]. Among them, Particle swarm optimization has been applied to Artificial Intelligence, Machine Learning and so on [10,11].

This paper is organized as follows. Shearlet is described in Sect. 2. In Sect. 3, the basic theory of particle swarm optimization is introduced. The new algorithm is presented in Sect. 4. Experimental results and analysis are shown in Sect. 5. In the end, the conclusion is summarized in Sect. 6.

© Springer Nature Singapore Pte Ltd. 2016
M. Gong et al. (Eds.): BIC-TA 2016, Part II, CCIS 682, pp. 120–126, 2016.
DOI: 10.1007/978-981-10-3614-9_16

2   Shearlet

As a special affine transform, shearlet is a kind of composite wavelet in $L^2(R^2)$ [5,6]. The decomposition of shearlet is shown in Fig. 1. Discrete shearlet transform can effectively separate the low and high frequency coefficients which would lay the foundation for subsequent processing. It owns good properties, such as sparsity, high sensibility to directions, multi-scale, and good localization property.

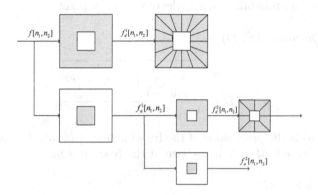

Fig. 1. Decomposition of shearlet

3   Particle Swarm Optimization

Particle swarm optimization (PSO) [10,11] is a population based stochastic optimization technique developed by Eberhart and Kennedy in 1995. The steps of the algorithm are as follows:

(1) Environment Initialization.
(2) Initialization: According to the characteristics of the problem, initialize a particle swarm P_0 size of N, and then randomly generate the initial position X_i and initial velocity v_i for each particle x_i.
(3) Calculation of Fitness: If the current value is superior to the individual optimal solution $pBest$ searched so far, update the current value to $pBest$. Otherwise, the value of $pBest$ remains unchanged.
(4) Determination of Overall Best Value: Choose the particle with the largest fitness value from the current population, and then set its fitness value as the overall best value $gBest$.
(5) Update the Position X_{id} and Velocity V_{id}.
(6) Terminate Condition: Judge whether the loop meets the terminate condition. If so, exit the loop and output the optimal solution. If it is not the case, then turn to step 3.

4 Multi-focus Image Fusion Algorithm Based on Shearlet and PSO

4.1 Introduction to Evaluation Criteria

1. Entropy (EN)

$$EN = -\sum_{i=0}^{i-1} P_i ln P_i \qquad (1)$$

where P_i is the probability of gray level i on each pixel.

2. Standard Deviation (STD)

$$STD = \sqrt{\frac{\sum_{i=0}^{N-1}\sum_{j=0}^{M-1}[f(x,y)-\mu]^2}{M \times N}} \qquad (2)$$

where $f(x,y)$ is the pixel value of the fused image at (x,y), denotes the mean value of the fused, $M \times N$ is the size of the fused image.

3. Average Grads (AG)

$$AG = \frac{1}{M \times N}\sum_{i=1}^{M-1}\sum_{j=1}^{N-1}\sqrt{\frac{(F(i,j)-F(i+1,j))^2 + (F(i,j)-F(i,j+1))^2}{2}} \qquad (3)$$

where $F(i,j)$ is the pixel value of image in row i, column j. M, N are the total row and total column. The larger the AG is, the clearer the fused image is.

4. Spatial Frequency (SF)

$$RF = \sqrt{\frac{\sum_{i=1}^{M}\sum_{j=2}^{N}[P(x_i,y_j)-P(x_i,y_{j-1})]^2}{M \times N}} \qquad (4)$$

$$CF = \sqrt{\frac{\sum_{i=2}^{M}\sum_{j=1}^{N}[P(x_i,y_j)-P(x_{i-1},y_j)]^2}{M \times N}} \qquad (5)$$

$$SF = \sqrt{RF^2 + CF^2} \qquad (6)$$

5. Mutual Information (MI)

$$MI(O,F) = \frac{EN_O + EN_F}{EN_{OF}} \qquad (7)$$

where EN_O, EN_F are the Entropy of original image and fused image, respectively. $O = f_A$ or $O = f_B$, $F = f$. EN_{OF} is the associated entropy which can be obtained based on the formula below.

$$EN_{OF} = -\sum_{i=1}^{M}\sum_{j=1}^{N} P(i, j)\log_2[P(i, j)] \tag{8}$$

where $P(i, j)$ is the possibility that pixel values (i, j) appear simultaneously. M, N are the total number of pixels in two images, respectively.

Besides, it can be seen that

$$MI = MI(f_A, f) + MI(f_B, f) \tag{9}$$

The large MI is, the better the result is.

6. Mean Cross Entropy (MCE)

$$\begin{cases} CE_{(f_A,f)} = \sum_{i=0}^{255} P_{f_A}(i)log|\frac{P_{f_A}(i)}{P_f(i)}| \\ CE_{(f_B,f)} = \sum_{i=0}^{255} P_{f_B}(i)log|\frac{P_{f_B}(i)}{P_f(i)}| \end{cases} \tag{10}$$

where f_A, f_B are the original images, and f is the fused image. Then MCE can be described as follows:

$$MCE = \frac{CE_{(f_A,f)} + CE_{(f_B,f)}}{2} \tag{11}$$

4.2   Multi-focus Image Fusion Based on Shearlet and PSO

The fusion framework of the proposed method is shown in Fig. 2.

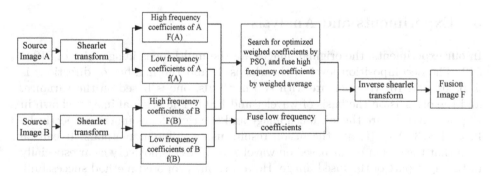

Fig. 2. Fusion framework of the proposed algorithm

The detail steps of our algorithm are described as follows:

(1) Image Registration: Register the source images before image fusion.

(2) Image Decomposition: Decompose the source images in both multi-scale and multi-direction by shearlet. Then the high frequency coefficients and low frequency coefficients are obtained.
(3) Process the Coefficients: The coefficients are processed by some certain fusion strategies.
(4) Image Reconstruction: Reconstruct the fused image by the inverse shearlet transform.

In the process of image fusion, the low frequency coefficients are processed based on the rule given below.

$$f_{low} = 0.5f_{A-low} + 0.5f_{B-low} \qquad (12)$$

In the proposed method, we choose weighting method to fuse the high frequency coefficients. Its formula is shown as follows:

$$f = \alpha f_A + (1 - \alpha)f_B \qquad (13)$$

where α is a weighted factor which is optimized by PSO algorithm.

In order to obtain a more comprehensive and accuracy fused image, three fitness functions are constructed as below.

$$fit_1() = \frac{(EN + SF + MI)}{\alpha} - \frac{STD}{\beta} \qquad (14)$$

where α, β are variable parameters. For the purpose of balancing the impact on fusion results of each evaluation index, here we set $\alpha = 2$, $\beta = 10$.

$$fit_2() = \frac{(MCE + AG) \times \gamma + SF}{2} \qquad (15)$$

where γ is a variable parameter.

5   Experiments and Analysis

In our experiments, the original images are the multi-focus images size of 512×512. The decomposition level of shearlet is 4, and the number of directions is 6, 6, 10, and 10. We compare with two methods, one is based on the variance, and the other is on the basis of wavelet and PSO. The original images shown in Fig. 3(a) and (b) are the left focus image and the right focus image, respectively. From Fig. 3(c) to (f) are the fusion results using different methods. It can be seen that the fusion result based on wavelet and PSO is not very clear especially in the right part of the fused image. However, our proposed method successfully reached a better performance in this experiment.

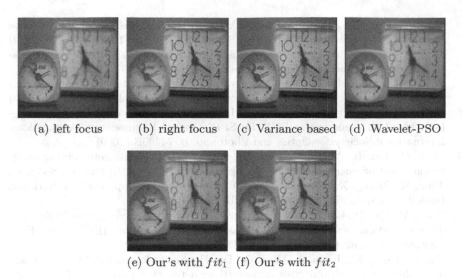

(a) left focus   (b) right focus   (c) Variance based   (d) Wavelet-PSO

(e) Our's with fit_1 (f) Our's with fit_2

Fig. 3. Experiment results

6   Conclusion

A novel multi-focus image fusion based on shearlet and PSO is proposed in this paper. Shearlet is an effective tool for image decomposition because of its multi-scale and multi-direction. Meanwhile, Particle swarm optimization, as a flexible optimizing tool with simple mechanism and strong search ability, has been successfully applied into the image fusion. Experimental results have proved the effectiveness and feasibility of our algorithm in image fusion.

Acknowledgments. The work was jointly supported by the National Natural Science Foundations of China under grant Nos. 61472302, 61272280, 41271447 and U1404620; The Program for New Century Excellent Talents in University under grant No. NCET-12-0919; The Fundamental Research Funds for the Central Universities under grant Nos. K5051203020, K5051303018, JB150313 and BDY081422; Natural Science Foundation of Shaanxi Province, under grant Nos. 2014JM8310 and 2010JM8027; The Creative Project of the Science and Technology State of Xi'an under grant No. CXY1441(1); The State Key Laboratory of Geo-information Engineering under grant No. SKLGIE2014-M-4-4.

References

1. Meek, T.R.: Multiresolution image fusion of thematic mapper imagery with synthetic aperture radar imagery. Technical report, DTIC Document (1999)
2. Rockinger, O.: Image sequence fusion using a shift-invariant wavelet transform. In: Proceedings of the International Conference on Image Processing, vol. 3, pp. 288–291. IEEE (1997)

3. Yang, Y., Huang, S., Gao, J., Qian, Z.: Multi-focus image fusion using an effective discrete wavelet transform based algorithm. Meas. Sci. Rev. **14**(2), 102–108 (2014)
4. Tian, J., Chen, L.: Adaptive multi-focus image fusion using a wavelet-based statistical sharpness measure. Signal Process. **92**(9), 2137–2146 (2012)
5. Easley, G., Labate, D., Lim, W.-Q.: Sparse directional image representations using the discrete shearlet transform. Appl. Comput. Harmon. Anal. **25**(1), 25–46 (2008)
6. Kutyniok, G., Shahram, M., Donoho, D.L.: Development of a digital shearlet transform based on pseudo-polar FFT. In: SPIE Optical Engineering+ Applications. International Society for Optics and Photonics, p. 74460B (2009)
7. Miao, Q., Liu, R., Wang, Y., Song, J., Quan, Y., Li, Y.: Remote sensing image fusion based on shearlet and genetic algorithm. In: Gong, M., Pan, L., Song, T., Tang, K., Zhang, X. (eds.) BIC-TA 2015. CCIS, vol. 562, pp. 283–294. Springer, Heidelberg (2015). doi:10.1007/978-3-662-49014-3_26
8. Gong, M., Cai, Q., Chen, X., Ma, L.: Complex network clustering by multiobjective discrete particle swarm optimization based on decomposition. IEEE Trans. Evol. Comput. **18**(1), 82–97 (2014)
9. Cai, Q., Gong, M., Ruan, S., Miao, Q., Du, H.: Network structural balance based on evolutionary multiobjective optimization: a two-step approach. IEEE Trans. Evol. Comput. **19**(6), 903–916 (2015)
10. Reyes-Sierra, M., Coello, C.C.: Multi-objective particle swarm optimizers: a survey of the state-of-the-art. Int. J. Comput. Intell. Res. **2**(3), 287–308 (2006)
11. Huang, R.: Improved artificial immune techniques for intrusion detection and pattern recognition. University of Liverpool, MA (2007)

Generalized Project Gradient Algorithm for Solving Constrained Minimax Problems

Cong Zhang$^{1(\boxtimes)}$, Limin Sun^1, and Zhibin Zhu^2

^{1} School of Mathematics and Information, Xinyang University, Xinyang 464000,
People's Republic of China
zhangmath@126.com
^{2} College of Mathematics and Computational Science,
Guilin University of Electronic Technology,
Guilin 541004, People's Republic of China

Abstract. In this work, constrained minimax problems are studied. By use of proposing a differentially auxiliary function and providing explicit search direction with the aid idea of generalized gradient project technique, a new algorithm with Armjio non-exact linear search is presented and its global convergence is obtained under arbitrary initial point condition.

Keywords: Constrained minimax problems · Generalized gradient project · Global convergence

1   Introduction

In this paper, it is proposed to consider the following constrained minimax problem:

$$
\begin{aligned}
\min \ & f_0(x) \\
\text{s.t.} \ & f_i(x) \le 0, i \in I \triangleq \{m+1, \cdots, l\}, \\
& f_i(x) = 0, i \in E \triangleq \{l+1, 2, \cdots, r\},
\end{aligned}
\tag{1}
$$

where $f_0(x) = max\{f_i(x), j \in J \triangleq \{1, 2, \cdots, m\}\}$, and $f_i(x)$, $i \in (J \cup I \cup E)$: $R^n \to R$ are continuously differentiable functions.

Due to the non-differentiability of the object function $f_0(x)$, We cannot use the classical gradient methods directly to solve such optimization problems [1–5]. However, by introducing an additional variable z, the minimax problem (1) can be reformulated as the nonlinear program in R^{n+1} as follows

$$
\begin{aligned}
\min \ & z \\
\text{s.t.} \ & f_i(x) \le z, i \in J, \\
& f_i(x) \le 0, i \in I, \\
& f_i(x) = 0, i \in E.
\end{aligned}
\tag{2}
$$

© Springer Nature Singapore Pte Ltd. 2016
M. Gong et al. (Eds.): BIC-TA 2016, Part II, CCIS 682, pp. 127–134, 2016.
DOI: 10.1007/978-981-10-3614-9_17

It is not difficult to know that the $K - T$ conditions of (2) at the point (x, z) are equivalent to

$$\sum_{i \in J \cup I \cup E} \lambda_i \nabla f_i(x) = 0, \quad \sum_{i \in J}^{m} \lambda_i = 1;$$
$$\lambda_i \geq 0, \ \lambda_i(z - f_i(x)) = 0, \ z - f_i(x) \geq 0, i \in J; \quad (3)$$
$$\lambda_i \geq 0, \ \lambda_i f_i(x) = 0, f_i(x) \leq 0, \ i \in I; f_i(x) = 0, i \in E.$$

Therefore, a pair (x, λ) satisfying (3) is called a stationary pair of (2), and x is said to be a stationary point of (1) with multiplier vector $\lambda = (\lambda_i, i \in J \cup I \cup E)$.

Since the 1960s, due to feature of simple construction and small amount of calculation, the generalized gradient project algorithm are currently considered among the most effective methods for solving nonlinear programming problems [7–9].

In this paper, we, introducing a differential auxiliary function

$$F(x, z, \lambda) = z - \sum_{i \in E \cup I_1} \left(\lambda_i f_i(x) - \tfrac{1}{2} f_i^2(x) \right) - \sum_{i \in J_1} \left(\lambda_i(z - f_i(x) - \tfrac{1}{2}(z - f_i(x))^2 \right)$$
$$- \sum_{i \in (J \cup I) \backslash (J_1 \cup I_1)} \tfrac{1}{2} \lambda_i^2,$$

$$(4)$$

where $J_1 \overset{\triangle}{=} J_1(x, z) = \{i \in J | z - f_i(x) \leq \lambda_i\}$, $I_1 \overset{\triangle}{=} I_1(x, z) = \{i \in I | - f_i(x) \leq \lambda_i\}$, present a generalized gradient project method to solve (1). Under some suitable assumptions, global convergence is obtained.

1.1   Description of Algorithm

For the sake of simplicity, we will denote the notations at $(x^k, z_k, \lambda^k) \in R^n \times R \times R^r$ as follows:

$$g_i(x^k, z_k) = \begin{cases} z_k - f_i(x^k), & z_k - f_i(x^k) > \lambda_i^k \text{ and } z_k - f_i(x^k) > 0, i \in J; \\ -f_i(x^k), & -f_i(x^k) > \lambda_i^k \text{ and } -f_i(x^k) > 0, i \in I \cup E; \\ 0, & \text{otherwise.} \end{cases}$$

$$G_k = G(x^k, z_k) = diag(g_i(x^k, z_k), i \in J \cup I \cup E).$$

$$(5)$$

$$A_{Jk} = \left(\begin{pmatrix} -\nabla f_i(x^k) \\ 1 \end{pmatrix}, i \in J \right), A_{IEk} = \left(\begin{pmatrix} -\nabla f_i(x^k) \\ 0 \end{pmatrix}, i \in I \cup E \right),$$
$$A_k = A(x^k, z_k) = (A_{Jk} \quad A_{IEk})$$

$$(6)$$

$$\bar{g}_i^k = \bar{g}_i(x^k, z_k) = \begin{cases} g_i(x^k, z_k), i \in J_{1k} \cup I_{1k} \cup E \overset{\triangle}{=} J_1(x^k, z_k) \cup I_1(x^k, z_k) \cup E, \\ 0, \qquad\qquad \text{otherwise.} \end{cases}$$

$$(7)$$

$$\bar{\lambda}_i^k = \begin{cases} \lambda_i^k, i \in J_{1k} \cup I_{1k} \cup E, \\ 0, \text{ otherwise.} \end{cases}$$

$$(8)$$

$$h_i^k = h_i(x^k, z_k) = \begin{cases} g_i^k, i \in J_{1k} \cup I_{1k} \cup E, \\ \lambda_i^k, \text{ otherwise.} \end{cases}$$

$$(9)$$

The following algorithm is proposed for solving problem (1).

Algorithm:

Step 1. Initialization and data: Given a starting point $(x^0, z_0, \lambda^0) \in R^n \times R \times R^r, t \in (0,1), k = 0;$

Step 2. Computation of the vector ρ_0^k which is important for the criterion of $K - T$ point:

Compute $\rho_0^k = (d_0^{kT}, s_0^{kT})^T$, where

$$P_k = P(x^k, z_k) = E_{n+1} - A_k(A_k^T A_k + G_k)^{-1} A_k^T, \quad B_k = B(x^k, z_k) = (A_k^T A_k + G_k)^{-1} A_k^T. \quad (10)$$

$$h^k = h(x^k, z_k, \lambda^k) = (h_i(x^k, z_k, \lambda^k), i \in I), \quad d_0^k = -P_k e_0 - B_k^T h^k, \quad e_0 = (0_{1 \times n} \ 1)^T. \quad (11)$$

$$v_0^k = B_k e_0 - (A_k^T A_k + G_k)^{-1} h^k. \quad (12)$$

$$s_0^k = -v_0^k + \overline{\lambda}^k - \overline{g}^k. \quad (13)$$

If $\rho_0^k = 0$, STOP.

Step 3. Computation of the search direction ρ^k: Obtain $\rho^k = (d^{kT}, s^{kT})^T$, where

$$d^k = d_0^k + B_k^T s_0^k, \quad v^k = v_0^k - (A_k^T A_k + G_k)^{-1} s_0^k, \quad s^k = -v^k + \overline{\lambda}^k - \overline{g}^k, \quad \rho^k = \begin{pmatrix} d^k \\ s^k \end{pmatrix}. \quad (14)$$

Step 4. The line search: Compute α_k, the first number α in the sequence $\{1, \frac{1}{2}, \frac{1}{4}, \frac{1}{8}, \ldots\}$ satisfying

$$F((x^k, z_k, \lambda^k) + \alpha \rho^k) \le F(x^k, z_k, \lambda^k) + \alpha t \nabla F^{kT} \rho^k \quad (15)$$

where ∇F^k denoting the gradient of the function (4):

$$\nabla F^k = \nabla F(x^k, z_k, \lambda^k) = \begin{pmatrix} \left(e_0 - A_k(\overline{\lambda}^k - \overline{g}^k)\right)_{(n+1) \times 1} \\ (-h(x^k, z_k, \lambda^k))_{m \times 1} \end{pmatrix}$$

Step 5. Update: Set $(x^{k+1}, z_{k+1}, \lambda^{k+1}) = (x^k, z_k, \lambda^k) + \alpha_k \rho^k$, $k := k + 1$, Go back to *step 2*.

2 Global Convergence of Algorithm

In this section, it is first shown that Algorithm is well defined, that is to say, it is possible to execute all the steps defined above. For this reason, we make the following general assumptions and let them hold throughout the paper.

H 2.1. *For all $(x, z) \in R^{n+1}$, the vectors*

$$\left\{ \begin{pmatrix} -\nabla f_i(x) \\ 1 \end{pmatrix}, i \in J(x, z), \begin{pmatrix} -\nabla f_i(x) \\ 0 \end{pmatrix}, i \in I(x, z) \cup E \right\}$$

are linearly independent, where $J(x, z) = \{i \in J | z - f_i(x) \le 0\} \cup J_1(x, z), I(x, z) = \{i \in J | -f_i(x) \le 0\} \cup I_1(x, z)$.

Lemma 2.1. *Under the assumption H 2.1, we have*

(i) $A_k^T P_k = G_k B_k$, $A_k^T B_k^T = E - G_k(A_k^T A_k + G_k)^{-1}$.
(ii) $(A_k^T A_k + G_k)$ *is a symmetric and positive definite matrix, and if*

$$x^k \to x^*, A_k \to A_*, G_k \to G_*, k \to \infty,$$

then $(A_*^T A_* + G_*)$ *symmetric and positive definite.*
(iii) $(\overline{\lambda}^k - \overline{g}^k)^T G_k = 0_{1 \times m}$.

Proof. The proof of this lemma $(i), (ii)$ is similar to that of Theorem $(1.1.9)$ in [6].

(iii) According to the definition of $\overline{\lambda}^k$ and $\overline{g}^k$, it is easy to see

$$(\overline{\lambda}^k - \overline{g}^k)_i = \lambda_i^k - g_i^k \geq 0, i \in J_1(x^k, z_k) \cup I_1(x^k, z_k) \cup E.$$

Correspondingly, the ith element of diagonal matrix G_k equal zero, i.e. $(G_k)_{ii} = 0$. While, for $i \in (J \cup I) \setminus (J_1(x^k, z_k) \cup I_1(x^k, z_k))$, we have $(\overline{\lambda}^k - \overline{g}^k)_i = 0$. Thereby,

$$(\overline{\lambda}^k - \overline{g}^k)^T G_k = 0.$$

The claim holds.

Lemma 2.2. *(i)* $e_0^T P_k e_0 \geq ||P_k e_0||^2$;
(ii) $-A_k^T d_0^k = G_k v_0^k + h^k$.

Proof. *(i)* From (10), it is clear that $e_0 = P_k e_0 + A_k(A_k^T A_k + G_k)^{-1} A_k^T$. Combining with Lemma 2.1, we get

$$\begin{aligned}
e_0^T P_k e_0 &= e_0^T P_k P_k e_0 + e_0^T P_k A_k(A_k^T A_k + G_k)^{-1} A_k^T e_0 \\
&= ||P_k e_0||^2 + e_0^T (A_k^T P_k)^T (A_k^T A_k + G_k)^{-1} A_k^T e_0 \\
&= ||P_k e_0||^2 + e_0^T (G_k B_k^T)^T (A_k^T A_k + G_k)^{-1} A_k^T e_0 \\
&= ||P_k e_0||^2 + (A_k^T e_0)^T \left((A_k^T A_k + G_k)^{-1} G_k (A_k^T A_k + G_k)^{-1} \right) (A_k^T e_0) \\
&\geq ||P_k e_0||^2
\end{aligned}$$

(ii) In view of the Lemma 2.1, we obtain from (11) that

$$\begin{aligned}
-A_k^T d_0^k &= A_k^T (P_k e_0 + B_k^T h^k) \\
&= A_k^T P_k e_0 + A_k^T B_k^T h^k \\
&= G_k B_k e_0 + (E - G_k(A_k^T A_k + G_k)^{-1}) h^k \\
&= G_k v_0^k + h^k
\end{aligned}$$

Lemma 2.3. $\nabla F_k^T \rho_0^k \leq -||P_k e_0||^2 - h^{kT}(A_k^T A_k + G_k)^{-1} h^k \leq 0.$

Proof. According to the definition of $F(x^k, z_k, \lambda^k)$, it is easy to verify that

$$\nabla F^k = \nabla F(x^k, z_k, \lambda^k) = \begin{pmatrix} \left(e_0 - A_k(\overline{\lambda}^k - \overline{g}^k)\right)_{(n+1)\times 1} \\ (-h(x^k, z_k, \lambda^k))_{m\times 1} \end{pmatrix}$$

From (11), (12) and (13), we have

$$\nabla F^{kT} \rho_0^k = - e_0^T P_k e_0 - (\overline{\lambda}^k - \overline{g}^k)^T A_k^T d_0^k - (B_k e_0)^T h^k$$
$$- h^{kT}(-B_k e_0 + (A_k^T A_k + G_k)^{-1} h^k + (\overline{\lambda}^k - \overline{g}^k))$$

It follows from Lemma 2.2(*ii*) that

$$\nabla F^{kT} \rho_0^k = - e_0^T P_k e_0 + (\overline{\lambda}^k - \overline{g}^k)^T (G_k v_0^k + h^k)$$
$$- (B_k e_0)^T h^k - h^{kT}(-B_k e_0 + (A_k^T A_k + G_k)^{-1} h^k + h^{kT}(\overline{\lambda}^k - \overline{g}^k))$$

Then, Combining with Lemma 2.1(*iii*) and Lemma 2.2(*i*), we deduce that

$$\nabla F^{kT} \rho_0^k = -||P_k e_0||^2 - h^{kT}(A_k^T A_k + G_k)^{-1} h^k \leq 0 \qquad (16)$$

Lemma 2.4. If x^k is not $K - T$ point of (1), then $\nabla F_k^T \rho^k < 0.$

Proof. From (13) and (14), we have

$$\rho^k = \rho_0^k + \begin{pmatrix} B_k^T s_0^k \\ (A_k^T A_k + G_k)^{-1} s_0^k \end{pmatrix}$$

So

$$\nabla F^{kT} \rho^k = \nabla F^{kT} \rho_0^k + (e_0 - A_k(\overline{\lambda}^k - \overline{g}^k))^T B_k^T s_0^k + (-h^k)^T (A_k^T A_k + G_k)^{-1} s_0^k$$
$$= \nabla F^{kT} \rho_0^k + (B_k e_0)^T - (\overline{\lambda}^k - \overline{g}^k)^T A_k^T B_k^T s_0^k - h^{kT}(A_k^T A_k + G_k)^{-1} s_0^k$$

In view of Lemma 2.1 (i)(iii), we, from (12) and (13), have

$$\nabla F^{kT} \rho^k = \nabla F^{kT} \rho_0^k + v_0^{kT} s_0^k - (\overline{\lambda}^k - \overline{g}^k)^T (E - G_k(A_k^T A_k + G_k)^{-1}) s_0^k$$
$$= \nabla F^{kT} \rho_0^k + v_0^{kT} s_0^k - (\overline{\lambda}^k - \overline{g}^k)^T s_0^k + (\overline{\lambda}^k - \overline{g}^k)^T G_k(A_k^T A_k + G_k)^{-1} s_0^k$$
$$= \nabla F^{kT} \rho_0^k - s_0^T s_0^k < 0.$$

Theorem 2.1. If $\rho_0^k = 0$, then x^k is a $K - T$ point of (1).

Proof. From $\rho_0^k = 0$, we have $\nabla F^{kT} \rho_0^k = 0$. Combining with (16), it follows that

$$P_k e_0 = 0, \ h^{kT}(A_k^T A_k + G_k)^{-1} h^k = 0. \qquad (17)$$

and thereby,

$$h^k = 0. \qquad (18)$$

Obviously, for $i \in \{i|i = 1, 2, \cdots, m, \; f_i(x^k) = z_k\} \cup \{i|i = m + 1, \cdots, l, \; f_i(x^k) = 0\}$, we have $\lambda_i^k = 0$. If $g_i(x^k, z_k) > \lambda_i^k$, then $\lambda_i^k = 0$, $g_i(x^k, z_k) > 0$.

It is easy to verify that

$$g_i(x^k, z_k) = 0, \; \lambda_i^k g_i(x^k, z_k) = 0, \; i \in E. \tag{19}$$

$$g_i(x^k, z_k) \geq 0, \; \lambda_i^k \geq 0, \; \lambda_i^k g_i(x^k, z_k) = 0, \; i \in J \cup I. \tag{20}$$

In addition, It follows from $\rho_0^k = 0$ that

$$s_0^k = 0, \; -v_0^k + \overline{\lambda}^k + \overline{g}^k = 0. \tag{21}$$

Again, from (18), (19), (20) and (21), we see

$$v_0^k = \overline{\lambda}^k = \lambda^k. \tag{22}$$

What's more, from (17), (18) and (22), we get $e_0 - A_k v_0^k = 0$, i.e.

$$\begin{pmatrix} 0_{n \times 1} \\ 1 \end{pmatrix} - \sum_{i \in J} \lambda_i^k \begin{pmatrix} -\nabla f_i(x^k) \\ 1 \end{pmatrix} - \sum_{i \in I \cup E} \lambda_i^k \begin{pmatrix} -\nabla f_i(x^k) \\ 0 \end{pmatrix} = 0, \tag{23}$$

which, combining with (19) and (20), implies x^k is a $K - T$ point of problem (1).

In order to present the global convergence of Algorithm, the following condition is necessary.

H 2.2. *The set* $\{(x, z, \lambda)|F(x, z, \lambda) \leq F(x^0, z_0, \lambda^0)\}$ *is bounded.*

According to assumption 2.2, there exists subset $K \subset \{1, 2, \cdots\}$, such that $x^k \to x^*$, $z_k \to z_*$, $\lambda^k \to \lambda^*$, $\forall k \in K$. Denote

$$g_i^* = g_i(x^*, z_*) = \begin{cases} z_* - f_i(x^*), & z_* - f_i(x^*) > \lambda_i^* \text{ and } z_* - f_i(x^*) > 0, i \in J; \\ -f_i(x^*), & -f_i(x^*) > \lambda_i^* \text{ and } -f_i(x^*) > 0, i \in I \cup E; \\ 0, & \text{otherwise.} \end{cases}$$

$G_* = G(x^*, z_*) = diag(g_i(x^*, z_*), i \in J \cup I \cup E)$, $B_* = (A_*^T A_* + G_*)^{-1} A_*$.

$P_* = E_{n+1} - A_* B_*$, $d_0^* = -P_* e_0 - B_* h^*$, $v_0^* = B_* e_0 - (A_*^T A_* + G_*)^{-1} h^*$.

$d* = d_0^* + B_* s_0^*$, $v^* = v_0^* - (A_*^T A_* + G_*)^{-1} s_0^*$, $s_0^* = -v_0^* + \overline{\lambda}^* + \overline{g}^*$.

Obviously, there exists $K_1 \subset K$, such that

$$\rho_0^k \to \rho_0^*, \quad \rho^k \to \rho^*, \quad \forall k \in K_1.$$

Theorem 2.2. *The algorithm either stops at $K - T$ point x^k of (1) in finite iteration, or generates an infinite sequence $\{x^k\}$ whose all accumulation points are $K - T$ points of (1).*

Proof. The first statement is obvious, the only stopping point being in step 2. Now, we suppose that an infinite sequence $\{x^k\}$ of points is generated by Algorithm. By contradiction, the accumulation point x^* of $\{x^k\}$ is not a $K - T$ point of (1). Similar to Lemma 2.4, we get $\nabla F^{*T} \rho^* < 0$. Combining with the continuity of ∇F, for k large enough, there exists $\overline{\alpha}_1 > 0$ and constant $a > 0$, such that

$$\nabla F((x^k, z_k, \lambda^k) + \alpha \rho^k)^T \rho^k \leq -a < 0. \tag{24}$$

where $\alpha \in [0, \overline{\alpha}_1]$. Taking into account (15) and Lemma 2.4, for k large enough, there exists $\overline{\alpha}_2 > 0$, such that

$$F(x^{k+1}, z_{k+1}, \lambda^{k+1}) \leq F((x^k, z_k, \lambda^k) + \alpha \rho^k) \tag{25}$$

where $\alpha \in [0, \overline{\alpha}_2]$.

Let $\overline{\alpha} = min\{\overline{\alpha}_1, \overline{\alpha}_2\}$. Again, by (24) and (25), one gets

$$F(x^{k+1}, z_{k+1}, \lambda^{k+1}) \leq F((x^k, z_k, \lambda^k) + \overline{\alpha} \rho^k)$$
$$= F(x^k, z_k, \lambda^k) + \overline{\alpha} \nabla F((x^k, z_k, \lambda^k) + \theta \overline{\alpha} \rho^k)^T \rho^k,$$

where parameter $0 < \theta < 1$. Further, for some constant k_0 and k large enough, we have

$$F(x^k, z_k, \lambda^k) \leq F(x^{k-1}, z_{k-1}, \lambda^{k-1}) - \overline{\alpha} a$$
$$\cdots \qquad \leq F(x^{k_0}, z_{k_0}, \lambda^{k_0}) - (k - k_0)\overline{\alpha} a \to -\infty, \ k \to \infty.$$

This is a contradiction, which shows that x^* is not a $K - T$ point of (1).

3   Numerical Experiments

In this section, we carry out numerical experiments based on the algorithm. The results show that the algorithm is effective.

During the numerical experiments, $\beta = 0.5, t = 0.2$.

Table 1. Numerical results for examples from Ref. [10]

No.	n	m	$l - m$	$r - l$	NG	FV	EPS
HS007	2	2	0	1	39	-5.87539	$0.10E - 5$
HS063	3	3	1	2	64	-3.93448	$0.10E - 5$
S378	10	8	0	3	157	$2.3339E + 3$	$0.10E - 3$

This algorithm has been tested on some problems from Ref. [10]. The results are summarized in Table 1. For each test problem, No. is the number of the test problem in [10], n the number of variables, m the number of object functions, $l - m$ the number of inequality constraints, $r - l$ the number of equality constraints, NIT the number of iterations, FV the final value of the objective function, and EPS the stopping criterion threshold ϵ. Execution is terminated if the norm of ρ_0^k is less than a constant $\epsilon > 0$.

Acknowledgment. This work was supported in part by the National Natural Science Foundation (11361018), the Natural Science Foundation of Guangxi Province (2014GXN SFFA118001), the Key Program for Science and Technology in Henan Education Institution (15B110008, 17A110030) and Huarui College Science Foundation (2014qn35) of China.

References

1. Han, S.P.: Variable matric methods for minimizing a class of nondifferentiable functions. Math. Program. **20**, 1–13 (1981)
2. Vardi, A.: A new minimax algorithm. J. Optim. Theory Appl. **75**, 613–634 (1992)
3. Husain, I., Jabeen, Z.: Continuous-time fractional minimax programming. Math. Comput. Model. **42**, 701–710 (2005)
4. Jian, J.B., Shi, L., Tang, C.M.: Perturbed SQP method with active set technology for unconstrained minimax problems. Appl. Math. J. Chin. Univ. **28**, 107–114 (2013)
5. Zhou, J.L., Tits, A.L.: Nonmonotone line search for minimax problems. J. Optim. Theory Appl. **76**, 455–476 (1996)
6. Jian, J.B.: Fast Algorithms for Smooth Constrained Optimization - Theoretical Analysis and Numerical Experiments, pp. 227–228. Science Press, Beijing (2010)
7. Rosen, J.B.: The gradient projection method for nonliear programming. Part 1. Linear constraints. SIAM J. Appl. Math. **8**, 181–217 (1960)
8. Gao, Z.Y., He, G.P.: A Generalized gradient project method for constrained optimization. Bull. Sci. Technol. **36**, 1443–1447 (1991)
9. Lai, Y.L., He, G.P., Gao, Z.Y.: Generalized gradient project method for nonlinear optimization. Sci. China **9**, 916–924 (1992)
10. Yu, Y.H., Gao, L.: Nonmonotone line search algorithm for constrained minimax problems. J. Optim. Theory Appl. **115**, 419–446 (2002)

A Real Adjacency Matrix-Coded Differential Evolution Algorithm for Traveling Salesman Problems

Hang Wei[1,2], Zhifeng Hao[1,3], Han Huang[4(✉)], Gang Li[1], and Qinqun Chen[2]

[1] School of Computer and Engineering, South China University of Technology,
Guangzhou, China
[2] School of Medical Information Engineering,
Guangzhou University of Chinese Medicine, Guangzhou, China
crwei@gzucm.edu.cn
[3] College of Science, Foshan University, Foshan, China
zfhao@fosu.edu.cn
[4] School of Software Engineering, South China University of Technology,
Guangzhou, China
hhan@scut.edu.cn

Abstract. Permutation-based combinatorial optimization problems have very wide application. Aim of the study is to design a real coding mechanism for evolutionary computing to solve permutation-based COPs. A real adjacency matrix-coded differential evolutionary algorithm (RAMDE) is proposed to solve traveling salesman problem (TSP): a classic COP. Considering TSP structure, a swarm of real adjacency matrices is adopted to represent individuals within population and arithmetical operators of DE execute in form of real matrices. Experimental results show that the proposed real adjacency matrix-coding mechanism is promising to extend DE for COPs.

Keywords: Real adjacency matrix-coding mechanism · Permutation-based combinatorial optimization problem (COP) · Differential evolution (DE) algorithm · Arithmetical operators · Traveling salesman problem (TSP)

1 Introduction

Permutation-based COPs appear in various domains [1]. Evolutionary algorithms (EAs) have been verified as effective alternatives for COPs [1–4]. Aim of the study is to design a real coding mechanism for COPs by evolutionary computation. Differential evolution (DE) is arguably one of the most powerful stochastic real-parameter optimization algorithms [5]. In order to apply DE for COPs with its powerful searching behavior in continuous space, a real adjacency matrix-coding mechanism is employed for TSP, which is NP-hard and widely applied [6]. Adopting a swarm of real adjacency matrices as data representation, structure of TSP can be described thoughtfully, so that satisfactory global

© Springer Nature Singapore Pte Ltd. 2016
M. Gong et al. (Eds.): BIC-TA 2016, Part II, CCIS 682, pp. 135–140, 2016.
DOI: 10.1007/978-981-10-3614-9_18

optimum could be found faster. Besides arithmetical operators of DE can be directly executed in form of real matrices, which makes the searching features in continuous space preserving.

In experiments, RAMDE outperformed state-of-the-art EAs with different data representation for TSP, such as ant colony system (ACS) [2] and set-based comprehensive learning particle swarm optimization(S-CLPSO) [3]. It illustrates that real matrix-coding mechanism imposed on DE is promising for COPs.

2   Real Adjacency Matrix-Coding Mechanism

2.1   TSP Prototype

TSP can be defined on a complete undirected graph $G = (V, E, D)$ if it's symmetric. Besides TSP can be defined on a complete directed graph if it's asymmetric [6]. The goal of TSP is to seek a Hamiltonian circuit T with the least costs. Vertex-set $V = \{1, 2, \ldots, n\}$, arc-set $E = \{<i, j>|i, j \in V\}$ and cost-set $D = \{d_{ij}|d_{ij} \geq 0; i, j \in V\}$ correspond to cities, paths between city i and city j and Euclidean distances of paths, respectively. Let $S = \{x = (v_1, v_2, \ldots, v_n)|(v_1, v_2, \ldots, v_n)$ is a permutaion of $V\}$ be the solution space of TSP. The cost of circuit is total length of arcs at solution x, so the value of objective function is the length of x.

$$f(x) = \sum_{i=2}^{n} d_{v_{i-1}v_i} + d_{v_n v_1} \tag{1}$$

2.2   Coding Mechanism for TSP

Considering entire association among vertices, individuals in population are represented as a swarm of real adjacency matrices.

$$W_k = (w_{ij})_{n \times n} \quad k = 1, 2, \ldots, NP \tag{2}$$

where n is number of vertices, w_{ij} represents the association weight between vertex v_i and vertex v_j or the decision weight of arc $<i, j>$, and NP is population size.

To map numeric search space into discrete solution space, decoding scheme is designed based on nearest neighbor heuristic for TSP. For choosing starting vertex v_s pseudo-random-proportional rule is employed according to standard deviation of association weights between the vertex $j(j = 1, 2, \ldots, n)$ and other vertices, denoted as $std(j)$. The value of $std(j)$ measures the difference of association weights between the vertex j and other vertices. The rule is applied as follows.

$$S = \begin{cases} argmax_{j \in J} std(j), & \text{if } q \leq q_0 \\ R & \text{otherwise} \end{cases} \tag{3}$$

where J is the set of vertices mutually exclusive chosen as starting vertices, q is a random number uniformly distributed in [0,1], q_0 is a parameter ($0 \leq q_0 \leq 1$), and R is a random variable selected according to the probability distribution given in Eq. (4).

$$p_j = \begin{cases} std(j)/\sum_{t\in J} std(j), & \text{if } t \in J \\ 0 & \text{otherwise} \end{cases} \tag{4}$$

Equations (3) and (4) are called as pseudo-random-proportional rule for sampling vertices as starting points, which favors vertices with great different weight between other vertices. Applied nearest neighbor heuristic, circuits are constructed correspondently to the chosen starting vertices. Here circuit T of minimal length is defined as a permutation of vertices $x = (v_1, v_2, \ldots, v_n)$ for solution to TSP in Eq. (5) and fitness of individual matrix $\mathbf{W}$ is defined as corresponding total length of $\mathbf{x}$ in Eq. (6).

$$x = \arg \min_{t=1,2,\ldots,n_0} f(x_t) \tag{5}$$

$$fit(W) = \min_{t=1,2,\ldots,n_0} f(x) \tag{6}$$

3   A Real Adjacency Matrix-Coded DE for TSP

3.1   Population Initializing

Considering some hints from distance matrix, one individual is initialized as reciprocal of distance matrix of the instance. To balance exploitation and exploration, other individuals are initialized randomly.

$$W_{k,ij} = \begin{cases} 1/d_{ij} & \text{if } k = 1; \ i,j = 1, 2, \ldots, N \\ lb + \lfloor rand \times (ub - lb) \rfloor & \text{if } k = 2, 3, \ldots, NP. \end{cases} \tag{7}$$

Where lb and ub are reciprocals of the longest and shortest arcs in instance respectively and rand is a *random* number uniformly distributed in [0,1].

3.2   Procedure of RAMDE

After encoding and initialization, iterations will be started. In iterations, DE operators are carried out in form of real matrices. If the best-so-far individual of the whole population W_{best} is replaced after iteration, a local search 3-opt [2] takes place for improvement. Algorithm 1 captures the framework of RAMDE (Fig. 1).

4   Experimental Studies

A series of experiments were implemented using TSP instances from TSPLIB [7]. Parameters are set as follows: $maxFEs$ is set as $(500 \times vertex - number)$ [4,5]; $q_0 = 0.9$ [3,4]; $F = 0.9$ [2], $CR = 0.9$ [5]; $NP = 5$ and $SR = 20\%$ according to experiments.

Algorithm 1. Procedure of RAMDE for TSP

Input :
 NP : *population size. maxFEs : max evaluation fitness times.* n_0 : *number of samp−ling circuits.* q_0 : *a parameter* $(0 \leqq q_0 \leqq 1)$ *of pseudo − random − proportional rule.*
Output : *best solution* **x** * *and its objective value.*
1 *Initialize population using Eq.* (7), $fe = 0$ *and* $\mathbf{W}_{best} = \mathbf{W}_1$
2 **for** $k \leftarrow 1$ *to* NP **do**
3 *if* **fit($\mathbf{w}_{k,G}$)** $<$ **fit($\mathbf{w}_{best}$)then**
4       $\mathbf{W}_{best} = \mathbf{W}_{k, G}$;
5   **end**
6 **end**
7 $fe = fe + NP$;
8 **while** $fe < maxFEs$ **do**
9 **for** $k \leftarrow 1$ *to* NP **do**
10   **Mutation** : *Generate donor matrix* $\mathbf{W}_k^{"}$ *via DE/best/2*
    $w_k^{"} = w_{best} + F(w_{r_1} - w_{r_2}) + F(w_{r_3} - w_{r_4})$(8)
11   **Crossover** : *Generate trial matrix* $\mathbf{W}_k^{"}$ *for the target matrix* $\mathbf{W}_k$
through binomial crossover in the following way :
    $$W^{"}{}_{k,ij} = \begin{cases} W_{k,ij}, \text{ if } rand \leq CR \\ W_{k,ij}, \text{ otherwise} \end{cases} \quad (9)$$
12   **Selection** : *Generate individual of next generation by greedy rule* :
    $$W_{k,G+1} = \begin{cases} W^{"}{}_{k,G}, \text{ if } fit(W^{"}{}_{k,G}) \leq fit(W_{k,G}) \\ W_{k,G}, \quad \text{ otherwise} \end{cases} \quad (10)$$
13   **if fit($\mathbf{W}_{k,G+1}$)** $\leq$ **fit($\mathbf{W}_{best}$) then**
14          $\mathbf{W}_{best} = \mathbf{W}_{k, G+1}$;
15   **end**
16   **end**
17   *If* $\mathbf{W}_{best}$, *is changed, the solution is brought to a local minimum using a tour improvement3 − opt.*
18    $fe = fe + NP$;
19 **end**
20 **return** *the fitness of individual* $\mathbf{W}_{best}$ *and its correspondent solution* **x**∗

4.1 Comparisons with Other EAs Using Different Data Representation

Furthermore, comparisons with other well-known EAs using different data representation approaches were carried out, such as ACS [2] and S-CLPSO [4]. 3-opt local search operators were imposed on the best-so-far individual in each iteration. The experimental results of large-mid scale instances were listed in Table 1. The proposed RAMDE outperformed ACS significantly and overtook S-CLPSO as well.

4.2 Analysis of the Convergent Characteristics of RAMDE

To demonstrate convergent characteristics of RAMDE, average FEs utilization of 12 instances were displayed in Table 2. Much fewer evaluation times were needed, which accounted for 0.13% to 22.58% of *maxFEs*. Computing complexity as $O(n^2)$ in decoding scheme would be made up largely. As fl1400 instance, a

Table 1. Comparing RAMDE with other EAs for TSP (over 50 runs)

Instance	Best known	Algorithm	Best	Average	Error
lin318	42029	RAMDE	42513	42513	1.15%
		ACS	48739	50690.38	20.61%
		S-CLPSO	42719	43518.4	3.54%
pcb442	50778	RAMDE	51396	51532.9	1.49%
		ACS	61879	66013.6	30.00%
		S-CLPSO		51577.7	1.57%
d493	35002	RAMDE	35642	35717.8	2.05%
		ACS	39050	40271.4	15.05%
		S-CLPSO		37028.83	5.79%
d657	48912	RAMDE	49953	50304.2	2.85%
		ACS	58405	59851.86	22.37%
		S-CLPSO		51799.53	5.90%
u724	41910	RAMDE	42885	43025.4	2.66%
		ACS	58405	59704.8	42.46%
		S-CLPSO		43373.3	3.49%
fl1400	20127	RAMDE	20455	20455	1.63%
		ACS	29376	30468	51.38%
		S-CLPSO	22141	22025.2	9.43%

Note: Error = 100% * (average-best known)/best known

Table 2. FEs utilization of RAMDE

Instance	maxFEs	Average FEs	FEs utilization	Instance	maxFEs	Average FEs	FEs utilization
eil51	25500	283.9	1.11%	lin318	159000	5022	3.16%
berlin52	26000	60	0.23%	pcb442	221000	5320.6	2.41%
st70	35000	412.8	1.18%	d493	246500	55662.3	22.58%
kroA100	50000	751.8	1.50%	d657	328500	72859.58	22.18%
lin105	52500	9343.5	17.80%	u724	362000	65007	17.96%
pr152	76000	2142	2.82%	fl1400	700000	880	0.13%

desired optimum could be found within 0.13% of *maxFEs* by RAMDE, while not by ACS or S_CLPSO.

5 Conclusion

In this paper, a real adjacency matrix-coding is proposed to extend DE for permutation-based COPs like TSP. Adopting a swarm of real adjacency matrices as data representation, structure of TSP can be described more thoughtfully, so that global optimum would be found within much less evaluation times. Moreover, arithmetical operators of DE can stay the same in form of real matrices. Hence searching features of DE in continuous space would be preserved to a large extent. By comparing performance of RAMDE, ACS and S-CLPSO for TSP, superior behavior of the real matrix-coding mechanism is clearly demonstrated, both on effect and efficiency. In future, its necessary to introduce some techniques such as machine learning to guide searching direction for faster optimization [8–11].

Acknowledgments. This work is financially supported by NSFC-Guangdong Joint Found (U1501254), Natural Science Foundation of China (61370102, 61202269, 61472089, 61572143, 61502108, 61502109), Natural Science Foundation of Guangdong province (2015 A030310312, 2014A030309013, 2014A030306050, 2014A030306004, 2014A030308 008), Key Technology Research and Development Programs of Guangdong Province (2015B010108006, 2015B010131015), Science and Technology Plan Project of Guangzhou City (2014Y2-00027), Opening Project of the State Key Laboratory for Novel Software Technology (KFKT2014B03, KFKT2014B23), the Fundamental Research Funds for the Central Universities, SCUT (2015PT022), Philosophy and social science project of Guangdong Provenience (GD14XYJ24), Guang dong High-level personnel of special support program (2014TQ01X664).

References

1. Onwubolu, G.C., Davendra, D.: Differential Evolution: A Handbook for Global Permutation-Based Combinatorial Optimization. Springer, Heidelberg (2009)
2. Dorigo, M., Gambardella, L.M.: Ant colony system: a cooperative learning approach to thetraveling salesman problem. IEEE Trans. Evol. Comput. 1(1), 53–66 (1997)
3. Chen, W., Zhang, J., Chung, H.H., et al.: A novel set-based particle swarm optimization method for discrete optimization problems. IEEE Trans. Evol. Comput. 14(2), 278–300 (2010)
4. Liu, Y., Chen, W.N., Zhan, Z.H., et al.: A set-based discrete differential evolution algorithm. In: IEEE International Conference on Systems, Man, and Cybernetics, pp. 1347–1352. IEEE press, Manchester (2013)
5. Das, S., Suganthan, P.N.: Differential evolution: a survey of the state-of-the-art. IEEE Trans. Evol. Comput. 15(1), 4–31 (2010)
6. Matai, R., Mittal, M.L., Singh, S.: Traveling Salesman Problem: An Overview of applications, Formulations, and Solution Approaches. Intech Open Access Publisher, Rijeka (2010)
7. TSPLIB. http://www.Iwr.uni_heidelberg.de
8. Zhou, A., Zhang, Q.: A surrogate-assisted evolutionary algorithm for mini max optimization. In: IEEE Congress on Evolutionary Computation, pp. 1–7. IEEE Press, Barcelona (2010)
9. Song, T., Pan, L.: Spiking neural P systems with request rules. Neurocomputing 193(12), 193–200 (2016)
10. Song, T., Liu, X., Zhao, Y., Zhang, X.: Spiking neural P systems with white hole neurons. IEEE Trans. Nanobiosci. (2016). doi:10.1109/TNB.2016.2598879
11. Song, T., Pan, Z., Wong, D.M., Wang, X.: Design of logic gates using spiking neural P systems with homogeneous neurons and astrocytes-like control. Inf. Sci. 372, 380–391 (2016)

A Hybrid IWO Algorithm Based on Lévy Flight

Xuncai Zhang, Xiaoxiao Wang, Guangzhao Cui, and Ying Niu[✉]

College of Electrical and Information Engineering,
Zhengzhou University of Light Industry,
No. 5 Dongfeng Road, Zhengzhou 450002, China
niuying@zzuli.edu.cn

Abstract. This paper presents a hybrid nature inspired metaheuristic algorithms, which derive from Invasive Weed Optimization (IWO) and Cuckoo Search (CS). Based on the novel and distinct qualifications of IWO and CS, we introduce a hybrid IWO algorithm and try to combine their excellent features in this extended algorithm. The efficiency of this algorithm both in the case of speed of convergence and optimality of the results are compared with IWO algorithm through a number of common multi-dimensional benchmark functions. Finally, experimental results show that the proposed approach can be successfully employed as a fast and global optimization method for a variety of theoretical or practical purposes.

Keywords: Particle swarm optimization · Cuckoo search · Lévy flight · Hybrid multi-objective optimization algorithm

1 Introduction

Optimization theory plays an important role in the field of science and engineering. Most of the applications of engineering like engineering design and communication engineering depend on optimization techniques that must be solved efficiently and effectively. Various optimization techniques are developed to handle real world problems. In the recent past, a wide range of practical problems have been solved by using metaheuristics approach as it produces the most suitable optimal solution with a reasonable computation [1]. Most of these algorithms are nature inspired [2], some of which have been proposed for optimization problems, such as Genetic Algorithm (GA) [3], Harmony Search (HS) [4], Ant Colony Optimization (ACO) [5], Imperialist Competitive Algorithm (ICA) [6] Artificial Bee Colony (ABC) [7] and Ant Lion Optimization [8].

In this article, a hybrid IWO algorithm based on Lévy flight of CS (HIWOLF) is proposed. This algorithm is merged the idea of intelligent swarming, social cooperation, competition, and reproduction in an optimization meta-algorithm. Invasive Weed Optimization is a novel ecologically inspired algorithm that mimics the process of weeds colonization and distribution. Despite its recent development, it has shown successful results in a number of practical applications like optimization and tuning of a robust controller [9], optimal positioning of

© Springer Nature Singapore Pte Ltd. 2016
M. Gong et al. (Eds.): BIC-TA 2016, Part II, CCIS 682, pp. 141–150, 2016.
DOI: 10.1007/978-981-10-3614-9_19

piezoelectric actuators [10], developing a recommender system [11], antenna configuration [12], analysis of electricity markets dynamics [13], machine learning [14], Biomedical Engineering [15–17], etc. Cuckoo search (CS) is inspired from the obligate brood parasitim of some cuckoo species in combination with the Lévy flight of some birds and fruit flies [15] and has been used in a large number of application like Economic dispatch (ED) system [18], virtualization technology [19], thermodynamic cycles [20], etc.

The rest of this article is organized as follows. Section 2 gives brief details of the standard IWO and Lévy flight of CS. Section 3 describes detailed explanation of HIWOLF algorithm. Section 4 presents some benchmark functions, and compares the results with IWO approach in the literatures. Finally, Sect. 5 discusses the conclusion and proposals for future work.

2   Preliminary Study

In this section, we provide the reader some details of the two algorithms, IWO and CS algorithms. Our aim is to fully prepare for below.

2.1   Invasive Weed Optimization

IWO is a novel population based numerical stochastic, derivative free optimization algorithm inspired from the biological growth of weed plants. It was first developed and designed by Mehrabian and Lucas in 2006 [9]. This technique is based on the colonizing behavior of weed plants. The IWO algorithm simply simulated natural behavior of weeds in colonizing and finding suitable place for growth and reproduction. The steps of the IWO algorithm are mentioned below:

Step 1: (Initialization) A certain number of weeds are randomly spread over in a small region of the search space. This initial population of each generation will be termed as $X = x_1, x_2, \cdots, x_m$.

Step 2: (Reproduction) Each weed produces a number of seeds depending on altering linearly from N_{min} to N_{max}, because highest ranked weed produces maximum number of seeds. The number of seeds can be computed using the Eq. (1) below,

$$N_{seeds} = \frac{F_i - F_{worst}}{F_{best} - F_{worst}}(N_{max} - N_{min}) + N_{min} \tag{1}$$

where F_i is the fitness of i_{th} weed. F_{worst} and F_{best} denote the worst and best fitness value in weed population.

Step 3: (Spatial Distribution) The produced seeds are spread across the neighborhood of the parent weed, and are added to the weed population. The varying standard deviation of iteration is described by Eq. (2),

$$N_{seeds} = (\frac{iter_{max} - iter}{iter_{max}})^n (\sigma_0 - \sigma_f) + \sigma_f \tag{2}$$

where $iter_{max}$ and $iter$ are the maximum number of iteration cycles assigned by the user and current iteration number, respectively. The σ_0 and σ_f are the predefined initial and final standard deviations, and n is the nonlinear modulation index.

Step 4: (Competitive Exclusion) When the maximum number of weeds in a colony is reached, each weed is allowed to produce seeds according to the mechanism mentioned in the Step 2. The produced seeds are then allowed to spread over the search area according to the Step 3. To begin with, when all seeds have found their position in the search area, they are ranked together with their parents. Next, weeds with worst fitness are eliminated to reach the maximum allowable population size P_{max} in a colony. The population control mechanism is also applied to their offspring until the stopping criterion is met, realizing competitive exclusion.

2.2   Invasive Weed Optimization

CS is one of the latest nature-inspired metaheuristic algorithms. This algorithm is not only because of the brood parasitic behavior of some cuckoo species, but also because of Lévy flights behavior of some birds [21], rather than simple isotropic random walks. Subsequent investigations have demonstrated that CS is a simple yet very promising population-based stochastic search technique by using Lévy flights random walk. Various studies have shown that fruit flies or Drosophila melanogaster explore their landscape using a series of straight flight path punctuated by a sudden 90 turn, leading to a Lévy-flight-style pattern. Such behavior has been applied to optimal search, and preliminary results show its promising capability [22]. Figure 1 shows an example of the Lévy flights path.

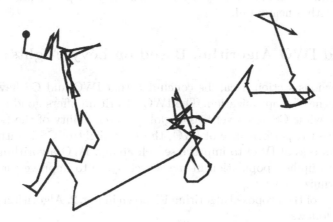

Fig. 1. Example of the Lévy flights path.

For simplicity in describing the CS, we introduce in three idealized rules: (1) Each cuckoo lays a egg at a time, and dumps it in a randomly chosen nest. (2)

The best nest with high quality of eggs (solutions) will be carried over to the next generation. (3) The number of available host nests is fixed, and a host can discover an alien egg with a probability $Pa \in [0, 1]$. In this case, the host bird can either get rid of the egg, or simple abandon the nest and build a new nest.

For minimization problem, the fitness value of a solution can be proportional to the value of its objective function. Other forms of fitness can be defined in a similar way in other evolutionary algorithm. The goal is to use the new and potentially better solutions (cuckoos) to replace worse solutions in the nests. When generating new solutions x^{t+1} for cuckoo i, a Lévy flight is performed using the following Eq. (3):

$$x^{t+1} = x^t + \alpha \oplus Levy(\lambda) \tag{3}$$

where $\alpha > 0$ is the step size which is related to the scales of the problem of interests. The product $\oplus$ means entry-wise multiplication. The above equation is essentially the stochastic equation for random walk. In general, a random walk is a Markov chain whose next status location only depends on the current location (the first term in the above Eq. (3)) and the transition probability (the second term).

The Lévy flight essentially provides a random walk, while the random step length is drawn from a Lévy distribution using the following Eq. (4). The distribution has an infinite variance with an infinite mean.

$$Levy(\lambda) \sim u = t^{-\lambda} \tag{4}$$

Studies show that Lévy flights can maximize efficiency of resource searches in uncertain environments [23]. Here the consecutive jumps/steps of a cuckoo essentially form a random walk process which obeys a power-law step-length distribution with a heavy tail.

3   Hybrid IWO Algorithm Based on Lévy Flights

From the previous section it can be concluded that IWO and CS have two different approaches for optimization. The IWO algorithm offers good exploration and diversity, while CS has a very good global search ability of the Lévy flight.

To improve the performance of IWO, the Lévy flight of CS is introduced in the update process of IWO to improve search ability. IWO algorithm first uses Lévy flights to update population in the search space to improve the ability of searching optimization.

A flowchart of the proposed algorithm is shown in Fig. 2. Algorithm procedure is defined as follows.

Step 1: Generate random population of N_0 solution;
Step 2: For *iter*=1 to the maximum number of generation;
    Step 2.1: Calculate fitness of each initialize individual;
    Step 2.2: Produce seeds according to Eq. (1);

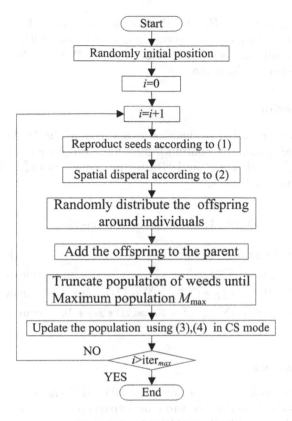

Fig. 2. Flowchart of HIWOLF algorithm.

Step 2.3: Randomly distribute generated seeds over search area according to Eq. (2);

Step 2.4: For each individual $w \in W$;

 Step 2.4.1: Randomly distribute the offspring around the parent individual w;

 Step 2.4.2: Add the offspring to the parent solution set W;

Step 2.5 If $(|W| = N) > M_{max}$;

 Step 2.5.1: Sort their fitness in the population W;

 Step 2.5.2: Truncate population of weeds with worse fitness until $N = M_{max}$;

Step 2.6 Update the population according to Eqs. (3), (4) in CS algorithm;

Step 3: Next *iter*;

4 Simulation Studies

In this section, several simulation studies are carried out to demonstrate merits of the proposed optimization algorithm. In the first step, the capability of the HIWOLF algorithm is demonstrated though three benchmark functions, "Sphere", "Griewank" and "Rastrigin".

As the second step, the HIWOLF algorithm is applied for finding optimal solution of the three high dimension continuous functions with the dimension of $d = 30Z$. The results are compared to a standard IWO to display the performance of the proposed algorithm.

4.1 Test Functions

Three studies are conducted to demonstrate ability of the HIWOLF algorithm in locating global minima of continues functions. Employed benchmark examples are "Sphere", "Griewank" and "Rastrigin" functions [9], which have some properties reported in Table 1.

Table 1. Optimization test functions

Problem	Objective functions	Sketch in 3D
sphere	$f(x) = \sum_{i=1}^{n} x_i^2$	convex
griewank	$f(x) = \frac{1}{4000} * (\sum_{i=1}^{n} x_i^2) - \prod \cos(\frac{x_i}{\sqrt{i}}) + 1$	convex
rastrigin	$f(x) = (\sum_{i=1}^{n} x_i^2 - 10\cos(2\Pi * x_i) + 10)$	convex

4.2 Test Functions

For the purpose of comparison between the HIWOLF and IWO algorithms, all the experiments are based on the same basic parameter settings, in which they are shown in Table 2. To facilitate the experimentation, we use the Matlab 7.0 to product simulation.

Table 2. The HIWOLF parameters values

Parameters	value
Number of initial population N_0	30
Number of maximum population N_{max}	50
Maximum number of iterations $iter_{max}$	2000
Problem dimension dim	30
Maximum number of seeds s_{max}	5
Minimum number of seeds s_{min}	2
Nunlinear modulation index n	3
Initial value of standard deviation $\sigma_{initial}$	10
Final value of standard deviation σ_{final}	0.001
Initial search area x_{ini}	$[-100, 100]$
Search Space Upper Bound Ub	100
Search Space Lower Bound Lb	-100

In this study, each experiment has been repeated 50 times, and the global best fitness of the 50 runs has been reported. For comparing the two algorithms, the change trends of the three test functions are shown in Figs. 3, 4 and 5.

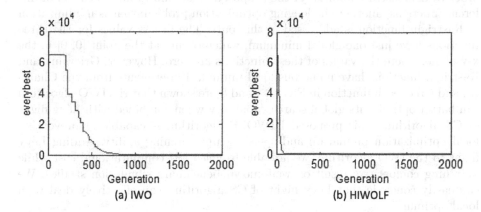

Fig. 3. The best solution of every generation with the two algorithms on Sphere.

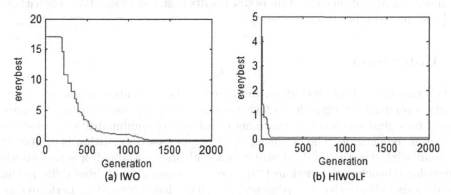

Fig. 4. The best solution of every generation with the two algorithms on Griewank.

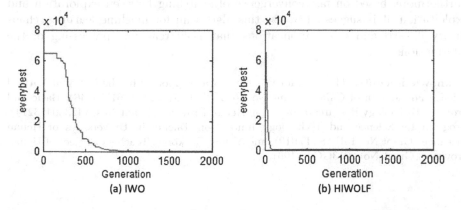

Fig. 5. The best solution of every generation with the two algorithms on Rastrigin.

For the three functions, Sphere function is a continuous, strongly convex function. Finding minima of the Griewank function is a challenging problem, which is the main reason for being a favorite benchmark for optimization algorithms. In order to demonstrate abilities of the proposed algorithm in minimization of different functions, another challenging optimization problem that is minimization of Rastrigin function is addressed in this part. The fitness values for the three functions have just one global minimum, which occurs at the point [0, 0] in the x-y plane, where the values of these functions are zero. However, Griewank and Rastrigin functions have numerous local minima. Experiments from the Charts (a) and (b) of each function in Figs. 3, 4 and 5 are shown that the IWO algorithm can batter optimize its global search capability when combined with Lévy flight of CS algorithm. This proposed HIWOLF algorithm is capable of preventing local optimization premature and speeding up searching ability. Adding Lévy flight to the IWO algorithm, we are able to get a low computational cost while obtaining competitive result on well-known benchmark simulation studies. We can easily conclude that Lévy flight of CS algorithm can effectively deal with local optimum.

By analyzing the above results, we can preliminarily conclude that the hybrid optimization algorithm can obtain better results than commonly IWO algorithm, and also provides better convergence.

5   Conclusion

In this paper, a hybrid IWO algorithm based on Lévy flights is a numerical stochastic optimization algorithm which includes some intelligent natural behaviors of biological systems like swarming collaborative communication, colonization, and competition. The performance of the proposed algorithm is evaluated by comparing it with standard evolutionary algorithm through a set of multi-dimensional benchmark functions ("Sphere", "Griewank", and "Rastrigin"). The simulations indicate that the proposed algorithm has outstanding performance in speed of convergence and precision of the solution for global optimization. Furthermore, based on fast convergence of switching between exploration and exploitation, it is suggested to use this algorithm for machine learning, chaos theory [25–31] and other applications that need real-time processing of the information.

Acknowledgments. The work for this paper was supported by the National Natural Science Foundation of China (Grant Nos. 61472371, 61472372, 61572446), Basic and Frontier Technology Research Program of Henan Province (Grant Nos. 142300413214), Program for Science and Technology Innovation Talents in Universities of Henan Province (Grant No. 15HASTIT019), and Young Backbone Teachers Project of Henan province (Grant No. 2013GGJS-106).

References

1. Ramu, N.Y., Ojha, A.K.: Solving nonlinear constrained optimization problems by invasive weed optimization using penalty function. In: IEEE International Advance Computing Conference (IACC), Gurgaon, pp. 1326–1330 (2014)
2. Yang, X.-S.: Metaheuristic optimization: algorithm analysis and open problems. In: Pardalos, P.M., Rebennack, S. (eds.) SEA 2011. LNCS, vol. 6630, pp. 21–32. Springer, Heidelberg (2011). doi:10.1007/978-3-642-20662-7_2
3. Holland, J.H.: Adoption in Natural and Artificial Systems. University of Michigan Press, Ann Arbor (1975)
4. Geem, Z.W., Kim, J.H., Loganathan, G.V.: A new heuristic optimization algorithm: harmony search. Simulation 76(2), 60–68 (2001)
5. Dorigo, M., Di Caro, G.: The ant colony optimization meta-heuristic. In: Corne, D., Dori-go, M., Glover, F. (eds.) New Ideas in Optimization. McGraw-Hill, England (1999)
6. Atashpaz-Gargari, E., Lucas, C.: Imperialist competitive algorithm: an algorithm for optimization inspired by imperialistic competition. In: Proceedings of the IEEE Congress on Evolutionary Computation, Singapore, pp. 4661–4667 (2007)
7. Karaboga, D.: An idea based on honey bee swarm for numerical optimization. Technical report-TR06, pp. 1–10 (2005)
8. Seyedali, M.: The ant lion optimizer. Adv. Eng. Softw. 83, 158–174 (2015)
9. Mehrabian, A.R., Lucas, C.: A novel numerical optimization algorithm inspired from weed colonization. Ecol. Inform. 1(4), 355–366 (2006)
10. Mehrabian, A.R., Yousefi-Koma, A.: Optimal positioning of piezoelectric actuators of smart fin using bio-inspired algorithms. Aerosp. Sci. Technol. 11, 174–182 (2007)
11. Sepehri-Rad, H., Lucas, C.: A recommender system based on invasive weed optimization algorithm. In: IEEE Congress on Evolutionary Computation, Singapore, pp. 4297–4304 (2007)
12. Dadalipour, B., Mallahzadeh, A.R., Davoodi-Rad, Z.: Application of the invasive weed optimization technique for antenna configurations. Prog. Electromagnet. Res. 79, 425–428 (2008). Loughborough
13. Sahraei-Ardakani, M., Roshanaei, M., Rahimi-Kian, A., Lucas, C.: A study of electricity market dynamics using invasive weed optimization. In: IEEE Symposium on Computational Intelligence and Games, Perth, Australia, pp. 276–282 (2008)
14. Xu, J.: Probe machine. IEEE Trans. Neural Netw. Learn. Syst. 27(7), 1405–1416 (2016)
15. Yang, J., Dong, C., Dong, Y.F., Liu, S., Pan, L.Q., Zhang, C.: Logic nanoparticle beacon triggered by the binding-induced effect of multiple inputs. ACS Appl. Mater. Interfaces 6(16), 14486–14492 (2014)
16. Shi, X.L., Lu, W., Wang, Z.Y., Pan, L.Q., Cui, G.Z., Xu, J., LaBean, T.H.: Programmable DNA tile self-assembly using a hierarchical sub-tile strategy. Nanotechnology 25(7), 1–12 (2014)
17. Shi, X.L., Wang, Z.Y., Deng, C.Y., Song, T., Pan, L.Q., Chen, Z.H.: A novel biosensor based on DNA strand displacement. PLoS ONE 9(10), 1–16 (2014)
18. Yang, X.S., Deb, S.: Cuckoo search via Lévy flights. In: World Congress on Nature Biologically Inspired Computing, India, pp. 210–214 (2009)
19. Dieu, N.V., Peter, S., Weerakorn, O.: Cuckoo search algorithm for non-convex economic dispatch. IET Gener. Transm. Distrib. 7(6), 645–654 (2013)
20. Sadiq, M.S., Abubakar, B., Aiman, H.E.: Cuckoo search based resource optimization of datacenters. Appl. Intell. 44(3), 489–506 (2016)

21. Manesh, M.H.K., Ameryan, M.: Optimal design of a solar-hybrid cogeneration cycle using Cuckoo Search algorithm. Appl. Therm. Eng. **102**, 1300–1313 (2016)
22. Tuba, M., Subotic, M., Stanarevic, N.: Modified cuckoo search algorithm for unconstrained optimization problems. In: Proceedings of the 5th European Conference on European Computing Conference, Republic of Serbia, pp. 263–268 (2011)
23. Walton, S., Hassan, O., Morgan, K., Brown, M.R.: Modified cuckoo search: a new-gradient free optimization algorithm. Chaos, Solitons Fractals **44**, 710–718 (2011)
24. Yang, X.S., Deb, S.: Engineering optimization by cuckoo search. Int. J. Math. Model. Numer. Optim. **1**(4), 330–334 (2010)
25. Sun, J.W., Shen, Y., Zhang, G.D., Xu, C.J., Cui, G.Z.: Combination-combination synchronization among four identical or different chaotic systems. Nonlinear Dyn. **73**(3), 1211–1222 (2013)
26. Junwei, S., Guangzhao, C., Yanfeng, W., Yi, S.: Combination complex synchronization of three chaotic complex systems. Nonlinear Dyn. **79**(2), 953–965 (2015)
27. Sun, J.W., Yin, Q., Shen, Y.: Compound synchronization for four chaotic systems of integer order and fractional order. EPL (Europhys. Lett.) **106**(4), 40005–40010 (2014)
28. Sun, J.W., Shen, Y.: Quasi-ideal memory system. IEEE Trans. Cybern. **45**(7), 1353–1362 (2015)
29. Song, T., Pan, L.: Spiking neural P systems with request rules. Neurocomputing **193**(12), 193–200 (2016)
30. Song, T., Pan, Z., Wong, D.M., Wang, X.: Design of logic gates using spiking neural P systems with homogeneous neurons and astrocytes-like control. Inf. Sci. **372**, 380–391 (2016)
31. Wang, X., Song, T., Gong, F., Pan, Z.: On the computational power of spiking neural P systems with self-organization. Sci. Rep. doi:10.1038/srep27624

Evolutionary Process: Parallelism Analysis of Differential Evolution Algorithm Based on Graph Theory

Xiaoqi Peng[1], Zhifeng Hao[2], Han Huang[3(✉)], Hongyue Wu[3],
and Fangqing Liu[3]

[1] School of Applied Mathematics, Guangdong University of Technology,
Guangzhou 510520, China
[2] School of Mathematics and Big Data, Foshan University, Foshan 528000, China
[3] School of Software Engineering, South China University of Technology,
Guangzhou 510006, China
hhan@scut.edu.cn

Abstract. Computation intelligence is becoming an essential technology during the development of human society. There are many family members in computation intelligence. Many researchers have already studied the mathematical inherent rules of these biology-inspired algorithms to found methods to improve the capacity of the algorithms. In the family of computation intelligence, differential evolution (DE) algorithm shows performance optimization ability. In order to explore the reason why DE could have stable and robust quality. We analyzed the parallelism of the evolutionary process in the iterative process of DE algorithm based on graph theory. By the knowledge of graph theory, it will directly exhibit the essential reason of differential evolution in the algorithm. The research will reveal that the superior DE algorithm have more extent parallelism ability than the elementary algorithm.

Keywords: Computation intelligence · Differential evolution · Parallel characteristic · Population · Graph theory

1 Introduction

After the industrial revolution, great changes have been taken place in people's life. Today, how to solve the problem faster and more effectively is the most important target that everybody pursued to. In order to get this target, many researches mimicked from nature then provided biology-inspired methods [1]. Biology-inspired methods are based on nature evolution and biological activities which contained evolutionary algorithms (EAs) [2], ant colony optimization (ACO) [3], particle swarm optimization (PSO) [4], differential evolution (DE) [5], etc. These novel random heuristic approaches had made great contribution to solve optimization problems. In this way, biology-inspired algorithms are widely used in industry or in people's daily life. Especially, DE has played an important role in many combinatorial optimization [6] problems.

© Springer Nature Singapore Pte Ltd. 2016
M. Gong et al. (Eds.): BIC-TA 2016, Part II, CCIS 682, pp. 151–162, 2016.
DOI: 10.1007/978-981-10-3614-9_20

With the biology-inspired methods widely used in combinatorial optimization problems, many researchers have explore the inherent rule of mathematic to these modern heuristic algorithms. They wonder if there will be a feature that will play an important part in the algorithm. If the researcher can find the inherent rule, it will greatly improve the performance of the algorithm. He and Yao [7] and his colleagues focused on the filed of the first hitting time of population to analysis the algorithm. Huang et al. [8] research the Runtime analysis based on average gain model further analysis the EA algorithm. Stutzle and Dorigo [9] proofed a short convergence of ACO algorithm, etc. Many researchers have made great contributions to the theory analysis of stochastic search algorithms, they help us stand on the shoulders of giants.

The differential evolution(DE) algorithm is one of the most simple and powerful stochastic optimizers in the current research field. DE algorithm has already successful used to various practical applications, such as image processing [10], machine learning [11], pattern recognition [12] and so on. Because the DE algorithm has superior optimize performance, more scholars focused on the DE algorithm from domestic to oversea. In decade years, the DE family of algorithms have been frequently developed more mature, some optimum DE algorithms had been researched out and applied, such as SaDE [13], EPSDE [14], MDE-pBX [15] and so on. Many experiments proved that the new DE algorithm is more outperformance than the classical DE algorithm.

There are many theory analyses of mathematic in the computation intelligence algorithm. The modern heuristic algorithms have already show the performance effect and continuous improvement until today. In this paper, we will focus on the parallelism inside the algorithm to discover the reason why the DE algorithm shows a great performance and the evolution of the DE algorithm made DE algorithm more effective. Like large railway station has more ability to transport passengers, the bigger the railway station is the more parallel characteristic the station will have. There will be more railways in the lager station. According to this phenomenon of human society we will analogy to the DE algorithm to explore why DE algorithm have powerful search capabilities. Some scholars have already research the parallel DE algorithm, such as Guo [16] and his colleagues focused parallel chaos differential evolution, Weber [17] and his partner research population structure of parallel global optimization, Wang [18] and his colleagues research parallel cooperative coevolutionary DE algorithm. These researchers from the external point of view to reveal the feature of the DE algorithm, they explore the advantage of the DE algorithm and make the algorithm get performance effect to the optimal value function. It is necessary to research more inherent characteristics to grasp the basic context of the DE algorithm.

In recent years, graph theory has showed its powerful ability of an important mathematical tool in widely field of subjects. It applied to the range from operational research and chemistry to genetics and linguistics [18]. And it also be used from geography to sociology and architecture. Particularly, graph theory play an important role in the field of electrical engineering [19]. Toady, graph theory has also emerged as a estimable mathematical discipline in its own right. Graph theory is an important tool that could connect computation intelligence with sociology which could help us to find effective internal information in the DE algorithm. In the evolutionary process of DE algorithm, to explore the diversity of population in the DE algorithm to make it more robust. With the discipline of graph theory, we can directly comprehended the course of evolution in DE algorithm. From the comparison between basic DE algorithm and senior DE algorithm we can get the main point is the parallelism that inside the DE algorithm.

The remainder of this paper is organized as follows. Section 2 provides the classical differential evolution algorithm to explain operating mechanism. Section 3 analysis parallelism of DE algorithm and will give the definition of vertexes and edges which are the basic element in the graph theory. Section 4 is the experiment and result of built a graph in DE algorithm and the result that could explore in the graph. Finally, Sect. 5 is the conclusion of the paper.

2   Classical Differential Evolution Algorithm

DE is one of the most basic intelligent algorithms of swarm evolutionary, so it will contain initialization and the cycle of stages of mutation, crossover, and selection. Generally, set the optimization problem as fellow.

$$\min f(x_1, x_2, \cdots, x_D). \tag{1}$$

Among them, D is the dimension of the problem.

2.1   Initialization

NP presents the population size, D is the dimension of the problem. So according to the formula (2) we can get the individual i.

$$x_{ij} = x_j^{\min} + rand() \cdot (x_j^{\max} - x_j^{\min}). \tag{2}$$

Among them, $i = 1, 2, \cdots, NP, j = 1, 2, \cdots, D$, the function of $rand()$ is the random number which obey uniform distribution in the interval (0,1).

2.2   The Mutation Strategy

Every vector x_i in the population is the target vector. The DE algorithm will have a mutation strategy to generate a donor vector v_i The common mutation formulas are as fellow.
DE/rand/1 [20]:

$$v_i = x_{r_1^i} + F \cdot (x_{r_2^i} - x_{r_3^i}). \tag{3}$$

DE/best/1 [21]:

$$v_i = x_{best} + F \cdot (x_{r_1^i} - x_{r_2^i}). \tag{4}$$

DE/current-to-best/1 [22]:

$$v_i = x_i + F \cdot (x_{best} - x_i) + F \cdot (x_{r_1^i} - x_{r_2^i}). \tag{5}$$

DE/best/2 [23]:

$$v_i = x_{best} + F \cdot (x_{r_1^i} - x_{r_2^i}) + F \cdot (x_{r_3^i} - x_{r_4^i}). \tag{6}$$

DE/rand/2 [24]:

$$v_i = x_{r_1^i} + F \cdot (x_{r_2^i} - x_{r_3^i}) + F \cdot (x_{r_4^i} - x_{r_5^i}). \tag{7}$$

Among them, $r_1^i, r_2^i, r_3^i, r_4^i, r_5^i \in \{1, 2, \cdots, NP\}$ and $r_1^i, r_2^i, r_3^i, r_4^i, r_5^i$ are mutually exclusive integers randomly chosen from the range [1,Np], and all are different from the index i. These indices are randomly generated a new one for each donor vector. The scaling factor F is a positive control parameter for scaling the difference vectors.

2.3   The Crossover Operation

The purpose of crossover operation is to generate new individuals. The donor vector mixes its components with the target vector. And after this operation form the trial vector $u_i = [u_{i1}, u_{i2}, \cdots, u_{iD}]$. The DE algorithms usually use two mainly kinds of crossover methods, exponential (or two-point modulo) and binomial (or uniform). We use the binomial crossover in this scheme. Binomial crossover is performed on each of the D variables whenever a randomly generated number between 0 and 1. If the random number is less than or equal to the CR value, we will do the crossover operation. The trial vector will be generated by the formula as fellow.

$$u_{ij} = \begin{cases} v_{ij}, & rand() \leq CR | j = j_{rand} \\ x_{ij}, & otherwise \end{cases} \tag{8}$$

There is a uniformly distributed random number j_{rand} generated in every trial vector. In that way, it will ensure that u_i gets at least one component from v_i for each vector in every generation.

2.4   The Selection Operation

Selection determines whether the target or the trial vector will survive to the next generation. If the new trial vector u_i yields an equal or lower value of the objective function, it replaces the corresponding target vector x_i in the next generation; otherwise, the target is retained in the population. The selection formula as fellow.

$$x_i = \begin{cases} u_i, & f(u_i) \leq f(x_i) \\ x_i, & otherwise \end{cases} \tag{9}$$

The basic process of the DE algorithm have been shown. We can find that the initialization part of the DE algorithm, the crossover operation and the selection of DE algorithm, these three parts in the DE algorithm general resemblance. The most difference of the DE family is the mutation strategy. It is the reason that some basic DE algorithms have different degree of ability. Furthermore, it also the point of view that we explore the parallel analysis in the DE algorithm. In the follow section, we will analysis the parallelism in different DE algorithm based on the method of graph theory.

3   Parallelism Analysis Based on Graph Theory

Compared with traditional algorithms in optimization problem. Biology-inspired methods, such an effective consequences for complex optimization problems, that traditional method will take long time to solve which people can not accept it. Investigated the foundation of why biology-inspired method could faster and more effectively, that is this evolutionary algorithm contained the characteristic of parallel inside the algorithm. The parallel optimization strategy in evolutionary algorithm is the main advantage which made a broader search scope. This important internal characteristics take effect of more accurate and effective information transfer between the individual in the population. Therefore, it is very necessary to explore the parallel features inside the algorithm, especially inside the differential evolution. It will provide theory support to reveal the internal and external performance of modern heuristic algorithms.

In order to described the parallel characteristic in DE directly. Parallelism in the algorithm is to show the inner characteristic in the biology-inspired methods. We will use graph theory to show the population structure in differential evolution which will discover the parallelism in differential evolution. Graph theory as an part of mathematic and computer science to research mathematical structure of graph. Because of the superiority that graph theory has. Such as the graph theory could be able to depict the process of differential evolution algorithm; The graph theory is a good supporter to express the parallel feature of differential evolutional algorithm; Finally, the graph theory has already reveal some mathematic and computer science problem, at the same time it show the principle and solution of the classical problem. All the above advantages illustrate the graph theory can intuitive showed the parallelism of differential evolution.

3.1   Graph Theory Description of Differential Evolution

The foundation points of graph theory is contained by vertices and edges in the graph. Some definitions and notations about the parallelism based on graph theory for differential evolution that will be given.

A graph is a pair $G = (V, E)$ of sets that satisfying $E \subseteq V \times V$ which contained the individuals of population and the iterative process in the differential evolution algorithm. The elements of V are the vertices of graph G that will represent the individual of the population in the differential evolution algorithms. The elements of E are the edges of the graph which represent the relationship of individual between the iteration.

Definition 1. Let $V_t = \{v_{t,1}, v_{t,2}, \cdots, v_{t,NP}\} (t = 1, 2, \ldots)$ be the vertex set which is the set of the solution in every iteration, every v represent one individual of population in one iteration, t is the number of iteration, NP is the number of individuals in the population. $v_i = \{v_{i,1}, v_{i,2}, \cdots, v_{i,D}\} (i = 1, 2, \cdots, NP)$ D is the dimension to the optimization problem.

Before the definition of edge, we will stipulate a criterion to determine the relationship between the two individuals. In this paper, we will use the value of cosine similarity $\cos(v_a, v_b)$ to represent the relationship between the two individual. As the formulate (10) shown below. Due to the properties of the cosine function, we know that if the value of the cosine similarity function is larger, the relationship of two individuals is closer and vice versa.

$$\cos(v_a, v_b) = \frac{\sum_{j=1}^{D} v_{aj} \cdot v_{bj}}{\sqrt{\sum_{j=1}^{D} v_{aj}^2} \cdot \sqrt{\sum_{j=1}^{D} v_{bj}^2}} \tag{10}$$

Definition 2. Let $E_t(t = 1, 2, \ldots)$ be the edge set of the individual relationship graph, t is the number of iteration. If the cosine similarity value $\cos(v_a, v_b)$ between two individual in the adjacent iterations process is more than a threshold, there will be a edge between the above two individuals. Besides that, if the cosine similarity value $\cos(v'_a, v'_b)$ between two individual in the adjacent iterations process is less than a threshold, there will be no edge between the above two individuals, that means the two individuals has no contact.

We had gave the essential definition of the graph which will present the process of the individual in the population of differential evolution. The individual and the relationship between them have a method to demonstrate. In this way, we can analysis the internal features in the algorithm which we can not directly discover.

3.2 Parallel Characteristic Analysis for Differential Evolution

Differential evolution has shown powerful stochastic optimizers of current interesting problem. Both the population structure and the ability of global optimization [26] are all reflected the parallelism inside this biology-inspired methods [27]. On the basis of the previous research and the analysis in this paper. We try to show the parallelism in the differential evolution by the graph theory with the vertexes presented by individual in the population and the edges expressed by the relation between two individuals in the evolutionary process. During the evolutionary process we will found the characteristics of the algorithm. To find if there has any process feature that could improve the searching capability of the algorithm.

Like other stochastic optimizers, DE could easily paralleled because each member of the population is evaluated individually [28]. In this paper, we try to use graph theory to show the parallelism inside the algorithm to discovered the internal feature in the algorithm. A path is a sequence of edges. In every iteration except the first iteration, there will be several edges that in the connection between the individuals. The number of the edges and the connection of the individual is to analysis to reveal the parallel feature. According to the definitions have descript, we will give the pseudo code of generate edges in differential evolution (Fig. 1).

Algorithm 1: The Algorithm of Generate Edges in Differential Evolution

Step 1. Initialize the population scale NP, the crossover rate CR, the scale factor F, initialize the iteration counter r: r = 0;

Step 2. According to the formula (2) initialize population V_r of NP with D-dimensional

individuals: $V_r = \{v_{1,r}, v_{2,r}, \cdots, v_{NP,r}\}$ with $v_{i,r} = \{x_{i,r}^1, x_{i,r}^2, \cdots, x_{i,r}^D\}$

// where v is the individual of the algorithm and v also the vertex of the graph

Step 3. Evaluate the objective function value of each individual in V_r,

   i.e. $f(v_{i,r}), i = 1, 2, \cdots, NP$;

Step 4. **while** the predefined termination criteria are not met **do**;
   for $i = 1 \to NP$ **do**
      Randomly select process;
      Generate a mutant vector according to the formula (3);
      Generate a trial vector according to the formula (8);
      Evaluate the objective function value of the generated trial vector, according to the formula (9) replaced the individual whose objective function value not achieved the demand;
   end for

Step 5: Produce new population $V_{r+1} = \{v_{1,r+1}, v_{2,r+1} \cdots, v_{NP,r+1}\}$

Step 6. Increase the iteration counter: r = r + 1;

Step 7. According to the formula (3) evaluate the cosine similarity
   for $i = 1 \to NP$
      for $j = 1 \to NP$
         $\cos(v_{i,r}, v_{j,r+1}) = \mu_{ij}$
      end for
   end for

Step 8. end while

Step 9. Until reach the termination conditions.

Fig. 1. Algorithm 1 is the pseudo code of generate edges in differential evolution.

A path is a sequence of edges and it also show the characteristic of the parallel in the relationship among the individuals. A path must have a starting point which disconnect with any individuals in the previous iteration. A new starting point means a new path generated. The number of paths will determine the ability of the parallelism in the algorithm. The pseudo code below will show the new starting point generated Fig. 2.

Algorithm 2: The Algorithm of Count Edges and Generate New Path

---

Step 1. Take the value of cosine similarity in algorithm 1

$$\mu_{r,ij}(r=1,\cdots,t; i=1,\cdots,NP; j=1,\cdots,NP);$$

Step 2. Initialize a **threshold value T, the number of iteration t;**

Step 3.for $r=1,2,\cdots,t$

    if $\mu_{r,ij} \geq T$

        generate a edge between $v_{i,r}, v_{j,r+1}$;

    else

        generate a new beginning of a path;

    end

  end

Fig. 2. Algorithm 2 is the pseudo code of generate the starting point of the new path.

4   Experiment and Results

This section will present the experiments and the results. The experiments are aimed to built a graph to explore in different DE algorithm. As the individuals in every iteration be the vertexes in the graph, and the relation between the individual in adjacent iterations be the edges that connected two individual. According to the above rule we will set a graph about the evolutionary process of DE algorithm. To discover the parallel features inside the algorithm. Gain an effective solution that could instructed the more senior the algorithm has more parallel features in the algorithm.

Referring to the literature [20–24], parameter settings of our experiments are as follows. In this paper we will compare two DE algorithm. One is the DE/rand/1, and the other one is DE/current-to-best/1/bin. In each algorithm we will set the population size NP for the DE variants has been kept equal to 100, and the problem dimension D is 30. And we will set the cross rate of the DE algorithm CR is 0.95, the scale factor F is 0.7. Each algorithm of function will run 25 times and gets the average results over multiple runs. In Above parameter set we will run the program to get the graph of DE algorithm evolutionary process.

After every iteration, it will be calculate the value of cosine similarity of each individual in adjacent. With the experiment of the diversity [25] that could control the premature convergence in the algorithm. Premature convergence will due to a decrease of diversity in search space that leads to ultimately fitness stagnation of the evolutionary process. So the diversity is also a sign to show the capacity of the algorithm. Therefore, as the result show in the experiment threshold of cosine similarity we will set be 0.5 in which the algorithm will have the best performance. The value of the cosine similarity will control the relation of each individual that is why the value of cosine similarity will reflect the number of the edge. If the threshold of the cosine similarity set too small, it will lead the graph has too much breakpoint. So that the graph will disconnect that it is difficult to explore the relationship of the individuals and the path of the graph will too short. On the other hand, if the threshold of the cosine similarity set too large, it will lead every individuals connect together. Too much connected edge in the graph will increase the complexity of analysis the parallelism of the algorithm, it may have increase the negative solution of no starting point of new path will appeared. In this situation, we could not get the information of parallelism because every edge will connect together (Tables 1 and 2).

Table 1. The distribution of the new path in DE/rand/1 algorithm

	iter1	iter2	iter3	iter4	iter5	iter6	iter7	iter8	iter9	iter10
pop1	-	-	-	-	-	-	-	*	-	-
pop2	*	-	-	-	-	-	-	-	-	-
pop3	-	-	-	-	-	-	-	-	-	-
pop4	*	*	-	-	*	-	*	-	-	-
pop5	*	*	*	-	-	*	-	-	-	-
pop6	-	-	-	*	-	-	-	*	-	-
pop7	*	*	-	*	-	-	*	*	-	-
pop8	*	*	-	-	-	-	-	-	-	-
pop9	-	-	*	*	-	-	-	-	-	-
pop10	*	-	*	-	-	-	-	-	-	-

Table 2. The distribution of the new path in DE/current-to-best/1/bin algorithm

	iter1	iter2	iter3	iter4	iter5	iter6	iter7	iter8	iter9	iter10
pop1	*	-	-	-	-	-	-	-	-	-
pop2	*	-	-	*	*	*	-	-	-	-
pop3	-	*	-	*	*	-	-	-	*	-
pop4	-	-	-	-	-	-	*	-	-	-
pop5	*	-	*	-	-	*	-	-	-	-
pop6	*	-	-	*	-	-	-	-	-	-
pop7	*	*	-	*	*	-	*	-	*	-
pop8	-	*	-	-	*	-	*	-	-	-
pop9	-	-	*	-	*	-	-	-	-	-
pop10	*	-	*	-	-	*	-	*	-	-

These two tables show the distribution of the starting point of the new path in the DE/rand/1 algorithm and the DE/current-to-best/1/bin algorithm. In the table, the row represents the number of previous iteration, the column represents the number of the individual which have been take the average value. The represents the value of cosine similarity of each individual in adjacent iteration larger than the threshold. The * represents the value less than the threshold, it also means the starting point of the new path.

With the experiment of the generation of vertexes and the relationship has been built to the edge. We now get the graph of evolutionary process in two DE algorithms. One is DE/rand/1 algorithm, and the other one is the DE/current-to-best/1/bin algorithm. The experiment of previous work have showed the DE/current-to-best/1/bin have more performance ability than the DE/rand/1 algorithm. As the solution of the starting point of the new path in the experiment shows below. Compared with the two tables we find that the DE/current-to-best/1/bin algorithm have more feature of parallelism which has more new path starting point. The parallelism of the DE/current-to-best/1/bin algorithm proofed it has better search ability than DE/rand/1 algorithm. It can be saw in the tables that senior algorithm reveal more staring point which is the beginning of the new path. We can also found that with the iteration number increased, the number of new path sharp dropped in DE/rand/1 algorithm. The algorithm which has outstanding performance ability will exist parallel features inside. The search ability is necessary to not only the biology-inspired method, but also the goal of the combinatorial optimization problems pursued.

5   Conclusion

In this paper, we have analyzed the parallelism in the evolutionary process of two DE algorithms based on graph theory to find the reason why different types of DE algorithms show different searching performance. We defined the vertexes which is presented by the individuals in the population and the edges which is expressed by the relation between two individuals in the contiguous evolutionary process. Make sure the evolutionary process will correspond the main idea of the graph theory. Compare to DE/rand/1 algorithm, the DE/current-to-best/1/bin algorithm shows more outstanding performance. And from the experiment of the parallelism tests in different DE algorithm, we find the DE/current-to-best/1/bin algorithm shows more parallel feature which reflected in the starting point of the new path in the graph. We believe that the more feature of parallel existed in the algorithm, the more performance ability will the algorithm have, so the future work will focus on expanding the parallelism analysis by graph theory on other algorithm.

Acknowledgments. This work is supported in part by NSFC-Guangdong Joint Found (U1501254), National Natural Science Foundation of China (61370102, 61472089, 61572143), Natural Science Foundation of Guangdong(2014A030306004, 2014A030308008), Science and Technology Planning Project of Guangdong (2013B 051000076, 2015B010108006, 2015B010131015), Guangdong Natural Science Funds for Distinguished Young Scholar (2014A030306050), the Fundamental Research Funds for the Central Universities, SCUT (2015PT022) and Guangdong High-level personnel of special support program (2014TQ01X664).

References

1. Yao, X.: An overview of evolutionary computation. J. Adv. Softw. Res. **3**(1), 12–29 (1996)
2. Eiben, A.E., Rudolph, G.: Theory of evolutionary algorithms: a bird eye view. J. Theoret. Comput. Sci. **229**, 3–9 (1999)
3. Dorigo, M., Sttzle, T.: Ant Colony Optimization, 1st edn. MIT Press, Cambridge (2004). (Chap. 4)
4. Eberhart, R.C., Kennedy, J.: A new optimizer using particle swarm theory. In: Proceedings of the Sixth International Symposium on Micro Machine and Human Science, vol. 1, pp. 39–43 (1995)
5. Storn, R., Price, K.: Differential Evolution-A Simple and Efficient Adaptive Scheme for Global Optimization Over Continuous Spaces. ICSI, Berkeley (1995)
6. Papadimitriou, C.H., Steiglitz, K.: Combinatorial Optimization: Algorithms and Complexity. Dover, New York (1998)
7. He, J., Yao, X.: From an individual to a population: an analysis of the first hitting time of population-based evolutionary algorithms. IEEE Trans. Evol. Comput. **6**, 495–511 (2002)
8. Huang, H., Xu, W.D., Zhang, Y.S., Lin, Z.Y., Hao, Z.F.: Runtime analysis for continuous (1+1) evolutionary algorithm based on average gain model. China Sci. Inf. Sci. **44**(6), 811–824 (2014)
9. Stutzle, T., Dorigo, M.: A short convergence proof for a class of ACO algorithms. IEEE Trans. Evol. Comput. **6**(4), 358–365 (2002)
10. Ugolotti, R., Cagnoni, S.: Differential evolution based human body pose estimation from point clouds. In: Proceeding of the Fifteenth Annual Conference on Genetic and Evolutionary Computation Conference, pp. 1389–1396. ACM, New York (2013)
11. Oh, S.K., Kim, W.D., Pedrycz, W., et al.: Design of K-means clustering-based polynomial radial basis function neural networks (pRBF NNs) realized with the aid of particle swarm optimization and differential evolution. Neurocomputing **78**(1), 121–132 (2012)
12. Okada, H.: Interval-valued differential evolution for evolving neural networks with interval weights and biases. In: IEEE Sixth International Workshop on Computational Intelligence and Applications (IWCIA), pp. 81–84. IEEE (2013)
13. Mallipeddi, R., Suganthan, P.N., Pan, Q.K., et al.: Differential evolution algorithm with ensemble of parameters and mutation strategies. Appl. Soft Comput. **11**(2), 1679–1696 (2011)
14. Langdon, W.B., Poli, R.: Evolving problems to learn about particle swarm optimizers and other search algorithms. IEEE Trans. Evol. Comput. **11**(5), 561–578 (2007)
15. Islam, S.M., Das, S., Ghosh, S., et al.: An adaptive differential evolution algorithm with novel mutation and crossover strategies for global numerical optimization. IEEE Trans. Syst. Man Cybern. Part B Cybern. **42**(2), 482–500 (2012)
16. Guo, Z., Cheng, B., Ye, M., et al.: A parallel chaos differential evolution algorithm. Hsi-An Chiao Tung Ta Hsueh/J. Xi'an. **41**(3), 299–302 (2007)
17. Weber, M.: Parallel global optimization: structuring populations in differential evolution. Stud. Comput. **121** (2010). ISBN: 978-951-39-4076-8
18. Wang, L., Lin, H.F., Teng, H.F.: Research on Parallel Cooperative Coevolutionary Differential Evolution Algorithm. Comput. Eng. **38**(04), 182–184 (2012)
19. Bondy, J.A., Murty, U.S.R.: Graph Theory. Springer, Heidelberg (2008)

20. Gibbons, A.: Algorithmic Graph Theory. Cambridge University Press, Cambridge (1985)
21. Storn, R., Price, K.: Differential evolution–simple and efficient heuristic for global optimization over continuous spaces. J. Global Optim. **11**(4), 341–359 (1997)
22. Price, K.V., Storn, R.M., Lampinen, J.A.: Differential Evolution-A Practical Approach to Global Optimization. Springer, Heidelberg (2005)
23. Mezura-Montes, E., Velzquez-Reyes, J., Coello Coello, C.A.: Modified differential evolution for constrained optimization. In: IEEE Congress on Evolutionary Computation, CEC 2006, pp. 25–32. IEEE (2006)
24. Gmperle, R., Mller, S.D., Koumoutsakos, P.: A parameter study for differential evolution. Adv. Intell. Syst. Fuzzy Syst. Evol. Comput. **10**, 293–298 (2002)
25. Qin, A.K., Huang, V.L., Suganthan, P.N.: Differential evolution algorithm with strategy adaptation for global numerical optimization. IEEE Trans. Evol. Comput. **13**(2), 398–411 (2009)
26. Weber, M., Neri, F., Tirronen, V.: Distributed differential evolution with explorative–exploitative population families. Genet. Program. Evol. Mach. **10**(4), 343–371 (2009)
27. Tsutsui, S.: Multi-parent recombination with simplex crossover in real coded genetic algorithms. In: GECCO 1999, pp. 657–664 (1999)
28. Schwefel, H.P.: Evolution and Optimum Seeking. Wiley, New York (1995)

A Mean Shift Assisted Differential Evolution Algorithm

Hui Fang[✉], Aimin Zhou, and Guixu Zhang

Shanghai Key Laboratory of Multidimensional Information Processing,
Department of Computer Science and Technology, East China Normal University,
Shanghai 200241, China
fhcmxfh@163.com, {amzhou,gxzhang}@cs.ecnu.edu.cn

Abstract. It is well known that Differential Evolution (DE) algorithm has been widely applied to solve global optimization problems during the last decades. DE is usually criticized for the slow convergence. To improve the algorithm performance, we propose an algorithm called MSDE that utilizes a local search operator based on mean shift. In MSDE, one offspring solution is generated by the mean shift based search operator, and the others are created by the DE search operator. A test suite of 12 benchmark functions with different characteristics are chosen to evaluate our approach. The experimental results suggest that MSDE can successfully improve the performance of DE and have a faster convergence rate on the given test suite.

Keywords: Differential evolution · Mean shift · Search operator · Global optimization

1 Introduction

In this paper, we consider the following continuous box-constrained global optimisation problem:

$$\min f(x)$$
$$\text{s.t. } x \in \Omega, \tag{1}$$

where $x = (x^1, x^2, \cdots, x^d)^T$ is a decision variable vector, $\Omega = [a^i, b^i]^d$ is the feasible region of the decision space, where $a^i < b^i$, $a^i \in R$ and $b^i \in R$ are the lower and upper boundaries of the decision space, respectively. $f(x) : \Omega \to R$ is a continuous mapping from the decision space to the objective space, and R is the objective space.

Differential evolution (DE) [1] is a population-based stochastic search technique, which has attracted much attention recently as an effective approach for solving global optimisation problems. It exhibits remarkable performance in diverse fields of science and engineering, such as cluster analysis [2], robot control [3], controller design [4], and graph theory [5]. Similar to traditional evolutionary algorithms (EAs) [6], the new individual in each generation is generated by mutation, crossover, and selection operators [7] in DE. Moreover, the

© Springer Nature Singapore Pte Ltd. 2016
M. Gong et al. (Eds.): BIC-TA 2016, Part II, CCIS 682, pp. 163–172, 2016.
DOI: 10.1007/978-981-10-3614-9_21

performance of the DE algorithm is sensitive to the mutation strategy and respectively control parameters such as the population size, scaling factor F, and crossover rate CR [8,9].

There are different strategies in improving the performance of DE during the past decades. The major works focus on adaptively setting the control parameters or choosing the search operators. Zhang proposed JaDE [10] which implements a new mutation strategy named DE/current-to-pbest. It uses an optional external archive to track the history information and updates the control parameters in an adaptive manner with generations. Qin and Suganthan proposed a self-adaptive approach called SaDE [11] which uses a learning strategy to self-adapt F and CR. Wang [12] introduced a novel method called CoDE for combining different trial vector generation strategies. The approach combines three well-studied trial vector generation strategies with three control parameter settings in a random way to generate trial vectors. Besides, Fan and Lampinen [13] proposed a trigonometric mutation operator to accelerate the DE convergence. Mezura-Montes et al. [14] proposed a novel mutation operator that can utilize information of the best parents and children.

In this paper, we propose a hybrid algorithm that uses both a mean shift based search operator and DE, denoted as MSDE. In each generation, one trial solution is generated by the mean shift based search operator, the others are created by the DE search operator. Mean shift [15] is a non-parametric feature-space analysis technique that can locate the maxima of a density function precisely without any function evaluation [16]. It can improve some promising solutions efficiently when the new trial solutions are constantly generated.

The rest of the paper is organized as follows. Section 2 presents the new algorithm MSDE. The algorithm framework and the search operator are introduced in detail. The experiment results and analysis are reported in Sect. 3. Finally, this paper is concluded in Sect. 4.

2   Proposed Algorithm

This section introduces the details of the newly proposed MSDE. In MSDE, the compose differential evolution (CoDE) is used as the DE search operator. In following, the algorithm framework is firstly given and the mean shift base search operator is presented.

2.1   Algorithm Description

In each generation, MSDE maintains

- a set of N solutions $\{x_1, x_2, \cdots, x_N\}$,
- their objective values $\{f(x_1), f(x_2), \cdots, f(x_N)\}$.

The main framework of MSDE is presented in Algorithm 1. It is basically a general CoDE framework and only several steps with the mean shift search operator are added. Its main components are explained as follows.

Algorithm 1. Main Framework of MSDE

---

1 Initialize the population $\{x_1, \cdots, x_N\}$ and evaluate them;

2 **while** *not terminate* **do**

3     $pop \leftarrow sort(pop,' ascend')$;

4     $x^* \leftarrow MS(pop)$;

5   **if** $f(x^*) < f(x_N)$ **then**

6 | Replace x_N by x^*.

7   **end**

8   **foreach** $i \in \{1, \cdots, N\text{-}1\}$ **do**

9   Generate three trial points y_1^i, y_2^i, y_3^i with the three trial vector generation strategies:

$$y_1^i = \begin{cases} x_{r1}^i + F \cdot (x_{r2}^i - x_{r3}^i) & if\ rand < C_r\ or\ i = i_{rand} \\ x^i & otherwise \end{cases}$$

$$y_2^i = \begin{cases} x_{r1}^i + F \cdot (x_{r2}^i - x_{r3}^i) + F \cdot (x_{r4}^i - x_{r5}^i) & if\ rand < C_r\ or\ i = i_{rand} \\ x^i & otherwise \end{cases}$$

$$y_3^i = \begin{cases} x^i + rand \cdot (x_{r1}^i - x^i) + F \cdot (x_{r2}^i - x_{r3}^i) & if\ rand < C_r\ or\ i = i_{rand} \\ x^i & otherwise \end{cases}$$

where the control parameters are randomly selected from [F = 1.0,Cr = 0.1], [F = 1.0,Cr = 0.9], [F =0.8,Cr = 0.2].

10   Evaluate the objective function values of the three trail points;

11   Let $y^* = \arg\min\limits_{y \in \{y_1^i, y_2^i, y_3^i\}} \hat{f}(y)$ be the offspring solution of x^i;

12   **if** $f(y^*) < f(x^i)$ **then**

13 | $x^i \leftarrow y^*$.

14   **end**

15   **end**

16 **end**

- *Population Initialization:* In *Line 1*, N solutions are uniformly sampled from the search space to form the initial population.
- *Stopping Condition:* The algorithm stops when the given maximum number of generations reaches the preset maximum value of generation G in *Line 2*.
- *Reproduction Procedure:* Part of the solutions are firstly generated by a search operator based on mean shift in *Line 4*. The MS operator will be introduced in detail later. Then a set of candidate solutions are created by CoDE in *Lines 8–15*. The three selected trial vector generation strategies and the parameters setting will be given in next section.
- *Selection Procedure:* In *Lines 5–7*, the new solution created by MS could replace the worst solution in generation if its objective function value is better. In *Lines 12–14*, the parent solution and the offspring solution will compete with each other and the winner will survive to the next generation.

The details of the MS operator will be discussed shortly in the following section.

2.2   Search Operator Based on Mean Shift

Mean shift is a non-parametric, iterative method introduced by Fukunaga and Hostetler [16] for seeking the mode of a density function represented by a set of samples. Its application domains include cluster analysis [17], visual tracking [18] and smoothing in computer vision and image processing [19]. There is no need to calculate the objective function values when we apply it to search optimal solutions. It has been proved that the minimization of the function value is equal to finding the point with the highest probability density in [20].

According to mean shift algorithm, given n data points x_i, $i = 1, ..., n$ in a d-dimensional space R^d, the multivariate kernel density estimate obtained with kernel $K(x)$ and bandwidth h is as follow:

$$\hat{f}_{h,K}(x) = \frac{1}{nh^d} \sum_{i=1}^{N} K\left(\left\|\frac{x - x_i}{h}\right\|^2\right). \tag{2}$$

To obtain the maxima of density function, the modes of the density function are located at the zeros of the gradient function $\hat{f}'(x) = 0$. The gradient of the density estimator is as follow:

$$\hat{\nabla} f_{h,K}(x) = \frac{1}{nh^d} \left[\sum_{i=1}^{N} g\left(\left\|\frac{x-x_i}{h}\right\|^2\right)\right] \left[\frac{\sum_{i=1}^{N} x_i g\left(\left\|\frac{x-x_i}{h}\right\|^2\right)}{\sum_{i=1}^{N} g\left(\left\|\frac{x-x_i}{h}\right\|^2\right)} - x\right]. \tag{3}$$

The first term is proportional to the density estimate at x computed with kernel $K(x)$ and the second term is the mean shift vector.

$$m_{h,g}(x) = \frac{\sum_{i=1}^{N} x_i g\left(\left\|\frac{x-x_i}{h}\right\|^2\right)}{\sum_{i=1}^{N} g\left(\left\|\frac{x-x_i}{h}\right\|^2\right)} - x. \tag{4}$$

The mean shift vector always points toward the direction of the maximum increase in the density and the new solution that we search for is the point with maximum density as follow:

$$x_{new} = \frac{\sum_{i=1}^{N} x_i g\left(\left\|\frac{x-x_i}{h}\right\|^2\right)}{\sum_{i=1}^{N} g\left(\left\|\frac{x-x_i}{h}\right\|^2\right)}. \tag{5}$$

The basic mean shift procedure, operated as follow is guaranteed to converge to a point where the gradient of density function is close to zero. Figure 1 shows the basic idea of mean shift.

It is noted that the bandwidth is the only parameter in the mean shift algorithm. In the standard method, the bandwidth represents the size of the window in which solutions can have impact on the initial point. It might not make any differences if the bandwidth is a constant value when the distances of all solutions are very small. Hence, using an adaptive bandwidth rather than the constant

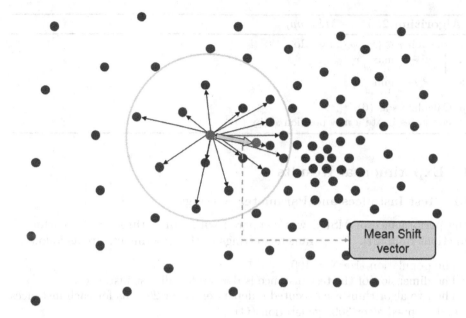

Fig. 1. An illustration of the search procedure based on mean shift

value would make some improvements in mean shift procedure. The adaptive bandwidth is calculated as follow:

$$s = \sqrt{\frac{1}{d}\sum_{j=1}^{d}(a^j - b^j)^2} \tag{6}$$

where a and b is the maximum and minimum values of the solutions in the current generation. d is the dimension of the solutions.

There are many types of kernel functions. Different kernels make different effects in imposing additional weights on the data points according to their distances to the shifting mean. Cheng [15] introduced two main kernel functions which have been frequently used in Mean shift researches, namely flat and Gaussian kernel. Compared to Gaussian kernels, flat kernel ignores the influence of the distance between two points. In the paper, Gaussian kernel is considered as follow:

$$g(x) = \frac{1}{\sigma\sqrt{2\pi}}e^{-\frac{1}{2}\left(\frac{x-\mu}{\sigma}\right)^2}. \tag{7}$$

It is obvious that μ and σ^2 play an important role in Gaussian kernel function. μ decides the position of function in the coordinate axes, whereas σ^2 decides the shape of a function, which can make effect on the weights put on the different solutions. We will discuss the influence of algorithm performance with the different setting strategies of σ^2 in next section.

The detailed algorithm framework of the search operator based on mean shift is shown in Algorithm 2.

Algorithm 2. $x^* \leftarrow MS(pop)$

1 **foreach** $x \in \{x_1, \cdots, x_N\}$ **do**
2 $\quad\quad a^j \leftarrow \max\limits_{i=1,\cdots,d} x_i^j$
3 $\quad\quad b^j \leftarrow \min\limits_{i=1,\cdots,d} x_i^j$

4 Calculate s as (6).
5 For x_1, estimate a new position x^* by (5).

3 Experimental Results

3.1 Test Instances and Parameter Settings

The performance of MSDE was compared with CoDE through 12 benchmark functions from [21]. The parameter settings of the experiments are as follows.

– The population size N = 100.
– The dimension of the test instance is d = 30 for all test instances.
– The two algorithms are executed independently for 20 runs for each instances and stopped after 3000 generations(G).

All the algorithms are implemented in Matlab R2010b and executed in Lenovo Thinkpad E430 with i5-3210 M CPU @ 2.50 GHz, 6.00 GB RAM, and Windows 7.

3.2 Experimental Results and Analysis

The statistical results of the mean values of the two algorithms after 1000, 2000 and 3000 generations over 20 runs are shown in Table 1. In the table, $\sim$, $+$,

Table 1. Mean values of the results obtained by the two comparison algorithms after 500, 1000, and 1500 generations over 20 runs for all the test instances.

	generation = 1000		generation = 2000		generation = 3000	
	MSDE	CoDE	MSDE	CoDE	MSDE	CoDE
f_1	5.28e−20(+)	6.52e−08	5.06e−43(+)	1.53e−19	4.03e−66(+)	3.05e−31
f_2	9.95e−11(+)	5.09e−05	2.84e−22(+)	2.53e−11	7.24e−34(+)	1.34e−17
f_3	2.95e−06(+)	6.25e−02	5.83e−15(+)	2.86e−07	6.10e−24(+)	1.11e−12
f_4	7.14e−07(+)	3.48e−01	2.11e−14(+)	1.88e−03	5.21e−22(+)	1.05e−05
f_5	1.35e+01(+)	2.21e+01	6.64e−04(+)	6.41e+00	9.07e−16(+)	4.18e−04
f_6	0.00e+00($\sim$)	0.00e+00	0.00e+00($\sim$)	0.00e+00	0.00e+00($\sim$)	0.00e+00
f_7	1.07e−02(+)	5.38e−02	1.41e−02(+)	2.99e−02	1.52e−02(+)	2.61e−02
f_8	1.97e−03(+)	1.02e−03	0.00e+00(+)	9.09e−14	0.00e+00($\sim$)	0.00e+00
f_9	9.49e+00(+)	2.54e+01	4.91e−12(+)	7.85e−05	0.00e+00($\sim$)	0.00e+00
f_{10}	5.81e−11(+)	6.97e−05	8.88e−16(+)	1.06e−10	8.88e−16(+)	4.62e−15
f_{11}	0.00e+00(+)	8.10e−06	0.00e+00($\sim$)	0.00e+00	0.00e+00($\sim$)	0.00e+00
f_{12}	5.05e−22(+)	5.44e−09	1.57e−32(+)	1.09e−20	1.57e−32(+)	4.26e−32

and − denote that the results obtained by MSDE are similar to, better than, or worse than that obtained by CoDE. It is noted that the performance of MSDE is better than CoDE on most test instances. The two algorithms both converge to the global optimal on f_6, f_8, f_9 and f_{11}, whereas do not perform well on f_7.

As is shown in Fig. 2, it is clear that the speed of convergence with MSDE is faster than that with CoDE throughout the process. Hence, appending special solutions created by the new search operator to the initial solutions generated from CoDE can help to find the optimal solution quickly in a large extent.

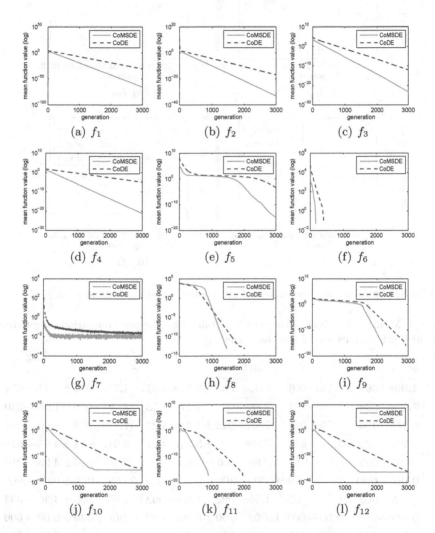

Fig. 2. The mean values of the best solutions found so far versus generations obtained by two algorithms over 20 runs for 12 test instances.

3.3 Sensitivity to Kernel Parameters

Kernel function plays an important part in the search strategy based on mean shift. The impact factor of each point is determined by the specific property of

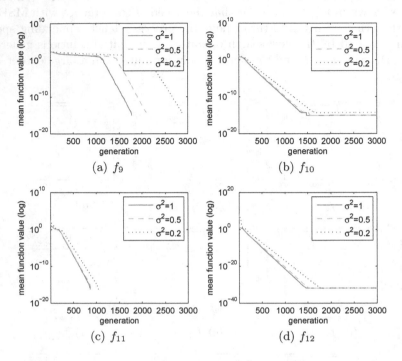

(a) f_9

(b) f_{10}

(c) f_{11}

(d) f_{12}

Fig. 3. The mean function values of different σ^2 versus generations on f_9–f_{12}

Table 2. Mean, Std. values of the results obtained by the two comparison algorithms after 3000 generations for 12 test instances.

	$\sigma^2=1$	$\sigma^2=0.5$	$\sigma^2=0.2$
f_1	**4.03e−066 ± 3.33e−066**	2.32e−063 ± 3.57e−063	1.78e−054 ± 1.34e−054
f_2	**7.24e−034 ± 4.32e−034**	2.88e−033 ± 1.17e−033	3.79e−030 ± 1.98e−030
f_3	**6.10e−024 ± 7.76e−024**	7.43e−023 ± 1.34e−022	7.93e−022 ± 1.09e−021
f_4	**5.21e−022 ± 3.54e−022**	7.50e−021 ± 3.74e−021	6.91e−018 ± 4.63e−018
f_5	9.07e−016 ± 2.15e−015	**1.79e−016 ± 3.15e−016**	2.16e−016 ± 4.25e−016
f_6	**0.00e+000 ± 0.00e+000**	**0.00e+000 ± 0.00e+000**	**0.00e+000 ± 0.00e+000**
f_7	**1.52e−002 ± 1.57e−002**	1.55e−002 ± 1.04e−002	7.40e−003 ± 4.36e−003
f_8	**0.00e+000 ± 0.00e+000**	**0.00e+000 ± 0.00e+000**	**0.00e+000 ± 0.00e+000**
f_9	**0.00e+000 ± 0.00e+000**	**0.00e+000 ± 0.00e+000**	9.86e−015 ± 3.82e−014
f_{10}	**8.88e−016 ± 0.00e+000**	**8.88e−016 ± 0.00e+000**	4.44e−015 ± 0.00e+000
f_{11}	**0.00e+000 ± 0.00e+000**	**0.00e+000 ± 0.00e+000**	**0.00e+000 ± 0.00e+000**
f_{12}	**1.57e−032 ± 2.81e−048**	**1.57e−032 ± 2.81e−048**	1.57e−032 ± 2.81e−048

the kernel. This section studies the influence of the algorithm performance with the different setting strategies of σ^2 in Gaussian kernel. We set $\sigma^2 = 0.2, 0.5$ and 1.0 respectively, and $f_9 - f_{12}$ are chosen for the study.

In Fig. 3, It is obvious that all of them perform well and obtain the optimal solutions. The detailed statistic results of the three different setting of σ^2 are shown in Table 2.

The algorithm with $\sigma^2 = 0.5$ and $\sigma^2 = 1$ reach the convergent stage faster than that with $\sigma^2 = 0.2$ in most test instances. Besides, the performance of $\sigma^2 = 1$ and $\sigma^2 = 0.5$ are similar on f_{10}, f_{11} and f_{12}. It can be seen that there is not much difference in the performance of MSDE among the three settings of σ^2.

4 Conclusion

This paper proposed a search strategy to improve the performance of the DE. An algorithm, named as MSDE, utilizes the mean shift search operator to choose some solutions and combines them with solutions generated from DE. In each generation, a point with the maximum density is created by mean shift operator and is added into the set of normal solutions, which can guides the population to the optimal solution efficiently. In this approach, the speed of convergence in this algorithm obtains a good improvement.

MSDE is applied to 12 test instances, and the experimental results suggest that MSDE can perform well on most functions and can get a faster convergence rate compared to CoDE. The analysis of the parameters in kernel function of mean shift is discussed and the experiential results shows that the value of σ^2 plays an important role in the performance of the algorithm.

The work reported in this paper is preliminary and there are still some further work that could be done in the future. A example is to study the efficiency of different kernel functions in the mean shift based search operator.

Acknowledgment. This work is supported by China National Instrumentation Program under Grant No. 2012YQ180132, the National Natural Science Foundation of China under Grant No. 61273313 and No. 61673180, and the Science and Technology Commission of Shanghai Municipality under Grant No. 14DZ2260800.

References

1. Das, S., Suganthan, P.N.: Differential evolution: a survey of the state-of-the-art. IEEE Trans. Evol. Comput. **15**, 4–31 (2011)
2. Das, S., Abraham, A., Konar, A.: Automatic clustering using an improved differential evolution algorithm. IEEE Trans. Syst. Man Cybern. Part A Syst. Hum. **38**, 218–237 (2008)
3. Neri, F., Mininno, E.: Memetic compact differential evolution for cartesian robot control. IEEE Comput. Intell. Mag. **5**, 54–65 (2010)
4. Wang, L., Li, L.P.: Fixed-structure controller synthesis based on differential evolution with level comparison. IEEE Trans. Evol. Comput. **15**, 120–129 (2011)

5. Greenwood, G.W.: Using differential evolution for a subclass of graph theory problems. IEEE Trans. Evol. Comput. **13**, 1190–1192 (2009)
6. Coello, C.A.C.: Theoretical and numerical constraint-handling techniques used with evolutionary algorithms: a survey of the state of the art. Computer Methods Appl. Mech. Eng. **191**, 1245–1287 (2002)
7. Whitley, D.: A genetic algorithm tutorial. Stat. Comput. **4**, 65–85 (1994)
8. Aalto, J., Lampinen, J.: A mutation adaptation mechanism for differential evolution algorithm. In: 2013 IEEE Congress on Evolutionary Computation, pp. 55–62. IEEE (2013)
9. Wei, Q., Qiu, X.: Dynamic differential evolution algorithm with composite strategies and parameter values self-adaption. In: 2015 Seventh International Conference on Advanced Computational Intelligence (ICACI), pp. 271–274. IEEE (2015)
10. Zhang, J., Sanderson, A.C.: JADE: adaptive differential evolution with optional external archive. IEEE Trans. Evol. Comput. **13**, 945–958 (2009)
11. Qin, A.K., Suganthan, P.N.: Self-adaptive differential evolution algorithm for numerical optimization. In: IEEE Congress on Evolutionary Computation, vol. 2, pp. 1785–1791. IEEE (2005)
12. Wang, Y., Cai, Z., Zhang, Q.: Differential evolution with composite trial vector generation strategies and control parameters. IEEE Trans. Evol. Comput. **15**, 55–66 (2011)
13. Fan, H.Y., Lampinen, J.: A trigonometric mutation operation to differential evolution. J. Global Optim. **27**, 105–129 (2003)
14. Mezura-Montes, E., Velázquez-Reyes, J., Coello, C.C.: Modified differential evolution for constrained optimization. In: 2006 IEEE International Conference on Evolutionary Computation, pp. 25–32. IEEE (2006)
15. Cheng, Y.: Mean shift, mode seeking, and clustering. IEEE Trans. Pattern Anal. Mach. Intell. **17**, 790–799 (1995)
16. Fukunaga, K., Hostetler, L.D.: The estimation of the gradient of a density function, with applications in pattern recognition. IEEE Trans. Inf. Theory **21**, 32–40 (1975)
17. Comaniciu, D., Meer, P.: Mean shift: a robust approach toward feature space analysis. IEEE Trans. Pattern Anal. Mach. Intell. **24**, 603–619 (2002)
18. Comaniciu, D., Ramesh, V., Meer, P.: Real-time tracking of non-rigid objects using mean shift. In: Proceedings IEEE Conference on Computer Vision and Pattern Recognition, vol. 2, pp. 142–149. IEEE (2000)
19. Comaniciu, D., Meer, P.: Mean shift analysis and applications. In: The Proceedings of the Seventh IEEE International Conference on Computer Vision, vol. 2, pp. 1197–1203. IEEE (1999)
20. Gong, W., Zhou, A., Cai, Z.: A multioperator search strategy based on cheap surrogate models for evolutionary optimization. IEEE Trans. Evol. Comput. **19**, 746–758 (2015)
21. Suganthan, P.N., Hansen, N., Liang, J.J., Deb, K., Chen, Y.P., Auger, A., Tiwari, S.: Problem definitions and evaluation criteria for the CEC 2005 special session on real-parameter optimization. KanGAL report 2005005 (2005)

Quantum-Behaved Particle Swarm Optimization Using MapReduce

Yangyang Li[✉], Zhenghan Chen, Yang Wang, and Licheng Jiao

Key Laboratory of Intelligent Perception and Image Understanding of Ministry of Education, Joint International Research Laboratory of Intelligent Perception and Computation, International Research Center for Intelligent Perception and Computation, Xidian University, Xi'an 710071, Shaanxi, China
lyy_791@163.com, yyli@xidian.edu.cn

Abstract. Quantum-behaved particle swarm optimization (short in QPSO) is an improved version of particle swarm particle (short in PSO), and the performance is superior. But for now, it may not always satisfy the situations. Nowadays, problems become larger and more complex, most serial optimization algorithms cannot deal with the problem or need plenty of computing cost. In this paper, we implement QPSO on MapReduce model, propose MapReduce quantum-behaved particle swarm optimization (short in MRQPSO), and realize QPSO parallel and distributed, which the MapReduce model is a parallel computing programming model. In the experiments, the test results show that MRQPSO is more advanced both on performance of solution and time than QPSO.

Keywords: Quantum-behaved particle swarm optimization · MapReduce · Distributed evolutionary computation · Cloud computing

1 Introduction

In recent years, many intelligent algorithms are facing with a serious difficulty the more and more large-scale data. Such as web content and bioinformatics data, the simple serial algorithms may be confused when processing these tough problems, needless to say some deceptive ones. In order to deal with hard optimization problems in real-word applications, distributed evolutionary algorithms (short in dEAs) have been blossomed rapidly. In the paper, it provides a comprehensive survey of the EAs and models and discuss the parallel and distributed genetic algorithms in different physical platforms.

The particle swarm optimization is an outstanding one of genetic algorithm [1–3]. This algorithm is proposed by Kennedy and Eberhart in 1995 in [4]. Depending on rapid convergence as well as good solution performance, the PSO has been attained increasing attention. However, the premature phenomenon as a drawback may influence the performance of solution. Focus on this shortcoming, Sun proposed the quantum-behaved particle swarm optimization in 2004 in [5] and presented a comprehensive analysis in [6]. Due to the quantum mechanics,

© Springer Nature Singapore Pte Ltd. 2016
M. Gong et al. (Eds.): BIC-TA 2016, Part II, CCIS 682, pp. 173–178, 2016.
DOI: 10.1007/978-981-10-3614-9_22

the QPSO avoids the particle fall in the local optimum greatly. Unfortunately, when the algorithm faces large-scale and complex problem, the increasing computational cost and the still existed premature phenomenon urge the original algorithm to be parallel.

In [7], MapReduce, as a tool to be adopted to implement dEAs, is proposed by Google in 2004. To respond the requirement of parallelization and distribution, this physical platform is very convenient to deploy an algorithm to update to be parallel. The programmers only need to consider the map function and reduce function, and the other details are provided by the model itself. Because of the convenience, the scholars can focus on the algorithms and problems, and appear many genetic algorithms through MapReduce to realize distributed, including the PSO [8].

In order to following this trend and enhancing the capabilities of a standard QPSO, the MapReduce quantum-behaved particle swarm optimization is developed. The MRQPSO transplants the QPSO on MapReduce model, makes the QPSO be parallel and distributed through partition the search space. The proposed MRQPSO decreases the time of same function evaluations, increases the performance of solution, and is more robust than QPSO.

2   The MRQPSO Algorithm

The particle swarm optimization algorithm [4] is one of the popular evolutionary algorithm. It has been attracted much attention because the merits of simple concept, rapid convergence and good quality of solution. However, this algorithm is bothered by some weakness, such as premature phenomenon. Focus on the short-coming of the PSO, Sun proposed an uncertain and global random algorithm, named quantum-behaved particle swarm optimization (short in QPSO), in 2004 in [5]. The new one put the search space into quantum space to let the particle can move to anywhere. Through this strategy, the premature phenomenon be improved to a certain degree.

Although the QPSO has a satisfy progress on premature phenomenon, it has not been prepared to challenge to the high-dimensional large-scale and complex problems, let alone the deceptive functions. Due to the particles of the QPSO fly discretely, they may miss the narrow area to search, where the global optimum is. And as the problem getting complex, the computational cost increases. So we implement the QPSO parallel and distributed by transplant the algorithm on MapReduce model, and named this algorithm MRQPSO.

The proposed MRQPSO partitions the search space into many subspace, then process the QPSO at every subspace independently. The mapper is called when the QPSO is start to work. After all the mappers finished the calculation, the reducer merges and integrates the immediate value, and output the solution. The space-partition help the particle distributed uniformly, which to ensure all areas have the particles fall in at the initialization phase. It is effective to avoid the particles overfly the narrow zone which the optimum may lies.

2.1 MRQPSO Map Function

Algorithm 1 shows the pseudocode of the map function of proposed MRQPSO, the mapper is called when a block starts a QPSO procedure. The input key/value pairs are denoted the massages of data block, which the key is the ID, the value is the string of search space. Then the mappers start to process the QPSO in every block independently, if a blocks procedure completed, another block will follow up immediately. Under ideal conditions, the number of mapper is larger, the single mapper process few procedures, the parallelization is fuller. However, the mapper would spend time to be started in fact. If the data is big enough, the starting time can be neglected, but in our experiments, it will influence the results more or less.

After being processed by mappers, the immediate key/value pairs change to denote the information of global best solution and optimum of current data block. And then the immediate key/value pairs are ready to transport to the reduce phase.

Algorithm 1. MRQPSO Map

```
( key1, value1 )=function mapper ( key, value ) {
//key is the ID of sub-space
//value is sub-space
while  (all data blocks are not completed){ do
    receive key and value;
    initialize the positions of all particles;
    process QPSO on the space in value;
    key1='sub-space';
    value1=obtained optimum and its optimal solution by QPSO on sub-space in
    value;
    output ( key1, value1 );
end while
```

2.2 MRQPSO Reduce Function

The reduce function is in charge of merging and integrating the information which the mapper emitted. As Algorithm 2 shows, the MRQPSOs reducer is to

Algorithm 2. MRCPSO Reduce

```
(key2, value2)=function reducer ( key1, list(value1) ) {
global best=1000000;
for each optimum value_i in list(value1) { do
    if  value_i ¡ global best { then
        global best = value_i;
    end if
end for
key2=problem;
value2=global best;
output (key2, value2)
```

select the minimum from all subspaces. The mappers produced and transported the immediate key/value pairs, the reducer receives them after all mappers completed their work. At the reduce phase, all blocks' global best solution and corresponding fitness are compared with each other, reducer selects and outputs the minimum of them finally.

3 Experiment Result and Analysis

To validate the proposed MRQPSO algorithm, we selected 8 functions to evaluate the ability of solving complex problems. The scalable optimization problems are proposed in the CEC 2013 Special Session on Real-Parameter Optimization [9], and we tested No.21–No.28 are denoted by F1–F8 respectively. All the test composition functions are in the same search range:$[-100, 100]^D$, and they are all minimization problem with global optimum zeros.

3.1 Compared Algorithms, Parameter Settings and Environment

We compared our proposed MRQPSO with original QPSO algorithm to test the optimization performance. Each function is run for 20 independent times and all the results are recorded in the following charts. All experiments are run for $2^{13} \times 900$ function evaluations. The population size is 10. The search space of MRQPSO is partitioned into 2^{11} blocks averagely.

All experiments are run on VMware Workstation virtual machines version 12.0.0: one processor, 1.0GB RAM. Hadoop version 1.1.2 is in Java 1.7 was used in MapReduce experiments; we used three virtual machines while serial algorithm used one. CPU is core i7. Programming language is Java.

3.2 Comparison with QPSO

The results of MRCPSO are compared with QPSO algorithm in Table 1. We show two columns for each item to compare two algorithms clearly. From the

Table 1. Comparison between MRQPSO and QPSO

Fun	Mean function value		St. d		Mean running time (ms)	
	MRQPSO	QPSO	MRQPSO	QPSO	MRQPSO	QPSO
F1	8.10E+01	4.45E+02	3.26E+01	1.51E+02	52098	60704
F2	9.07E+01	3.15E+02	2.09E+01	2.22E+02	57123	71371
F3	3.65E+02	4.97E+02	7.50E+01	2.60E+02	58311	72962
F4	1.09E+02	2.14E+02	1.75E+00	2.07E+01	942736	1811935
F5	1.12E+02	2.11E+02	2.62E+00	2.42E+01	903781	1739438
F6	1.08E+02	2.40E+02	1.09E+00	7.87E+01	982763	1855480
F7	2.37E+02	5.80E+02	5.08E+01	6.09E+01	970225	1945936
F8	1.14E+02	5.81E+02	5.16E+00	2.60E+02	76354	104103

comparison, MRQPSO has a better solution on complexity functions on all items. Because the search space has been partitioned, MRQPSO can get a lower fitness while QPSO be caught in a worse local optimum. In general, the MRQPSO has a better performance on mean value and standard derivation, this suggests the MRQPSO is more capable to search for the optimum and can improve the premature phenomenon of the original QPSO in some ways, and more robust and steady than original QPSO in high-dimension.

The notable advantage is efficiency. From this chart, the MRQPSO is more effective on function convergence, and the more time spend, the more the advantage is. That is because our data blocks which contain several sub-space are run on two different visual machine independently. Normally, the mapper start to work will cost some time. When a problem is so simple that the serial algorithm processes fast, the outstanding benefit of rapid convergence may weaken, such as F1–F3. But when search time gets longer, the mapper starting time even can be negligible, such as F4–F7, the MRQPSO programs running time reduced to half than the QPSO.

To summarize, we can discover that the MRQPSO has better solution performance and cost less running time. The performance of MRQPSO is superior stabilize to QPSO, it is a strong performer at complex problems. It is more suitable and effective for large-scale complex problems, and it is owned to the search space-partition, every sub-space can be explored. When the QPSO is cheated by the deceived functions, MRQPSO gets the global optimum or a smaller local optimum. At the same time, MRQPSO is more efficient than QPSO, and this benefit from the parallelization.

4 Conclusion

This paper developed a MRQPSO algorithm and implemented serial QPSO into the MapReduce model, achieved parallelization and distribution of QPSO. The proposed method was applied to solve the composition benchmark functions, and got a satisfactory solution basically. Moreover, the MRQPSO was compared with the QPSO, the results showed us the parallel one outperformed the serial one whether in search ability, quality of solution or time. The MRQPSO can be considered as a suitable algorithm to solve large-scale and complex problems.

Acknowledgments. This work was supported by the National Natural Science Foundation of China (Nos. 61272279, 61272282, 61371201, and 61203303), the National Basic Research Program (973 Program) of China (No. 2013CB329402), the Program for Cheung Kong Scholars and Innovative Research Team in University (No. IRT-15R53), and the Fund for Foreign Scholars in University Research and Teaching Programs (the 111 Project) (No. B07048).

References

1. Gong, Y., Chen, W., Zhan, Z., Zhang, J., Li, Y., Zhang, Q., Li, J.: Distributed evolutionary algorithms, their models: a survey of the state-of-the-art. Appl. Soft Comput. **34**, 286–300 (2015)

2. Umbarkar, A., Joshi, M.: Review of parallel genetic algorithm based on computing paradigm and diversity in search space. ICTACT J. Soft Comput. **3**, 615–622 (2013)
3. Johar, F.M., Azmin, F.A., Suaidi, M.K., Shibghatullah, A.S., Ahmad, B.H., Salleh, S.N., Aziz, M.Z.A.A., Md Shukor, M.: A review of genetic algorithms and parallel genetic algorithms on graphics processing unit (GPU). In: Proceedings of the 2013 IEEE International Conference on Control System, Computing and Engineering, 264–269 (2013)
4. Kennedy, J., Eberhart, R.C.: Particle swarm optimization. In: Proceedings of the IEEE International Conference on Neural Networks, pp. 1942–1948 (1995)
5. Sun, J., Feng, B., Xu, W.B.: Particle swarm optimization with particles having quantum behavior. In: Proceedings of the IEEE Congress on Evolutionary Computation, pp. 325–331 (2004)
6. Sun, J., Fang, W., Wu, X., Palade, V., Xu, W.: Quantum-behaved particle swarm optimization: analysis of individual particle behavior and parameter selection. Evol. Comput. **20**(3), 349–393 (2012)
7. Dean, J., Ghemawat, S.: MapReduce: simplified data processing on large clusters. Commun. ACM **51**(1), 107–113 (2008)
8. McNabb, A.W., Monson, C.K., Seppi, K.D.: Parallel PSO using MapReduce. In: IEEE Congress on Evolutionary Computation (CEC), pp. 7–14 (2007)
9. Liang, J.J., Qu, B.Y., Suganthan, P.N., Hernndez-Daz, A.G.: Problem definitions and evaluation criteria for the cec 2013 special session on real-parameter optimization. Technical report 201212, Computational Intelligence Laboratory, Zhengzhou University, Zhengzhou China and Technical Report, Nanyang Technological University, Singapore, January 2013

Dynamic Fitness Landscape Analysis on Differential Evolution Algorithm

Shuling Yang[1], Kangshun Li[1(✉)], Wei Li[1,2], Weiguang Chen[1], and Yan Chen[1]

[1] College of Mathematics and Informatics, South China Agricultural University,
Guangdong Province 510642, People's Republic of China
likangshun@sina.com
[2] School of Information Engineering, Jiangxi University of Science and Technology,
Jiangxi 341000, People's Republic of China

Abstract. Dynamic fitness landscape analyses mainly try to figure out the performance of evolutionary algorithms through some simple graphs and effective data. In this paper, we focus on one of evolutionary algorithms named as differential evolution (DE) algorithm. Six benchmark functions we selected because of different properties are involved in our experiments using metrics of dynamic fitness landscape analyses to test. According to experimental results, they shows obviously that differential evolution algorithm can calculate low dimension of benchmark functions and is very hard to handle high dimension. When a benchmark function becomes more and more complicate within higher dimension, sometimes differential evolution algorithm can get good results, but most of time there is no result at all. Dynamic fitness landscape analyses truly obtain experimental results and more details as differential evolution algorithm.

Keywords: Dynamic fitness landscape analyses · Differential evolution algorithm · Benchmark functions

1   Introduction

As we all know, there are different evolutionary algorithms including Evolutionary Strategy (ES), Genetic Algorithm (GA), Particle Swarm Optimization (PSO), Differential Evolution (DE) and so on. And recently, some new evolutionary algorithms are proposed such as Ant Colony Optimization (ACO), Artificial Immune System (AIS), Estimation of Distribution Algorithm (EDA), Cultural Algorithm (CA). Besides, there are some not very popular but promising evolutionary algorithms like Artificial Fish Swarm Algorithm (AFSA), Group Search Optimization (GSO). Differential evolution (DE) proposed by Storn and Price in 1997 is an algorithm which optimizes a problem by attempting to improve a candidate solution with regard to a given measure of quality [12]. DE is calculated for multidimensional real-data functions but does not require for the optimization problem to be differentiable as traditional optimization methods such as gradient descent and quasi-newton methods. DE can therefore also be

© Springer Nature Singapore Pte Ltd. 2016
M. Gong et al. (Eds.): BIC-TA 2016, Part II, CCIS 682, pp. 179–184, 2016.
DOI: 10.1007/978-981-10-3614-9_23

used on optimization problems that are not even continuous, are noisy, change over time [8].

Fitness landscape analyses include static fitness landscape analyses and dynamic fitness landscape analyses. Here, we are going to try to use dynamic fitness landscape to analyze behaviors and performance of differential evolution algorithm. Recently, fitness landscape characterisation can help understand the search process and its probability of success for search-based software testing problems [9]. Climbing combinatorial fitness landscapes mainly try to go towards a better understanding of the intensification stages of metaheuristics by comparing different climbing strategies and evaluate the behavior of classical climber variants on combinatorial fitness landscapes of different properties including dimension, ruggedness and neutrality level [10]. Further more, fitness landscape is also applied in biological world. For example, fitness was broadly correlated with the predicted fraction of correctly folded transfer RNA (tRNA) molecules, thereby revealing a biophysical basis of the fitness landscape [11].

The structure of this paper is arranged as follows: Sect. 2 describes two metrics of dynamic fitness landscape analyses we are going to employ in experiments. Experimental results will show in Sect. 3. And in Sect. 4, we conclude our work and give some future work which may be meaningful to improve this study.

2   Fitness Landscape Analysis

Fitness landscape analyses are very popular to apply in different areas. In fact, there are two kinds of fitness landscape analyses which one of them is named as static fitness landscape analysis and another on is dynamic fitness landscape analysis. Here, differential evolution algorithm which is one of evolutionary algorithms is discussed. Therefore, two methods of dynamic fitness landscape analysis will be used in this paper.

2.1   Dynamic Severity

Dynamic severity measures the relative strength of the landscape change by comparing the landscape before and after a change. It will show a difference if the optimum moves a long or a short way from its current position for the evolutionary search. And dynamic severity is aimed at measuring this dynamic property which can be done using several notation [3]. Here, the corresponding dynamic optimization problem is defined as follows

$$f_s(k) = \max_{x \in S} f(x, k), \forall k \geq 0 \tag{1}$$

which $f_s(k)$ is the temporarily highest fitness, S is the search space and k is the landscape time. The solution trajectory of $f_s(k)$ reads

$$x_s(k) = arg f_s(k), \forall k \geq 0 \tag{2}$$

Therefore, dynamic severity is given as

$$\eta(k+1) = \parallel x_S(k+1) - x_S(k) \parallel \qquad (3)$$

Then, the time average severity is

$$\eta = \lim_{K \to} \sum_{K=0}^{K-1} \eta(k) \qquad (4)$$

In this paper, we are going to analyze changes of differential evolution algorithm using dynamic severity.

2.2 Ruggedness

Ruggedness was used in quantifying for constrained continuous fitness landscapes [2]. Random walk which includes the length T and the step size t_s to calculate for ruggedness on dynamic fitness landscape [3]. Given a random walk on the fitness landscape [4] as

$$x(j+1) = x(j) + t_s \times rand \qquad (5)$$

Here, we set the step size is 10% of the problem's domain named as micro ruggedness $(FEM_{0.1})$ and macro ruggedness $(FEM_{0.5})$ means 50% of the problem's domain [5]. This is the fitness value as time series:

$$f(j,k) = f(x(j),k), j = 1, 2, \ldots, T \qquad (6)$$

where k is time. And $r(t_L, k)$ is defined as the spatial correlation which can be obtained from the autocorrelation function of the time series with time lag t_L. Random walk correlation function is defined as follows:

$$r(t_L, k) = \frac{\sum_{j=1}^{T-t_L} (f(j,k) - \bar{f}(k))(f(j+t_L, k)) - \bar{f}(k)}{\sum_{j=1}^{T} (f(j,k) - \bar{f}(k))^2} \qquad (7)$$

where $\bar{f}(k) = \frac{1}{T} \sum_{j=1}^{T} f(j,k)$ and $T \gg t_L > 0$. The spatial random walk correlation function measures the correlation between different segments of the fitness landscape for a fixed k [3].

2.3 Success Rate

The success rate (SRate) is calculated by the number of successful runs that reach a solution within the fixed accuracy level of the global optimum divided by the total number of runs [6]. The range of the Success rate is from 0 to 1. If the value equals to 1, that means there is not failure time. The formula shows as follows:

$$SRate = \frac{ST}{ST + FT} \qquad (8)$$

where ST and FT equal to success times failure times respectively.

3   Experiments and Results

Table 1 shows results of ruggedness and success rate which are calculated by metrics of dynamic fitness landscape according to differential evolution algorithm for six benchmark functions. When benchmark functions are very complicated, we can see values of ruggedness are not stable which means it is hard to find optimum because of existing deceived values or local optimum. From Figs. 1, 2, 3, 4, 5 and 6, they show results of dynamic severity and optimum. It is very clear that when dynamic severity changes frequently, we can not get the optimum of each benchmark function. For example, in Fig. 4, before 20 times, dynamic severity seems to change quickly, at the same time, different evolution algorithm is seeking the global optimum. When dynamic severity of Salomon converged, the optimum is also converged.

Table 1. Dynamic fitness landscape metrics according to differential evolution algorithm for 6 benchmark functions.

Function	Definition	D	$r_{FEM_{0.1}}$	$r_{FEM_{0.5}}$	SRate
Ackley	$f_{ack}(x) = -20exp$ $(-0.2\sqrt{\frac{1}{D}\sum_{i=1}^{D}x_i^2}) - exp$ $(\sum cos(2\pi x_i)) + 20 + e$	2	0.000	0.000	0.667
Quadric (Schwefel 1.2)	$f_{qdr}(x) = \sum_{i=1}^{D}(\sum_{i}^{j=1}x_j)^2$	2	0.013	0.011	0.762
Rastrigin	$f_{ras}(x) =$ $\sum_{i=1}^{D}(x_i^2 - 10cos(2\pi x_i) + 10)$	2	0.349	0.602	0.905
Salomon	$f_{sal}(x) =$ $-cos(2\pi\sqrt{\sum_{i=1}^{D}x_i^2}) +$ $0.1\sqrt{\sum_{i=1}^{D}x_i^2} + 1$	2	0.858	0.862	0.750
Schwefel 2.22	$f_{sch2.22}(x) = \sum_{i=1}^{D}|x_i|$ $+ \prod_{i=1}^{D}|x_i|$	2	0.614	0.629	0.837
Schwefel 2.26	$f_{sch2.26}(x) =$ $-\sum_{i=1}^{D}(x_i sin(\sqrt{|x_i|}))$	2	0.466	0.474	0.967

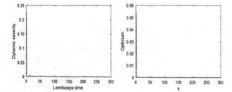

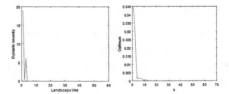

Fig. 1. Dynamic severity and optimum of Ackley function.

Fig. 2. Dynamic severity and optimum of Quadric function.

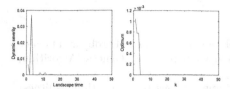

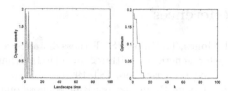

Fig. 3. Dynamic severity and optimum of Rastrigin function.

Fig. 4. Dynamic severity and optimum of Salomon function.

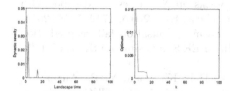

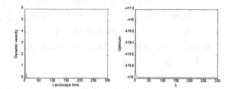

Fig. 5. Dynamic severity and optimum of Schwefel 2.22 function.

Fig. 6. Dynamic severity and optimum of Schwefel 2.26 function.

4   Conclusion

Actually, fitness landscape can be used in many different areas. In this paper, we use dynamic fitness landscape metrics to try to analyze properties of differential evolution algorithm: dynamic severity as an evolutionary search measure and a ruggedness measure as entropy. We can see when the optimum moves different distance no matter a long way or a short way, it shows the relative strength of the landscape change by comparing the landscape before and after a change. Here, we try to use metrics of dynamic fitness landscape analyses to figure out properties and performance of differential evolution algorithm. It is clear when a benchmark function is very complicate, results of ruggedness seems to be very chaotic and can not be stable until finding optimum. As for dynamic severity, it changes location frequently because it is aimed at measuring the relative strength of the landscape change.

Obviously, there is still a lot of work to do in the future. First, there are many other metrics of dynamic fitness landscape which can evaluate performance of evolutionary algorithms. Secondly, we just focus on integral performance of differential evolution algorithm. Actually, we can also pay attention to different operators and parameters.

Acknowledgments. This work is supported by the National Natural Science Foundation of China with Grant No. 61573157, the Fund of Natural Science Foundation of Guangdong Province of China with Grant No. 2014A030313454 and the Key Project of Natural Statistical Science and Research with the Grant No. 2015LZ30, the National Natural Science Foundation of China with the Grant No. 61561024 and 61562038.

References

1. Jones, T., Forrest, S.: Fitness distance correlation as a measure of problem difficulty for genetic algorithms. In: 6th International Conference on Genetic Algorithm, San Francisco, pp. 184–192 (1995)
2. Shayan, P., Frank, N.: Ruggedeness quantifying for constrained continuous fitness landscapes. In: Evolutionary Constrained Optimization, India, pp. 29–50 (2015)
3. Hendrik, R.: Dynamic fitness landscape analysis. Indian J. Med. Sci. 336–339 (2013). India
4. Nowak, S., Krug, J.: Analysis of adaptive walks on NK fitness landscapes with different interaction schemes. J. Stat. Mech. Theor. Exp. **2015**, 1742–5468 (2015)
5. Malan, K.M., Engelbrecht, A.P.: Particle swarm optimisation failure prediction based on fitness landscape characteristics. In: IEEE Symposium on Swarm Intelligence, pp. 1–9 (2014)
6. Suganthan, P. N., Hansen, N., Liang, J. J., Deb, K., Chen, Y. P., Auger, A., Tiwari, S.: Problem definitions and evaluation criteria for the CEC: special on real-parameter optimization. Technical report, Nanyang Technological University, Singapore (2005)
7. Storn, R., Price, K.: Differential evolution - a simple, efficient heuristic for global optimization over continuous spaces. J. Global Optim. **11**, 341–359 (1997)
8. Rocca, P., Oliveri, G., Massa, A.: Differential evolution as applied to electromagnetics. IEEE Antennas Propag. Mag. **55**, 38–49 (2011)
9. Aleti, A., Moser, I., Grunske, L.: Analysing the fitness landscape of search-based software testing problems. Autom. Softw. Eng. 1–19 (2016)
10. Basseur, M., Goeffon, A.: Climbing combinatorial fitness landscapes. Appl. Soft Comput. **30**, 688–704 (2015)
11. Li, C., Qian, W., Maclean, C.J., Zhang, J.: The fitness landscape of a tRNA gene. Science **352**, 837–840 (2016)
12. Differential Evolution from Wikipedia. https://en.wikipedia.org/wiki/Differential_evolution

Improving Artificial Bee Colony Algorithm with Historical Archive

Yalan Zhou[1], Jiahai Wang[2,3]($\boxtimes$), Shangce Gao[4], Xing Yang[2], and Jian Yin[2,3]

[1] College of Information, Guangdong University of Finance & Economics, Guangzhou 510320, China
[2] Department of Computer Science, Sun Yat-sen University, Guangzhou 510006, China
[3] Guangdong Province Key Laboratory of Big Data Analysis and Processing, Guangzhou 510006, China
wjiahai@hotmail.com
[4] Faculty of Engineering, University of Toyama, Toyama-shi 930-8555, Japan

Abstract. In this study, an artificial bee colony with historical archive (HAABC) is proposed to help ABC escape from stagnation situation. The proposed framework keeps track of the search history and stores excellent successful solutions into an archive. Once stagnation is detected in scout bees phase of ABC, a new individual is generated by utilizing the historical archive. Experimental results on 28 benchmark functions show that the proposed framework significantly improves the performance of basic ABC and five state-of-the-art ABC algorithms.

Keywords: Artificial bee colony · Scout bees phase · Historical archive

1 Introduction

Artificial bee colony (ABC) algorithm [1] is a relatively new swam intelligence algorithm. It is shown in [2,3] that the best ABC variants are competitive with recent state-of-the-art algorithms, which establishes ABC algorithms as serious competitors in continuous optimization. ABC has been successfully applied to various scientific and engineering fields [4,5].

The general algorithmic structure of ABC contains three phases: employed bees phase, onlooker bees phase and scout bees phase. In scout bees phase, an stagnated individual, which has not been improved for a predefined threshold *limit*, is abandoned. Then, a scout produces a new individual randomly in the predefined search scope. This way may be impossible to help the individual escape from stagnation situation because the quality of a randomly generated individual can not be guaranteed.

In this study, an artificial bee colony with historical archive (HAABC) is proposed to keep track of the search history and store excellent successful solutions into an archive. In scout bees phase, a new individual is generated utilizing the archive in the proposed framework. This way is able to prevent the algorithm from searching in the poor regions. Thus the algorithm has a high chance of moving to a new promising region.

© Springer Nature Singapore Pte Ltd. 2016
M. Gong et al. (Eds.): BIC-TA 2016, Part II, CCIS 682, pp. 185–190, 2016.
DOI: 10.1007/978-981-10-3614-9_24

2   Proposed HAABC Framework

To guide the algorithm toward the most promising regions in the search space, the proposed HAABC keep track of the search history and collect these excellent successful solutions in terms of their diversity and fitness into an archive. Once stagnation is detected in scout bees phase, an individual is generated by utilizing previous excellent successful solution in archive to increase the probabilities of generating successful solution at next iteration. The proposed HAABC framework is showed in Fig. 1.

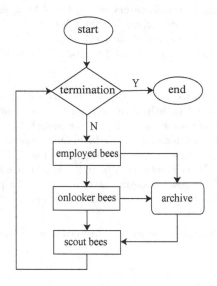

Fig. 1. HAABC framework

Each individual in ABC is denoted as $X_i = [x_{i,1},\ x_{i,2},\ \cdots,\ x_{i,D}]$, where $i = 1, 2, \cdots, NP$, NP is the number of population.

A historical archive scheme using an ordered list can be depicted by Fig. 2.

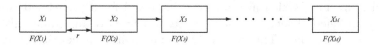

Fig. 2. Historical archive data structure – an ordered list

An archive can be formally defined as follows:

$$\mathbf{AR} = \{X_1, X_2, ..., X_M | Fit(X_1) \geq Fit(X_2) \geq ... \geq Fit(X_M);$$
$$\forall i_1 \neq i_2, crowd(X_{i_1}, X_{i_2}) = 0\} \tag{1}$$

where $X_1, X_2, \ldots, X_M$ are the solutions in historical archive; M is the maximum number of solutions in historical archive; $Fit(X_i)$ is the fitness value of X_i; $crowd(X_{i_1}, X_{i_2})$ denotes whether X_{i_1} and X_{i_2} are crowded, X_{i_1} and X_{i_2} are in crowded distance and denoted by $crowd(X_{i_1}, X_{i_2}) = 1$, while X_{i_1} and X_{i_2} are in safe distance and denoted by $crowd(X_{i_1}, X_{i_2}) = 0$.

In the ideal case, the decision space can be divided into M equal subregions and each population member can locate an optima in each subregion. For obtaining equal subregions, each of the D dimensions is divided into T divisions. An appropriate value for T can be obtained as follows:

$$T^D = M \Rightarrow T \approx \lfloor e^{\frac{\ln M}{D}} \rfloor \tag{2}$$

This ensures that each subregion can theoretically be represented by at least one archive member thus covering the extreme case when the multimodal function has global optima, one in each subregion.

Then, niche distance of each dimension can be calculated as follows:

$$v_j = (x_j^{max} - x_j^{min})/T \tag{3}$$

where $j = 1, 2, ..., D$.

The niching distance defined above using Manhattan distance metric in each dimension. Finally, $crowd()$ of two archive members X_{i_1} and X_{i_2} are defined based on the niching distance as follows:

$$crowd(X_{i_1}, X_{i_2}) = \begin{cases} 1, & \text{if } |x_{i_1,j} - x_{i_2,j}| < \alpha \cdot v_j, \forall j \in \{1, 2, ..., D\} \\ 0, & \text{otherwise} \end{cases} \tag{4}$$

HAABC generates new solution at scout bees phase as follows:

$$v_{i,j} = x_{A,j} + \phi_i \cdot (x_{i,j} - x_{k,j}). \tag{5}$$

where ϕ_i is a rand number in the range $[-1, 1]$, X_A is selected from archive using a roulette wheel selection based on fitness value, X_k ($k \neq i$) is a randomly selected solution in current population.

3 Experimental Results

Firstly, the proposed framework is incorporated into basic ABC ($NP = 100$, $limit = 200$), and comparisons of HAABC ($NP = 100$, $limit = 100$, $M = 10$, $\alpha = 0.2$) with basic ABC on 28 benchmark functions at $10D$, $30D$ and $50D$ from CEC 2013 [6]. Then, the proposed framework is incorporated into five advanced ABC variants. A maximum number of $10^4 \times D$ function evaluations (FEs) are allowed in each run of an algorithm. And each algorithm is tested 51 times independently on each function. The paired Wilcoxon's rank-sum test [7] is conducted at the 5% significance level to show the significant difference of performance between two algorithms. The result of the test is represented as

Table 1. Statistics of performance comparisons of HAABC with basic ABC algorithm for CEC2013 functions at 10D, 30D and 50D.

Algorithm at 10D	$w/t/l$	R+	R−	p-value	$\alpha = 0.05$	$\alpha = 0.1$
HAABC vs basic ABC	13/10/5	287.5	90.5	0.016788	**Yes**	**Yes**
Algorithm at 30D	$w/t/l$	R+	R−	p-value	$\alpha = 0.05$	$\alpha = 0.1$
HAABC vs basic ABC	13/8/7	282.5	123.5	0.07168	No	**Yes**
Algorithm at 50D	$w/t/l$	R+	R−	p-value	$\alpha = 0.05$	$\alpha = 0.1$
HAABC vs basic ABC	15/8/5	294.5	111.5	0.03684	**Yes**	**Yes**

$w/t/l$, which means that one algorithm is significantly better than, similar to and worse than the corresponding competitor on w, t, and l functions, respectively. To identify differences between a pair of algorithms on all problems, the multiproblem Wicoxon rank-sum test [8,9] is carried out.

The statistics summarizing the performance comparisons are showed in Table 1. The results in column $w/t/l$ show that HAABC significantly outperforms basic ABC on most of functions. It is clear that HAABC obtains higher $R+$ values than $R-$ values in all cases. Further, p-value at the significance level $\alpha = 0.05$ and $\alpha = 0.1$ are compared, the results are marked with 'Yes' to indicate there is a significant difference, otherwise marked with 'No'. For the functions at $10D$ and $50D$, according to the Wilcoxon test at $\alpha = 0.05$, there are significant differences between HAABC and basic ABC. According to the Wilcoxon test at $\alpha = 0.1$, there are significant differences between HAABC and basic ABC in all cases. The overall results of Table 1 clearly show that the proposed HAABC framework can significantly improve the performance of basic ABC.

The propose HAABC framework is applied to five advanced ABC variants (i.e., Composite ABC [2], GABC [10], IABC [11], ILABC [12], OCABC [13]). Table 2 provides the statistics summarizing the performance comparisons. The results in column $w/t/l$ show that HAABC significantly outperforms the corresponding advanced ABC variants on most functions. From the multiproblem Wilcoxon test, it is clear that HAABC obtains higher $R+$ values than $R-$ values in all cases. It means that HAABC is better than its corresponding advanced ABC variants for all functions. Additionally, for the functions at all dimensions, the p values are less than 0.05 in four cases (except in Composite ABC case). These results indicate that HAABC variants are significantly better than most of its corresponding ABC variants according to both single problem and multiproblem Wilcoxon statistical analysis.

To conclude, HAABC framework can improve the performance of the advanced ABC variants. It means that the proposed framework can cooperate with other different kinds of modifications to further improve the performance of ABC.

Table 2. Statistics of performance comparisons of HAABC with advanced ABC variants for CEC 2013 functions at 10D, 30D and 50D.

Algorithm at 10D	w/t/l	R+	R−	p-value	$\alpha = 0.05$	$\alpha = 0.1$
HAComposite ABC *vs* Composite ABC	4/21/3	237.5	140.5	≥ 0.2	No	No
HAGABC *vs* GABC	14/14/0	330.5	47.5	0.00032	Yes	Yes
HAIABC *vs* IABC	15/12/1	305.5	72.5	0.004055	Yes	Yes
HAILABC *vs* ILABC	17/10/1	318.5	59.5	0.001192	Yes	Yes
HAOCABC *vs* OCABC	11/16/1	355.5	22.5	8.76E−06	Yes	Yes
Algorithm at 30D	w/t/l	R+	R−	p-value	$\alpha = 0.05$	$\alpha = 0.1$
HAComposite ABC *vs* Composite ABC	11/14/3	263.5	142.5	0.17457	No	No
HAGABC *vs* GABC	16/12/0	308.5	69.5	0.003107	Yes	Yes
HAIABC *vs* IABC	17/11/0	355	51	0.000244	Yes	Yes
HAILABC *vs* ILABC	16/11/1	330.5	47.5	0.00032	Yes	Yes
HAOCABC *vs* OCABC	13/14/1	309	97	0.014598	Yes	Yes
Algorithm at 50D	w/t/l	R+	R−	p-value	$\alpha = 0.05$	$\alpha = 0.1$
HAComposite ABC *vs* Composite ABC	9/14/5	269.5	136.5	0.13449	No	No
HAGABC *vs* GABC	17/10/1	354	52	0.000274	Yes	Yes
HAIABC *vs* IABC	17/10/1	358	48	0.000172	Yes	Yes
HAILABC *vs* ILABC	17/10/1	349	57	0.000473	Yes	Yes
HAOCABC *vs* OCABC	12/16/0	305	101	0.019114	Yes	Yes

4 Conclusion

In HAABC, an archive is used to save successful solutions as history information. Once a solution is not improved for *limit* times, which would be abandoned and replaced by a new solution. The new solution is generated by both information in historical archive and current solutions. Experimental results on benchmark functions show that the proposed framework significantly improve performance of the considered ABC algorithms.

Acknowledgments. This work is supported by Foundation for Distinguished Young Talents in Higher Education of Guangdong, China (Yqgdufe1404), and Program for Characteristic Innovation Talents of Guangdong (2014KTSCX127), and the National Natural Science Foundation of China (61472453, 61673403).

References

1. Karaboga, D., Basturk, B.: A powerful and efficient algorithm for numerical function optimization: artificial bee colony (ABC) algorithm. J. Global Optim. **39**(3), 459–471 (2007)
2. Aydin, D.: Composite artificial bee colony algorithms: from component-based analysis to high-performing algorithms. Appl. Soft Comput. J. **32**, 266–285 (2015)
3. Liao, T., Aydin, D., Stutzle, T.: Artificial bee colonies for continuous optimization: experimental analysis and improvements. Swarm Intell. **7**(4), 327–356 (2013)

4. Karaboga, D., Gorkemli, B., Ozturk, C., Karaboga, N.: A comprehensive survey: artificial bee colony (ABC) algorithm and applications. Artif. Intell. Rev. **42**(1), 21–57 (2014)
5. Bansal, J., Sharma, H., Jadon, S.: Artificial bee colony algorithm: a survey. Int. J. Adv. Intell. Paradigms **5**(1–2), 123–159 (2013)
6. Suganthan, P.N., Liang, J.J., Qu, B.Y., Alfredo, G.H.D.: Problem definitions and evaluation criteria for the CEC 2013 special session on real-parameter optimization. Technical report, vol. 201212. Zhengzhou University and Nanyang Technological University (2013)
7. Wilcoxon, F.: Individual comparisons by ranking methods. Biometrics **1**(6), 80–83 (1945)
8. Garca, S., Fernndez, A., Luengo, J., Herrera, F.: Advanced nonparametric tests for multiple comparisons in the design of experiments in computational intelligence and data mining: experimental analysis of power. Inf. Sci. **180**(10), 2044–2064 (2010)
9. Derrac, J., Garca, S., Molina, D., Herrera, F.: A practical tutorial on the use of nonparametric statistical tests as a methodology for comparing evolutionary and swarm intelligence algorithms. Swarm Evol. Comput. **1**(1), 3–18 (2011)
10. Zhu, G., Kwong, S.: Gbest-guided artificial bee colony algorithm for numerical function optimization. Appl. Math. Comput. **217**(7), 3166–3173 (2010)
11. Wang, H., Wu, Z., Zhou, X., Rahnamayan, S.: Accelerating artificial bee colony algorithm by using an external archive. In: 2013 IEEE Congress on Evolutionary Computation, pp. 517–521. IEEE Press (2013)
12. Gao, W.-F., Huang, L.-L., Liu, S.-Y., Dai, C.: Artificial bee colony algorithm based on information learning. IEEE Trans. Cybern. **45**(12), 2827–2839 (2015)
13. Gao, W.-F., Liu, S.-Y., Huang, L.-L.: A novel artificial bee colony algorithm based on modified search equation and orthogonal learning. IEEE Trans. Cybern. **43**(3), 1011–1024 (2013)

Recent Advances in Evolutionary Programming

Jing Yu and Lining Xing[✉]

School of Information Systems and Management,
National University of Defense Technology, Changsha 410073, Hunan, China
xing2999@qq.com

Abstract. In this paper, we provide an overview of some recent advances in evolutionary programming. We mainly discuss the principle and technical method of design for classical evolutionary programming and improving evolutionary programming (IEP). IEP has included many types of improving methods to solve realistic problems: fast evolutionary programming, self-adaptive Cauchy evolutionary programming, mixed mutation strategy in evolutionary programming, parallel evolutionary programming, Quality of Transmission (QoT) aware evolutionary programming algorithm, shifting classical evolutionary programming, and surrogate-assisted evolutionary programming. The above methods and some issues related to the future development of evolutionary programming are discussed in this paper.

Keywords: Evolutionary programming (EP) · Fast EP · Self-adaptive Cauchy EP · Mixed mutation strategy · Parallel EP · Surrogate-assisted EP

1 Introduction

Evolutionary computation (EC) is the study of computational systems that use ideas and obtain inspiration from natural evolution and adaptation EC was originally divided into four branches [1–3, 11–13]: evolution strategy (ES), evolutionary programming (EP), genetic algorithm (GA), and genetic programming (GP). EP is one of the main branches of EC, and mainly seeks the global optimal solution of a particular function and encodes for decimal coding through individual variation to produce a new individual, that is the new individual is generated using the rules of the evolutionary algorithm affected by the mutation operator.

There are three major operations in a generic evolutionary algorithm: crossover, selection, and mutation. For the evolution of offspring, the most essential operation is gene mutation, which plays a decisive role. The algorithm of the mutation operator of the evolutionary algorithm includes Gaussian mutation, the Cauchy operator, and the Lévy operator.

Fogel (1992) proceeded with continuous solution space discretization and using natural spatial discretization again proved the convergence of EP. He successfully applied it to numerical optimization and neural network training topics.

© Springer Nature Singapore Pte Ltd. 2016
M. Gong et al. (Eds.): BIC-TA 2016, Part II, CCIS 682, pp. 191–203, 2016.
DOI: 10.1007/978-981-10-3614-9_25

Back and Schwefel (1993) proposed adaptive mutation EP. Experiments in their paper [15] showed that this proposed method was superior when compared with methods that did not have its advantages, such as classical EP (CEP) using Gaussian mutation.

Given a standard Gaussian distribution expectation of zero and variance one, the search step length was shorter than that applicable to a local search. When the search point was near to the local optimal value, it was easy to fall into the local optimal solution to the problem. To address this problem, Yao and Liu (1997, 2002) proposed fast EP (FEP) using Cauchy mutation. Increasing the search step length allowed the method to achieve the global optimal solution of the problem quickly.

In recent years, EP has remained a very active area of research. In 2004, for example, Lee and Yao proposed introducing a mutation operator base on Lévy probability distribution into evolutionary planning to better solve the sparse peak distribution function of the optimization problem. However, its Lévy operator makes the method so complex that its scope of application is small. In 2008, Fang Jun et al. combined the Cauchy distribution and Gaussian distribution with t-distribution by changing the degrees of freedom and controlling its mutation operation. By changing the degrees of freedom n control its mutation operation. The simulation experiment shows its superiority.

The remainder of this paper is organized as follows: In Sect. 2, we introduce CEP in detail. In Sect. 3, we describe the characteristics and algorithms of a variety of improving EPs (IEP), including FEP, SAEP, and MEP, followed by the summary and future development in Sect. 4.

2   Classical Evolutionary Programming

Initially, Fogel [20] proposed CEP to solve practical problems. Then, to address the real optimization problem, they introduce the normal distribution function. Compared with the genetic algorithm, EP places greater emphasis on its own development, thus it has the advantages of simple description, flexible use, high efficiency, strong robustness, and a limited number of conditions. In this section, we briefly introduce the components of CEP and its algorithm.

2.1   Constituent Elements

There are five basic stages in this algorithm:

(1) Initial population
The initial population is assumed to consist of a single individual. The population consists of chromosomes. Each individual is essentially a chromosome and every path represented by chromosome is a sequence of nodes or genes generated randomly.

(2) Fitness calculation

In biology, fitness represents the degree to which the species is adapted to its living environment in the natural world. It is used to measure the global optimal solution of the individual in EP and evaluate the degree of individual adaptation. The fitness calculation function F is usually a positive function.

For optimization problems $\max f(x)$, the fitness function can be expressed as follows:

$$Fit(x) = f(x) - f_{inf}.$$

For $\min f(x)$, the fitness function is

$$Fit(x) = f_{sup} - f(x).$$

(3) Mutation

The mutation operation simulates the mutation of biological gene location. The diversity of a population is improved by the mutation operation in EP under individual coding rules, for which the position of the corresponding gene is mutated according to the mutation probability so that offspring with new characteristics are generated. The mutation operation in CEP mainly includes uniform mutation, non-uniform mutation, and normal mutation.

(4) Selection

The selection operation is the process of selecting appropriate individuals from the parent and transitional individual, according to a certain rule. This process simulates the evolutionary theory of "survival of the fittest." Generally, the operation, based on the individual fitness evaluation function, chooses individuals with higher fitness values. It can ensure that good genetic individuals can be selected for the next generation because the search direction of the algorithm is in the direction of the global optimal solution and in a relatively short time, the solution can converge to the global optimal.

2.2   The Algorithm of CEP

The algorithm of CEP can be described as follows:

(1) Generate an initial population of μ individuals and set $t = 1$. Each individual is taken as a pair of real-valued vectors, $(x_i, \eta_i), \forall i \in 1, \cdots, \mu$, where x_i are objective variables and η_i are standard deviations for Gaussian mutations.
(2) Evaluate the fitness score for each individual $(x_i, \eta_i), \forall i \in 1, \cdots$, in the population based on the objective function $f(x_i)$.
(3) Each parent $(x_i, \eta_i), i = 1, \cdots, \mu$ creates a single offspring:

$$x_i^{'}(j) = x_i(j) + \eta_i(j)N_j(0, 1) \tag{1}$$

$$\eta_i^{'}(j) = \eta_i(j)exp(\tau^{'} N(0, 1) + \tau N_j(0, 1)), \tag{2}$$

where $x_i(j)$, $x_i^{'}(j)$, $\eta_i(j)$, and $\eta_i^{'}(j)$ denote the j-th component of the vectors x_i, $x_i^{'}$, η_i, and $\eta_i^{'}$, respectively, and $N(0, 1)$ denotes normally distributed mean zero and standard deviation one, $N_j(0,1)$ indicates that a new random number is generated under the condition of normally distributed mean zero and standard deviation one for each value of j. The parameters τ and τ' are commonly set to $(\sqrt{2\sqrt{n}})^{-1}$ and $(2\sqrt{n})^{-1}$, respectively.

(4) Calculate the fitness of each offspring $(x_i, \eta_i), \forall i \in 1, \cdots, \mu$.
(5) Each individual (x_i, η_i) and its offspring (x_i', η_i') are one group. q candidates are chosen uniformly at random from the group. For each comparison, if the individuals fitness is not smaller than the candidates fitness, it receives a "win."
(6) Select μ individuals from (x_i, η_i) and $(x_i', \eta_i'), \forall i \in 1, \cdots, \mu$, which should have the most "wins" to be parents of the next generation.
(7) Stop if the halting criterion is satisfied; otherwise, $k = k + 1$ and go to Step (3).

3   Improving Evolutionary Programming

The improvement of EP can be summed up in the following two aspects:

(1) the new offspring population is generated by variation
(2) selecting new population from the variation of the population and the parent generation.

Next, we will introduce some improving evolutionary programmings based on the above two aspects.

3.1   Fast Evolutionary Programming

One disadvantage of CEP is its slow convergence to or near to an optimal solution, and we found that using Gaussian mutation in CEP is one of the reasons for this. Its search step is not sufficiently large when using Gaussian mutation, and the individual may jump out of the local optimum. However, using a large search step makes it easy to miss an optimal solution. Thus, how to select a suitable sized search step is an essential problem.

For this problem, an FEP was proposed. Yao et al. [14] showed that FEP is very good at searching in a large neighborhood, whereas CEP is better at searching in a small local neighborhood. Thus, we consider how to determine a global optimum using FEP.

We consider Gaussian mutation as an example to show necessity of a large search step. The Gaussian density function f^G with a normal distribution of expectation zero and variance σ^2 is

$$f^G(x) = \frac{1}{\sigma\sqrt{2\pi}} b^{-\frac{x^2}{2\sigma^2}}, \quad -\infty < x < +\infty. \tag{3}$$

The probability of generating a point near the global optimum x^* is as follows [19]:

$$P^G(|x - x^*| \le \varepsilon) = \int_{x^*-\varepsilon}^{x^*+\varepsilon} f^G(x) dx, \tag{4}$$

where ε is the neighborhood size and σ is the step size of the Gaussian mutation, and $\varepsilon > 0$, $\sigma > 0$.

To evaluate the impact of σ in $P^G(|x - x^*| \leq \varepsilon)$, we consider the derivation of (4):

$$\frac{\partial}{\partial \sigma} P^G(|x - x^*| \leq \varepsilon) = \frac{2\varepsilon}{\sigma^2 \sqrt{2\pi}} e^{-\frac{(x^* - \varepsilon + \delta)^2}{\sigma^2}}. \tag{5}$$

$$(\frac{(x^* - \varepsilon + \delta)^2}{\sigma^2} - 1)$$

Therefor, we hold that:

$$\begin{cases} \frac{\partial}{\partial \sigma} P^G(|x - x^*| \leq \varepsilon) > 0, \, if \, \sigma < |x^* - \varepsilon + \delta| \\ \frac{\partial}{\partial \sigma} P^G(|x - x^*| \leq \varepsilon) < 0, \, if \, \sigma > |x^* - \varepsilon + \delta| \end{cases} \tag{6}$$

Similar analysis of Cauchy distribution with scale parameter $t(t > 0)$, we fined that:

$$\begin{cases} \frac{\partial}{\partial \sigma} P^C(|x - x^*| \leq \varepsilon) > 0, \, if \, t < |x^* - \varepsilon + \delta| \\ \frac{\partial}{\partial \sigma} P^C(|x - x^*| \leq \varepsilon) < 0, \, if \, t > |x^* - \varepsilon + \delta| \end{cases} \tag{7}$$

where the density function is

$$f^C(x) = \frac{1}{\pi} \frac{1}{t^2 + x^2}, \quad -\infty < x < +\infty.$$

Based on the above results, Yao et al., based on Cauchy mutation, proposed a fast yet effective evolutionary optimization algorithm - FEP. Compared with the CEP, FEP would be less effective than CEP when the search point is near the small neighborhood of the global optimum. The core deference between FEP and EP is that Cauchy mutation is more likely to generate larger jumps than Gaussian mutation. The numerical experiments in the literature [11] verify the superiority of FEP.

3.2 Self-adaptive Cauchy Evolutionary Programming

In 2004, Lee and Yao [10] generalized EP with mutations based on the Lévy probability distribution, with which one can extend and generalize FEP because the Cauchy probability distribution is a special case of the Lévy probability distribution. The Lévy probability distribution differs from the Gaussian distribution in that the Lévy distribution, like the Cauchy distribution, has an infinite second moment. The Lévy probability distribution has an infinite second moment and is, therefore, more likely to generate an offspring that is further away from its parent than the commonly employed Gaussian mutation. Moreover, by adjusting the parameter in the distribution, the probability density can be adjusted, and then the variation in the mutation. Based on the characteristics of the Lévy distribution, Lee and Yao proposed an EP algorithm using adaptive as well as non-adaptive Lévy mutations.

Based on the characteristics of the Lévy distribution, the authors proposed an EPself-adaptive Cauchy EP (ACEP)Based on the current point and optimization point, we can adjust the parameters r of ACEP gradually by optimizing the functions at a period and determine the optimal solution quickly.

3.3   Mixed Mutation Strategy in EP

Various mutation operators have been proposed in EP. However, each operator may be efficient in solving a subset of problems, but fails for another subset. The idea of mixing various mutation operators as one mutation operator may be possible to integrate their advantages. In 2005, He and Yao [8] proposed the mixed strategy, which is described as follows: An individual chooses one mutation strategy s from its strategy set based on the selection probability $p(s)$ for each generation. This probability distribution is called a mixed strategy distribution in game theory. The key problem is to determine a good, and if possible, optimal, mixed probability $p(s)$ for every individual.

He and Yao proved that this mixed strategy solves problems more efficiently than CEP, which usually uses a single mutation strategy because none of the single mutation operators can solve all problems efficiently, regardless of how powerful they are This paper has confirmed this point.

Now, we introduce the mutation of the mixed strategy in detail.

A mixed strategy using Gaussian and Cauchy mutations
First, we briefly introduce the following two mutation operators:

Gaussian Mutation:

$$x_i^{t+1}(j) = x_i^t(j) + \sigma_i^{t+1}(j)N_j(0,1), \tag{8}$$

where $N_j(0,1)$ is Gaussian random variable for every j.

Cauchy Mutation:

$$x_i^{t+1}(j) = x_i^t(j) + \sigma_i^{t+1}(j)C_j(0,1), \tag{9}$$

where $C_j(0,1)$ is Cauchy random variable for every j.

The output of an individual is defined by how far an individual moves during a successful mutation. Let x_i^t be the parent individual and x_i^{t+1} its offspring through a mutation strategy, then the output is

$$o(x_i^{(t+1)}) = \begin{cases} \max_1^n\{|x_i^{t+1}(j) - x_i^t(j)|\}, & if \ f(x_i^{t+1}) < f(x_i^t) \\ 0, & otherwise \end{cases} \tag{10}$$

The output of strategy s_1 is defined by

$$o^{(t+1)}(s_1) = \max_i\{o(x_i^{(t+1)})\}, \tag{11}$$

where $x_i^{(t+1)}$ is generated by applying strategy s_1.

When considering the effects of historical strategies, the output 11 is modified as follows:

$$\bar{o}(t+1) = \begin{cases} o^{(t+1)}(s_1), & if \ o^{(t+1)}(s_1) \geq \alpha \cdot o^{(t)}(s_1), \\ \alpha \cdot o^{(t)}(s_1), & otherwise \end{cases} \tag{12}$$

where $\alpha \in [0, 1]$ is a controlling parameter, which could store the size of previous output.

Then, the payoff of players could be defined as follows:

$$\pi_1(s_1, s_2) = \frac{o(s_1)}{o(s_2)};$$

$$\pi_2(s_1, s_2) = \frac{o(s_2)}{o(s_1)}.$$

To avoid the denominator, $o(s_2)$ or $o(s_1)$, equaling zero, some measures should be taken. A feasible method is to add a controlling parameter β:

$$\pi_1(s_1, s_2) = \begin{cases} \beta & if \ \frac{o(s_1)}{o(s_2)} \leq \beta \\ \frac{1}{\beta} & if \ \frac{o(s_1)}{o(s_2)} \geq \frac{1}{\beta} \\ \frac{o(s_1)}{o(s_2)} & otherwise, \end{cases} \tag{13}$$

where $\beta \in [0, 1]$. When $\beta = 0$, the payoff will be infinitely large, and $= 1$ means that the payoffs of s_1 and s_2 both equal one.

Now we can define the strategy profile as $s = (s_1, s_2)$, and the mixed probability distribution $p(s)$ can be calculated as

$$p_1(s_1) = \frac{\pi_1(s_1, s_2)}{\pi_1(s_1, s_2) + \pi_2(s_1, s_2)}.$$

3.4   Parallel Evolutionary Programming

For some very difficult and large problems, EP usually requires a long time to determine adequate solutions. Riessen et al. proposed designing a faster EP by dividing a large task into smaller and easier tasks, and running a number of EPs simultaneously on multiple processors to solve each task to reduce the time needed. Based on this idea, Riessen et al. [17] presented two parallel structures for the EP Net algorithm population parallelism and individual parallelism.

Population parallelism takes advantage of the independence of each member of the ANN population to train a number of individuals concurrently. Individual parallelism takes advantage of the independence of the nodes within an ANN. The connection weights between several node-pairs can be altered simultaneously [17,18].

Figures 1 and 2 show the PEP net parallel architectures. Next, we introduce two frequently used architectures that take advantage of individual parallelism with the use of helper processors.

Farmer/Worker Architecture. To generate a global population, the farmer transmits the subpopulation to the workers. The workers control the generation of a population running under the selection, mutation, replacement, and completion testing performed on its subpopulation. Upon completion of all of the required generation operations, workers send back their subpopulations. When all evolved subpopulations have been received by the farmers, the run is complete.

The communication cost is not the problem; communication is mainly concentrated at the beginning and end of a run. The communication populations cost relative to the number of generations is minimal. Workers are independent of each other; there is no communication between workers. The farmer/workers parallelism uses population parallelism and simultaneously, workers perform the EPNet algorithm rather than using individual parallelism. By contrast, the farmer/workers/farmer parallelism uses both population and individual parallelism.

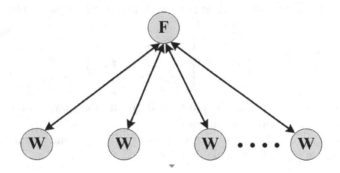

Farmer/Worker Parallelism

Fig. 1. Farmer/worker architecture

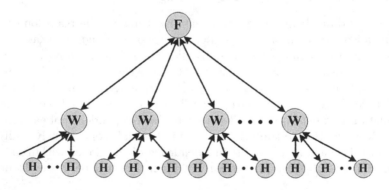

Farmer/Worker/Helper Parallelism

Fig. 2. Farmer/worker/helper architecture

Farmer/Worker/Helper Architecture. The farmer/worker/helper architecture takes advantage of population and individual parallelism. A farmer and workers in similar missions to those under the structure of the farmers and workers. Workers are assigned a group of helpers.

Helpers have two tasks: the initial MBP training of the entire population and any modified random search training performed on any individual.

The latter of these tasks represents the individual parallelism employed by the farmer/worker/helper architecture. This form of parallelism aids cooperation to achieve a common goal. MBP training assistants work independently without communicating with each other.

To assist the worker with MBP training, each helper is assigned a single ANN from the worker's subpopulation. The helpers are also called upon by the MRS operator, and work cooperatively and communicate partial results. For each helper allocation of a region, only the helper is allowed to change.

Communication among helpers is via the worker to reduce the amount of communication necessary and allow the workers to keep a consistent copy of the ANN. The overall communication architecture is greater than the farmer/workers architecture, thus it is necessary to offset this cost calculation.

3.5   QoT Aware Evolutionary Programming Algorithm

In 2013, Bhanja et al. [7] presented an EP algorithm to solve the quality of transmission (QoT) aware dynamic routing and wavelength assignment (DRWA) problem in transparent optical networks using wavelength division multiplexing (WDM).

At the core of QoT aware EP is the selection of the fitness function (fitness calculation). The fitness function for the problem in [7] is formulated as follows:

$$f_\chi = W_\chi (\Sigma_{j=1}^{k_\chi - 1} C_{g\chi(j), g\chi(j+1)} + \Sigma_{(i,j) \in E} H_{ij\chi} + \sigma^2_{sig-ase(\chi)} + \sigma^2_{sig-shot(\chi)} + \sigma^2_{thermal} + \sigma^2 sig - demu\chi(\chi)).$$

Experimental results in [7] show that the proposed algorithm also performs better than other existing work in the literature, [8,9,21], and this programming algorithm together with the novel wavelength ordering assignment technique can also be used for real-time applications for a network load less than 90 erlang.

3.6   Shifting Classical Evolutionary Programming

In 2013, Alipouri et al. [5] presented a modification to classical EP by shifting strategy parameters: shifting classical EP (SCEP).

It is known that when one of the strategy parameters is a large value, adding it to the related variable causes abrupt changes in that related variable and an iterative result may be far from the optimum point. This problem slows down the rate of the related iteration.

The main problem is the constant, repeated addition of small or large step sizes to individuals, which stagnates the algorithm. Therefore, in place of omitting small and large step sizes, the algorithm can simply avoid repetition. To implement this idea, Alipouri et al. [5] proposed that the algorithm occasionally rotates the strategy parameters. With rotation, the advantages and disadvantages of one species shift to another species, that is, species individuals occasionally share their gathered information with each other. By implementing this idea, the variable gives its own strategy parameter to its neighbor, which avoids the repetition of adding very fast or slow steps to only one variable. Using this method, each individual can share its large or small step size with other individuals. This prevents variables from extending further out of the optimal search space.

The most essential part (3) in SCEP is as follows: (the other steps are similar to those of CEP)

(3) Each parent $(x_{i,i})$, $i \in 1, \dots,$, creates a single offspring $(x'_{i,i})$ by: for $j = 1, \cdots, n$

$$a = int(rand \times n)$$
$$if \ (rand > R_C)$$
$$\quad \eta_i = shifting(\eta_i, a)$$
$$end$$
$$x'_i(j) = x_i(j) + \eta_i(j)N_j(0,1)$$
$$\eta'_i(j) = \eta_i(j)exp(\tau'N(0,1) + \tau N_j(0,1))$$

shifting: the function that shifts strategy parameter a times;
a: the number of shifting which is chosen randomly;
$int(\cdot)$: rounds to near integer value;
rand: generates a uniform random number in $[0,1]$.

3.7 Surrogate-Assisted Evolutionary Programming Algorithm

In 2013, Regis [6] proposed a surrogate-assisted EP algorithm for constrained expensive black-box optimization that can be used for high-dimensional problems with many black-box inequality constraints. Compared with other methods, this does not use a penalty function, and it builds surrogates for the objective and constraint functions.

Below is pseudocode for the proposed surrogate-assisted EP for optimization problems with black-box inequality constraints. Unlike many previous evolutionary algorithms for constrained problems, this method does not use a penalty function. Instead, it treats each inequality constraint separately and builds a surrogate model for each constraint function using all previously sampled points (both feasible and infeasible points).

As in EP in the previous section, the main input to this algorithm is the optimization problem:

$$\min f(x)$$

s.t.

$$x \in \mathbb{R}^d$$

$$g_i(x) \leq 0, i = 1, 2, \cdots, m$$

$$a \leq x \leq b$$

together with a simulator that yields the values of $f(x), g_1(x), \cdots, g_m(x)$ for any input $x \in \mathbb{R}^d$. The proposed surrogate-assisted $(+) - EP$ uses two additional parameters: ν, the number of trial offspring generated for each parent, and $p_m ut$, the probability of perturbing a coordinate of a parent solution when generating a trial offspring.

Surrogate-assisted $(\mu + \mu) - EP$ for constrained black-box optimization

(1) Set generation counter $t = 0$ and set the initial population: $P(0) = (x_1(0), \sigma_1(0)), \cdots, (x_\mu(0),_\mu(0))$, where $\sigma_i(0) = \sigma_{init}$.

(2) Evaluate the objective and constraint functions at the points in $P(0)$: For each $i = 1, \cdots, \mu$, run the simulator to determine $f(x_i(0)), g_1(x_i(0)), \cdots, g_m(x_i(0))$.

(3) While the termination criteria are not satisfied

(3.1) Fit or update surrogates $s_t^0, s_t^1, \cdots, s_t^m$ for the objective and constraint functions $f, g_1, \cdots, g_m$, respectively, using all available function values from previous simulations.

(3.2) For $i = 1, \cdots, \mu$

(3.2(a)) For $j = 1, \cdots, \nu$, generate

$$(x_{ij}'(t), \sigma_{ij}'(t)) = Mutate((x_i(t),_i(t)), p_{mut}).$$

(3.2(b)) Evaluate the surrogates of the objective and constraint functions at the points in

$$P_i'(t) = \{(x_{i1}'(t), \sigma_{i1}'(t)), \cdots, (x_{i\nu}'(t), \sigma_{i\nu}'(t))\} :$$

For $j = 1, \cdots, \nu$, calculate

$$s_t^0(x_{ij}'(t)), s_t^1(x_{ij}'(t)), \cdots, s_t^m(x_{ij}'(t))$$

(3.2(c)) $(x_i'(t), \sigma_i'(t)) = Select(P_i'(t))$.

(3.2(d)) Evaluate the objective and constraint functions at the selected point: Run the simulator to determine $f(x_i'(t), g_1(x_i'(t)), \cdots, g_m(x_i'(t))$.
End

(3.3) $P(t+1) = Select(P(t) \bigcup P'(t))$,
where

$$P'(t) = \{(x_i'(t), \sigma_i'(t)), \cdots, (x_\mu'(t), \sigma_\mu'(t))\}.$$

(3.4) Increment generation counter: $t \leftarrow t + 1$.
End

(4) Return the best solution found.

4   Research and Outlook

(1) Model theory research: Research into the evolutionary mechanism is key to biological evolution. Additionally, the rules of EP, algorithm performance, convergence, and complexity analysis also require further research.
(2) Algorithm study: Some of the IEP algorithms have been reserved more meticulous, such as the algorithm in Sect. 3.7, but also need to improve their universality.
(3) Multi-objective optimization: Recently, multi-objective evolutionary algorithms have inspired the interest of researchers in EP, in particular, multi-objective optimization problems, such as those proposed in [4] for the graphic processing method. Therefore, research into the EP algorithm of the multi-objective optimization problem has important research significance.
(4) Application research: We could pay more attention to some areas not covered, such as the high-dimensional function, multi-objective optimization, constrained optimization, and stochastic optimization problems.

Acknowledgment. This research is supported by the National Natural Science Foundation of China (No. 71331008), the Program for New Century Excellent Talents in University, Foundation for the Author of National Excellent Doctoral Dissertation of PR China (2014-92), the Youth Training Program for Innovation and Entrepreneurship Platform of Science and Technology at Hunan Province, the Outstanding Youth Fund Project of Hunan Provincial Natural Science Foundation (S2015J5050), the Top-notch Innovative Talents Training Plan of National University of Defense Technology, the Outstanding Youth Fund Project of National University of Defense Technology (JQ14-05-01), the Fundamental Research Funds for the Central Universities (531107050772) and Shenzhen Basic Research Project for Development of Science and Technology (JCYJ20160530141956915).

References

1. Schwefel, H.P.: Numerical Optimization of Computer Models. Wiley, Chichester (1981)
2. Holland, J.H.: Adaptation in Natural and Artificial Systems. University of Michigan Press, Ann Arbor (1975)
3. Fogel, L.J., Owens, A.J., Valsh, M.J.: Artificial Intelligence Through Simulated Evolution. Wiley, New York (1966)
4. Shelokar, P., Quirin, A.: Three-objective subgraph mining using multiobjective evolutionary programming. J. Comput. Syst. Sci. **80**, 16–26 (2013)
5. Alipouri, Y., Phoshtan, J.: A modification to classical evolutionary programming by shifting strategy parameters. Appl. Intell. **38**(2), 175–192 (2013)
6. Regis, R.G.: Evolutionary programming for high-dimensional constrained expensive black-box optimization using radial basis functions. IEEE Trans. Evol. Comput. **18**(3), 326–347 (2014)
7. Bhanja, U., Mahapatra, S., Roy, R.: An evolutionary programming algorithm for survivable routing and wavelength assignment in transparent optical networks. Inf. Sci. **222**, 634–647 (2013)

8. He, J., Yao, X.: A game-theoretic approach for designing mixed mutation strategies. In: Wang, L., Chen, K., Ong, Y.S. (eds.) ICNC 2005. LNCS, vol. 3612, pp. 279–288. Springer, Heidelberg (2005). doi:10.1007/11539902_33
9. Saminadan, V., Meenakshi, M.: In-band crosstalk performance of WDM optical networks under different routing and wavelength assignment algorithms. In: Pal, A., Kshemkalyani, A.D., Kumar, R., Gupta, A. (eds.) IWDC 2005. LNCS, vol. 3741, pp. 159–170. Springer, Heidelberg (2005). doi:10.1007/11603771_19
10. Lee, C.Y., Yao, X.: Evolutionary programming using mutations based on the Lévy probability distribution. IEEE Trans. Evol. Comput. **8**(1), 1–13 (2004)
11. De Jong, K.A.: Genetic algorithms: a 10 year perspective. In: Proceedings the First International Conference on Genetic Algorithms, pp. 169–177. Lawrence Erlbaum Associates, Hillsdale (1985)
12. Fraser, A.: Simulation of genetic systems by automatic digital computers: I. Introduction. Aust. J. Biol. Sci. **10**, 484–491 (1957)
13. Koza, J.R.: Genetic Programming: On the Programming of Computers by Means of Natural Selection. The MIT Press, Cambridge (1992)
14. Yao, X., Liu, Y., Lin, G.: Evolutionary programming made faster. IEEE Trans. Evol. Comput. **3**(2), 82–102 (1999)
15. Bäck, T., Schwefel, H.P.: An overview of evolutionary algorithms for parameter optimization. Evol. Comput. **1**(1), 1–23 (1993)
16. Yao, X., Liu, Y.: Fast evolution strategies. Control Cybern. **26**(3), 467–496 (1997)
17. Riessen, G.A., Williams, G.J., Yao, X.: PEPNet: parallel evolutionary programming for constructing artificial neural networks. In: Angeline, P.J., Reynolds, R.G., McDonnell, J.R., Eberhart, R. (eds.) EP 1997. LNCS, vol. 1213, pp. 35–45. Springer, Heidelberg (1997). doi:10.1007/BFb0014799
18. Tongchim, S., Yao, X.: Parallel evolutionary programming. In: Proceedings of the 2004 Congress on Evolutionary Computation (CEC 2004), Portland, Oregon, USA, June 2004, pp. 1362–1367 (2004)
19. Hunt, R.A.: Calculus with Analytic Geometry. Harper and Row Publishers, Inc., New York (1986). 322 p., 10225299
20. Fogel, L.J.: Artificial Intelligence Through Simulated Evolution. Wiley, New York (1966)
21. Ramamurthy, B., Datta, D., Feng, H., Heritage, J.P., Mukherjee, B.: Impact of transmission impairments on the teletraffic performance of wavelength-routed optical networks. J. Lightwave Technol. **17**(10), 1713–1723 (1999)
22. Fogel, D.B.: Evolving Artificial Intelligence. University of California, San Diego (1992)
23. Back, T., Schwefel, H.P.: An overview of evolutionary algorithms for parameter optimization. Evol. Comput. **1**(1), 1–23 (1993)
24. Schwefel, H.P.: Evolution and Optimum Seeking. Wiley, New York (1995)
25. Yao, X., Liu, Y., Lin, G.: Evolutionary programming made faster. IEEE Trans. Evol. Comput. **3**(2), 82–102 (1999)
26. Liu, Y., Yao, X.: How to control search step size in fast evolutionary programming. In: Proceedings of the 2002 IEEE Congress on Evolutionary Computation, pp. 652–656. IEEE Press, USA (2002)

Application of Discrete Ant Colony Optimization in VRPTW

Qinhong Fu[1], Kang Zhou[2(✉)], Huaqing Qi[2], and Tingfang Wu[3]

[1] School of Math and Computer,
Wuhan Polytechnic University, Wuhan 430023, Hubei, China
fuqinhong@foxmail.com
[2] Department of Economics and Management,
Wuhan Polytechnic University, Wuhan 430023, Hubei, China
zhoukang_wh@163.com, qihuaqing@sohu.com
[3] Key Laboratory of Image Information Processing and Intelligent Control,
School of Automation, Huazhong University of Science and Technology,
Wuhan 430074, Hubei, China
tfwu@hust.edu.cn

Abstract. The classical ant colony algorithm for vehicle routing problem with time windows (VRPTW) has problems of low efficiency, slow convergence and prematurity. And the discrete ant colony optimization (DACO) is proposed for these problem. It adopts the one-dimensional discrete coding that can make the data structure simpler and bring in faster convergence speed. In addition, self-convergence mode is used to calculate the optimal vehicle number rather than setting the optimal vehicle number at the beginning, which makes the algorithm more flexible and accelerates the convergence speed effectively. The time window and vehicle load are not considered in the optimization process, when ants complete the whole process and then the path is explained, this move not only expands the ant search scope but also improves the efficiency of the algorithm. The above highlights make the most of the self-adaptation and self-regulating mechanism, which effectively reduces the probability of the local optimal solution at the same time. Experimental results for Solomon benchmark test problems indicate that DACO outperforms both in reducing time and space complexity in the premise of not affecting the accuracy. Thus proves DACO is effective and feasible in solving the VRPTW.

Keywords: Vehicle routing problem · Time windows · Discrete ant colony optimization

1 Introduction

The Vehicle Routing Problem (VRP) is a well known optimization problem and it has received a lot of attention in operational research literature [1–3]. Besides, VRP still belongs to NP-hard problems. The efficiency of algorithm is not so

© Springer Nature Singapore Pte Ltd. 2016
M. Gong et al. (Eds.): BIC-TA 2016, Part II, CCIS 682, pp. 204–218, 2016.
DOI: 10.1007/978-981-10-3614-9_26

high that it is hard to get the optimal solution in the limited time when the scale of the problem is to a certain extend. The vehicle routing problem with time windows (VRPTW) is the basis of VRP by adding time window constraints. The VRPTW can be described as the problem of designing least cost routes for a fleet of vehicles from one depot to a set of geographically scattered points, the routes must be designed in such a way that each point is visited only once by exactly one vehicle within a given time interval; all routes start and end at the depot. And the total demands of all points on one particular route must not exceed the capacity of the vehicle. Due to the limitations of service time, VRPTW is more fit for the actual logistics distribution mode, so it is widely used in the field of logistics and transportation. Therefore, to solve the vehicle routing problem with time windows is of great significance in practical research.

Since VRPTW is still a NP-hard problem, exact algorithm is difficult to solve it, so the heuristic algorithm is used to solve the problem. In recent years, many scholars have extensively researched VRPTW by heuristic algorithms and evolutionary algorithms. However a heuristic algorithm often achieves better results. In [2–7], Li proposed ant colony optimization (ACO) and tested the ability of optimization for the algorithm through numerical computation, which gives encouraging results to solve VRPTW. Hu et al. designed a hybrid ant colony optimization and applied it to VRPTW [8–12]. Pang presented an adaptive heuristic path construction algorithm and gave the simulation analysis [13–19]. Baños et al. developed a mix of modern heuristic algorithm for multi-objective vehicle routing problem with time windows and got the optimal solution [20–27]. These studies have a certain degree of improvement on the algorithm. But the effect of improving the convergence rate is not particularly obvious; slowness is still the bottleneck of ant colony algorithm in large-scale application of optimization problems.

This paper adopts a new idea to study the discrete ant colony optimization (DACO) on VRPTW. The proposed algorithm combines the characteristics of the improved/exchange method and the interactive optimization method. Improvements have made as follows. Firstly, ant colony algorithm is discretized and improved on the basis of classical ant colony algorithm. Secondly, the limitation of time window is not considered in the process of optimization which makes the search scope more extensive. Moreover, the vehicle load is not taken into account in advance, so that ants make full use of self sensitive sense of smell to broadly searching, after completing the whole process then considering the limitations of the vehicle load. Finally, to avoid falling into local optimum early, the number of vehicles is not given and the upper limit of the vehicle is even considered, so as to give full play to the adaptive characteristics of ants and self-regulating mechanism. Experimental results indicate that the proposed algorithm can solve the local optimal problem and the accuracy is greatly improved, so is the efficiency.

2   Problem Formulation

The VRPTW is defined on a graph (N, A). The node set N consist of the set of customers, denoted by C, and the nodes 0 and $n + 1$, which represent the depot. The number of customers $|C|$ will be denoted n and the customers will be denoted by $1, 2, \ldots, n$. The arc set A corresponds to possible connections between the nodes. No arc terminates at node 0 and no arc originates at node $n + 1$. All routes start at 0 and end at $n + 1$. A cost c_{ij} and travel time t_{ij} are associated with each arc $(i, j) \in A$ of the network. The travel time t_{ij} includes a service time at customer i. The set of identical vehicles is denoted by V. Each vehicle has a given capacity q and each customer a demand d_i, $i \in C$. At each customer, the start of the service must be within a given time interval, called a time window, $[a_i, b_i]$, $i \in C$. Vehicles must also leave the depot within the time window $[a_0, b_0]$ and return during the time window $[a_{n+1}, b_{n+1}]$. A vehicle is permitted to arrive before the opening of the time window, and waits at no cost until service becomes possible, but it is not permitted to arrive after the latest time window. Since waiting time is permitted at no cost, we may assume without loss of generality that $a_0 = b_0$; that is, all routes start at time 0.

The model contains two types of decision variables. The decision variable X_{ij}^k (defined $\forall(i, j) \in A, \forall k \in V$) is at equal to 1 if vehicle k drives from node i to node j, and 0 otherwise. The decision variable (defined $\forall i \in N, \forall k \in V$) denotes the time vehicle k, starts service at customer i, $i \in C$. If vehicle k does not service customer i, has no meaning. We may assume that $S_0^k = 0, \forall k, S_{n+1}^k$ and denotes the arrival time of vehicle k at the depot. The objective is to design a set of minimal cost routes, one for each vehicle, such that all customers are serviced exactly once. Hence, split deliveries are not allowed. The routes must be feasible with respect to the capacity of the vehicles and the time windows of the customers serviced. The VRPTW can be stated mathematically as:

$$\min \sum_{k \in V} \sum_{(i,j) \in A} c_{ij} X_{ij}^k \tag{1}$$

The following formulate are used to illuminate the constraints and definitions

$$\sum_{k \in V} \sum_{(i,j) \in A} X_{ij}^k = 1, \forall i \in C \tag{2}$$

$$\sum_{i \in C} d_i \sum_{j \in N} X_{ij}^k \leq q, \forall k \in V \tag{3}$$

$$\sum_{j \in N} X_{0j}^k = 1, \forall k \in V \tag{4}$$

$$\sum_{i \in N} X_{ih}^k - \sum_{j \in N} X_{hj}^k = 0, \forall h \in C, \forall k \in V \tag{5}$$

$$\sum_{i \in N} X_{i,n+1}^k = 1, \forall k \in V \tag{6}$$

$$X_{ij}^k(S_i^k + t_{ij} - S_j^k) \leq 0, \forall (i,j) \in A, \forall k \in V \qquad (7)$$

$$a_i \leq S_i^k \leq b_i, \forall i \in N, \forall k \in V \qquad (8)$$

$$X_{ij}^k \in \{0,1\}, \forall (i,j) \in A, k \in V \qquad (9)$$

The objective function (1) states that costs should be minimized. Constraint set (2) states that each customer must be assigned to exactly one vehicle, and constraint set (3) states that no vehicle can service more customers than its capacity permits. Constraint sets (4)–(6) are the flow constraints requiring that each vehicle k leaves node 0 once, leaves node h, $h \in C$ if and only if it enters that node, and returns to node $n + 1$. Note that constraint set (6) is redundant, but is maintained in the model to underline the network structure. The arc (0, $n + 1$) is included in the network, to allow empty tours. More precisely, we permit an unrestricted number of vehicles, but a cost c_v is put on each vehicle performing an empty tour, i.e., to each vehicle not used. This is done by setting $c_{0,n+1} = -c_v$. That is, the more there are empty tours, the lower is the total cost. The value of c_v is sufficiently large to primarily minimize the number of vehicles and secondarily minimize travel costs. Nonlinear constraint set (7) states that vehicle k cannot arrive at j before $S_i^k + t_{ij}$ if it travels from i to j. Constraint set (8) ensures that all time windows are respected and (9) is the set of integrality constraints.

3   Discrete Ant Colony Optimization for VRPTW

In this paper, ant colony optimization (ACO) is first discretized and the mathematical model is re-conceived. Then, algorithm steps are redesigned according to the defects of ACO, eventually forming a discrete ant colony optimization (DACO). In this algorithm, the path expression method is used to represent the coding of the individual ants and the movement of ants corresponds to a transformation of the path code. In fact, each ant represents a possible paths.

3.1   Design for DACO

(1) Coding method. A sequence of feasible paths is used as the coding of individual ants; it is the most direct, simple and logical method. For example, 0-1-2-4-3-0-5-8-7-6-9-0 can be directly expressed as (0 1 2 4 3 0 5 8 7 6 9 1), which means there are two paths that start from the city 0 (distribution center) and finally back to the city 0.

(2) State transition probability. Each ant chooses the next city under the mutual influence of synergy and visibility, meanwhile, the elements of tabu list and related attributes of ants are updated. The selection formula is calculated as follows:

$$p_{ij}^k(t) = [\tau_{ij}(t)]^\alpha [\eta_{ij}(t)]^\beta / \sum ([\tau_{ij}]^\alpha \times [\eta_{ij}(t)]^\beta | j \in allowed_k) \qquad (10)$$

Where $\eta(t) = 1/d_{ij}$ is a heuristic function [16] and it means the extent to which ants move from the element (city) i to the element (city) j; $allowed_k$

is the optional city set, besides, $allowed_k = C\text{-}tabu_k$; α refers to the heuristic factor and there will be pheromone left in the process of searching, which affects the next step of ants to find the best decision. The greater the α is, the more powerful this effect is. Hence, ants will move toward the path of higher pheromone concentration, which leads to too strong collaboration. The algorithm is easy to fall into the local optimal. β means to the expectation heuristic factor that refers to the influence degree of the path that ants see to the optimization process. If β is too large, algorithm is easy to full into a greedy rule.

(3) Pheromone update formula. Information changes with time and the update formula is as follows:

$$\tau_{ij}(t+n) = (1-\rho) \times \tau_{ij}(t) + \Delta\tau_{ij}(t); \Delta\tau_{ij}(t) = \sum(\Delta\tau_{ij}^k(t)|k = 1, 2, \ldots, m) \tag{11}$$

Where m is the number of ants; ρ is the information volatile factor, in order to prevent the pheromone enhanced continuously, we set its value among $[0, 1)$. $\Delta\tau_{ij}(t) = \sum(\Delta\tau_{ij}^k(t)|k = 1, 2, \ldots, m)$, it refers to the pheromone increment from i to j in the current iterations and before iteration start its value is 0. When the ant k went through (i, j) in this cycle, then $\Delta\tau_{ij}^k = Q/L_k$ (global optimization); and 0, otherwise. Q is a constant and represents a total concentration of pheromone that the ant runs the whole Journey; L_k is the total path length of ant k at the end of each loop.

(4) The objective function. In this paper, the smaller the value of the objective function is, the better the ant search path is. The formula for calculating the objective function value is:

$$f(x_i(t)) = \sum_{j=0}^{N} d(x_{i(j)}, x_{i(j+1)}) \tag{12}$$

Where x_i is the path i; $x_{i(j)}$ is the city j in the path i; $d(x_{i(j)}, x_{i(j+1)})$ is the distance between j and $j + 1$; N is the number of cities in the path.

(5) The establishment of the initial population. This paper assumes that the distribution center has been set up, and the default for the city 0, all ants can be placed in the distribution center, there is no need to disrupt the initial city of ants.

3.2   The Innovation Points of DACO

Ant colony algorithm has excellent performance in solving VRPTW, but the searching time is long and the efficiency is low. Moreover, it is easy to converge to the local optimal solution, so it is restricted to be further popularized and applied. The reasons are as follows.

(1) For low efficiency problems. In the process of optimization, the restriction of time windows makes the ant colony algorithm have a large amount of computation in the construction process of each feasible solution, which increases

the time complexity of the algorithm. Such as the TSP problem is $O(m - n^2)$, where m is the number of iterations of algorithm, n is the scale of the problem. Moreover, the complex algorithm design will contain a great deal of judgments which are likely to cause that some high-quality feasible solutions are unreachable or have small probability to be found.

(2) For premature problem. Since the ant colony algorithm is a heuristic algorithm, actually, heuristic algorithm is a kind of greedy strategy. This is also objectively determines that the better or the best feasible solution which does not comply with the greedy strategy will be missed, especially along with the increasing of iterations, the results of algorithm will be stagnant and even fall into local optimal.

It can be seen from the above analysis that the traditional ant colony algorithm has some limitations. Therefore, this paper proposes the improved ant colony algorithm to overcome the above problems, the solution is as follows.

a. Ignore the time windows
In the process of program implementation, if time window constraints is considered in advance, the program will be very lengthy and the efficiency will be reduced obviously. In addition, considering the time windows will largely reduce search scope and weak the original search mechanism at the same time. Therefore, this algorithm proposes a new idea to solve the problem: we do not consider the time windows until an explanation of the code is adding in the later stages of the algorithm.

The idea effectively solves the problem of local optimum, and makes the objective function do not directly effect the optimal choice of ants but just have a certain impact. Through a large number of experiments, it is proved that the efficiency of the algorithm can be greatly improved if we ignore the time windows in the optimization process.

b. Ignore the vehicle load
The optimization process has ignored the time windows, at this point, it is very likely to find the feasible solution in early period but the feasible solution is maybe infeasible solution after joining time windows, thereby greatly reducing the effectiveness of the algorithm. In addition, it also needs to go through two filter to get the feasible solution if the time window takes into account, which greatly reduces its running speed. Therefore, the time windows and the vehicle load can be considered as a one-time which can improve the effectiveness of the algorithm.

The idea effectively avoids the local optimum, because the path can not be directly used as a feasible solution but needs to be explained later. And the later explanation interrupts the continuity of searching path, which do not make ants into local optimum but maintain a wide range of search.

c. Open the number of vehicles
In the traditional vehicle routing problem, the maximum number of vehicles can be set to avoid the infeasible solution that caused by the number of vehicles.

But this approach will make some good paths become infeasible solutions and be abandoned due to the restrictions of the number of vehicles. Therefore, this paper puts forward the strategy of opening the number of vehicles, so that the algorithm can make full use of the self adaptation of ants to converge the number of vehicles. Experiments show that the solution found in this way is better and the number of vehicles will not more than the maximum value as long as a reasonable set of iterations.

3.3   Algorithm Process of DACO

The detailed steps are described below.

Step 1. Initialization of DACO. Set parameters in DACO and initialize the pheromone of the network.

Step 2. Tabu status. Assign all ants to the distribution center and initialize the pointer to the tabu list.

Step 3. Update the route of ants. Ants select the next city by means of transition probabilities, update the tabu list until the tabu list is filled.

Step 4. Explain the path of ants. Redefine the code by time windows and vehicle load limits and if the service to the next city can meet above restrictions, then the next city is served; otherwise the vehicle returns to the dispatch center.

Step 5. Pheromone updating. The increments of pheromone is updated by the step 4, find out the optimal solution in the current iteration and compared it with the previous iteration then retain the best solution.

Step 6. Update the information of each path. Calculate for each edge: $\tau_{ij}(t+n) = \rho^*\tau_{ij}(t) + \tau_{ij}(\rho \in (0,1))$; Set $t = t + n$; Set $N_c = N_c + 1$; Set $\tau_{ij} = 0$.

Step 7. DACO termination. Check the DACO termination conditions ($N_c < N_{cmax}$ and not all the ants choose the same path). If algorithm meets the termination conditions, DACO comes to an end; otherwise, goto step 2 and continue DACO search.

4   Simulation Results and Analysis

4.1   Experimental Environment

In order to verify the correctness and effectiveness of the algorithm, this paper selects 20 points to test. The proposed algorithm (DACO) was developed in C++ programming language and tested in a computer with an Intel Core 2.5 GHz microprocessor with 4 GB of RAM memory and operating system Windows 7 Ultimate 64 bits (i5-3210M). The experimental results are obtained by platform VC++.

4.2 Analysis and Setting of Experimental Parameters

In the discrete ant colony optimization, the number of ants (m) and iterations (N_c) have a certain effect on the stability and the search depth of the algorithm. Therefore, we should optimize and set this two parameters at first. In addition, through many experiments and researches, the information heuristic factor (α) is the relatively important parameters. If the α is larger, the previous path is more likely to be chosen by the ant and the random search probability becomes smaller; otherwise, algorithm is easy to fall into local optimum. The expected heuristic factor (β) is expected to reflect the relative importance of the heuristic information to guide the search. If the β is larger, the ant more easily choose local shortest path; otherwise, algorithm is easy to fall into local optimum. Similarly, the value of ρ directly affects the global search ability and convergence speed of the algorithm. When the value of ρ is too large, the possibility of repeated search is large too, which affects randomness and global search ability; otherwise, the convergence rate will decrease.

By reading literature and summary, we can see that the parameters of m and N_c, adjusted according to the scale of the problem, are not sufficient to affect the global convergence of the algorithm and global search ability, therefore they belong to the peripheral parameters. And α, β, ρ and other parameters which belong to the core parameters have a great impact on the performance of the algorithm. So this paper makes a deep discussion about the optimal configuration of those parameters. When the other parameters have reached the optimal state, the pheromone amount (Q) has little effect on the objective function value, so its value is usually set to 100.

a. Setting the number of ants

In order to ensure the validity of the experimental results, we set the initial value of the parameters $N_c = 1500$, $Q = 100$. The other three parameters α, β and ρ both take two groups, one group is $\alpha = 0.7$, $\beta = 1.6$, $\rho = 0.8$, and the other group is $\alpha = 0.8$, $\beta = 1.8$, $\rho = 0.6$. m starts from 10 and each increment is 10, every time the experiment repeats 30 times and the optimal value of each experiment is recorded, and then get the average of 30 experiments. According to the experimental results, the effect of m on the objective function is shown in Fig. 1.

From Fig. 1 we can see that both (a) and (b) show when $m < 50$, the curve tends to decline precipitously but the quality of optimal solution is rising; when $m = 50$, the average value of the optimal solution is the best and the curve gradually tends to be stable; when $m > 50$, although the optimal solution can also be obtained, the running time of the algorithm increases and the improvement of the algorithm can work. Therefore, the optimal value of m is 50.

b. Setting the number of iterations

When the value of m is determined, the other parameters remain the same but the N_c needs to be optimized. N_c starts from 200 and each increment is 200, every time the experiment repeats 30 times and the optimal value of each experiment is recorded, and then get the average of 30 experiments. In Table 1,

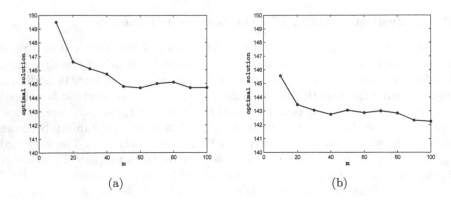

Fig. 1. The relationship between m and optimal solution

Table 1. The relationship between N_c and optimal solution

m	N_c	BestR	
		group1	group2
50	200	145.99	145.27
50	400	144.59	144.13
50	600	143.88	143.29
50	800	143.10	143.52
50	1000	142.71	142.98
50	1200	143.28	142.68
50	1400	142.75	142.72
50	1600	143.08	142.46
50	1800	142.45	142.60
50	2000	142.56	142.50

"BestR" indicates the optimum tested by DACO. According to the experimental results, the effect of N_c on the objective function is shown in Table 1 (the group1 is $\alpha = 0.7$, $\beta = 1.6$, $\rho = 0.8$, the group2 is $\alpha = 0.8$, $\beta = 1.8$, $\rho = 0.6$).

As shown From the two groups of different parameters in Table 1, when $N_c < 1000$, the quality of optimal solution has been improved. Furthermore, there is no stagnation phenomenon with the increasing of iterations, which shows that the optimal solution has not been obtained; when $N_c = 1000$, the value of optimal solution is close to the convergence and the data is also present a stable trend. Considering the performance of the computer, the operating speed and so on, the optimal of N_c is set to 1000 times.

c. Setting the information heuristic factor

When the value of m and N_c are determined, the other parameters remain the same but the α needs to be optimized. In the two different groups, α both starts from 0.1 and each increment is 0.1, every time the experiment repeats 30 times and the optimal value of each experiment is recorded, and then get the average of 30 experiments. According to the experimental results, the effect of α on the objective function is shown in Fig. 2.

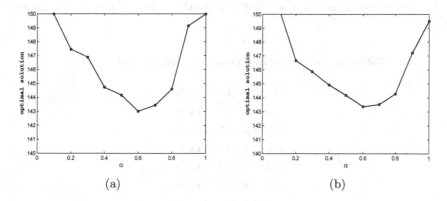

(a)   (b)

Fig. 2. The relationship between α and optimal solution

It can be seen from the trend of the curve in Fig. 2 that the optimal solution has been improved fast and maintains in the initial stage of which α increases from 0.1 to 0.6. The algorithm gets the optimal solution when $\alpha = 0.6$. But with the increasing of α, the optimal solution gradually reduces and is not stable. Hence, from the performance of optimal solution, α is 0.6.

d. Setting the expected heuristic factor

When the value of m, N_c and α are determined, the other parameters remain the same but the β needs to be optimized. β starts from 1 and each increment is 0.1, every time the experiment repeats 30 times and the optimal value of each experiment is recorded, and then get the average of 30 experiments. According to the experimental results, the effect of β on the objective function is shown in Table 2.

Table 2. The relationship between β and optimal solution

α	0.6	0.6	0.6	0.6	0.6	0.6	0.6	0.6	0.6	0.6	0.6
β	1.0	1.1	1.2	1.3	1.4	1.5	1.6	1.7	1.8	1.9	2.0
BestR	148.45	146.96	145.42	145.35	145.02	143.76	143.69	143.51	143.03	143.54	143.97

Table 2 shows that as β increases, the average value of the optimal solution is improved in the initial stage, thereafter basically maintained at the same level. When $\beta = 1.8$ the optimal solution is best, but the optimal solution is gradually degraded along with the value of β continuous increasing, so the value of β is set to 1.8.

e. Setting the information volatile factor

When the value of m, N_c, α and β are determined, the other parameters remain the same but the ρ needs to be optimized. ρ starts from 0.1 and each increment is 0.1, every time the experiment repeats 30 times and the optimal value of each experiment is recorded, and then get the average of 30 experiments. According to the experimental results, the effect of ρ on the objective function is shown in Table 3.

Table 3. The relationship between ρ and optimal solution

α	β	ρ	BestR
0.6	1.8	0.1	143.98
0.6	1.8	0.2	145.55
0.6	1.8	0.3	143.34
0.6	1.8	0.4	145.13
0.6	1.8	0.5	144.16
0.6	1.8	0.6	143.24
0.6	1.8	0.7	143.4
0.6	1.8	0.8	143.82
0.6	1.8	0.9	144.48

From the relationship between ρ and the optimal solutions, we can know that although the optimal solution is better when $\rho = 0.3$, but its performance is not stable. Because just a slight deviation will make the value of the objective function have a large fluctuation. Instead, the number of the optimal solution is relatively dense which shows that the performance of the program is very stable when $\rho = 0.6$. Therefore, the optimal value of ρ is 0.6.

4.3   The Stability Analysis of the Algorithm

A good algorithm must be stable, that is to say, fluctuations in the value of each calculation is smaller. In order to describe the stability of the algorithm, the following formula is used to calculate the standard deviation:

$$\sigma = \sqrt{\frac{1}{N} \sum_{i=1}^{N} (x_i - \mu)^2} \tag{13}$$

Among them, x_1, x_2, x_3, ..., x_n are all real numbers, μ is the arithmetic average and σ is the standard deviation. As shown in Fig. 3, it depicts a graph of city scale and standard deviation and the maximum fluctuation value through a large number of experimental data.

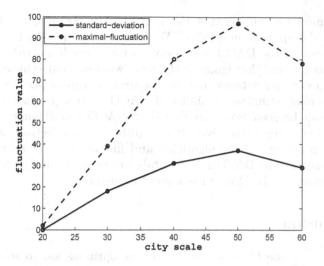

Fig. 3. The relationship between city scale and standard deviation

From Fig. 3 we can see that as city scale increases, the value of standard deviation and maximum fluctuation are also increased. And it is a normal phenomenon from a practical point of view, after all, with the increase of city scale the feasible solution will also be a substantial increase. When the city size equal to 50, the standard deviation gradually tends to be stable, the curve instead begin to decline with the increase of city size, which indicates that the algorithm is fluctuate in the acceptable range. So it is proved that the algorithm has better stability and it can solve a certain scale of VRPTW.

4.4 Experimental Comparison Between DACO and Tabu Search Algorithm

In order to show the advantages of DACO, the experiment respectively tests the two algorithms in the scale of 25, 50 and 100. The algorithm is repeated 30 times and records optimal solution, average and variance based on considering the exist of random factor in membrane algorithm. The experimental results are shown in Table 4. In Table 4, "BestR" indicates the optimal solution, "Avg" means the average value of the test, and "Vari" indicates the variance of the test.

Table 4. Comparison Results of DACO and Tabu Search Algorithm

Scale	BestR		Avg		Vari	
	DACO	Tabu	DACO	Tabu	DACO	Tabu
25	212.14	235.51	221.33	281.24	6.95	6.87
50	471.62	473.09	489.41	514.33	18.37	39.61
100	1298.78	1341.93	1308.26	1356.28	15.92	24.21

From Table 4 we can see that the DACO is better than the tabu search algorithm in the application of VRPTW. It can be seen From the BestR that the performance of the DACO is superior to tabu search algorithm in average optimum thus proving that ignoring the time windows and vehicle load limits, DACO has greater advantages than tabu search. It can be seen from the Avg that the searching optimization ability of DACO is stronger than Tabu search; and it also can be seen from the Vari that DACO can expand the scope of search space and increase the diversity of solutions, thus effectively avoiding the premature convergence of the algorithm and finding a better solution. Above mentioned results show DACO is more stable than the tabu search in terms of stability, in other words, DACO has a good robustness.

5   Conclusion

In this paper, we use the discrete ant colony optimization to solve VRPTW and put forward the new ideas that do not consider the time windows and the vehicle load limit until an explanation of the code is added to the later stage of the algorithm. This strategy makes the algorithm significantly improved in the search accuracy and the efficiency of algorithm. In addition, DACO also solves the common problem in the VRPTW that algorithm easily falls into local optimum. Compared with the Tabu search algorithm, the results show that the DACO is an effective algorithm to solve the VRPTW.

The future research is mainly on improving and optimizing the encoding and decoding process of the algorithm, and striving for the realization of using less time to solve VRPTW under the premise of ensuring the accuracy, and further enhancing the operational efficiency of the algorithm. Secondly, applying DACO to other fields, such as image processing, fault diagnosis and job shop scheduling and thereby expanding the scope of its application. At the same time, analyzing the parameters of the algorithm so that its performance can be played to the best state. Finally, it can be further studied in combination with genetic algorithm, tabu search algorithm, fish swarm algorithm, bee colony algorithm and glowworm swarm optimization algorithm and so on.

Acknowledgments. This work was supported by National Natural Science Foundation of China (Grant No. 61179032), the Special Scientific Research Fund of Food Public Welfare Profession of China (Grant No. 201513004-3) and the Research and Practice Project of Graduate Education Teaching Reform of Wuhan Polytechnic University (YZ2015002).

References

1. Dorigo, M., Maniezzo, V., Colorni, A.: The ant system: optimization by a colony of cooperating agents. IEEE Trans. Syst. **26**(1), 1–13 (1996)
2. Li, Q.L.: Application of ant colony algorithm to vehicle routing problem with time windows. Math. Pract. Theor. **36**(10), 173–178 (2006)

3. Ling, Q., Zhang, Y.Z.: A hybrid ant colony optimization and its application to vehicle routing problem with time windows. Bio-inspired Comput. Appl. **98**(98), 101–107 (2012)
4. Pang, K.W.: An adaptive parallel route construction heuristic for the vehicle routing problem with time windows constraints. Expert Syst. Appl. **38**(9), 11939–11946 (2011)
5. Ba, R., Ortega, J., Gil, C.: A hybrid meta-heuristic for multi-objective vehicle routing problems with time windows. Comput. Ind. Eng. **65**(2), 286–296 (2013)
6. Pan, L.J.: Study on Vehicle Routing Problem with Time Windows and algorithms. Central South University, Changsha (2012)
7. Stutzle, T.: MAX-MIN ant system. Future Gener. Comput. Syst. **16**(8), 889–914 (2000)
8. Gambardella, L.M., Dorigo, M.: An ant colony system hybridized with a new local search for the ordering problem. Informs J. Comput. **12**(3), 237–255 (2000)
9. Kima, B.I., Kimb, S., Sahoo, S.: Waste collection vehicle routing problem with time windows. Comput. Oper. Res. **33**, 3624–3642 (2006)
10. Cho, Y.-H.: An efficient Global optimization of neural networks by using hybrid method. Theory Appl. 807–812 (2007)
11. Wei, L., Wang, J., Zeng, J.: VRPTW problem solving multi-objective fuzzy preference ant coltny algorithm. Appl. Res. Comput. **28**(12), 4495–4499 (2011)
12. Bansal, S., Goel, R., Mohan, C.: Use of ant colony system in solving vehicle routing problem with time window constraints. Adv. Intell. Syst. Comput. **236**, 39–50 (2014)
13. Shi, C., Wang, X., Ge, X.: Research on multi-objective vehicle routing problems with time windows. Comput. Eng. Appl. **45**(34), 21–24 (2009)
14. Veen, B., Emmerich, M., Yang, Z., Bäck, T., Kok, J.: Ant colony algorithms for the dynamic vehicle routing problem with time windows. In: Ferrández Vicente, J.M., Álvarez Sánchez, J.R., Paz López, F., Toledo Moreo, F.J. (eds.) IWINAC 2013. LNCS, vol. 7931, pp. 1–10. Springer, Heidelberg (2013). doi:10.1007/978-3-642-38622-0_1
15. Sandhya, S., Katiyar, V.: An enhanced ant colony system for solving vehicle routing problem with time window. Int. J. Comput. Appl. **73**(12), 27–31 (2013)
16. Krishnanand, K., Ghose, N.: Glowworm swarm optimization for simultaneous capture of multiple local optima of multi-modal functions. Swarm Intell. **3**, 87–124 (2009)
17. Balseiro, S.R., Loiseau, I., Ramonet, J.: An ant colony algorithm hybridized with insertion heuristics for the time dependent vehicle routing problem with time windows. Comput. Oper. Res. **38**(6), 954–966 (2011)
18. Yunfei, Y., Xiaodong, L., Kang, S., Yongle, C.: An improved ant colony algorithm to solve vehicle routing problem with time windows. In: Huang, D.-S., Bevilacqua, V., Prashan, P. (eds.) ICIC 2015. LNCS, vol. 9225, pp. 11–22. Springer, Heidelberg (2015). doi:10.1007/978-3-319-22180-9_2
19. Pan, L.: Solving multidimensional 0–1 knapsack problem by p systems with input and active membranes. J. Parallel Distrib. Comput. **65**(12), 1578–1584 (2005)
20. Pan, L., Mario, J.: Computational complexity of tissue-like P systems. J. Complex. **26**(3), 296–315 (2010)
21. Pan, L.: Spiking neural P systems: an improved normal form. Theoret. Comput. Sci. **411**(6), 906–918 (2010)
22. Zhang, H., Guo, N., Mao, J., Wang, H.: A improved pareto of ant colony algorithm to solve the vehicle routing problem with time windows. Adv. Mater. Res. **1030**, 1941–1944 (2014)

23. Song, T., Pan, L.: Spiking neural P systems with request rules. Neurocomputing **193**(12), 193–200 (2016)
24. Song, T., Liu, X., Zhao, Y., Zhang, X.: Spiking neural P systems with white hole neurons. IEEE Trans. Nanobiosci. (2016). doi:10.1109/TNB.2016.2598879
25. Song, T., Pan, Z., Wong, D.M., Wang, X.: Design of logic gates using spiking neural P systems with homogeneous neurons and astrocytes-like control. Inf. Sci. **372**, 380–391 (2016)
26. Wang, X., Song, T., Gong, F., Pan, Z.: On the computational power of spiking neural P systems with self-organization. Sci. Rep. **6**, 27624 (2016). doi:10.1038/srep27624
27. Shi, X., Wu, X., Song, T., Li, X.: Construction of DNA nanotubes with controllable diameters and patterns by using hierarchical DNA sub-tiles. Nanoscale **8**, 14785–14792 (2016). doi:10.1039/C6NR02695H

Differential Evolution Algorithm with the Second Order Difference Vector

Xinchao Zhao[1(✉)], Dongyue Liu[1], Xingquan Zuo[2], Huiping Liu[1], and Rui Li[1]

[1] School of Science,
Beijing University of Posts and Telecommunications, Beijing 100876, China
zhaoxc@bupt.edu.cn
[2] School of Computer Science,
Beijing University of Posts and Telecommunications, Beijing 100876, China

Abstract. DE is challenging to maintain a balance between exploration and exploitation behaviors, and also the neighborhood and direction information of the difference vector is not completely utilized. In this paper, a completely novel DE variant, SODE, is proposed with the second order difference information, which is introduced to DE for even more fully utilizing the heuristic direction information. The second order difference information also enriches the neighborhood structure and enlarges the neighborhood domain with more heuristic information. Preliminary experimental results show that SODE is better than, or at least comparable to, the classical first order DE algorithms in terms of convergence performance and accuracy.

Keywords: Differential evolution · Second order DE · Difference vector

1 Introduction

Differential evolution is a simple, yet very efficient evolutionary algorithm for many complex optimization problems, which was proposed by Price and Storn [1]. It has been proved that DE has a series of advantages, such as lower computational complexity, higher robustness and simplicity. It is used to find the satisfactory or approximate solutions for optimization problems and real-world applications [2,3]. Because basic and difference vectors are randomly chosen from the current population, which does not utilize any neighborhood structure and/or beneficial direction information to guide the individuals toward the potential promising regions. This drawback will increase the possibility of being trapped in local optimum.

Consequently, in order to apply DE successfully to solve optimization problems and alleviate its disadvantages, various DE variants and a trial and error search for the strategies are proposed by many researchers and engineers. Fan and Lampinen [4] proposed a trigonometric mutation operator to enhance the performance of DE algorithm. This modification enables the algorithm to get a better trade-off between convergence rate and robustness. Sun et al. [5] proposed a hybrid of DE and estimation of distribution algorithm, called DE/EDA.

© Springer Nature Singapore Pte Ltd. 2016
M. Gong et al. (Eds.): BIC-TA 2016, Part II, CCIS 682, pp. 219–228, 2016.
DOI: 10.1007/978-981-10-3614-9_27

They designed DE algorithm from a new aspect, which utilizes local information and global information respectively. Three different learning strategies for
conventional DE, one is for selecting the base vector and the other two are for
constructing the difference vector was proposed by Wang and Xiang [6]. Zhao
et al. [7] proposed a new hybrid differential evolution with simulated annealing
and self-adaptive immune operation which introduced simulated annealing idea
to escape from possible local optimum attraction. Wei et al. [8] proposed a new
constraint differential evolution framework which can be applied to most constraint differential evolution variants. Zhang and Sanderson [9] proposed a new
differential evolution algorithm to improve optimization performance by implementing a mutation strategy: DE/current-to-best with optional external archive
and updating control parameters in an adaptive manner.

This paper proposed the second order differential evolution algorithm. The
major contribution are as follows. This idea is executed by making use of the
beneficial exploration direction of individual and employing different mutation
strategies for these groups. It produces the even more beneficial search moves to
promote the detection of promising regions.

- Proposing the concept of the second order difference vector and the algorithmic
  model: this concept is based on the strategies - DE/rand/1 and DE/best/1;
- The second order difference vectors are associated with each individual, which
  can be individually updated according to its current status.

2   Classical Differential Evolution

In this section, the basic operations of differential evolution will be introduced to
better understand our new algorithm proposed in Sect. 4. DE is an optimization
algorithm based on the principles of natural evolution, using a population P with
individuals encoded in floating point, indicated as Eq. (1).

$$P^G = [X_1^G, X_2^G, \ldots \ldots X_{N_P}^G] \tag{1}$$

where $X_{i,j}^G$ denotes the j-th component of the i-th individual in the population
of the G-th generation as in (2).

$$X_i^G = [X_{i,1}^G, X_{i,2}^G \ldots \ldots, X_{i,D}^G] \qquad i = 1, 2, \cdots N_p \tag{2}$$

Four main steps in DE are initialization, mutation, crossover and selection.

2.1   Initialization

The initial population is usually randomly generated according to a uniform
distribution within the search space constrained by the lower bound and the
upper bound of the optimization problem, where D is the dimension of the
variable. It is shown as in (3).

$$X_{i,j} = X_j^{\min} + rand(0,1)(X_j^{\max} - X_j^{\min}) \qquad i = 1, 2, \cdots, N_p, j = 1, 2, \cdots, D \tag{3}$$

2.2 Mutation Operation

At each generation G, DE employs mutation operation to produce a mutant vector V_i^G based on the current parent population individual X_i^G. The notation DE/a/b/c is used for distinguishing these strategies. "a" means the mutated vector; "b" denotes the number of the used difference vectors; "c" specifies the crossover scheme. The most frequently used mutation strategies of DE algorithm are given as Eqs. (4)–(9) [13]. The best vector in generation G is denoted as X_{best}^G.

$$DE/rand/1 : V_i = X_{r1} + F(X_{r2} - X_{r3}) \tag{4}$$

$$DE/best/1 : V_i = X_{best} + F(X_{r2} - X_{r3}) \tag{5}$$

$$DE/best/2 : V_i = X_{best} + F(X_{r2} - X_{r3} + F(X_{r4} - X_{r5}) \tag{6}$$

$$DE/rand/2 : V_i = X_{r1} + F(X_{r2} - X_{r3}) + F(X_{r4} - X_{r5}) \tag{7}$$

$$DE/current - to - best/1 : V_i = X_i + F(X_{best} - X_i) + F(X_{r2} - X_{r3}) \tag{8}$$

$$DE/rand - to - best/1 : V_i = X_{r1} + F(X_{best} - X_{r1}) + F(X_{r2} - X_{r3}) \tag{9}$$

where $i = 1, 2, \cdots, N_p$, $r_k \in [1, N_p]$, $k = 1, 2, \ldots, 5, k \neq i$ are different random integers, and they are also different from vector index i. The scaling parameter F is usually in [0.4, 1] and it is used to adjust the exploration or exploitation step size. Equations (5), (6) generate a new individual around the current best solution to exploit the current neighborhood. In order to enlarge the exploring region, Eqs. (7)–(9) provide two difference vectors which are randomly selected to obtain a new solution. In this way, the population diversity can be maintained and more heuristic information can be utilized.

2.3 Crossover Operation

When the mutation operation is completed, crossover operation is applied to each target vector V_i^G and the parent individual X_i^G. Then the parent vector is mixed with the target vector to create a trial vector U_i^G. The uniform crossover used in the classical DE is given by (10):

$$U_{i,j}^G = \begin{cases} V_{i,j}^G, & rand \leq CR \, or \, j = j_{rand} \\ X_{i,j}^G, & otherwise \end{cases} \tag{10}$$

where j_{rand} represents a random integer in $[1, N_p]$, which ensures that the trial vector gets at least one component from the mutant vector V_i^G. $CR \in [0, 1]$ is the crossover probability.

2.4 Selection Operation

Selection operator contains a greedy mechanism according to their fitness of the trial vector and the parent individual. Then the better one, whose fitness is higher, is selected to survive for next generation. This operation is shown as in (11) for minimization.

$$X_i^{G+1} = \begin{cases} U_i^G, f(U_i^G) \leq f(X_i^G) \\ X_i^G, otherwise \end{cases} \tag{11}$$

The above three basic steps repeat until the termination condition is met and a final candidate solution is obtained.

3   SODE Algorithm

The new second order differential evolution algorithm, SODE, is proposed. The second order difference vector is introduced to even better utilize the search direction information and the direction information of difference vectors. The research motive for the preliminary results provided in this paper is not to propose a superior DE variant with an excellent performance, but to propose a second order differential evolution algorithm model for the possible novel sub-branch in the swarm intelligence and evolutionary computation.

3.1   The Second Order Difference Vector Mechanism

The usually and widely used mutation operations, DE/rand/1 and DE/best/1, are adopted as analytic model strategies in this paper. It is said to be the most successful and widely used scheme. However, the available heuristic direction information of second order difference vector is not utilized efficiently. In order to efficiently utilize the direction information and the search status of the current population, the second order difference vector mechanism, which is based on the two classical mutation strategies, is indicated as in (12)–(16).

$$d^G = X_{r1}^G - X_{r2}^G \tag{12}$$

$$d_1^G = X_{best}^G - X_{r3}^G \tag{13}$$

$$d_2^G = X_{r4}^G - X_{worst}^G \tag{14}$$

$$dr^G = d^G + \lambda(d_1^G - d_2^G) \tag{15}$$

$$V_i^G = X_k^G + F \cdot dr^G \tag{16}$$

$$V_i^G = X_{best}^G + F \cdot dr^G \tag{17}$$

where r1, r2, r3, r4 are different random integers in $[1, N_p]$ and $r1 \neq r2$. Scaling parameter F is set as 0.5. Difference vectors in (12)–(14) are the same as the classical DE algorithm. The term of $(d_1^G - d_2^G)$ in (15) is the second order difference vector, which is used to slightly modify the difference vector d^G constructs the mutant vectors as in (16) and (17). They are associated with each individual, which can be individually updated according to its current status and the remaining historic information. The second order difference vector in (15) also aims to enlarge the exploring region and reduce the possibility of being trapped in the local optimum when it is introduced to the first order difference vector d^G. Parameter λ is set as 0.5. Then the proposed new mechanism is added to the mutation operations - DE/rand/1 as in (16) and DE/best/1 as in (17).

4   Performance Comparison and Analysis

In order to initially evaluate the performance of the proposed second difference strategy, 8 benchmark functions [4,10,11] with dimensions D = 30 are chosen and four DE algorithms are adopted.

4.1   Benchmark Functions

Functions f_1–f_4 are unimodal functions. f_5–f_8 are multimodal functions and the number of local minima increases exponentially with the increase of problem dimension. They are described in Table 1.

Table 1. Benchmark functions

Benchmark functions	Initial range
$f_1(x) = \sum\limits_{i=1}^{D} x_i{}^2$	$[-100, 100]^D$
$f_2(x) = \sum\limits_{i=1}^{D} \|x_i\| + \prod\limits_{i=1}^{D} \|x_i\|$	$[-10, 10]^D$
$f_3 = \sum\limits_{i=1}^{D} (\lfloor x_i + 0.5 \rfloor)^2$	$[-100, 100]^D$
$f_4 = 0.1\{10\sin^2(3\pi x_1) + \sum\limits_{i=1}^{D-1} (x_i - 1)^2[1 + 10\sin^2(3\pi x_{i+1})]$ $+(x_D - 1)^2[1 + \sin^2(2\pi x_D)]\} + \sum\limits_{i=1}^{D} u(x_i, 5, 100, 4)$	$[-50, 50]^D$
$f_5 = 418.98288727243369D - \sum\limits_{i=1}^{D} (x_i \sin(\sqrt{\|x_i\|}))$	$[-500, 500]^D$
$f_6 = -20\exp[-0.2\sqrt{\frac{1}{D}\sum\limits_{i=1}^{D} x_i^2}] - \exp(\frac{1}{D}\sum\limits_{i=1}^{D} \cos(2\pi x_i) + 20 + e)$	$[-32, 32]^D$
$f_7 = \frac{\pi}{D}\{10\sin^2(\pi y_1) + \sum\limits_{i=1}^{D-1} (y_i - 1)^2 \cdot [1 + 10\sin^2(\pi y_{i+1})] + (y_D - 1)^2\}+$ $\sum\limits_{i=1}^{D} \mu(x_i, 5, 100, 4), y_i = 1 + \frac{1}{4}(x_i + 1)$	$[-50, 50]^D$
$f_8 = \sum\limits_{i=1}^{D}\left(\sum\limits_{k=0}^{k\,\max} [a^k \cos(2\pi b^k(x_i + 0.5))]\right) - D\sum\limits_{k=0}^{k\,\max} [a^k \cos(2\pi b^k - 0.5)]$ $a = 0.5, b = 3, k\,\max = 20$	$[-0.5, 0.5]^D$

4.2 Parameters Setting

Parameters are set as follows except for the special instructions.

- Number of independent runs: RUN = 30
- Population size: SIZE = 50
- Benchmark dimension: D = 30
- The maximal function evaluation numbers: MAXFUNNUM = 100000

The classical DE has two other parameters: scale factor F and crossover probability CR. In order to remain the algorithms being modified as simple as possible, F and CR are initialized to 0.5 for all algorithm variants [12,13]. The involving parameter λ is also simply initialized as 0.5.

4.3 Simulation Results and Comparison Analysis

In this paper, we propose the second order difference vector differential evolution. The new proposed algorithm is analyzed and verified with different algorithm variants and various benchmark functions.

1. Algorithms for comparison:

In order to show the performance of the proposed algorithm, four DE algorithms are chosen to compare each other, which are described as follows:

- DE1: differential evolution using generation strategy "DE/rand/1;
- DE2: differential evolution using generation strategy "DE/best/1";
- SODE1: adding the second order difference vector to "DE/rand/1";
- SODE2: adding the second order difference vector to "DE/best/1".

2. Results analysis and performance comparison:

All of the above algorithms are executed 30 independent runs on 8 functions. The first row is five different values and the first column represents the test functions for the experiments. In order to clearly observe the final numeric comparison, the items of min, median, mean and std are presented, in which "min", "median", "mean" and "std" are the minimal, median, average and standard deviation of all the final results in 30 runs. Observed from Table 2, it can be found that SODE1 outperforms DE1 and SODE2 performs much better than DE2. Algorithm SODE1 has smaller function values on 7 from 8 functions than DE1 except for f3 and algorithm SODE2 has better performance for all functions than DE2, which indicate the excellent enhancement for the proposed strategy. For 4 unimodal functions, SODE1 performs better on 3 functions than DE1 and SODE2 performs better on 4 functions than DE2. For 4 multimodal functions, both of SODE1 and SODE2 perform better on 4 functions. These results sufficiently indicate that the second order difference vector greatly benefits the search for the optimization process.

Table 2. Performance comparison among four DEs

Fun	Items	DE1	DE2	SODE1	SODE2
f1	Min	3.33E-10	5.45E-13	2.29E-13	1.84E-59
	Median	8.91E-10	1.20E-07	8.39E-13	5.95E-58
	Mean	1.15E-09	1.82E-04	9.07E-13	1.52E-57
	Std	1.03E-09	5.11E-04	4.92E-13	2.99E-57
f2	Min	5.69E-06	3.00E-11	2.34E-08	8.74E-32
	Median	1.52E-05	1.48E-07	5.29E-08	7.98E-31
	Mean	1.55E-05	1.61E-04	5.47E-08	1.08E-30
	Std	6.30E-06	8.56E-04	1.57E-08	9.87E-31
f3	Min	0	2	0	0
	Median	0	11	0	0
	Mean	0	19.4	0	0
	Std	0	31.8072	0	0
f4	Min	4.20E-10	1.39E-07	2.36E-12	1.35E-32
	Median	2.32E-09	2.7259	7.76E-12	1.35E-32
	Mean	3.74E-09	4.5146	9.40E-12	2.85E-32
	Std	3.34E-09	5.7491	6.56E-12	8.23E-32
f5	Min	1.04E+03	1.42E+03	2.93E+03	3.55E+02
	Median	4.22E+03	2.28E+03	3.81E+03	9.48E+02
	Mean	4.01E+03	2.43E+03	3.77E+03	9.00E+02
	Std	1.01E+03	5.76E+02	3.64E+02	2.70E+02
f6	Min	4.94E-06	2.52E-08	1.91E-07	4.44E-15
	Median	9.93E-06	2.408	2.63E-07	7.99E-15
	Mean	1.02E-05	2.454	2.84E-07	0.0447
	Std	3.58E-06	1.4283	6.35E-08	0.2447
f7	Min	1.03E-10	1.57E-06	1.28E-12	1.57E-32
	Median	6.36E-10	2.9988	6.42E-12	1.57E-32
	Mean	7.31E-10	3.2482	8.73E-12	0.0242
	Std	4.64E-10	2.5935	7.08E-12	0.0802
f8	Min	1.14E-02	1.2041	5.74E-04	0
	Median	1.93E-02	4.3804	9.05E-04	0
	Mean	2.05E-02	4.3848	9.01E-04	3.10E-04
	Std	6.98E-03	1.8121	1.82E-04	1.36E-03

In general, SODE1 performs better than DE1 which indicates that the second order difference vector has significant influence on the convergence ability and ac-curacy. The fact of SODE2 being better than DE2 indicates that the second order difference vector has significant influence on the expansion of population diversity. These progressive phenomena verify the excellent effects of the proposed second order difference information strategy.

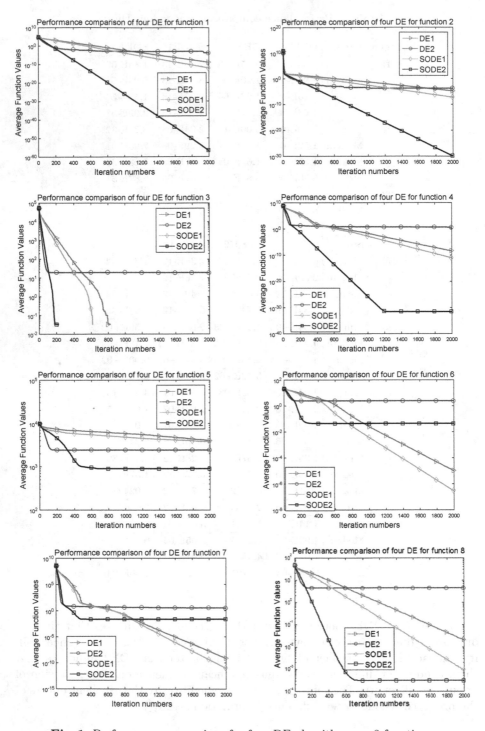

Fig. 1. Performance comparison for four DE algorithms on 8 functions

3. Online evolving performance comparison and analysis:

The online performance comparison among four DE algorithms is shown as Fig. 1, which furthermore supports the previous numerical results and the related analysis. Observed from Fig. 1, SODE1 based on DE1 algorithm performs better for 7 from 8 benchmarks for the final results and SODE2 based on DE2 performs better for all the functions. When function f3 is considered for SODE1 and DE1, SODE1 has faster convergent speed than that of DE1 although they have the same final results. The evolving lines of SODE1 and SODE2 decline faster than DE1 and DE2 and they steadily obtains even better function values than the classical DE algorithms for all the functions. What's more, it can be seen that DE1, DE2 suffer from frequent premature convergence for several functions significantly. In general, SODE1 and SODE2 present more robust performance and faster convergence speed when the second order difference information is considered, which shows the necessity and validity of the proposed strategy.

5   Conclusion

In this paper, a completely novel DE variant, SODE, is proposed and investigated with the second order difference vector, which effectively extends the current research scope of the classical (first order) DE algorithms. It aims at further efficiently utilizing the direction information of difference vector and the search statuses of the current population to refine solution and to enhance the adaptability of DE search mechanism. It is possible to spark even more interesting and challenging research topics in future. This strategy has distinct advantage and has a significant effect on avoiding premature convergence efficiently. The experimental results show that its competitive optimization performance is better than other classical algorithms and indicate the proposed strategies' effects and cooperation.

How to more fully utilize the second order difference information of DE algorithm deserves extensive research.

Acknowledgment. This research is partially supported by National Natural Science Foundation of China (61375066, 61374204, 11471052).

References

1. Storn, R., Price, K.: Differential evolution: a simple and efficient heuristic for global op-timization over continuous spaces. J. Glob. Optimi. **11**, 341–359 (1997)
2. Wang, Y., Li, B., Weise, T.: Estimation of distribution and differential evolution cooperation for large scale economic load dispatch optimization of powers systems. Inf. Sci. **180**, 2405–2420 (2010)
3. Zhang, M., Luo, W., Wang, X.: Differential evolution with dynamic stochastic selection for constrained optimization. Inf. Sci. **178**, 3043–3074 (2008)
4. Fan, H.Y., Lampinen, J.: A trigonometric mutation operation to differential evolution. J. Glob. Optim. **27**, 105–129 (2003)

5. Sun, J.Y., Zhang, Q.F., Tsang, E.P.K.: DE/EDA: a new evolutionary algorithm for global optimization. Inf. Sci. **169**, 249–262 (2005)
6. Wang, Y.X., Xiang, Q.L.: Exploring new learning strategies in differential evolution algorithm. In: IEEE Congress on Evolutionary Computation, pp. 204–209 (2008)
7. Zhao, X.C., Lin, W.Q., Yu, C.C., Chen, J., Wang, S.G.: A new hybrid differential evolution with simulated annealing and self-adaptive immune operation. Comput. Math. Appl. **66**, 1948–1960 (2013)
8. Wei, W.H., Wang, J.H., Tao, M.: Constrained differential evolution with multi-objective sorting mutation operators for constrained optimization. Appl. Soft Comput. **33**, 207–222 (2015)
9. Zhang, J.Q., Sanderson, A.C.: JADE: adaptive differential evolution with optional external archive. IEEE Trans. Evol. Comput. **13**, 945–958 (2009)
10. Leung, Y.W., Wang, Y.P.: An orthogonal genetic algorithm with quantization for global numerical optimization. IEEE Trans. Evol. Comput. **5**, 41–53 (2001)
11. Yao, X., Liu, Y., Lin, G.M.: Evolutionary programming made faster. IEEE Trans. Evol. Comput. **3**, 82–102 (1999)
12. Tasgetiren, M.F., Pan, Q.K., Suganthan, P.N., Liang, Y.C.: A differential evolution algorithm with variable parameter search for real-parameter continuous function optimization. In: IEEE Congress on Evolutionary Computation, pp. 1247–1254 (2009)
13. Vesterstrom, J., Thomsen, R.: A comparative study of differential evolution, particle swarm optimization, and evolutionary algorithms on numerical benchmark problems. In: IEEE Congress on Evolutionary Computation, vol. 2, pp. 1980–1987 (2004)

Multi-objective Optimization

Biomimicry of Plant Root Foraging
for Distributed Optimization:
Models and Emergent Behaviors

Hanning Chen[✉], Xiaodan Liang, Maowei He, and Weixing Su

Tianjin Polytechnic University, Tianjin 300160, China
perfect_chn@hotmail.com

Abstract. Terrestrial plants have evolved remarkable adaptability that enables them to sense environmental stimuli and use this information as a basis for governing their growth orientation and root system development. In this paper, we explain the foraging behaviors of plant root and develop simulation models based on the principles of adaptation processes that view root growing as optimization. This provides us with novel models of plant root foraging behavior and with new methods for global optimization. This model is instantiated as a novel bio-inspired optimization model, which adopts the root foraging, memory and communication, and auxin-regulated mechanisms of the root system. We perform comprehensive simulation to demonstrate that the proposed model exhibit the property identified by natural plant root system. That is, in order to be able to climb noisy gradients in nutrients in soil, the foraging behaviors of root system is social and cooperative that is analogous to animal foraging behaviors.

Keywords: Plant root growth · Foraging · Global optimization · Swarm intelligence · Bio-inspired computing

1 Introduction

Logically, such optimal foraging principles have led scientists in the field of optimization theory to exploit the analogy between searching a given problem space for an optimal solution and the natural search process of foraging for food [1]. In recent years a considerable amount of natural foraging strategies has inspired natural computing paradigms in optimization area, prominent examples being ant colony system (ACS) [2], particle swarm optimization (PSO) [3], and artificial bee colony algorithm (ABC) [4]. In these optimization models, communication strategies are also applied for cooperatively foraging in groups of animals.

Although foraging behavior is typically considered as a feature of animals, this definition does not exclude the responses of other organisms, including plants [5]. However, Because of their specific lifestyle, the areas where plants can access to forage for resources are confined to those which can be explored by growth [6]. This is the major difference between plant growth and animal foraging. Obviously,

© Springer Nature Singapore Pte Ltd. 2016
M. Gong et al. (Eds.): BIC-TA 2016, Part II, CCIS 682, pp. 231–240, 2016.
DOI: 10.1007/978-981-10-3614-9_28

efficient searching of the soil for the nutrients and water is principal to the survival of each plant species in the earth. Therefore, plant roots have evolved the ability to both sense myriad factors in their local environment and use this information to drive changes in growth direction and root system development [7].

Plant root growth is marked by a diversity of adaptation to continuous changes in environment, including increased lateral branching, root biomass, root length and uptake capacity. Particularly, all these developmental events require correct auxin transport and signaling [8]. Plants also adjust root demography and the length per unit mass of roots in response to heterogeneity [5]. Many studies have implied that plants are optima foragers, but there is little experimental evidence built on this assumption and only a handful of studies that explicitly develop optimality models for plant foraging [9].

The objective of this paper is to present a new optimization model based on principles from plant root growth and foraging behaviors, which will be called the root system growth Optimization (RSGO). We utilize the optimal foraging theory perspective in formulating our RSGO model for global numerical optimization. The proposed model is presented by modeling of the root foraging, memory and communication, and auxin-regulated mechanisms of the root system. In the proposed algorithm emulating the distributed optimization process represented by the activity of plant root growth, several efficient ways to search for space optimization problems is proposed. The local search and global search using root branching and elongation (tropism) both controlled by auxin concentration during the foraging process are implemented. The random walk of lateral roots and root tip death mechanisms are also developed to keep the diversity and efficiency of the model. In order to illustrative the inherent adaptive mechanism in the proposed model of root system growing, the root tropic growth, auxin controlled population dynamic, and root system structure formulation are simulated based on RSGO model in this paper. The simulation results capture some important aspects of the dynamics of root growth that some plant biologists believe takes place in nature.

2   Root Foraging

2.1   Root Growth Responds to Nutrition Gradient in Soil

In keeping with their functions as the main nutrients foraging organ of plant, roots are highly sensitive to the availability of essential resources in the soil. Indeed, plant roots from different species are able to sense multiple environmental nutrition gradients and exert different responses by adjusting their growth direction to promote exploration of nutrition rich areas. This directional growth response is called tropism [10]. Plant roots display different tropisms, namely gravitropism, phototropism, hydrotropism, thigmotropism, thermotropism, electrotropism, magnetotropism and chemotropism, in response to the gradient of environmental gravity, light, water (moisture gradient), touch (mechanical stimuli), temperature, electric fields, magnetic fields, and chemicals, respectively [11].

2.2 Root Memory and Communication

Plant biologists are now realizing that previous experience also greatly influences plant behaviors through conditioning [8]. Plants exhibit memory, altering their behaviors depending upon their previous experiences or the experiences of their parents. For examples, plant competitors in the soil with uniform nutrient distribution exhibit obvious reduction in root system breadth and spatial segregation; while plant competitors in the soil with heterogeneous nutrient distribution reduce their root growth modestly, which indicating that plants integrate information about both neighbor and resource distribution in determining their root foraging behaviors.

2.3 Auxin-Regulated Root System Development

Auxin is involved in lateral root initiation and development. For example, auxin local accumulation in Arabidopsis root pericycle cells adjacent to xylem vessels, triggers lateral root initiation by re-specifying these cells into lateral root founder cells [12]. Root branching is an extremely flexible means to rapidly adjust the overall surface of the root system and plants have evolved efficient control mechanisms. Auxin transport into the regions where lateral root initiate also seems crucial for the regulation of root branching, including when and where to start lateral root formation, and during which the development of primordia can be arrested for a certain time [13].

3 Root System Growth for Optimization

3.1 Auxin Concentration

In the RSGO model, the plant root system is defined to consist of a collection of root tips, which is represented as:

$$RS = \left\{ \theta_i^t | i = 1, 2, \ldots, P^t; t = 1, 2, \ldots, T \right\} \tag{1}$$

where

$$\theta_i^t = \left\langle x_i^t, f_i^t, n_i^t, \alpha_i^t, \varphi_i^t \right\rangle \tag{2}$$

denotes a single root tip; P^t denotes the root tips' number at time t; T is the final time of the root system growing process; θ_i^t has its own position x_i^t, fitness f_i^t, nutrient n_i^t, and the auxin α_i^t which depends on f_i^t and n_i^t that control this root tip to forage (elongate), branch or die at time t. If it is foraging, the root tip moves with an orientation φ_i^t as an angle formed by the root axis.

At the initial stage $t = 0$, a number of P root tips are randomized in the D-dimensional space. In mathematical terms, the position and heading angle of the ith root tip is represented as $x_i = (x_{i1}, x_{i2}, \ldots x_{iD})$ and $\varphi_i = (\varphi_{i1}, \varphi_{i2}, \ldots \varphi_{i(D-1)})$ respectively. Here $x_{id} \in [l_d, u_d]$, $d \in [1, D]$, l_d, u_d are the lower and upper bounds for the dth dimension, respectively. In each growing time step t, the root tip i will forage for nutrient and its nutrient n_i^t can be updated by:

$$n_i^{t+1} = \begin{cases} n_i^t + 1 & if\ f_i^{t+1} < f_i^t \\ n_i^t - 1 & else \end{cases} \tag{3}$$

In initialization stage, nutrients of all root tips are zero. During the root growth, for each tip in the root system, if the new tip position is better than the last one, it is regarded that this root tip will gain nutrient from the environment and the nutrient is added by one. Otherwise, the root tip loses nutrient in the foraging process and its nutrient is reduced by one.

Then the auxin concentration α_i^t, which combines the health and energy states of the ith root tip, is manipulated according to the following equations:

$$health_i^t = \frac{f_i^t - f_{worst}^t}{f_{best}^t - f_{worst}^t} \tag{4}$$

$$energy_i^t = \frac{n_i^t - n_{worst}^t}{n_{best}^t - n_{worst}^t} \tag{5}$$

$$\alpha_i^t = \xi \frac{health_i^t}{\sum\limits_{j=1}^{Pt} health_j^t} + (1 - \xi) \frac{energy_i^t}{\sum\limits_{j=1}^{Pt} energy_j^t}, \ \xi \subset [0, 1] \tag{6}$$

where f_{worst}^t / f_{best}^t and n_{worst}^t / n_{best}^t are the current worst/best fitness and nutrient of the whole root system at time t.

In each cycle of roots growth process, all root taps are sorted by auxin concentration values defined above. That is, the strong root taps have higher probability to be selected as main roots for branching. The number of main roots is computed as:

$$S_m^t = P^t \times Cr \tag{7}$$

where S_m^t is the size of selected main root group, P^t is the total number of root tips and Cr is the selection probability. The other $S_l^t = P^t - S_m^t$ root tips are considered as lateral roots.

3.2   Root Branching

Then a threshold $BranchG$ is compared with the auxin concentration value of each main root to determine whether it performs branching:

$$\begin{cases} branching & if\ \alpha_i^t > BranchG \\ nobranching & otherelse \end{cases} \tag{8}$$

If θ_i^t is selected as main root and its auxin concentration is enough to conduct branching, the branching number wi of θ_i^t is determined by:

$$S_i^t = \lceil R_1 \alpha_i^t (S_{max} - S_{min}) + S_{min} \rceil \tag{9}$$

where S_{max} and S_{min} are the maximum and minimum of the new growing tips, and R_1 is a random distribution coefficient. Considering growth direction of θ_i^t as reference angle, the searching space of its all branches is divided into Smax subzones and the angle of new growing tips (i.e. the new root branches of θ_i^t) is randomly falling within one of these subzones. Then these new branching tips will grow as:

$$\varphi_j^{t+1} = \varphi_i^t + \lambda_j \varphi_{max}/S_{max} \tag{10}$$

$$x_j^{t+1} = x_i^t + R_2 l_{max} H(\varphi_j^{t+1}) \tag{11}$$

where $j \subseteq [S_{min}, S_i^t]$ is the root branch index of root tip θ_i^t, $\lambda_j \subseteq [1, S_{max}]$ is the selecting subzone number of the root branch x_j^{t+1}, φ_{max} is the maximum growing turning angle, which is limited to π, R_2 is random value between 0 and 1, l_{max} is the maximum of root elongation length, and $\varphi_j^{t+1} = (h_{j1}^{t+1}, h_{j2}^{t+1}, \ldots, h_{jD}^{t+1}) \in R^D$ is a Polar to Cartesian coordinates transform function, which can be calculated as:

$$\begin{aligned} h_{j1}^{t+1} &= \prod_{p=1}^{D-1} \cos(\varphi_{jp}^{t+1}) \\ h_{jk}^{t+1} &= \sin(\varphi_{j(k-1)}^{t+1}) \prod_{p=j}^{D-1} \cos(\varphi_{jp}^{t+1}) \\ h_{jD}^{t+1} &= \sin(\varphi_{j(D-1)}^{t+1}) \end{aligned} \tag{12}$$

3.3 Tropisms

In RSGO model, two typical tropisms, namely hydrotropism and gravitropism, are realized. Firstly, the effect of gravitropism depends on the communication mechanism in root system. That is, a half of main roots will grow toward the best position with most moisture among the root system, given by:

$$x_i^{t+1} = x_i^t + R_3(x_{best}^t - x_i^t) \tag{13}$$

where $i \subseteq [1, S_m^t/2]$, R_3 is random value in the range (0 1), and x_{best}^t is the best position in the root tip group.

Considering the hydrotropism depends on the root memory, the rest of main roots will grow along their original directions as:

$$x_i^{t+1} = x_i^t + R_4 l_{max} H(\varphi_i^t) \ if \ x_i^t > x_i^{t-1} \tag{14}$$

where $i \subseteq [S_m^t/2, S_m^t]$, l_{max} is the maximum of root elongation length, and R_4 is random value in the range (0 1).

3.4 Random Walk of Lateral Roots

During each foraging bout, all the lateral root tips will perform random walk, which are thought to be the most efficient foraging strategy for randomly distributed nutrition [14]. At the tth iteration, each lateral root tip generates a random head angle and a random elongation length, given by:

$$\varphi_i^{t+1} = \varphi_i^t + R_5 \varphi_{max} \tag{15}$$

$$x_i^{t+1} = x_i^t + R_6 l_{max} H(\varphi_i^{t+1}) \tag{16}$$

where $i \subseteq [0, S_l^t]$, R_5 and R_6 are random values in the range (0 1), φ_{max} is the maximum growing turning angle, and l_{max} is the maximum of root elongation length.

3.5 Root Tip Death

Lower auxin concentration represents that a root tip did not get as many nutrients during its lifetime of foraging and hence is not as active and thus unlikely to continue to grow. Then in each cycle of roots growth process, all root tips with auxin values less than zero die and will be simply eliminated from the root group.

4 Root Growth Simulation in RSGO Model

4.1 Root Tropic Growth: Gravitropism Versus Hydrotropism

We simulated the directional root growth behaviors, namely the hydrotropism and gravitropism of RSGO model, on 2D Sphere and Griewank's landscapes, respectively (shown as in Figs. 1 and 2). In both cases, the simulations were carried out on three independent scenarios, namely the hydrotropic response without gravitational force, the gravitational force without hydrotropic response, and both tropic responses exist. In each simulation, only one tip is initialized at $(-3, -3)$ as main root (represented as the red lines in the figures), which is the unique one can branch lateral roots (represented as the green lines in the figures) in its whole life-cycle.

The growth trajectories, which only consider hydrotropic response in RSGO model, in 2D Sphere and Griewank's landscapes are shown in Figs. 1(a) and 2(a), respectively. From Figs. 1(a) and 2(a), we can observe that underlying hydrotropic rule in RSGO, the root tips climb the moisture gradients through increasing the number of branches and elongation of roots. It can be obviously observed that the hydro-tropic rule in RSGO is a typical local search strategy that is well documented by empirical studies in both plants and animals: when there are multiple types of a resource with different costs and benefits, organisms are expected to select among these re-sources in a way that maximizes benefits and minimizes costs.

From the growth trajectories in Figs. 1(b) and 2(b), we can observe that the root tips move throughout both the unimodal and multimodal landscapes (defined by Sphere and Griewank, respectively) through the gravitational force in RSGO model. That is, the gravitational force designed in RSGO is the global search strategy that makes each tip a social forager to maximize the performance of the root system as a whole, rather than their own individual performance.

Figures 1(c) and 2(c) illustrate the root growth trajectories under the influence of both tropisms. In this simulation, gravitropism interferes with

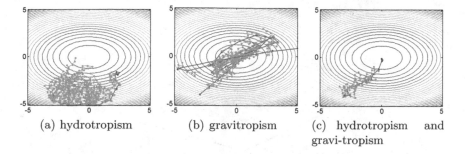

(a) hydrotropism   (b) gravitropism   (c) hydrotropism   and
gravi-tropism

Fig. 1. Simulation on 2-dimensional Sphere considering

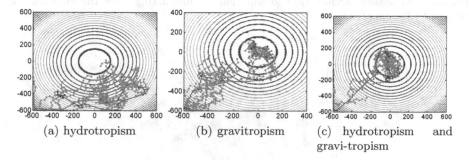

(a) hydrotropism   (b) gravitropism   (c) hydrotropism   and
gravi-tropism

Fig. 2. Simulation on 2-dimensional Griewang considering

hydrotropism, which provides an understanding of how roots sense multiple environmental cues and exhibit different tropic responses. That is, the hydrotropic rule in RSGO encourages exploitation ability, while the gravitational force designed in RSGO improves exploration ability. This shared and divergent mechanism that mediating the two tropisms is important because it permits the root system to refine its foraging behaviour adaptively. At the beginning of the simulation, the root tips start exploring the search space. In that manner, the main root does not waste much time before finding the promising region that contains the global optimum, because the gravitational force designed in RSGO improves exploration ability. On the other hand, by the hydrotropic rule in RSGO, the main root slows down near the optimum and increases the number of branches in order to pursue the more and more precise solutions.

4.2 Root System Structure Formulation

Modeling of root architecture is helpful in linking knowledge gained at the level of the individual root to that of the entire root system. Conceptually, root system architecture can be modeled in different ways, depending on the goals, actual knowledge and parameterization of the different processes available. Here, the root system is represented by the developmental processes of the root system. This results in a three dimensional set of connected branching points,

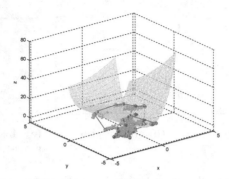

Fig. 3. Root system architecture formulation by interacting with the environment defined by Rosenbrock

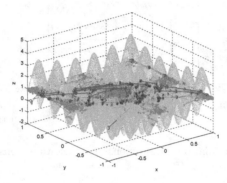

Fig. 4. Root system architecture formulation by interacting with the environment defined by Rastrigin

representing the roots and their tips, each characterized by properties such as age, root type, angle, length and foraging ability that defined in RSGO model.

We simulated the root-soil interactions and the dynamics of rhizosphere in RSGO model, on 3D Rosenbrock, Rastrigin and Griewank's landscapes, respectively (shown as in Figs. 3, 4 and 5). From the simulation results, we can observe that root system architecture is flexible and can alter as a result of prevailing soil conditions. This flexibility arises due to the modular structure of roots which enables root deployment in zones or patches rich in moisture or nutrients. Although the relationship between root foraging precision and scale remain elusive, it can be clearly observed that the root systems allocated more of their new root growth into the nutrient-rich zones, while less of their new root growth into the nutrient-poor zones in all three simulation cases.

That is, the RSGO rules enable the root system place their new roots with more precision.

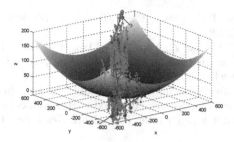

Fig. 5. Root system architecture formulation by interacting with the environment defined by Griewank

5 Conclusions

In this paper, we adopt the optimal foraging theory perspective in formulating our simulation model for root foraging behaviors. The optimal root foraging behaviors and root growth controlling by auxin are combined in our model. Next, the proposed model is instantiated as an optimization algorithm called RSGO that emulates the distributed optimization process represented by the activity of plant root growth. We validate the model on several widely-used benchmark functions and briefly discuss that the principle of a number of emerging characteristics, namely the root tropic growth, auxin controlled population dynamic, and root system structure formulation, which are valid for both model and plant root system. Based on this comprehensive analysis of RSGO performance, we believe RSGO has a great potential of being applied to a variety of complex real-world problems. Indeed, there is ongoing research that is studying this now.

References

1. El-Abd, M.: Performance assessment of foraging algorithms vs. evolutionary algorithms. Inf. Sci. **182**(1), 243–263 (2012)
2. Socha, K., Dorigo, M.: Ant colony optimization for continuous domains. Eur. J. Oper. Res. **185**(3), 1155–1173 (2008)
3. Kennedy, J.: The particle swarm as collaborative sampling of the search space. Adv. Complex Syst. **10**, 191–213 (2007)
4. Akay, B., Karaboga, D.: A modified artificial bee colony algorithm for real-parameter optimization. Inf. Sci. **192**(1), 120–142 (2012)
5. McNickle, G.G., Clair, C.C.S., Cahill Jr., J.F.: Focusing the metaphor: plant root foraging behavior. Trends Ecol. Evol. **24**(8), 419–426 (2009)
6. de Kroon, H., Mommer, L.: Root foraging theory put to the test. Trends Ecol. Evol. **21**, 113–116 (2006)
7. Falik, O., Reides, P., Gersani, M., Novoplansky, A.: Root navigation by self inhibition. Plant Cell Environ. **28**, 562–569 (2005)
8. Karban, R.: Plant behaviour and communication. Ecol. Lett. **11**, 727–739 (2008)
9. Kembel, S.W., Cahill, J.F.: Plant phenotypic plasticity belowground: a phylogenetic perspective on root foraging trade-offs. Am. Nat. **166**, 216–230 (2005)

10. Gilroy, S., Masson, P.H. (eds.): Plant Tropisms. Blackwell Publishing, Ames, Oxford, Victoria (2008)
11. Rubio, G., Walk, T.C., Ge, Z., Yan, X.L., Liao, H., Lynch, J.: Root gravitropism and below-ground competition among neighbouring plants: a modelling approach. Ann. Bot. **88**, 929–940 (2002)
12. Dubrovsky, J.G., Sauer, M., Napsucialy-Mendivil, S., Ivanchenko, M.G., Friml, J., Shishkova, S., Celenza, J., Benková, E.: Auxin acts as a local morphogenetic trigger to specify lateral root founder cells. Proc. Natl. Acad. Sci. USA **105**, 8790–8794 (2008)
13. Hodge, A., Berta, G., Doussan, C., Merchan, F., Crespi, M.: Plant root growth, architecture and function. Plant Soil **321**(1–2), 153–187 (2009)
14. Banks, A., Vincent, J., Phalp, K.: Natural strategies for search. Nat. Comput. **8**, 547–570 (2009)

Adaptive Bacterial Foraging Algorithm and Its Application in Mobile Robot Path Planning

Xiaodan Liang, Maowei He, and Hanning Chen[(✉)]

Tianjin Polytechnic University, Tianjin 300160, China
lxdtjpu@163.com, perfect_chn@hotmail.com

Abstract. This work considered the utilization of biomimicry of bacterial foraging strategy to develop an adaptive control strategy for mobile robot, and proposed a bacterial foraging approach for robot path planning. In the proposed model, robot that mimics the behavior of bacteria is able to determine an optimal collision-free path between a start and a target point in the environment surrounded by obstacles. In the simulation studies, a test scenario of static environment with different number obstacles is adopted to evaluate the performance of the proposed method. Simulation results show that the robot which reflects the bacterial foraging behavior can adapt to complex environments in the planned trajectories with both satisfactory accuracy and stability.

Keywords: Robot path planning · Bacterial foraging behaviors · Swarm intelligence · Adaptation

1 Introduction

The goal of robot path planning is to find an optimal, collision-free trajectory between two points in a working environment composed of many obstacles [1]. The optimality of the path is usually measured by the traveling time and penalty for obstacle avoidance of the mobile robot. Generally global planning methods complemented with local methods are used for indoor missions since the environments are known or partially known; for outdoor applications, local planning methods are more suitable because of the scant information of the environment.

Recently, the interest in using evolutionary algorithms (EA) and swarm intelligence (SI) for robot path planning is increasing. Up to now, the genetic algorithm and bacterial foraging optimization are used in mobile robots trajectory planning, generally when the environment description is given [2,3]. Although the heuristic EA and SI approaches can not guarantee optimal performance on all engineering problems, however, they can find optimal solution faster than most classical methods [4].

This work uses a recently developed BFO [5] based search model, namely the self-adaptive bacterial foraging optimization (SABFO) [6], to create optimal collision-free trajectories for mobile robot. Instead of the simple description

© Springer Nature Singapore Pte Ltd. 2016
M. Gong et al. (Eds.): BIC-TA 2016, Part II, CCIS 682, pp. 241–246, 2016.
DOI: 10.1007/978-981-10-3614-9_29

of chemotactic behavior in original bacterial foraging optimization (BFO) algorithm, SABFO also incorporates the adaptive search strategy, which allows each bacterium strikes a good balance between exploration and exploitation during algorithmic execution by tuning its run-length unit self-adaptively. In the experiments, two cases study of static environment with obstacles are presented and evaluated. Simulation results show the adaptation of the bacterial robot in different environments in the planned trajectories.

2 Self-adaptive Bacterial Foraging Optimization

In the SABFO algorithm, an "individual run-length unit" to the ith bacterium of the colony was introduced and each bacterium can only modify the search behavior of itself by using the current status of its own. In this way, not only the position (solution vector) but also the run-length unit of each bacterium undergoes evolution, respectively. In the foraging process of SABFO model, each bacterium displays alternatively two distinct search states:

(1) *Exploration state*, during which the bacterium employs a large run-length unit to explore the previously unscanned regions in the search space as fast as possible.
(2) *Exploitation state*, during which the bacterium uses a small run-length unit to exploit the promising regions slowly in its immediate vicinity.

Table 1. Pseudocode for dynamic self-adaptive strategy.

1	**For** (each bacterium i) IN PARLLEL
2	**IF** (*Criterion-I*) then
3	$C^i(t+1) = C^i(t+1)/\alpha$;
4	$\varepsilon^i(t+1) = \varepsilon^i/\beta$;
5	**ELSE IF** (*Criterion-II*) then
6	$C^i(t+1) = C_{intial}$; //exploration
7	$\varepsilon^i(t+1) = \varepsilon_{intial}$
8	**ELSE**
9	$C^i(t+1) = C^i(t)$;
10	$\varepsilon^i(t+1) = \varepsilon^i(t)$;
11	**END IF**
12	**END FOR INPARALLEL**

Each bacterium in the colony has to permanently maintain an appropriate balance between Exploration and Exploitation states by varying its own run-length unit adaptively. In SABFO, the adaptation of the individual run-length unit is done by taking into account two decision indicators: a fitness improvement (finding a promising domain) and no improvement registered lately (current domain is food exhausted). The criteria that determine the adjustment of individual run-length unit and the entrance into one of the states (i.e. Exploitation and Exploration) are the following:

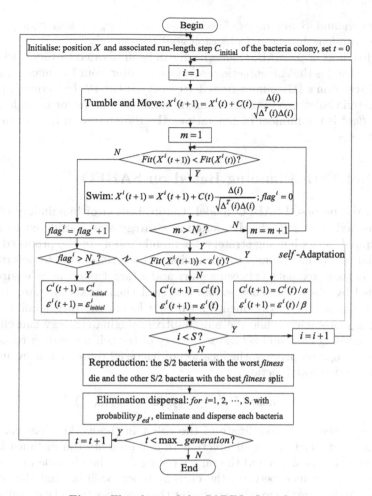

Fig. 1. Flowchart of the SABFO algorithm

- *Criterion-1:* if the bacterium discovers a new, promising domain, the run-length unit of this bacterium is adapted to another smaller one. Here "discovers a new promising domain" means this bacterium registers a fitness improvement beyond a certain precision from the last generation to the current.
- *Criterion-2:* if the bacterium's current fitness is unchanged for a number Ku (user-defined) of consecutive generations, then augment this bacterium's run-length unit and this bacterium enters Exploration state. This situation means that the bacterium searches on an un-promising domain or the domain where this bacterium focuses its search has nothing new to offer.

This self-adaptive strategy is given in pseudocode in Table 1. Where t is the current generation number, $C_i(t)$ is the current run-length unit of the ith bacterium, $\varepsilon_i(t)$ is the required precision in the current generation of the ith bacterium, α and β are user-defined constants, $C_{inintial}$ and $\varepsilon_{initial}$ are the initialized run-length unit and precision goal respectively.

The flowchart of the SABFO algorithm can be illustrated by Fig. 1, where S is the colony size, t is the chemotactic generation counter from 1 to max-generation, i is the bacterium's ID counter from 1 to S, X^i is the *ith* bacterium's position of the bacteria colony, N_s is the maximum number of steps for a single activity of swim, $flag^i$ is the number of generations the *ith* bacterium has not improved its own fitness.

3   Robot Path Planning Based on SABFO

Based on the proposed SABFO model, the utilization of biomimicry of bacterial chemotaxis and self-adaptive foraging strategy was considered to develop a bio-inspired path planning strategy for mobile robot. In the proposed model, a bacterial robot that mimics the behavior of bacteria is able to determine an optimal collision-free path between a start and a target point in an environment surrounded by obstacles. That is, the bacterial chemotaxis mechanism enable the robot explore the environment and finally locate the target point without colliding any obstacles; while the self-adaptive foraging strategy can efficiently save the traveling time and actuators' energy of the self navigating robot.

In the navigation process, the location of bacterial robot can be evaluated as a multi-objective cost function:

$$\text{Minimize}\ \ f(x^t) = w_1 f_g(x^t) + w_2 f_o(x^t) \tag{1}$$

where x represents the coordinate of the robot in the working environment, t is the time step, f_g is the goal function that represents the distance between the current robot position and the target point, f_o is the obstacle function that represents the distance between the current robot position and the obstacles nearby, w_1 and w_2 are the weight parameter that specifies the relative importance of achieving obstacle avoidance and reaching the goal.

4   Simulation Results

In this experiment, the proposed planning method is evaluated against an ideal 2-dimension square working area. The 2D Sphere function [7] with the global minimum (i.e., the goal point) at [25, 25] is used for the goal function that is given by:

$$f_g(x,y) = (x - 25)^2 + (y - 25)^2 \quad x, y \in [0, 30] \tag{2}$$

In this work, Gaussian function of unity height [8] was taken to represent an obstacle. Then the obstacle function can be formulated as a composition of a number of Gaussian functions and can be formulated as:

$$f_o(x,y) = \max_{i=1}^{n} \exp(-0.8 \times ((x - x_i^o)^2 + (y - y_i^o)^2)) \tag{3}$$

where n is the number of the obstacles in the working environment and $(x_i^o y_i^o)$ is the position of the ith obstacle. It should be note that the use of the maximum of all the Gaussian functions ensures that each obstacle position is represented independent of the others. x_i and y_i are generated randomly at the initialization process. In simulation process, x_i and y_i can change automatically after specific cycles or in specific phases.

Since the more obstacles the more environmental complexity, obstacle function, namely f_o with 20 obstacles, is evaluated in our experiment. The landscapes of f_o is shown in Fig. 2. Figure 2(b) shows the contour plots of the final working environments combining the goal and obstacle function, along with the initial position and goal position.

The parameters of SABFO is set as $S = 1$, $C_{initial} = 0.1$, $\varepsilon_{initial} = 100$, $K_u = 100$, $\alpha = \beta = 10$, and the maximum generation is 1000.

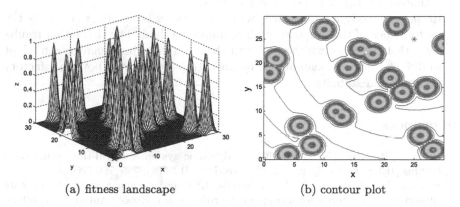

(a) fitness landscape   (b) contour plot

Fig. 2. Fitness landscape and contour plot of the obstacle function 2 with initial (square) and goal (star) positions

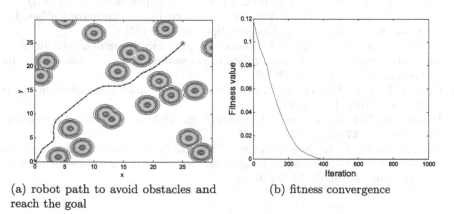

(a) robot path to avoid obstacles and   (b) fitness convergence
reach the goal

Fig. 3. Simulation results

The simulation results on tested case 2 with 20 obstacles are illustrated in Fig. 3(a). Although the environment is complex in this case, the robot using bacterial foraging strategy was able to find the target point without colliding into any obstacles. The Fig. 3(b) shows that the robust convergence of path planning is obtained.

5   Conclusions

(1) This work proposed a bacterial foraging approach for robot path planning based on bacterial foraging algorithm. In the proposed path planning model, the bacterial chemotaxis mechanism enable the robot explore the environment and finally locate the target point without colliding any obstacles, while the self-adaptive foraging strategy can efficiently save the traveling time and actuators' energy of the self navigating robot.
(2) In the case study, a test scenario with 20 obstacles is adopted to evaluate the performance of the proposed path planning method. The simulation results show that the robot which mimics the bacterial foraging behavior can adapt to different environments in the planned trajectories with both satisfactory accuracy and stability.

References

1. Willms, A.R., Yang, S.X.: An efficient dynamic system for real-time robot-path planning. IEEE Trans. Syst. Man Cybern.-Part B **36**(4), 755–766 (2006)
2. Ioannidis, K., Sirakoulis, G.C., Andreadis, I.: Cellular ants: a method to create collision free trajectories for a cooperative robot team. Robot. Auton. Syst. **59**(2), 113–127 (2011)
3. Gemeinder, M., Gerke, M.: GA-based path planning for mobile robot systems employing an active search algorithm. Appl. Soft Comput. **3**, 149–158 (2003)
4. Chen, H.N., Zhu, Y.L., Hu, K.Y.: Discrete and continuous optimization based on multi-swarm coevolution. Nat. Comput. **9**(3), 659–682 (2010)
5. Badamchizadeh, M.A., Nikdel, A., Kouzehgar, M.: Comparison of genetic algorithm and particle swarm optimization for data fusion method based on Kalman filter. Int. J. Artif. Intell. **5**(10), 67–78 (2010)
6. Chen, H.N., Zhu, Y.L., Hu, K.Y.: Adaptive bacterial foraging optimization. Abstr. Appl. Anal. **2011**, 1–27 (2011)
7. Rashedi, E., Nezamabadi-Pour, H., Saryazdi, S.: GSA: a gravitational search algorithm. Inf. Sci. **179**(13), 2232–2248 (2009)
8. Badamchizadeh, M.A., Nikdel, A., Kouzehgar, M.: Comparison of genetic algorithm and particle swarm optimization for data fusion method based on kalman filter. Int. J. Artif. Intell. **5**(10), 67–78 (2010)

A Novel Hierarchical Artificial Bee Colony Optimizer and Its Application for Model-Based Prediction of Droplet Characteristic in 3D Electronic Printing

Maowei He and Hanning Chen[✉]

Tianjin Polytechnic University, Tianjin 300160, China
hemaowei@hotmail.com, perfect_chn@hotmail.com

Abstract. This paper presents a novel optimization algorithm, namely hierarchical artificial bee colony optimization (HABC), which employs a pool of optimal foraging strategies to extend the classical artificial bee colony framework to cooperative and hierarchical fashion. The higher-level species can be aggregated by the subpopulations from lower level. In the bottom level, each subpopulation employing the canonical ABC method searches the part-dimensional optimum in parallel. At the same time, the comprehensive learning method with crossover and mutation operator is applied to enhance the global search ability between species. Furthermore, HABC is applied in predicting the droplet characteristic based on lumped element modeling methods. The simulation results demonstrate that the effectiveness of the proposed method.

Keywords: Hierarchical cooperative optimization · Artificial bee colony · Lumped element modeling · 3D electronic printing

1 Introduction

The application of swarm intelligence (SI) for solving complex optimization problems in engineering has gained significant attention in the literature [1]. Artificial bee colony algorithm (ABC), due to its simple arithmetic and good robustness, is one of the most popular members of the family of SI, which simulates the social foraging behavior of a honeybee swarm [2]. However, facing up complex problems, similar to other SI algorithms, ABC algorithm suffers from the following drawbacks [3]: (1) the solution search equation of ABC works well in global exploration but is poor in the exploitation process. (2) When dealing with the problems with incremental dimension, the information exchange of each individual is restricted in a random dimension, resulting in a slow convergence rate. (3) Due to the random selection of the neighbor bee and dimensions, food sources with higher fitness are not utilized, influencing the ability of global search.

Comparing with the huge in-depth studies of other evolutionary [4,5], how to improve the diversity of swarm or overcome the local convergence of ABC is still

© Springer Nature Singapore Pte Ltd. 2016
M. Gong et al. (Eds.): BIC-TA 2016, Part II, CCIS 682, pp. 247–253, 2016.
DOI: 10.1007/978-981-10-3614-9_30

a challenging issue Thus, this paper presents a novel hierarchical optimization algorithm, namely HABC, to extend the topology of original ABC algorithm from flat (one level) to hierarchical (multiple levels), which adopting cooperative evolutionary strategies.

Moreover, we investigate an interesting real-world application of the HABC scheme to solve the optimal droplet property prediction (ODPP) problem, which focusing on minimizing the error between the desired droplet volume/velocity and simulated droplet volume/velocity. A typical analytical model - lumped element modeling method C is adopted to simulate the droplet formation process. The advantage of this method is its simpler structure with the sufficient simulation accuracy. After setting a series of desired droplet characteristics, a grid search method is applied to determine the parameters of printhead driving waveform.

2   Hierarchical Artificial Bee Colony Algorithm

The flowchart of the HABC is shown in Fig. 1.

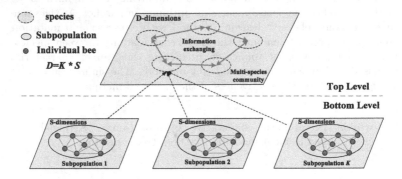

Fig. 1. Hierarchical optimization model

2.1   Hierarchical Multi-population Optimization Model

HABC contains two levels, namely the bottom level and top level. In the bottom level, with the variables decomposing strategy, each subpopulation employs the canonical ABC method to search the part-dimensional optimum in parallel. In each iteration, K subpopulations in the bottom level generate K best solutions, which are constructed into a complete solution species that update to the top level. In the top level, the multi-species community adopts the information exchange mechanism based on crossover operator, by which each species can learn from its neighborhoods in a specific topology.

2.2   Variables Decomposing Approach

The purpose of this approach is to obtain finer local search in single dimensions inspired by the divide-and-conquer approach.

Step1. The simplest grouping method is permitting a D-dimensional vector to be split into K subcomponents, each corresponding to a subpopulation of s-dimensions, with M individuals (where $D = K * s$). The jth subpopulation is denoted as P_j.

Step2. Construct complete evolving solution *Gbest*, which is the concatenation of the best subcomponents' solutions P_j by fowling:

$$Gbest = (P_1.g, P_2.g, P_j.g...P_K.g) \tag{1}$$

$P_j g$ represents the personal best solution of the jth subpopulation.

Step3. For each component P_j, $j \in [1...K]$, do the following:

At employed bees' phase, for each individual $X_i, i \in [1... M]$, Replace the i-th component of the *Gbest* by using the i-th component of individual X_i Calculate the new solution fitness: $f(newGbest(P_1.g, P_2.g, X_i, ...P_k.g))$. If $f(newgbest) < f(Gbest)$, then G*best* is replaced by *newGbest*

Random Grouping of Variables. To increase the probability of two interacting variables allocated to the same subcomponent [6], we adopt the same random grouping scheme by dynamically changing group size. The probability of placing two interacting variables into the same subcomponent becomes higher, over an increasing number of iterations.

2.3   The Information Exchange Mechanism Based on Crossover Operator Between Multi-species

In the top level, we adopt crossover operator with a specific topology to enhance the information exchange between species.

Step 1. Select elites to the best-performing list (BPL)

A set of competent individuals from current species P_j's neighborhood (i.e. ring topology) are selected to construct the best-performing list (BPL) with higher fitness have larger probability to be selected. The size of BPL is equal with the number of current species P_j. These individuals are regarded as elites. The selection operation tries to mimic the maturing phenomenon in nature, where the generated offspring will become more suitable to the environment by using these elites as parents.

Step 2. Crossover and mutation between species

To produce well-performing individuals, parents are selected from the BPL's elites only for the crossover operation. The tournament selection scheme is used. Firstly, two enhanced elites are selected randomly. Then, the one with better fitness value is viewed as parent. Another parent is selected in the same way. Two offspring are created by performing crossover on the selected parents.

3 Optimal Droplet Property Prediction (ODPP) Problem

3.1 Lumped Element Modeling of Printhead

A classical LEM is given to simulate jetting characteristics of PZT printhead, as shown in Fig. 2. Model structure shows that the energy converts from electrical energy to mechanical energy, then to fluidic/acoustic energy, and finally to kinetic energy. The droplet generator structure can be characterized by equivalent acoustic mass (representing stored kinetic energy) and acoustic compliance (representing stored potential energy), in which the corresponding equivalent circuit models are supported by various fluid mechanisms [7–9].

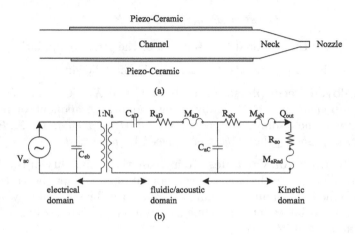

Fig. 2. Schematic overview of lumped-element modeling for PZT printhead

3.2 Optimal Prediction Model for Droplet Properties

In Fig. 3, a novel optimal prediction model for searching the appropriate combination of waveform parameters is proposed in this work.

In mathematical terms, the driving waveform includes nine adjustable parameters: two rising times T_{R1} and T_{R2}, two falling times T_{F1} and T_{F2}, two dwell times T_{w1} and T_{w2}, two voltage magnitude V_1 and V_2, and one gap time T_g. Actually, the rising or falling times of the trapezoidal pulse is fixed as *0.3us*. Therefore, there are still five adjustable parameters in the driving waveform. Moreover, the driving waveform can be parameterized as a vector with five dimensions $M = [T_{w1}, V_1, T_g, T_{w2}, V_2]^T$.

Then, to evaluate the error between the predictive droplet volume and velocity and the desired droplet volume and velocity, the ODPP problem can be defined as:

$$Minimize\ \mathrm{I} = w_1(U - U_{t\arg et})^2 + w_2(S - S_{t\arg et})^2 \tag{2}$$

where U is the predictive droplet volume, S is the predictive droplet velocity, U_{target} is the desired droplet volume, S_{target} is the desired droplet velocity, w_1 and w_2 are the user-defined weighs, and $w_1 + w_2 = 1$.

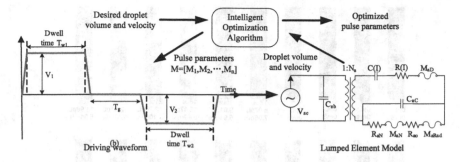

Fig. 3. The optimal prediction model for the appropriate combination of waveform parameters

3.3 Prediction Results

Here, we give an illustrative example to show the optimization effect. The desired droplet volume and velocity are $12pL$ and $5\,\text{m/s}$, respectively. We choose the weighting as $w = [0.8\ 0.2]$. The proposed HABC, ABC, CMA-ES, PSO and GA are all tested as the intelligent optimization algorithms in the optimal prediction system. The value of iterations is set as 6000.

The fitness values obtained by all involved algorithms after 6000 iterations are listed in Table 1. It is obvious that HABC has a better performance in local search than other five algorithms. HABC is the fastest one for finding satisfactory results within relatively few generations.

Table 1. Fitness values obtained by all involved algorithms

Algorithm	Fitness
HABC	0.0027
ABC	0.0219
CMA-ES	0.0115
PSO	0.0301
GA	0.0399

The dynamic effect of jetting characteristics driven by HABC is shown in Fig. 4. The jetting characteristics satisfy the specified desired conditions quite well. Meanwhile, almost no satellite droplet emerges after jetting the main droplet.

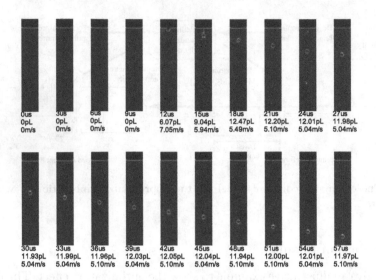

Fig. 4. A sequence of pictures of droplet falling from nozzle (obtained by HABC algorithm)

4   Conclusions

This paper proposes a hierarchical artificial bee colony algorithm, namely HABC. Main idea is extending single artificial bee colony (ABC) algorithm to hierarchical and cooperative mode by combining the multi-population cooperative co-evolution approach based on vector decomposing strategy and the comprehensive learning method To prove the effectiveness and robustness of the proposed algorithms using different strategies, HABC has been compared with ABC, CMA-ES, PSO and GA on the real-world optimal droplet property prediction problem.

References

1. Qiu, X., Lau, H.Y.K.: An AIS-based hybrid algorithm for static job shop scheduling problem. J. Intell. Manuf. **25**(3), 489–503 (2014)
2. Karaboga, D., Basturk, B.: A powerful and efficient algorithm for numerical function optimization: artificial bee colony (ABC) algorithm. J. Glob. Optim. **39**(3), 459–471 (2007)
3. Karaboga, D., Basturk, B.: Artificial bee colony (ABC) optimization algorithm for solving constrained optimization problems. In: Melin, P., Castillo, O., Aguilar, L.T., Kacprzyk, J., Pedrycz, W. (eds.) IFSA 2007. LNCS (LNAI), vol. 4529, pp. 789–798. Springer, Heidelberg (2007). doi:10.1007/978-3-540-72950-1_77
4. Banharnsakun, A., Achalakul, T., Sirinaovakul, B.: The best-so-far selection in artificial bee colony algorithm. Appl. Soft. Comput. **11**(2), 2888–2901 (2011)
5. Gao, W., Liu, S., Huang, L.: A novel artificial bee colony algorithm based on modified search equation and orthogonal learning. IEEE Trans. Cybern. **43**(3), 1011–1024 (2013)

6. Karaboga, D., Akay, B., Ozturk, C.: Artificial bee colony (ABC) optimization algorithm for training feed-forward neural networks. In: Torra, V., Narukawa, Y., Yoshida, Y. (eds.) MDAI 2007. LNCS (LNAI), vol. 4617, pp. 318–329. Springer, Heidelberg (2007). doi:10.1007/978-3-540-73729-2_30
7. Prasad, S., Horowitz, S., Gallas, Q., Sankar, B., Cattafesta, L., Sheplak, M.: Two-port electroacoustic model of an axisymmetric piezoelectric composite plate. In: Proceedings of the 43rd AIAA/ASME/ASCE/AHS Structures, Structural Dynamics, and Materials Conference, AIAA Paper 2002–1365, AIAA, Denver, Colo, USA, April 2002
8. Blackstock, D.T.: Fundamentals of Physical Acoustics. Wiley, New York (2000)
9. White, F.M.: Fluid Mechanics. McGraw-Hill, New York (1979)

Research on Network-on-Chip Automatically Generate Method Based on Hybrid Optimization Mapping

Chao Li[1] and Yuqiang Chen[2(✉)]

[1] School of Computer, Guangdong University of Science and Technology,
Dongguan, Guangdong, China
superman_87@163.com
[2] Department of Computer Engineering, Dongguan Polytechnic,
Dongguan, Guangdong, China
chenyuqiang@126.com

Abstract. To solve underperforming particle swarm optimization algorithm for the optimization problem of discrete and easy to fall into local optimum problem in network on chip mapping algorithm, a hybrid optimization mapping Algorithm based on particle swarm optimization and genetic algorithm is proposed. It will implement separately GA and PSO operations by the two groups, by the superior individuals from GA algorithm instead of the initial random particles from PSO algorithm, which not only maintains the diversity of the group but also improves search efficiency. Simulation results based on NS-2 show that the Network-on-Chip from the automatic generation tools based on hybrid optimization mapping algorithm have a good performance in network latency, throughput, and link bandwidth optimization comparing the results of the random mapping under the same amount of computation scale.

Keywords: Hybrid algorithm · Particle swarm optimization algorithm · Genetic algorithm · Average network delay model · NS-2

1 Introduction

Along with the rapid development of semiconductor integrated technology, the transistor feature sizes rapidly shrinking, more and more complex function circuit is integrated into a single silicon wafer. Interconnect system delay, power consumption and optimize are the key factor restricting the performance of the system. Network on chip (NOC), adopting global asynchronous local synchronization network, came into being as a new type of integrated circuit architecture [1], whose core idea is to computer network technology transplanted to chip design, solve the complicated problem of communication effectively. Now, there is little study of NOC automation design and general also complete it in manual design by borrowing the synchronization design tools. The lacking of automation software seriously hindered the NOC used in the practical application [2]. At the

© Springer Nature Singapore Pte Ltd. 2016
M. Gong et al. (Eds.): BIC-TA 2016, Part II, CCIS 682, pp. 254–264, 2016.
DOI: 10.1007/978-981-10-3614-9_31

same time, the NoC mapping is an extremely important part of the NoC automation design, because the good or bad results of mapping will affect directly on the performance of the network. In view of the NoC mapping problem, researchers have proposed many excellent algorithms [3–8]. While it belongs to the NP-hard problem, there is no best algorithm to get the best optimal mapping. IN this paper, the objective function of mapping to link bandwidth priority built on the NoC platform based on the 2D-Mesh topology structure. Then, the genetic hybrid particle swarm optimization algorithm for mapping is introduced and the design of the automatic generation of NoC is completed. By analyzing their characteristics of the particle swarm optimization (PSO) algorithm and the genetic algorithm (GA), the local tracking and global optimal particle operation has great randomness in PSO algorithm. Insteading of the initial random particles in PSO algorithm by GA algorithm of fine individual, the retention of particles is fine and maintain the diversity of the population. This algorithm combines the advantages of both, which have the characteristics of rapid convergence, good optimization effect. When expanding the scale of the system, significantly in terms of performance and efficiency of the algorithm is superior to the particle swarm algorithm and genetic algorithm, as much as possible to reduce the link bandwidth requirements of the system.

2 Related Works

2.1 NoC Automatic Generation Platform

Application oriented NOC to automatically generate methods generally fall into two kinds, one kind is to map specific application to rule on the NOC structure, another method is to customize automatically irregular NOC according to the specific application. This system adopts the rules of the 2D-Mesh topology, which is the earliest and the most studied in NoC topology. In the 2D-Mesh structure, each IP core is connected to a router, which is connected by physical channel and each physical channel contains two one-way communication links. In addition, communication between IP cores can only through the router. A 4×4 2D-Mesh topology is shown in Fig. 1(a). The packets from the router in the network, according to the routing ways, enter into an input port and output from a different port. Routers usually have five I/O port - the East, West, South, North and Local. The local port is used to connect to the local IP core and the others four ports is used to connect respectively the four adjacent routers. As shown in Fig. 1(b) [9].

In this paper, the goal of automatic generation NoC is mainly to realize the link bandwidth requirements minimized. The minimum link bandwidth means minimum traffic demand, traffic and communication power consumption.

2.2 PSO-GA

In PSO algorithm, each solution of optimization problem is seen as a "particle". All the particles correspond to an adaptive value determined by the optimization

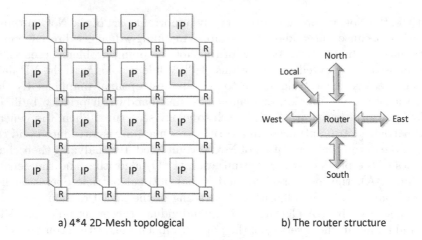

a) 4*4 2D-Mesh topological   b) The router structure

Fig. 1. NoC platform.

function. The merits of the particles are usually determined by the corresponding adaptive value size. Each particle's velocity vector decide the next direction and distance of the flight, each iteration is through following two extreme values to update their status: the first is the individual particles best solutions and another is the global best solutions which are found by the whole population.

$$v_{ij}(t+1) = w * v_{ij}(t) + c_1 r_1(t)(p_{ij}(t) - x_{ij}(t)) + c_2 r_2(t)(p_{gj}(t) - x_{ij}(t)). \quad (1)$$
$$x_{ij}(t+1) = x_{ij}(t) + v_{ij}(t+1). \quad (2)$$

Explain: the subscript j means the j dimension of particles, the subscript i means the ith particle, t means the t generation of particle, c_1, c_2 is accelerate constants, which is values generally between 0 and 2, and $r_1 \sim U(0,1)$, $r_2 \sim U(0,1)$ are two random function, they are independent of each other. By the particle update equations can know, c_1 mainly adjust the step length of direction of the particle to its own historical best position, and c_2 mainly adjust the step length of direction of the particle to the global best position. Particles search the solution space by following the current optimum particles.

The particles in PSO have the focus trend from the best location of their own history to the optimal position of group history, leading to rapid convergence of particle population. It is easy to make particles trapped in local optimum, precocious or stagnation phenomenon [10]. At the same time, the parameters has a great influence on the performance of PSO algorithm [11]. In order to solve the above problems, from the perspective of mixed strategy, this paper proposes a new genetic hybrid particle swarm optimization algorithm (PSO-GA) [12–15]. Genetic algorithm, using iterative probability mechanism, reflects the global search ability, and has a good scalability, easy to combine with other algorithms, but its search speed is slow. Rules of particle swarm algorithm are simple, easy to fall into local optimum. This article will try to combine both, trying to solve complex on-chip network mapping a NP-hard problem.

2.3 Representing Method

Using particle swarm genetic algorithm, the key problem is the representation method of the particles of PSO and the chromosome of GA. It means we must find a proper corresponding relationship between the PSO particles and PSO individual coding. Because, in the process of NoC mapping, different IP core node cannot be mapped to the same topology resources and randomly generated particles in PSO can't satisfy the constraint conditions, in order to represent the particles reasonable in the process of mapping, literature [4] put forward a new method of particle: represent the resources node location of N IP cores in 2D-Mesh network topology using a 1 dimension array by the order from left to right. The ith position values are the location of the ith a relative map IP core, and the initial position of 1 of each array. For example, a code values (1 2 3 4 6) contains 6 IP core map to 2×3 topology structure to obtain the array (a d b e c f). Because the NoC is a 2×3 2D-Mesh, we can translate the array of ID into a 2×3 matrix $\begin{pmatrix} a & d & b \\ e & c & f \end{pmatrix}$, it shows that IP core a is mapped to 2D-Mesh area 1, IP core d is mapped to the area 2, area 1~6 with the corresponding the rule 2×3 2D-Mesh. For GA, the chromosome coding using real number coding way, crossover and compile the variation cannot be carried out in accordance with the traditional genetic algorithm. Because of the traditional parents crossover method can produce illegal solution. Using a kind of unconventional intersection method, as shown in Fig. 2, the father A and the father B needs to cross, assuming that cross for after the second position, the son of A father first inherits the previous two genes, then inherits father B gene in sequence, and the inherited genes from the parent A no longer inherited from parent B in succession. The son of parent B is in the same way.

$$\text{Sun A} \quad 14|2536 \quad \text{Sun A} \quad 14|2635$$
$$\text{Sun B} \quad 26|4351 \quad \text{Sun B} \quad 26|1453$$

Fig. 2. Crossover operation.

3 Hybrid Optimization Algorithm

The hybrid optimization algorithm is an algorithm based on PSO algorithm and GA algorithm. It implements separately GA and PSO operations by the two groups, by the superior individuals from GA algorithm instead of the initial random particles from PSO algorithm, which not only maintains the diversity of the group but also improves search efficiency.

3.1 Problem Description

NoC mapping decides the mapping relation of each IP core and corresponding resource nodes in the NoC topology. Generally it needs consider some constraints, such as delay, bandwidth, power consumption etc. As shown in Fig. 2, Based on the application characteristics (AGC) that exist in the practical application and the rules of a structure of the NoC topology structure, resource nodes in the NoC topology with the IP core of AGC one-to-one correspondence, the result of mapping make sure that meet specific constraint conditions and make the whole piece on the performance of the network to achieve the optimal [16,17].

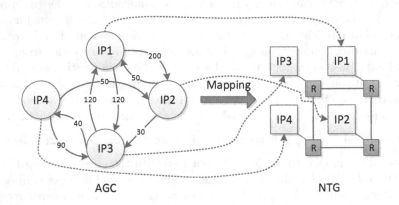

Fig. 3. AGC and NTG.

Definition 2 $n * n$ matrix first:

(1) The distance matrix $D = [d_{ij}]$ indicates the Manhattan distance between IP core i and IP core j. In Fig. 3, the Manhattan distance matrix $\mathbf{D} =$
$$\begin{bmatrix} 0 & 1 & 1 & 2 \\ 1 & 0 & 1 & 2 \\ 1 & 2 & 0 & 1 \\ 2 & 1 & 1 & 0 \end{bmatrix}$$, namely the fixed Manhattan distance between i and j.

(2) The traffic matrix $W = [w_{hk}]$ means the traffic matrix between the IP core h and IP core k in application characteristics. In Fig. 3, the traffic matrix
$$W = \begin{bmatrix} 0 & 200 & 120 & 0 \\ 50 & 0 & 30 & 0 \\ 120 & 0 & 0 & 40 \\ 0 & 50 & 90 & 0 \end{bmatrix}$$, with 0 indicates traffic of no arc connection
between the IP core.

(3) Define the set $N = \{1, 2 \ldots n\}$, with $\prod_N$ record collection of n all arranged.

So, mapped to slice on the Manhattan distance between two IP core network and the product of traffic between two IP core is $d_{ij} \times w_{\Omega(i)\Omega(j)} + d_{ji} \times w_{\Omega(i)\Omega(j)}$, which is equal to the power consumption of data transmission between any two IP core requirements. Therefore, NoC mapping problem is equivalent to looking for resources to the mapping relationship between node R and IP core function

$\Omega(v)$ to make the whole NoC the lowest power consumption:

$$\min\{\sum_{i=1}^{n}\sum_{j=1}^{n}d_{ij} \times w_{\Omega(i)\Omega(j)}\}. \tag{3}$$

Formula (3) problem can be transformed to find a permutation $p \in \prod_N$, makes:

$$Z_{mapping} = \min\{\sum_{i=1}^{n}\sum_{h=1}^{n}\sum_{j=1}^{n}\sum_{k=1}^{n}d_{ij}whkx_{ih}x_{jk}\}. \tag{4}$$

At the same time, the above formula must meet the following constraints:

$$\sum_{i=1}^{n}x_{ih} = 1 \quad (h = 1, 2, \dots, n).$$

$$\sum_{h=1}^{n}x_{ih} = 1 \quad (i = 1, 2, \dots, n).$$

$$x_{ih} = \begin{cases} x_{ih} = 1, & V_i \rightarrow R_i \\ x_{ih} = 0, & otherwise \end{cases}.$$

3.2 Algorithm Implementation

First, initial two populations (P1, P2 (initial blank), let P1 with genetic algorithm (selection, crossover, mutation), choose a percentage of the outstanding individual as a particle swarm initial population P2 (position and velocity update) of particle swarm optimization (PSO), adding some random new individual to keep the balance of population. After N iterations, finally find out the optimal solution. Based on genetic hybrid particle swarm optimization algorithm flow diagram, as shown in Fig. 4.

Algorithm detailed steps are as follows:

1. The initial population. Randomly generated a certain number of initial populations P1 and genetic algorithm applied to the population. Initialize the population P2 is empty and the particle swarm algorithm is applied to the population.
2. Calculate population P1 fitness function value. Conclusion according to the mapping problem description to decide power priority target function as fitness function, calculate the fitness of each monomer. Its fitness value corresponds with the power consumption size under some kind of mapping results. If reach the number of iterations, go to the step7.
3. Divide the population. According to the size of the fitness, the individuals are sorted in the population p1. Selected gene in p1 is relatively good individual. Proportion ϕ is selected added to the group of P2 as the particles of P2.
4. Improve population p2 individuals. Particle swarm optimization (PSO) algorithm is used to P2 of population, updating P2 each particle in the population

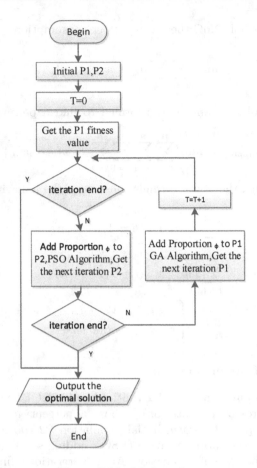

Fig. 4. PSO-GA flow chart.

according to the optimal history of the individual and the global optimal position. Then, we obtain a new species P2. Calculate the updated population P2 all particle fitness function, determine whether to the number of iterations, if meet, go to the step 7.

5. The newly added proportion ϕ randomly particle.
6. Improve population p1 individuals. Population p1 optimization using genetic algorithm, according to the selection, crossover and mutation obtain a new generation of populations p1, increase a number of iterations, transfer to step2 continue to cycle.
7. Output the optimal solution, the algorithm is to end.

4   Experiment and Result Analysis

This paper simulates automatically generated NOC based on the NS2 and analyzes its performance under different mapping algorithm [18,19].

This paper presents a network model of 8×8, used to simulate the automatically generated NOC under the condition of multi-core. In order to simplify the model, the modeling process of nodes are all the same in addition to address. Resource nodes are indicated by S $(0 \ldots n-1)$, routing nodes indicated by R $(0 \ldots m-1)$, m and n indicate the node number. Each IP core has sending and receiving ability, Buffer is considered infinite, but the inside of the router buffer is limited. The link of modeling needs to consider link delay and link maximal bandwidth. The packet size (micro) is 4 bytes and link delay is 10 Ms. Each node of the data transfer rate are sent according to their traffic, such as IP1 sent to IP2 the amount of data for 200, then set IP1 sending rate of 2 MByte/s.

In this paper, after the simulation, we obtain the Trace file, and then use awk text-processing tool to deal with it. Under different mapping results, the relationship between the average network delay, throughput and time is obtained, then, mapped it by using graphical tools gnuplot.

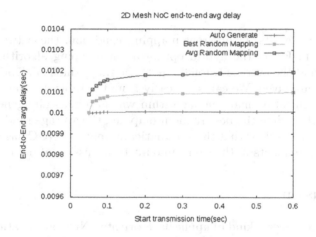

Fig. 5. Network latency contrast figure.

In order to facilitate comparison, three different topology mapping results are drawn in a picture by gnuplot.

Under the condition of different mapping, the network average delay is shown in Fig. 5. For testing the automatic generation advantage of network mapping results, using the same routing strategy, it compared with the best random map and the average random mapping. The average network delay is equal to the average of the whole network packet delay, awk is written to calculate the average network delay. Tcl script selects 11 time points to get the average delay in the process of network transmission. Comparison results showed that the same communication task, with the method of hybrid optimization mapping algorithm is used to map the topological structure of network delay time shortest, and relatively stable, and the best random mapping results are better than the

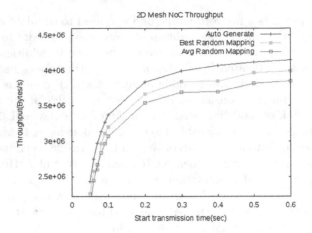

Fig. 6. Network throughput contrast figure.

average random results. In different mapping condition, the network throughput as shown in Fig. 6, the hybrid optimization mapping algorithm, the best random map and the average throughput of the three kinds of algorithm of random mapping are given. We can see clearly from the table, the same task, with the hybrid optimization mapping algorithm way automatically generated NOC throughput better than the best random map and the average random mapping network. The results show that the automatically generate NOC has less network bandwidth requirements in the same amount transmission of data.

5   Conclusion

This paper introduces a kind of application oriented NOC automatic generation process and put forward a hybrid optimization mapping algorithm. This algorithm combined with particle swarm algorithm convergence speed and the characteristics of strong global search ability of the genetic algorithm to realize NoC mapping. The NoC is automatically generated by writing the program, including NoC mapping automatically. Through NS2 simulation, compared to the average network delay under different mapping result performance, throughput, and network bandwidth, etc. The experimental results show that the hybrid optimization mapping algorithm method, in terms of total link bandwidth requirements significantly is lower than that of random mapping results link bandwidth needed for the total amount. Apparently, with the improved particle swarm optimization algorithm of automatic generation NOC method can generate NoC meet the design requirements.

Acknowledgements. The work is supported in part by Department of Education of Guangdong Province under Grant 2015KTSCX162, 2015KTSCX163.

References

1. Yakovlev, A., Vivet, P., Renaudin, M. Advances in asynchronous logic: from principles to GALS & NoC, recent industry applications, and commercial CAD tools. In: Proceedings of the Conference on Design, Automation and Test in Europe. EDA Consortium, pp. 1715–1724 (2013)
2. Rezaei, A., Zhao, D., Daneshtalab, M., et al.: Shift sprinting: fine-grained temperature-aware NoC-based MCSoC architecture in dark silicon age. In: Proceedings of the 53rd Annual Design Automation Conference. ACM, p. 155 (2016)
3. Chen, Y., Hu, J., Ling, X.: Topology and mapping co-design for complex communication systems on wireless NoC platforms. In: Proceedings of 2013 IEEE 8th Conference on Industrial Electronics and Applications, pp. 1442–1447 (2013)
4. Palaniveloo, V.A., Ambrose, J.A., Sowmya, A.: Improving GA-based NoC mapping algorithms using a formal model. In: Proceedings of 2014 IEEE Computer Society Annual Symposium on VLSI. IEEE, pp. 344–349 (2014)
5. Li, Z., Liu, Y., Cheng, M.: Solving NoC mapping problem with improved particle swarm algorithm. In: Proceedings of 2013 the Sixth International Conference on Advanced Computational Intelligence, pp. 12–16 (2013)
6. Wang, J., Li, L.I., Wang, Z., et al.: Energy-efficient mapping for 3D NoC using logistic function based adaptive genetic algorithms. Chin. J. Electron. $23(2)$, 254–262 (2014)
7. Sepúlveda, M.J., Chau, W.J., Gogniat, G., et al.: A multi-objective adaptive immune algorithm for multi-application NoC mapping. Analog Integr. Circ. Sig. Process. $73(3)$, 851–860 (2012)
8. Sepúlveda, M.J., Chau, W., Strum, M., et al.: Multi-objective artificial immune algorithm for security-constrained multi-application NoC mapping. In: Proceedings of the 14th Annual Conference Companion on Genetic, evolutionary computation, pp. 1449–1450 (2012)
9. Ling, S.H., Iu, H.H.C., Leung, F.H.F.: Improved hybrid particle swarm optimized wavelet neural network for modeling the development of fluid dispensing for electronic packaging. IEEE Trans. Ind. Electron $55(9)$, 3447–3460 (2008)
10. Dos Santos Coelho, L., Herrera, B.M.: Fuzzy identification based on a chaotic particle swarm optimization approach applied to a nonlinear yo-yo motion system. IEEE Trans. Ind. Electron $54(6)$, 3234–3324 (2007)
11. Bao, Y., Hu, Z., Xiong, T.: A PSO and pattern search based memetic algorithm for SVMs parameters optimization. Neurocomputing 117, 98–106 (2013)
12. Martínez-Soto, R., Castillo, O., Aguilar, L.T.: Type-1 and Type-2 fuzzy logic controller design using a Hybrid PSO-GA optimization method. Inf. Sci. 285, 35–49 (2014)
13. Khansary, M.A., Sani, A.H.: Using genetic algorithm (GA) and particle swarm optimization (PSO) methods for determination of interaction parameters in multicomponent systems of liquid-liquid equilibria. Fluid Phase Equilib. 365, 141–145 (2014)
14. Martínez-Soto, R., Castillo, O., Aguilar, L.T., et al.: A hybrid optimization method with PSO and GA to automatically design Type-1 and Type-2 fuzzy logic controllers. Int. J. Mach. Learn. Cybern. $6(2)$, 175–196 (2015)
15. Yu, S., Zhang, J., Zheng, S., et al.: Provincial carbon intensity abatement potential estimation in China: a PSO-GA-optimized multi-factor environmental learning curve method. Energy Policy 77, 46–55 (2015)

16. Song, T., Pan, L.: Spiking neural P systems with request rules. Neurocomputing (2016). doi:10.1016/j.neucom.2016.02.023
17. Pimpalkhute, T., Pasricha, S.: An application-aware heterogeneous prioritization framework for NoC based chip multiprocessors. In: Fifteenth International Symposium on Quality Electronic Design. IEEE, pp. 76–83 (2014)
18. Wang, X., Song, T., Gong, F., Zheng, P.: On the computational power of spiking neural P systems with self-organization. Scientific reports. doi:10.1038/srep27624
19. Reddy, T.N.K., Swain, A.K., Singh, J.K., et al.: Performance assessment of different Network-on-Chip topologies. In: Proceedings of 2014 2nd International Conference on Devices, Circuits and Systems, pp. 1–5 (2014)

Evolutionary Algorithms for Many-Objective Ground Station Scheduling Problem

Zhongshan Zhang[1]([✉]), Lining Xing[1], Yuning Chen[2], and Pei Wang[1]

[1] College of Information System and Management,
National University of Defense Technology, Changsha, China
zhongshanzhang@outlook.com, xing2999@qq.com, peigongliu@hotmail.com
[2] Department of Computer Science and Technology,
University d'Angers, Angers, France
cyn_nudt@hotmail.com

Abstract. The task planning of satellite-ground time synchronization (SGTSTP) is a complex many-objective ground station scheduling problem. In this paper, we first provide a mathematical formulation of SGT-STP. To solve this problem, we propose a decomposition-and-integration (DI) based method. In DI method, the plan horizon is evenly divided into many disjoint plan periods and all time windows are distributed to each period, based on which the task planning problem turns into a multi-period 0-1 programming problem. Then we embed DI method into evolutionary algorithm framework and propose DI based evolutionary many-objective algorithm (DI-EMOA). At last, the computational results show that the DI-EMOAs have obvious performance promotion compared with heuristic algorithm.

Keywords: Many-objective optimization · Decomposition and integration · Scheduling · Evolutionary algorithm

1 Introduction

Satellite-ground time synchronization (SGTS), realized by building the satellite-ground communication link, is a core operation in global navigation satellite system (GNSS) [1]. In this context, an optimization problem which is called task planning of satellite-ground time synchronization (SGTSTP) problem arises. SGTSTP is a complex problem due to its over-constrained nature [2–4]. Compared to those traditional ground station problems, SGTSTP is a multi-objective optimization problem. In practical applications, a heuristic algorithm called first in-first served (FIFS) algorithm was often used. In this paper, we attempt to solve SGTSTP using evolutionary algorithms (EAs).

2 Problem Formulation

We first introduce a number of notations that are useful for the problem formulation as follows.

© Springer Nature Singapore Pte Ltd. 2016
M. Gong et al. (Eds.): BIC-TA 2016, Part II, CCIS 682, pp. 265–270, 2016.
DOI: 10.1007/978-981-10-3614-9_32

t_{begin}: plan begin time
t_{end}: plan end time
$planHorizon$: $planHorizon = [t_{begin}, t_{end}]$
S: satellite set, $S = \{1, ..., s, ...\}$, whose number of elements is n_s.
M: antennas set, $M = \{1, ..., m, ...\}$, whose number of elements is n_m.
$V_{(s,m)}$: time window set, $V_{(s,m)} = \bigcup_{h=1,...,H_{sm}} [tw_{sm}^{start(h)}, tw_{sm}^{end(h)}]$. H_{sm} expresses the number of time windows between s and m in $planHorizon$.
t: SGTS task, which refers to the operation that requires ground-to-satellite communications, it can be defined by the following tetrad.

$$\{antenna, satellite, begintime, endtime\} = \{t_s, t_m, t^{start}, t^{end}\}$$

T: task set, it is defined as follows.

$$T = \bigcup_{i=1,...,I_{sm}} [t_{sm}^{start(i)}, t_{sm}^{end(i)}] = \bigcup_{l=1,...,L_m} [t_m^{start(l)}, t_m^{end(l)}] = \bigcup_{o=1,...,O_s} [t_s^{start(o)}, t_s^{end(o)}]$$

I_{sm} expresses the number of tasks between satellite s and antenna m. L_m expresses the number of tasks of antenna m. The O_s expresses the number of tasks of satellite s. Besides, $t_m^{end(l)} \leq t_m^{start(l+1)} t_s^{end(o)} \leq t_s^{start(o+1)}$.

σ_m: set-up time of antenna. In this paper, we assume that $\sigma_m = 0, \forall m \in M$.
ϕ_m: service ability of antenna. We assume that $\phi_m = 1, \forall m \in M$.
ν_s: service ability of satellite. In this paper, we assume that $\nu_s = 1, \forall s \in S$.
η_t: the shortest task duration.

Optimization objectives:

$$\max \quad avg_{duration} = \sum_{s \in S} md_s / n_s \tag{1}$$

$$\min \quad avg_{interval} = \sum_{s \in S} mI_s / n_s \tag{2}$$

$$\min \quad sd_{duration} = \sqrt{\sum_{s \in S} (md_s - avg_{duration})^2 / n_s} \tag{3}$$

$$\min \quad sd_{interval} = \sqrt{\sum_{s \in S} (mI_s - avg_{interval})^2 / n_s} \tag{4}$$

where,

$$mD_s = \sum_{o=1}^{O_s} (t_s^{end(o)} - t_s^{start(o)}) / O_s \tag{5}$$

$$mI_s = \sum_{o=1}^{O_s} (t_s^{start(o+1)} - t_s^{end(o+1)}) / O_s \tag{6}$$

Clearly, the SGTSTP is a many-objective problem (MaOP) since the objective number of SGTSTP is more than 3. These objectives could be of different scale, they are normalized with a set of parameters during computing. As observed in [5,6], such normalization can avoid solution method bias to any of the four objectives.

3 Decomposition-and-Integration Based Evolutionary Algorithms for SGTSTP

3.1 Description of Method

SGTSTP is a mixed integer nonlinear programming (MINLP) problem. As we know, the evolutionary algorithm (EA) is the popular method in solving MaOPs. However, it is difficult to use EAs. Given the challenges, we propose a decomposition-and-integration based method (DIM) for the SGTSTP as shown in Fig. 3. This method basically divides the task planning process into three main procedures: decomposition, planning and integration.

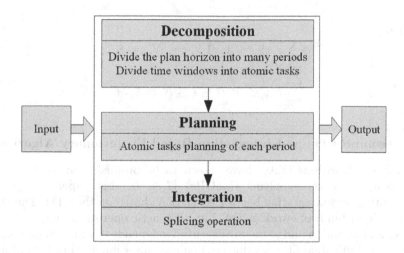

Fig. 1. Decomposition-and-integration based solution method

In the decomposition step, DIM divides the whole plan horizon into a number of plan periods with equal length ($pLength$), which are assigned with a set of time windows. A decomposed time window is associated with a pre-planning task (called "atomic task").

After decomposing, the task planning problem in each period is a combinatorial optimization problem (called single period task planning problem (SPTP)) which consists of selecting a subset of atomic tasks in order to satisfy the system objectives. The SPTP problem can be formulated as a 0-1 integer programming problem (Z-OLIP), which is a typical NP-hard problem. It should be noted that the SPTP of each period is independent and there is no influence in different periods.

The last step of DIM is to splice some adjacent tasks based on the solution of the SPTP. Two adjacent atomic tasks $t1$ and $t2$ can be spliced if they satisfy the following condition:

$$(t1_s = t2_s) \cap (t1_m = t2_m) \cap (t1^{end} = t2^{start})$$

Let N be the number of periods, nt^i_{sm} be the atomic task of period i. Let x^i_{sm} be the decision variable such that:

$$x^i_{sm} = \begin{cases} 1, nt^i_{sm} \text{ is selected} \\ 0, \text{otherwise} \end{cases}$$

Then we use the following matrix $\mathbf{T}^i_{sm}$ to express the atomic tasks of period i. Let $\sum \oplus$ be the splicing operation. The final planning scheme T can be aggregated with the following formula.

$$T = \sum_{i=1}^{N} \oplus \mathbf{T}^i_{sm} \tag{7}$$

subject to:

$$\sum_{m \in M} x^i_{sm} \leq 1, \forall 1 \leq i \leq N, s \in S \tag{8}$$

$$\sum_{s \in S} x^i_{sm} \leq 1, \forall 1 \leq i \leq N, m \in M \tag{9}$$

3.2 Decomposition-and-Integration Based Evolutionary Algorithms

Evolutionary algorithms (EAs) have shown to be promising in solving many-objective optimization problems (MaOPs) [7,8]. In this paper, we propose decomposition-and-integration based EAs (DIEA) based on the DIM. The DIEA has same algorithm framework as EA, but all genetic operations, e.g., selection, crossover and mutation and so on, are executed independently in each period, and moreover the individual fitness value is calculated after integration operation.

Given that SGTSTP is a many-objective optimization problem, evolutionary many-objective algorithm (EMOA) is a straightforward framework. In this paper, we propose a decomposition-and-integration based EMOA (DI-EMOA). In literature, MOEA/D and NSGA3 are typical and primary algorithms.

4   Computational Experiment

4.1   Test Bed Description

A computational experiment was carried out based on compass system of China, and the instance parameters are shown in Table 1.

4.2   Computational Results

All algorithms have been run for one time and we obtain the results as follows. Figures 2 and 3 show the value path plot of all obtained solutions by all algorithms in each instance, the Objective No. (1, 2, 3, 4) express respectively the objectives of (1) to (4).

Table 1. Simulation parameters

Parameters	Setting values	
	NSGA3	MOEA/D
t_{begin}		2016-01-01 00:00:00 UTC
t_{end}		2016-01-08 00:00:00 UTC
η_t		30 min
$pLength$		30 min, 60 min
$\lambda_i = (i = 1, 2, 3, 4)$		(250, 0.0125, 1, 0.04)
Antennas	Three antennas in each station of Beijing, Sanya and Kashi	
Navigation constellation	Walker24/3/2 constellation	
Crossover probability	0.8	0.8
Mutation probability	0.2	0.2
Population size	364	455
Iterations	200	200
Neighborhood vectors	-	20

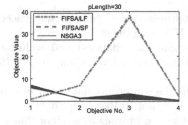 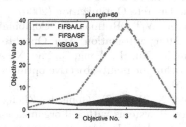

Fig. 2. Value path plot of obtained solutions by DI-NSGA3 in large scale instance

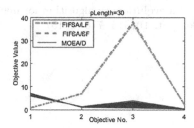 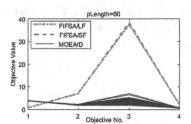

Fig. 3. Value path plot of obtained solutions by DI-MOEA/D in large scale instance

We can make the following observations:

It can be seen from Figs. 2 and 3 that the solutions obtained by DI-EMOAs outperform obviously those solutions obtained by FIFSAs for each $pLength in$ objective No. 2, 3 and 4, but have worse performance in objective No. 1. In our opinion, the reason of above phenomenon is that the DI method divided the time windows and decreased the potential task duration, which leads to smaller objective No. 1.

5 Conclusion

In this paper, we investigated the SGTSTP, which is a complex many-objective ground station scheduling problem. We proposed to handle it using a decomposition-and-integration method (DI), which transforms the task planning problem into a multi-period 0-1 programming problem. Based on the DI, we developed DI-EMOA to solve this MaOP. At last, the computational result showed that the DI-EMOAs have obvious performance promotion.

References

1. Shusen, T.: The Engineering of Satellite Navigation and Positioning, vol. 2. National Defense Industry Press, Beijing (2010)
2. Barbulescu, L., Watson, J.-P., Whitley, L.D., Howe, A.E.: Scheduling space-ground communications for the air force satellite control network. J. Sched. **7**, 7–34 (2004)
3. Pemberton, J.C., Galiber, F.: A constraint-based approach to satellite scheduling. In: Presented at the DIMACS Workshop on Constraint Programming and Large Scale Discrete Optimization (2000)
4. Scherer, W.T., Rotman, F.: Combinatorial optimization techniques for spacecraft scheduling automation. Ann. Oper. Res. **50**, 525–556 (1994)
5. Yuan, Y., Xu, H., Wang, B., Yao, X.: A new dominance relation-based evolutionary algorithm for many-objective optimization. IEEE Trans. Evol. Comput. **20**, 16–37 (2015)
6. Wang, X., Song, T., Gong, F., Zheng, P.: On the computational power of spiking neural P systems with self-organization. Sci. Rep. doi:10.1038/srep27624
7. Deb, K., Jain, H.: An evolutionary many-objective optimization algorithm using reference-point-based nondominated sorting approach. IEEE Trans. Evol. Comput. **18**, 577–601 (2014)
8. Zhang, X., Tian, Y., Jin, Y.: A knee point-driven evolutionary algorithm for many-objective optimization. IEEE Trans. Evol. Comput. **19**, 761–776 (2015)

Indicator-Based Multi-objective Bacterial Foraging Algorithm with Adaptive Searching Mechanism

Lianbo Ma[1](✉), Xu Li[2], Tianhan Gao[1], Qiang He[3], Guangming Yang[1], and Ying Liu[1]

[1] College of Software, Northeastern University, Shenyang, China
malb@swc.neu.edu.cn, {gaoth,yanggm}@mail.neu.edu.cn, 20603877@qq.com
[2] Benedictine University, Lisle, IL, USA
46272589@qq.com
[3] College of Computer Science and Engineering,
Northeastern University, Shenyang, China
heqiangcai@gmail.com

Abstract. Derived from the social foraging behavior of E. coli bacteria and the general adaptive concentration searching strategy, this paper proposes and develops a novel indicator-based multi-objective bacterial colony foraging algorithm (I-MOBCA) for complex multi-objective or many-objective optimization problems. The main idea of I-MOBCA is to develop an adaptive and cooperative model by combining bacterial foraging, adaptive searching, cell-to-cell communication and preference indicator-based measure strategies. In this algorithm, each bacteria can adopt its run-length unit to appropriately balance exploitation and exploration states, and the quality of position or solution is calculated on the basis of the binary quality indicator to determine the Pareto dominance relation. Our algorithm uses Pareto concept and preference indicator-based measure to determine the non-dominated solutions in each generation, which can essentially reduce the computation complexity. With several mathematical benchmark functions, I-MOBCA is proved to have significantly better performance over compared algorithms for solving some complex multi-objective optimization problems.

Keywords: Preference indicator · Adaptive searching · Bacterial forging algorithm · Multi-objective optimization

1 Introduction

In a multi-objective optimization scenarios, the goal of decision makers is often to find a best potential tradeoff between multiple objectives that are conflicting to each other [1]. Accordingly these objectives should be handled simultaneously, and they are generally called multi-objective optimization problems (MOPs) (usually two or three objectives) or many-objective optimization problems (MaOPs) (usually more than three objectives). Obviously, the MOPs or

© Springer Nature Singapore Pte Ltd. 2016
M. Gong et al. (Eds.): BIC-TA 2016, Part II, CCIS 682, pp. 271–277, 2016.
DOI: 10.1007/978-981-10-3614-9_33

MaOPs are more difficult to be tackled over single-objective ones because there is no single solution available for them but a set of Pareto-optimal solutions (PS) that indicate a trade-off among the objectives.

For solving of MOPs, over the past decades, many evolutionary algorithms (EA) and swarm intelligence (SI) algorithms have been proposed and developed, such as artificial bee colony algorithms (ABC) [2], artificial immune systems (AIS) [3] and bacterial foraging optimization (BFO). Currently, these nature-inspired paradigms have already been widely applied in real-world multi-objective optimizations. The aim of this work is to look to optimization and the bacterial search, and to develop more bacterially-realistic and efficient multi-objective optimization model.

Recently the bacterial foraging models and algorithms have received more and more attention, due to its research potential in optimization application. Among them, bacterial foraging optimization (BFO) is a successful population-based algorithm that draws inspiration from the foraging behavior of E. coli bacteria [4]. Until now, BFO has been developed widely, and as a problem-solving technique, the main strength of BFO is its deliberate exploitation ability, which compares favorably with other population-based algorithms [4]. Although BFO is relatively efficient and widely used in the single-objective optimization domain, there are few work to apply BFO and its variants in solving the MOPs. Compare to the huge in-depth studies of other EA and SI algorithms, such as non-dominated sorting strength genetic algorithm II (NSGAII) [5], and improved strength Pareto evolutionary algorithm (SPEA2) [6], on MOPs, how to improve the approximation to Pareto-optimal front (PF) w.r.t balance diversity and convergence is still a challenging task in MO optimization.

The motivation of this paper is to propose a quality indicator-based bacterial foraging algorithm called I-MOBFA for solving the MOPs, which combines with bacterial foraging rules (chemotaxis, cell-to-cell communication, and self-adaptive searching) and preference indicator-based multi-objective strategies. The main algorithmic concept is to integrate preference information about continuous generalizations of the dominance relation into the multi-objective search. By incorporating this hybridization, the I-MOBFA not only allows adaptation to arbitrary preference information and optimization scenarios, but also does not need any diversity preservation techniques, in contrast to Pareto-based paradigms [5].

The rest of the paper is given as follows. Section 2 describes the bacterial social foraging rules in BFO model. In Sect. 3, the quality indicator-based measure is defined and the proposed algorithm derived from the BFO model is deliberately designed. Section 4 presents the experimental studies over our proposed algorithms. Section 5 outlines the conclusions.

2 Enhanced Bacterial Foraging Optimization Model

In our proposed enhanced BFO model, the most significant foraging operation w.r.t bacterial chemotaxis is enhanced over the original BFO by re-defining:

(1) the bacterial self-adaptive searching at individual-level and (2) the bacterial cell-to-cell communication mechanism at colony-level. This model essentially extends the basic BFO to a self-adaptive and cooperative foraging model by incorporating below detailed strategies:

- **Self-adaptive searching**

Generally, an efficient foraging individual in the searching process strives to exploit finely in promising areas as well as to explore thoroughly to distant areas potentially better than the current one. In our self-adaptive searching, each bacterium is about to consistently adjust its own run-length unit adaptively according to following rules:

Rule-1: if a bacterium enters into a nutrient-rich area, its run-length unit is adjusted dynamically to a smaller one. In other words, if the fitness improvement of a bacterial in this so-called 'nutrient-rich' or 'promising' area reaches a certain precision criterion defined from last generation, then following Rule-1, this bacterium's searching is turned into the exploitation phase.

Rule-2: if the bacteriums fitness has not been improved for a certain number of evolutionary generations, then its run-length unit is augmented accordingly, which also means that this bacterium turns into the exploration phase.

The detailed pseudocode of the self-adaptive searching strategy is listed in Algorithm 1.

Algorithm 1. The self-adaptive searching strategy

1: **for** each bacterium i **do**
2:     **if** $Rule-1$ is $satisfied$ **then**
3:         $L_i(t+1) = L_i(t)/\tau$
4:         $\delta_i(t+1) = \delta_i(t)/\tau$
5:     **else if** Criterion-2 **then**
6:         $L_i(t+1) = L^{initial}$
7:         $\delta_i(t+1) = \delta_i(initial)$
8:     **else**
9:         $L_i(t+1) = L_i(t)$
10:        $\delta_i(t+1) = \delta_i(t)$
11:    **end if**
12: **end for**

- **Cell-to-cell communication**

The cell-to-cell communication aims to improve the efficiency of information sharing between foraging bacteria. Specifically, the turning direction of a bacterial turns is determined by the combined information of itself and its colony members as following:

$$A_i(t) = mA_i(t-1) + \lambda_1 R_1 \|X_{p_i} - X_i(t-1)\| + \lambda_2 R_2 \|X_{s_i} - X_i(t-1)\|, \quad (1)$$

where A_i is the turning direction at the tth iteration, where m is the inertia coefficient, X_{p_i} is the best position in its historical experience, X_{s_i} is the best position ever searched by the bacterial colony, λ_1 and λ_2 are the learning factors to adjust the impact degree of the cognitive and social components, R_1 and R_2 are random numbers uniformly falling in the scope of $[0, 1]$.

- **Enhanced chemotaxis**

By applying the self-adaptive searching in each chemotactic step, the swim amplitude of a bacterium can be adjusted self-adaptively by varying chemotactic step-size L_i dynamically to enable it towards a desired direction, which is specified determined by the cell-to-cell communication based A_i:

$$X_i(t) = X_i(t-1) + L_i(t-1)A_i(t-1), \tag{2}$$

3 The I-MOBFA Algorithm

3.1 Fitness Assignment Based on Quality Indicator

- **Binary quality indicator**

As depicted in [1], the quality indicator is a performance metric that transforms a Pareto set approximation to a real number. Especially the binary additive ε-indicator is developed to calculate the comparative quality of two Pareto set approximations relatively to each other. This method aims to provide the minimum distance by which a Pareto set approximation can be translated in each dimension in objective space such that another approximation is weakly dominated. Mathematically, this indicator can be defined as:

$$I_{s+}(A, B) = min\forall x^2 \in B, \exists\, x^1 \in B : f_i(x^1) - \varepsilon \le f_i(x^2)\, for\ i \in 1, 2, ..., m, \tag{3}$$

where i donates the fitness indexes, m is the number of objectives.

- **Fitness assignment**

This fitness assignment is re-defined by I_{s+} indicator representing the Pareto dominance relation, as below:

$$Fit_{I\varepsilon+}(i) = \sum -e^{-I_{\varepsilon+}(j-i)/(c-s)}, \tag{4}$$

where i and j donates the fitness indexes, $Fit_{I\varepsilon+}(i)$ is assigned to the new fitness. This indicator can be directly employed to measure to determine dominance relation in the multi-objective optimization.

3.2 Implantation of the I-MOBFA Algorithm

By integrating the complexity degree of these strategies, the procedure of I-MOBFA algorithm is given in Algorithm 2.

Algorithm 2. Pseudocode of the I-MOBFA algorithm

Input: - S: colony size
     - N: maximum number of iteration
     - k: zooming factor
Output: P_o : $Paretosetapproximation$ STATE Initialization: Initialize bacterial colony P with S individuals; Set the current iteration counter MaxIter=0.
1: Fitness assignment: Calculate the indicator-based fitness of each bacterium;
2: Bacterial foraging rules: Iterate the following steps:

    (1) According to self-adaptive searching strategy, each bacterium adjusts its run-length unit.
    (2) According to cell-to-cell communication, the swimming direction is determined.
    (3) Each bacterium implements enhanced chemotaxis operation

3: Termination: If MaxIter ¿ N is met, then set Po to the set of the non-dominated individuals in P, then stop.
4: Output the best solution achieved

4 Benchmark Test

4.1 Test Functions and Experimental Setup

Six benchmark functions are selected to access the performance of the proposed algorithm, including three bi-objective ZDT benchmarks (i.e., ZDT1, ZDT2 and ZDT6) and two tri-objective DTLZ instances (i.e., DTLZ1, DTLZ2 and DTLZ6) [7]. In addition, two performance metrics for multi-objective optimization are employed: (1) convergence metric- IGD metric; (2) spread metric Δ. The detailed information about these two performance metrics can be referred in [5].

Two state-of-the-art Pareto-based algorithms including NSGA-II [5], and SPEA2 [6] are compared with the proposed I-MOBFA. The common parameter configure for these three algorithms are set as following: the population size is 50, the maximum iteration number is set to 2000. For other related parameters in SPEA2 and NSGA-II, they keep the same with their original references [5,6]. For I-MOBFA, the zoom factor k is set to 10 empirically.

4.2 Computation Results and Analysis

Tables 1 and 2 report computational results achieved by I-MOBFA, NSGA-II and SPEA2 in 20 runs on two-objective and tri-objective test functions, respectively, in terms of mean, best and standard deviation of the IGD-metric and Δ-metric values.

From Tables 1 and 2 where the IGD values obtained by each algorithm on two-objective and tri-objective problems, it can be clearly observed that I-MOBFA finds the best computational results in terms of mean, best and standard deviation on most test instances. Specifically, for comparison in term of IGD, I-MOBFO perform most powerfully on ZDT1, ZDT6, DTLZ1, DTLZ2 and DTLZ6. Only on ZDT2, I-MOBFA performs a little worse than NSGAII, still

Table 1. Comparative performance by all algorithms on 30-D ZDT1, ZDT2, and 10-D ZDT6.

Benchmarks		ZDT1			ZDT2			ZDT3		
		I-MOBFA	NSGAII	SPEA2	I-MOBFA	NSGAII	SPEA2	I-MOBFA	NSGAII	SPEA2
IGD	Mean	**6.12e−3**	2.15e−2	8.21e−3	7.93e−4	**2.64e−4**	4.44e−3	**1.13e−3**	5.46e−3	1.42e−2
	Best	**5.83e−4**	6.42e−3	9.55e−4	1.11e−4	**6.88e−5**	1.02e−4	**5.22e−4**	6.18e−4	5.83e−3
	Std	**5.57e−3**	6.82e−2	6.42e−3	**1.73e−3**	6.72e−3	8.12e−3	2.03e−2	**4.03e−3**	3.42e−2
Δ	Mean	**5.33e−1**	7.03e−1	6.52e−1	**4.21e−2**	2.22e−1	5.12e−2	**1.52e−2**	5.22e−2	1.93e−1
	Best	8.21e−2	1.05e−1	**8.01e−2**	7.93e−3	8.11e−2	**7.11e−3**	**8.78e−3**	1.00e−2	6.28e−2
	Std	**1.52e−1**	5.32e−1	2.04e−1	**2.66e−2**	7.42e−2	7.32e−2	**2.45e−2**	1.94e−1	5.04e−1

Table 2. Comparative performance by all algorithms on 30-D ZDT1, ZDT2, and 10-D ZDT6.

Benchmarks		ZDT1			ZDT2			ZDT3		
		I-MOBFA	NSGAII	SPEA2	I-MOBFA	NSGAII	SPEA2	I-MOBFA	NSGAII	SPEA2
IGD	Mean	**1.45**	1.03e+1	1.11e+1	**6.43e−3**	2.21e−2	8.02e−2	**1.31e−2**	8.32e−2	7.21e−2
	Best	**6.22e−1**	5.73	8.31	**1.42e−3**	7.12e−3	1.31e−2	**7.42e−3**	1.13e−2	1.42e−2
	Std	**7.61e−1**	2.56	1.73	**4.63e−3**	3.52e−2	**1.53e−2**	1.53e−2	1.67e−2	4.56e−1
Δ	Mean	**1.89e−1**	2.64e−1	2.38e−1	**2.45e−1**	2.63e−1	5.77e−1	**2.62e−1**	2.94e−1	5.11e−1
	Best	5.53e−1	**5.42e−2**	5.45e−2	**2.53e−1**	4.14e−1	**2.04e−1**	6.67e2	6.94e−1	8.33e−2
	Std	**1.12e−1**	2.56e−1	5.33e−1	**1.94e−2**	5.21e−1	4.11e−2	**2.00e−1**	2.53e−1	4.54e−1

better than SPEA2. For comparison in term of spread metric, I-MOBFA is significantly superior to its counterparts on ZDT2, ZDT6, DTLZ2 and DTLZ6. Especially for the more complex DTLZ6, the proposed I-MOBFA exhibit obviously better approximation than NSGA-II and SPEA2 in terms of both convergence metric and spread metric. Overall, from aforementioned computational results a distinct conclusion can be outlined that the proposed I-MOBFA has great potential to tackle complex multi-objective problems.

5   Conclusion

In order to apply bacterial colony algorithm to solve multi-objective problems efficiently, this paper proposes a new indicator-based bacterial foraging algorithm called H-MOBFA based on the enhanced BFO model and the quality indicator-based measure. Specifically, In the proposed enhanced BFO model, the most important contributions are: (1) to define the bacterial self-adaptive searching that dynamically balances the exploration and exploitation phases at individual-level; (2) to define the bacterial cell-to-cell communication mechanism that improves the efficiency of information sharing at colony-level; (3) to define the Pareto dominance relation by incorporating the quality indicator-based fitness assignment mechanism. To prove the effectiveness of the proposed paradigm, the I-MOBFA has been compared experimentally with the NSGAII and SPEA2 on both two-objective and tri-objective benchmarks. Computation results reveal the proposed I-MOBFA has a great potential of being applied to a variety of complex multi-objective problems.

Acknowledgment. This work is supported by National Natural Science Foundation of China under Grant No. 61503373 and Natural Science Foundation of Liaoning Province under Grand 2015020002.

References

1. Zitzler, E., Künzli, S.: Indicator-based selection in multiobjective search. In: Yao, X., et al. (eds.) PPSN 2004. LNCS, vol. 3242, pp. 832–842. Springer, Heidelberg (2004). doi:10.1007/978-3-540-30217-9_84
2. Akay, B.: Synchronous and asynchronous pareto-based multi-objective artificial bee colony algorithms. J. Global Optim. **57**(2), 415–445 (2013)
3. Gong, M., Jiao, L., Du, H., Bo, L.: Multiobjective immune algorithm with nondominated neighbor-based selection. Evol. Comput. **16**(2), 225–255 (2008)
4. Muller, S.D., Marchetto, J., Airaghi, S., Kournoutsakos, P.: Optimization based on bacterial chemotaxis. IEEE Trans. Evol. Comput. **6**(1), 16–29 (2002)
5. Deb, K., Pratap, A., Agarwal, S., Meyarivan, T.: A fast and elitist multiobjective genetic algorithm: NSGA-II. IEEE Trans. Evol. Comput. **6**(2), 182–197 (2002)
6. Zitzler, E., Laumanns, M., Thiele, L.: SPEA2: improving the strength pareto evolutionary algorithm (2010)
7. Zhang, Q., Liu, W., Li, H.: The performance of a new version of MOEA/D on CEC09 unconstrained mop test instances. In: IEEE Congress on Evolutionary Computation, CEC 2009, 203–208 (2009)

Applying K-means Clustering and Genetic Algorithm for Solving MTSP

Zhanqing Lu[1], Kai Zhang[1,2], Juanjuan He[1,2(✉)], and Yunyun Niu[3]

[1] School of Computer Science, Wuhan University of Science and Technology,
Wuhan 430081, China
hejuanjuan@wust.edu.cn
[2] Hubei Province Key Laboratory of Intelligent Information Processing
and Real-time Industrial System, Wuhan 430081, China
[3] School of Information Engineering,
China University of Geosciences, Beijing 100083, China

Abstract. In this paper, a new algorithm is designed to solve Multiple Traveling Salesman Problem (MTSP) that avoiding the path intersection among the traveling salesmen. There are three objectives in this problem including the shortest path of every salesman, the balance of each salesmans task and avoiding the crosses of each routes. We combine the K-means algorithm and genetic algorithm. K-means algorithm is designed to divide all points into several subsets and choose the start city for the genetic algorithm, and then using GA to process every subsets in parallel. This method not only achieve these multiple objectives, but also use much less time, since we have divided all the points into several parts and make them calculated at the same time.

Keywords: MTSP · K-means · Genetic algorithm · Parallel computing

1 Introduction

Over the years, there have been a lot of researches on multiple traveling salesman problem (MTSP), but they are all about vehicle path on the road [1]. If the way of transportation becomes unmanned aerial vehicle (UAV), there is a problem needed to consider. The path intersections of traveling salesman should be avoided, that can avoid collisions of UAV. UAV can be applied to military and civil fields, such as reconnaissance and surveillance in war, extinguishing fire, spraying pesticides and delivering goods.

At present, the researches on MTSP have rarely mentioned the problem of avoiding crosses of paths. Applying these algorithms to UAV delivery will cause collisions. Moreover, most genetic algorithms for MTSP set some virtual points in order to translate MTSP to TSP [4,5]. But, if the scale of cities is large, the efficiency of the algorithm will decrease rapidly [6].

There have been many attempts to use GAs for clustering, it is also observed that these methods search faster than some of the other evolutionary algorithms

© Springer Nature Singapore Pte Ltd. 2016
M. Gong et al. (Eds.): BIC-TA 2016, Part II, CCIS 682, pp. 278–284, 2016.
DOI: 10.1007/978-981-10-3614-9_34

used for clustering [7]. The searching capability of genetic algorithms is exploited in order to search for appropriate cluster centers in the feature space such that a similarity metric of the resulting clusters is optimized [8]. There also have been attempt to use parallel method for TSP in order to increase efficiency [9]. Over the years, varieties of intelligent algorithms have been introduced: Neural Networks [10–12], genetic algorithm, clustering. Artificial neural network algorithm is a kind of pattern matching algorithm which simulates biological neural network and genetic algorithm simulates the processing of biological evolution [13–16].

Combining all these perspectives, in this paper, we designed a new algorithm which combines K-means algorithm and genetic algorithm. The purpose of K-means algorithm is preprocessing the points on MTSP. We divide the points into m clusters according to the distribution of them, and find the center point as the start point of genetic algorithm. Finally, GA is used to process every point cluster in parallel. In this case, a large scale problem is divided into several small problems by our algorithm, and genetic algorithm shows very high performance solving small scale TSP (or other combinatorial optimization). We have carried out several tests on our algorithm using many examples, and the results show that most of the problems mentioned above can be solved.

2   Multiple Traveling Salesman Problem

MTSP is an extension of TSP, which is also a NP problem. The multiple traveling salesman problem is to discuss how m salesmen visit a set of n locations, each of them is visited exactly only once while minimizing the total distance traveled by the salesmen. That is:

$$\text{Min} \sum_{i=1}^{m} \left(\sum_{j=1}^{k_i} d(v_j, v_{j+1}) + d(v_j, v_0) \right) \tag{1}$$

In formula (1), m is the number of travel agents. $K_i \epsilon(1, m)$ is the number of cities to be passed. $d(v_j, v(j+1))$ represents the distance of city j to $j+1$.

The optimal route of MTSP problem consists of M closed loop. Therefore, in this study, the MTSP translate into MTSP. The way to get the minimum total distance is getting the mining distance of every close loop. The formula is

$$\text{Min} \left(\sum_{j=1}^{k_i} d(v_j, v_{j+1}) + d(v_j, v_0) \right). \tag{2}$$

3   The Implementation of Our Algorithm

K-means to Preprocessing the Points

Our k-means algorithm divides all points into several subsets according to the Similarity of Euclidean distance.

Steps of the algorithm are:

(1) Choosing k points randomly from the n points as the initial cluster centers.
(2) For each sample i, calculate the cluster that it should belong to:

$$C^{(i)} := \arg \min_j ||x^{(i)} - U_j||^2 \tag{3}$$

(3) Re-calculate the mean of j cluster:

$$M_j := \frac{\sum_{i=1}^{m} 1\{C^{(i)} = j\}x^i}{\sum_{i=1}^{m} 1\{C^{(i)} = j\}} \tag{4}$$

(4) Repeat step (2) and step (3), until the objective function J(C, U) converge [19].

In the MTSP, there are always so many cities, and the city may be unevenly distributed. When the start point is fixed, the routes of all salesmen may cross. If the salesman is replaced by the UAV, it is dangerous because of the possible crash. So this algorithm is designed to choose one center point as the start point for genetic algorithm. In the k-means algorithm the mean M_i of all the clusters have been calculated. Now we can get the start point P for GA.

First the means M_0 of $M_i(i = 1, \ldots, K)$ is calculated:

$$M_0 = \frac{\sum_{i=1}^{K} M_i}{K} \tag{5}$$

Then select the nearest point P to the center point M_0.

Genetic Algorithm

When the problem is decomposed into a set of easier sub-problems, the scale of the population is smaller. Genetic algorithm is suitable for these sub-problems. In this algorithm we use parallel multiple threads to run multiple small scale GA in order to improve the efficiency [20], [21], with the cross probability Pc $= 0.9$, mutation probability is Pm $= 0.1$.

The Step of Our Algorithm

There are so many researches on TSP that is realized by GA. But, Sometimes the scale of point are large, and they are non-uniform distributed. The purpose of processing the points is to find k routes that are not crossed. The scale of points becomes smaller. Using genetic algorithm is a good choice. The steps of our algorithm are:

Step 1: K-means clusters all the cities of MTSP, cities are clustered into $C^{(i)}$ (i is the number of classes), and $M_{(i)}$ ($i = 1, \ldots, i, \ldots, k$) is the center of each the cluster ($M_{(i)}$ is not a point in $C^{(i)}$);

Step 2: Get the means $M_{(0)}$ of all center points $M_{(i)}$, the x coordinate of $M_{(0)}$ is $\frac{\sum_{i=0}^{c} x_i}{k}$, the y coordinate of $M_{(0)}$ is $\frac{\sum_{i=0}^{c} y_i}{k}$, then calculate the distance of every point in the MTSP problem, choose the point which has the shortest distance as the start point of every cluster.

Step 3: $C^{(i)}$ (i = 1, 2, ..., k) is seen as a small scale TSP. They are solved by using parallel GA algorithm.

The key of our algorithm is to divide the problem into some of the subproblems by using clustering processing and get the center point, in order to reduce the complexity of the problem.

4   Result and Discussion

4.1   Result

We have test on some TSP instances, and the following figures are the results we get. For The eil51 TSP problem, we set K = 4 (K is the count of salesman). Figure 1(a) shows four paths that are not crossed clearly, and the program running time is only 484 ms. And In the ch130 TSP we set K = 5, the result is shown in Fig. 1(b). The five paths are not crossed too. The data proves the validity of our algorithm.

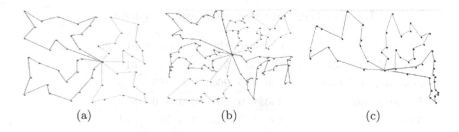

(a)   (b)   (c)

Fig. 1. The result of eil51, ch130 and att48

In Table 1, some results are listed including the total distance and the time that cost.

4.2   Discussion

In this passage, an algorithm which combines K-means and GA to solve MTSP problem is proposed. And we have compared it with GA without K-means. The following table shows the data.

GA which is used in our algorithm is compared with our algorithm. Here, set K-1 virtual points which translate MTSP to TSP like most research do. In Table 2, some data are listed to compare them. Obviously, our algorithm gets better result. As is known that when MTSP translate to TSP by using virtual points, if the scale of city become larger, the efficiency of the algorithm will reduce. It is seen in the table, when we set the same population scale and iteration number, our algorithm is much faster than the traditional GA algorithm that is used for processing MTSP. When our algorithm has got the best result, GA algorithm still needs some time to converge.

Table 1. The instances of our test

Example	Number of points	Distance (m)	Time (ms)	The count of salesman
Ulysses16	16	74	203	$K = 2$
ulysses22	22	78	250	$K = 2$
att48	48	38617	617	$K = 3$
eil51	51	518	484	$K = 4$
st70	70	791	4497	$K = 3$
eil76	76	656	2830	$K = 4$
kroE100	100	30714	7206	$K = 5$
eil101	101	787	3707	$K = 5$
bier127	127	156790	13061	$K = 6$
ch130	130	7927	13851	$K = 5$
ch150	150	8767	10782	$K = 6$
kroB150	150	38940	7172	$K = 7$
a280	280	2358	8862	$K = 7$

Table 2. The comparison of our algorithm and GA

Algorithm	Our algorithm			GA and start point is fixed		
The scale of cities	22	32	51	22	32	51
Scale of population	200	180	200	200	180	200
Iterative number	400	480	600	400	480	600
Time (ms)	250	265	484	375	784	872
Total distance (m)	78	403	514	105	1040	1180
Get best result	Yes	Yes	Yes	No	No	No
Avoid path intersection	Yes	Yes	Yes	No	No	No
The number of salesman	2	3	4	2	3	4

5   Conclusion

In this passage, a new algorithm is proposed, in order to solve MTSP problem. Combining k-means algorithm with GA, the goals are almost achieved: the shortest paths, balancing of tasks and avoiding crosses of paths. K-means algorithm is used for preprocessing the points in MTSP and GA calculates the shortest path.

What is more, after the preprocessing of k-means, the problem is broken down into several small problems. Compared with the traditional GA algorithm that deal with the MTSP, our algorithm is not only more efficient, but also avoiding the path inter-section among traveling salesmen which can be applied to designing route for UAV.

Acknowledgment. This work was supported by the National Natural Science Foundation of China (Grant Nos. 61472293, 61502012, 60974112 and 91130034), Natural Science Foundation of Hubei Province (2015CFB335), and the Beijing Natural Science Foundation (4164096).

References

1. Jin, S.: The model and algorithm of city vehicles logistic tours. Comput. Eng. Appl. **22**, 38–40 (2002)
2. Lawler, E.L., Lenstra, J.K., Shmoys, D.B.: The Traveling Salesman Problem. Wiley, Chichester (1985)
3. Alves, R.M.F., Lopes, C.R.: Using genetic algorithms to minimize the distance and balance the routes for the multiple traveling salesman problem. Evol. Comput. **41**, 44–51 (2015). IEEE
4. Shengping, J.: A hybrid genetic algorithm to solve TSP and MTSP. J. Wuhan Univ. Technol. **26**, 839–842 (2002)
5. Wang, C.: The modelling of the optimal routes for the disaster inspection. J. An-hui Inst. Mech. Electr. Eng. (2000)
6. Zhang, K., Yang, S., Li, L., Qiu, M.: Parallel genetic algorithm with OpenCL for traveling salesman problem. In: Pan, L., Păun, G., Pérez-Jiménez, M.J., Song, T. (eds.) BIC-TA 2014. CCIS, vol. 472, pp. 585–590. Springer, Heidelberg (2014). doi:10.1007/978-3-662-45049-9_96
7. Krishna, K., Murty, M.N.: Genetic K-means algorithm. IEEE Trans. Syst. Man Cybern. Part B Cybern. **29**, 433 439 (1999)
8. Maii, U., Bandyopadhyay, S.: Genetic algorithm-based clustering technique. J. Pattern Recogn. **33**, 1455–1465 (2000)
9. Li, L., Zhang, K., Yang, S., He, J.: Parallel hybrid genetic algorithm for maximum clique problem on OpenCL. In: Gong, M., Pan, L., Song, T., Tang, K., Zhang, X. (eds.) BIC-TA 2015. CCIS, vol. 562, pp. 653–663. Springer, Heidelberg (2015). doi:10.1007/978-3-662-49014-3_58
10. Song, T., Zeng, X., Liu, X.: Asynchronous spiking neural P systems with rules on synapses. Neurocomputing **151**, 1439–1445 (2015)
11. Zhang, X., Pan, L., Pun, A.: On universality of axon P systems. IEEE Trans. Neural Netw. Learn. Syst. **26**, 2816–2829 (2015)
12. Pan, L., Wang, J., Hoogeboom, H.J.: Spiking neural P systems with astrocytes. Neural Comput. **24**, 805–825 (2012)
13. Liu, X., Li, Z., Liu, J., Liu, L., Zeng, X.: Implementation of arithmetic operations with time-free spiking neural P systems. IEEE Trans. NanoBiosci. **14**, 617–624 (2015)
14. Zeng, X., Zhang, X., Song, T., Pan, L.: Spiking neural P systems with thresholds. Neural Comput. **26**, 1340–1361 (2014)
15. Xu, J.: Probe machine. IEEE Trans. Neural Netw. Learn. Syst. **27**, 1405–1416 (2016)
16. Zhang, X., Ye, T., Cheng, R., Jin, Y.: An efficient approach to non-dominated sorting for evolutionary multi-objective optimization. IEEE Trans. Evol. Comput. **19**, 201–213 (2015)
17. Torkey, F.A., Ramadan, M.A.: An efficient enhanced k-means clustering algorithm. J. of Zhejiang Univ. Sci. A **7**, 1626–1633 (2006)

18. Kanungo, T., Mount, D.M., Netanyahu, N.S.: An efficient k-means clustering algorithm: analysis and implementation. IEEE Trans. Pattern Anal. Mach. Intell. **24**, 881–892 (2002)
19. Huang, Z.: A fast clustering algorithm to cluster very large categorical data sets in data mining. In: Research Issues on Data Mining & Knowledge Discovery (1998)
20. Song, T., Zheng, P., Wong, D.M., Wang, X.: Design of logic gates using spiking neural P systems with homogeneous neurons and astrocytes-like control. Inf. Sci. **372**, 380–391 (2016)

A Multi-objective Optimization Algorithm Based on Tissue P System for VRPTW

Wenbo Dong[1], Kang Zhou[1(✉)], Huaqing Qi[2], Cheng He[3], Jun Zhang[1], and Bosheng Song[4]

[1] School of Math and Computer, Wuhan Polytechnic University, Wuhan 430023, Hubei, China
dongwb7@foxmail.com, zhoukang_wh@163.com, jzhang111@msn.com
[2] Department of Economics and Management, Wuhan Polytechnic University, Wuhan 430023, Hubei, China
qihuaqing@sohu.com
[3] Key Laboratory of Image Information Processing and Intelligent Control, Huazhong University of Science and Technology, Wuhan 430074, Hubei, China
chenghehust@gmail.com
[4] School of Automation, Huazhong University of Science and Technology, Wuhan 430074, Hubei, China

Abstract. Vehicle routing problem with time windows has an important practical significance, but it is NP-Hard problem. In order to solve the problem, an optimization algorithm based on P system is proposed. The encoding of glowworm's location is considered as evolutionary object and discrete glowworm evolution mechanism and variable neighborhood evolution mechanism are used as sub-algorithms. In this paper, the motion equations and related motion rules of glowworm algorithm are improved to optimize the performance of the algorithm. Meanwhile, in order to enlarge the search area of solution space and improve the precision, the variable neighborhood evolution mechanism is redesigned. Cell communication rules are used to exchange information between cells. Moreover, this paper introduced the concept of Pareto dominance to evaluate the advantages and disadvantages of the object, as a result, this method returns not a single non-dominated solution but a set of no-dominated solutions. At last, by solving the different Solomon numerical examples and simulation results show that the algorithm is easier to jump out of local optimal both achieves very good results in the number of vehicles and distance cost, besides, generates a lot of new solutions which are different from the database. This algorithm has the features of faster convergence rate and accurate precision, and it is competitive with other heuristic or metaheuristic algorithms in the literature.

Keywords: Tissue P system · Discrete glowworm evolution mechanism · Multi-objective VRPTW · Variable neighborhood evolution mechanism · Cell communication rules · Pareto

© Springer Nature Singapore Pte Ltd. 2016
M. Gong et al. (Eds.): BIC-TA 2016, Part II, CCIS 682, pp. 285–301, 2016.
DOI: 10.1007/978-981-10-3614-9_35

1   Introduction

Membrane computing (MC) aims to research the calculation model which is abstract by biological cells and tissue or organ which is made up of cells. MC has many characteristics, such as distributed, parallel and uncertainty [1], it is proposed by Gheorghe Păun, also known as P system [2]. Roughly speaking, there are three types of P systems, that is, cell-like P systems, tissue-like P systems, and neuron-like P systems [3–6]. They provide distributed parallel and nondeterministic computing devices. Membranes delimit space to different regions, and objects evolve according to evolution rules in each region [7–9]. Evolutionary Computation (EC) is based on Darwin's theory of evolution, it is a type of self-organizing, self-adaption and self-learning artificial intelligent techniques that simulate evolutionary process and mechanism, mainly includes Genetic algorithm (GA), evolutionary strategy and swarm intelligence optimization represented by particle swarm optimization, ant colony optimization and so on. MC and EC are important branch in the field of natural computation, EC has a very wide applications, and MC has the solid theoretical foundation, it has importance significant and broad prospects to explore the intersection of EC and MC. MA is a hybrid optimization algorithm that combines with concepts and principles of the membrane system structure, evolution rules and calculation mechanism and it is also a bridge between MC and practical application [10,11]. A large number of studies have shown that many MC models have the computation ability as the Turing machine in theory, and even beyond the limitations of Turing machine [12]. Therefore, because of many advantages, MC develops very rapidly, and now is one of research hotspot in the field of intelligent optimization [13,14]. Even MC attracts the attention of many scholars in the world, there are relatively few papers about this question in Chinese literatures. And many articles are focusing on studying the theory of MC, the research of MA is not thorough, a lot of research has great value in theory, but it is not very good to be applied in practical problems, how to apply it in all kinds of practical engineering problems, for example, Vehicle routing problem with time windows (VRPTW), is important question in the field of MC.

VRPTW is an NP-hard problem that can be applied to many distribution systems, such as logistics distribution, electric power dispatching problems, postal deliveries and bus routing problem, etc. In the literature, many heuristic or meta-heuristic approaches have been proposed for solving VRPTW. At present, the method can be divided into two types: exact algorithm and heuristic algorithm [15]. With the enlargement of customers, The calculation of the exact algorithm will show exponential growth. The scholars mainly concentrate on the heuristic algorithm now, such as genetic algorithm [16], ant colony optimization [17] and tabu search algorithm [18] and so on [19,20] are all used to solve VRPTW. Glowworm Swarm Optimization algorithm (GSO) is a new type of intelligent bionic swarm optimization algorithm [21], Now studies of GSO for continuous optimization problems are not sufficient, but primary studies have shown its good performance [22]. Discrete Glowworm Swarm Optimization algorithm (DGSO) has been successfully to solve the TSP [23] and VRP [24], and shows strong vitality. However, GSO is a global search algorithm, it suffers a shortcoming of precision, and variable neighborhood evolutionary mechanism (VNEM) is a kind of local search algorithm which has strong ability of local search [25], so VNEM is introduced to do local-search for the chromosome in every generation of the evolution process, this can make up the weakness of GSO in its local-search and this improves the convergence of the algorithm. The new algorithm provides not only with strong global search capability of GSO, but also with strong local search capability of VNEM.

According to the above mentioned problems and the characteristics of P system, an optimization algorithm based on P system is proposed in this paper. The algorithm employs a tissue P system which consists of three cells as computing framework, two of these cells use discrete glowworm evolution mechanism (DGEM) and variable neighborhood evolution mechanism (VNEM) as a sub-algorithm, another cell is used as the output cell. So, the algorithm is also called PDVA. In the system, the three cells are placed in the same environment, every cell have different functions and they encode the glowworm's location in the cells, and they are able to use this to predict where each glowworm is standing. So the encoding of glowworm's location is considered as evolutionary object. Transport rules are adopted as a way to achieve the information communication between cells or cells and environment. Furthermore, In order to improve the performance of DGEM, the motion equations of the glowworm and related algorithms are improved. Meanwhile, in order to enlarge the search area of solution space and improve the precision, the VNEM is redesigned. This paper introduced the concept of Pareto dominance to evaluate the advantages and disadvantages of the object, as a result, this method returns not a single non-dominated solution but a set of no-dominated solutions, which provides powerful decision support to the decision-maker. Our algorithm is tested by Solomon's benchmark problems. Compared with the best known solutions in the literature, our algorithm is competitive in terms of its solution quality, and it is proved to be an effective method for solving multi-objective VRPTW, and shows a unique high efficiency.

2   Model Formulation

Multi-objective VRPTW can be defined as a set of identical vehicles denoted by V, and a directed graph $G = (C, A)$, which consist of a set of customers, C. The vehicles are located at the depot. It is assumed that there is no limitation on the number of vehicles that can be used, but in order to facilitate the model formulation the maximum possible size of the fleet is denoted by K. The actual number of vehicles will be found after solving the model that it would be equal to the number of routes in the traffic network. Let us assume there are $N + 1$ customers, $C = \{0, 1, 2, ..., N\}$ and for simplicity, depot is denoted as customer 0. A route is defined as staring from depot, going through a number of customers and ending at the depot. Every customer in the network must be visited only once by one of the vehicles, since each vehicle has a limited capacity $q_k(k = 1, ..., K)$, and each customer has a varying demand m_i, q_k must be greater than or equal to the summation of all demands on the route traveled by that vehicle k. On the other hand, any customer i must be serviced within a predefined time interval $[e_i, l_i]$, limited by an earliest arrival time (e_i) and latest arrival time (l_i). Vehicle arriving later than the latest arrival time are penalized while those arriving earlier than the earliest arrival time incur waiting. Assuming waiting time is permitted at no cost. The objective is to determine a feasible route schedule which minimizes the number of vehicles and the total travel distance [26, 27].

In order to formulate the model, other following notations are defined: $d_{ij} = distance$ from customer i to customer j; $Q = $ maximum load of the vehicle; $q_i = $ demand of customer i; $t_i = $ arrive time of customer i; $t_{ij} = $ travel time from i to j; $st_i = $ service time at i; $w_i = $ waiting time at i; x_{ijk} is equal to 1 if vehicle k drives from i to j and 0 otherwise [28].

Therefore, after establishment of target levels which represent optimistic aspiration levels for each objective, this multi-objective problem is formulated as a goal programming model. Hence, the following goals, in accordance with the above mentioned objectives, are defined:

$$min f_1 = \sum_{k=1}^{K} \sum_{i=0}^{n} \sum_{j=0}^{n} d_{ij} x_{ijk} \tag{1}$$

$$min f_2 = \sum_{j=0}^{n} \sum_{k=1}^{K} x_{0jk} \tag{2}$$

Subject to:

$$\sum_{i=1}^{n} q_i y_{ik} \leq Q; \forall k \in I \tag{3}$$

$$\sum_{i=0}^{n} x_{ijk} = y_{jk}; j = 1, 2, \cdots, n; \forall k \in I \tag{4}$$

$$\sum_{j=0}^{n} x_{ijk} = y_{jk}; i = 1, 2, \cdots, n; \forall k \in I \tag{5}$$

$$\sum_{k=1}^{K} y_{ik} = \begin{cases} 1 & i = 1, 2, \cdots, n; \forall k \in I \\ K & i = 0 \end{cases} \tag{6}$$

$$\sum_{i \in S} \sum_{j \in S} x_{ijk} \leq |s| - 1; \forall S(2 \leq |S| \leq n - 1) \subseteq V/0 \tag{7}$$

$$t_i + t_{ij} + st_i + w_j \leq t_j; i, j = 0, 1, \cdots, n; \forall k \in I \tag{8}$$

$$e_i \leq t_i \leq l_i; i = 1, 2, \cdots, n \tag{9}$$

Constraints (1) and (2) refer to goals 1 and 2. Constraint (3) is the capacity constraint. Constraints (4) and (5) define that every customer node is visited only once by one vehicle. Constraints (6)–(7) secures every route starts and ends at the central depot. Constraints (8)–(9) define the time window.

3 Multi-objective Optimization Algorithm Based on Tissue P System

It is not ideal to use DGEM or VNEM [25] to solve multi-objective VRPTW, so a tissue P system is designed to combine DGEM and VNEM for solving multi-objective VRPTW together. This algorithm has overcome the disadvantage of DGEM effectively, meanwhile, it has enhanced the capability of overall searing and local optimum jumping from VNEM. At the same time, this system also need a cell which can be dedicated to output the optimal solution, so this paper designed a tissue P system whose degree is three. The tissue P system can be described as the follow:

$$\prod = (O, \sigma_1, \sigma_2, \sigma_3, syn, i_0)$$

where:

(1) $O = \{x_1, x_2, \cdots, x_{NP}\}$, $x_i(i = 1, 2, \cdots, NP)$ is an integer string – that is the positional encoding of glowworm, NP is the number of integer string.
(2) $syn = \{(2,3), (3,1), (3,2)\} \subseteq \{1,2,3\} \times \{1,2,3\}$ is the channel sets between cells, among them, using two-way channel between cell 2 and 3, using one-way channel between cell 3 and 1.
(3) $i_0 = 1$ represents that cell 1 is output cell.
(4) $\sigma_i(i = 1, 2, 3)$ represents a cell, it can be represented by following multi-tuple

$$\sigma_i = (Q_i, s_{i,0}, w_{i,0}, R_i)$$

where:

a. $Q_i = (s_{i,0}, s_{i,1}, \cdots, s_{i,t_{max}})$, $s_{i,j}$ is the state of σ_i at j times of iterations in cell B, t_{max} is the maximal number of iterations.
b. $s_{i,0} \in Q_i$ is initial state, $w_{i,0} = \{x_{i,1}^0, x_{i,2}^0, \cdots, x_{i,NP_i}^0\}$ is the initial object sets in the cell, NP_i is the number of objects.
c. R_i represents rule sets, including the evolution rules and communication rules whose function is transfer an object from one cell to another.

Figure 1 shows the network structure of tissue P system. Environment contains three cells, they are marked with label 1, 2 and 3 respectively. The arrow in Fig. 1 represents the channel and communication direction between interconnected cells. There is a two-way channel between cells 2 and 3 which provides a platform for information exchanges and sharing. There is a one-way channel from the cell 3 to 1. Only cell 1 could transport object from the cell to the environment through one-way channel.

In this paper, the object in cell is an integer string – that is, the positional encoding information of glowworm; Each cell used their evolution rules to evolve object; Cells achieve information exchange and share through communication channels in the process of evolution, and cells use evolutionary mechanism to evolve object, then turn it to the corresponding cells through communication rules, used to guide the next calculation.

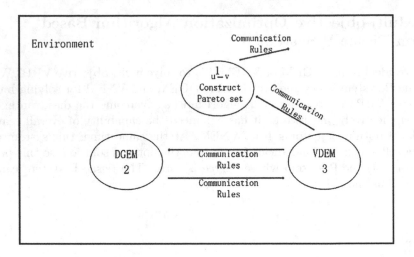

Fig. 1. Tissue P System with a degree of three

3.1 Objects

In the cells, the location encoding of glowworm is taken into account as an evolutionary object, it is represented by an integer string, the length is the number of customers. Each point in the string is the integer node number originally assigned to that customer. The sequence of the points in the string is the order for visiting these customers. It can be represented as $(c_1, c_2, \cdots, c_i, \cdots, c_n)$, where $c_i \in [1, n]$.

In the beginning, a certain number of objects are randomly generated in cell 2. In the process of calculation, cell 1 keeps record the current optimal object the system have found so far, namely E_{best}. E_{bset} is a maximum value of the system in the beginning.

3.2 Evolution Mechanism in Cell 1

Cell 1 is the output cell and when the system stops running, it should returns a set of Pareto non-dominated solutions. In the cell, there is a object rewrite rules, $[u \rightarrow v]$, the rule runs suggests that: u is replaces by v. The main functions of the cell is: Comparing u and E_{best}, where u is an object transferred from cell 3, E_{best} is the global optimal object stored in cell 1. If $u \succ E_{best}$, E_{best} is replaced by u; Otherwise, u is discarded to the environment.

3.3 Evolution Mechanism in Cell 2

In cell 2, the sub-algorithm is DGEM, in which this paper redefines glowworms' motion equation and its related algorithms. These definitions reflect a more realistic evolution process, and they greatly improve the computing efficiency.

(1) A decoding operator based on greed construction method

In order to improve the efficiency of decoding, this paper proposes a kind of decoding operator based on greed construction method. When decoding a sequence, the system only need to insert the customers into the path as much as possible, if a customer does not satisfy the constraints of time window or capacity, the system will open up a new path to service him. In this way, until all the customer are serviced. This decoding method can make the decoded path and encoded path are consistent, and the number of vehicles can be dynamically obtained in the process of decoding. It can achieve the automatic optimization of the number of vehicles, without the need to set the number of vehicles in advance. For example, there is a string 361857294, it is decoded as: route 1, $0 \rightarrow 3 \rightarrow 6 \rightarrow 0$; route 2, $0 \rightarrow 1 \rightarrow 8 \rightarrow 5 \rightarrow 7 \rightarrow 0$; route 3, $0 \rightarrow 2 \rightarrow 9 \rightarrow 4 \rightarrow 0$.

(2) The innovation of distance between the glowworms

The differences between the two codes are the superposition of differences of corresponding customers. Therefore, how to depict the differences between the two codes is a key problem that to design distance between glowworm individuals. Because the actual difference between the two customer points is the actual distance between the two customers, therefore, in order to better describe and reflect the actual distance between glowworm individuals, in this paper, the actual differences between the two customers is arc distance of the two customers. From this the new distance between two glowworms is designed.

Assuming that there are two codes, where i and j denotes glowworm respectively, t is a certain time. So, the difference degree of encoding can be defined according to the following form:

$$\delta_{ij}(t) = \frac{\sum\limits_{k=1}^{n} d_{ij}(t,k)}{M} \tag{10}$$

where $d_{ij}(t,k)$ is arc distance between i and j, k is the current dimension; M is the sum of the maximum in each row in the weight matrix; Therefore, $\delta_{ij}(t) \in [0,1]$.

Based on the above definition of the difference degree, the calculation formula of distance between i and j can be designed as follows:

$$Dist_{ij}(t) = c \times \delta_{ij}(t) \tag{11}$$

where c is a constant, $\delta_{ij}(t)$ is the difference degree of encoding.

The definition of distance reflects the actual differences between the two codes, and it lays a foundation for the following design of location update rules too.

(3) The innovation of the location update rules

In the literature [27], glowworm's location update did not reflect the moving length of the glowworm fly to the moving object. In order to inherit the concept of step of GSO in the process of discretization, this paper designed the flight step length 's' based on the concept of the distance between the glowworm individuals, update rules are given which indicate that glowworms fly to the moving objects and their step length is s.

In the movement phase, system randomly generates an array $r(s) = (r_1, r_2, \cdots, r_s)$ whose length is s, where $r_i \neq r_j (i, j \in [1, n])$. For glowworm $x = (x_1, x_2, \cdots, x_n)$, moving object $y = (y_1, y_2, \cdots, y_n)$ and a random number r_k in $r(s)$, the position encoding update is as follows:

$$temp = x[r_k]; x[r_k] = y[r_k]; x[y[r_k]] = temp, \tag{12}$$

where $k \in [1, s]$. The code update methods inherited the position update formula of GSO. According to the distance between glowworm x and y, the distance x fly to y is 's' in each iteration step, and then the differences of encoding between x and y will be reduced s units correspondingly. After a certain iterative process, the encoding between x and y will tend to be more consistent, that is to say, x fly to the position where y stay on.

3.4   Evolution Mechanism in Cell 3

In cell 3, the sub-algorithm is VNEM. The purpose of VNEM is making the object u to be a local optimal object, and transfer the g_{best} (global solution) to the cell 2 and 1 to guide the next operation. The concrete operation steps are described as follows: will u as the initial evolution object, and select one at random from the following three kinds of neighborhood operations, and the neighborhood search is performed to improve object. Finally, after evolution operations, the new object will be transported to the cell 1 and 2 at the same time.

Evolutionary operation:

(1) Exchange: Let us assume there are two different numbers a and b which are generated randomly, exchange encoding two numbers represent.
(2) Inversion: Let us assume there are two different numbers a and b which are generated randomly, invert encoding between there two numbers.
(3) Insert: Let us assume there is a number b which is generated randomly, it will be inserted into the front of encoding.

3.5   Cell Communication Rules

Cell-to-cell communication rules provide good foundation for information exchange and share, and they are implemented through the channel between the cells. In the tissue P system, there are the following three kinds of communication rules to improve the function of system.

Rule 1: $(2, u/v, 3)$

This is a two-way transport rule between cell 2 and cell 3. The result of the execution is that: object u is transferred from cell 3 to cell 2, and object v is transferred from cell 2 to cell 3.

Rule 2: $(3, u/\lambda, 1)$

This is a one-way transport rule between cell 3 and cell 1. The result of the execution is that: object u is transferred from cell 3 to cell 1, where λ is a null object.

Rule 3: $(1, v/\lambda, 0)$

This is a one-way transport rule between cell 1 and the environment. The result of the execution is that: object v is transferred from cell 1 to the environment, where λ is a null object.

In tissue P system, DGEM is adopted to improve the objects in cell 2. Then object u in cell 2 is transported to the cell 3 through rule 1, it will be optimized by VNEM in cell 3. The new object v which is improved will be transported to the cell 2 and cell 1 through rule 1 and rule 2. And then cell 2 continue to perform the following steps to optimize the v. In cell 1, v and E_{best} are compared, if $v > E_{best}$, v is added to the Pareto non-dominated solutions and the rewrite rule defined in cell 1 begin to execute to replace the original, i.e. $E_{best} \leftarrow v$; otherwise, v will be discarded to the environment. This internal transfer relationship provides a co-evolution mechanism for system, and it is helpful to enhance the convergence performance and optimization capacity of the system.

3.6 Stop and Output

Stop condition: the maximal number of iteration.

Output: Pareto non-dominated solutions set.

3.7 P System Steps

In this section, the steps of P system are described as follows:

Algorithm 1. P System Steps

Step 1. Built the tissue P system as shown in Fig. 1; Initialize a certain number of glowworms in cell 2 to form the populations; And set the following parameters: maximum number of iterations, $l_i(0)$, $r_d^i(0)$, γ, r_s, ρ, β, s, n_t.

Step 2. Determine whether meet the stop condition. If meet, the system stops running; Otherwise, continue to step.

Step 3. Object evolution in the cell. Cell 2 performs evolution operations on its internal objects. After the evolution, the object u_i which is in cell 2 is transported to cell 3 through the cell channel. It can achieve the information communication among the cells.

Step 4. Continue to optimize u_i use VNEM in cell 3, and then the new object v_i is transported to cell 2 and cell 1 by cell communication rules.

Step 5. Continue to execute the steps of cell 2, and then begin to optimize u_{i+1}.

Step 6. Cell 1 begin to built Pareto non-dominated solution sets. Comparing u and E_{best}, where u is an object transferred from cell 3, E_{best} is the global optimal object stored in cell 1. If $u \succ E_{best}$, u will join the Pareto non-dominated solutions and replace the original E_{best}; Otherwise, u will be discarded to the environment.

Step 7. Determine whether meet the stop condition. If meet, the system stops running; Otherwise, go to step 3.

Step 8. Store the Pareto non-dominated solution sets in a file.

---

4   Experimental Analysis

In order to test the correctness and validity of algorithm, and make the results more comparable and compelling, the paper uses benchmark instances to test the proposed algorithm. Research data mainly come from the international recognized VRPTW database. There are three different size of data sets (25, 50 and 100) in database. Each data set contains 56 test problems, and they were divided into six categories: C1, C2, R1, R2, RC1, RC2. Problems in sets R1 and R2 have the customers' locations generated randomly over a square. Problems in sets C1 and C2 have the clustered customers whose time windows generated based on a known solution. Problems in set RC1 and RC2 have a combination of randomly placed and clustered customers. Problems in sets R1, C1 and RC1 have narrow time windows and a small capacity of the vehicle, while problems in sets R2, C2 and RC2 have larger time windows and a larger capacity of the vehicle.

Computer processor: AMD A6-3420M APU with Radeon (tm) HD Graphics 1.5 GHz; Computer RAM: 4 GB; Operating system: Windows 7 64-bit; Programming software: VC 6.0; Programming language: C/C++.

The following are the parameters of the algorithm: $\rho = 0.6$, $\gamma = 0.7$, $\beta = 0.05$, $n_t = 20$, $l_0 = 15$, $r_0 = 7$, $iteration = 200$, $population\ size = 100$.

4.1   Simulation Experiment

In this section, some relative examples in the database are simulated. There are 25, 50 and 100 customers of six type problems in the database. The results are shown in Table 1.

As can be seen from Table 1, the proposed algorithm can solve the multi-objective VRPTW very well. The algorithm returns a lot new solutions which are different from the reference solutions, and they are Pareto solutions which provide powerful decision support to the decision-maker. In some numerical examples, there is a single Pareto solution, that is to say, vehicles and total distance achieve the optimal at the same time.

As can be seen from Table 1, this algorithm returns a single non-dominated solution in some instances, this section provides an in-depth analysis of these situations based on the numerical examples. In the process of simulation, we found that some examples with the distribution of the number of vehicles increase (decrease) as the total distance corresponding decrease (increase), while there are other examples with the distribution of the number of vehicles increase (decrease)

Table 1. The non-dominated solutions of PDVA

Instances	Best known		PDVA		Instances	Best known		PDVA		Instances	Best known		PDVA	
	V	C	V	C		V	C	V	C		V	C	V	C
R103.25	5	454.6	4	473.4	C101.100	10	827.3	10	828.9	RC104.100	-	-	11	1307.1
			5	455.7				9	1050.1					
R103.50	9	772.9	8	853.1	C103.100	10	826.3	10	1155.3	RC106.100	-	-	15	1583.7
			5	455.7				9	1030.1					
R105.25	6	530.5	5	556.7	C201.50	3	360.2	2	485.5	RC201.25	3	360.2	2	432.3
			6	531.5				3	361.7					
R108.100	-	-	11	1048.4	C202.25	2	214.7	1	223.3	RC201.50	5	684.8	3	919.2
			6	531.5				2	215.5				4	880.8
R109.25	5	441.3	4	460.5	C202.50	3	360.2	2	403.8	RC201.100	9	1261.8	7	1539.9
R111.25	5	428.8	4	429.7	C203.25	2	214.7	1	223.3	RC202.50	3	338	1	551.6
													2	376.1
R112.100	-	-	11	1089.4	C203.50	3	359.8	2	414.3	RC202.100	8	1092.3	5	1519.9
													6	1412.1
R201.25	4	463.3	2	523.7	C204.25	2	213.1	1	213.9	RC203.25	3	326.9	1	432.5
R201.50	6	791.9	4	879.3	C205.25	2	214.7	1	297.5	RC203.50	4	555.3	2	715.5
								2	215.5				3	626.4
R201.100	8	1143.2	7	1375.4	C205.50	3	359.8	2	444.1	RC203.100	-	-	4	1269.8
								3	361.7				5	1187.1
R202.25	4	410.5	2	457.9	C206.25	2	214.7	1	285.4	RC204.25	3	299.7	1	327.5
R202.50	5	698.5	3	826.1	C206.50	3	359.8	2	484.5	RC204.50	3	444.2	2	482.9
								3	361.4					
R202.100	-	-	5	1328.8	C207.25	2	214.5	1	274.7	RC204.100	-	-	3	1084.9
			6	1245.9									4	932.1
R203.25	3	391.4	2	400.4	C207.50	3	359.6	2	427.1	RC205.25	3	338	2	386.2
R203.50	5	605.3	2	766.8	C208.25	2	214.5	1	229.8	RC205.50	5	630.2	3	910.2
			3	689.7										
R203.100	-	-	4	1123.1	R211.100	—	-	3	975.1	RC205.100	7	1154	6	1634.2
			5	1066.7				4	913.5					
R204.25	2	355	1	388.6	R211.50	3	535.5	2	585.6	RC206.25	3	324	1	482.0
R204.100	-	-	3	875.4	R211.25	2	350.9	1	361.7	RC206.50	5	610	3	717.2
R205.25	3	393	1	504.5	R210.100	-	-	4	1092.1	RC207.25	3	298.3	2	308.6
			2	405.9				5	1050.9					
R205.50	4	690.1	3	746.7	R210.50	4	645.6	2	806.4	RC207.50	4	558.6	2	786.6
								3	629.9				3	599.7
R205.100	-	-	4	1154.2	R210.25	3	404.6	1	516.0	RC207.100	-	-	4	1336.3
			5	1156.7				2	413.6				5	1212.6
R206.25	3	374.4	1	413.2	R207.25	3	361.6	1	398.0	RC208.50	-	-	2	535.8
R206.50	4	632.4	2	780	R209.100	-	-	4	1071.7	RC208.100	-	-	3	1192.9
			3	701.6				5	1065.6				4	947.1
R206.100	-	-	4	1089.4	R209.50	4	600.6	2	724.3	R209.25	2	370.7	1	418.3
			5	1043.3				3	673.2					
R207.50	-	-	2	626.7	R208.50	-	-	2	508.6	R208.100	-	-	3	815.9

Note: '-' represents that there is no reference solution in the database

as the total distance corresponding increase (decrease). Figure 2 shows the relationship between vehicles and total distance. So when there is a positive correlation between vehicles and total distance, the algorithm will return a single non-dominated solution.

As shown in Fig. 2, in R201, there is a negative relationship between vehicles and total distance. Each vertical bar said in the current number of vehicles, the different iterative values of total distance. The number of vehicles increased from 7 to 10, and the total distance is reduced from 1478.19 to 1326.31; In RC101, there is a positive relationship between vehicles and total distance. The number

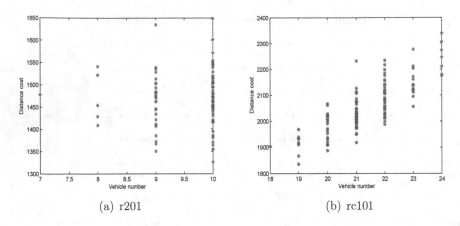

(a) r201   (b) rc101

Fig. 2. R201 (a) and RC101 (b) solution set distribution

of vehicles increased from 7 to 10, and the total distance is reduced from 1478.19 to 1326.31; In RC101, there is a positive relationship between vehicles and total distance. The number of vehicles reduced from 24 to 19, and the total distance is reduced from 2173.59 to 1835.95.

4.2 Performance Analysis of PDVA

In order to test the performance of the algorithm, we begin to study the performance of the algorithm from the following two aspects.

(1) Compared with other algorithms

Table 2 shows comparison results of some examples.

As can be seen from Table 2, compared with several numerical tests in varied scales and position of points, the result shows that our algorithm can search multiple Pareto solutions. When the problem's size is 25, the algorithm can find out the optimal solutions of different kinds of examples, some solutions as compared with the reference solution are Pareto solutions, or they have the same number of vehicles, but the error is less than 0.5%. It also can be seen from table that when the number of vehicles is same, the difference of their path is at about 1, but they have the same path, so we have reason to believe that this might be caused by the system error, therefore, we think those solutions are optimal solutions. Compared with other types, R2, C2, RC2 type problems are more likely to be found a Pareto sets. When the problem's size is 50, the algorithm can find the optimal solution of problems, some solutions have been greatly improved. Some Pareto solutions which are different from the reference solutions are generated in R1, R2, C2 and RC2 type problems. The error of other instances is less than 0.5%. When the problem's size is 100, although this algorithm can find out some Pareto solutions which are different from the reference solutions, such as, R2, C1 and RC2, however, the algorithm seem to be

Table 2. Performance analysis

Instances	Size	Best known			P D V A		
		Source [30]	n	c	n	c	DEV
R101	25	KDMSS	8	617.1	8	618.3	0.19
R102	25	KDMSS	7	547.1	7	548.1	0.18
R201	25	CR+KLM	4	463.2	4	478.2	3.23
R202	25	CR+KLM	4	410.5	4	411.2	0.17
C101	25	KDMSS	3	191.3	3	191.8	0.26
C102	25	KDMSS	3	190.3	3	190.7	0.21
C201	25	CR+L	2	214.7	2	215.5	0.37
C202	25	CR+L	2	214.7	2	215.5	0.37
RC101	25	KDMSS	4	461.1	4	462.1	0.22
RC102	25	KDMSS	3	351.8	3	352.7	0.26
RC201	25	CR+L	3	360.2	3	361.3	0.31
RC202	25	CR+KLM	3	338.0	3	338.8	0.23
R102	50	KDMSS	11	909.0	11	967.9	6.47
R103	50	KDMSS	9	772.9	9	773.2	0.03
R205	50	IV+C	4	690.1	4	733.9	6.34
R206	50	IV+C	4	632.4	4	687.3	8.68
C106	50	KDMSS	5	362.4	5	363.2	0.22
C107	50	KDMSS	5	362.4	5	363.2	0.22
C206	50	CR+KLM	3	359.8	3	361.4	0.44
C207	50	CR+KLM	3	359.6	3	389.9	8.43
RC104	50	KDMSS	5	545.8	5	546.5	0.13
RC108	50	KDMSS	6	598.1	6	599.1	0.17
RC202	50	IV+C	5	613.6	5	755.6	23.14
R101	100	KDMSS	20	1637.7	20	1714.3	4.68
R102	100	KDMSS	18	1466.6	18	1636.2	11.56
R202	100	KLM	4	1091.2	4	1092.1	0.08
R206	100	KLM	3	833.0	3	940.1	12.85
C101	100	KDMSS	10	827.3	10	828.9	0.19
C103	100	KDMSS	10	826.3	10	828.06	0.21
C205	100	CR+KLM	3	586.4	3	654.8	11.66
C206	100	CR+KLM	3	586.0	3	588.9	0.49
RC105	100	IV	16	1590.3	16	1611.6	1.34
RC108	100	IV	11	1114.2	11	1156.5	3.79
RC201	100	KLM	9	1261.8	9	1542.2	22.22
RC202	100	IV+C	8	1092.3	8	1325.8	21.37

Note: "DEV" represents deviation.

insufficient in other types. Such as in R1 type, although this algorithm can find the optimal number of vehicles, but the path value deviation is 4.68%~11.56%; In C2 type, some numerical examples can be found the optimal number of vehicles and the error of path is 11.66%. Some numerical examples are not be solved very well. In RC1 type, the solutions which the algorithm can find are worse than reference solutions, so you can see that the performance of algorithm for solving RC1 needs to be improved.

(2) The time-consuming of PDVA

There is no doubt that the time-consuming is a very important one in all the judgement elements of the algorithm. In this section, in order to verify the search capability of the algorithm, a statistical result of the average time is presented, it can be seen in Fig. 3.

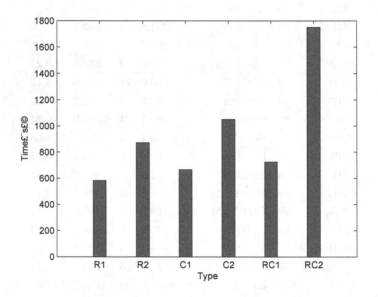

Fig. 3. The average time of PDVA for various types of problems

As can be seen from Fig. 3, it is the most time-consuming to solve RC2 type problem, followed by C2, R2, RC1, C1, the relatively shortest time-consuming to R1. From the space distribution of customers to analyze, it is mainly because the distribution of customers is clustered and evenly distributed, so it is the most time-consuming for solving RC type problems. While the distribution of customers in R type problems is evenly distributed, so the time-consuming is shortest; From the service window of customers to analyze, it is mainly because the time window of RC2, C2 and R2 is wide, it is more flexible to do routing arrangement, so it takes a longer time to calculate.

From the experimental results, the algorithm is sensitive to data sets and it will show different robustness according to the different type of data sets. The dispersion of data sets and the width of time window can affect the performance of the algorithm. C1, R1 and RC1 these three kind of problems have smaller load of the vehicle and their time window is narrow, so the customers each vehicle can service are less; On the contrary, C2, R2 and RC2 these three kind of problems have larger load of the vehicle and their time window is wide, so each vehicle can service more customers.

5 Conclusion

Structure design is a very important research topic in the field of optimization algorithm. In this work, this paper presents an optimization algorithm based on tissue P system. The algorithm employs a tissue P system which consists of three cells as computing framework, two of these cells uses DGEM and VNEM as sub-algorithms, another cell is used as the output cell. Transport rules are adopted as a way to achieve the information communication between cells or cells and environment. DGEM and VNEM are redesigned and improved to enhance the performance of the algorithm. Tissue P system greatly improve the computational efficiency using parallel computing model and cell membrane rules. Finally, a number of Solomon examples of different sizes are tested. And the experimental results show that our algorithm is very competitive with the classical algorithms described in the literature.

Further research may include investigations into scalable methods for large VRPTW or other types of optimization problems. The vehicle routing problem with time window considered in our paper has one depot and hard time window. Other types of VRPTW, such as multi-depot vehicle routing problem with time window [29], vehicle routing problem with soft time window, can be tested by our algorithms with some changes. On the other hand, the influence of other characters of P system on the performance of approximate algorithms should be considered in the future, for example, choosing rules in a non-deterministic manner. Spiking neural P systems see e.g. [31–35], can be considered as a further candidate to design neural-like computing models to solve vehicle routing problem.

Acknowledgments. This project was supported by National Natural Science Foundation of China (Grant No. 61179032), the Special Scientific Research Fund of Food Public Welfare Profession of China(Grant No. 201513004-3) and the Research and Practice Project of Graduate Education Teaching Reform of Wuhan Polytechnic University (YZ2015002).

References

1. Zhang, G.X., Pan, L.Q.: A survey of membrane computing as a new branch of natural computing. Chin. J. Comput. **33**(2), 208–214 (2010)
2. Păun, G.: Computing with membranes. J. Comput. Syst. Sci. **61**(1), 108–143 (2000)

3. Pan, L.Q., Martin-Vide, C.: Solving multidimensional 0-1 knapsack problem by P systems with input and active membranes. J. Parallel Distrib. Comput. **65**(12), 1578–1584 (2005)
4. Pan, L.Q., Pérez-Jiménez, M.J.: Computational complexity of tissue-like P systems. J. Complex. **26**(3), 296–315 (2010)
5. Zhang, X.Y., Wang, S., Niu, Y.Y., Pan, L.Q.: Tissue P systems with cell separation: attacking the partition problem. Sci. China Inf. Sci. **54**(2), 293–304 (2011)
6. Pan, L.Q., Zeng, X.X., Zhang, X.Y.: Time-free spiking neural P systems. Neural Comput. **23**, 1320–1342 (2011)
7. Zhang, X.Y., Luo, B., Fang, X.Y., Pan, L.Q.: Sequential spiking neural P systems with exhaustive use of rules. BioSystems **108**, 52–62 (2012)
8. Song, T., Pan, L.Q., Wang, J., Venkat, I., Subramanian, K.G., Abdullah, R.: Normal forms of spiking neural P systems with anti-spikes. IEEE Trans. Nanobiosci. **11**(4), 352–360 (2012)
9. Song, T., Pan, L.Q., Paun, G.: Asynchronous spiking neural P systems with local synchronization. Inf. Sci. **219**, 197–207 (2013)
10. Song, T., Pan, L.Q., Paun, G.: Spiking neural P systems with rules on synapses. Theoret. Comput. Sci. **529**, 82–95 (2014)
11. Zhang, X.Y., Zeng, X.X., Luo, B., Pan, L.Q.: On some classes of sequential spiking neural P systems. Neural Comput. **26**, 974–997 (2014)
12. Pan, L.Q., Daniel, D.P., Perez-Jimenez, M.J.: Computation of Ramsey numbers by P systems with active membranes. Int. J. Found. Comput. Sci. **22**(1), 29–38 (2011)
13. Peng, H., Jiang, Y., Wang, J.: Membrane clustering algorithm with hybrid evolutionary mechanisms. J. Softw. **26**(5), 1001–1012 (2015)
14. Ma, X.J., Zhao, Y.F.: Research on the Heuristic algorithm of VRPTW based on membrane computing. J. Wuhan Univ. Technol. **35**(2), 83–89 (2013)
15. Pan, L.J.: Vehicle routing problem with time windows and its algorithms. Central South University (2012)
16. Ursani, Z., Essam, D., et al.: Localized genetic algorithm for vehicle routing problem with time windows. Appl. Soft Comput. **11**(8), 5375–5390 (2011)
17. He, X.F., Ma, L.: Quantum-inspired ant colony algorithm for vehicle routing problem with time windows. Syst. Eng. - Theory Pract. **33**(5), 1255–1261 (2013)
18. Lang, M.X., Hu, S.J.: Study on the tabu search algorthm for vehicle routing problem. J. Ind. Eng. Eng. Manag. **18**(1), 81–84 (2004)
19. Liu, F.-H.F., Shen, S.Y.: A route-neighborhood-based metaheuristic for vehicle routing problem with time windows. Eur. J. Oper. Res. **118**, 485–504 (1999)
20. Wang, J.: Differential evolution hybrid algorithm for vehicle routing problem with time windows. Comput. Eng. Appl. **49**(2), 24–28 (2013)
21. Krishnand, K.N., Ghose, D.: Glowworm swam optimisation: a new method for optimizing multi-modal functions. Int. J. Comput. Intell. Stud. **1**(1), 93–119 (2009)
22. Krishnand, K.N., Ghose, D.: Glowworm swarm based optimization algorithm for multimodal functions with collective robotics applications. Multiagent Grid Syst. **2**(3), 209–222 (2006)
23. Dong, W.B., Zhou, K.: Adaptive neighborhood search's DGSO applied to travelling saleman problem. Commun. Comput. Inf. Sci. **562**, 125–137 (2015)
24. Su, Y.: Study of Modern Heuristic Algorithm for the Vehicle Routing Problem with Constraints. Xidian University (2014)
25. Liu, S.X., Liu, L.: Variable neighborhood search for solving vehicle routing problems with backhauls and time windows. J. Northeast. Univ. (Nat. Sci.) **29**(3), 316–319 (2008)

26. Tan, K.C., Chew, Y.H., Lee, L.H.: A hybrid multiobjective evolutionary algorithm for solving vehicle routing problem with time windows. Comput. Optim. Appl. **34**, 115–151 (2006)
27. Song, X.Y., Zhu, J.Y.: Hybrid differential evolution algorithm for vehicle routing problem with time windows. Comput. Sci. **41**(12), 220–225 (2014)
28. Niu, Y., He, J., Wang, Z.: A P-based hybrid evolutionary algorithm for vehicle routing problem with time windows. Math. Probl. Eng. **2014**(3), 1–11 (2014)
29. Crevier, B., Cordeau, J.F., Laporte, G.: The multi-depot vehicle routing problem with inter-depot routes. Eur. J. Oper. Res. **176**, 756–773 (2007)
30. VRPTW. http://web.cba.neu.edu/~msolomon/problems.htm
31. Song, T., Pan, L.: Spiking neural P systems with request rules. Neurocomputing **193**(12), 193–200 (2016)
32. Song, T., Liu, X., Zhao, Y., Zhang, X.: Spiking neural P systems with white hole neurons. IEEE Trans. Nanobiosci. (2016). doi:10.1109/TNB.2016.2598879
33. Song, T., Pan, Z., Wong, D.M., Wang, X.: Design of logic gates using spiking neural P systems with homogeneous neurons and astrocytes-like control. Inf. Sci. **372**, 380–391 (2016)
34. Wang X., Song T., Gong F., Pan Z.: On the computational power of spiking neural P systems with self-organization, Scientific reports. doi:10.1038/srep27624
35. Shi, X., Wu, X., Song, T., Li, X.: Construction of DNA nanotubes with controllable diameters and patterns by using hierarchical DNA sub-tiles. Nanoscale. doi:10.1039/C6NR02695H

The Subideal Version of the SOI-Algorithm and Its Application

Haifeng Sang[1,2(✉)] and Qingchun Li[1]

[1] College of Mathematics and Statistics, Beihua University, Jilin 132013, China
[2] School of Mathematics, Jilin University, Changchun 130012, China
sanghaifeng2008@163.com

Abstract. The coordinates of the empirical points are known with only limited precision, typically up to a permitted tolerance ε. In this paper, we present an algorithm which computes stable border bases of the ideal $I \cap J$, where I is the approximately vanishing ideal of an empirical point set, and J is the vanishing ideal of an exact point set. This algorithm is the subideal version of the SOI-Algorithm and it can be applied to the production allocation problem in the Algebraic Oil Research Project.

Keywords: SOI-Algorithm · Vanishing ideals · Subideal border bases

1 Introduction

Let $P = \mathbb{R}[x_1, \ldots, x_n]$ be a polynomial ring. Given a set of distinct points $\mathbb{X} \subset \mathbb{R}^n$, it is well-known that the set of all polynomials vanishing at $\mathbb{X}$ constitutes a radical zero-dimensional ideal, denoted by $\ell(\mathbb{X})$, which is called the vanishing ideal of $\mathbb{X}$.

If $\mathbb{X}$ is a set of empirical points, representing real-world measurements, then the coordinates are known only imprecisely. Roughly speaking, if $\widetilde{\mathbb{X}}$ is another set of points and each point of $\widetilde{\mathbb{X}}$ is different by less than the uncertainty from the corresponding element of $\mathbb{X}$, then these two sets can be regarded as equivalent. In recent years, authors have great interest in the problem about describing vanishing ideals of sets of empirical points. Sauer [1] considered a method, suitable for numerical computations, which computes a low-degree algebraic variety containing the input points. Heldt et al. [2] introduced the numerically stable AVI-Algorithm which computes a set of polynomials that almost vanish at the given points and almost form a border basis. Abbott et al. [3] presented the SOI-Algorithm which computes the stable border bases for vanishing ideals of sets of empirical points. Fassino [4] gave us the NBM-Algorithm, which computes the almost vanishing polynomials for the sets of empirical points.

In the industrial production, we usually deal with the given data. Some data are derived from tests, so these data inevitably exist errors. The others are summarized from the production practice for many years and they can be seen as the exact data. These point sets whose points can be discussed the exact points and the empirical points are called semi-empirical point sets.

© Springer Nature Singapore Pte Ltd. 2016
M. Gong et al. (Eds.): BIC-TA 2016, Part II, CCIS 682, pp. 302–309, 2016.
DOI: 10.1007/978-981-10-3614-9_36

In modeling physical systems, we may want to impose certain vanishing conditions on the model equations we are constructing. Suppose that the polynomial set $F = \{f_1, f_2, \ldots, f_m\} \subseteq \mathbb{R}[x_1, \ldots, x_n]$ represents the vanishing conditions we want to impose. Using Hilbert's Nullstellensatz, what we are looking for is the intersection of the approximately vanishing ideal of an empirical point set $\mathbb{X}^\varepsilon$ with a given ideal $J = \langle F \rangle$.

Therefore, it is useful to construct stable border bases of the intersection of the approximately vanishing ideal of an empirical point set with a given ideal J. And it can be applied to an actual industrial problem such as the Algebraic Oil Research Project (see [5–7]).

The algorithm (see [1–4]) produce a set of polynomials which vanish approximately at the given data points, but we do not demand that there exists a nearby set of points at which these polynomials vanish exactly. We want to construct approximate interpolation polynomials which vanish ε-approximately at the empirical points and they are contained in the vanishing ideal generated by the exact points. So these algorithms are not suitable for computing the almost vanishing polynomials of semi-empirical point sets. Therefore it is necessary to study the almost vanishing polynomials for semi-empirical point sets. The algorithm for computing the subideal border bases of zero-dimensional ideals can be applied for computing the almost vanishing polynomials for semi-empirical point sets. That is, we compute the intersection of the approximate vanishing ideal of the empirical points with the vanishing ideal of the exact points and we can deal with so-called commingled production problem (see [6,7]).

This paper is organized as follows. In Sect. 2 we introduce the preliminary definitions and notation we shall use. The main result, the subideal version of the SOI-Algorithm for computing the almost vanishing polynomials of semi-empirical point sets, is presented in Sect. 3. In Sect. 4 we provide some examples for the production allocation problem in the Algebraic Oil Research Project.

2 Notation and Preliminaries

In this section, we will settle the key notation used throughout the paper and give some background results. We shall assume that the reader has some familiarity with the theory of exact and approximate border bases (see [2,8–10], Sect. 6.4 of [11,12]). First, we recall some concepts about the polynomial ring $P = \mathbb{K}[x_1, \ldots, x_n]$ (see [10,11]).

Definition 1. *Let $\mathbb{X} = \{p_1, \ldots, p_s\} \subset \mathbb{R}^n$ be a non-empty finite set of points and let $G = \{g_1, \ldots, g_k\}$ be a non-empty finite set of polynomials.*

1. *The ideal $l(\mathbb{X}) = \{f \in P \mid f(p_i) = 0, \ \forall p_i \in \mathbb{X}\}$ is called the vanishing ideal of $\mathbb{X}$.*
2. *The $\mathbb{K}$ linear map $eval_\mathbb{X} : P \to \mathbb{K}^s$ defined by $eval_\mathbb{X}(f) = (f(p_1), \ldots, f(p_s))$ is called the evaluation map associated to $\mathbb{X}$. For brevity, we write $f(\mathbb{X})$ to denote $eval_\mathbb{X}(f)$.*
3. *The evaluation matrix of G associated to $\mathbb{X}$, written as $M_G(\mathbb{X}) \in Mat_{s \times k}(\mathbb{K})$, is defined as having entry (i, j) equal to $g_j(p_i)$, i.e., whose columns are the images of the polynomials g_j under the evaluation map.*

Definition 2. *Let $\mathbb{T}^n$ be the monoid of power products of P and let $\mathcal{O}$ be a nonempty subset of $\mathbb{T}^n$. The set $\mathcal{O}$ is called an order ideal if $\mathcal{O} = \overline{\mathcal{O}}$, where $\overline{\mathcal{O}}$ is the set of all power products in $\mathbb{T}^n$ which divides some power product of $\mathcal{O}$.*

Next, we recall the definitions of empirical point and of admissible perturbation (see [3,12]).

Definition 3. *Let $p = (c_1, \ldots, c_n)$ be a point in $\mathbb{R}^n$ and $\varepsilon = (\varepsilon_1, \ldots, \varepsilon_n) \in \mathbb{R}_+^n$.*

1. *The pair (p, ε) is called an empirical point in $\mathbb{R}^n$. We shall denote it also by p^ε. The point p is called the specific value and ε is called the tolerance of p^ε.*
2. *A point $\widetilde{p} = (\widetilde{c}_1, \ldots, \widetilde{c}_n) \in \mathbb{R}^n$ is called an admissible perturbation of p if $|c_i - \widetilde{c}_i| < \varepsilon_i$ for each $1 \le i \le n$.*
3. *Let $\mathbb{X}^\varepsilon = \{p_1^\varepsilon, \ldots, p_s^\varepsilon\}$ be a set of empirical points which share the same tolerance ε, and let $\mathbb{X} = \{p_1, \ldots, p_s\}$ be its specific value. A set of points $\widetilde{\mathbb{X}} = \{\widetilde{p}_1, \ldots, \widetilde{p}_s\}$ is called an admissible perturbation of $\mathbb{X}$ if each point $\widetilde{p}_i$ is an admissible perturbation of p_i.*
4. *Let a set $\mathbb{X}^\varepsilon = \{p_1^\varepsilon, \ldots, p_s^\varepsilon\}$ of empirical points be given with specific values $p_i = (c_{i,1}, \ldots, c_{i,n})$. Let e be the following error indeterminates*

$$e = (e_{1,1}, \ldots, e_{s,1}, e_{1,2}, \ldots, e_{s,2}, \ldots, e_{1,n}, \ldots, e_{s,n}).$$

Then the set $\mathbb{X}(e) = \{p_1(e_1), \ldots, p_s(e_s)\}$ where $p_k(e_k) = (c_{k,1} + e_{k,1}, \ldots, c_{k,n} + e_{k,n})$ is called the generic perturbation of $\mathbb{X}$.

Finally, we recall some concepts about the subideal border bases (see [5]).

Definition 4. *Let $F = \{f_1, \ldots, f_m\} \subset P \backslash \{0\}$, I be a zero-dimensional ideal, and $\mathcal{O} \subset \mathbb{T}^n$ be an order ideal whose residue classes form a $\mathbb{K}$-vector space basis of P/I.*

1. *For $i = 1, \ldots, m$, let $\mathcal{O}_i \subseteq \mathcal{O}$ be an order ideal. Then the set $\mathcal{O}_F = \mathcal{O}_1 \cdot f_1 \cup \cdots \cup \mathcal{O}_m \cdot f_m$ is called an F-order ideal. Its elements, i.e. products of the form tf_i with $t \in \mathcal{O}_i$ will be called F-terms.*
2. *If $\mathcal{O}_F = \mathcal{O}_1 \cdot f_1 \cup \cdots \cup \mathcal{O}_m \cdot f_m$ is an F-order ideal whose residue classes form a $\mathbb{K}$-vector space basis of $J/(I \cap J)$, we say that the ideal I has an $\mathcal{O}_F$-subideal border basis.*

Definition 5. *Let $F = \{f_1, \ldots, f_m\} \subset P \backslash \{0\}$, and let $\mathcal{O}_F = \mathcal{O}_1 \cdot f_1 \cup \cdots \cup \mathcal{O}_m \cdot f_m$ be a F-order ideal. We write $\mathcal{O}_F = \{t_1 f_{\alpha_1}, \ldots, t_\mu f_{\alpha_\mu}\}$ with $\alpha_i \in \{1, \ldots, m\}$.*

1. *The set of polynomials $\partial \mathcal{O}_F = (x_1 \mathcal{O}_F \cup \cdots \cup x_n \mathcal{O}_F) \backslash \mathcal{O}_F$ is called the border of $\mathcal{O}_F$.*
2. *Let $\partial \mathcal{O}_F = \{b_1 f_{\beta_1}, \ldots, b_\nu f_{\beta_\nu}\}$. A set of polynomials $G = \{g_1, \ldots, g_\nu\}$ is called an $\mathcal{O}_F$-subideal border prebasis if $g_j = b_j f_\beta - \sum_{i=1}^\mu c_{ij} t_i f_{\alpha_i}$ with $c_{1j}, \ldots, c_{\mu j} \in \mathbb{K}$ for $j = 1, \ldots, \nu$.*
3. *An $\mathcal{O}_F$-subideal border prebasis G is called an $\mathcal{O}_F$-subideal border basis of an ideal I if G is contained in I and the residue classes of the elements of $\mathcal{O}_F$ form a $\mathbb{K}$-vector space of $J/(I \cap J)$.*

The following proposition provides the motivation for the name of subideal border bases.

Proposition 1. *Let* $F = \{f_1, \ldots, f_m\} \subset P \backslash \{0\}$, $J = \langle F \rangle$, $\mathcal{O}_F = \{t_1 f_\alpha, \ldots, t_\mu f_\alpha\}$ *be an F-order ideal where* $\alpha_i \in \{1, \ldots, m\}$ *and* $t_i \in \mathcal{O}_\alpha$, *and let* $\partial \mathcal{O}_F = \{b_1 f_\beta, \ldots, b_\nu f_\beta\}$ *be its border and* $G = \{g_1, \ldots, g_\nu\}$ *be an* $\mathcal{O}_F$-*subideal border basis of an ideal* I. *Then* G *generates the ideal* $I \cap J$.

3   The Subideal Version of SOI-Algorithm

Definition 6. *Let* $M \in F^{r \times c}$. *We define* M_k, *the homogeneous component of degree* k *of* M, *to be the matrix whose* (i, j) *entry is the homogeneous component of degree* k *of* (i, j) *entry of* M.

Given $\nu \in F^{r \times 1}$ and a full rank matrix $M \in F^{r \times c}$, with $r \geq c$, define $\alpha \in F^{c \times 1}$ and $\rho \in F^{r \times 1}$ as follows:

$$\alpha = (M^T M)^{-1} M^T \nu, \qquad \rho = \nu - M\alpha. \tag{1}$$

Proposition 2. *Let* $r, c \in \mathbb{N}$ *with* $r \geq c$, *let* ν *be a vector in* $F^{r \times 1}$ *and* M *be a full rank matrix in* $F^{r \times 1}$. *Let* $\alpha \in F^{r \times 1}$ *and* $\rho \in F^{r \times 1}$ *be defined by (1). Then the homogeneous components of degrees 0 and 1 of* α *are*

$$\alpha_0 = (M_0^T M_0)^{-1} M_0^T \nu_0, \qquad \alpha_1 = (M_0^T M_0)^{-1} (M_0^T \nu_1 + M_1^T \nu_0 - M_0^T M_1 \alpha_0 - M_1^T M_0 \alpha_0)$$

and the homogeneous components of degrees 0 and 1 of ρ *are*

$$\rho_0 = \nu_0 - M_0 \alpha_0, \qquad \alpha_1 = \nu_1 - M_0 \alpha_1 - M_1 \alpha_0.$$

Proposition 3. *Let* $\mathbb{X}^\varepsilon$ *be a set of* s *distinct empirical points, and let* $\mathcal{O}_F = \{t_1 f_\alpha, \ldots, t_s f_\alpha\}$ *be a quotient basis for* $\ell(\mathbb{X})$ *which is stable w.r.t.* $\mathbb{X}^\varepsilon$. *Then, for each admissible perturbation* $\tilde{\mathbb{X}}$ *of* $\mathbb{X}^\varepsilon$, *the vanishing ideal* $\ell(\mathbb{X})$ *has an* $\mathcal{O}_F$-*subideal border basis* G. *Furthermore, if* $\partial \mathcal{O}_F = \{b_1 f_\beta, \ldots, b_\nu f_\beta\}$ *is the border of* $\mathcal{O}_F$ *then* G *consists of* ν *polynomials of the form*

$$g_j = b_j f_\beta - \sum_{i=1}^{s} \alpha_{ij} t_i f_\alpha \quad \text{for } j = 1, \ldots, \nu$$

where the coefficients $\alpha_{ij} \in \mathbb{R}$ *satisfy the linear systems*

$$(b_j f_\beta)(\tilde{\mathbb{X}}) = \sum_{i=1}^{s} \alpha_{ij} (t_i f_\alpha)(\tilde{\mathbb{X}}).$$

We present the subideal version of SOI-Algorithm which computes the stable F-order ideal $\mathcal{O}_F$ and stable subideal border bases of ideal I. The strategy for computing $\mathcal{O}_F$ is the following. As in the Buchberger-Möller algorithm (see [14,15]) the set $\mathcal{O}_F$ is built stepwise: initially $\mathcal{O}_F$ comprises just the smallest candidate in $F \cup \partial F$ according to a fixed term ordering σ which is used only as a computational tool; then at each iteration, a new polynomial tf is considered. Let D_ε be the domain of the perturbed set $\widetilde{\mathbb{X}}(e)$. If the evaluation matrix $M_{\mathcal{O}_F \cup \{tf\}}(\widetilde{\mathbb{X}}(\delta))$ has full rank for all $\delta \in D_\varepsilon$, then tf is added to $\mathcal{O}_F$; otherwise tf is added to the corner set of the F−order ideal.

Algorithm 1. Subideal Version of the SOI(SSOI)-Algorithm
Input. A finite set $\mathbb{X}^\varepsilon = \{p_1^\varepsilon, \ldots, p_s^\varepsilon\}$ of s empirical points, a polynomial set $F = \{f_1, \ldots, f_m\} \subset P \backslash \{0\}$, an ideal $J = \langle F \rangle$, a term ordering σ and $\gamma \geq 0$ (see Theorem 10).
Output. A stable F−order ideal $\mathcal{O}_F$ and a stable $\mathcal{O}_F$-subideal border basis G.

Let $L = [t_1 f_{\alpha_1}, \ldots, t_\nu f_{\alpha_\nu}]$ be the list of all F-terms in $F \cup \partial F$ with their leading terms ordered decreasingly $w.r.t.$ σ. Let $tf = \min_\sigma(L)$ and delete it from L. Consider the following sequence of instructions.

Step 1. Initialize $\mathcal{O}_F = \{tf\}$ and $C = [\ ]$. Let M_0 and M_1 be the homogeneous components of degrees 0 and 1 of the evaluation vector $(tf)(\mathbb{X}(e))$.
Step 2. If $L = \emptyset$, then go to Step 7. Otherwise, let $tf = \min_\sigma(L)$ and delete it from L.
Step 3. Let ν_0 and ν_1 be the homogeneous components of degrees 0 and 1 of the evaluation vector $\nu = (tf)(\mathbb{X}(e))$. Compute the vectors

$$\rho_0 = \nu_0 - M_0 \alpha_0, \quad \rho_1 = \nu_1 - M_0 \alpha_1 - M_1 \alpha_0$$

with

$$\alpha_0 = (M_0^T M_0)^{-1} M_0^T \nu_0, \quad \alpha_1 = (M_0^T M_0)^{-1}(M_0^T \nu_1 + M_1^T \nu_0 - M_0^T M_1 \alpha_0 - M_1^T M_0 \alpha_0).$$

Step 4. Let $C_t \in \mathbb{R}^{s \times sn}$ be such that $\rho_1 = C_t e$. Let k be the maximum integer such that the matrix $\widehat{C}_t$, formed by selecting the first k rows of C_t, has minimum singular value $\widehat{\sigma}_k$ greater than $\|\varepsilon\|$. Let $\widehat{\rho}_0$ be the vector comprising the first k elements of ρ_0 and let $\widehat{C}_t^+$ be the pseudoinverse of $\widehat{C}_t$. Compute $\widehat{\delta} = -\widehat{C}_t^+ \widehat{\rho}_0$.
Step 5. If $\|\widehat{\delta}\| > (1 + \gamma)\sqrt{s}\|\varepsilon\|$, then adjoin the vector ν_0 as a new column of M_0 and the vector ν_1 as a new column of M_1. Append the polynomial tf to $\mathcal{O}_F$, and add to L those elements of $\{x_1 tf, \ldots, x_n tf\}$ which are not multiples of an element of L or C. Continue with Step 2.
Step 6. Otherwise append tf to the list C, and remove from L all multiples of tf. Continue with Step 2.
Step 7. If $\#\mathcal{O}_F = s$, then for each $tf \in \partial \mathcal{O}_F$, solve the linear system

$$M_{\mathcal{O}_F}(\mathbb{X})Y = (tf)(\mathbb{X}) \tag{2}$$

to obtain a set G of polynomials. Return $(\mathcal{O}_F, G)$. Otherwise, return "Failure".

Proposition 4. *Algorithm 1 stops after finite steps. If γ satisfies $\sup_{\delta \in D_\varepsilon} \|\rho_{2+}(\delta)\| \leq \gamma \sqrt{s}\|\varepsilon\|^2$, then $\mathcal{O}_F$ is an F−order ideal stable $w.r.t.$ the empirical set $\mathbb{X}^\varepsilon$. In particular, when $\#\mathcal{O} = s$ then $\ell(\mathbb{X})$ has a corresponding stable $\mathcal{O}_F$-subideal border basis $w.r.t.$ $\mathbb{X}^\varepsilon$.*

Note that in order to implement Algorithm 1 a value of γ has to be chosen even if an estimate of $\sup_{\delta \in D_\varepsilon} \|\rho_{2+}(\delta)\|$ is unknown. Since we consider small perturbations $\widetilde{\mathbb{X}}$ of the empirical set $\mathbb{X}^\varepsilon$, in most cases $\rho_0 + \rho_1(\delta)$ is a good linear approximation of $\rho(\delta)$ for every $\delta \in D_\varepsilon$. For this reason $\sup_{\delta \in D_\varepsilon} \|\rho_{2+}(\delta)\|$ is small and a value of $\gamma \ll 1$ can be chosen to obtain a polynomial set $\mathcal{O}_F$ stable w.r.t. $\mathbb{X}^\varepsilon$.

4   Applications and Examples

In the Algebraic Oil Research Project (see [6,7]), suppose that a multi-zone well consists of two zones A and B. (The Fig. 1 gives a schematic representation of a two-zone well).

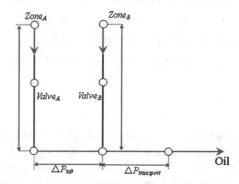

Fig. 1. Schematic representation of a two-zone well.

During so-called commingled production, the two zones are interacting and influence each other. Let the indeterminate x_A represent the valve position of zone A and x_B the valve position of zone B. Here $x_i = 0$ means that the valve is closed and $x_i = 1$ represents a fully opened valve position. We write the total production $p_{AB} = p_A + p_B + q_{AB}$ where q_{AB} is a polynomial which measures the interaction of the two zones and p_A, p_B are polynomials which measure the production of zone A and B. Assume that suitable production polynomials p_A and p_B have been constructed during suitable well tests. Hence q_{AB} can be computed via the subideal version of the SOI-Algorithm by applying it to the ideal $J = \langle x_B p_A, \ x_A p_B \rangle$.

Let us illustrate the application of the subideal version of the SOI-Algorithm by the following examples.

Example 1. In the ring $P = \mathbb{R}[x, y, z]$, let $\{(0, 1, 1), (1, 1, 0), (1.01, 0, 0.98), (2.03, 1.04, 0.97), (0, 1.97, 1.03)\}$ be the semi-empirical point set, $\sigma = \mathbf{DegLex}$ and $\varepsilon = 0.03 \cdot (1, 1, 1)$. Then we want to compute an F-order ideal $\mathcal{O}_F$ about the points of $\mathbb{X} = \{(1.01, 0, 0.98), (2.03, 1.04, 0.97), (0, 1.97, 1.03)\}$. The border basis of the exact points $\{(0,1,1),(1,1,0)\}$ is $F = \{f_1 = x + z - 1, f_2 = y - 1, f_3 = xz, f_4 = yz - z, f_5 = z^2 - z\}$ and the ideal $J = \langle F \rangle$.

Using the subideal version of the SOI-Algorithm, we obtain that the stable F-order ideal $\mathcal{O}_F = \{f_1, f_2, yf_2\}$ and the stable subideal border basis G:

$$g_1 = xf_1 - 1.0011f_2 - 2.0212f_1 + 0.5399yf_2,$$
$$g_2 = xf_2 - 1.0405f_2 - 0.0308f_1 + 0.5286yf_2,$$
$$g_3 = xyf_2 - 0.0414f_2 - 0.0418f_1 + 0.0216yf_2,$$
$$g_4 = yf_1 - 1.0198f_2 - 1.0301f_1 + 0.5029yf_2,$$
$$g_5 = y^2f_2 + 0.0190f_2 + 0.0192f_1 - 1.9799yf_2,$$
$$g_6 = zf_1 + 0.0098f_2 - 0.9701f_1 - 0.0059yf_2,$$
$$g_7 = zf_2 - 0.9793f_2 + 0.0007f_1 - 0.0258yf_2,$$
$$g_8 = yzf_2 + 0.0012f_2 + 0.0012f_1 - 1.0306yf_2,$$
$$g_9 = f_3 + 0.0146f_2 - 0.9850f_1 + 0.0080yf_2,$$
$$g_{10} = f_4 - 0.9793f_2 + 0.0007f_1 - 0.0258yf_2,$$
$$g_{11} = f_5 - 0.0048f_2 + 0.0149f_1 - 0.0140yf_2.$$

5   Conclusion

In the industrial production, we usually deal with semi-empirical point sets. Therefore we present an algorithm which computes stable border bases for the ideal of semi-empirical points. That is, we can compute stable border bases for the ideal $I \cap J$, where I is the approximately vanishing ideal of an empirical point set, and J is the vanishing ideal of an exact point set. This algorithm can be applied to the production allocation problem in the Algebraic Oil Research Project.

Acknowledgments. This work is supported by Jilin Province Department of Education Science and Technology Research Project under Grants 2015131 and 2015156.

References

1. Sauer, T.: Approximate varieties, approximate ideals and dimension reductions. Numer. Algorithms **45**, 295–313 (2007)
2. Heldt, D., Kreuzer, M., Pokutta, S., Poulisse, H.: Approximate computation of zero-dimensional polynomial ideals. J. Symb. Comput. **44**, 1566–1591 (2009)
3. Abbott, J., Fassino, C., Torrente, M.: Stable border bases for ideals of points. J. Symb. Comput. **43**, 883–894 (2008)
4. Fassino, C.: Almost vanishing polynomials for sets of limited precision points. J. Symb. Comput. **45**, 19–37 (2010)
5. Kreuzer, M., Poulisse, H.: Subideal border bases. Math. Comput. **80**, 1135–1154 (2011)
6. The algebraic oil research project. http://www.fim.uni-passau.de/algebraic-oil

7. Kreuzer, M., Poulisse, H., Robbiano, L.: From oil fields to Hilbert schemes. In: Robbiano, L., Abbott, J. (eds.) Approximate Commutative Algebra. Springer, Berlin (2010)
8. Kehrein, A., Kreuzer, M.: Characterizations of border bases. J. Pure Appl. Algebra **196**, 251–270 (2005)
9. Kehrein, A., Kreuzer, M., Robbiano, L.: An algebraists view on border bases. In: Bronstein, M., Cohen, A.M., Cohen, H., Eisenbud, D., Sturmfels, B., Dickenstein, A., Emiris, I.Z. (eds.) Solving Polynomial Equations. Springer, Berlin (2005)
10. Kreuzer, M., Robbiano, L.: Computational Commutative Algebra 1. Springer, Berlin (2008)
11. Kreuzer, M., Robbiano, L.: Computational Commutative Algebra 2. Springer, Berlin (2008)
12. Stetter, H.J.: Numerical Polynomial Algebra. SIAM, Philadelphia (2004)
13. Mourrain, B., Ruatta, O.: Relation between roots and coefficients, interpolation and application to system solving. J. Symb. Comput. **33**, 679–699 (2002)
14. Möller, H.M., Buchberger, B.: The construction of multivariate polynomials with preassigned zeros. In: Calmet, J. (ed.) EUROCAM 1982. LNCS, vol. 144, pp. 24–31. Springer, Heidelberg (1982). doi:10.1007/3-540-11607-9_3
15. Abbott, J., Bigatti, A., Kreuzer, M., Robbiano, L.: Computing ideals of points. J. Symb. Comput. **30**, 341–356 (2000)

A Diversity Keeping Strategy
for the Multi-objective Examination
Timetabling Problem

Yu Lei[✉], Jiao Shi, and Kun Zhang

School of Electronics and Information, Northwest Polytechnical University,
ADD: 127 West Youyi Road, Xi'an 710072, Shaanxi, China
leiy@nwpu.edu.cn

Abstract. This paper presents a diversity keeping strategy for examination timetabling problems. In this paper, the examination timetabling problem is considered as a two-objective optimization problem while it is modeled as a single-objective optimization problem generally. Within the NNIA framework, a diversity-keeping strategy which consists of an elitism group operator and an extension optimization operator to ensure a sufficient number of solutions in the pareto front. The proposed algorithm was tested on the most widely used un-capacitated Carter benchmarks. Experimental results prove that the proposed algorithm is a competitive algorithm.

Keywords: Examination timetabling problem · Multi-objective optimization · NNIA · Diversity-keeping strategy

1 Introduction

The examination timetabling problem has long been a challenging area for researchers in the fields of operational research and artificial intelligence, especially at the time that the Toronto benchmark dataset stated by Carter et al. [1]. The problem has been more difficult because universities are recruiting more students into a larger variety of courses with an growing number of combined degree courses [2]. In the past 40 years there are many methods that have been applied to this problem. The represented techniques include constraint-based techniques [2,3], population based techniques including genetic algorithms [4], graph coloring techniques [5,6], ant colony optimization [7], scatter search [8], local search methods including tabu search [9] and simulated annealing [10,11], variable neighborhood search [12], hybrid and hyper-heuristic approaches [5] and so on. Generally, this problem is modeled as a single-objective optimization problem, only the number of clashes is considered by researchers. To evaluate the quality of one feasible timetable, a function evaluating the average cost for per student based on soft constraints has been proposed. It can be presented as follows:

$$fitness = \left(\sum_{s=0}^{4} \omega_s \times N_s \right) \Big/ S \tag{1}$$

© Springer Nature Singapore Pte Ltd. 2016
M. Gong et al. (Eds.): BIC-TA 2016, Part II, CCIS 682, pp. 310–315, 2016.
DOI: 10.1007/978-981-10-3614-9_37

where $\omega_s = 2^s (s = 0, 1, 2, 3, 4)$ is the weight that represents the importance of scheduling exams with common students either 4, 3, 2, 1, or 0 timeslots away in one timetable, and N_s is the number of students involved in the violation of the soft constraint. S is the total number of students in the problem. For this reason that equation (1) emphasizes the most important indicators that is whether the exams in the timetable are allocated throughout the timetable equally, we use this function as one of the objectives in our algorithm. The two objectives of our algorithm optimized are described as follows:

$$\min \begin{cases} f_1 = |P| \\ f_2 = \left(\sum_{s=0}^{4} \omega_s \times N_s \right) \Big/ S \end{cases} \tag{2}$$

The ETTP is a semiannual or annual problem for colleges and is studied by many operational research widely due to its complexity and utility. There have been proposed a large range of approaches to solve the problem and discussed in the existing literature. These approaches can be classified into the following broad categories [13]: graph-based sequential techniques, Local search-based techniques, population-based techniques, multi-criteria techniques, and hyper-heuristics.

In summary, during the recent years, there are an increasing number of excellent algorithms almost all of these algorithms were tested on either benchmark datasets or in real applications, which had made quite good achievements. In this paper, we also proposed a multi-objective optimization algorithm, named Nondominated Neighbor Immune Algorithm (NNIA) in [14]. NNIA adopts an immune inspired operator, a nondominated neighbor-based selection technique, two heuristic search operators, and elitism. It indicates that NNIA is an effective method for solving MOPs by a number of experiments [15,16]. Due to its good performance, we will adopt the framework of NNIA with some modifications, which will be described in the following section. The contribution of this paper is that solve this task by using multi-objective optimization technique.

2 Diversity Keeping Operators

2.1 Elitism Group Strategy

Although the local search can intensify the optimization results, the discrete optimization is different from the continuous optimization that a small disturbance in decision domain may probably let individuals transform irregularly even result in deterioration. As such, in order to avoid this phenomenon we put forward the novel local search exploitation with an extra elitism group to save nondominated solutions in every generation. However normal population is just offering a space of updating the nondominated solutions. In our algorithm we also introduce a corresponding elitism strategy and a crowded selection optimization mechanism, the details will be introduced in next part.

The local search operators are applied after the strategy of extension and optimization of the elitism group. The operators avoid an objective in an individual deterioration, then minimize the other objective and get the new elitist solutions mixed with original elitist solutions to conduct the nondominated sorting. The frontier may extend to the two different directions as far as possible according to the operators. The local search is searching vertically between two objectives in order which is shown as Fig. 1(a). It indicates that one objective is optimized prior and then the other, shown as the rout A or rout B of the individual i in the figure.

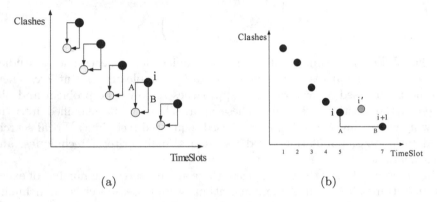

(a)   (b)

Fig. 1. Diversity keeping operators: (a) Elitism group local search, (b) The computation of congestion degree

2.2 Extension Optimization Strategy

Due to the normal selection and mutation operators are make a little contribution to the nondominated elitism group, we present a strategy to extend and optimize the elitism group based on the congestion degree which is shown in Fig. 1(a). Compute the difference of timetable length between every individual and its right side one. If the D-value is 1, then extend a time period of this individual and randomly select some exams into the time period. We can get a uniform frontier by this means. As is shown in the Fig. 1(b), the crowding degree of individual i is the length of the line segment AB. Assume that the crowding degree of individual i is 2, according to our theory, expend the individual i and get i, then put it into the original elitism group. Finally, we take Local Search operators to the generations after extending the time periods.

3 Experimental Analysis

Our algorithm is programmed in Matlab and simulations are performed on a 2.8 GHz Core Personal Computer. We use 8 un-capaciteted benchmark examinations timetabling datasets proposed by Carter et al. [17] to evaluate the effectiveness of our algorithm. As no dataset is designed to evaluate the multi-objective timetabling algorithms, we just use the datasets used in the single objective

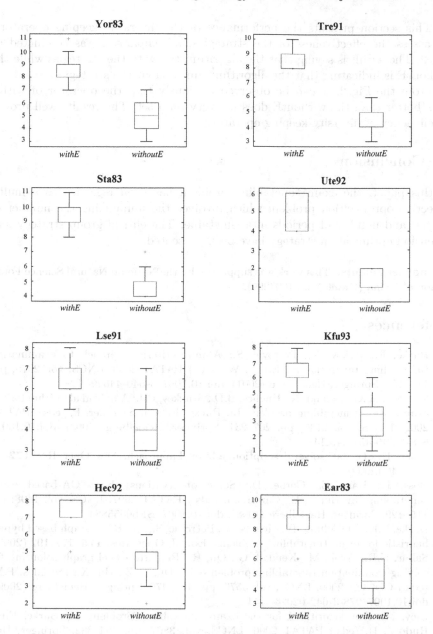

Fig. 2. Performance comparison for MOEA with and without diversity-keeping strategy

to evaluate the feasibility and reasonableness of our algorithm. The parameter settings are presented in Table 2. The population size is 100 and the maximum iteration is 100.

This section presents the performance of the diversity- keeping operators. To assess the effectiveness of the strategies, a comparison was conducted as Fig. 2. The withE is saying that the algorithm run with the strategies while the withoutE is indicating that the algorithm run without the strategies.

From the Fig. 2, it can be observed obviously that the operator of withE does better than the withoutE does in every data set. The results well proved theefficiency of diversity-keeping operator.

4   Conclusion

In this paper, the exam timetabling problem has been regarded as a multi-objective optimization problem which involves the minimizing the number of clashes and number of periods in a timetable. The elitism group strategy and extension optimization strategy have been presented.

Acknowledgments. This work was supported by the National Natural Science Foundation of China (Grant No. 61603299).

References

1. Burke, E., Bykov, Y., Petrovic, S.: A multicriteria approach to examination timetabling. In: Burke, E., Erben, W. (eds.) PATAT 2000. LNCS, vol. 2079, pp. 118–131. Springer, Heidelberg (2001). doi:10.1007/3-540-44629-X_8
2. Merlot, L.T.G., Boland, N., Hughes, B.D., Stuckey, P.J.: A hybrid algorithm for the examination timetabling problem. In: Burke, E., Causmaecker, P. (eds.) PATAT 2002. LNCS, vol. 2740, pp. 207–231. Springer, Heidelberg (2003). doi:10.1007/978-3-540-45157-0_14
3. Mller, T.: ITC2007 solver description: a hybrid approach. Ann. Oper. Res. **172**(1), 429–446 (2009)
4. Ross, P., Hart, E., Corne, D.: Some observations about GA-based exam timetabling. In: Burke, E., Carter, M. (eds.) PATAT 1997. LNCS, vol. 1408, pp. 115–129. Springer, Heidelberg (1998). doi:10.1007/BFb0055884
5. Burke, E.K., McCollum, B., Meisels, A., Petrovic, S., Qu, R.: A graph based hyper-heuristic for exam timetabling problems. Eur. J. Oper. Res. **176**, 177–192 (2007)
6. Sabar, N.R., Ayob, M., Kendall, G., Qu, R.: Roulette wheel graph colouring for solving examination timetabling problems. In: Du, D.-Z., Hu, X., Pardalos, P.M. (eds.) COCOA 2009. LNCS, vol. 5573, pp. 463–470. Springer, Heidelberg (2009). doi:10.1007/978-3-642-02026-1_44
7. Eley, M.: Ant algorithms for the exam timetabling problem. In: Burke, E.K., Rudová, H. (eds.) PATAT 2006. LNCS, vol. 3867, pp. 364–382. Springer, Heidelberg (2007). doi:10.1007/978-3-540-77345-0_23
8. Mansour, N., Isahakian, V., Ghalayini, I.: Scatter search technique for exam timetabling. Appl. Intell. **34**, 299–310 (2011)
9. De Smet G.: ITC2007 examination track, practice and theory of automated timetabling (PATAT 2008), Montreal, pp. 19–22 (2008)
10. Burke, E.K., Bykov, Y., Newall, J.P., Petrovic, S.: A time-predefined local search approach to exam timetabling problems. IIE Trans. Oper. Eng. **36**(6), 509–528 (2004)

11. Thompson, J., Dowsland, K.: A robust simulated annealing based examination timetabling system. Comput. Oper. Res. **25**, 637–648 (1998)
12. Qu, R., Burke, E.K.: Hybrid variable neighbourhood hype-heuristics for exam timetabling problems. In: Proceedings of the MIC2005: The Sixth Meta-heuristics International Conference, Vienna, Austria (2005)
13. Burke, E.K., Kingston, J., de Werra, D.: Applications to timetabling. In: Gross, J., Yellen, J. (eds.) Handbook of Graph Theory, pp. 445–474 (2008)
14. Gong, M., Jiao, L., Du, H., Bo, L.: Multiobjective immune algorithm with non-dominated neighbor-based selection. Evol. Comput. **16**(2), 225–255 (2008)
15. Yang, D., Jiao, L., Gong, M., Feng, J.: Adaptive ranks and K-nearest neighbour list based multiobjective immune algorithm. Comput. Intell. **26**(4), 359–385 (2010)
16. Yang, D., Jiao, L., Gong, M., Liu, F.: Artificial immune multi-objective sar image segmentation with fused complementary features. Inf. Sci. **181**(13), 2797–2812 (2011)
17. Burke, E., Elliman, D., Ford, P., Weare, R.: Examination timetabling in British universities: a survey. In: Burke, E., Ross, P. (eds.) PATAT 1995. LNCS, vol. 1153, pp. 76–90. Springer, Heidelberg (1996). doi:10.1007/3-540-61794-9_52

A Grid-Based Decomposition for Evolutionary Multiobjective Optimization

Zhiwei Mei[1], Xinye Cai[1(✉)], and Zhun Fan[2]

[1] College of Computer Science and Technology,
Nanjing University of Aeronautics and Astronautics,
Nanjing 210016, Jiangsu, People's Republic of China
{zwmei,xinye}@nuaa.edu.cn
[2] Department of Electronic Engineering, School of Engineering, Shantou University,
Shantou, Guangdong, People's Republic of China
zfan@stu.edu.cn

Abstract. Decomposition based multiobjective evolutionary algorithms (MOEAs) decompose a multiobjective optimization problem into a set of scalar objective subproblems and solve them in a collaborative way. Commonly used decomposition approaches are originated from mathematical programming and the direct use of them may not suit MOEAs due to their population-based property. This paper proposes a grid-based decomposition MOEA (G-MOEA/D). A grid has an inherent property of reflecting the information of convergence, diversity, and neighborhood structures among the solutions, which is very suitable for population-based MOEAs. The extensive experiments are conducted to compare G-MOEA/D with other state-of-art MOEAs. The results show that G-MOEA/D is very competitive with or superior to the compared algorithms.

Keywords: Evolutionary multiobjective optimization · Decomposition · Neighborhood

1 Introduction

Multiobjective optimization problems (MOPs) involve the optimization of more than one objective function simultaneously. Due to the conflicting nature of objectives, there is usually no single optimal solution but a set of Pareto optimal solutions, which represent the best trade-off between different objectives. The set of such solutions is called *Pareto set* (*PS*) and the image of *PS* on the objective vector space is called *Pareto front* (*PF*) [13].

Over the past decades, a wide range of multiobjective evolutionary algorithms (MOEAs) have been proposed to approximate the PFs [3–5,8,14]. MOEAs can be further categorized into domination-based (e.g., [7]), indicator-based (e.g., [1,2,17]) and decomposition-based (e.g., [9,10,15]) approaches. Multiobjective evolutionary algorithm based on decomposition (MOEA/D) [15] is a representative approach in decomposition-based MOEAs. Three commonly-

© Springer Nature Singapore Pte Ltd. 2016
M. Gong et al. (Eds.): BIC-TA 2016, Part II, CCIS 682, pp. 316–321, 2016.
DOI: 10.1007/978-981-10-3614-9_38

used decomposition approaches (Weighted Sum (WS), Tchebycheff (TCH) and Penalty-based Boundary Intersection (PBI)) [13] have been applied in the original MOEA/D [15]. WS, TCH and PBI are originated from mathematical programming and the direct use of them may not be well suited to the decomposition-based MOEAs due to their population-based nature [12].

In this paper, we propose a grid-based decomposition MOEA (G-MOEA/D), in which a grid system is combined with an improved ϵ-constraint decomposition approach to better suit decomposition-based MOEA framework. A grid-based decomposition (GD) is used where one objective function is selected to be optimized while all the other objective functions are converted into constraints by setting up both upper and lower bounds.

2   Main Idea and Algorithm

2.1   The Setup of a Grid System

In GD, each objective is divided into K intervals within the ideal and nadir points. Therefore, the width of each interval is

$$d_j = (z_j^{nad} - z_j^* + 2 \times \sigma)/K. \tag{1}$$

The grid location of x along the j-th objective $g_j(x)$ can be calculated as

$$g_j(x) = \lceil (f_j(x) - z_j^* + \sigma)/d_j \rceil, \tag{2}$$

where $\lceil . \rceil$ denotes the ceil function, $g_j(x)$ is the grid-coordinate of solution x and $f_j(x)$ is the value of j-th objective function. A small positive number σ is introduced to ensure that g_j is greater than 0 and less than or equal to K.

2.2   Grid-Based Decomposition

The grid-based decomposition approach for k-th subproblem of l-th objective can be defined as follows.

$$
\begin{aligned}
\text{minimize} \quad & f_l(x) && \text{for all} \quad l = 1, \dots, m, \\
\text{subject to} \quad & g_j(x) = k_j && \text{for all} \quad j = 1, \dots, m, j \neq l, \\
& k_j \in \{1, \dots, K\}, \\
& x \in \Omega.
\end{aligned}
\tag{3}
$$

where K is a division parameter which determines the number of grids. With K intervals on each objective, the grids decompose an MOP into $m \times K^{m-1}$ subproblems.

In general, the k-th subproblem of l-th objective contains a solution set $S_l(k)$ (k is a $(m-1)$-dimensional vector), which can be defined as:

$$S_l(k) = \{x | g_1(x) = k_1, \dots, g_{l-1}(x) = k_{l-1}, g_{l+1}(x) = k_{l+1}, \dots, g_m(x) = k_m\}, \tag{4}$$

subject to $l \in \{1, \dots, m\}$ $k \in \{1, \dots, K\}^{m-1}$.

To use the grid locations for mating selection in MOEAs, the Grid Neighbor is defined for convenience as follows.

Definition 1 (Grid Neighbor). *A set of grid neighbors of solution x with neighborhood distance T is defined as*

$$GN(x,T) = \{x^* | \max_{j=1,\ldots,m} (|g_j(x) - g_j(x^*)|) \leq T, x, x^* \in R^m\}. \qquad (5)$$

2.3   The Main Framework of G-MOEA/D

Algorithm 1.
Input:

(1) an MOP;
(2) a stopping criterion;
(3) N: the population size of P;
(4) T: the maximum grid distance for neighborhood;
(5) K: the number of the intervals in each objective.

Output: A solution set P;
Step 1: Initialization:

Step 1.1: Generate an initial population $P = \{x^1, \ldots, x^N\}$ randomly;
Step 1.2: Approximate the ideal and nadir points;
Step 1.3: Initialize the grid system: GS(P);
Step 1.4: Set $gen = 0$.

Step 2: Reproduction:

Step 2.1: Generate an empty set $Q = \varnothing$;
For each solution $x \in P$ do
Step 2.2: Obtain the neighboring solutions as the mating pool of x:

$$NS = \begin{cases} GN(x,T), & rand < \delta, \\ \{x^1, \ldots, x^N\}, & otherwise. \end{cases} \qquad (6)$$

Step 2.3: Select two solutions x^k and x^l from NS randomly; and generate an offspring y from x, x^k and x^l by DE operators; then y is added to Q.
End for

Step 3: Update of the ideal and nadir points:

Step 3.1: $gen = gen + 1$;
Step 3.2: $P = P \cup Q$;
Step 3.3: update ideal and nadir point.

Step 4: Update of the grid system:

Step 4.1: $\bar{P} = \{x | x \in P \wedge \exists j \in \{1, \ldots, m\}, f_j(x) > z_j^{nad}\}$;
Step 4.2: $P = P \backslash \bar{P}$;
Step 4.3: Update the grid system: GS(P).

Step 5: Grid-based selection:

Step 5.1: If $|P| < N$, randomly select $N - |P|$ solutions from $\bar{P}$ and add them to P. Otherwise, $P = \text{GBS}(P)$.

Step 6: Termination:

Step 6.1: If the stopping criterion is satisfied, terminate the algorithm and output P. Otherwise, go to **Step 2**.

In Step 1.1, a population P is initialized randomly. In Step 1.2, Step 3.3 and Step 3.4, the ideal and nadir points are approximated based on P. The ideal point is updated by the minimum of each objective in P and the nadir point is updated by the maximum of each objective in the nondominated solutions in P.

In Step 5, N solutions are selected from P by grid-based selection, which include decomposition-based ranking and lexicographic sorting, presented in Algorithm 1. In the decomposition-based ranking, each solution set $S_l(k)$ for the k-th subproblem of l-th objective is ranked based on grid-based decomposition defined in Eq. (3). After ranking all the m objectives, each solution x has m ranks, saved in $R(x) = (r_1(x), \ldots, r_m(x))$. In the lexicographic sorting, $R(x)$ is sorted in an ascending order and saved in $R'(x)$. Then, each solution $x \in P$ is ranked in lexicographic order based on $R'(x)$ and the first N solutions are selected.

Algorithm 2. Grid-based Selection (GBS)

    Input : Q: the current population.
    Output: An elite population P.
    /* Decomposition-based Ranking   */
1 **foreach** $x \in Q$ **do**
2 | initialize $R(x) = \{r_1(x), \ldots, r_m(x)\} = \{0, \ldots, 0\}$;
3 **end**
4 **for** $l = 1$ **to** m **do**
5 | **forall** *subproblems* $S_l(k)$ **do**
6 | | **if** $S_l(k) \neq \varnothing$ **then**
7 | | | $[S', I] = sort_l(S_l(k));$ // sort $S_l(k)$ by f_l and I is the ranks
8 | | | **foreach** $x \in S_l(k)$ **do** $r_l(x) = I(x);$
9 | | **end**
10 | **end**
11 **end**
    /* Lexicographic Sorting   */
12 **foreach** $x \in Q$ **do** $R'(x) = sort(R(x));$
    /* sort all $x \in Q$ based on $R'(x)$ in lexicographic order   */
13 $Q = \text{LEXICOGRAPHIC-SORT}(Q);$
14 $P = Q(1 : N);$ // select first N solutions

---

3   Experimental Studies and Discussions

UF benchmark suite is used in our experimental studies. For UF1 to UF7, population size is set to 300, $K = 180$ and neighborhood distance is 5. For UF8 to UF10, population size is 600, $K = 30$ and neighborhood distance is 1. Function evaluations is set to 300,000 for each test instance. Each algorithm is run 30 times independently for each test instance.

G-MOEA/D is compared with five MOEAs: MOEA/D-DE (WS, TCH or PBI) [11], MSOPS-II [9] and NSGA-II [6]. The performance of six algorithms in terms of IGD [16] is presented in Table 1. G-MOEA/D is significantly better than other compared algorithms on most of the test problems, except for UF3, UF8 and UF10.

Table 1. Performance comparisons of G-MOEA/D with five classical MOEAs on UF problems in terms of the mean and standard deviation values of IGD.

Instance		G-MOEA/D	MOEA/D-DE			MSOPS-II	NSGA-II
			WS	TCH	PBI		
UF1	mean	**2.072E-03**	6.113E-02†	2.439E-03†	2.394E-03†	7.023E-02†	8.390E-02†
	std	5.063E-05	1.399E-02	5.026E-04	7.929E-04	5.731E-03	1.187E-02
UF2	mean	**5.191E-03**	5.442E-02†	1.118E-02†	3.532E-02†	5.707E-02†	3.272E-02†
	std	1.276E-03	1.102E-02	3.263E-03	3.582E-02	2.137E-02	2.355E-03
UF3	mean	**1.832E-02**	1.252E-01†	2.539E-02	4.670E-02†	3.141E-01†	7.031E-02†
	std	1.367E-02	3.208E-02	2.157E-02	3.615E-02	1.784E-02	1.163E-02
UF4	mean	**4.077E-02**	3.431E-01†	6.767E-02 †	6.177E-02†	5.393E-02†	7.606E-02†
	std	7.424E-04	4.382E-03	2.849E-03	3.588E-03	2.545E-03	1.370E-02
UF5	mean	**1.446E-01**	3.026E-01†	2.901E-01†	3.674E-01†	3.429E-01†	6.793E-01†
	std	2.713E-02	3.446E-02	4.636E-02	1.476E-01	1.004E-01	1.006E-01
UF6	mean	**6.140E-02**	2.731E-01†	1.868E-01†	3.792E-01†	2.960E-01†	3.207E-01†
	std	3.085E-02	1.451E-01	1.361E-01	2.329E-01	2.346E-01	7.719E-02
UF7	mean	**2.634E-03**	3.514E-01†	4.067E-03†	6.088E-03†	3.858E-02†	3.504E-01†
	std	1.441E-04	4.038E-03	9.467E-04	4.618E-03	6.747E-03	8.797E-03
UF8	mean	5.846E-02	5.359E-01‡	6.213E-02†	**2.401E-02**‡	1.902E-01†	2.671E-01†
	std	1.259E-02	5.586E-02	7.577E-03	7.142E-04	4.524E-03	5.537E-02
UF9	mean	**4.530E-02**	3.653E-01†	6.111E-02†	9.091E-02†	2.344E-01†	1.840E-01†
	std	3.002E-02	3.942E-02	3.914E-02	5.620E-02	3.507E-02	7.033E-02
UF10	mean	9.121E-01	4.066E-01‡	4.971E-01‡	5.632E-01‡	**2.438E-01**‡	6.630E-01‡
	std	1.542E-01	6.183E-02	4.517E-02	1.081E-01	1.205E-01	6.928E-02

Wilcoxon's rank sum test at a 0.05 significance level is performed between G-MOEA/D and each of the other competing algorithms. † and ‡ denotes that the performance of the corresponding algorithm is significantly worse than or better than that of G-MOEA/D, respectively. The best mean is highlighted in boldface

4   Conclusion

This paper proposed a novel grid-based decomposition approach to better fit decomposition-based MOEAs. The proposed G-MOEA/D is compared with five MOEAs and the experimental results show that G-MOEA/D outperforms the compared algorithms in most test problems.

References

1. Bader, J., Zitzler, E.: Hype: an algorithm for fast hypervolume-based many-objective optimization. Evol. Comput. **19**(1), 45–76 (2011)
2. Beume, N., Naujoks, B., Emmerich, M.: SMS-EMOA: multiobjective selection based on dominated hypervolume. Eur. J. Oper. Res. **181**(3), 1653–1669 (2007)
3. Coello Coello, C.A.: Evolutionary multiobjective optimization: a historical view of the field. IEEE Comput. Intell. Mag. **1**(1), 28–36 (2006)
4. Coello Coello, C.A., Lamont, G.B., Van Veldhuizen, D.A.: Evolutionary Algorithms for Solving Multi-Objective Problems, 2nd edn. Springer, New York (2007). ISBN 978-0-387-33254-3
5. Deb, K.: Multi-Objective Optimization using Evolutionary Algorithms. Wiley, Chichester (2001)
6. Deb, K., Agrawal, S., Pratab, A., Meyarivan, T.: A Fast Elitist Non-Dominated Sorting Genetic Algorithm for Multi-Objective Optimization: NSGA-II. KanGAL report 200001, Indian Institute of Technology, Kanpur, India (2000)
7. Deb, K., Pratap, A., Agarwal, S., Meyarivan, T.: A fast and elitist multiobjective genetic algorithm: NSGA-II. IEEE Trans. Evol. Comput. **6**(2), 182–197 (2002)
8. Fonseca, C.M., Fleming, P.J.: An overview of evolutionary algorithms in multiobjective optimization. Evol. Comput. **3**(1), 1–16 (1995)
9. Hughes, E.: MSOPS-II: A general-purpose many-objective optimiser. In: IEEE Congress on Evolutionary Computation, CEC 2007, pp. 3944–3951, September 2007
10. Hughes, E.J.: Multiple single objective pareto sampling. In: Proceedings of the 2003 Congress on Evolutionary Computation (CEC 2003), vol. 4, pp. 2678–2684. IEEE Press, Canberra, December 2003
11. Li, H., Zhang, Q.: Multiobjective optimization problems with complicated Pareto sets, MOEA/D and NSGA-II. IEEE Trans. Evol. Comput. **13**(2), 284–302 (2009)
12. Liu, H., Gu, F., Zhang, Q.: Decomposition of a multiobjective optimization problem into a number of simple multiobjective subproblems. IEEE Trans. Evol. Comput. **18**(3), 450–455 (2014)
13. Miettinen, K.: Nonlinear Multiobjective Optimization. Kluwer Academic Publishers, Boston (1999)
14. Tan, K., Yang, Y., Goh, C.: Multiobjective evolutionary algorithms and applications: Algorithms and applications (2006)
15. Zhang, Q., Li, H.: MOEA/D: a multiobjective evolutionary algorithm based on decomposition. IEEE Trans. Evol. Comput. **11**(6), 712–731 (2007)
16. Zhang, Q., Zhou, A., Jin, Y.: RM-MEDA: a regularity model-based multiobjective estimation of distribution algorithm. IEEE Trans. Evol. Comput. **12**(1), 41–63 (2008)
17. Zitzler, E., Künzli, S.: Indicator-based selection in multiobjective search. In: Yao, X., et al. (eds.) PPSN 2004. LNCS, vol. 3242, pp. 832–842. Springer, Heidelberg (2004). doi:10.1007/978-3-540-30217-9_84

Multi-objective Evolutionary Algorithm for Enhancing the Robustness of Networks

Zheng Li$^{(\boxtimes)}$, Shanfeng Wang, and Wenping Ma

Key Laboratory of Intelligent Perception and Image Understanding
of Ministry of Education, Xidian University, Xian 710071, China
330645132@qq.com

Abstract. Networks can represent many real-world complex systems. Systems like internet, power grids and fuel distribution networks need to be robust and capable of surviving from failures or intentional attacks. In recent years, the measurements node-robustness and link-robustness have attracted many researchers, and some researchers use different methods to enhance one of them or both of them. In this paper, we put forward a new method which is to use a multi-objective evolutionary algorithm to enhance both these two kinds of robustness of networks against attacks. We define two objective functions which represent node-robustness and link-robustness respectively. Experiments show that our algorithm can find a good balance between improving node-robustness and link-robustness.

Keywords: Complex networks · Node-robustness · Link-robustness · Multi-objective optimization

1 Introduction

With the development of the science and technology, more and more complex systems appear and need to be researched. Networks can represent many real-world complex systems such as collaboration networks, the World-Wide-Web, power grids, biological networks, and social networks. Networks could be modeled as graphs, where nodes (or vertices) represent the objects and edges represent the interactions among these objects. The area of complex networks has attracted many researchers from different fields such as physics, mathematics, biology, and sociology. Some complex systems usually involve practical situations [1], for example, the security of the infrastructure in modern society is of great importance. Systems like internet, power grids, transportation and fuel distribution networks need to be robust and can survive from random failures or intentional attacks. Thus, the robustness of networks is very important to guarantee the security of network systems [2]. Therefore, in the past decade, the robustness of different kinds of network structures has been studied intensively. Researchers have proposed several ways to define the robustness of a network. Generally, a network can be regard as a robust one if its function is not affected

© Springer Nature Singapore Pte Ltd. 2016
M. Gong et al. (Eds.): BIC-TA 2016, Part II, CCIS 682, pp. 322–327, 2016.
DOI: 10.1007/978-981-10-3614-9_39

by the attacks to nodes or links, which can be either random or malicious. Schneider et al. [3] proposed the measurement of node-robustness to optimize node-robustness. Buesser et al. in Reference [4] proposed a simulated annealing algorithm. Louzada et al. in Reference [5] proposed a smart rewiring method for this problem. Besides, in Reference [6], a suitable memetic algorithm with a local search operator was designed to improve the robustness. Another measurement named link-robustness was proposed by Zeng and Liu [7]. A method to improve the link-robustness was proposed by swapping the connections of two randomly chosen edges. In order to design robust networks resistant to more realistic attack condition, it is not enough to consider just one of these measurements. As a result, it is important to take both the node-robustness and link-robustness into account. In [7], the authors found that optimizing one measurement could not improve another one. In other word, optimizing node-robustness and link-robustness simultaneously is contradictory. Multi-objective evolutionary algorithm should be considered for this problem. Therefore, NSGA-II proposed by Deb [8] is a good choice. Because NSGA-II is one of the most popular multi-objective evolutionary algorithms and it has several advantages when compared with others. NSGA-II has a fast nondominated sorting approach with lower computational complexity and it has a better astringency in result. Whats more, NSGA-II includes an elitist strategy and it preserves the diversity by proposing the conception of crowding-distance. In this paper, we design a method which includes NSGA-II and a local search operator to improve both the node-robustness and link-robustness of networks by keeping the degree distribution and the connectivity of single node unchanged. BA network [9] is used to test our method and the experiment results demonstrate that our proposed method can find a balance between optimizing two measurements.

2 Related Theories

In this section, in order to make it easier to understand our method, we will introduce the related theories of our method briefly, including node-robustness and link-robustness.

A. Node-Robustness and Link-Robustness

In a recent work [3], adapted from the percolation theory, Schneider et al. focused on the evolution of the largest component (connected subgraph) when one repeatedly removes the highest-degree vertices in the network, and proposed a new measure R_n to weigh the network node-robustness, which is defined as

$$R_n = \frac{1}{N} \sum_{q=1/N}^{1} s(q) \qquad (1)$$

where $s(q)$ is the fraction of nodes in the largest connected cluster after removing qN nodes. The normalization factor $1/N$ ensures that the robustness of networks with different sizes can be compared.

Link-robustness index R_l is proposed in [7], which is based on the highest edge-betweenness attack strategy. It is defined as

$$R_l = \frac{1}{E} \sum_{q=1/E}^{1} s(q) \tag{2}$$

where E is the total number of links. This measure captures the network response to any fraction of link removal.

3   Our Method

Multi-objective Optimization Model

In this paper, we design a method to improve both the node-robustness and link-robustness of networks by keeping the degree distribution and the connectivity of single node unchanged. In the objective function, the node-robustness and link-robustness are evaluated respectively as two objectives which are optimized by NSGA-II. This method can get a Pareto-optimal front which includes a series of best solutions in both two objectives.

Introduction of Our Algorithm

In this algorithm, the initialization of population is in a classical method. In the initialization, since we need to keep invariant the number of links and the degree of each node, each chromosome is generated by randomly adjusting a fraction of edges in the initial network. To adjust the edges, the swap operation proposed in [3] is employed; that is, the connections of two randomly chosen edges which have no common nodes are swapped. The crossover operator and local search operator are as the same as the method in Reference [6]. Then, the nondominated sorting approach [8] is employed to select chromosomes based on both their node-robustness and link-robustness. At last, the function of replacing the chromosomes which is from NSGA-II [8] is based on rank and crowding distance. Initially the population size is reached, and each front is added one by one until addition of a complete front which results in exceeding the population size. At this point, the chromosome in that front is added subsequently to the population based on crowding distance.

4   Experiment Results

A. Experiment Dataset

In this section, the network is generated by the BA model [9]. The population size is set to 100. The parameters p_c and p_l are set to 0.5 and 0.8, respectively. The parameter α is equal to 0.9 because of priori knowledge in Reference [6]. And the BA networks with 100 nodes is used to test the performance of our algorithm, where $N_0 = 3$ and $M_0 = 2$. 100 independent runs are conducted on the networks and then the results are reported in Fig. 1. As can be see, our algorithm can get a series of pareto solutions.

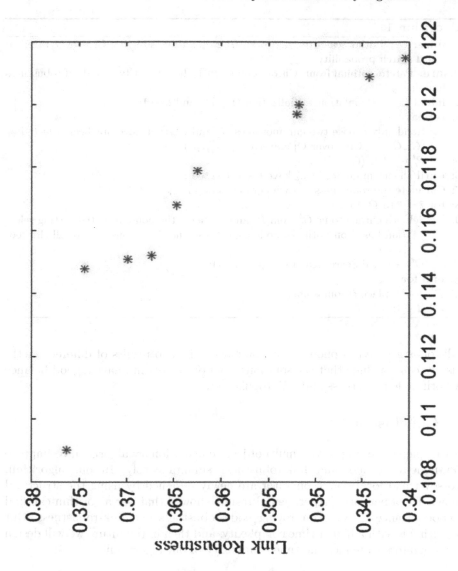

Fig. 1. The result of our method.

B. Comparison

$MA - RSF_{MA}$ [6] is one of memetic algorithms for optimizing just the node-robustness of scale-free networks against malicious attacks. We use this algorithm to optimize the same BA network and then the maximum node-robustness in result is equal to 0.1905 which is better than the final node-robustness of our method. The link-robustness of the networks after being optimized is equal to 0.2201 which is less than the link-robustness of our solutions. It shows that although this method can improve node-robustness, but it cannot improve the

---

Algorithm 1

Require: G_0: Initial scale-free network; Ω: Population size; p_c: Crossover rate; p_l: Local search probability;

Ensure: Pareto-optimal front: Chromosomes with the highest two kinds of robustness found;

1: initial $P^1 \leftarrow$ Population_Initialization (Ω, G_0) and $t \leftarrow 1$;
2: **repeat**
3:     Randomly choose two chromosomes G_i^t and G_j^t that have not been selected;
4:     $(G_i^t, G_j^t) \leftarrow$ Crossover_Operator $(G_{ci}^t, G_{cj}^t, p_c)$
5:     $P_c^t \leftarrow P_c^t \cup (G_i^t, G_j^t)$
6: **until** all chromosomes in P_t have been selected
7: Calculate the robustness of each chromosome in p_c^t;
8: **for** $i = 1$ to Ω **do**
9:     Select a chromosome G^t from P^t and P_c^t using the nondominated sorting selection based on both the node-robustness and link-robustness of all chromosomes;
10:     $G^t \leftarrow$ Local_Search_Operator (G^t, p_t, α);
11: **end for**;
12: $P^{t+1} \leftarrow$ replace_chromosome(P^t);
13: $t \leftarrow t + 1$;

---

link-robustness synchronously. By comparing the two results of different methods, we can conclude that the solutions from our algorithm have a good balance in both node-robustness and link-robustness.

5   Conclusion

In this paper, we proposed a multi-objective evolutionary algorithm to improve the node-robustness and link-robustness simultaneously. In our algorithm, crossover and local search operator are newly designed by using the structural knowledge of network. Experimental results showed that our algorithm can find a good balance between improving node-robustness and link-robustness. Our algorithm is with a higher time complexity, and then in the future we will design new operators to reduce the time complexity of our algorithm.

References

1. Girvan, M., Newman, M.E.J.: Community structure in social and biological networks. Proc. Natl. Acad. Sci. U.S.A. **99**(12), 7821–7826 (2002)
2. Crucitti, P., Latora, V., Marchiori, M., et al.: Error and attack tolerance of complex networks. Nature **406**(6794), 542 (2000)
3. Schneider, C.M., Moreira, A.A., Andrade Jr., J.S., Havlin, S., Herrmann, H.J.: Mitigation of malicious attacks on networks. Proc. Natl. Acad. Sci. U.S.A. **108**(10), 3838–3841 (2011)
4. Buesser, P., Daolio, F., Tomassini, M.: Optimizing the robustness of scale-free networks with simulated annealing. In: Dobnikar, A., Lotrič, U., Šter, B. (eds.) ICANNGA 2011. LNCS, vol. 6594, pp. 167–176. Springer, Heidelberg (2011)

5. Louzada, V.H.P., Daolio, F., Herrmann, H.J., Tomassini, M.: Smart rewiring for network robustness. J. Complex Netw. **1**, 150–159 (2013)
6. Zhou, M., Liu, J.: A memetic algorithm for enhancing the robustness of scale-free networks against malicious attacks. Phys. A Stat. Mech. Appl. **410**(12), 131–143 (2014)
7. Zeng, A., Liu, W.: Enhancing network robustness for malicious attacks. Physics **85**(6), 3112–3113 (2012)
8. Deb, K., Pratap, A., Agarwal, S., et al.: A fast and elitist multiobjective genetic algorithm: NSGA-II. IEEE Trans. Evol. Comput. **6**(2), 182–197 (2002)
9. Albert, R., Barabási, A.L.: Statistical mechanics of complex networks. Rev. Mod. Phys. **74**, 47–97 (2002)

Multi-objective Optimization with Nonnegative Matrix Factorization for Identifying Overlapping Communities in Networks

Hongmin Liu[1], Hao Li[2(✉)], and Wei Zhao[3]

[1] School of Computer Science and Technique, Henan Polytechnic University,
Jiaozuo 454000, China
[2] Key Laboratory of Intelligent Perception and Image Understanding,
Xidian University, Xi'an 710071, China
omegalihao@gmail.com
[3] School of Computer Science and Technology, Xidian University,
Xi'an 710071, China

Abstract. Community structure is one of the most important properties existing in complex networks, and community detection in complex networks is an intensively investigated problem in recent years. In real-world networks, a node is usually shared by several overlapping communities. The problem of detecting overlapping communities is much more complicated than the hard-partition problem. In this paper, a multi-objective immune algorithm with nonnegative matrix factorization as local search module (MOIA-Net) is proposed to uncover overlapping communities in networks. The proposed algorithm simultaneously optimizes two criteria, negative ratio association and ratio cut, to achieve a preferable soft-partition in networks. It adopts a nonnegative matrix factorization strategy as local search procedure to enhance the search ability. Experiments on synthetic networks show the efficiency of the proposed algorithm.

Keywords: Complex network · Overlapping community detection · Multi-objective optimization · Nonnegative matrix factorization

1 Introduction

A lot of real-world networks typically have a common feature that a group of nodes probably share common properties. The groups of nodes are usually called clusters or communities. The task of community detection problem (CDP) is to find good communities that can divide the network reasonably. It has attracted attention of many researchers in various areas and many approaches have been proposed [5, 14].

However, some aspects of community detection are quite challenging and still unsolved. One of the questions is how to detect the overlapping communities. The overlapping feature means that a node in the network can belong to more

© Springer Nature Singapore Pte Ltd. 2016
M. Gong et al. (Eds.): BIC-TA 2016, Part II, CCIS 682, pp. 328–333, 2016.
DOI: 10.1007/978-981-10-3614-9_40

than one community. This feature is quite common in real-world networks, e.g., in the network of our real life. One person can be both a scientist and a photographer, so he should be assigned to both of these two communities. Most of traditional algorithms fail to find the overlapping communities [10]. There are some specific algorithms proposed to solve the overlapping problem [8]. LFM algorithm proposed by [7] is based on the local optimization of a fitness function. Community structure is revealed by peaks in the fitness histogram. It can detect the overlapping and hierarchical communities both. Nonnegative Matrix Factorization (NMF) has emerged as a powerful tool for data analysis with enhanced interpretability. Researches have tried to apply NMF algorithms to solve the overlapping community detection problem [10,12]. However, most of these NMF-based algorithms need to set the number of community in advance. This can be quite improper in real-world networks because the number of communities is unknown before.

In this paper, we proposed a multi-objective optimization algorithm to solve the overlapping community detection problem. The algorithm adopts a multi-objective immune algorithm to simultaneously optimize two new objectives, non-negative ratio association (NRA) [1] and ratio cut (RC) [13]. The negative ratio association measures the links with-in communities and the ratio cut measures the links connecting different communities. A new coding method suitable for the overlapping conditions with variable community numbers is proposed. We use the framework of nondominated neighbor immune algorithm (NNIA) [4], which is a quite effective multi-objective optimization algorithm, to optimize the two objectives simultaneously. A NMF strategy is used as the local search procedure to enhance the search ability of the multi-objective immune algorithm.

2   Proposed Multi-objective Immune Algorithm for Overlapping Community Detection

In this section, we first present the framework of the proposed algorithm, termed as MOIA-Net. In MOIA-Net, there are three populations named dominant population D_k, active population A_k, and the clone population C_k. The dominant population is the external population to store nondominated individuals. The active population is selected from D_k according to a measure called crowding-distance. The clone population is obtained by applying proportional cloning operator to the active population.

2.1   Objective Functions

We use two criteria Ratio Association (NRA) and Ratio Cut (RC) [13] to measure the partition results. We now first give the definition of them and then show how they can be used in a multi-objective optimization approach to find communities. In [1], the authors proposed a criteria called RA to measure the quality of community structure. It is defined as follows:

$$RA = \sum_{c=1}^{K} \frac{C(V_c, V_c)}{|V_c|}, \tag{1}$$

where $C(V_1, V_2) = \sum_{i \in V_1, j \in V_2} A_{ij}$. K is the number of communities, $|V_i|$ is the number of nodes in community i. RA aims to maximize within-cluster association relative to the size of cluster. In our algorithm, in order to guarantee that the objective function is to be minimized instead of being maximized, we transform the RA to NRA as follows:

$$NRA = -\sum_{c=1}^{K} \frac{C(V_c, V_c)}{|V_c|}. \tag{2}$$

The other function RC [13] tries to minimize the links between communities, which is defined as follows:

$$RC = \sum_{c=1}^{K} \frac{C(V_c, \bar{V}_c)}{|V_c|}, \tag{3}$$

where $\bar{V}_c = V - V_c$ represents the set of nodes which are outside subset V_c.

2.2   The NMF Local Search Operator

We use a Nonnegative Matrix Factorization as local search strategy to update the results after the hypermutation operator. We know that each normalized row of W expresses a soft-membership distribution over communities given a certain node. Therefore if we want to use NMF as a local search operator, we need to convert the membership matrix into the W and H. A denormalization strategy is used here.

$$\hat{M}_{ij} = \frac{M_{ij} \sum_i A_{ij}}{\sum_{ij} A_{ij}} \tag{4}$$

$$then, \quad W_{ij} = \frac{b\hat{M}_{ij}}{\sum_{ij} \hat{M}_{ij}} \quad H = W', \tag{5}$$

where A is the adjacency matrix and b is the sum of W in the last iteration. Because the networks are undirected, we can get H by transposing W according to [12].

3   Experimental Results

3.1   Parameters Settings

The parameter settings are listed in Table 1. Some of parameters are from NNIA algorithm including $gens$, n_D, n_A, n_C, p_c, p_m. These parameters follow the rules of parameter settings in NNIA.

Table 1. Some parameters in the algorithm.

Parameter	Meaning	Value
$gens$	Maximum number of iterations	20
n_D	Maximum size of dominate population	200
n_A	Maximum size of active population	50
n_C	Number of cloning population	200
p_c	Probability of recombination	0.3
p_m	Probability of hypermutation	0.1

In the experiments, we select the values that have good results for most problems and the experiments show that the proposed algorithm is quite robust to parameters. These parameters settings in Table 1 are fixed for all experiments in the paper. Users can apply the algorithm to networks using the same parameter settings. In our paper, Normalized Mutual Information (NMI) [3] is used to evaluate the proposed method.

3.2   Experiments on Synthetic Networks

In this section, we would conduct a quantitative evaluation of the ability of MOIA-Net to identify community structure. We first apply our algorithm on two computer-generated benchmark graphs.

First, we use an extension of the classic GN benchmark network proposed by [6] to access the algorithm's performance with the degree of fuzziness in the network. This benchmark data consists of 128 nodes with 4 communities and each community has 32 nodes. The average degree of nodes is 16 and a mixing parameter μ controls the module cohesiveness of the network. We generate 30 realizations of the networks according to the rules of the benchmark network. Different algorithms are performed in these different networks and the average values are computed.

The NMI performance of our algorithm is shown in Fig. 1. We can see that when we make the network fuzzier by increasing the parameter μ, the NMI has not changed greatly. When $\mu = 0.45, 0.5$, the NMI is not good being 0.94 and 0.50 respectively, for the community structure is little cohesive. For comparison we also provide the NMI performance of some other methods: MOGA-Net [9], FM algorithm [2], Infomap algorithm [11], and the NMF [10] algorithm. For the NMF algorithm, we set the original community number as half of the number of nodes. In the figure, we can see that the performance of MOIA-Net is quiet competitive. Through the experiments we can conclude that the proposed algorithm have a competitive performance when dealing with the networks which have no overlapping structure.

Next, we would check how MOIA-Net performs on networks with a higher degree of community overlap. However, there is little work on evaluate algorithms on graphs with overlapping community structure for the lack of

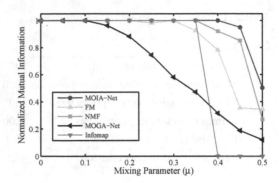

Fig. 1. Compare the *NMI* performance of our algorithm against MOGA-Net, NMF, Infomap, and FM algorithms in dealing with the extension of GN benchmark networks.

benchmark graphs. Fortunately, [6] have addressed the problem. They proposed a new kind of benchmark graphs. LFR is not a specific network, but a specification to create new networks. Under the specification one can design networks with scale-free degree and community size distributions and overlapping degree. There are ten parameters needed to make a LFR network. We want to see how the performance of MOIA-Net varies with the fraction of overlapping nodes.

In our experiments we mainly consider the overlapping aspect of networks, so we make the number of overlapping nodes as a variant and the mixing parameter is fixed at 0.1. Among these 11 networks, we choose the network with 200 overlapping nodes to show the community structure. In Fig. 2 the network is shown at the community-level where a pie chart mean communities of the network. There are 49 communities and the size of each pie denotes the number of nodes belonging to this community. For the overlap exists in network, different communities share nodes. The lines between pies means the overlapping relationship between these two communities.

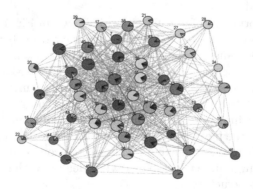

Fig. 2. The LFR network with 200 overlapping nodes. Each pie denotes one community, the line between two communities means there are overlapping nodes between them.

4   Concluding Remarks

In this paper, we have presented a multi-objective optimization method named MOIA-Net to detect the overlapping communities in networks. Unlike the traditional evolutionary algorithms for community detection problem, the proposed algorithm not only obtains the membership of a node in multiple communities, but also quantifies how strongly that node belongs to each of the communities. Experiments on several artificial networks show that the proposed algorithm is quite competitive with the traditional community detection algorithms and has the ability to uncover the overlapping communities in networks.

References

1. Angelini, L., Boccaletti, S., Marinazzo, D., Pellicoro, M., Stramaglia, S.: Identification of network modules by optimization of ratio association. Chaos **17**(2), 023114 (2007)
2. Clauset, A., Newman, M.E., Moore, C.: Finding community structure in very large networks. Phys. Rev. E **70**(6), 066111 (2004)
3. Danon, L., Diaz-Guilera, A., Duch, J., Arenas, A.: Comparing community structure identification. J. Stat. Mech. **2005**(09), P09008 (2005)
4. Gong, M., Jiao, L., Du, H., Bo, L.: Multiobjective immune algorithm with nondominated neighbor-based selection. Evol. Comput. **16**(2), 225–255 (2008)
5. Gong, M., Ma, L., Zhang, Q., Jiao, L.: Community detection in networks by using multiobjective evolutionary algorithm with decomposition. Phys. A **391**(15), 4050–4060 (2012)
6. Lancichinetti, A., Fortunato, S.: Benchmarks for testing community detection algorithms on directed and weighted graphs with overlapping communities. Phys. Rev. E. **80**(1), 016118 (2009)
7. Lancichinetti, A., Fortunato, S., Kertész, J.: Detecting the overlapping and hierarchical community structure in complex networks. New J. Phys. **11**(3), 033015 (2009)
8. Palla, G., Derényi, I., Farkas, I., Vicsek, T.: Uncovering the overlapping community structure of complex networks in nature and society. Nature **435**(7043), 814–818 (2005)
9. Pizzuti, C.: A multi-objective genetic algorithm for community detection in networks. In: Proceedings of IEEE International Conference on Tools with Artificial Intelligence, pp. 379–386 (2009)
10. Psorakis, I., Roberts, S., Ebden, M., Sheldon, B.: Overlapping community detection using bayesian non-negative matrix factorization. Phys. Rev. E **83**(6), 066114 (2011)
11. Rosvall, M., Bergstrom, C.T.: Maps of random walks on complex networks reveal community structure. Proc. Natl. Acad. Sci. USA **105**(4), 1118–1123 (2008)
12. Tan, V.Y., Févotte, C.: Automatic relevance determination in nonnegative matrix factorization. In: Proceedings of Signal Processing with Adaptive Sparse Structured Representations (2009)
13. Wei, Y.C., Cheng, C.K.: Ratio cut partitioning for hierarchical designs. IEEE Trans. Comput. Aided Des. Integr. Circuits Syst. **10**(7), 911–921 (1991)
14. Zhang, P., Moore, C., Newman, M.: Community detection in networks with unequal groups. Phys. Rev. E **93**(1), 012303 (2016)

Magnetic Bacterial Optimization Algorithm for Mobile Robot Path Planning

Hongwei Mo[1], Lifang Xu[2(✉)], and Chaomin Luo[3]

[1] Automation College, Harbin Engineering University, Harbin 150001, China
honwei2004@126.com
[2] Engineering Training Center, Harbin Engineering University, Harbin 150001, China
mxlfang@163.com
[3] Department of Electrical and Computer Engineering, University of Detroit Mercy,
Detroit 48208-2576, USA
luoch@udmercy.edu

Abstract. Autonomous navigation of robots is a promising research field due to its extensive applications. In recent years, more and more heuristic methods are applied in robot path planning. This paper proposes a new heuristic algorithm for path planning-magnetic bacterial optimization algorithm (MBOA). In the path planning algorithm based on MBOA, magnetosomes are mapped to the nodes in the path of robot. Simulation results show that the proposed algorithm is suitable for the problem of path planning and has better performance than some classical heuristic methods.

Keywords: Magnetic bacterial algorithm · Path planning · Mobile robot

1 Introduction

Path planning is one of the most important problems of robot navigation. Many classical methods such as road-map method (RM) [1], subgoal method (SG) [2] had been proposed. But these classical approaches commonly have difficulty in path planning with complex environments due to their high cost of computation. In recent years, nature inspired methods such as Genetic Algorithms (GAs), Particle Swarm Optimization (PSO), Ant Colony Optimization (ACO), Biogeography Based Optimization (BBO) were developed for solving the path planning problem.

Magnetic Bacteria Optimization Algorithm (MBOA) is a new intelligent optimization algorithm [3]. The algorithm is inspired by magnetic bacteria with magnetosomes in their bodies, which can make them move along the magnetic field lines. Experiment results have shown that the MBOA can effectively solve the optimization problems [4–6]. In this paper, we proposed a robot path planning algorithm based on MBOA. The paper is organized as follows. In Sect. 2, the process of MBOA for path planning is described. In Sect. 3, experiments and discussion are given. Section 4 is conclusion.

© Springer Nature Singapore Pte Ltd. 2016
M. Gong et al. (Eds.): BIC-TA 2016, Part II, CCIS 682, pp. 334–339, 2016.
DOI: 10.1007/978-981-10-3614-9_41

2 Path Planning Based on Magnetic Bacteria Optimization Algorithm

The basic definition and process of MBOA is referred to [3]. When the MBOA is used to solving optimization problem, a candidate solution is seemed as a cell. In this paper, it is used to optimize the robot path, the number of cells corresponds to the number of paths. Each path consists of grids with no obstacles from start node to target node. The dimensions L of the ith cell are the effective points produced in environment, that is, the points covered in area with no obstacles. Each cell use the start point as the current node, select the next node by the value of L dimensions vector. The process is as follows:

Suppose $X_i = (x_{i,1}, x_{i,2}, ..., x_{i,n})$ as the n dimensions vector of the ith cell, and $X_{i,j} \in (0, 1)$. Taboo search is used in order not to repeat the same trajectory. Taboo mobile strategy sets taboo list to save nodes in a path. Suppose the taboo list of the path represented by the ith cell as $Dist_i$, the start point as the current point, and save it to the taboo list $Dist_i$. Assume the points set of neighborhood domain of start point $Next[i]$, where the number of the points which have no obstacles on the connection line with the current node is n, then in local search, the selection method of next node of the current point is:

$$l = (int)(X_i) \tag{1}$$

$$next = Next[l] \tag{2}$$

where m is the integer between [0, n-1], and then save the node $next$ in $Dist_i$. And this node is used as the current node for the next search, until the target node is added into the tabu list. The optimal solution in the algorithm corresponds to the solution which has the shortest length of paths.

The procedure of path planning based on MBOA is as follows:

Step1. Load the environment map, set the start node and the target node of the path, extract the effective point, that is, the barrier free point, save the environmental information, set the maximum number of iterations.

Step2. Initialization of the parameters of the MBOA including the magnetic field strength values B, energy function parameters C_1, C_2 and the total number of cells N. Initialize randomly $X_i = (x_{i,1}, x_{i,2}, ..., x_{i,n})$, the number of initialization iterations C is 0, the number of initializtion cells m is 0.

Then each cell is generated as follows:

$$x_{i,j} = x_{\min,j} + rand(0, 1) \times (x_{\max,j} - x_{\min,j}) \tag{3}$$

where $i = 1, 2..., N, j = 1, 2, ..., n$. $x_{max,j}$ and $x_{min,j}$ are upper and lower bounds for the dimension j, respectively. $rand(0, 1)$ is a random number between 0 and 1.

Step3. Set the start node as the current node, select the next node by roulette selection according to the fitness of feasible grids in the neighborhood domain of the current node. And each selected node is saved in list. Each node will be checked in order to avoid repeatation. If it is not in the list, then it is saved in the list. Otherwise, it is given up. The roulette selection will continue in the left grids till target node. Calculate the cost of path.

2.1   Interaction Distance

Interaction distance is used to calculate the interaction energy for generating the magnetosomes of cells. The distance $d_{i,r}$ of two cells x_i and x_r calculated as follows:

$$d_{i,r} = x_i - x_r \tag{4}$$

Thus, we can get a $N \times n$ distance matrix $D = [D_1, D_2, ..., D_N]'$, where i and r is mutually different integer indices from $\{1, 2, ..., N\}$, and r is randomly chosen one. N is the size of cell population.

2.2   MTSs Generation

Based on the distances among cells, the interaction energy e_i between two cells based on (4) is defined as

$$e_{i,j}(t) = \left(\frac{d_{i,j}(t)}{1 + c_1 \times norm(D_i) + c_2 \times d_{p,q}(t)} \right)^3 \tag{5}$$

where t is the generation index, c_1 and c_2 are constants. $norm(D_i)$ is the Euclidean length of vector D_i. $d_{p,q}$ is randomly selected from D_p. p is randomly chosen integer indices from$\{1, 2, ..., N\}$. $q \in \{1, 2, ..., n\}$ stands for one randomly chosen integer. n is the dimensions of a cell. $D_{i,r}$ stands for the Euclidean distance between two cells x_i, x_r.

After obtaining interaction energy, the moments m_i are generated as follows [11]:

$$M_i(t) = \frac{E_i(t)}{B} \tag{6}$$

where B is a constant named magnetic field strength.

Then the total moments of a cell is regulated as follows:

$$x_{i,j}(t) = x_{i,j}(t) + m_{r,q}(t) \times rand \tag{7}$$

where $m_{r,q}$ is randomly chosen from m_i. $rand$ is a random number in interval (0,1).

Step4. $m = m + 1$, if $m < M$, if not satisfied, then return to Step3.

Step5. The path values of all cells are compared to save the minimum path value.

Step6. The expansion of the magnetic body, the replacement process of the magnetic body, the replacement of the lower torque value of the magnetic bodies of the solution.

After moments generation, evaluate the population according to cells fitness, then the moments are regulated as follows:

$$X_i(t+1) = X_{best}(t) + (X_{best}(t) - X_i(t)) \times rand \tag{8}$$

Otherwise,

$$X_i(t+1) = X_i(t) + (X_{best}(t) - X_r(t)) \times rand \tag{9}$$

X_{best} is the best cell in the current generation. $rand$ is a random number in interval $(0,1)$. r is randomly chosen from $\{1, 2, ..., N\}$.

After the moments migration, evaluate the population according to cells' fitness, some worse moments are replaced by the following way

$$X_i(t+1) = m_{r,q}(t) \times ((rand(1,n) - 1) \times rand(1,n)) \tag{10}$$

where $m_{r,q}$ is randomly chosen from M_r. r is randomly chosen from $\{1, 2, ..., N\}$. $q \in \{1, 2, ..., n\}$ stands for one randomly chosen integer. $rand(1,n)$ is a random vector with n dimensions in interval $(0,1)$.

Step7. Evaluate the population according to cells' fitness after replacement, if the output to meet the optimal solution, then stop, otherwise return to Step2.

3   Experiments and Discussion

In this section, MBOA is compared with PSO and BBO on the problem of robot path planning.

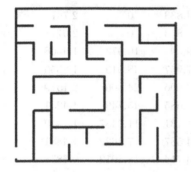
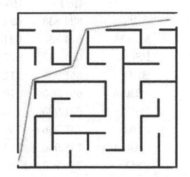

Fig. 1. Environment map   **Fig. 2.** Resulted path by MBOA

The algorithm parameters are set as follows: PSO: the number of particles is $M = 30$, the inertia factor is the linear dynamic adjustment and the maximum value is 0.8, the minimum value is 0.4, the acceleration constant is $C1 = C2 = 0.5$. BBO: the number of habitat $M = 30$, the maximum variation rate of $M_{max} = 0.3$. MBOA: cell number $M = 30$, magnetic field intensity value $B = 10$, energy factor $C1 = C2 = 0.5$. In addition, the tabu search algorithm is also applicable to the MBOA algorithm and PSO algorithm. The environment map used in the simulation experiment is shown in Fig. 1. The environment (a) is mapped from a real work space. There some tables and chairs and some other obstacles. The red point in the map is injected after the map was generated. The environment (b) is a simple maze as a map.

In the experiments, under the environment (a), MBOA is better than that of the BBO algorithm. Under the environment (b), BBO and MBOA converge in the 20th generation and 13th generation, respectively. The data in the Table 1

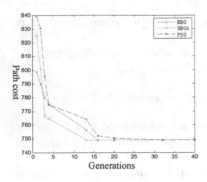
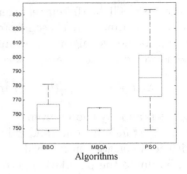

Fig. 3. Convergence   **Fig. 4.** Time cost

Table 1. Path cost under different environments of three algorithms

Environment map	Algorithms	minimum value (px)	Average value (px)	Maximum value (px)	Standard deviation	Planning time (s)
(a)	BBO	624.833	624.833	624.833	0	2.7074
	MBOA	624.833	624.833	624.833	0	2.9718
	PSO	624.833	627.979	669.09	10.973	1.4508
(b)	BBO	651.905	711.816	797.957	48.919	1.8555
	MBOA	651.905	670.063	716.506	24.606	2.1579
	PSO	651.905	714.204	801.685	45.749	1.4231
(c)	BBO	748.966	759.082	781.131	11.0487	1.2449
	MBOA	748.966	754.176	764.587	7.3622	1.4881
	PSO	748.966	786.947	833.714	18.5012	0.6878

also shows that MBOA can find better path value than the other two algorithms (Fig. 2).

In Figs. 3 and 4, the convergence, time cost and the variance of the three algorithms.

4   Conclusion

In the paper, we proposed an new robot path planing algorithm based on Magnetic Bacteria Optimization Algorithm. It is tested under three different environments to show its performance. It is compared with the other two nature inspired algorithms including PSO and BBO. Experimental results show that the proposed MBOA is suitable for path planning and has better performance in the respect of convergence. In future, we will use the MBOA to the problem of dynamic environment.

References

1. Rantanen, M.T., Juhola, M.: A configuration deactivation algorithm for boosting probabilistic road-map planning of robots. Int. J. Autom. Comput. **9**(2), 155–164 (2012)
2. Singh, N.N., Chatterjee, A., Chatterjee, A., Rakshit, A.: A two-layered subgoal based mobile robot navigation algorithm with vision system and IR sensors. Emerg. Res. Artif. Intell. Comput. Intell. Commun. Comput. Inf. Sci. **237**, 325–334 (2011)
3. Mo, H.W.: Research on magnetotactic bacteria optimization algorithm. In: The Fifth International Conference on Advanced Computational Intelligence (ICACI 2012), Nanjing, pp. 423–427 (2012)
4. Mo, H.W., Xu, L.F.: Magnetotactic bacteria optimization algorithm for multimodal optimization. In: IEEE Symposium on Swarm Intelligence (SIS), Singapore, pp. 240–247 (2013)
5. Mo, H.W., Liu, L.L., Xu, L.F., Zhao, Y.Y.: Performance research on magnetotactic bacteria optimization algorithm based on the best individual. In: The sixth International Conference on Bio-inspired Computing(BICTA2014), Wuhan, China, pp. 318–322 (2014)
6. Mo, H.W., Geng, M.J.: Magnetotactic bacteria optimization algorithm based on best-rand scheme. In: 6th Nature and Biologically Inspired Computing, Porto Portugal, pp. 59–64 (2014)

Pattern Recognition

A Simple Deep Feature Representation for Person Re-identification

Shengke Wang, Lianghua Duan, Yong Zhao, and Junyu Dong[(✉)]

Department of Computer Science and Technology,
Ocean University of China, 238 Songling Road, Qingdao 266100, China
{neverme,dongjunyu}@ouc.edu.cn, 1160050472@qq.com,
yongzhao.ouc@gmail.com

Abstract. Person re-identification (Re-ID) aims to match persons across non-overlapping camera views at different time. Typical person Re-ID models include two critical components: feature representation and metric learning. Due to the large variations in a persons appearance by different poses, viewpoints, illumination and occlusions, metric learning is always a necessary part in person Re-ID. In this paper, we propose a Deep person Feature Representation (DFR) learning framework based on a classification-oriented convolution neural network, and the DFR is directly used to calculate cosine distance for the similarity measure while with-out explicit metric learning. In the framework, Batch Normalization (BN) is applied before the ReLU layer to accelerate the convergence process, and with dropout strategy the DFR is only 64-dimension which makes the feature representation more effective and less noisy. Experiments demonstrate that our approach achieves the state-of-the-art results on most of the challenging datasets, especially on dataset of the largest scale CUHK03.

Keywords: Person re-identification · Deep learning · Distance measure · Metric learning

1 Introduction

The problem of person re-identification focuses on the verification of two pedestrian image shots by various cameras, or a single camera in different time, still remains a challenging problem in computer vision due to the complicated diversifications in pose, occlusion, illumination, viewpoint and image resolution across different camera views (See Fig. 1).

To solve this problem, many traditional methods have been proposed, such as [1–5]. Procedures of these approaches can be summarized as: (1) extract the pedestrian images hand-crafted features; (2) calculate the distance of given image pairs through a metric learning process. However, manual features are usually vulnerable to representation, and metric learning may waste time while the improvement seems slim. Hence, people have been searching for the new

© Springer Nature Singapore Pte Ltd. 2016
M. Gong et al. (Eds.): BIC-TA 2016, Part II, CCIS 682, pp. 343–354, 2016.
DOI: 10.1007/978-981-10-3614-9_42

Fig. 1. Examples of several datasets: CUHK03 (first row), CUHK01 (second row) and VIPeR (third row). Image pairs denote the same person.

methods for this problem. With the deep learning getting more and more popular in some domain, especially in computer vision, using Convolution Neural Network (CNN) [6–11] for person re-identification problem becomes more important. Most noteworthy is that [6] proposed a deep learning architecture, and obtained good performance, which can learn the feature and similarity metric simultaneously.

In this paper, we propose a deep feature representation (DFR) learning framework with convolution neural networks to learn the pedestrian features. And then, we take Cosine similarity as our similarity measures to calculate images similarity directly. The DFR is only 64-d which reserving more useful information but less noises. We have tested our DFR learning framework on several public person Re-ID datasets, and the results show that our method is superior to previous work both on the process time and the accuracy.

2   Related Work

2.1   Person Re-identification with CNN

Convolution Neural Network has shown the good performance in person Re-ID problem. In DeepReID [8], Li et al. first used CNN with two special layers to address the problems of viewpoint and pose variations. [12] used a Siamese architecture to deal with the variations of different images. [6] proposed an improved deep learning structure for person re-identification, using the Cross-Input Neighborhood Difference to learn the relationships between the two views. [13] proposed deep transfer metric learning (DTML) to transfer cross-domain visual knowledge into target dataset, increasing the robust of method. [9] investigated the combination and complementary of a multi-color space hand-crafted features and deep feature with a feature fusion Network (FFN). [14] applied constrained deep metric learning for re-identification with a full-connected layers replacing the process of metric learning, and got the good single-shot result on CUHK01 [15] dataset. Since most of those use a pair image as input, they need amounts of time to train CNN and process data. Compared with others, our deep feature representation (DFR) learning structure use single image as input, simplifying the process but also improving the performance.

2.2 Metric Learning and Similarity Measure

For an given image pair in person Re-ID problem, people would like to learn a distance metric to reduce the distance of matched images and enlarge the distance of mismatched images [2–4,7,14,16,17]. Typical metric learning methods including: Fisher discriminant analysis (FDA), local Fisher discriminant analysis (LFDA) [12], marginal Fisher analysis (MFA) [18], and cross-view quadratic discriminant analysis (XQDA) [19]. According to a survey on metric learning [20], the dominant position of metric learning has been occupied by a global Mahalanobis metric. The distance or similarity between image pair (x, y) can be defined as:

$$d_M(x, y) = \sqrt{(x - y)^T M (x - y)}. \tag{1}$$

Where x, y are feature vectors, M is a positive semi-definite matrix. Metric learning has long improved the performance, but the cost of promotion is worth discussing. We believe that the process of metric learning would be redundant that may waste time even reduce the accuracy if the feature representation is so efficient that can be used directly. Except for metric learning, there are many distance strategy to calculate images similarity, such as Euclidean distance, Cosine distance, Mahalanobis distance, etc. In our work, we experiment our features on several metric learning methods, the promotion is tiny. Therefore, we design our methods without metric learning process. After several experiments, We choose Cosine similarity as our similarity metric method.

3 Our Method

In the previous deep learning works, there were usually taking as CNN input as two images, and applying PCA to reduce the learned features dimensions to 256 or 512, then learning a metric with a complex process, and calculating image pairs distance through Euclidean Distance measure in the end. So from the global perspective, the previous methods are very complicated. In this paper, we propose a simple method to solve the person Re-ID problem. The basic framework of our method includes two parts: (1) Feature Network (FN), images of pedestrians are put into a classification CNN to capture the discriminating information of different person automatically (See Fig. 2 green box). The learned CNN model

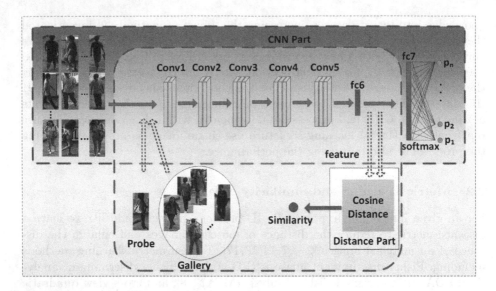

Fig. 2. The overview of our method. For the person re-identification problem, we first train a classification CNN for feature extraction (green box), then calculate images similarity by a Distance part (red box). (Color figure online)

can be used to extract the distinguishing feature representation of different persons with various appearance in different poses, viewpoints and illumination etc. (2) Matching, a matching procedure is applied to the architecture, we propagate the test dataset images in the learned network for-ward and utilize the fc6 layers output as the images feature, and then put it in Distance part to calculate the similarity of image pairs (See Fig. 2 red box).

3.1   CNN Structure for Feature Extraction

The quality of features impact the matching result directly. We use a very deep classification network to extract the pedestrian feature for two reasons: (1) among visual recognition tasks solved by CNN, the classification problem is the foundation of complex tasks; (2) a growing number of problem that using the classification network are getting good performance. According to the Microsoft research, the deeper the CNNs structure the better the result. Hence, we design our Feature Network (FN) modeled on VGG16 [21] which have a deeper network structure and have been achieved state-of-the-art performance on ImageNet dataset.

However, person re-identification problem cant use the original VGG Network directly because of pedestrian images are usually small and not a fixed-size. Inspired by [10,13], we design the network for fitting the person Re-ID problem that using the bodys aspect ratio. Whats more, we use the Batch Normalization (BN) strategy before the ReLU layer referenced in [9], which has proven that the BN can accelerate the convergence process and avoid manually tweaking the

Table 1. The structure details of our proposed FN

Name		Kernel size/ stride/ pad	Output size
Input			$3 \times 144 \times 56$
conv1	(conv+BN+ReLU) *2	3/ 1/ 1	$64 \times 144 \times 56$
	Maxpool1	2/ 2/ 0	$64 \times 72 \times 28$
conv2	(conv+BN+ReLU) *2	3/ 1/ 1	$128 \times 72 \times 28$
	Maxpool2	2/ 2/ 0	$128 \times 36 \times 14$
conv3	(conv+BN+ReLU) *3	3/ 1/ 1	$256 \times 36 \times 14$
	Maxpool3	2/ 2/ 0	$256 \times 18 \times 7$
conv4	(conv+BN+ReLU) *3	3/ 1/ 1	$512 \times 18 \times 7$
	Maxpool4	2/ 2/ 0	$512 \times 9 \times 4$
conv5	(conv+BN+ReLU) *3	3/ 1/ 1	$512 \times 9 \times 4$
	Maxpool5	2/ 2/ 0	$512 \times 5 \times 2$
fc6	FC+ReLU+Dropout		64
fc7	FC		N

initialization of weight and biases. In order to improve the robust of our CNN framework, we use Dropout strategy [22], which is wide used in the CNNs train step, dropout some neurons be-fore processing the last full connected layer. It must be pointed out that our Deep person Feature Representation (DFR) is only 64-d that is much smaller than previous method, retained more effective identity information but less noise. Detailed FN structures are listed in Table 1 (N denote that the numbers of each datasets train set, FC means a full connected layer, conv+BN+ReLU means that it consists of a convolution layer, a Batch Normalization layer and a ReLU layer).

3.2   Cosine Distance Measure

In our work, we use Cosine similarity as our similarity measure.

Let $A = (a_1, a_2, \cdots, a_{64})$, $B = (b_1, b_2, \cdots, b_{64})$, respectively, represent the two features extracted by our FN from two images, the similarity of two images can be denote as:

$$Similarity = cos\left(\theta\right) = \frac{A \bullet B}{\|A\|\|B\|} = \frac{\sum_{i=1}^{64} A_i B_i}{\sqrt{\sum_{i=1}^{64} A_i^2}\sqrt{\sum_{i=1}^{64} B_i^2}}. \qquad (2)$$

Higher values indicate a higher similarity of two images.

3.3   Experiments

We implemented our Feature Network (FN) architecture using the Caffe [23] deep learning framework. 40k iteration of network training converge in roughly 10 h on NVIDIA Titan x GPUs on CUHK03 [8], and finetune on other dataset expend 3–5 h for 15k iteration. In this section, we report a comprehensive evaluation of our method by comparing it to the state-of-the-art approach on various datasets (CUHK03 [8], CUHK01 [15], VIPeR [24], PRW [25]) and we then analyze the effects of distance measure, feature dimension, Batch normalization and Dropout strategy. The Cumulative Matching Characteristic (CMC) curves are multi-shot results which is more difficult than single-shot.

3.4   Implement Details

When operating the Feature Network (FN), we employ mini-batch stochastic gradient descent (SGD) for faster back propagation and smoother convergence [26]. In each iteration of training phase, the mini-batch is 50 images, learning rate =0.01, and decreased by every 20000 iteration. We train CUHK03 dataset firstly due to its the largest dataset and then finetune it on other datasets. The dataset and protocols are followed at Table 2 (# means the number of, ID means the identity of person, FN means our Feature Network, Tr means train, Val means validation, Pb and Gal means the probe and gallery dataset for test). With the procedure of FN accomplished, we propagate the probe and gallery data forward and save the fc6 layers output as the images feature. Followed by Cosine distance measure, we calculate the image pairs similarity straightly without any idle operation. We test proposed method on CUHK03, CUHK01 and VIPeR dataset which are challenging and reprehensive for person re-identification problem.

3.5   Experiments on CUHK03

The CUHK03 [8] data set has more than 14,000 images of 1467 subjects, captured by five different pairs of surveillance cameras. Each identity has 10 images approximately. Following the protocol, we randomly partition 1467 pedestrians into non-overlap FN set, Test sets. We use 21009 train images and 5252 validation images to train our classification Network, 50k iteration late, the accuracy of classification can up to 99.8%. Based on the learned model, we evaluate the test set to illustrate the efficiency of proposed method. We compare our approach against traditional methods including KISSME [27], LOMO-XQDA [2] and eSDC [5], and deep learning methods including FPNN [8], SIR+CIR [28], RME [3] and

Table 2. Statistics of the datasets and evaluation protocols

Dataset	#ID	#FN			#Test	
		#FN ID	#Tr images	#Val images	#Pb ID	#Gal ID
CUHK03	1467	1367	21009	5252	100	100
CUHK01	971	486	1552	388	485	485
VIPeR	632	316	506	126	316	316
PRW	932	482	10000	4893	450	450

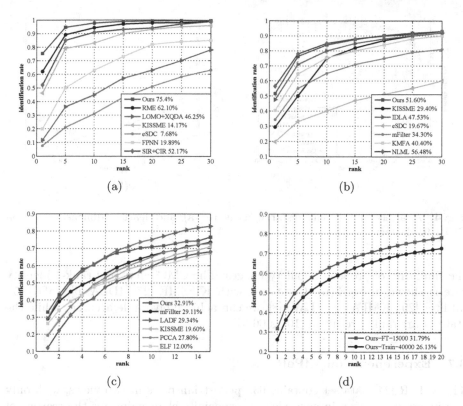

Fig. 3. CMC curves on datasets: (a) CUHK03 dataset with 100 test IDs: Our method get the state-of-the-art result. (b) CUHK01 dataset with 485 test IDs: We achieved favorable accuracy. (c) VIPeR dataset: Our method win the best while has a wide gap with the sate-of-the-art result 47.8%. (d) PRW dataset with 450 test IDs: We obtained 31.79% accuracy in this new dataset.

DGD [10] which gained the previously best performance on CUHK03 with rank-1 matching up to 75.3%. The CMC curves and the rank-1 identification rates are shown in Fig. 3(a). From picture, we can see our method is superiority over others both traditional methods and new methods of using CNN. We achieve the state-of-the-art result with rank-1 accuracy up to 75.4%. Most of all, our method is simpler than DGD which needs several adjustments.

3.6 Experiments on CUHK01

The CUHK01 [15] data set contains 971 subjects captured from two cameras view in a campus environment. We set the number of individuals in the train split to 486 and test split to 485. As described in Sect. 4.1, we initialize the Feature Network by the model pre-trained on CUHK03 dataset, and then finetune the FN on CUHK01. After 1,5K iteration, we extract the features of probe and gallery dataset using the trained model, followed by the Cosine Distance, we can get

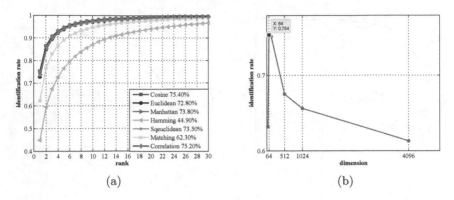

Fig. 4. Analysis of different distance measure (a) and feature dimension (b) on CUHK03 dataset

the similarity of probe and gallery images. The CMC curve and rank-1 identity rate is shown in Fig. 3(b). Compared with KISSME [27], IDLA [6], eSDC [5], mFilter [29], KMFA [4], NLML [8], we can achieve favorable accuracy while the state-of-art rank-1 result in [10] is 66.6%.

3.7   Experiments on VIPeR

The VIPeR [24] data set contains 632 pedestrian pairs in two views, with only one image per person in each view, is especially challenging for the reasons of viewpoint and low-solutions. Based on the protocol, we finetune the dataset using the CUNHK03 datasets model, after the 1.5K iteration, the result compared with mFilter [29], LADF [30], PCCA [31], eSDC [5], KISSME [27], SSCDL [32] is drawn in Fig. 3(c). Our method win the best while has a wide gap with the sate-of-the-art result 47.8% in [16].

3.8   Experiment on PRW

The PRW [25] dataset is an extension of the Market-1501 dataset [33] that contains 11,816 wild video frames captured by 6 cameras and 34,304 pedestrians are annotated by hand-drawn with an ID ranging from 1 to 932. Due to shot in wild, the phenomenon of variation in pose, occlusion, illumination, viewpoint and image scale across different pedestrian images is more serious which makes person re-identification harder. We use annotated bounding boxes as pedestrian images, as we know, we are first to do this due to the PRW is the new dataset that was released recently. Compared with training dataset directly, we finetune the dataset based on the model that trained for CUHK03. The CMC curve and rank-1 accuracy is plotted in Fig. 3(d). We obtained 31.79% top-1 accuracy.

3.9   Analysis

Distance Measure. We use the Cosine distance measure to calculate the image pairs similarity while variation of distance measure influence the result. To understand the powers of Cosine distance measure, we compare the performance with other six strategies using the same CUHK03 image feature. The result is shown in Fig. 4(a). From the figure, we can see that the Cosine distance measure is most suitable for our 64-d features, however, the Euclidean distance measure used mostly get the third due to the Euclidean distance measure cant considerate the correlation between the components, and the multiple components of a single feature can interfere with the results. Compared to the Euclidean distance measure, the Cosine similarity is more attention to the difference of the two vectors in the direction, fit into our 64-d features.

Feature Dimension. In our work, we set the f6 layers output to 64-d, achieved the state-of-the-art on CUHK03 dataset. To further certify the superiority of our choice, we analyze the results with varying feature dimension on the CUHK03 dataset with the same Cosine distance measure. Figure 4(b) shows the CMC result and the rank-1 matching rate from our experiment. From the picture, we find that the result becomes well with the dimension decreasing, but if the dimension is under 64, the performance would diminish rapidly. The optimal performance was obtained when dimension is set to 64.

Batch Normalization and Dropout. Our method achieve such a good result, to a large extent depends on the Batch Normalization (BN) and Dropout strategy. The former is proposed to overcome the shortcomings of the difficulty of training in deep learning, the latter is presented by Hinton that with a probability of 50% setting the output of hidden layer to 0 which will no longer working

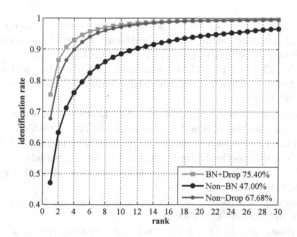

Fig. 5. Comparison of BN and dropout strategy on CUHK03 dataset

for the forward or backward process, such randomness can increase the capacity of network generalization. To understand the contribution of BN and Dropout we experiment the performance on CUHK03 dataset under the same conditions except that the BN and Dropout layer exist or not. Its quite striking that the BN strategy improved the performance by 30% at rank-1 while the result with Dropout strategy increased by 28% (see Fig. 5).

4   Conclusion

Using the CNN that can collect the available information automatically with the BP strategy. In this paper, we present an effective way of feature extraction for person re-identification called Feature Net (FN). The feature extracted by FN is low-dimension but valid for calculating the similarity of two images. Whats more, we employ the simple but useful Cosine distance measure as the similarity measure method directly, saving the time while performing excellently. Experiment on four challenging and common person re-identification datasets (CUHK03 [8], CUHK01 [15], VIPeR [24], PRW [25]), we beat the most method individually, demonstrate the robust of our method, especially on CUHK03 dataset we obtain the state-of-the-art result with rank-1 accuracy of 75.4% with a simple but effective approach.

Acknowledgments. This work is supported by the Natural Science Foundation of China (NSFC) Grants 61301241, 61403353, 61303145, 61501417 and 61271405; Natural Science Foundation of Shandong (ZR2015FQ011; ZR2014FQ023); China Postdoctoral Science Foundation funded project (2016M590659); Qingdao Postdoctoral Science Foundation funded project(861605040008); The Fundamental Research Funds for the Central Universities (201511008, 30020084851).

References

1. Chen, D., Yuan, Z., Hua, G., Zheng, N.: Similarity learning on an explicit polynomial kernel feature map for person re-identification. In: Conference on Computer Vision and Pattern Recognition, pp. 1565–1573 (2015)
2. Liao, S., Hu, Y., Zhu, X., Li, S.Z.: Person re-identification by local maximal occurrence representation and metric learning. In: Computer Vision and Pattern Recognition, pp. 2197–2206 (2015)
3. Paisitkriangkrai, S., Shen, C., Hengel, A.: Learning to rank in person re-identification with metric ensembles. Computer Science (2015)
4. Xiong, F., Gou, M., Camps, O., Sznaier, M.: Person re-identification using kernel-based metric learning methods. In: Fleet, D., Pajdla, T., Schiele, B., Tuytelaars, T. (eds.) ECCV 2014. LNCS, vol. 8695, pp. 1–16. Springer, Heidelberg (2014). doi:10.1007/978-3-319-10584-0_1
5. Zhao, R., Ouyang, W., Wang, X.: Unsupervised salience learning for person re-identification. **9**(4), 3586–3593 (2013)
6. Ahmed, E., Jones, M., Marks, T.K.: An improved deep learning architecture for person re-identification. In: Computer Vision and Pattern Recognition (2015)

7. Huang, S., Lu, J., Zhou, J., Jain, A.K.: Nonlinear local metric learning for person re-identification. Computer Science (2015)
8. Li, W., Zhao, R., Xiao, T., Wang, X.: Deepreid: deep filter pairing neural network for person re-identification. In: IEEE Conference on Computer Vision and Pattern Recognition, pp. 152–159 (2014)
9. Wu, S., Chen, Y.C., Li, X., Wu, A.C., You, J.J., Zheng, W.S.: An enhanced deep feature representation for person re-identification. In: IEEE Winter Conference on Applications of Computer Vision, pp. 1–8 (2016)
10. Xiao, T., Li, H., Ouyang, W., Wang, X.: Learning deep feature representations with domain guided dropout for person re-identification (2016)
11. Ding, S., Lin, L., Wang, G., Chao, H.: Deep feature learning with relative distance comparison for person re-identification. Pattern Recogn. **48**(10), 2993–3003 (2015)
12. Pedagadi, S., Orwell, Velastin, S., Boghossian, B.: Local fisher discriminant analysis for pedestrian re-identification. In: IEEE Conference on Computer Vision and Pattern Recognition, pp. 3318–3325 (2013)
13. Hu, J., Lu, J., Tan, Y.P.: Deep transfer metric learning. In: IEEE Conference on Computer Vision and Pattern Recognition, pp. 325–333 (2015)
14. Shi, H., Zhu, X., Liao, S., Lei, Z., Yang, Y., Li, S.Z.: Constrained deep metric learning for person re-identification. Computer Science (2015)
15. Li, W., Wang, X.: Locally aligned feature transforms across views. **9**(4), 3594-3601 (2013)
16. Yang, Y., Liao, S., Lei, Z., Li, S.Z.: Large scale similarity learning using similar pairs for person verification. In: AAAI (2016)
17. Yi, D., Lei, Z., Li, S.Z.: Deep metric learning for practical person re-identification, pp. 34–39. Computer Science (2014)
18. Yan, S., Dong, X., Zhang, B., Zhang, H.J., Yang, Q., Lin, S.: Graph embedding, extensions: a general framework for dimensionality reduction. IEEE Trans. Pattern Anal. Mach. Intell. **29**(1), 40–51 (2007)
19. Liao, S., Hu, Y., Zhu, X., Li, S.Z.: Person re-identification by local maximal occurrence representation and metric learning. In: Computer Vision and Pattern Recognition, pp. 2197–2206 (2015)
20. Bellet, A., Habrard, A., Sebban, M.: A survey on metric learning for feature vectors and structured data. Computer Science (2013)
21. Simonyan, K., Zisserman, A.: Very deep convolutional networks for large-scale image recognition. Computer Science (2015)
22. Hinton, G.E., Srivastava, N., Krizhevsky, A., Sutskever, I., Salakhutdinov, R.R.: Improving neural networks by preventing co-adaptation of feature detectors. Comput. Sci. **3**(4), 212–223 (2012)
23. Jia, Y., Shelhamer, E., Donahue, J., Karayev, S., Long, J., Girshick, R., Guadarrama, S., Darrell, T.: Caffe: Convolutional architecture for fast feature embedding. Eprint Arxiv, pp. 675–678 (2014)
24. Gray, D., Brennan, S., Tao, H.: Evaluating appearance models for recognition, reacquisition, and tracking (2007)
25. Zheng, L., Zhang, H., Sun, S., Chandraker, M., Tian, Q.: Person re-identification in the wild (2016)
26. Bottou, L.: Stochastic gradient descent tricks. In: Montavon, G., Orr, G.B., Müller, K.-R. (eds.) NN: Tricks of the Trade. LNCS, vol. 7700, pp. 421–436. Springer, Heidelberg (2012). doi:10.1007/978-3-642-35289-8_25
27. Hirzer, M.: Large scale metric learning from equivalence constraints. In: IEEE Conference on Computer Vision and Pattern Recognition, pp. 2288–2295 (2012)

28. Wang, F., Zuo, W., Lin, L., Zhang, D., Zhang, L.: Joint learning of single-image and cross-image representations for person re-identification
29. Zhao, R., Ouyang, W., Wang, X.: Learning mid-level filters for person re-identification. In: IEEE Conference on Computer Vision and Pattern Recognition, pp. 144–151 (2014)
30. Li, Z., Chang, S., Liang, F., Huang, T.S. Cao, L., Smith, J.R.: Learning locally-adaptive decision functions for person verification. In: IEEE Conference on Computer Vision and Pattern Recognition, pp. 3610–3617 (2013)
31. Mignon, A., Jurie, F.: PCCA: a new approach for distance learning from sparse pairwise constraints. In: IEEE Conference on Computer Vision and Pattern Recognition, pp. 2666–2672 (2012)
32. Liu, X., Song, M., Tao, D., Zhou, X., Chen, C., Bu, J.: Semi-supervised coupled dictionary learning for person re-identification, pp. 3550–3557 (2014)
33. Zheng, L., Shen, L., Lu, T., Wang, S., Wang, J., Tian, Q.: Scalable person re-identification: a benchmark. In: IEEE International Conference on Computer Vision, pp. 1116–1124 (2015)

A Common Strategy to Improve Community Detection Performance Based on the Nodes' Property

Wei Du and Xiaochen He[✉]

School of Public Policy and Administration, Center for Administration Complexity
Science, Xi'an Jiaotong University, Xi'an 710049, China
duwei@mail.xjtu.edu.cn, hexiaochen121vip@163.com

Abstract. In order to improve community detection results, a novel strategy based on the nodes' property is put forward for the detecting algorithm. For a given community structure of a network, the value of the modularity will be changed when a node is moved from one community to another. Accordingly, this new strategy re-adjusts the affiliation between a node and its community to get the bigger value of the modularity. The results of community detection for some classic networks, which from Ucinet and Pajek networks, indicate that the new algorithm achieves better community structure (bigger value of modularity) than other methodologies based on modularity, such as Girvan and Newman's algorithm, Newman's algorithm, Aaron's algorithm and Blondel's algorithm.

1 Introduction

The modularity Q defined by Girvan and Newman in [1,2] is the milestone of community structure study and a suitable criterion for community structure measurement, although there are still some arguments. Currently, community structure detecting methods have been the hot spot in many domains and disciplines. The current algorithms are taking the detection of community structure based on modularity as an optimization process for the objective function of modularity. Since a network with n nodes has $\sum_{k=1}^{n} \frac{1}{k!} \sum_{j=1}^{k} \binom{k}{j} j^n$ different possible community structures, detecting community structure in networks suffers from an NP hard problem. Theoretically, all of these detecting algorithms are hard to get the optimization solution. In order to get bigger modularity value, most of these algorithms pay more attention to change the strategies of merging or partitioning the community (especially in the late of algorithm execution), and seldom consider the nodes locating in different community may impact on the community structure and the modularity value. For a given division community structure, this paper discusses the influence that the network node in different community may have, and put forward a simple mechanism based on this idea to modify the current the community structure detection algorithms [3-8].

© Springer Nature Singapore Pte Ltd. 2016
M. Gong et al. (Eds.): BIC-TA 2016, Part II, CCIS 682, pp. 355–361, 2016.
DOI: 10.1007/978-981-10-3614-9_43

2   The Algorithm

For a given network $G(V, A)$, where $V = \{v_1, v_2, \ldots v_n\}$ represents the set of n nodes in the network, and the connections between nodes are represented by an $n \times n$ adjacency matrix $A = (a_{ij})$ for $i, j = 1, 2, \ldots, n$, if i and j are connected, then the entry $a_{ij} = 1$, otherwise $a_{ij} = 0$. We assume there are no-self connections; that is, $a_{ii} = 0$ for $i = 1, 2, \ldots, n$. $\tau(V)$ is one of possible community structure. Where $\tau(V) = \{V_1, V_2, \ldots, V_m\}$, $V_i \subset V$, $V_i \neq \Phi$, for $i = 1, 2, \ldots, m$, $\cup_{i=1}^{m} V_i = V$, $V_i \cap V_j = \Phi$, $i \neq j$, and V_i represents community i. Girvan and Newman defined the modularity Q as:

$$Q = \sum_{p=1}^{m} [e_{pp} - (\sum_{q=1}^{m} e_{pq})^2] \tag{1}$$

where $e_{pq} = \frac{\|A_{pq}\|}{2\|A\|}$, $e_{pp} = \frac{\|A_{pp}\|}{2\|A\|}$ and $\|A\| = \frac{1}{2} \sum_{j=1}^{n} \sum_{j=1}^{n} a_{ij}$ is the total number of links in the network, $\|A_{pp}\| = \frac{1}{2} \sum_{i \in V_p} \sum_{j \in V_q} a_{ij}$, $a_{ij} \in A$. $\|A_{pp}\|$ denotes the number of links within V_p; $\|A_{pq}\|$ is the total degree of the nodes in community V_p.

For the community structure $\tau(V)$, Fig. 1 shows node i located in community V_p, where $k_{ip} = \frac{\sum_{j \in V_p} a_{ij}}{2\|A\|}$, $k_{iq} = \frac{\sum_{j \in V_q} a_{ij}}{2\|A\|}$, $\sum_{j \in V_p} a_{ij}$ and $\sum_{j \in V_q} a_{ij}$ represents the denotes the number of links of node i within V_p and V_q separately. If remove

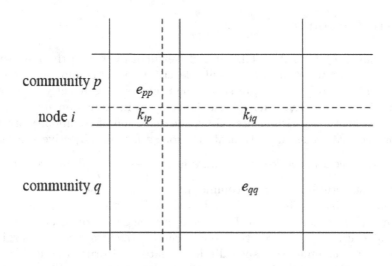

Fig. 1. The relationship between node i and the communities.

node i from community p and set it as an independent community, the change of modularity can be computed by:

$$\Delta Q_{p\to i} = (e_{pp} - (\sum_{j=1}^{m} e_{pj})^2) + (0 - k_i)^2 - (e_{pp} + 2k_{ip} - (\sum_{j=1}^{m} e_{pj} + k_i)^2) \quad (2)$$

$$= -2k_{ip} + 2k_i \sum_{j=1}^{m} e_{pj}$$

Then merge node i into the community q, the change of modularity can be computed by:

$$\Delta Q_{i\to q} = (e_{qq} + 2k_{iq} - (\sum_{j=1}^{m} e_{qj} + k_i)^2) - (e_{qq} - (\sum_{j=1}^{m} e_{qj})^2) - (0 - k_i)^2 \quad (3)$$

$$= 2k_{iq} - 2k_i \sum_{j=1}^{m} e_{qj}$$

If combine the above two operations together, i.e. remove the node i from community p and placed it in another community q, the gain of the modularity will be:

$$\Delta Q = \Delta Q_{p\to i\to q} = \Delta Q_{p\to i} + \Delta Q_{i\to q} = 2k_{iq} - 2k_{ip} + 2k_i(\sum_{j=1}^{m} e_{pj} - \sum_{j=1}^{m} e_{qj}) \quad (4)$$

Obviously, if $\Delta Q > 0$, then the node i located in community q is more suitable than in community p, and if the degree of node i $d_i = 1$ or $\Delta Q < 0$, the node i will stay in its original community p.

The above analysis has discussed the effect by moving one node from one community to another community, while moving more nodes will have the similar effect because ΔQ can be superposed. In this paper, we mainly focus on moving nodes one by one. For a community structure of a network, which is obtained by a detecting algorithm, such as Newman's algorithm, Bodel's algorithm, and so on, a common strategy based on the above discussion to modify the recent community detecting algorithms can be described as following briefly:

This new algorithm is performed based on the existing community structure $\tau(V) = \{V_1, V_2, ..., V_m\}$. Hence it can be used to improve the detection result acquired by any other detecting algorithm. Because the network has been separate to m community, the new algorithm at most explores $n \times m$ times. Due to $m \ll n$, the computational complexity of the new algorithm will not exceed $O(n^2)$. But the complexity of the most existing community structure detection algorithms is mostly $O(n^2)$. Therefore the new algorithm cannot increase the computational complexity of original algorithm significantly.

3   Experimental Results

In this section, four other algorithms are compared with the new algorithm: G algorithm, N Algorithm, A Algorithm, B Algorithm. We use a similarity

---

Algorithm: the framework of the new algorithm based on the node's property

1: Input: $COM(c)$,which is the node set in community c, $c = 1, 2, \ldots m$;
2: repeat
3: for each node i in $COM(p)$ do
4: computer $\Delta Q_{p \to i \to q}$ according to Eq. 4;
5: $\Delta Q_{\bar{q}'} \leftarrow \max_q \Delta Q_{p \to i \to q}$;
6: if $\Delta Q_{\bar{q}'} > 0$
7: move node i from $COM(p)$ to $COM(\bar{q}')$
8: end if
9: end for
10: until $c = m$
11: Output: COM

---

measurement Normalized Mutual Information (NMI) to estimate the efficiency of the modified algorithm by calculating the similarity between detecting community structure and actual community structure generated by computer. And we use 11 different sets of computer-generated data as the experimental test data, with the mixing parameter μ ranging from 0 to 0.5. For each μ, the corresponding NMI are generated by the average of 10 independent runs. Figures 2, 3 and 4 shows the average NMI for A algorithm, N algorithm, B algorithm and their modified algorithm when the mixing parameter increases from 0 to 0.5. The experiments show that the detecting results of modified algorithm are always superior to the results of the three original algorithm.

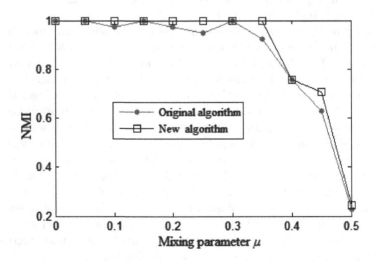

Fig. 2. The relationship between node i and the communities.

In order to analyze the applicability of the new algorithm, we tested the dolphins network, the lesmis network and some standard networks available in

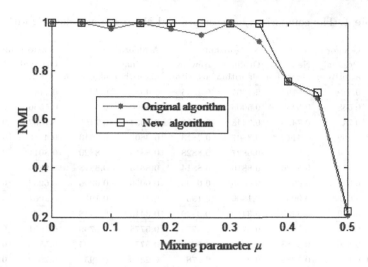

Fig. 3. The relationship between node i and the communities.

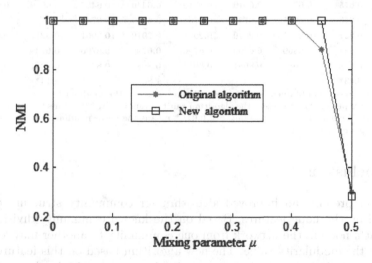

Fig. 4. The relationship between node i and the communities.

the social network analysis software, Pajek and Ucinet. The modularity's values of the community structure detecting results using these four typical algorithms are shown in the column "Original algorithm" in Table 1 separately. And the corresponding results for the algorithm are shown in column "New algorithm" in Table 1. All the t-test results show the new algorithm has significantly improved the original algorithms.

Table 1. The comparison between original algorithm and new algorithm

Network	G algorithm		N algorithm		A algorithm		B algorithm	
	Original algorithm	New algorithm	Original algorithm	New algorithm	Original algorithm	New algorithm	Original algorithm	New algorithm
Dolphins	0.519	0.5194	0.4955	0.4955	0.4955	0.4955	0.5188	0.5233
lesmis	0.538	0.5481	0.5006	0.5498	0.5006	0.5498	0.5556	0.5556
Drugnet	0.74	0.7426	0.7448	0.7455	0.7454	0.7455	0.7067	0.7067
Zachary	0.409	0.4112	0.3807	0.3813	0.3807	0.3813	0.4188	0.4188
1crn	0.874	0.8766	0.8827	0.8828	0.8819	0.8820	0.8011	0.8039
ADF073	0.883	0.8826	0.8810	0.8814	0.8815	0.8818	0.8354	0.8354
B	0.632	0.6323	0.6096	0.6096	0.6096	0.6096	0.6234	0.6261
BKHAM	−0.002	0.000	0.1800	0.196	0.1800	0.196	0.2067	0.2067
BKOFF	0.339	0.3439	0.3413	0.3429	0.3413	0.3478	0.3676	0.3676
c	0.556	0.5683	0.5778	0.5778	0.5778	0.5799	0.5651	0.5772
cc	0.556	0.5683	0.5778	0.5778	0.5778	0.5799	0.5578	0.5643
CENPROD	0.11	0.1288	0.2746	0.278	0.2893	0.2951	0.2902	0.2902
dnet	0.6	0.612	0.6548	0.6576	0.6548	0.6554	0.6499	0.6499
GR353	0.675	0.675	0.6519	0.6519	0.6440	0.6457	0.6616	0.6815
GR360	0.673	0.6731	0.6739	0.6761	0.6739	0.6746	/	/
KAPTAIL	0.227	0.2481	0.2910	0.2961	0.2910	0.2961	0.3215	0.3215
merza3	0.681	0.6809	0.6796	0.6796	0.6796	0.6796	0.6139	0.6139
nooy	0.808	0.8081	0.8081	0.8081	0.8081	0.8081	0.8081	0.8081
T-test	3.43**		1.64+		1.83*		2.14*	

G algorithm result is obtained by Ucient 6.212, the values of the modularity were calculated to three decimal places. "/" represent the algorithm can't obtain result. *** means the corresponding $p < 0.001$; ** means the corresponding $p < 0.01$; * means the corresponding $p < 0.05$; + means the corresponding $p < 0.1$.

4 Conclusions

This paper presents an improved algorithm for community structure detecting based on the node features. Based on the known community division, the movement a node in the network from one community to another may lead the change of the modularity value. The new algorithm based on this feature readjusts the affiliation of node and community in order to obtain the maximum modularity value, i.e. the new community structure. According to the experiments of representative detection algorithm for classic network data, we believe that our improved algorithm can optimize the community detection result of original algorithm furthermore, and obtain a greater modularity with no significant computation increscent.

References

1. Newman, M.E.J.: Fast algorithm for detecting community structure in networks. Phys. Rev. E **69**(6), 066133 (2004)
2. Girvan, M., Newman, M.E.J.: Community structure in social and biological networks. Proc. Natl. Acad. Sci. U.S.A. **99**(12), 7821–7826 (2002)

3. Fortunato, S., Barthélemy, M.: Resolution limit in community detection. Proc. NatL. Acad. Sci. U.S.A. **104**(1), 36–41 (2007)
4. Li, Z., Zhang, S., Wang, R., Zhang, X., Chen, L.: Quantitative function for community detection. Phys. Rev. E **77**(2), 257–260 (2008)
5. Newman, M.E.J., Barabàsi, A.L., Watts, D.J.: The Structure and Dynamic of Networks. Princeton University Press, Princeton (2006)
6. Santo, F.: Community detection in graphs. Phys. Rep. **486**(3–5), 75–174 (2010)
7. White, S., and Smyth, P.: A spectral clustering approach to finding communities in graphs. In: SIAM International Conference on Data Mining. Newport Beach, California (2005)
8. Clauset, C., Newman, M.E.J., Moore, C.: Finding community structure in very large networks. Phys. Rev. E **70**, 264–277 (2004)

HVS-Inspired Dimensionality Reduction Model Based on Factor Analysis

Zhigang Shang$^{(\boxtimes)}$, Mengmeng Li, and Yonghui Dong

School of Electrical Engineering, Zhengzhou University, 100 Science Avenue,
Zhengzhou 450001, China
zhigang_shang@zzu.edu.cn, limengmeng1014@163.com, zzudongyonghui@163.com

Abstract. A biologically inspired dimensionality reduction model is proposed to solve the high dimension data dimensionality reducing and classifying problem. The model is inspired from the Human Visual System (HVS). As in that work, in order to utilize its dimension reduction characteristics we first apply factor analysis to simulate the dimension reduction process from the retina to Lateral Geniculate Nucleus (LGN) to remove redundant irrelevant variables. The common factors obtained are then used to calculate the factor scores and they are regarded as new features to characterize the original features. Finally the new features classified by kSVM. The proposed model is tested in numerical experiments on eight different data sets and the experimental results suggest that the model is effective.

Keywords: Biologically inspired · HVS · Dimensionality reduction · LGN · Factor analysis · kSVM

1 Introduction

With the rapid development of internet technologies, the data generated in many different areas such as biomedical, electronic commerce, network communications usually has a very high dimension, so the high-dimensional data processing becomes a hot research field of data mining and has caught broad attention in the research community over the past few years. Thus it is of great significance to study how to solve the course of dimensionality [1]. Data dimensionality reduction [2] is central in this process. The so-called data dimensionality reduction is to map the samples from high dimensional space to low dimensional space by linear or nonlinear mapping and obtain a meaningful low dimensional representation of the original high dimensional data. Dimensionality reduction can reduce the curse of dimensionality and remove some unrelated features in high dimension space, so as to promote the classification, visualization and compression of high dimensional data.

Aim at data dimensionality reduction problem, a lot of researches have been conducted and many algorithms have been proposed in recent years, such as the widely used unsupervised data analysis method: Principal Component Analysis

© Springer Nature Singapore Pte Ltd. 2016
M. Gong et al. (Eds.): BIC-TA 2016, Part II, CCIS 682, pp. 362–372, 2016.
DOI: 10.1007/978-981-10-3614-9_44

(PCA) [3], widely used supervised data analysis method: Linear Discriminant Analysis (LDA) [4], Non-Negative Matrix Factorization (NMF) [5] and manifold learning based algorithm: Isometric Mapping (ISOMAP) [6], Locally Linear Embedding (LLE) [7] and Laplacian Embedding (LE) [8].

As we all know, the processing of visual information of the HVS [9] is hierarchical. The ascending pathway consisted of the retina, LGN [10] and the visual cortex is the most important visual pathway. The visual signals collected from the retina are sent to LGN. LGN uses fewer neurons than before to arrange them under categories layer by layer, and this can be seen as a dimension reduction process. Finally well-arranged low dimensional signals are sent to the primary visual cortex. As a visual attention mechanism [11] of human beings, LGN processing reveals the specific perception mode of the eye. It helps the HVS to quickly filter the redundant information and accurately extract the effective information from the complex scene. The powerful information filtering ability, which can help to save computing resources, greatly improves the accuracy and robustness of the system [12].

Inspired by this biological information processing mechanism, a new biologically inspired [13] dimensionality reduction model based on LGN information processing mechanism is proposed. In consideration of its dimension reduction characteristics, factor analysis [14] is used to simulate the dimension reduction process from the retina to LGN to remove redundant irrelevant variables. The high dimensional mapping characteristics of the kernel SVM [15] can help to effectively solve the classification problem of the nonlinear independent feature sets, so it is used to simulate the dimension reduction process from LGN to the visual cortex. Numerical examples on different data sets are provided to verify the validity of the proposed model. The results show that the model can perform well on data dimensionality reduction and the classification accuracy after the dimensional reduction remains as high as the original all features model basically.

The rest of this paper is organized as follows. Section 2 introduces the HVS model and our proposed HVS-inspired model. Section 3 presents the experiments and simulation results analysis. Finally, the discussion and future work of the paper is concluded in Sect. 4.

2 Models

2.1 HVS Model

Human obtain external image information by HVS. It will cause the complex physio-logical and psychological changes in human when the light radiation stimulates the human eye, and this feeling is the visual. As an signal processing system, the HVS is non-uniform and non-linear. External signals are firstly received and preprocessed by the retina and then they are transported to LGN. Finally the visual cortex receives and processes them further. In the HVS process, the signal is constantly extracted and the spatial and temporal integration is also carried out [16]. The following subsections describe these three regions.

The Retina. The light-sensing cells of the retina is related to the visual. The optical structure of the eye firstly receives the external light stimulation and realizes the conversion from optical to electrical [17]. A large amount of information is extracted in this process and transmitted to the LGN by the axon of the ganglion cell.

LGN. LGN is the sensory relay structure of the thalamus, which is responsible for the signal relay and transmission. It plays a key role to shunt the signals and organize them into different groups in the information processing of central nervous system [18]. LGN has three main functions: Receive the signal from the retina and grouping them under categories; Transmit the signals to the visual cortex and receives the feedback from it; Signal whitening [19].

The Visual Cortex. Visual cortex is responsible for visual perception in HVS. Most of the neurons which are related to perception and cognition are located in the cerebral cortex. The processing of signal is gradually completed from the low-level visual cortex to the advanced [20].

The above HVS model is shown in Fig. 1, in which P, m and M are the numbers of the neuron in different regions.

2.2 Factor Analysis and the Proposed HVS-inspired Model

The idea of factor analysis was derived from the study of the students' test scores by a British psychologist C.E. Spielman in 1904. It uses the idea of dimensionality reduction. It can reflect most of the information of the original signal with less number of factors, and the explanation for the common factors practical significance is reasonable and easy. So it has been widely used in many fields at present [21].

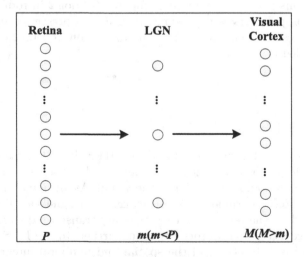

Fig. 1. Overview of the HVS model.

Without loss of generality, a general model of factor analysis can be defined as follows:

$$X_i = \mu_i + a_{i1}F_1 + \cdots + a_{im}F_m + \varepsilon_i. \tag{1}$$

where $X_i\,(i = 1, 2, \cdots, p) \in X$ is one variable of the sample X; the common factors of the X are $F_j\,(j = 1, 2, \cdots, m; m \leq p)$; ε_i is the special factor (random error) of X_i; a_{ij} is the loads of X_i in the common factor F_j and it reflects different degree of importance of common factors on the variables under different value.

Communality of the variable is a common index to measure the effect of factor analysis and reflects the degree of explanation of the variance of all common factors to the original variable. It can be described as follows:

$$C_i = a_{i1}{}^2 + \cdots + a_{ij}{}^2 + \cdots + a_{im}{}^2. \tag{2}$$

where C_i is the communality of the variable X_i.

Variance contribute rate of one common factor reflects the explanatory of the common factor to all the original total variation and usually is used to measure the relative importance of common factors. The greater the variance contribution of a factor, the more important it is [22]. It can be described as follows:

$$VC_j = a_{1j}{}^2 + \cdots + a_{ij}{}^2 + \cdots + a_{pj}{}^2. \tag{3}$$

where VC_j is the variance contribution rate of the jth factor.

The calculating formula of the cumulative variance contribute rate is shown as follows.

$$CVC_n = \sum_{j=1}^{n} VC_j. \tag{4}$$

where CVC_n is the cumulative variance contribution rate of the first n factors.

Inspired by the above HVS model, a new data reduction model is proposed. The number of neurons in the area of the retina is much larger than that in LGN, because the signal is arranged under categories layer by layer. Although this arrangement mechanism has not been thoroughly researched clearly in the scientific community, one thing for sure is that some higher correlated features may be clustered together and some redundant irrelevant features may be filtered out through this process. So this signal transmission process can be seen as dimensionality reduction process and factor analysis is a good way to simulate it. Both factor analysis and PCA can reduce the dimension effectively. The reason we choose factor analysis rather than PCA is that PCA focuses on explaining the total variance of variables and find the best principal component that can be expressed as a linear combination of the input variables [23]. In contrast, factor analysis is a statistical technique to extract common factors from the variables and its purpose is to represent the input variables as a linear combination of the factors. It focuses on explaining the covariance between the variables and finds the hidden representative factors in many variables. Some feature variables with the same nature are grouped into one same factor to reduce the number of variables. This process mechanism is much more like the HVS model.

Similar to the original HVS model, the proposed model consists of three layers: the data layer, the FA layer and the kSVM layer. It is shown graphically in Fig. 2, in which N is the number of the samples and P, m and M are the numbers of the feature dimension in different layers. The following subsections describe each layer.

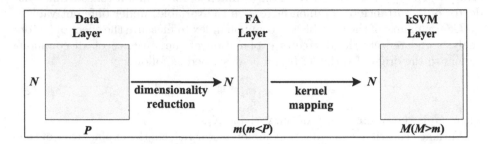

Fig. 2. Overview of the proposed inspired model.

Data Layer. The data layer receives and preprocesses the input signals, then transfers them to the next layer.

Factor Analysis (FA) Layer. FA layer obtains the signal data from the last layer. In consideration of the advantage of factor analysis, it is used to analyze the data to determine the number of public factors. This process is equivalent to simulate the shunting and grouping mechanism of LGN to reduce the dimension of the data, so that the high dimensional complex data become simple and easy to explain.

kSVM Layer. kSVM layer uses the rise-dimensional mechanism of the kernel mapping to map the low dimension signal to the high dimension space and uses the SVM to carry on the classification.

The dimensionality reduction algorithm based on HVS-inspired model is shown in Algorithm 1.

The calculation process of the inspired model proposed in this paper can be summarized as following five steps:

(1) **Data normalization.** In order to acquire the exact experimental result, data normalization is carried out to remove the unit limit of the data.
(2) **Stepwise factor analysis.** The original sample matrix is analyzed by the stepwise factor analysis. Each step realizes the purpose of characterizing several features by using a common factor and they will be deleted in the next step to reconstruct the sample matrix until the exact number of common factors are obtained. There may be several cases in this process: When the step number is m, the loads on the remaining features of the mth factor are all relatively high, then the number of public factors should be m; When the step number is m, the loads on the remaining features of the mth factor are

---

Algorithm 1. Dimensionality Reduction Algorithm based on HVS-inspired Model

Input: Data set and labels: $X_{N \times P}$, $y_{N \times 1}$;

Output: Factor scores: $FX_{N \times n}$;

1: Initialize $m = 1$, the number of common factors $n = 0$;

2: **while** $m \leq P$ **do**

3:    Stepwise factor analysis of X; obtain the loads of X in different common factors a_l

4:    **if** $a_{lj} < 0.2, (l = m + 1, m + 2, \cdots, P; j \in \{1, 2, \cdots, l\}; j_{max} = l - 1)$
      or $a_{lj} \geq 0.2, (l = m; j = 1, 2, \cdots, m)$ **then**

5:       $n = m$;

6:    **else** $n = b + m - 1$;

7:    **end if**

8: **end while**

9: Calculate the factor scores FX as the new feature space by factor analysis of X under the common factors number n;

---

all relatively low, the number of common factors should be $b + m - 1$; When the step number is greater than m and the common factors of the remaining features in each step after the mth step just only have one high load, the number of common factors should be m.

(3) **Factor analysis.** Analysis the original data by factor analysis using the number of common factors obtained above. Then the cumulative variance contribution rate of the common factors and the factor scores of all samples are obtained.

(4) **kSVM classification.** Factor scores are used as new features to reconstruct the sample matrix and it is considered as the input of kSVM to be classified.

(5) **Results recording and analysis.** The output accuracy of kSVM is recorded and analyzed.

3   Experiments and Results

In order to investigate the application properties of the proposed model method in different data sets, related numerical experiments are carried out. All of the calculations in this paper are using MATLAB software programming. The experimental conditions is: Intel Xeon E5-2680 v2 @ 2.80 GHz/CPU 16 GB (DDR3 1866 MHz)/Windows 7/MATLAB R2014a.

So as to make a full comparison of the experimental results, we make a diversity of the sample size and the number of features as far as possible. So seven different artificial data sets and a real data set are selected to carry out the experiment. The real tumor data set originate in the texture analysis of 174 pieces of Magnetic Resonance images of patients with two kinds of posterior fossa tumors (medulloblastomas and ependymomas) provided by the Magnetic Resonance Department, the first Affiliated Hospital of Zhengzhou University. 42 texture features obtained constitute its feature space. The detailed information of the data set is shown in Table 1.

Table 1. Data sets used in our experiments

Data set	Class	Sample	Variable
Ionosphere	2	351	32
Landsat	6	2000	36
Spambase	2	4601	57
Sonar	2	208	60
Musk	2	6589	166
USPS	10	7291	526
Isolet	26	7797	617
Real tumor	2	174	42

Firstly, each data set is processing through the stepwise factor analysis, thus the number of common factors and cumulative variance contribution of them are obtained. The results are recorded in Table 2.

Table 2. Results of stepwise factor analysis

Data set	Variable	Common factor	Cumulative variance contribute rate (%)
Ionosphere	32	7	60.40
Landsat	36	2	84.03
Spambase	57	46	60.82
Sonar	60	10	68.00
Musk	166	13	74.12
USPS	526	12	72.66
Isolet	617	28	68.32
Real tumor	42	3	86.58

As can be seen from Table 2, for most of data sets, the original high dimensional features can be characterized by less common factors through using factor analysis, which undoubtedly achieved the goal to reduce data dimension greatly.

Cross validation is used in the numerical experiments. Seventy percent of the samples in each data set are randomly selected as the training set and the remaining thirty percent as the test set. In order to comprehensively analyze the effectiveness of the proposed model, the experiments with original full features, LDA and PCA features are chosen to carry out experiments as contrast. Twenty random samples are implemented to be experimented respectively, and the results are shown in Fig. 3.

The experimental results show that the classification performance with fewer common factors is acceptable. In the Ionosphere, Spambase, Sonar, Landsat and Musk data set, the classification accuracies of the common factors are quite

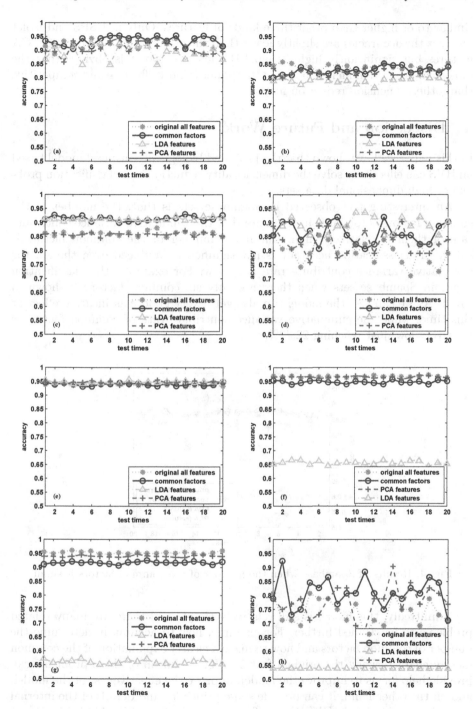

Fig. 3. Comparison of classification accuracies of original all features and common factors on different sets. (a) Ionosphere. (b) Landsat. (d) Sonar. (f) USPS. (g) Isolet. (h) Real tumor.

similar to or higher than other three kinds of features. Only in USPS and Isolet data set the accuracies are slightly lower than the original full features and PCA features but significantly higher than LDA features. So It is obvious that the biological inspired model proposed in this paper is more effective and competitive than other dimension reduction method.

4   Discussion and Future Work

In this paper we have shown that the proposed biologically-inspired model based on HVS can effectively solve the dimensionality reduction and classification problem of high dimensional data sets.

An interesting fact observed in Spambase sets is that, the number of the common factors is too large if we ensure that the cumulative variance contribute rate of them is relatively high. But if the number of the common factors is small, the classification accuracy is not significantly reduced even though the cumulative variance contribute rate is so low. For example, the classification result in Spambase sets when there are only six common factors is shown in Fig. 4. As we can see, the model can also get a very good classification effect at this time, while the cumulative variance contribute rate of common factors is relatively low, just reaching 22.47%.

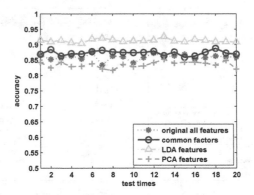

Fig. 4. Results of Spambase when the number of the common factors is small.

Admittedly, this model is still relatively simple and there are many related problems to be studied further. For example, how to accurately determine the number of common factors and how to make a clearer explanation of the common factors characterizing the original features. The solution of these problems can provide help for us to improve the model, improve the effectiveness of the model, and on the other hand, it can provide some principles and details of the internal operation mechanism in HVS. So our first step in the future would likely attempt to model intermediate level process more accurately and what we lean towards future enhancements are biologically realistic.

Acknowledgments. The work is supported by National Nature Science Foundation of China (U1304602) and Colleges and Universities Major Scientific Research Funded Projects of Henan Province (15A120016). The authors thank the Magnetic Resonance Department, the first Affiliated Hospital of Zhengzhou University for data providing and marking.

References

1. Indyk, P.: Approximate nearest neighbors: towards removing the curse of dimensionality. Theory Comput., 604–613 (2015)
2. Chang, C.: Data dimensionality reduction. In: Hyperspectral Data Processing: Algorithm Design and Analysis, pp. 168–199. Wiley (2013)
3. Jolliffe, I.T.: Principal Component Analysis. Springer, New York (2002)
4. Xanthopoulos, P., Pardalos, P.M., Trafalis, T.B.: Linear discriminant analysis. In: Xanthopoulos, P., Pardalos, P.M., Trafalis, T.B. (eds.) Robust Data Mining, pp. 237–280. Springer, New York (2013)
5. Hoyer, P.O.: Non-negative matrix factorization with sparseness constraints. Neurocomputing **80**(1), 38–46 (2004)
6. Saul, L.K., Roweis, S.T.: Think globally, fit locally: unsupervised learning of low dimensional manifolds. J. Mach. Learn. Res. **4**(2), 119–155 (2003)
7. Roweis, S.T., Saul, L.K.: Nonlinear dimensionality reduction by locally linear embedding. Science **290**(5500), 2323–2326 (2000)
8. Belkin, M., Niyogi, P.: Laplacian Eigenmaps for dimensionality reduction and data representation. Neural Comput. **15**(15), 1373–1396 (2003)
9. Wang, B., Wang, Z., Liao, Y., et al.: HVS-based structural similarity for image quality assessment. In: International Conference on Signal Processing, pp. 1194–1197 (2008)
10. Dacey, D.M., Liao, H.W., Peterson, B.B.: Melanopsin-expressing ganglion cells in primate retina signal color and irradiance and project to the LGN. Nature **433**(7027), 749–754 (2005)
11. Gozli, D.G., Moskowitz, J.B., Pratt, J.: Visual attention to features by associative learning. Cognition **133**(2), 488–501 (2014)
12. Frintrop, S. (ed.): VOCUS: A Visual Attention System for Object Detection and Goal-Directed Search. LNCS (LNAI), vol. 3899. Springer, Heidelberg (2006). doi:10.1007/11682110
13. Hong, Q., Xi, X., Li, Y.: Biologically inspired visual model with preliminary cognition and active attention adjustment. IEEE Trans. Cybern. **45**(11), 2612–2624 (2015)
14. Mulaik, S.A.: Foundations of Factor Analysis. Chapman Hall/CRC, New York (2009)
15. Dong, S., Sun, D., Tang, B., et al.: A fault diagnosis method for rotating machinery based on PCA and Morlet kernel SVM. Math. Prob. Eng. **2014**(10), 805–808 (2014)
16. Kerr, D., Mcginnity, T.M., Coleman, S., et al.: A biologically inspired spiking model of visual processing for image feature detection. Neurocomputing **158**, 268–280 (2015)
17. Masland, R.H.: The fundamental plan of the retina. Nat. Neurosci. **4**(9), 877–886 (2001)
18. Lee, H., Kirkby, L., Brott, B.K., et al.: Synapse elimination and learning rules coregulated by MHC Class I H2-Db. Nature **509**(7499), 195–200 (2014)

19. Dasog, M., Koirala, K., Liu, P., et al.: EMG bandwidth used in signal whitening. In: 2013 39th Annual Northeast Bioengineering Conference (NEBEC), pp. 189–190. IEEE (2013)
20. Bienenstock, E.L., Cooper, L.N., Munro, P.W.: Theory for the development of neuron selectivity: orientation specificity and binocular interaction in visual cortex. J. Neurosci. Official J. Soc. Neurosci. $2(1)$, 32–48 (2015)
21. Maccallum, R.C., Widaman, K.F., Zhang, S., et al.: Sample size in factor analysis. Psychol. Methods $4(1)$, 84–99 (1999)
22. Anderson, T.W., Rubin, H.: Statistical Inference in Factor Analysis, pp. 111–150. University of California, Berkeley (2015)
23. Liu, X., Jiang, B., Gu, W., et al.: Temporal trend and climate factors of hemorrhagic fever with renal syndrome epidemic in Shenyang city China. BMC Infect. Dis. $11(1)$, 1–6 (2011)

Human Face Reconstruction from a Single Input Image Based on a Coupled Statistical Model

Yujuan Sun[1], Muwei Jian[2], and Junyu Dong[2(✉)]

[1] School of Information and Electrical Engineering, Ludong University, Yantai, China
[2] Department of Computer Science and Technology, Ocean University of China, Qingdao, China
{jianmuwei,dongjunyu}@ouc.edu.cn

Abstract. In this paper, the similar characteristics of human face has been used to relax the numbers of the input into one single face image, and reconstruct the 3D shape based on a couple statistical model. Moreover the lighting conditions of the single input image can be different from that of the training database. The experiment results have demonstrated the effectiveness of the proposed method.

Keywords: Three dimensional reconstruction · Coupled statistical model · Human face

1 Introduction

In general, the scene depth information has been lost when the two-dimensional images are captured. Hence reconstructing the three-dimensional shape of the object from one single image is a difficult and challenging issue. However, in reality there are many objects with similar characteristics, such as face, rocks, grasses and other nature objects. These similar characteristics can be used to relax the reconstruction problem and reduce the numbers of the input images.

In this paper, an algorithm has been proposed to reconstruct the 3D shape of human face from a single face image based on a coupled statistical model. First, an initial training database is built, which includes three dimensional shapes and albedo of different human faces. Then, a new training database can be generated by relighting the initial database, and the lighting parameters for relighting are estimated from the input face image. At last, a coupled statistical model has been built using the new training database based the similarity of different human faces.

2 Related Works

Photometric stereo is a hot research problem in the field of computer vision [1–3]. Andrew Y. Ng published several related papers [4–6] about 3D depth reconstruction from one single image; their methods can create 3D models,

© Springer Nature Singapore Pte Ltd. 2016
M. Gong et al. (Eds.): BIC-TA 2016, Part II, CCIS 682, pp. 373–378, 2016.
DOI: 10.1007/978-981-10-3614-9_45

which were quantitatively accurate as well as visual pleasing, but is far from detailed reconstruction. For accurate reconstructing the 3D shape of the object, some researchers focused on reconstructing the object with similar shapes. In [7], a 3D reconstruction method was presented by estimating the parameters of the principal components for human head. In [8], an efficient two-dimensional to three-dimensional integrated face reconstruction approach was introduced to reconstruct a personalized 3D face model from a single frontal face image. Later, a novel method for 3D face shape recovery was proposed by exploiting the similarity of faces [9]. Reference [10] reconstructed the 3D human face in real time from a coarse depth image. But these methods required that the single input image had a desired, uniform illumination, and without significantly shadow on the face.

Reference [11] used a coupled statistical model to reconstruct the 3D shape of the human face. The coupled statistical model is similar to the active appearance model (AAM). Based on the lighting estimation method in [10], this paper proposed an improved method to reconstruct the 3D shape of human face from a single input image via the coupled statistical model, and the input image can be captured in any lighting conditions.

3   The Proposed Method

Reference [11] can only reconstruct the 3D shape from a single input image when lighting conditions are similar with the sample database. If the lighting conditions of the input image is inconsistent with that of the sample in database, the error of the reconstructed result will be largely increased. In this section, a new framework for the coupled statistical model has been proposed, which can accurately reconstruct the 3D shape of the single face image. The framework of the improved coupled statistical model is shown in Fig. 1.

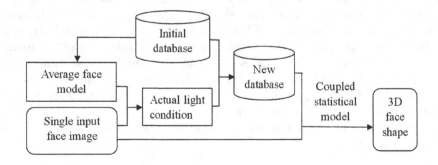

Fig. 1. The new framework of the improved coupled statistical model.

In Fig. 1, the initial database contains the aligned training samples. Based on the average face model of the training samples, the lighting parameter (actual lighting condition in Fig. 1) of the single input image can be estimated using the method in [10]. With the estimated lighting parameter l, the new database can be built:

$$\begin{cases} t_k^a = a_k n_k l, \, k = 1, 2, \ldots, N \\ t_k^h = h_k, \quad i = 1, 2, \ldots, N \end{cases} \tag{1}$$

where, t_k^a and t_k^h are the face image and the height map of the new database, respectively; n_k is the face surface normal computed from the height map. In Eq. (1), t_k^a and t_k^h are regarded as the sample pair in the new database, which has the same light condition with that of the input image.

3.1 Building the Coupled Statistical Model Based on the New Training Database

The coupled statistical model includes the image model and height model of human face, and the building of the two models and the association method will be introduced in detail.

The image model is built as in Eq. (2):

$$\begin{aligned} A &= [a_1 - \bar{a}, a_2 - \bar{a}, \ldots, a_N - \bar{a}] \\ \bar{a} &= \frac{1}{N} \sum_{k=1}^{N} a_k, \, k = 1, 2, \ldots, N \end{aligned} \tag{2}$$

where $\bar{a}$ is the average face A is the image matrix, and a_k is one image of the new training database. Then PCA method is used to obtain a set of orthogonal vectors, which can be computed by using covariance of the image matrix, which is defined as

$$M = AA^T \tag{3}$$

where M are called the data covariance matrix. The eigenvector of the data covariance matrix can be represented by M^a. Then a new input image of human face can be represented using the linear combination of eigenvectors in M^a. The minimum variance solution is

$$b^a = (M^a)^T (\breve{a} - \bar{a}) \tag{4}$$

where b^a is the parameter vector, and it represents the different contribution of each eigenface in M^a for the synthesis of the input face image.

Similar with the minimum variance solution of the human image, the height map $\breve{h}$ of the new input human face can be presented using the eigenface of the height covariance matrix M^h.

$$b^h = (M^h)^T (\breve{h} - \bar{h}) \tag{5}$$

After connecting the b_k^a and b_k^h, the parameter series will be generated according to

$$b_k^c = \begin{bmatrix} \Lambda b_k^a \\ b_k^h \end{bmatrix} = \begin{bmatrix} \Lambda((M^a)^T (t_k^a - \bar{a})) \\ (M^h)^T (t_k^h - \bar{h}) \end{bmatrix} \tag{6}$$

where, Λ is a diagonal matrixwhich represents different relative weights between the intensity face image and its height map. Since the parameter vectors of b_k^a and b_k^h represent different types of data (one is the intensity image, and the other is the height map), it needs to set a scale to connect the two parameter vectors. By using the method in [11], Λ is set to $\Lambda = rI$, where I is the identity matrix, and r^2 is the ratio of the variance between the height map and intensity value of the human face.

Then PCA method is also employed to extract the principal components (b^c) of parameter series b_k^c, and b^c can be written as

$$b_k^c = Cc = \begin{bmatrix} \Lambda b_k^a \\ b_k^h \end{bmatrix} c \tag{7}$$

where, C is the eigenvectors of b^c the matrix of C^a represents the principal eigenvectors (assume S rows) of the image matrixand C^h represents the principal eigenvectors (assume T rows) of the height matrix, respectively. c is the parameter vector of b^c, which need to be estimated according to the input face image.

Suppose that the single input face image is $\breve{t}^a$, which can be represented as

$$\breve{t}^a = \bar{a} + M^a \breve{b}^a = \bar{a} + M^a C^a c \Rightarrow \breve{b}^a = C^a c \tag{8}$$

By estimating the parameter vector of c, the height map of human face can be computed according to Eq. (17):

$$\breve{h}_a = \bar{h} + M^h C^h c \tag{9}$$

3.2   Experimental Results and Analysis

In order to verify the effectiveness of the proposed method, the images in BU3D [12] face databases have been used in our experiments. Figures 2 and 3 show the reconstructed 3D face shapes based on BU3D database from one single input image with no shadow and self-shadow respectively. The image in the first column of Figs. 2 and 3 is the single input image; the second column represents the G.T (ground truth) of the 3D face shape; the results in the third column are the reconstructed 3D face shapes of Ref. [11]; and the results in the last column are the reconstructed 3D face shapes of the proposed algorithm. It can be seen that the reconstructed results of the proposed method are good with the input image with no shadow or self-shadow, but some artifacts or deformations exist in the results of the third column in Fig. 3 (the results of [11]), especially around the nose or eyes.

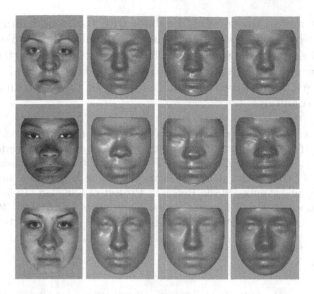

Fig. 2. The reconstructed 3D face shapes based on BU3D database (the input single image with no shadow).

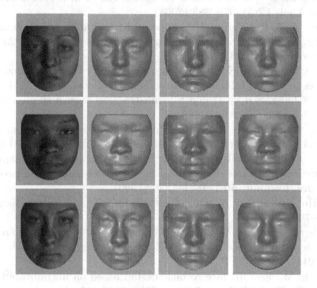

Fig. 3. The reconstructed 3D face shapes based on BU3D database (the input single image with selfshadow).

4 Conclusions

In this paper, an effective method of reconstructing 3D shape from a single human face image has been proposed. By estimating the lighting parameter of the input face image, the training database with the same lighting condition with the input image has been built. Then by building the coupled statistical model, the 3D shape of the single input face image can be reconstructed. Since lighting parameter of the training database can be kept identical with that of the input image, the proposed method is robust for the input image with the different light conditions.

Acknowledgments. This work was supported by National Natural Science Foundation of China (61601427, 61602229); Natural Science Foundation of Shandong Province (ZR2015 FQ011; ZR2014FQ023); China Postdoctoral Science Foundation funded project (20 16M590659); Qingdao Postdoctoral Science Foundation funded project (861605040 008) and Applied Basic Research Project of Qingdao (16-5-1-4-jch); The Fundamental Research Funds for the Central Universities (201511008, 30020084851); and Technology Cooperation Program of China (ISTCP) (2014DFA10410).

References

1. Jian, M., Dong, J., Lam, K.M.: A fast self-adaptive method for correcting non-uniform illuminatoin for 3D reconstruction. Comput. Ind. **64**(9), 1229–1236 (2013)
2. Shen, L., Bai, L.: 3D Gabor wavelets for evaluating SPM normalization algorithm. Med. Image Anal. **12**(3), 375–383 (2008)
3. Georghiades, A.S.: Recovering 3-D shape and reflectance from a small number of photographs. In: 14th Eurographics Workshop on Rendering, pp. 230–240. Eurographics Association (2003)
4. Saxena, A., Chung, S.H., Ng, A.Y.: Learning depth from single monocular images. In: Advances in Neural Information Processing Systems, pp. 1161–1168 (2005)
5. Saxena, A., Chung, S.H.: 3-D depth reconstruction from a single still image. Int. J. Comput. Vis. **76**(1), 53–69 (2008)
6. Saxena, A., Sun, M., Ng, A.Y.: Learning 3D scene structure from a single still image. IEEE Trans. Pattern Anal. Mach. Intell. **31**(5), 824–840 (2009)
7. Atick, J.J., Griffin, P.A., Redlich, A.N.: Statistical approach to shape from shading: reconstruction of three-dimensional face surfaces from single two-dimensional images. Neural Comput. **8**(6), 1321–1340 (1996)
8. Jiang, D., Hu, Y.: Efficient 3D reconstruction for face recognition. Neural Comput. **38**(6), 787–798 (2005)
9. Kemelmacher-Shlizerman, I., Basri, R.: 3D face reconstruction from a single image using a single reference face shape. IEEE Trans. Pattern Anal. Mach. Intell. **33**(2), 394–405 (2011)
10. Sun, Y., Jian, M.: Fast 3D face reconstruction based on uncalibrated photometric stereo. Multimedia Tools Appl. **74**(11), 3635–3650 (2015)
11. Castelan, M., Smith, W.A.P.: A coupled statistical model for face shape recovery from brightness images. IEEE Trans. Image Proc. **16**(4), 1139–1151 (2007)
12. Yin, L., Wei, X., Sun, Y., et al.: A 3D facial expression database for facial behavior research. In: 7th International Conference on Automatic Face and Gesture Recognition, pp. 211–216 (2006)

Research on Micro-blog New Word Recognition Based on MapReduce

Chaoting Xiao[1,3], Jianhou Gan[2(✉)], Bin Wen[1], Wei Zhang[3],
and Xiaochun Cao[3]

[1] Yunnan Normal University, Kunming, Yunnan, China
xiaochaoting@gmail.com, wenbin@ynnu.edu.cn
[2] Key Laboratory of Educational Informatization for Nationalities,
Yunnan Normal University, Ministry of Education, Kunming, Yunnan, China
ganjh@ynnu.edu.cn
[3] Institute of Information Engineering, Chinese Academy of Sciences, Beijing, China
wzhang.cu@gmail.com, caoxiaochun@iie.ac.cn

Abstract. New word discovery possesses a significance in NLP. This paper first reduces noise to the corpus of micro-blog and employ the new filtering algorithm to filter the candidate words, then improves the traditional mutual information and adjacency entropy method respectively and put forward enhancement of mutual information and relative adjacency entropy. In terms of multi-feature massive data generated by a large-scale corpus to recognize the new words, the MapReduce parallel computing model is exploited to extract three features such as, enhancement of mutual information, relative adjacency entropy and background document frequency, to improve the parallelization. With the extracted three features, the feature vectors of the candidate words are formed, and a SVM model can be trained by training the labelled corpus. The experiments show that the proposed method shortens the time required by the whole recognition process. In addition, compared with the existing methods, the F-value reaches 86.98%.

Keywords: New words recognition · NLP · Enhancement of mutual information · Relative adjacency entropy · MapReduce · SVM

1 Introduction

In the process of Chinese word segmentation, new word recognition is quite difficult. Sproat and others pointed out that 60% errors of Chinese word segmentation are caused by new words [1]. Now, many new words are spreading via micro-blog. New words such as, '(family)', '(Geyou repose)' and '(Beijing repose)', etc., have been created. Micro-blog text contains a considerable proportion of new words. The linguists have concluded according to the statistics that the average annual production of new words is more than 800 [2]. In the field of new word recognition, there is no definition for 'new word'. Based on

© Springer Nature Singapore Pte Ltd. 2016
M. Gong et al. (Eds.): BIC-TA 2016, Part II, CCIS 682, pp. 379–387, 2016.
DOI: 10.1007/978-981-10-3614-9_46

existing research, people think that new word should have the following properties. From the perspective of word itself, it should be an independent word. From the perspective of appearing frequency, the new word should be widely adopted. Even in corpus, the new word should have a high frequency of appearance in many documents and is used by numerous people. From the perspective of time, the word has just appeared within a certain period of time [3]. Sui and others [4] extracted the words with close relationship through computing the static union rate among the words after word segmentation of corpus. Then they used the grammar rule and field features to get the field terms with high confidence. The rule only has the features of field, so it is not suitable for other corpora. Sornlertlamvanich and others used decision-tree model to train the new word recognition model, with a precision result of 85% [5]. Unfortunately, it is not suitable for large-scale corpus. Peng [6] and others used the CRF model of combining lexical features and field knowledge to extract the new words. At the same time, they added the discovered new words into the dictionary to enhance the recognition effect of the model. The method improves the accuracy of word segmentation but costs a long time. Liu [7] and others applied the left & right information entropy and likelihood rate (LLR) to determine the word boundary to extract the candidate new words. The extracted features of the method are less and the precision rate is not high. Zifang [8] and others extracted new words based on word's internal model and combined with mutual information, IWP and position-word probability. The proposed mutual information is not suitable for multi-strings and there are limitations. Li and other scholars [9] employed word frequency, word probability, etc., to train a SVM model and consider the new recognition from the perspective of classification. The limitation of the method is that it cannot recognize the low-frequency new words, thus it will produce a lot of garbage strings. Xiaobao [10] and others iteratively used the mutual information, left (right) entropy, left (right) adjacency right (left) average entropy, etc., to obtain the candidate list of new words. Then they used a Chinese collocation library to filter the list to get new words. The multi-strings will be divided into two substrings in the calculation. This will affect the results of recognizing the new words. Wang [11] and others researched the new words from the internet based on time series information and used the combination between dynamic feature and statistical method. Shuai and others [12] proposed a filter method for stop word and iterative context entropy algorithm which can use to recognize new words. Su [13] and others proposed to improve the adjacency entropy with a weighted adjacency entropy to optimize and improve the performance. Li [14] and others were used the internal word probability, mutual information, word frequency and word probability rule as the features to train the SVM model, but the precision rate was only 61.78%. Due to the problems of slow speed caused by the above methods, as well as the low precision rate when recognizing new words. We firstly reduces the noise in the micro-blog corpus. Then we use N-Gram statistical method to extract new word candidates based on a word segmentation. We propose a new filtering algorithm and combines it with the stop word list launched by Harbin Institute of Technology to filter the candidates. Then, a SVM classifier will be trained by multiple eigenvalues which were obtained through enhancement of mutual information, relative adjacency entropy and background document frequency method in MapReduce. At last, with the trained SVM model for recognizing the new words of micro-blog of test set. The method improves the speed of new word training recognition model which is caused by the multi-featured massive data of large-scale corpus. Meanwhile, the proposed method can also improve the precision rate of new word recognition.

2   New Word Discovery Method Based on Micro-blog Contents

2.1   Preprocessing of Corpus

Micro-blog has a strong randomness in the word use and grammar, which causes a large number of noisy data. Based on analysis to micro-blog corpus, we can find that, '@', [expression] and URL links exist in most of the micro-blog content. These noisy data have great influences to the generation of candidate words. We eliminates these noisy data through the method of building regular expression of the micro-blog data.

2.2   Filtering Algorithm

We introduce N-gram algorithm for Preprocessing of the micro-blog corpus data. These candidate new words contain many garbage strings, so they need to be filtered. Therefore, we proposes a filtering algorithm of combing news corpus and stop words. The pseudocode is shown in Algorithm 1, where N is the news corpus. W stands for the candidate new word set of micro-blog. T is the stop word list and NL means the candidate new word set after filtering.

Algorithm 1. Filtering algorithm based on news corpus and stop word list:

Input: N,W,T
Output: NL
  1: NL = Φ
  2: **for** each g in W **do**
  3:     **if** g$\in$ N || T **then**
  4:        W = W - g
  5:     **else**
  6:        NL = NL - g
  7:     **end if**
  8: **end for**
  9: **Return:** NL

---

3   Feature Selection of Candidate New Words

We need to use the statistical method to quantify the features of these candidate new words. We use mutual information [10] to measure internal coagulation. Meanwhile, we also use information entropy [10] and background document frequency to measure external freedom degree.

3.1   Internal Coagulation

Traditional mutual information formula [10] only gives the calculation formula of two character string, which can only be applied to the two character new words. For the multi-character string, We proposes an enhanced mutual information which is suitable for the multi-word strings. The definition is as follows.

$$C(S) = \log_2 \frac{P(S_1 \cdots S_n)}{[\prod\limits_{i=1}^{n} (\frac{F(S_i)}{W} - P(S_1 \cdots S_n))]^{\frac{2}{n}}}, \tag{1}$$

where W is the total words of micro-blog corpus and P is the frequency of string in the corpus. The larger the value is, the more possible the expression will be a potential new word.

3.2   External Freedom Degree

We proposes a relative adjacency entropy. In our opinion, the string with a higher word probability than its substring will be regarded as a new word. For string $W = \{w_1 w_2 \cdots w_n\}$ and its longest substring $W_{left} = \{w_1 w_2 \cdots w_{n-1}\}$ and $W_{right} = \{w_2 w_3 \cdots w_n\}$. We subtract the substring's adjacency entropy which is taking the weight from the adjacency entropy, and take the minimum of relative adjacency entropy. The definition is as follows.

$$C_L(\omega) = \frac{1}{n} \sum_{a_i \in \alpha} C(a_i, \omega) \log \frac{C(a_i, \omega)}{n}, \tag{2}$$

$$C_r(\omega) = \frac{1}{n} \sum_{b_i \in \beta} C(b_i, \omega) \log \frac{C(\omega, b_i)}{n}, \tag{3}$$

where, $n = \sum_{a_i \in \alpha} C(a_i, \omega) = \sum_{b_i \in \beta} C(\omega, b_i)$

The adjacency entropy after taking the weight and relative adjacency entropy are defined as follows.

$$C_r(\omega) = \lambda C_r(\omega) - (1 - \lambda) C_r(\omega_{left}), \tag{4}$$

$$C_L(\omega) = \lambda C_L(\omega) - (1 - \lambda) C_L(\omega_{right}). \tag{5}$$

The minimum formula of relative adjacency entropy is defined as:

$$C(\omega) = \min\{C_L(\omega), C_r(\omega)\}. \tag{6}$$

From the above definitions, we can conclude that the character strings only used in the fixed context and the relative adjacency entropy is small.

3.3 Background Document Frequency

Considering from the perspective of human memory, new words have never appeared in previous memories. We use a large-scale background corpus to simulate the human memory. If the frequency of the string in foreground corpus is much larger than that in the large-scale background corpus, the string is likely to be a new word. The formula of the relevant frequency ratio of string ω in X and Y of two corpora is as follows.

$$\sigma(\omega; X, Y) = \frac{f(\omega, X)}{f(\omega, Y)}, \tag{7}$$

where $f(\omega, X)$ and $f(\omega, Y)$ are the corresponding frequencies of ω in X and Y of corpora, X is the foreground corpus and Y is the background corpus.

4 Parallel Implementation of New Word Feature Quantization Algorithm

4.1 Parallel Implementation of Background Document Frequency Algorithm

In order to improve the coupling efficiency of the multi-features, we calculate the word frequencies in X and Y corpus respectively. The overall system diagram is shown in Fig. 1.

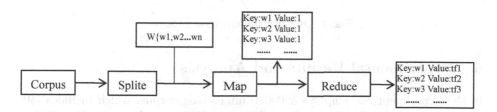

Fig. 1. Parallelization of string frequency

4.2 Parallelization of Relative Adjacency Entropy

The context entropy can be classified as the left and right entropy respectively. Their algorithm are similar. The overall process is shown in Fig. 2.

4.3 Multi-feature Data Coupling

After obtaining the feature data of the candidate new word (such as: the enhanced mutual information, the relative adjacency entropy and the background document frequency), we need to couple the multiple feature data which can form feature vector. The overall process is shown in Fig. 3.

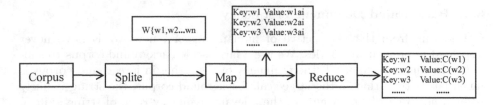

Fig. 2. Parallelization of relative adjacency entropy

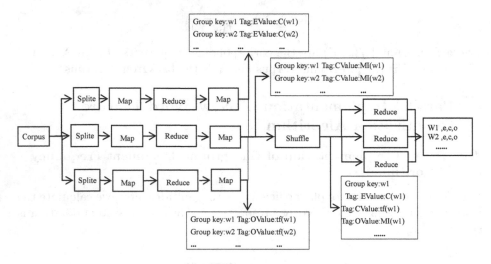

Fig. 3. Overall parallelization process

5   Experimental Results and Analysis

In the experiment, we employs 5200000 micro-blog corpus, which includes 591 micro-blog of 2009, 60795 micro-blog of 2010, 763027 micro-blog of 2011, 1699484 micro-blog of 2012, 1782335 micro-blog of 2013, 681449 micro-blog of 2014 and 198925 micro-blog of 2015. We make the micro-blog from 2009 to 2013 as the background corpus. We let the micro-blog of 2014 and 2015 be the foreground corpus. The preliminary results have a total of 13273 words. In relative adjacency entropy algorithm, we set the weight to be 0.62.

5.1   Methods and Standards

The specific definitions of the measurements are as follows.

$$R = \frac{New\ word\ number\ recognized\ by\ system}{New\ word\ number\ to\ be\ recognized}, \tag{8}$$

$$P = \frac{New\ word\ number\ with\ correct\ recognition}{New\ word\ number\ with\ recognition}, \tag{9}$$

$$F - measure = \frac{(\beta^2 + 1) \times P \times R}{\beta \times P + R}(\beta = 1). \tag{10}$$

In formula (8), R means the recall rate of the recognized new word. In formula (9), P means the precision rate of the recognized new word. In formula (10), the F value is the harmonic mean of the precision rate and the recall rate. These measurements can comprehensively reflect the overall performance of the new word recognition.

5.2 Experimental Results and Analysis

Comparing the advantages and disadvantages between the proposed method S (MI+E+BF+F) and previous methods, the specific experimental results are as shown in Table 1. In Table 1, S represents the SVM classifier which includes different candidate word features. MI represents the mutual information which is the enhanced mutual information. E means the information entropy. BF is background document frequency and F represents filtering algorithm. We can conclude from the experiment that both the precision rate and recall rate of the enhanced mutual information are improved when comparing S (MI+F) with S (MI*+F). Similarly, both the precision rate and recall rate of S (E*+F) are higher than that of S (E+F). Via the comparison between S (MI*+E*+BF+F) and S (MI*+E*+BF), we can observe that the new word recognition accuracy without the filtering algorithm is lower. According to the results, the combination of three features improves the precision rate, recall rate and F value of micro-blog new word recognition when comparing with traditional method S (MI+E+BF+F). The final F value is 86.98%.

Table 1. Experimental results of micro-blog new word recognition under different features

Features	Precision rate	Recall rate	F-measure
S(MI+F)	41.72	55.86	47.77
S(MI*+F)	45.13	57.36	50.52
S(E+F)	51.17	60.32	55.37
S(E*+F)	59.62	67.35	63.25
S(MI+E+BF+F)	76.95	86.54	81.46
S(MI*+E*+BF+F)	83.1	91.25	86.98
S(MI*+E*+BF)	80.32	87.63	83.82

The parallelization algorithm sets the processing speed under the node of one, three and six sets. We obtain the operation situation of micro-blog corpora with different size. We count the time spent by the system when recognizing the new words. The results are shown in Fig. 4.

Unit: Hour

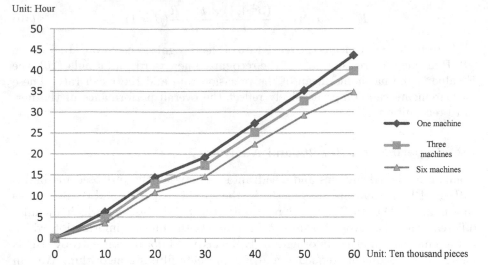

Fig. 4. Operation speed chart on micro-blog new word recognition

6   Conclusions

This paper proposes a new filtering algorithm aiming at recognizing new words in the micro-blog content, and put forward the enhanced mutual information and relative adjacency entropy method. After experimental verification, the parallelization shortens the overall time of new word recognition. The precision rate and recall rate of micro-blog new word recognition are improved by the SVM classification model with the features generated from the above methods. The proposed method can achieve very good classification and recognition performance. In the future, we will try to fully explore the effective features which can further improve the performance of the micro-blog new word recognition task.

Acknowledgements. The research is supported by a National Nature Science Fund Project with No. 61262071 and Key Project of Applied Basic Research Program of Yunnan Province No. 2016FA024.

References

1. Sproat, R., Emerson, T.: The first international Chinese word segmentation bake-off. In: Proceedings of the Second SIGHAN Workshop on Chinese Language Processing, vol. 17, pp. 133–143. Association for Computational Linguistics (2003)
2. Dexin, Z.: There will be no fish if the water is too clear - my normative view on new words. J. Peking Univ.: Philos. Soc. Sci. **5** (2000)
3. Huang, X., Li, R.F.: Discovery method of new words in blog contents. Mod. Electron. Tech. **36**(2), 144–146 (2013). (in Chinese)
4. Sui, Z.F., Chen, Y.R., Wu, Y.F., et al.: The research on the automatic. Term Extr. Domain Inf. Sci. Technol. [EB/OL] (2013)

5. Sornlertlamvanich, V., Potipiti, T., Charoenporn, T.: Automatic corpus-based Thai word extraction with the C4.5 learning algorithm. In: Proceedings of the International Conference on Computational Linguistics, Saarbrcken, pp. 802–807 (2011)
6. Peng, F., Feng, F., McCallum, A.: Chinese segmentation, new word detection using conditional random fields. In: Proceedings of the 20th International Conference on Computational Linguistics. Association for Computational Linguistics, p. 562 (2004)
7. Liu, T., Liu, B.Q., Xu, Z.M.: Automatic domain-specific term extraction and its application in text classification. Acta Electronica Sinica **35**(2), 328 (2007)
8. Zifang, L., Xiufeng, J.: New word recognition based on internal model of word. Comput. Mod. **11**, 56–58 (2010)
9. Li, H., Huang, C.N., Gao, J.: The Use of SVM for Chinese New Word Identification. In: Proceedings of First International Joint Conference on Natural Language Processing, pp. 723–732 (2004)
10. Xiaobao, Z., Huaping, Z.: New word recognition based on iterative algorithm. Comput. Eng. **40**(07), 154–158 (2014)
11. Wang, M., Lin, L., Wang, F.: New word identification in social network text based on time series information. In: IEEE International Conference on Computer Supported Cooperative Work in Design, pp. 552–557. IEEE (2014)
12. Shuai, H., Min, Z., Yiqun, L., et al.: New word recognition based on micro-blog contents. Pattern Recogn. Artif. Intell. **27**(2), 141–145 (2014)
13. Su, Q.L, Liu, B.Q.: Chinese new word extraction from MicroBlog data. In: International Conference on Machine Learning, Cybernetics, pp. 1874–1879. IEEE (2013)
14. Li, C., Xu, Y.: Based on support vector and word features new word discovery research. In: Yuan, Y., Wu, X., Lu, Y. (eds.) ISCTCS 2012. CCIS, vol. 320, pp. 287–294. Springer, Heidelberg (2013). doi:10.1007/978-3-642-35795-4_36

A Memetic Kernel Clustering Algorithm for Change Detection in SAR Images

Yangyang Li[✉], Gao Lu, and Licheng Jiao

Key Laboratory of Intelligent Perception and Image Understanding of Ministry of Education, International Research Center for Intelligent Perception and Computation, Joint International Research Laboratory of Intelligent Perception and Computation, Xidian University, Xian 710071, Shaanxi, China
lyy_791@163.com, yyli@xidian.edu.cn

Abstract. For SAR images change detection problem, a memetic kernel clustering algorithm (MKCA) is proposed. SAR image change detection problem as an optimization problem can solved by kernel clustering method. In this paper, the kernel function can transform nonlinear data into a high dimensional feature space, and increases the probability of the linear separability of the patterns within the transformed space and simplifies the associated data structure. Meanwhile local learning operators are designed to further enhance the ability of global exploration and promote performance of classification. Finally, to evaluate this method, the performance of the proposed method has been compared with some classical clustering algorithms for change detection in SAR (synthetic aperture radar) images. The experiments showed that the proposed algorithm can reduce the number of missed alarms and false alarms. So the proposed algorithm can effectively separate the unchanged area and the changed area.

Keywords: Kernel clustering · Memetic algorithm · Image change detection · SAR image

1 Introduction

In remote sensing applications, change detection is the process aimed at identifying differences in the state of a land cover by analyzing a pair of images acquired on the same geographical area at different times [1,2]. But there are two major difficulties associated with SAR image change detection, which are the removal of speckle noise and the registration of information between images [3]. If accurate registration between images were not achieved, spurious differences will be detected merely because the land surface properties at wrong locations are evaluated instead of real changes at the same location between one time and another [4]. The result is that the misregistration of two images will significantly affect the change detection accuracy since change analysis is generally performed on a pixel-by-pixel basis. So both an intensive preprocessing phase and the development of effective data analysis techniques capable of dealing with speckle noise

© Springer Nature Singapore Pte Ltd. 2016
M. Gong et al. (Eds.): BIC-TA 2016, Part II, CCIS 682, pp. 388–393, 2016.
DOI: 10.1007/978-981-10-3614-9_47

are required [5]. In this paper, the log-ratio (LR) operation is applied to the two multitemporal images.

In the present work, we propose the memetic kernel cluster algorithm (MKCA) for change detection in SAR images. Kernel function can transform nonlinear data into a high dimensional feature space, and increases the probability of the linear separability of the patterns within the transformed space and simplifies the associated data structure. Local learning operator is applied to the individuals and refines capabilities of search algorithms. So the local learning operators have high opportunities to apply every point to clustering center and obtain optimal classification results.

2   The Description of MKCA for Change Detection

Unsupervised change detection techniques mainly use the analysis of change data which are constructed using multitemporal images [6]. In this paper, a memetic kernel clustering method for SAR image change detection is proposed to analyze the difference image of two satellite images acquired from the same area coverage but at two different time instances. Our clustering methods are developed based on the LR difference image. Figure 1 shows the overall structure of the proposed approach.

Considered two SAR images I_1 and I_2 acquired on the same geographical area at two times. Let I_d be the LR difference image computed from the two considered images. $I_1(x)$ is the gray level of a pixel on position on the first SAR image, $I_2(x)$ is the gray level of a pixel on position on the second SAR image, and $I_d(x)$ is the gray level of a pixel on position x on I_d. Figure 1 shows the overall structure of the proposed approach.

The major elements of our proposed approach are presented as follows.

(1) Computing difference image

Considered the influence of the presence of speckle noise, the LR operation is used to generate the difference image in this paper.

(2) Kernel k-means algorithm

Kernel k-means algorithm was described in detail in [7]. Given difference image dataset $I_d(x) = \{x_1, x_2, \cdots, x_N\}, x_i \in i^d$, and the dataset of N points is represented by the set P, d is dimension, the purpose of kernel k-means is to partition the I_d dataset into $k = 2$ disjoint clusters $C = \{C_1, C_2\}$. The best clustering results is that patterns from same cluster are as similar as possible and patterns from different clusters differ as far as possible. Kernel function φ is applied to map data into a nonlinear high-dimensional space $H : \varphi : i^d \rightarrow H, x_i \rightarrow \varphi(x_i)$, where $x_i = [x_{i,1}, x_{i,2}, \cdots, x_{i,d}]^T$ and $\varphi(x_i) = [\varphi_1(x_i), \varphi_2(x_i), \cdots, \varphi_H(x_i)]^T$. Cluster centers $m_i(i = 1, 2, \cdots, k)$ are mapped into feature space is $m_i^{\varphi}(i = 1, 2, \cdots, k)$. By applying the mapping, Inner product of two dots $x_i^T \cdot x_j$ is mapped into $\varphi(x_i)^T \cdot \varphi(x_j)$. The dot

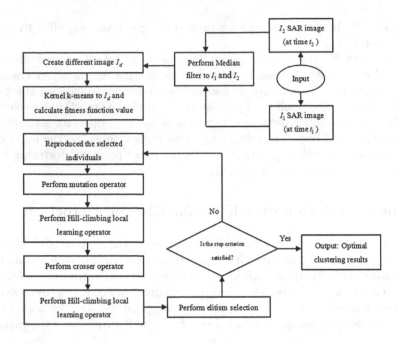

Fig. 1. Overall structure of our proposed approach.

product in the transformed space can be calculated through the kernel function $K(x_i, x_j) = \varphi(x_i)^T \cdot \varphi(x_j)$ in the input space i^d. In this paper, we use Gaussian kernel function.

(3) Memetic algorithm

The memetic kernel clustering algorithm is provided in Fig. 1. Note that local learning operator can guide the process of evolution. It enhance the genotype to influence the better results which is replaced the locally improved individual back into population to compete for reproductive opportunities [10]. In order to maximize the fitness function, we choose local search algorithms as local learning operator to improve the capability of the searching and optimize the fitness function. After the mutation and crossover operators performance, the hill-climbing local learning methods [11] are cooperated to the two operators to further enhance the ability of global exploration and overcome premature convergence effectively.

(4) Mutation operator, Crossover operator and Elitism selection operator

Mutation operator and crossover operator is cooperated to our algorithm, and these two operators will increase enough diversity for population. Elitism selection can help the algorithm to select the solution more quickly and enhance the global convergence.

(5) Termination criterion

In this paper, the degrees of no assign of improvement can be employed as a termination criterion. For example, we set $\epsilon = 10^{-5}$ as the stop threshold and $e = 10$ as the degrees of no assign of improvement. In other words, if the change of the best values of objective function between current generation and former generation is less than ϵ, it will be called the index of no assign of improvement for one time ($e = 1$), otherwise $e = 0$. If the index $e = 10$, that means there is no improvement between two adjacent generations continuously for 10 times, the termination criterion is satisfied.

3 Experimental Results

In order to test the effectiveness of the proposed method-MKCA, we compare its performance with other two clustering algorithms which are k-means [6] and kernel k-means [7] over SAR image datasets. In the following experiments, we performed 30 independent runs on each test problem.

The first dataset is a section of size 290×350 pixels of two SAR images acquired by a RADARSAT SAR sensor and provided by Defense Research and Development Canada Ottawa [8].

The second dataset is a section of two SAR images acquired by Radarset-2 over an area near Yellow River Estuary in China. The original size of these two SAR images acquired in June 2008 and June 2009 by Radarsat-2 is 7666×7692.

In this paper, the parameters used in MKCA are set as follows: the population size is 50; mutation probability is 0.1; crossover probability is 0.8; the index of no assign of improvement $e = 10$; and the stop threshold $\epsilon = 10^{-5}$. In order to make a quantitative evaluation of the effectiveness of MKCA, the number of missed alarms, the number of false alarms and error detection rate are selected to quantitatively evaluate the results [8,9]. The number of change pixels is denoted as C_0, and the number of change pixels is denoted as C_1. Thus the change detection truth number of change pixels is $C_r = \{C_0 \cap C_c\}$, the number of change detection false alarms (unchanged pixels wrongly classified as changed) is $C_f = C_c - C_r$ and the number of change detection missed alarms (changed

Table 1. Change detection results (in number of pixels).

Datasets	Comparison algorithm	C_f	C_m	C_z	P
Ottawa	K-means	6103	3633	9736	9.59%
	Kernel k-means	4740	1028	5768	5.68%
	MKCA	3921	1291	5212	5.13%
Yellow River Estuary	K-means	14709	212	14921	10.66%
	Kernel k-means	10102	482	10584	7.56%
	MKCA	6223	136	6359	4.54%

pixels that undetected)) is $C_m = C_0 - C_r$. So the total number of error classified pixels is $C_z = C_f + C_m$, and the percentage error classification is $P = \frac{C_z}{C_0 + C_1}$. Table 1 summarizes the quantitative results obtained by comparing the reference map with the change detection maps yielded applying the proposed technique and classical change detection algorithms.

In Table 1, it is obviously seen that total error detection rate P of MKCA is far less than other two algorithms. And the number of change detection missed alarms C_m of MKCA is least among three algorithms.

4 Conclusions

This paper has presented a memetic kernel clustering algorithm (MKCA) for change detection in SAR images. The change detection problem based on clustering approach is viewed as an optimization problem, which can solve by MKCA in this paper. The proposed method optimizes the fitness function with memetic algorithm, and it maximizes the fitness function relating to the kernel k-means objective function through local learning methods Finally it will get better clustering results than other classical clustering algorithms. From the experimental results, we can see that the proposed algorithm can promote performance of classification. Therefore MKCA can effectively solve the image change detection problem. So in our future work, we should develop more novel local learning method to enhance the ability of global exploration and optimize the objective function. We can try to apply memetic algorithm to other fields, such as image segmentation.

Acknowledgments. This work was supported by the National Natural Science Foundation of China (Nos. 61272279, 61272282, 61371201, and 61203303), the Program for New Century Excellent Talents in University (No. NCET-12-0920), the National Basic Research Program (973 Program) of China (No. 2013CB329402), the Program for Cheung Kong Scholars and Innovative Research Team in University (No. IRT-15R53), and the Fund for Foreign Scholars in University Research and Teaching Programs (the 111 Project) (No. B07048).

References

1. Richards, J.A., Jia, X.: Remote Sensing Digital Image Analysis: An Introduction, 4th edn. Springer, Berlin (2005)
2. Ghosh, S., Bruzzone, L., Patra, S., et al.: A context-sensitive technique for unsupervised change detection based on Hopfield-type neural networks. IEEE Trans. Geosci. Remote Sens. **45**(3), 778–789 (2007)
3. Cihlar, J., Pultz, T.J., Gray, A.L.: Change detection with synthetic aperture radar. Int. J. Remote Sens. **13**(3), 401–414 (1992)
4. Townshend, J.R.G., Justice, C.O., Gurney, C., et al.: The impact of misregistration on change detection. IEEE Trans. Geosci. Remote Sens. **30**(5), 1054–1060 (1992)
5. Tzeng, Y.C., Chiu, S.H., Chen, K.S.: Automatic change detections from SAR images using fractal dimension. In: IEEE International Conference on Geoscience and Remote Sensing Symposium (IGARSS 2006), pp. 759–762 (2006)

6. Celik, T.: Unsupervised change detection in satellite images using principal component analysis and k-means clustering. IEEE Geosci. Remote Sens. Lett. **6**(4), 772–779 (2009)
7. Schlkopf, B., Smola, A., Mller, K.-R.: Nonlinear component analysis as a kernel eigenvalue problem. Neural Comput. **10**(5), 1299–1319 (1998)
8. Gong, M.G., Cao, Y., Wu, Q.D.: A neighborhood-based ratio approach for change detection in SAR Images. IEEE Geosci. Remote Sens. Lett. **9**(2), 307–311 (2011)
9. Bruzzone, L., Prieto, D.F.: Automatic analysis of the difference image for unsupervised change detection. IEEE Trans. Geosci. Remote Sens. **38**(3), 1171–1182 (2000)
10. Le, M.N., Ong, Y.-S., Jin, Y., et al.: Lamarckian memetic algorithms: local optimum and connectivity structure analysis. Memetic Comput. **1**(3), 175–190 (2009)
11. Liang, R.S., Jiang, Y.F., Bian, R.: Ordered hill climbing search for heuristic planning. In: International Conference on Information Engineering and Computer Science (ICIECS 2009), pp. 1–4 (2009)

Collaborative Rating Prediction Based on Dynamic Evolutionary Heterogeneous Clustering

Jianrui Chen, Uliji[✉], Hua Wang, and Chunxia Zhao

College of Science, Inner Mongolia University of Technology,
Hohhot 010051, Inner Mongolia, China
ulji@imut.edu.cn

Abstract. Collaborative filtering based clustering has been proved to have many advantages. In this paper, a novel heterogenous dynamic evolutionary clustering is presented. Firstly, the items and users are regarded as heterogenous individuals in the network. According to the dynamic network model, they are clustered into several groups. Secondly, item-based collaborative filtering is adopted in each cluster. Similarity between individuals only in the same cluster are computed not for all individuals in the system. The target rating is calculated according to the item-based collaborative filtering in its cluster. Diverse simulations show the efficiency of our proposed methods. Moreover, the presented methods gain better prediction results than two existing better algorithms.

Keywords: Recommender systems · Prediction rating · Collaborative filtering · Dynamic evolutionary clustering

1 Introduction

In recent years, online social networks such as Facebook, Twitter, Taobao, Google have become an important part of our daily life. They provide us with abundant online contents, which makes it very time-consuming to find our needed information. This is often referred as the information overload problem. And in order to solve it, much attention has been paid attention to design efficient recommendation algorithms. User-based (UCF) and item-based collaborative filtering (ICF), collaborative filtering algorithm based on matrix decomposition [1], collaborative filtering (CF)-based methods [2] are the most representative ones. And these algorithms have been proved to be effective in helping users to find items that fit their personal tastes best from a large catalog of choices [3].

In spite of this, there are still many challenging research problems. For example, traditional recommendation techniques in recommender systems mainly focus on improving recommendation accuracy, but it ignores a proper balance between accuracy and diversity. The purpose of clustering technique is to reduce dimensionality. In [4,5], Gong et al. proposed a multi-objective recommendation model to solve this problem. And in their paper, a clustering technique

M. Gong et al. (Eds.): BIC-TA 2016, Part II, CCIS 682, pp. 394–399, 2016.
DOI: 10.1007/978-981-10-3614-9_48

is employed to improve the computational efficiency. Sarwar et al. presented and experimentally evaluated a new approach in improving the scalability of recommender systems by using clustering techniques [6]. Xue et al. proposed a novel framework for collaborative filtering which combines the strengths of memory-based approaches and model-based approaches in order to enable recommendation by groups of closely related individuals [7]. Honda et al. considered a new approach, user-item clusters are extracted one by one in a sequential manner via a structural balancing technique, used in conjunction with SFCE extraction method [8]. Ba et al. proposed a new approach combining the clustering algorithm with SVD algorithm which is widely used in the domain of image-processing into collaborative filtering algorithm. The users are gathered into clusters according to the attributes, e.g., gender, age, and occupation. Then the user-product rating matrix is decomposed and recombined into a new rating matrix to calculate the similarity between any two users [9,10]. Recently, there are many dynamic evolutionary clustering algorithms are proposed due to their low time complexity and high clustering performance [11–14].

The rest of the paper is organized as follows. Algorithm description is given in Sect. 2. Section 3 shows simulation results. Section 4 concludes the paper.

2   Algorithm Description

Supposed there are N users and M items. 80% ratings are known and 20% ratings are to be predicted. In this section, a dynamic evolutionary heterogenous clustering algorithm is proposed for prediction ratings in recommender systems. Firstly, the users and items are clustered into several communities. Secondly, K nearest neighbors in the sub-cluster are calculated. Thirdly, the ratings are predicted based on item-based collaborative filtering.

2.1   Dynamic Evolutionary Heterogenous Clustering

In most references, the similarity is firstly calculated to cluster the items and users. However, in this paper, only the score matrix is adopted to gather users and items into groups.

Items and users are regarded as the heterogeneous individuals in networks. In refs. [12–14], they have presented dynamic evolutionary clustering algorithms for networks. In order to reduce the complexity, the edges between users and edges between items are not calculated. Here, only the information between user and item is adopted. Heterogeneous individuals are roughly divided into several clusters according to the adjacent matrix. Supposed there are N users and M items in the network. V is the individual set containing users and items. S is an $N \times M$ score matrix. S_{ij} denotes the i-th user rating of the j-th item. In order to obtain the adjacent matrix of network, the following definition is given:

$$A = \begin{bmatrix} \mathbf{0}_{N \times N} & S_{N \times M} \\ (S^T)_{M \times N} & \mathbf{0}_{M \times M} \end{bmatrix}.$$

Here $\mathbf{0}$ is a zero matrix. A is an $N + M$ dimension square matrix.

The dynamic evolutionary clustering rule is: users and items with higher ratings are regarded as in the same cluster. For this reason, the users and items in the same cluster would have similar interest. For prediction rates in recommendation systems, the dynamic evolutionary clustering model is constructed as follows.

$$x_i(k+1) = x_i(k) + K_1 \sum_{j \in J_i} sin(x_j(k) - x_i(k)) + K_2 \sum_{j \notin J_i} sin(x_j(k) - x_i(k)).$$

(1)

$x_i(k)$ denotes state of the i-th node at k iteration step. $x_i(k+1)$ denotes state of the i-th node at $k+1$ iteration step. $J_i = \{j | A_{ij} \geq 3, j = 1, \cdots, M\}$. Parameter $K_1 > 0$ and it's role is to make the items and users with higher ratings evolve together. Parameter $K_2 < 0$ and it's role is to make the items and users with lower ratings evolve far away.

Each individual in the constructed network updates its state in every step according to Eq. (1). Eventually, the states of all individuals in network would be stable. The state values in nearby range would be divided into the same cluster.

2.2   Item-Based Collaborative Filtering

The similarity between items are calculated only for each cluster not for all items in the network. For example, if there are five clusters, then there are five similarity sub-matrixes. One sub-matrix is for one cluster. The computational complexity is reduced largely. At the prediction stage, for each prediction rating would be calculated in its cluster as follows:

$$r_{u,i} = \frac{\sum_{j \in N_i} (\sharp_i sim)_{ij} \times R_{u,j}}{\sum_{j \in N_i} |(\sharp_i sim)_{ij}|}.$$

(2)

$\sharp i$ is cluster number of the i-th individual. Denote the similarity matrix for $\sharp i$ cluster as $\sharp_i sim$. Here, cosine [15], person correlation [16] and adjusted cosine [17] are considered. From the $\sharp i$ cluster, the optimal similar items are singled out as the K nearest neighbors, denoted as N_i.

2.3   Algorithm Flow

In this paper, Collaborative Filtering Rating Prediction based on Dynamic Evolutionary Heterogeneous item Clustering (denoted as $DEHC - CFi$) algorithm is proposed. The main steps of $DEHC - CFi$ are given as follows.

- Step1. Find clusters of items according to Eq. (1).
- Step2. Calculate similarity between items in each cluster based on cosine, correlation and adjusted cosine.
- Step3. Predict the ratings based on item collaborative filtering according to formula (2).

Our main innovation is in Step 1. The proposed method is more efficient than the other algorithms with clustering. This is because our method does not require the number of clusters.

3   Simulation Results

All the algorithms is coded in Matlab 2013a, the experiments have been executed on Intel(R) Xeon(R) CPU E5-2680 v2 @ 2.80 GHz, 64 GB memory. The operating system is Windows Server 2008 R2 Enterprise.

3.1   Evaluation Metric

Evaluation metric RMSE (Root Mean Square Error) is adopted to test the efficiency of our proposed algorithm.

$$RMSE = \sqrt{\frac{\sum_{i=1}^{n}(r_{ui} - \hat{r}_{ui})^2}{n}}. \tag{3}$$

Here, $\hat{r}_{ui}$ is the estimated value of user u rating of item i. r_{ui} is the real value of user u rating of item i. n is the number of ratings in test set. Then, prediction ratings are rounded integer.

We use the popular dataset in the field of recommender systems, Movielens (ML-100k, http://grouplens.org/datasets/movielens/). This data set consists of 100,000 ratings (1–5) from 943 users on 1682 movies.

To test our proposed method is efficient, two algorithms are compared. They are collaborative filtering without cluster and collaborative filtering with K-means cluster algorithm.

Here, $DEHC - CFi$ is our proposed method based on item. CFi denotes global collaborative filtering based on item. $Kmeans - CFi$ denotes collaborative filtering based on item with $Kmeans$ cluster algorithm.

Figure 1 gives the comparing RMSE results on CFi, $Kmeans - CFi$ and our $DEHC - CFi$. We can see that RMSE of our $DEHC - CFi$ is slightly lower than $Kmeans - CFi$ and CFi. And the algorithms with cluster are more efficient than CFi without cluster.

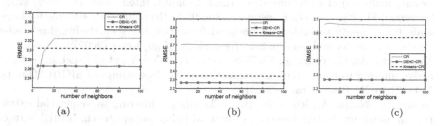

| (a) | (b) | (c) |

Fig. 1. Comparing results on CFi, $Kmeans - CFi$ and our $DEHC - CFi$. (a) Similarity based on *cosine*. (b) Similarity based on *correlation*. (c) Similarity based on *adjustedcosine*.

4   Conclusion

A heterogenous dynamic evolutionary clustering collaborative filtering prediction rating method is proposed in this paper. Firstly, the users and items are regarded as individuals in the network. Dynamic evolutionary clustering algorithm is generated for recommender systems. The individuals states update according to the constructed network model. Individuals with similar state values are divided into the same cluster according to the stable states. Secondly, in each cluster, item-based collaborative filtering is proposed. Comparing with several acknowledgement algorithms from several angles, our presented algorithm is more efficient in terms of accuracy. Online recommendation algorithms are in demand, we would further consider online dynamic evolutionary prediction ratings in future.

Acknowledgment. This work is supported by National Natural Science Foundation of China (No. 11261034, 71561020, 61503203, 11326239); Higher school science and technology research project of Inner Mongolia (NJZY13119); Natural Science Foundation of Inner Mongolia (2015MS0103, 2014BS0105).

References

1. Gai, L.I., Lei, L.I., Polytechnic, S.: Collaborative itering algorithm based on matrix decomposition. Comput. Eng. Appl. **47**, 4–7 (2011)
2. Cai, Y., Leung, H., Li, Q., Min, H., Tang, J., Li, J.: Typicality-based collaborative filtering recommendation. IEEE Trans. Knowl. Data Eng. **2**, 97–104 (2010)
3. Niu, J., Wang, L., Liu, X., Yu, S.: Fusing user and item information to deal with data sparsity by using side information in recommendation systems. J. Netw. Comput. Appl. **70**, 41–50 (2016)
4. Wang, S., Gong, M., Ma, L., Cai, Q., Jiao, L.: Decomposition based multiobjective evolutionary algorithm for collaborative filtering recommender systems. In: IEEE Congress on Evolutionary Computation (CEC), pp. 672–679. IEEE Press, Beijing (2014)
5. Zuo, Y., Gong, M., Zeng, J., Ma, L.: Personalized recommendation based on evolutionary multi-objective optimization. IEEE Comput. Intell. Mag. **10**, 52–62 (2015)
6. Sarwar, B.M., Karypis, G., Konstan, J., Riedl, J.: Recommender systems for large-scale E-commerce: scalable neighborhood formation using clustering. In: Conference on Computer and Information Technology, Hong Kong (2002)
7. Xue, G.R., Lin, C., Yang, Q., Xi, W.S., Zeng, H.J., Yu, Y., et al.: Scalable collaborative filtering using cluster-based smoothing. In: Proceedings of SIGIR 2006, pp. 114–121. ACM Press, Brazil (2005)
8. Honda, K., Notsu, A., Ichihashi, H.: Collaborative filtering by sequential extraction of user-item clusters based on structural balancing approach. In: IEEE International Conference on Fuzzy Systems, pp. 1540–1545. IEEE Press, Fuzz-IEEE (2009)
9. Liao, C.L., Lee, S.J.: A clustering based approach to improving the efficiency of collaborative filtering recommendation. Electron. Commer. Res. Appl. **18**, 1–9 (2016)
10. Ba, Q., Li, X., Bai, Z.: Clustering collaborative filtering recommendation system based on SVD algorithm. In: 2013 4th IEEE International Conference on Software Engineering and Service Science (ICSESS), pp. 963–967. IEEE Press, Beijing (2013)

11. Shao, J., He, X., Bohm, C., Yang, Q., Plant, C.: Synchronization-inspired partitioning and hierarchical clustering. IEEE Trans. Knowl. Data Eng. **25**, 893–905 (2013)
12. Wu, J., Jiao, Y.: Clustering dynamics of complex discrete-time networks and its application in community detection. Chaos **24**, 033104 (2014)
13. Wu, J., Zhang, L., Li, Y., Jiao, Y.: Partition signed social networks via clustering dynamics. Phys. A **443**, 568–582 (2016)
14. Chen, J., Wang, H., Wang, L., Liu, W.: A dynamic evolutionary clustering perspective: Community detection in signed networks by reconstructing neighbor sets. Phys. A **447**, 482–492 (2016)
15. Salton, G., McGill, M.: Introduction to Modern Information Retrieval. McGraw-Hill, New York (1983)
16. Breese, J.S., Heckerman, D., Kadie, C.: Empirical analysis of predictive algorithms for collaborative filtering. In: Proceedings of the Fourteenth Conference on Uncertainty in Artificial Intelligence, pp. 43–52. Morgan Kaufmann Publishers Inc., (1998)
17. Shardanand, U., Maes, P.: Social information filtering: algorithms for automating "word of mouth". In: Proceedings of the SIGCHI Conference on Human Factors in Computing Systems, pp. 210–217. ACM Press (1995)
18. Sideris, T.C.: Ordinary differential equations and dynamical systems. Atlantis Press **18**, 189–194 (2013)

Improving Sample Optimization with Convergence Speed Controller for Sampling-Based Image Matting

Liang Lv[1], Han Huang[1], Zhaoquan Cai[2], and Yihui Liang[1(✉)]

[1] School of Software Engineering, South China University of Technology,
Guangzhou 510006, China
yihuiliangchn@gmail.com
[2] College of Huizhou, Huizhou 516007, Guangdong, China

Abstract. Image matting is a core and challenging operator when processing images or videos. Its aim is to accurately extract the foreground region from an image. In this paper, we explore sampling-based image matting. The key optimization problem of sampling-based image matting is how to search the best foreground-background sample pair for every undetermined pixel. It is termed as the "sample optimization problem". Many sample optimization algorithms have been proposed for improving the efficiency of searching the best foreground-background sample pair. However, they fail when premature convergence is occurred. This paper presents a new sample optimization algorithm, which is based on convergence speed controller (CSC). The CSC is a general algorithm strategy. It can be embedded into algorithms and enhance the performance of the algorithms by maintaining the convergence speed and preventing premature convergence. By comparing with existing sample optimization algorithms, the experimental results show that our algorithm is competitive and effective to search the best sample pair and improve the performance of sampling-based image matting.

Keywords: Image matting · Sample optimization · Premature convergence · Convergence speed controller

1 Introduction

Image matting originated in film and video production [1]. Its goal is to determine which pixels of undetermined region belong to the foreground region. In general, this process is based on user-provided extra information, which can be obtained by a trimap [2]. In the literature, the matting methods are mainly classified into propagation-based methods and sampling-based methods.

In this study, we focus on sampling-based methods. The basic assumption of these methods is: the region of every undetermined pixel can be accurately estimated by a pair of foreground-background pixels from known regions. Therefore, sampling-based methods attempt to sampling some pixels from known regions

© Springer Nature Singapore Pte Ltd. 2016
M. Gong et al. (Eds.): BIC-TA 2016, Part II, CCIS 682, pp. 400–406, 2016.
DOI: 10.1007/978-981-10-3614-9_49

and search the best foreground-background sample pair for every undetermined pixel. The best foreground-background sample pair is defined as it can accurately estimate the region of current undetermined pixel. Earlier methods were based on local sampling [2,3]. They constructed sample set by sampling some known foreground and background pixels from nearby regions of every undetermined pixel. In general, the size of the sample set is not huge. The best sample pair can be found by brute-force method. However, since the limitation of the sampling rule, the best foreground-background pixels are not always in constructed sample set. This is called as the missing problem. In order to avoid missing the best foreground-background pixels, the global sampling method [4] was proposed to collect all known foreground and background pixels around the boundary of undetermined region. The global sampling method can effectively solve the missing problem. However, the time cost of searching the best sample pair for every undetermined pixel grows rapidly. Therefore, how to search the best sample pair within an acceptable time cost becomes a key optimization problem of sampling-based methods. The random search algorithm [4] and the particle swarm optimization (PSO) [5] have been used to solve the sample optimization problem. The experimental results proved that they can obtain more accurate matting results than local sampling methods. However, premature convergence is the major obstacle of these algorithms. Once premature convergence is occurred, their performance will degrade sharply.

In this study, we use the convergence speed controller (CSC) [6,7] to enhance the performance of sample optimization algorithm. We embed the CSC into existing particle swarm optimization [5] for verifying whether the CSC can improve the efficiency of sample optimization algorithm. This new sample optimization algorithm is called as CSCPSO algorithm.

2   Sample Optimization Problem

Image matting is based on a linear combination equation, where the undetermined pixel's color is combined by a foreground color and a background color. As shown in Expression (1).

$$I_k = \alpha_k F + (1 - \alpha_k)B. \tag{1}$$

where I_k is the color of the kth undetermined pixel, $k = 1, 2, \ldots, N_u$. N_u is the number of undetermined pixels. α_k is called as the foreground opacity of the kth undetermined pixel. F is a known foreground color. B is a known background color. I_k can be directly obtained from the image. In sampling-based methods, F and B are the optimized variables. They are used for calculating the α_k by Expression (2). The range of α_k is in $[0, 1]$. If $\alpha_k = 1$, it indicates that the kth undetermined pixel is a foreground pixel. If $\alpha_k = 0$, it indicates that the kth undetermined pixel is a background pixel. The best foreground-background colors can accurately estimate current undetermined pixel's region. Sampling-based methods attempt to obtain the best foreground-background colors by sampling some known pixels. Once the sample sets are constructed, the next step is to search the best foreground-background sample pair for every undetermined pixel. It is referred to as "sample optimization problem".

$$\hat{\alpha} = \frac{(I_k - B)(F - B)}{\|F - B\|^2} \tag{2}$$

In this study, we adopt a classic evaluation model [4] to distinguish the qualities of various foreground-background sample pairs. It is based on spatial and color characteristics. Formally, for a candidate foreground-background sample pair (F^i, B^j), its evaluation value is calculated by Expression (3).

$$f\left(F^i, B^j\right) = f_c\left(F^i, B^j\right) + f_s\left(F^i\right) + f_s\left(B^j\right) \tag{3}$$

where F^i is the ith foreground sample in foreground sample set, B^j is the jth background sample in background sample set. $f_c()$ is the color evaluation function. A smaller f_c indicates that the candidate sample pair (F^i, B^j) can better explain current undetermined pixel's color. $f_s()$ is the spatial evaluation function. A smaller $f_s()$ indicates that the F^i or B^j is spatially closer to current undetermined pixel. Therefore, a smaller $f()$ value indicates that the quality of the current sample pair (F^i, B^j) is better. The detailed formulation of $f_c()$ and $f_s()$ is introduced in [4].

3   Particle Swarm Optimization with Convergence Speed Controller

According to above description, every undetermined pixel needs to find the best foreground-background sample pair in sample sets. Therefore, the sample optimization problem can be regarded as a large-scale optimization problem, where the best sample pairs of all undetermined pixels will be searched at the same time. In particular, for an image with N_u undetermined pixels, we can construct a $2N_u$ dimensional search space. The formulation of every position is shown in Expression (4)

$$X = (x_1, \ldots, x_j, \ldots, x_{2N_u}), j = 1, \ldots, 2N_u \tag{4}$$

where $x_1, x_3, \ldots, x_{2N_u-1}$ are chosen from $\{1, \ldots, N_F\}$, $x_2, x_4, \ldots, x_{2N_u}$ are chosen from $\{1, \ldots, N_B\}$. N_F and N_B are the sizes of foreground sample set and background sample set. Every odd dimensional value represents a foreground sample. Every even dimensional value represents a background sample. A adjacent pair of odd dimensional value and even dimensional value represents a candidate sample pair for an undermined pixel. Therefore, Every position is an overall solution for all undetermined pixels. In this study, we attempt to embed convergence speed controller (CSC) into particle swarm optimization (PSO) [5] to solve the large-scale sample optimization problem. CSC includes two rules and the corresponding trigger conditions [6,7], which can improve performance of algorithm by maintaining the convergence speed and preventing premature convergence. Next, the detailed implementation will be described.

Condition 1 is designed for checking whether the convergence speed of PSO is too fast and the population diversity is lost. This phenomenon is referred to as premature convergence. If the condition 1 is met, rule 1 is carried to slow the convergence speed and recover the diversity by randomly regenerating the population in search space. Condition 1 is shown in Expression (5).

$$cos\left(X_a, X_b\right) > t1 \tag{5}$$

where X_a and X_b are two randomly selected individuals in current population. They are $2N_u$ dimensional vectors. $cos()$ is their cosine similarity. If this value is greater than the threshold $t1$, it indicates the population diversity is lost.

Condition 1 and rule 1 can prevent premature convergence at the appropriate moment. However, the convergence speed of PSO may become very slow when the high-quality solution is not found. Therefore, in order to accelerate the convergence speed of PSO under this circumstances, condition 2 and rule 2 are designed. The condition 2 is shown in Expression (6).

$$\frac{Value_{gBest} - Value_{lgBest}}{Value_{lgbest}} < t2 \tag{6}$$

where $Value_{gBest}$ is the evaluation value of the historical best position of current population, $Value_{lgBest}$ is the evaluation value of the historical best position of the population before p generations. p is a period parameter. Condition 2 is used to measure the convergence speed of PSO within p generations. If the condition 2 is met, it indicates that the convergence speed of PSO is too slow. Rule 2 will be carried to accelerate the convergence speed, which is shown below.

$$X_{i,j} = gBest_j + Norm(0, \frac{N_F + N_B - 1}{D}) \tag{7}$$

where $X_{i,j}$ is the jth dimensional value of ith individual, $i = 1, 2, \ldots, N_p, j = 1, 2, \ldots, 2N_u$. N_p is the size of population. $gBest$ is the historical best position of the current population. $Norm(0, \frac{N_F+N_B-1}{D})$ is an adaptive normal random number. The parameter D is a multiple of P. In order to avoid producing infeasible solution, the integer part of $X_{i,j}$ will be preserved. In addition, if a dimensional value of the individual is over boundary, it will be modified into the original value.

As we have discussed, every individual of population obtains a group of the candidate sample pairs of all undetermined pixels. In order to distinguish the qualities of various individuals, we adopt a evaluation function, which is based on the evaluation model [4]. For the ith individual, $i = 1, 2, \ldots, N_p$, its evaluation value was calculated by:

$$\varepsilon\left(X_i\right) = \sum_{j=1}^{N_u} f\left(X_{i,2j-1}, X_{i,2j}\right) \tag{8}$$

where $f()$ is the expression (3). A smaller $\varepsilon()$ indicates that the quality of current individual is better.

4   Experiments and Results

The aim of the experiments was to prove that the CSCPSO algorithm can effectively search high-quality foreground-background sample pairs, thereby improving the matting quality of sampling-based image matting. Existing random search algorithm [4] and particle swarm optimization [5] were used to compare.

In order to avoid missing the best foreground-background pixels, the global sampling method [4] was adopted to construct the sample sets. For a fair comparison, only the sample optimization step was replaced with different sample optimization algorithms. Other steps kept unchanged. A public test set was used to as the input images [8], which obtains twenty-seven suit images. In addition, the maximum iteration number of the proposed CSCPSO algorithm kept same with [5]. The parameters $t1$, $t2$ and p were set to 0.9, 0.001 and 150, which is conducive to find higher-quality sample pairs.

Table 1. Comparisons of the mean squared error

No	Random	PSO	CSCPSO	No	Random	PSO	CSCPSO
Image_1	0.01390	0.00125	0.00184	*Image_15*	0.00925	0.00388	0.00412
Image_2	0.00702	0.00823	0.00189	*Image_16*	0.08049	0.06230	0.05170
Image_3	0.01300	0.00421	0.00398	*Image_17*	0.01092	0.00258	0.00395
Image_4	0.10017	0.02010	0.01637	*Image_18*	0.01164	0.00381	0.00328
Image_5	0.01580	0.00220	0.00206	*Image_19*	0.00618	0.00094	0.00110
Image_6	0.01022	0.00267	0.00242	*Image_20*	0.00445	0.00194	0.00218
Image_7	0.01565	0.00257	0.00205	*Image_21*	0.02250	0.00484	0.00455
Image_8	0.05726	0.01232	0.01520	*Image_22*	0.01115	0.00194	0.00314
Image_9	0.01254	0.00250	0.00247	*Image_23*	0.00449	0.00376	0.00332
Image_10	0.00812	0.00311	0.00309	*Image_24*	0.00629	0.00445	0.00381
Image_11	0.01297	0.00404	0.00437	*Image_25*	0.02496	0.01550	0.02241
Image_12	0.00486	0.00282	0.00213	*Image_26*	0.04748	0.02544	0.02455
Image_13	0.05717	0.02158	0.02010	*Image_27*	0.02088	0.01633	0.01579
Image_14	0.00460	0.00200	0.00255				

The quantitative comparisons among matting results of different sample optimization algorithms are shown in Table 1. This is based on mean squared error (MSE). The MSE is a quantitative metric, which is used to measure the difference between the experimental matting result and the true matting result. A smaller MSE indicates that the experimental matting result is closer to the true matting result. By observing the MSEs of different algorithms, we found that the MSEs of the CSCPSO algorithm are smaller than the values of the random search algorithm on all test images. It indicates that the performance of

CSCPSO algorithm is higher the random search algorithm in sample optimization step. Besides, the MSEs of the CSCPSO algorithm are also smaller than the values of the particle swarm optimization on seventeen test images. Therefore, the experimental results can prove that the convergence speed controller (CSC) can enhance the performance of sample optimization algorithm and improve the accuracy of sampling-based image matting.

5   Conclusion

The sample optimization problem is the key optimization problem of sampling-based image matting. Its aim is to find the best foreground-background sample pairs for all undetermined pixels within an acceptable time cost. In this study, in order to improve the efficiency of sample optimization algorithm, we embedded the convergence speed controller into particle swarm optimization to maintain the convergence speed and prevent premature convergence. By comparing with the existing sample optimization algorithms. The experimental results show that the proposed CSCPSO algorithm is competitive and effective to solve the sample optimization problem.

Acknowledgments. This study was funded by National Natural Science Foundation of China (61370 102, 61170193, 61370185), Guangdong Natural Science Foundation (2014A03030 6050, S2012010009865, S2013010013432, S2013010015940), the Fundamental Research Funds for the Central Universities, SCUT (2015PT022), Science and Technology Planning Project of Guangdong Province (2011B090400041, 2012B01010 0039, 2012B040305011, 2012B010100040, 2015B010129015). Education and Science Programs of Guangdong Province (11JXZ012, 14JXN065), Discipline Construction Programs of Guangdong Province (2013LYM00874), Distinguished Young Scholars Fund of Department of Education (No. Yq2013126).

References

1. Fieldling, R.: Animation. In: The Technique of Special Effects Cinematography (1970)
2. Rhemann, C., Rother, C., Gelautz, M.: Improving color modeling for alpha matting. In: BMVC (2008)
3. Gastal, E.S.L., Oliveira, M.M.: Shared sampling for real-time alpha matting. Comput. Graph. Forum **29**, 575–584 (2010)
4. He, K., Rhemann, C., Rother, C., Tang, X., Sun, J.: A global sampling method for alpha matting. In: Computer Vision and Pattern Recognition (CVPR), pp. 2049–2056 (2011)
5. Lv, L., Huang, H., Cai, Z.Q., Hu, H.: Using particle swarm large-scale optimization to improve sampling-based image matting. In: Conference on Genetic and Evolutionary Computation, pp. 957–961 (2015)
6. Ye, S.J., Huang, H., Xu, C.J.: Enhancing the differential evolution with convergence speed controller for continuous optimization problems. In: Conference on Genetic and Evolutionary Computation, pp. 161–162 (2014)

7. Xu, C.J., Huang, H., Lv, L.: An adaptive convergence speed controller framework for particle swarm optimization variants in single objective optimization problems. In: IEEE International Conference on Systems, Man, and Cybernetics, pp. 2684–2689 (2015)

8. Rhemann, C., Rother, C., Wang, J., Gelautz, M., Kohli, P., Rott, P.: A perceptually motivated online benchmark for image matting. In: Computer Vision and Pattern Recognition (CVPR) (2009)

An Improved Extraction Algorithm About Disease Spots

Lu Xiong[✉], Dongbo Zhang, and Kangshun Li

Department of Computer Science, Guangdong University of Science and Technology,
Dongguan, Guangdong, China
317771184@qq.com

Abstract. This paper designs two histogram segmentation method based on evolutionary algorithm, which combined with the analysis of image of maize diseases and insect pests, with full consideration of color and texture characteristic of the lesion of pests and diseases, the image color and gray composed of two tuples to build a two-dimensional histogram, solves the problem of one-dimensional histograms cannot be clearly divided into target and background bimodal distribution, and improved the traditional two-dimensional histogram application in pest damage lesion extraction.

Keywords: Crop diseases and insect pests · Evolutionary algorithm · Disease spot extraction

1 Introduction

In recent years, as the country pay more attention on the problem of "agriculture, countryside and farmers", "precision agriculture" concept gradually on the rise. The new ideal of using information technology and computer technology to assist farmers to carry out agricultural production has been put on the agenda. In order to solve the problem of fuzziness and subjectivity in the detection and identification of crop diseases and insect pests, graphics and image processing technology is introduced into the field of agricultural pests identification and control. Image classification and recognition technology of crop pests and diseases is the application of image processing technology in the field of crop diseases and insect pests identification [1], The image classification and recognition technology will be able to rely on computer image obtain a large amount of information, as the basis for the diagnosis of diseases and insect pests, can make up for the shortcomings of traditional diagnostic techniques, which has the characteristics of less input parameters, fast diagnosis, high accuracy and good real-time performance, so it has important significance for the timely provision of the necessary information and the prevention and treatment of diseases and insect pests of agricultural workers.

Research on the diagnosis and image recognition of crop diseases and insect pests on machine vision in foreign countries should be carried out earlier

© Springer Nature Singapore Pte Ltd. 2016
M. Gong et al. (Eds.): BIC-TA 2016, Part II, CCIS 682, pp. 407–412, 2016.
DOI: 10.1007/978-981-10-3614-9_50

[2–4]. As early as 1985, Related researchers identified disease spot by the shape characteristic of grain. In recent years, with the development of computing power, especially the development of pattern recognition and image processing, computer vision technology has been developed. The experimental results show that the research has high recognition efficiency.

2   Evolutionary Algorithm

Evolutionary algorithm is an iterative search algorithm proposed by Holland in 1975. Evolutionary algorithm [5,6] is based on Darwin's theory of biological evolution, which is the nature of biological evolution, the nature of the population to be integrated into the algorithm, so that the algorithm is intelligent and parallel. At the same time, the reasonable design evolution algorithm can effectively avoid the local optimization problem in the process of solving the problem, and the algorithm has strong robustness. Evolutionary algorithm essentially is a kind of probability of random search, but with adaptive, refer to the "survival of the fittest, the survival of the fittest" evolutionary ideas.

The algorithm gives a fitness value of each individual in the population, which represents the survival probability of the individual in the process of biological evolution. The higher fitness of the individual, then the probability of its entry into the next generation of reproduction is high. The optimal solution of the individual with the highest fitness value is obtained by genetic decoding.

3   Analysis of Diseases and Pest of Crop

3.1   Analysis of Image Gray

The gray images of crop diseases and insect pests include many features of the image. Among them, the gray histogram can be generalized to represent the gray statistical information of the image [7], and can get the description information for a particular type of image. As shown in Fig. 1, in order to analyze the image of the corn big spot for the analysis of the target, the original image gray level 256 gray level, the use of gray scale histogram for the analysis of pests and diseases. It takes the maize big spot disease image as the analysis target, carries on histogram the original image to 256 gray level, uses the gray histogram to carry on the analysis. From the visual angle of analysis, leaf disease has obvious

Fig. 1. Analysis of gray of big spot disease image. (Color figure online)

characteristics of the external position through the observation. The gray value of disease spot are significantly higher than that of no symptoms around the lesion area. From the point of view of statistical information, it can be found that the gray value of the image of the maize spot disease showed a single peak distribution, and in the 100 areas of gray value change significantly, the frequency of rapid decline.

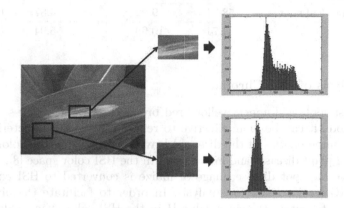

Fig. 2. Gray histogram distribution characteristics of large spot disease image.

Table 1. Gray information of plant diseases and insect pests image

Image type	Mean value	Mean square error	Entropy	Energy
No symptoms of image	147.67	13.87	5.82	0.019
Big spot disease	109.30	30.27	6.80	0.012
Cochliobolus heterostrophus	125.11	43.41	7.01	0.010
Gray leaf spot	127.28	32.63	6.85	0.011
Cercospora leaf spot	146.01	26.39	6.64	0.012
Anthrax	147.14	32.11	6.90	0.009

The infection process of the leaf of crops is the pathogen invading the local side and gradually outward to form the green spot which differ in size, color and shape. The lesion and healthy leaf area in the color difference, and this difference in gray image performance as gray inhomogeneity. As shown in Fig. 2, analysis showed that lesion location of gray values broadly distributed in more than 100, and no symptom location of gray values broadly distributed below 100. It is obvious that Gray mean value of pest lesion position in the image is higher than that of the disease-free area from Tables 1 and 2.

Table 2. Chroma information of image of plant diseases and insect pests

Types of spot	Mean value	Mean square error	Entropy	Energy
No symptoms image	67.34	2.76	3.11	0.153
Big spot disease	63.77	11.94	4.58	0.069
Cochliobolus heteostrophus	55.16	10.46	5.01	0.041
Gray leaf spot	75.98	21.85	6.13	0.017
Cercospora leaf spot	58.54	9.22	4.87	0.044
Anthrax	44.74	10.99	5.04	0.038

3.2 Analysis of HSI Chroma

General pest spots will appear yellow, red brown, brown and other strange colors. Therefore, it can be more effective to reflect the visual characteristics and statistical characteristics of the diseased leaves by analyzing the color value of the image of plant diseases and insect pests in the HSI color space [8]. As shown in Fig. 3 the big spot disease image of maize is converted to HSI color space from the RGB color space for analysis. In order to facilitate the observation and analysis, to obtain the color value H in the HSI color space, calculate the conversion image I which is divided into 256 levels. The position of disease spot in converting image I has obvious external dissimilarity compared to disease-free position, and the bimodal phenomenon can be observed in the statistical histogram.

Fig. 3. Analysis of HSI chroma of big spot disease. (Color figure online)

4   The Segmentation Scheme of Spot Disease Based on Genetic Algorithm

4.1 The Combination of Genetic Algorithm and Chroma-Gray Histogram

Threshold segmentation is an effective method of image segmentation, and the ideal situation of threshold segmentation is the statistical histogram of the image to be bimodal, and the valley in the histogram is used as the segmentation threshold to separate the object and background [9]. But in most cases, the image histogram is not the bimodal form, more is a single peak or multi-peak shape, this will make the selection of the threshold of the histogram segmentation is difficult. Two dimensional histogram i, j respectively represent the image of the two indicators. Taking the frequency of two tuples(i, j) as the vertical coordinate to establish 3D information coordinate of image. Set the frequency of two tuples(i, j) f_{ij}, in which, respectively, corresponding to the gray value of the pixel and the right pixel gray value, the joint probability density is defined as the formula (1)

$$p_{ij} = \frac{f_{ij}}{M \times N} \tag{1}$$

Where, $M \times N$ is the size of image. In order to form the gray level co-occurrence matrix, which represents the gray spatial variation. Two dimensional histogram is divided into four regions by using two thresholds (t, s).

In the previous section of pest damage image analysis, we can know, Lesion location in the image gray value characteristics and no symptom location gray value feature has a obvious gap, but single gray-scale information cannot be well determine the location of the lesion in the image, also prone to regional misjudgment of the situation. Therefore, this study proposed a segmentation method based on chroma-gray histogram. The chroma value is divided into K, the chroma of non green area is divided in $[t, K - 1]$, the gray value is divided into L. Count the frequency of two tuples(i, j) which consisting of chroma value and gray value. The distribution probability of the region 0 and region 1 are represented by P_0 and P_1 after threshold (t, s) segmentation. Formulas (2) and (3) are used to represent the distribution probability of the two region.

$$p_0 = \sum_{i=0}^{t} \sum_{j=0}^{s} p_{ij} \tag{2}$$

$$P_1 = \sum_{i=t+1}^{K-1} \sum_{j=s+1}^{L-1} P_{ij} \tag{3}$$

Area 0 is defined as the background region, and the region 1 is the target area. The region 2 and region 3 are negligible noise points and scattered points. Expressed as a formula 4

$$P_0 + P_1 \approx 1 \tag{4}$$

Thus, in a two-dimensional histogram, the distance measure defined by Region 0 and region 1 can be expressed as a formula (5)

$$\delta_B(t, s) = P_0(\xi_0 - \xi)^2 + P_1(\xi_1 - \xi)^2 \tag{5}$$

Where, ξ_0, ξ_1 is mean value of element of region 0 and 1. ξ is Population mean value. Figure out the value of (t^*, s^*) as the threshold of image segmentation when δ_B is the largest value.

5 Summary

First of all, this paper analyzes the data of maize diseases and pests damage image, in terms of both gray and chroma space of image in global and local statistical characteristics of the data analysis, taking differences in lesion location to obtain and disease-free position of the color, texture, etc. as pest image segmentation and extraction of the lesion. According to the analysis of plant diseases and insect pests image, gray image and the HSI color space of color image composed of two tuples to build a two-dimensional histogram, to better describe the distribution of pixel, to solve the one-dimensional histograms cannot be clearly divided into target and background bimodal distribution situation, and improve the using traditional two-dimensional histogram in pest damage lesion extraction. Finally, experimental results show that the algorithm of lesion region extraction is effective, and discuss the weight matrix parameters setting effect of experimental results. Through comparison with the traditional Otsu algorithm, EM clustering algorithm, indicating the applicability of the algorithm of crop disease, insect and pest image, at the same time, through comparative tests with Gauss MRF and tsrg algorithm, the algorithm in the spot region extraction effect of the superiority.

Acknowledgements. The work is supported in part by Department of Education of Guangdong Province under Grant 2015KQNCX193, the National Natural Science Foundation of China with the Grant No. 61573157, the Fund of Natural Science Foundation of Guangdong Province of China with the Grant No. 2014A030313454, and Natural Science Foundation of Guangdong Province of China (2015A030313408).

References

1. Wang, J., Zhang, W., Liu, L., Huang, S.: Summary of crop diseases and pests image recognition technology. Comput. Eng. Sci. **36**(7), 1363–1370 (2014)
2. Keagy, P.M., Schatzki, T.F.: Machine recognition of weevil damage in wheat radiographs. Proc. SPIE Int. Soc. Opt. Eng. **70**(6), 108–119 (1993)
3. Ridgway, C., Davies, R., Chambers, J.: Imaging for the High-Speed Detection of Pest Insects, Other Contaminants in Cereal Grain in Transit: 2001 Sacramento
4. Zayas, I.Y., Flinn, P.W.: Detection of insects in bulk wheat samples with machine vision. Trans. Asae **41**(3), 883–888 (1998)
5. Zhang, J., Zhan, Z.H., Lin, Y.: Evolutionary computation meets machine learning: a survey. IEEE Comput. Intell. Mag. **6**(4), 68–75 (2011)
6. Kavetha, M.J.: Coevolution evolutionary algorithm: a survey. Int. J. Adv. Res. Comput. Sci. **04**(04) (2013)
7. Yang, J., Liu, C.: Research on color space and its transformation in digital image processing. J. Shangqiu Vocat. Techn. College **8**(2), 25–27 (2009)
8. Wang, Y.: Research on key technology of the image segemention, Jiangnan University (2008)
9. Liang, Y., Pang, R., Zhu, Y.: Two dimensional Otsu line segmentation method for gray level images. Comput. Eng. Appl. **48**(33), 178–182 (2012)

Fine-Grained Image Categorization with Fisher Vector

Xiaolin Tian$^{(\boxtimes)}$, Xin Ding, and Licheng Jiao

Key Laboratory of Intelligent Perception and Image Understanding of Ministry of Education, International Research Center of Intelligent Perception and Computation, International Collaboration Joint Lab in Intelligent Perception and Computation, Xidian University, Xi'an 710071, Shaanxi Province, China
xltian@mail.xidian.edu.cn

Abstract. Fine-grained image categorization is a categorization task, where classifying objects should be the same basic-level class and have similar shape or visual appearances. Generally, the bag-of-words (BoW) model is popular in image categorization. However, in BoW model, the feature quantization for image representation is also a lossy process, which severely limits the descriptive power of the image representation. Fisher vectors employ soft assignments and reduce information loss due to quantization by calculating the gradient for each parameter separately, which have been shown to outperform other global representations on most benchmark datasets. In this paper, the acquired template is represented by Fisher Vector (FV). Combing FV with improved spatial pyramid matching (SPM) respectively, we use an approach, i.e., FV+SPM, to obtain feature representation. Experimental results show that our method outperforms state-of-the-art categorization approaches on the Caltech-UCSD Birds dataset.

Keywords: Image categorization · Fisher vector · Template matching

1 Introduction

Fine-grained image categorization aims to achieve a categorization task, where classifying objects should have similar shape or visual appearances and belong to the same basic-level class [1–3]. Unlike the basic-level categorization, fine-grained categorization needs more local information, and the obtained feature should be more discriminative and characteristic.

Fine-grained categorization requires an algorithm to discriminate delicate differences among highly similar object classes. Traditional the bag-of-words (BoW) approach does not meet the requirements of fine-grained categorization. When we construct BoW model, fine-grained image categorization can produce more redundant words than the general image categorization, which will increase computation complexity. Moreover, BoW model doesn't describe direction information, and Fisher vector (FV) avoids this default and can best fit image data. Recently, the performance of template matching has been greatly

© Springer Nature Singapore Pte Ltd. 2016
M. Gong et al. (Eds.): BIC-TA 2016, Part II, CCIS 682, pp. 413–419, 2016.
DOI: 10.1007/978-981-10-3614-9_51

increased by FV which codes higher order statistics of local features. In this paper, fine-grained image categorization with FV [4] based on template matching is implemented. We extract feature points of the training samples, and establish Gaussian mixture model (GMM) to approximate the distribution of samples. Accordingly, we can obtain the FV feature by the derivation of the GMM [5–7].

The FV represents the entire distribution feature of image, so that the scale and orientation of object in an image need not be specifically processed. We introduce spatial information based on improved spatial pyramid matching (SPM) [8]. Spatial pyramid is gathered on different spatial resolution in partially disordered images. SPM achieves the statistics on different levels, and it mainly reflects on statistical feature of information distribution.

The remaining part of this paper is organized as follows: Sect. 2 discusses related work. Section 2 describes the FV and GMM. Section 3 describes templates and feature representation. Section 4 describes image coding based on SPM. Experiment results are described in Sect. 5, and Sect. 6 concludes this paper.

2 The FV and Gaussian Mixture Model

In this section, we introduce the Fisher Vector (FV) and establishment of GMM. We first describe the principle of the Fisher Kernel (FK) [9] and how to build GMM.

Let $X = \{x_t, t = 1, 2, \ldots, T\}$ be a sample set of local feature descriptors, T is the number of the samples. X can be described as the following gradient vector [9]:

$$G_\lambda^X = \frac{1}{T}\nabla_\lambda \log \mu_\lambda(X) \tag{1}$$

where μ_λ is likelihood function, i.e., $p(X|\lambda)$, with the parameter λ and $G_\lambda^X \in R^M$. We can use the following equation to measure the distance between the sample X and the sample Y:

$$K(X,Y) = G_\lambda^{X'} F_\lambda^{-1} G_\lambda^Y \tag{2}$$

Since F_λ is positive semi-definite, it is reversible. Using the Cholesky decomposition $F_\lambda^{-1} = L_\lambda' L_\lambda$, and F_λ is the Fisher information matrix:

$$F_\lambda = E_{x \sim \mu_\lambda}\left[\nabla_\lambda \log \mu_\lambda(x)\, \nabla_\lambda \log \mu_\lambda(x)'\right] \tag{3}$$

Assuming that the above feature distribution is independent and governed by the mixture Gaussian distribution, we can use K Gaussian distributions to express these independent distributions. Let the parameter $\lambda = \{w_i, \mu_i, \sum_i i = 1, 2, \ldots, K\}$, we can obtain the value of logarithm:

$$p(x_t|\lambda) = \sum_{i=1}^{K} w_i p_i(x_t|\lambda) \tag{4}$$

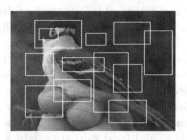

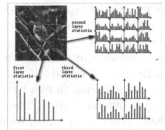

Fig. 1. Acquisition of the templates   **Fig. 2.** Construction of SPM

$$p_i\left(x|\lambda\right) = \frac{\exp\left\{-\frac{1}{2}\left(x - \mu_i\right)'\sum_i^{-1}\left(x - \mu_i\right)\right\}}{\left(2\pi\right)^{D/2}\left|\sum_i\right|^{1/2}} \tag{5}$$

where p_i in the Eq. 4 expresses Gaussian distribution, and w_i represents linear combination coefficients, and $\sum_{i=1}^{N} w_i = 1$. In the Eq. 5, D is the dimension of feature vectors. And then, we can calculate the partial derivatives of the Eq. 4, and compute its gradient to obtain FV of an image. Assuming that the dimension of sample feature is D-dimension and K number of Gaussian is selected, the dimension of FV feature is $(2 \times D + 1) \times K$ dimension. After the FV is obtained [10,11], we use L2-normalization [12] to replace Kernel and power normalization in each dimension.

3   Templates and Feature Representation

A feature difference response diagram [13] is obtained by randomly matching between image templates and one image [2,13] in our method. Through statistics of the response diagram, we can acquire the final image encoding. After we obtain training image samples, acquisition of the templates are carried out in training samples [2,13]. For each training image A, if it has S different feature types (e.g. RGB, SIFT, HOG, et al.) [14,15], they are described as $\{A^s\}_{s=1}^{S}$. A template image is represented as $T = \left(\{A^s\}_{s=1}^{S}, \{r, s\}\right)$. Each set of r and s represent location information of the template in the image. The template acquisition is shown in Fig. 1. We extract feature points of the training samples, and establish GMM. We represent each template with the obtained GMM, based on which FV of each template can be obtained [16–18].

4   Image Coding Based on SPM

In the SPM procedure, the image is divided into different levels, i.e., layer 0, layer 1, and layer 2. Then, we deal with statistical image information respectively. The process is shown in Fig. 2. The first layer has 4 blocks, the second layer has 16, and the layer i has blocks $2^i \times 2^i$. Statistical information at different levels in different blocks is concatenated and normalized, which form the final image statistics.

Considering computational complexity, we employ the statistical information from two layers of Pyramid [19]. At the layer 0, we take the three biggest similarity of response diagram from a block. The same processing step is carried out in each block of different layers. The three locations with biggest similarity values should have a certain distance, which is beneficial for whole statistics of a block. We can obtain statistical distribution of whole and local similarity, which represent response vector of a template on the image [20]. Finally, we joint response vectors of all the templates. Matching is carried out using the same template sets, then the statistic feature of each image is obtained.

5   Experiments

The proposed method is implemented in MATLAB (Version R2010a) on a machine with an Intel core i5-5200 CPU, 8 GB memory and Microsoft Windows 7 operating system.

We use Caltech-UCSD Birds dataset (CUB-200) as test set, which is widely used in the fine-grained image categorization. CUB-200 dataset contains 200 bird images. Each category contains 15 training images and 10 to 25 test images. We use a part of the image library [21] and verify our categorization performance. We only consider 13 categories of birds from the Black Capped Vireo to the Downy Woodpecker.

CUB-200 dataset has a coarse segmentation, and we use this segmentation in the training samples. We first take out the target from images as a new training sample set, and get a template in the selected target image. In our experiments, we select templates with five sizes, i.e., WH = [20 20; 50 50; 100 100; 50 80; 80 50], where WH is width and height of a template.

Firstly, images are segmented in the training sample by SLIC super-pixel segmentation. Since images have been segmented roughly in this dataset, we can use the segmented target regions. So the number of super-pixel blocks is initialized 150 blocks, and we extract RGB features of each image. These RGB feature points are used to establish GMM. Figure 3 show that the number of GMM has an effect on algorithm performance.

In order to discuss how the number of GMM influences on the algorithm, we fix other parameters. In experiments, we randomly select six different locations in each training samples, so that we get $13 \times 15 \times 5 \times 6 = 5850$ templates, which is expressed by FV coding with power normalization and L2-normalization. Finally, we use 1×13 vectors in SPM model that represents the matching result of each template. When the number of GMM is fewer, it is more difficult to obtain the accurate feature distribution; When the number of GMM is larger, the feature point is fewer and this will cause the average accuracy rate to decline. So, we select five GMM in our experiments.

Figure 4(a) shows response diagram of a template in an image, where we consider the three maximum similarity values with a certain distance. The distance

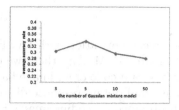

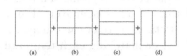

Fig. 3. The relation of algorithm performance and number of GMM

Fig. 4. Formation of 1×13 vector

among the three points with maximum similarity values should larger than 0.1 times the width (height). In Fig. 4(b), the image is divided into 2×2 blocks, and we only consider the maximum similarity value of each block; In Fig. 4(c), the image is divided into top, middle and bottom part. We only consider the maximum similarity value of each block. The processing procedure of Fig. 4(d) is similar to Fig. 4(c). Finally, we can get a vector with thirteen dimensions, which represent the coding of a template in an image. We extract only the RGB feature and use coding method based on the SPM model. The number of templates, randomly selected from each training image, has great influence on image coding. Figure 5 shows how the number of templates affects algorithm performance.

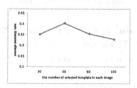

Fig. 5. The relation of number of template and algorithm performance

Table 1. Comparison of classification results

Algorithms	MAP
cSIFT+SPM	37.12%
MKL	37.02%
Birdlet	40.25%
CF+AF	39.76%
Ours(FV+SPM)	**40.30%**

Our model runs 46 min 30 s, in which the feature extraction only takes 2 min 10 s and FV representation based on SPM takes 44 min 20 s. For accurately describing image information, FV representation based on SPM is implemented by two traverses in our experiments, so that it takes most of the time. In addition, we achieve two other models: FV+VQ (Vector Quantization) and FV+LLC (locality-constrained linear coding). Figure 5 shows the relation of number of KNN and algorithm performance, where the codebook size of the two models is 200×200.

The compared methods include: cSIFT + SPM [8], MKL [2], Birdlet [22], and CF+AF [18,23]. We use confusion matrix and mean average precision (MAP) as evaluation criteria, and the classification results are shown in Table 1. From Table 1, we know that our method improves classification performance compared with other methods.

6   Conclusion

In this paper, we implement fine-grained image categorization with FV. Firstly, we discuss about Fisher Kernel and how to create GMM. And then, we obtain the statistic feature of each image. Finally, we obtain code of an image based on SPM. After matching each template and image and obtain response diagram of similarity, the spatial hierarchical statistics is obtained for coding image. Finally, image categorization is carried out using SVM. Compared with other methods, our method generally improves the accuracy rate of categorization.

Acknowledgment. This work was supported by the National Natural Science Foundation of China under Grant 61571342, 61573267, 61473215, and National Basic Research Program of China under Grant 2013CB329402.

References

1. Biederman, I., Subramaniam, S., Bar, M., et al.: Subordinate-level object classification reexamined. Psychol. Res. **62**(2–3), 131–153 (1999)
2. Branson, S., Wah, C., Schroff, F., Babenko, B., Welinder, P., Perona, P., Belongie, S.: Visual recognition with humans in the loop. In: Daniilidis, K., Maragos, P., Paragios, N. (eds.) ECCV 2010. LNCS, vol. 6314, pp. 438–451. Springer, Heidelberg (2010). doi:10.1007/978-3-642-15561-1_32
3. Hillel, A., Weinshall, D.: Subordinate class recognition using relational object models. In: NIPS, pp. 73–80 (2006)
4. Yang, J., Yu, K., Gong, Y., et al.: Linear spatial pyramid matching using sparse coding for image classification. In: CVPR, pp. 1794–1801 (2009)
5. Sivic, J., Zisserman, A.: Video google: a text retrieval approach to object matching in videos. In: CVPR, pp. 1470–1478 (2003)
6. Zheng, W., Gong, S., Xiang, T.: Associating groups of people. In: BMVC, pp. 23.1–23.11 (2009)
7. Yao, B.B., Bradski, G., Li, F.F.: A codebook-free, annotation-free approach for fine-grained image categorization. In: CVPR, pp. 3466–3473 (2012)
8. Lazebnik, S., Schmid, C., Ponce, J.: Beyond bags of features: spatial pyramid matching for recognizing natural scene categories. In: CVPR, pp. 2169–2178 (2006)
9. Sánchez, J., Perronnin, F., Mensink, T.: Image classification with the Fisher Vector: theory and practice. Int. J. Comput. Vis. **105**(3), 222–245 (2013)
10. Perronnin, F., Sánchez, J., Mensink, T.: Improving the fisher kernel for large-scale image classification. In: Daniilidis, K., Maragos, P., Paragios, N. (eds.) ECCV 2010. LNCS, vol. 6314, pp. 143–156. Springer, Heidelberg (2010). doi:10.1007/978-3-642-15561-1_11
11. Perronnin, F., Dance, C.: Fisher kernels on visual vocabularies for image categorization. In: CVPR, pp. 1–8 (2007)
12. Zhang, J., Marszalek, M., Lazebnik, S., et al.: Local features and kernels for classification of texture and object categories: a comprehensive study. Int. J. Comput. Vis. **73**(2), 213–238 (2005)
13. Liu, H., Su, Z.: Template-based multiple codebooks generation for fine-grained shopping classification, retrieval. In: ICDH, pp. 293–298 (2014)
14. Lowe, D.G.: Distinctive image features from scale-invariant keypoints. Int. J. Comput. Vis. **60**(2), 91–110 (2004)

15. VandeSande, K., Gevers, T., Snoek, C.: Evaluating color descriptors for object and scene recognition. IEEE Trans. Pattern Anal. Mach. Intell. **32**(9), 1582–1596 (2010)
16. Hiremath, P.S., Pujari, J.: Content based image retrieval using color, texture, shape features. In: ADCOM, pp. 780–784 (2007)
17. Yu, J., Qin, Z., Wan, T., et al.: Feature integration analysis of bag-of-features model for image retrieval. Neurocomputing **120**, 355–364 (2013)
18. Li, L.J., Su, H., Xing, E., Li, F.F.: Object bank: a high-level image representation for scene classification and semantic feature sparsification. In: NIPS, vol. 26, no. 6, pp. 719–729 (2010)
19. Maji, S., Bourdev, L., Malik, J.: Action recognition from a distributed representation of pose, appearance. In: CVPR, pp. 3177–3184 (2011)
20. Coates, A., Lee, H.: An analysis of single-layer networks in unsupervised feature learning. In: AISTATS, pp. 215–233 (2011)
21. Farrell, R., Oza, O., Zhang, N., Birdlets, et al.: Subordinate categorization using volumetric primitives and pose-normalized appearance. In: ICCV, pp. 809–818 (2011)
22. Yao, B.B., Khosla, A., Li, F.F.: Combining randomization, discrimination for fine-grained image categorization. In: CVPR, pp. 1577–1584 (2011)
23. Welinder, P., Branson, S., Mita, T., et al.: Caltech-UCSD birds 200. Technical report, Caltech (2010)

Analysis of SNP Network Structure Based on Mutual Information of Breast Cancer Susceptibility Genes

Shudong Wang[1], Shanqiang Zhang[1(✉)], Shanshan Li[3], Xinzeng Wang[1],
Sicheng He[1], Yan Zhao[1], Xiaodan Fan[1], Fayou Yuan[1], Xinjie Zhu[1],
and Yun Jiang[2]

[1] College of Computer and Communication Engineering,
China University of Petroleum, Qingdao 266580, Shandong, China
zhangsq@s.upc.edu.cn
[2] School of Computer Science and Information Engineering,
Chongqing Technology and Business University, Chongqing 400067, China
[3] Bihai Water Service Company of Qingdao West Coast New Economic District,
Qingdao 266555, Shandong, China

Abstract. Genome-wide association studies (GWAS) are used to identify diseases associated with single nucleotide polymorphisms (SNPs).
But many existing methods did not consider the interactions among
SNPs while SNPs form a network in complex interrelated ways. In our
research, we attempted to establish case and control mutual information networks based on simulation data of breast cancer associated gene
BRCA2. By constructing the network and comparing the network statistics, the average degree of network is found to clearly distinguish the
case and control groups. Starting from the network structure, we put
forward a method to find "structural key SNPs", and got four structural
key SNPs. Two out of these four SNPs are pre-assigned causal SNPs in
BRCA2. A large number of simulative experiments and results illustrate
the feasibility of our proposed method.

Keywords: Genome-wide association studies (GWAS) · Complex network · Mutual information · Network statistics · SNP-SNP interaction

1 Introduction

Genome-wide association studies (GWAS) aim to find the association relationships between genes and complex diseases at the whole genome level. It was
firstly proposed by Risch and Merikangas [1] in 1996 and has been widely used
in detecting causal genes of complex diseases in recent years. Many causal genes
has been detected through different methods of GWAS. In 2011, it is used the
method named Taq-Man to identify SNP locus rs3803662 of gene TOX3 related
to causal type and histological classification in [2]. In 2012, Ghoussaini identified three risk susceptibility loci rs2823093, rs10771399 and rs1292011 associated with breast cancer, and rs10771399 had been verified to be important

M. Gong et al. (Eds.): BIC-TA 2016, Part II, CCIS 682, pp. 420–430, 2016.
DOI: 10.1007/978-981-10-3614-9_52

in the development of breast cancer and bone metastases in [3]. After that, in 2013, Kong proposed a method based on independent component analysis in gene expression data of breast cancer and obtained 35 genes closely related to breast cancer [4]. Although many causal genes associated complex diseases have been detected, many methods did not consider the interactions among SNPs. In our research, we considered the complex relationships and used the complex networks to describe the complex interactions, which have been used to design powerful computing models [8–12].

Based on simulation data of breast cancer susceptibility genes, we transform the data into genotyping data and establish mutual information using approaches from [5–7] network of case and control groups with many thresholds. As well, six statistics features of the two networks have been compared, which are average path length, average clustering coefficient, average degree, modularity measure, average betweenness and network density. It is found that suitable value to the threshold by these comparison and find that average degree can distinguish the networks of the case and control groups significantly. We use the the average degree of suitable thresholds to establish the networks and find SNPs that are different in case and control groups as "structural key SNPs".

2   Preliminary Knowledge

2.1   Mutual Information Network

Traditional methods of modeling network are mainly used to represent the process of gene expression and interaction [13], but reverse modeling [14] uses various methods of data analysis to discover the relationship between the factors. Compared to the former, reverse modeling is on the basic of the data and tries to estimate the network from the data. Once the network is established, the result of the data expression can be predicted from the network.

With the study of biological networks in [15–17], correlations among elements are described more and more accurately, such as Pearson correlation coefficient [18] and Spearman correlation coefficient [19]. Mutual Information is a method to measure correlation based on the entropy of information. In this paper, networks are established based on mutual information to analyze the difference between case and control groups.

We use original data and transform these data into a vector matrix, each row for a vector. Let X and Y be two vectors from this vector matrix. By $H(X,Y)$ it is denoted the joint entropy of X and Y, which is the uncertainty measure of the binary random variables, defined as:

$$H(X,Y) = \sum_{x,y} p(x,y) log \frac{1}{p(x,y)}, \tag{1}$$

where $p(x,y)$ is the frequency when X and Y appear at the same time. On the basis of this definition, the mutual information is defined as follows:

$$I(X;Y) = H(X) + H(Y) - H(X,Y), \tag{2}$$

The bigger $I(X;Y)$ is, the greater correlation between X and Y is. $I(X;Y) = 0$ indicates that X and Y are independent. Thus, the mutual information expresses the correlations between the two vectors of SNPs.

2.2   The Statistics of Network

Here is a brief introduction to the statistics of complex network involved, more details can be found from [20]. Let $G = (V, E)$ be a complex network with n nodes, where $V = \{1, 2, 3, \ldots, n\}$ and E are the set of nodes and the set of edges in the network G respectively, $m = |E|$ is the number of edges.

(1) Average Path Length (L)

In the network, the distance, denoted by d_{ij} between nodes i and j is defined as the number of edges in the shortest path connecting the two nodes. Average path length (L) is defined as the average distance of all the pairs of nodes:

$$L = \frac{1}{0.5n(n-1)} \sum_{i>j} d_{ij}. \tag{3}$$

(2) Average Clustering Coefficient (C)

Clustering coefficient, denoted by C_i is defined as the ratio of the number of triangles connected to node i to the number of triples connected to node i, namely:

$$C_i = \frac{N_i}{M_i}, \tag{4}$$

where N_i is the number of triangles connected to the node i and M_i is the number of triples connected to the node i. Average clustering coefficient (C) is the average of clustering coefficient of all the nodes.

(3) Average Degree (K)

Degree of the node is defined as the number of other nodes connected to the node, and the network degree is the average of all nodes.

(4) Modularity Measure (Q)

Modularity measure is to measure the strength of the network community structure. It was first proposed by Newman [21]. Modularity measure (Q) is defined as:

$$Q = \sum_i Q_i = \sum_i (e_{ij} - a_i^2) \tag{5}$$

where a_i is the sum of the elements in the i_{th} row (or column), representing the proportion of the edges connected to the i_{th} community on all sides. By e_{ij}, it represents the proportion of edges that are connected to i community and j community on all sides. The size of the modularity measure depends mainly on the distribution of nodes in the network. It can be used to measure the quality of network community classification. The closer that the value is to one, the better quality the partition has. So it is possible to get the best community division by maximizing modularity measure.

(5) Average Betweenness (B)

Betweenness of the node i is defined as the ratio of the number of shortest paths through node i to the number of all shortest paths, which is defined as:

$$B_i = \frac{S_i}{S}, \tag{6}$$

where S_i is the number of shortest paths through node i, and S is the number of all shortest paths. Average betweenness is the average of all nodes.

(6) Network Density (D)

Density is a measure of the completeness of the network. It is defined as the ratio of the number of edges in the network to all possible edges, denoted by

$$D = \frac{2m}{n(n-1)}. \tag{7}$$

3 Data Sources

The data files of BRCA2 contain 88 SNPs from HapMap. The hap file is a file of known haplotypes, with one row for a SNP and one column for one haplotype. The legend file is for the SNP markers, this file has four columns with one row for each SNP, and the columns should contain an ID for each SNP, the base pair position of each SNP, base represented by 0 and base represented by 1. The map file contains the fine-scale recombination rate across the region, and this file has three columns with one line for each SNP [22].

In these files, some data are all 0 or all 1 and these data should be deleted from the original data, because we focus on the structure of gene networks and these data make no contribution to network structure. We get the remaining data of 45 SNPs as source database, which are placed in the same directory as the HAPGEN2 binary file. Running HAPGEN2 software with programming codes:

```
./hapgen2   -m BRCA2.map -l BRCA2.legend -h BRCA2.hap -o BRCA2.out
-dl 31821690 1 1.5 2.25 31834646 0 2 4 -n 1000 1000.
```

The simulation is performed with data of 1000 groups of case and 1000 groups of control. Two disease SNPs are randomly simulated, at positions 31821690 and 31834646, with heterozygote risks 1.5 and 2, homozygote risks 2.25 and 4 respectively. The out files contain the results of the simulation.

It is used the gen file with 45 rows, and every row having the data creating by one SNP of 1000 groups. The columns contain the ID, rs id of the marker, the base pair and 0 or 1 data. We delete the first five columns and transform this file into a vector matrix by representing one row as a vector. Every three numbers represent one individual at one vector, we use one of 0, 1, 2 numbers to represent one genotype to transform data of 0 and 1 to the data of 0, 1 and 2 to get the final vector matrix for later calculation.

4   Method and Results

4.1   The Selection of Threshold

We take each row as a vector to calculate the mutual information of every two vectors based on (2), with the maximum value 0.63 and the minimum value 0. We set a threshold and select SNPs whose mutual information is over the threshold as close SNPs and take these SNPs as nodes to create networks. Analyze and compare six statistics of the network: average path length (L), average clustering coefficient (C), average degree (K), modularity measure (Q), average betweenness (B) and network density (D). Each statistic reflects the characteristics of the network and represents the variation of the mutual information between two SNPs. We take steps of 0.01 from 0 to 0.63 and calculate value of the network statistics for each threshold shown in Fig. 1.

With analysis above, lines of network density (D) and average clustering coefficient (C) in the case and control groups interweave together, they cannot distinguish the case and control groups.

As we can see from Fig. 1, when $0 <$ threshold < 0.21, average betweenness (B) has similar changing tendency in the case and control groups. When the threshold $0.21 <$ threshold < 0.63, average betweenness (B) decreases and it is higher in case group than control group. It shows that with the increase of mutual information threshold, the number of network edges decreases, and the number of nodes also decreases.

About average path length (L), it can distinguish these two groups when $0.2 <$ threshold < 0.4, but the threshold range is limited.

About the average degree (K), it can be found that there is a big difference in a long range of threshold of case and control groups. And the average degree (K) is rising along with the increase of threshold, this can be correspond to the isolated points in the network.

- When the threshold $0 <$ threshold < 0.2 or $0.43 <$ threshold < 0.63, modularity measure (Q) in the two groups rises gradually, but the changes are almost the same, and when $0.2 <$ threshold < 0.43, there is a great difference in the two groups.
- When threshold > 0.62, there is only a fully coupled network of two nodes in the case and control groups, so the value of average clustering coefficient (C) and average path length (L) are both one.
- When the threshold is still increasing, the network is isolated, and the value of average clustering coefficient (C) and average path length (L) are missing, and average degree (K), modularity measure (Q), average betweenness (B) became zero.

In summary, network density (D) and average clustering coefficient (C) cannot distinguish the case and control groups, while average path length (L) and average betweenness (B) can distinguish these two groups, but the threshold range is limited. However, average degree can distinguish these two groups in a large range of threshold, so average degree is chosen for distinction between

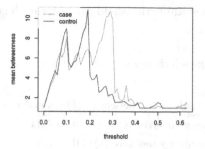

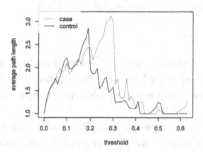

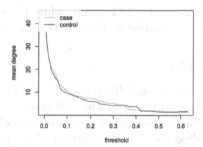

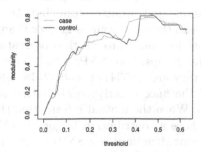

Fig. 1. Comparison of four statistics between case and control group networks for gene BRCA2 with different thresholds, the abscissa standing for the threshold, the ordinate for the respective statistics, red for case and blue for control (Color figure online)

two groups. We get the suitable threshold range for each statistic of the network shown in Table 1.

Table 1. Threshold range which can distinguish the case and control groups of four statistics.

Statistic of the network	Threshold range
average degree (K)	0.09-0.34
modularity measure (Q)	0.2-0.28
average path length (L)	0.2-0.3
average betweenness (B)	0.21-0.3

From Table 1, every statistic has a different threshold range, but they have a common region. Combined with Figure 1, we choose 0.27 for the best threshold, it can mostly distinguish the case and control groups. We create the complex network when threshold is 0.27.

As seen from Fig. 2, the network structures of these two groups are significantly different. In the control group, there is a lot of isolated points and it has a weak connection. But in the case group, many isolated points are no longer isolated and it has a closer connection. There are 36 out of 45 connected points and nine isolated points in the control group, while the same indicators in the case group are 39 and six. It indicates that our threshold 0.27 is suitable.

4.2   Structural Key SNPs

Structure determines function, and difference of function is determined by difference of the structure. In this paper, the difference is refined to each node. Average degree can be fine to distinguish case and control groups, so we choose average degree (K) to describe the difference of SNPs in the case and control groups.

Structural key SNPs are SNPs that have greater contributions to network structure, including positive and negative contributions. Positive contribution refers that degree of node in the case group is greater than control group. Otherwise we call negative contribution. Through the observation of Fig. 3, compared with the case and control groups. Four SNPs which have the max positive contribution are obtained, they are rs9534174, rs4942448, rs9534262 and rs206146. Two SNPs which have the max negative contribution are obtained, they are rs4942448 and rs206146. When the mutual information threshold is set to 0.27, we choose SNPs which have a contribution larger than three as structural key SNPs, and then we get four structural key SNPs shown in Table 2.

Based on the result shown in Table 2, we get four structural key SNPs, they are rs9534174, rs4942448, rs9534262 and rs206146. In these four structural key SNPs, rs4942448 and rs9534262 are the causal SNPs we set up in advance. These experiments and results illustrate that our method is effective.

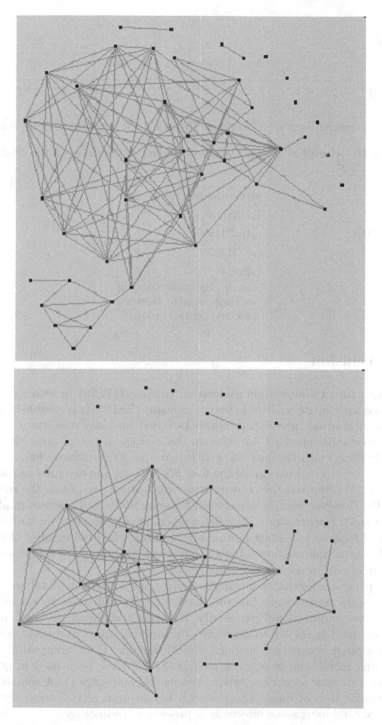

Fig. 2. The mutual information network of gene BRCA2 for case and control groups respectively at threshold = 0.27, first figure for the case group and the second for the control group

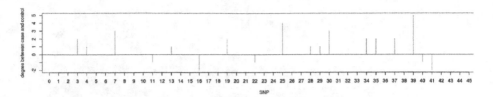

Fig. 3. The contributions of SNPs on gene BRCA2 to the network structure at t = 0.27

Table 2. The selected SNPs and the corresponding contribution on the condition of threshold = 0.27.

Structural key SNPs	Δd
rs9534174	3
rs4942448	4
rs9534262	3
rs206146	5

Δd is the difference of average degree between case and control groups

5   Conclusion

This paper uses Genome-wide association studies (GWAS) to identify diseases associated with single nucleotide polymorphisms (SNPs). It is established a case and control mutual information networks based on simulation data of breast cancer associated gene BRCA2, wherein the average degree of network is found to clearly distinguish the case and control groups. As results, we identified four structural key SNPs with two of the four SNPs being pre-assigned causal SNPs in BRCA2. We compare the network structure statistics to obtain the structural key SNPs. However, finding association between SNPs and diseases in all chromosome needs further study. Through numerical experiments, we find that the number of samples will affect mutual information: when the number of samples is small, mutual information is higher, but when the number of samples is large, mutual information decreases gradually.

This paper argues that, few samples could cause incomplete database without enough specific individuals, but too much samples will cause redundancy and increase the computational complexity. It is still a challenge to use neural-like computing models [23–30] to determine the suitable upper and lower bounds.

Bio-inspired computing models, mainly include DNA computing models [31,32] and membrane computing models [33–35] have been used in gene signal detection, such as nuclear export signals [36] and ultra DNA signals [37] in recent works. It is of interest to use such bio-inspired models to analyze SNP Networks, combining some information processing technology.

Acknowledgment. This work was supported by National Natural Science Foundation of China (61402187, 61502535, 61572522 and 61572523), China Postdoctoral Science Foundation funded project (2016M592267), Natural Science Foundation Project of CQ CSTC (No.cstc2012jjA40059), and Fundamental Research Funds for the Central Universities (R1607005A).

References

1. Risch, N., Merikangas, K.: The future of genetic studies of complex human diseases. Sci. **273**(5281), 1516–1517 (1996). AAAS Weekly Paper Edition
2. Yuyan, M., Yanmei, Y., Huilong, C.: Relationship between genotype of rs3803662 locus in TOX3 gene and clinical and pathological characteristics of breast cancer. Pract. Oncol. J. **25**(6), 501–505 (2011)
3. Ghoussaini, M., Fletcher, O., Michailidou, K., et al.: Genome-wide association analysis identifies three new breast cancer susceptibility loci. Nat. Genet. **44**(3), 312–318 (2012)
4. Wei, K., Chenxi, H., Xiaoyang, M.: Reliability feature extraction of breast cancer gene expression data based on ICASSO. Acta Universitatis Medicinalis Anhui **48**(10), 1252–1255 (2013)
5. Szymczak, S., Igl, B.W., Ziegler, A.: Detecting SNP-expression associations: a comparison of mutual information and median test with standard statistical approaches. Stat. Med. **28**(29), 3581–3596 (2009)
6. Liu, Z., Lin, S.: Multilocus LD measure and tagging SNP selection with generalized mutual information. Genet. Epidemiol. **29**(4), 353–364 (2005)
7. Zhang, W., Shang, J., Li, H.: SIPSO: selectively informed particle swarm optimization based on mutual information to determine SNP-SNP interactions. Springer, Berlin (2016)
8. Song, T., Pan, L.: Spiking neural P systems with request rules. Neurocomput. **193**(12), 193–200 (2016)
9. Song, T., Liu, X., Zhao, Y., Zhang, X.: Spiking neural P systems with white hole neurons. IEEE Trans. Nanobiosci. (2016). doi:10.1109/TNB.2016.2598879
10. Song, T., Pan, Z., Wong, D.M., Wang, X.: Design of logic gates using spiking neural P systems with homogeneous neurons and astrocytes-like control. Inf. Sci. **372**, 380–391 (2016)
11. Wang, X., Song, T., Gong, F., Pan, Z.: On the computational power of spiking neural P systems with self-organization. Sci. Rep. **6**, 27624 (2016). doi:10.1038/srep27624
12. Shi, X., Wu, X., Song, T., Li, X.: Construction of DNA nanotubes with controllable diameters and patterns by using hierarchical DNA sub-tiles. Nanoscale **8**, 14785–14792 (2016). doi:10.1039/C6NR02695H
13. Mani, R., St Onge, R.P., Giaever, G.: Defining genetic interaction. Proc. Natl. Acad. Sci. U.S.A. **105**(9), 3461–3466 (2008)
14. Wang, S., Li, K., Xu, X.: Structural characteristics of gene networks for colon cancer. In: IEEE International Conference on Signal Processing, Piscataway, NJ, pp. 1–6 (2011)
15. Baranzini, S.E., Galwey, N.W., Wang, J.: Pathway and network-based analysis of genome-wide association studies in multiple sclerosis. Hum. Mol. Genet. **18**(11), 2078–2090 (2009)
16. Bowers, P.M., O'Connor, B.D., Cokus, S.J.: Utilizing logical relationships in genomic data to decipher cellular processes. FEBS J. **272**(20), 5110–5118 (2005)

17. Cabrol, S.: Network properties of complex human disease genes identified through genome-wide association studies. Plos One **4**(11), e8090 (2009)

18. Benesty, P.J., Chen, J., Huang, Y.: Pearson correlation coefficient. In: Benesty, P.J., Chen, J., Huang, Y. (eds.) Noise Reduction in Speech Processing, pp. 1–4. Springer, Berlin (2009)

19. Artusi, R., Verderio, P., Marubini, E.: Bravais-Pearson and Spearman correlation coefficients: meaning, test of hypothesis and confidence interval. Int. J. Biol. Markers **17**(2), 148–151 (2002)

20. Werhli, A.V., Grzegorczyk, M., Husmeier, D.: Comparative evaluation of reverse engineering gene regulatory networks with relevance networks, graphical Gaussian models and Bayesian networks. Bioinf. **22**(20), 2523–2531 (2006)

21. Newman, M.E.: Modularity and community structure in networks. Proc. Nat. Acad. Sci. **103**(23), 8577–8582 (2006)

22. Su, Z., Marchini, J., Donnelly, P.: HAPGEN2: simulation of multiple disease SNPs. Bioinf. **27**(16), 2304–2305 (2011)

23. Song, T., Zou, Q., Zeng, X., Liu, X.: Asynchronous spiking neural P systems with rules on synapses. Neurocomput. **151**(3), 1439–1445 (2015)

24. Song, T., Wang, X., Zhang, Z., Chen, Z.: Homogenous spiking neural P systems with anti-spikes. Neural Comput. Appl. **24**(7–8), 1833–1841 (2014)

25. Song, T., Wang, X.: Homogeneous spiking neural P systems with inhibitory synapses. Neural Process. Lett. **42**(1), 199–214 (2015)

26. Song, T., Liu, X., Zeng, X.: Asynchronous spiking neural P systems with anti-spikes. Neural Process. Lett. **42**(3), 633–647 (2015)

27. Song, T., Liu, X., Zhao, Y., Zhang, X.: Spiking Neural P Systems with White Hole Neurons. IEEE Trans. Nanobiosci. (2016, in press)

28. Song, T., Zheng, P., Wong, M.D., Wang, X.: Design of logic gates using spiking neural P systems with homogeneous neurons and astrocytes-like control. Inf. Sci. **372**, 380–391 (2016)

29. Zhang, X., Wang, B., Pan, L.: Spiking neural P systems with a generalized use of rules. Neural Comput. **26**(12), 2925–2943 (2014)

30. Zeng, X., Zhang, X., Song, T., Pan, L.: Spiking neural P systems with thresholds. Neural Comput. **26**(7), 1340–1361 (2014)

31. Shi, X., Wang, Z., Deng, C., Song, T., Pan, L., Chen, Z.: A novel bio-sensor based on DNA strand displacement. PloS ONE **9**, e108856 (2014)

32. Wang, X., Song, T., Wang, Z., Yansen, S., Liu, X.: MRPGA: motif detecting by modified random projection strategy and genetic algorithm. J. Comput. Theor. Nanosci. **10**, 1209–1214 (2013)

33. Song, T., Pan, L., Wang, J., Venkat, I., Subramanian, K.G., Abdullah, R.: Normal forms of spiking neural P systems with anti-spikes. IEEE Trans. NanoBiosci. **4**(11), 352–359 (2012)

34. Song, T., Pan, L.: Spiking neural P systems with rules on synapses working in maximum spikes consumption strategy. IEEE Trans. NanoBiosci. **14**(1), 37–43 (2015)

35. Song, T., Pan, L.: Spiking neural P systems with rules on synapses working in maximum spiking strategy. IEEE Trans. NanoBiosci. **14**(4), 465–477 (2015)

36. Tingfang, W., Zhang, Z., Gong, F., Song, T., Chen, Z., Zhang, P., Zhao, Y.: NES-REBS: a novel nuclear export signal prediction method using regular expressions and biochemical properties. J. Bioinf. Comput. Biol. **3**, 1650013 (2016)

37. Shi, X., Li, X., Song, T., Chen, Z.: A universal fast colorimetric method for DNA signal detection. J. Nanomater. (2016)

Novel Image Deconvolution Algorithm Based on the ROF Model

Su Xiao[(✉)]

School of Computer Science and Technology, Huaibei Normal University,
Huaibei 235000, China
csxiaosu@163.com

Abstract. The ROF (Rudin-Osher-Fatemi) model is one of the most successful and widely used models in image deconvolution. However, efficiently solving this model is usually impractical because of its non-smoothness. To solve the ROF model quickly and accurately to improve image deconvolution, a novel algorithm based on the splitting Bregman method and the two-step iterative thresholding method (2-SITM) is presented. The ROF model is decomposed into several sub-problems using the split Bregman method. These sub-problems are then solved by corresponding methods to obtain their closed-form solutions. To compute the denoising sub-problem, the 2-SITM is introduced. Compared with the popular iterative thresholding method, the 2-SITM is conducive to improving the performance of the presented algorithm. In an experiment, uniform-blurry images are restored by the 2-SITM to verify its effectiveness. Results also show the superior performance of the presented algorithm to some similar state-of-the-art algorithms.

Keywords: Image deconvolution · ROF model · Splitting Bregman method · Denoising sub-problem · Two-step iterative thresholding method (2-SITM)

1 Introduction

Removing the blur and noise in a degraded image is no easy task because of the ill-poseness of image deconvolution. To eliminate the adverse effects of ill-posedness problem, image deconvolution is generally modeled as a global optimization problem. Among the variety of deconvolution models, the ROF model may be the most successful in preserving the edges of restored images [1]. However, because of the non-smoothness of the total variation (TV) term of the objective function, solving the ROF model effectively, rapidly, and accurately is a key problem. Therefore, quickly restoring images with high quality is the main criteria for evaluating the performances of deconvolution algorithms based on the ROF model. Aside from image deconvolution, the ROF model has also been applied in many other fields, such as image denoising [2] and image inpainting [3]. The ROF model is originally presented by Rudin et al. [4], and is a popular powerful tool. To solve the ROF model, Rudin et al. applied the time marching

© Springer Nature Singapore Pte Ltd. 2016
M. Gong et al. (Eds.): BIC-TA 2016, Part II, CCIS 682, pp. 431–440, 2016.
DOI: 10.1007/978-981-10-3614-9_53

method to its Euler-Lagrange (EL) equation. However, because of the nonlinear and non-smooth term of the EL equation of the ROF model, the convergence of the time marching method cannot be guaranteed. Moreover, the constraint on the stability of the time-step makes slows down the computation of the EL equation of the ROF model. To improve the convergence of the EL equation and to reduce its computational complexity, Chan et al. [5] introduce the dual variables to replace the outliers of the EL equation of the ROF model, and then alternately estimate the primal variables and dual variables using Newton linearization technology. Computing the EL equation of the ROF model is inefficient in large-scale data (e.g., images), which reduces the quality of image deconvolution. To solve the ROF model efficiently and to eliminate the effect of its non-smoothness, Wang et al. [6] presented an image deconvolution algorithm based on variable splitting and alternating minimization. The ROF model is reformulated into a half-quadratic optimization problem. The solutions for this problem are obtained by alternately computing its primal sub-problem and dual sub-problem. Wangs algorithm has speed advantage compared with many similar image deconvolution algorithms because obtaining the closed-form solutions of these two sub-problems is easy, and solving the primal sub-problem can be accelerated with the help of fast Fourier transform (FFT). However, the rate of convergence of the alternating minimization used by Wang et al. to restore images is still not fast enough. Alternating direction minimization (ADM) is used in the algorithm presented by Chan et al. [7] to solve the ROF model. In ADM, the ROF model is first inverted into an equivalent unconstrained convex optimization problem. This convex optimization problem is then decomposed into a series of sub-problems. By alternately and iteratively computing these sub-problems, the global optimal solution of the ROF model can be approached. Simulated results show that compared with alternating minimization, ADM can improve the speed of image deconvolution and obtain better restored results. When solving non-smooth convex optimization problems (e.g., ROF model), many image deconvolution algorithms, including some of the algorithms mentioned above, use variable splitting technology as a key step. The primary role of variable splitting is to introduce new variables, which can decouple the smooth component and non-smooth component of the ROF model. Combining variable splitting with other methods to generate more efficient methods is easy; the most famous of this method may be the split Bregman method (SBM) [8]. SBM has been widely used in many fields, such as image denoising [9], image inpainting [10], and compressed sensing [11], because of its many advantages. Cai et al. [12] introduce SBM into image deconvolution to solve the l_2-l_1 optimization problem. The advantages of Cais algorithm are simplicity, high-efficiency, and high-accuracy, which are also shown by other image deconvolution algorithms based on SBM. The speed of SBM-based deconvolution algorithms depends mostly on time performance in computing the denoising sub-problem. The most common method for the denoising sub-problem is the iterative thresholding method [13], but its main drawback is slow convergence speed. To improve the convergence of the iterative thresholding method, Wright et al. [14] introduce warm starting for the initialization and continuation method to update parameters. However, Wrights research fails to solve completely the convergence problem of the iterative thresholding method. Bioucas-dias et al. [15] present a novel 2-SITM; when this method is compared with the iterative thresholding method, the result of each iteration depends on the results of two previous iterations, instead of the result of the previous one iteration. The 2-SITM is faster and more accurate than the iterative thresholding method in solving the denoising sub-problem.

SBM and the 2-SITM both have many advantages, but combining these methods to solve image deconvolution problems has not been reported yet. Based on the above discussion, this paper presents a novel image deconvolution algorithm based on SBM and 2-SITM. SBM is used to decompose the ROF model into a series of sub-problems, and 2-SITM is applied to the denoising sub-problem. The rest of paper is arranged as follows. Section 2 presents the algorithm in detail, including solving the denoising sub-problems by 2-SITM. Experimental results are shown in Sect. 3. A group of experiments is conducted in this section to show the validity of the presented algorithm and evaluate the performance of it. Conclusions are drawn in Sect. 4.

2   Presented Algorithm

The ROF model can be expressed as:

$$\min_{u} \frac{||Hu - g||_2^2}{2} + \mu||\nabla u||_1, \tag{1}$$

where $u \in R^N$, $H \in R^{M \times N}$, and $g \in R^M$ represent sharp image, blur operator, and degraded image, respectively; $||\cdot||_1$ and $||\cdot||_2$ are l_1-norm and l_2-norm, respectively; $\nabla \in R^{L \times N}$ denotes the gradient operator, $||\nabla u||_1$ is the TV-regularized term; and $\mu > 0$ is a constant. The ROF model is a powerful tool, but non-smoothness makes the numerical computation a very difficult problem, and slows down early deconvolution algorithms based on the ROF model. Efficiently solving the ROF model was made possible by variable splitting methods. As a combination of the Bregman iterative method and variable splitting, SBM inherits the advantages of these two methods. To address the non-smoothness of the ROF model, SBM first converts it into a constrained convex optimization problem:

$$\min_{u,v} \frac{||Hu - g||_2^2}{2} + \mu||v||_1$$
$$s.t. \quad v = \nabla u, \tag{2}$$

where $v \in R^L$ is the dual variable, then decomposes the problem (2) into the following sub-problems:

$$u^{k+1} = \underset{u}{\operatorname{argmin}} ||Hu - g||_2^2 + \gamma||v^k - \nabla u - d^k||_2^2, \tag{3}$$

$$v^{k+1} = \underset{v}{\operatorname{argmin}} \frac{\gamma}{2}||v - \nabla u^{k+1} - d^k||_2^2 + \mu||v||_1, \tag{4}$$

$$d^{k+1} = d^k + (\nabla u^{k+1} - v^{k+1}), \tag{5}$$

where k denotes the iterations. The solutions to the original problem, i.e., the ROF model, can be obtained by iteratively and alternately solving these sub-problems. Evidently, Eq. (5) can be directly computed. For u, the objective function of problem (3) is smooth. Thus,

$$u^{k+1} = (H^T H + \gamma \nabla^T \nabla)^{-1} (H^T g + \gamma \nabla^T c^k), \tag{6}$$

where $c^k = v^k - d^k$. Given that image deconvolution involves large-scale data processing, the computational efforts of the matrix multiplication and the matrix inversion of Eq. (6) are very large, which makes the fast computation of u^{k+1} sub-problem impossible. Therefore, FFT is employed in Eq. (6) to obtain:

$$u^{k+1} = F^{-1} \left(\frac{F(H)^* \otimes F(g) + \gamma F(\nabla)^* \otimes F(c^k)}{F(H)^* \otimes F(H) + \gamma F(\nabla)^* \otimes F(\nabla)} \right), \tag{7}$$

where F represents FFT; F^{-1} represents the inversion of FFT; $(\cdot)^*$ denotes complex conjugate; and $\otimes$ denotes the dot product. With the help of FFT, the time complexity of the matrix multiplication and the matrix inversion of Eq. (6) are both $O(n\log n)$.

2.1   Solving Denoising Sub-problem (4)

Directly computing the denoising sub-problem in Eq. (4) is impossible because of the l_1-norm. If the iterative thresholding method is applied to the sub-problem (4), the results are:

$$v^{k+1} = (1 - \lambda)v^k + \lambda \Psi_{\mu/\gamma}(\nabla u^{k+1} + d^k), \tag{8}$$

where the constant $\lambda > 0$; $\Psi_{\mu/\gamma}$ denotes the denoising operator, e.g., the thresholding function [16]. Although the solution of denoising sub-problem (4) can be obtained using Eq. (8), it is slow and the precision of the result is low. To improve the iterative thresholding method, 2-SITM is presented. The effectiveness of this method has been theoretically and experimentally proved. Therefore, this paper applies 2-SITM in literature [15] to the denoising sub-problem (4).

For the following convex optimization problem:

$$\min_x \frac{||Ax - y||_2^2}{2} + \delta \Phi(x), \tag{9}$$

where x and y are arbitrary vectors; A is a linear operator; the constant $\delta > 0$; and $\Phi(x)$ denotes TV or l_1 regularized term. The 2-SITM solution given in literature [15] is:

$$\begin{cases} x^1 = \Psi_\delta(x^0 + A^T(y - Ax^0)) \\ x^{i+1} = (1 - \alpha)x^{i-1} + (\alpha - \beta)x^i + \beta \Psi_\delta(x^i + A^T(y - Ax^i)) \end{cases}, \tag{10}$$

where the constants $\alpha > 0$, $\beta > 0$; and i denotes iterations. We let $x = v^{k+1}$, $A = I$ (identity matrix), and $y = \nabla u^{k+1} + d^k$ and $\delta = \mu/\gamma$. Equation (10) can be expressed as:

$$\begin{cases} v^{k+1,1} = \Psi_{\mu/\gamma}(\nabla u^{k+1} + d^k) \\ v^{k+1,i+1} = (1-\alpha)v^{k+1,i-1} + (\alpha - \beta)v^{k+1,i} + \beta\Psi_{\mu/\gamma}(\nabla u^{k+1} + d^k) \end{cases} \quad (11)$$

Equation (11) is the two-step thresholding solution of the denoising sub-problem (4).

2.2   Description of the Presented Algorithm

Based on Eqs. (5), (7) and (11), the presented algorithm is summarized as follows:

(1) **Input:** v^0, d^0; γ, μ
(2) **Output:** u^{k+1}
(3) **for** $k = 0$ to k_{max}.
    (a) computing u^{k+1} by Eq. (7)
    (b) **if** $|J(u^{k+1})|/|J(u^k)| < \epsilon$
        i. stop iteration
    (c) **end**
    (d) computing $\tilde{v}^k = \Psi_{\mu/\gamma}(\nabla u^{k+1} + d^k)$
    (e) computing v^{k+1} by 2-SITM
    (f) computing d^{k+1} by Eq. (5)
(4) **end**

where 2-SITM is as follows:

(1) **Input:** $v^{k+1,0}$, $\tilde{v}^k$; α, β
(2) **Output:** $v^{k+1,i+1}$ (i.e. v^{k+1})
(3) $v^{k+1,1} = \tilde{v}^k$
(4) **for** $i = 0$ to i_{max}.
    (a) $v^{k+1,i+1} = (1-\alpha)v^{k+1,i-1} + (\alpha - \beta)v^{k+1,i} + \beta\tilde{v}^k$
(5) **end**

In the presented algorithm, J denotes the objective function of the ROF model, ϵ is a small constant, and $\Psi_{\mu/\gamma}(\nabla u^{k+1} + d^k)$ denotes the component-wise application of the following soft-thresholding function:

$$soft((\nabla u^{k+1} + d^k)_j, \mu/\gamma) = sign((\nabla u^{k+1} + d^k)_j)max(|(\nabla u^{k+1} + d^k)_j| - \mu/\gamma, 0) \quad (12)$$

to $\nabla u^{k+1} + d^k$, where $(\nabla u^{k+1} + d^k)_j$ $(j = 1, 2, \cdots, P)$ denotes the jth element of $\nabla u^{k+1} + d^k$, and $sign$ denotes the signum function. The time complexity of $\Psi_{\mu/\gamma}(\nabla u^{k+1} + d^k)$ is $O(n)$ because the soft function computes $\nabla u^{k+1} + d^k$ component-by-component.

Cai et al. [12] and Setzer [17] proved the convergence of the SBM applied to the ROF model. Proof of 2-SITM is also given in literature [15]. Details are provided in relevant literature. Therefore, the convergence of the presented algorithm can be guaranteed.

3   Experimental Results

The images shown in Fig. 1 are used as the sharp images with 256×256 resolutions. To create the degraded images shown in Fig. 2, the sharp images are first convolved with an averaging filter with a size of 15×15. The images are then perturbed by Gaussian noise with a standard variance of 1e-3. In Fig. 2, signal-to-noise ratio (SNR) is defined as $10 \times lg(||u||_2^2/||u^{k+1} - u||_2^2)$. The presented algorithm and the algorithms in literature [6,7,12,15] are used to restore the degraded images. The results are shown in Fig. 3 and Tables 1 and 2. To obtain the time in Table 2, each algorithm is run 10 times. The average time is then adopted. The parameters of the presented algorithm are as follows: $\mu = 7.5$, γ=7.5e-7, $\alpha = 1.95$, $\beta = 3.8$, ϵ=1e-5, $k_{max} = 10$, $i_{max} = 10$; the default settings of the algorithms in literature [6,7,12,15] are adopted.

The data and images in Fig. 3 and Tables 1 and 2 demonstrate the effectiveness of the presented algorithm. These images also show that the presented algorithm is superior to the algorithms in literature [6,7,12,15] in terms of speed and the quality of the restored images. As an image deconvolution algorithm based on sparse representation, the Cai algorithm fails to overcome its inherent weaknesses, which resulted in visually blurred restored images. By contrast, the algorithms based on the ROF model can accurately reconstruct the edges of restored images. Hence, they obtain better experimental results in both visual

(a)   (b)   (c)   (d)

Fig. 1. Sharp images. (a) boat with 256×256 resolution; (b) house with 256×256 resolution; (c) livingroom with 512×512 resolution; and (d) pirate with 512×512 resolution.

(a)   (b)   (c)   (d)

Fig. 2. Degraded images. (a) SNR = 5.81 dB; (b) SNR = 6.72 dB; (c) SNR = 6.46 dB; and (d) SNR = 8.01 dB

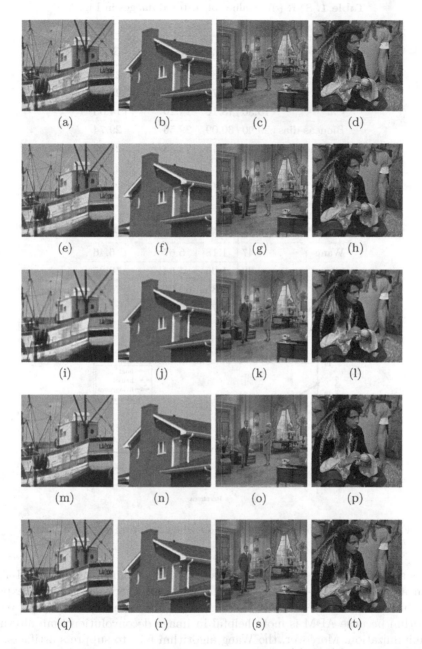

Fig. 3. Restored images obtained by each algorithm. (a) to (d) Restored images obtained using the Wang algorithm [6]; (e) to (h) restored images obtained using the Chan algorithm [7]; (i) to (l) restored images obtained using the Cai algorithm [12]; (m) to (p) restored images obtained using the Bioucas-dias algorithm [15]; and (q) to (t) restored images obtained using the presented algorithm.

Table 1. SNR (dB) values of restored images in Fig. 3.

Algorithms	SNR (dB)			
	Boat	House	Livingroom	Pirate
Wang	23.32	24.88	22.60	22.68
Chan	25.87	29.79	26.89	25.59
Cai	15.30	18.10	14.20	14.63
Bioucas-dias	29.90	30.09	29.56	29.74
Prestned	30.01	31.13	29.83	29.97

Table 2. Average time (s) of restoring the images in Fig. 3.

Algorithms	Time (s)			
	Boat	House	Livingroom	Pirate
Wang	1.47	1.18	5.67	6.46
Chan	2.32	1.05	4.64	10.25
Cai	23.72	19.35	69.06	76.98
Bioucas-dias	1.13	0.76	5.18	4.63
Presented	0.58	0.65	4.08	4.22

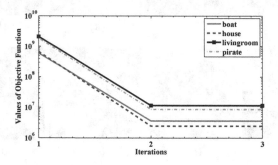

Fig. 4. Values of the objective function when restoring degraded images.

effects and SNR. Among the ROF model based algorithms, the presented algorithm and the Bioucas-dias algorithm outperform other algorithms in experiment because of 2-SITM. The Chan algorithm has advantages over the Wang algorithm because ADM is more helpful in image deconvolution than alternating minimization. Moreover, the Wang algorithm fails to suppress artifacts. To validate the convergence of the presented algorithm when restoring degraded images, the variation values of $||Hu^{k+1} - g||_2^2/2 + ||\nabla u^{k+1}||_1$ (i.e., the objective function of the ROF model) are illustrated in Fig. 4. With a few iterations, the objective function converges with the minimizer, i.e., the presented algorithm is convergent.

4 Conclusion

In this paper, SBM and 2-SITM are used to solve the ROF model. A novel image deconvolution algorithm is presented based on this model. SBM decouples the ROF model into three sub-problems, and takes only a few iterations to compute these sub-problems to obtain the solution of the ROF model. Compared with the iterative thresholding method, 2-SITM can solve the denoising sub-problem more efficiently. By restoring degraded images, the effectiveness of the presented algorithm is proved. The experimental results also show that the presented algorithm outperforms some state-of-the-art image deconvolution algorithms. Future work should be focused on the use of the presented algorithm to solve the l2-l1 optimization problem.

Acknowledgments. This work is supported by Anhui Provincial Natural Science Foundation (No. 1608085QF150).

References

1. Cai, F., Dong, B., Osher, S., Shen, Z.: Image restoration: total variation, wavelet frames, and beyond. J. Am. Math. Soc. **25**, 1033–1089 (2012)
2. Micchelli, C.A., Shen, L., Xu, Y., Zeng, X.: Proximity algorithms for the L1/TV image denoising model. Adv. Comput. Math. **38**, 401–426 (2013)
3. Papafitsoros, K., Schonlieb, C.B.: A combined first and second order variational approach for image reconstruction. J. Math. Imaging Vis. **48**, 308–338 (2014)
4. Rudin, L.I., Osher, S., Fatemi, E.: Nonlinear total variation based noise removal algorithms. Physica D: Nonlinear Phenomena **60**, 259–268 (1992)
5. Chan, T.F., Golub, G.H., Mulet, P.: A nonlinear primal-dual method for total variation-based image restoration. SIAM J. Sci. Comput. **20**, 1964–1977 (1999)
6. Wang, Y., Yang, J., Yin, W., Zhang, Y.: A new alternating minimization algorithm for total variation image reconstruction. SIAM J. Imaging Sci. **1**, 248–272 (2008)
7. Chan, S.H., Khoshabeh, R., Gibson, K.B., Gill, P.E., Nguyen, T.Q.: An augmented lagrangian method for total variation video restoration. IEEE Trans. Image Process. **20**, 3097–3111 (2011)
8. Goldstein, T., Osher, S.: The split Bregman method for L1-regularized problems. SIAM J. Imaging Sci. **2**, 323–343 (2009)
9. Liu, X., Huang, L.: A new nonlocal total variation regularization algorithm for image denoising. Math. Comput. Simul. **97**, 224–233 (2014)
10. Cheng, Q., Shen, H., Zhang, L., Li, P.: Inpainting for remotely sensed images with a multichannel nonlocal total variation model. IEEE Trans. Geosci. Remote Sens. **52**, 175–187 (2014)
11. Yang, Y., Moller, M., Osher, S.: A dual split Bregman method for fast l^1 minimization. Math. Comput. **82**, 2061–2085 (2013)
12. Cai, J.F., Osher, S., Shen, Z.: Split Bregman methods and frame based image restoration. Multiscale Model. Simul. **8**, 337–369 (2009)
13. Daubechies, I., Defrise, M., De Mol, C.: An iterative thresholding algorithm for linear inverse problems with a sparsity constraint. Commun. Pure Appl. Math. **57**, 1413–1457 (2004)

14. Wright, S.J., Nowak, R.D., Figueiredo, M.A.T.: Sparse reconstruction by separable approximation. IEEE Trans. Sig. Process. **57**, 2479–2493 (2009)
15. Bioucas-Dias, J.M., Figueiredo, M.A.T.: A new TwIST: two-step iterative shrinkage/thresholding algorithms for image restoration. IEEE Trans. Image Process. **16**, 2992–3004 (2007)
16. Ma, Z.: Sparse principal component analysis and iterative thresholding. Ann. Stat. **41**, 772–801 (2013)
17. Setzer, S.: Operator splittings, Bregman methods and frame shrinkage in image processing. Int. J. Comput. Vis. **92**, 265–280 (2011)

Nucleic Acid Secondary Structures Prediction with Planar *Pseudoknots* Using Genetic Algorithm

Zhang Kai[1], Li Shangyi[1,2], He Juanjuan[1,2(✉)], and Niu Yunyun[3]

[1] School of Computer Science, Wuhan University of Science and Technology,
Wuhan 430081, China
hejuanjuan@wust.edu.cn
[2] Hubei Province Key Laboratory of Intelligent Information Processing
and Real-time Industrial System, Wuhan 430081, China
[3] School of Information Engineering, China University of Geosciences,
Beijing 100083, China

Abstract. Nucleic acid nanotechnology offers many methods to fold into a variety of complex and functional nanostructures. These self-assemble scaffolds are valuable in various applications, such as molecular programming, sensing, drug delivery and nanofabrication. However, existing algorithms are typically lacking on predicting pseudoknots structure fast and accurately. This paper proposes a novel genetic algorithm to predict nucleic acid secondary structure including pseudoknots. The length of continues base pairs stacking and free energy are considered to evaluate individuals. Furthermore, the performance of our algorithm is compared with RNAStructure using PseudoBase benchmark instances, and the results show that our algorithm outperforms on accuracy and efficiency.

Keywords: Secondary structure prediction · Genetic algorithm · Pseudoknots · Minimum free energy

1 Introduction

In the past few decades, DNA and RNA molecules have also shown great potential as a design medium for the construction of nanostructures and the programmed assembly, such as nanostructure design [1,2], molecular computing [3,4], DNA chips [5]. These self-assemble scaffolds are valuable in various applications, such as molecular programming, sensing, drug delivery and nanofabrication [6]. In these fields, it is very important to design efficient search algorithms to predict nucleic acid secondary structures.

The secondary structure can be divided into sub-structures that are either pseudoknot free or pseudoknotted [7–9]. In the last decade, several comparative sequence analyses, dynamic programming [10–12], grammars, and bio-inspired

© Springer Nature Singapore Pte Ltd. 2016
M. Gong et al. (Eds.): BIC-TA 2016, Part II, CCIS 682, pp. 441–447, 2016.
DOI: 10.1007/978-981-10-3614-9_54

computing [13–15]. Methods have been used to predict the pseudoknots structure. However, accurate prediction is still an ongoing challenge, being an NP-complete problem [16–21].

In this paper, we propose an efficient genetic algorithm to predict nucleic acid secondary structure with planar pseudoknots. By using complementary base pair map-ping, the algorithm encodes the nucleic acid secondary structure and uses the mini-mum free energy and base pairs stacking as fitness function. Moreover, the performance of our algorithm compared with RNA structure method using PseudoBase benchmark instances. The comparison result shows that our algorithm is more accurate and competitive with higher sensitivity and specificity values.

2   Problem Definition

Single-stranded nucleic acid molecules can fold to reduce their energy and form a stable secondary structure like double helix, hairpin, internal loops, bulge, pseudoknots etc. The stability of the duplex structure is based on the perfect fit of $G{\equiv}C$ and A=T (in DNA) or A=U (in RNA) base pairs into the WatsonCCrick double helix structure. For a given sequence $X = 5' - x_1 x_2 \ldots x_n - 3'$ of length n, the secondary structure defined to be a set S of ordered pairs (i, j), several constraints must be satisfied:

Constraint 1. Base pairs Constraint: If $(i,j){\epsilon}S$, then $\{x_i, x_j\}{\epsilon}\{\{A,T\}, \{G,C\}\}$ in DNA; If $(i,j){\epsilon}S$, then $\{x_i, x_j\}{\epsilon}\{\{A,U\}, \{G,C\}, \{U,G\}\}$in RNA;

Constraint 2. No share bases Constraint: If (i,j) and (i,k) belong to S, then $j = k$; If (i,j) and (k,j) belong to S, then $i = k$;

Constraint 3. Threshold requirement for hairpins: If (i,j) belongs to S, then $j - i > \theta$, for a fixed value $\theta \geq 3$; i.e. there must be at least θ unpaired bases in a hairpin loop.

Constraint 4. Stacking requirement for stems: If base pairs $(x_i, x_j), (x_i+1, x_j+1), \ldots (x_j + n, x_j + n){\epsilon}P$ and form a stem, then $n \geq 3$; i.e. stems must contain $n(n \geq 3)$ base pairs.

3   Genetic Algorithm for Secondary Structure Prediction

3.1   Encoding

Given a DNA / RNA string $X = 5' - x_1 x_2 \ldots x_n - 3'$ of length n, $M(X)$ is the one to one mapping of base-pairs of X, $M(X) = (m_1, m_2, m_i, m_n)$. If x_i bonds with x_j, the value of mi are assigned to j and the value of m_j is assigned to i. If x_i do not bond with any other bases, the value of m_i is assigned to i itself. The sequence of Mengo-PKB is

$5' - ACGUGAAGGCU ACGAU AGUGCCAG - 3'$.

Definition 1 (Positive Bond). A base pairs (x_i, x_j) is Positive Bond if and only if they are bonded above the nucleic acid backbone, and the bond could not intersect any other existing above positive bonds.

Definition 2 (Negative Bond). A base pairs (x_i, x_j) is Negative Bond if and only if they are bonded below the nucleic acid backbone, and the bond could not intersect any other existing below negative bonds.

Definition 3 (Invalid Bond). If a base pair (x_i, x_j) intersects with another existing positive bond, it could not to be assigned a positive bond. Then the algorithm should check whether the base pair could be assigned negative bond. If a base pair (x_i, x_j) is neither Positive Bond nor Negative Bond, instead, it is an Invalid Bond.

3.2 Fitness Function Evaluation

Among the exponential possibilities of secondary structure for a given nucleic acid sequence, the most stable nucleic acid structure is the structure of minimum free energy. Stacks are almost the only structure stabilizing elements, because base pair stacking is contribution with substantial negative free energy, while loops are often contribution with positive free energy including hairpin loop, bulge, internal loop and multi-brunch loop.

Let $M(X) = (m_1, m_2, m_i, m_n)$ be a candidate individual. Firstly, our algorithm statistics continuous base-pair stacking, then the results are sorted in descending order. Secondly, every mi should be assigned positive bond or negative bond from the largest continuous base-pair stacking to the smallest. After all positive bonds and negative bonds are clearly assigned, the invalid bonds would be neglected. The fitness function is the accumulation of free energy and continuous base-pair stacking. The fitness function be calculated as following:

$$f(x) = a \times \sum ConBP^2 + (-1) \times \sum \Delta G \qquad (1)$$

3.3 Population Initialization

Our algorithm proposes an effective method to generate a group of high quality random sequences. Firstly, a linked list LA consisted of original indexes of bases is created. Secondly, linked list array LB[n] consisted of indexes of complementary bases is created.

Step 1: Choose a base index i from linked list LA randomly;

Step 2: Choose a complementary index j from linked list LB(i) randomly. If selected j is null, base i should be alone and mi should be assigned to i itself, then index i should be marked visited and remove from LA; Otherwise, (i, j) is a base pair, both i and j should be marked visited and remove from LA. m_i should be assigned to j and m_j should be assigned to i;

Step 3: If linked list LA is not empty, jump to step 1; otherwise, until all the m_i have been visited and assigned, the algorithm outputs the initial candidate individual $M(X)$.

3.4   Crossover Operator

The algorithm adopts two points crossover operator to generate new offspring. First, two points i and j are selected randomly for each RNA molecule. Moreover, a crossover probability P_{ran} is generated randomly. If P_{ran} is larger than the given $P_{crossover}$, the sections from i to j will be exchanged, and other sections should be copied to offspring individuals directly.

3.5   Mutation Operator

As we know, mutation operator can maintain variability of the population and avoid trapping in local optimum. In this algorithm, two points p and q are chosen randomly. If the random probability P_{ran} is larger than given $P_{mutation}$, the individual should mutate.

4   Result and Discussion

In order to verify the performance of our algorithm, we compare the results obtained by our algorithm against *RNAStructure*. To evaluate the predictions of both algorithms, we compute sensitivity and specificity over all base-pairs in the test set *PseudoBase*. Let S_{real} be the true structure and S_{pred} be the predicted structure, we define these metrics in the standard fashion as

$$Sen = \frac{TP}{TP + FN} \qquad Spec = \frac{TP}{TP + FP} \tag{2}$$

Where

TP = bases paired in S_{pred} that are in S_{real}
FP = bases paired in S_{pred} but not in S_{real}
FN = bases paired in S_{real} but not in S_{pred}

Pseudoknots test lib *PseudoBase* includes over 200 records of *Pseudoknots* obtained in the past 25 years through crystallography, NMR, mutational experiments, and sequence comparisons. We choose 29 nucleic acid sample with length from 24 to 134, The comparison results are shown in Table 1.

Obviously, our algorithm is more competitive than *RNAStructure* with higher sensitivity and specificity values on most *PseudoBase* benchmark instances. In addition, when the length is less than 50, our algorithm achieves 100% sensitivity and specificity, that means the predicted structures are is identical with the real structures.

For the instance HPeV1, the result of our algorithm shows more continues stacking base pairs and free energy than *RNAStructure*. Moreover, the Sensitivity and Specificity of our algorithm reach 100% separately, while the Sensitivity value of *RNAStructure* is 81.82%.

For the instance *PEMV*, the Sensitivity and Specificity of our algorithm reach 100% and 71.43% separately, while the values of *RNAStructure* are 60% and 100%. Obviously, the result of our algorithm shows more continues stacking base pairs and free energy than *RNAStructure*.

Table 1. The comparison of our algorithm and GA

Name	Length	RNAStructure		Our algorithm	
		Sen	Spec	Sen	Spec
Mengo_PKB	24	42.86%	60.00%	100.00%	100.00%
BMV3_UPD-PK4	26	66.67%	60.00%	100.00%	100.00%
T4-gene32	28	63.64%	87.50%	100.00%	100.00%
HAV_PK2	29	62.50%	83.33%	100.00%	100.00%
Ec_PK1	30	36.36%	44.44%	100.00%	100.00%
SBWMV1_UPD-PKc	31	45.46%	55.57%	100.00%	91.67%
HAV_PK1	33	58.33%	87.50%	100.00%	92.30%
HPeV1	35	81.82%	100.00%	100.00%	100.00%
BSBV3_UPD-PKb	36	50.00%	100.00%	100.00%	100.00%
TEV_PK1	37	45.46%	62.50%	81.82%	100.00%
CABYV	39	0.00%	0.00%	100.00%	100.00%
IPCV1	40	62.50%	55.56%	100.00%	100.00%
PEMV	41	60.00%	100.00%	100.00%	71.43%
ScYLV	42	62.50%	83.83%	65.50%	83.33%
Ec_PK3	46	64.29%	100.00%	100.00%	100.00%
SRV1_gag/pro	52	0.00%	0.00%	50.00%	50.00%
EIAV	54	50.00%	35.71%	60.00%	60.00%
BaEV	62	0.00%	0.00%	40.00%	40.00%
VMV	68	50.00%	41.18%	92.86%	76.47%
SESV	70	42.11%	32.00%	57.89%	78.57%
JEV	77	50.00%	41.67%	65.00%	59.10%
MVEV	80	55.56%	37.04%	61.11%	55.00%
WBV	82	73.68%	53.85%	94.74%	75.00%
FCiLV3	109	81.08%	93.75%	83.87%	81.58%
AMV3	113	87.18%	82.93%	82.05%	88.89%
BBMV3	116	82.05%	82.05%	53.85%	58.33%
RSV	128	74.36%	76.32%	74.36%	74.36%
CVV3	129	89.19%	78.57%	78.38%	80.56%

5   Conclusion

We propose a nucleic acid secondary structure prediction genetic algorithm that includes *Pseudoknots*. The free energy and continues base pairs stacking are used as fitness function. The algorithm provides effective initialization population, selection, crossover and mutation operators, which are the most important processes for genetic algorithm. Moreover, the performance of our algorithm is compared with *RNAStructure* method using 28 *PseudoBase* benchmark instances, and the comparison result shows that our algorithm is more accurate and competitive with higher sensitivity and specificity values.

Acknowledgment. This work was supported by the National Natural Science Foundation of China (Grant Nos. 61472293, 61502012, 60974112 and 91130034), Natural Science Foundation of Hubei Province (2015CFB335), and the Beijing Natural Science Foundation (4164096).

References

1. Ishikawa, J., Furuta, H., Ikawa, Y.: RNA Tectonics (tectoRNA) for RNA nanostructure design and its application in synthetic biology. J. Wiley Interdisc. Rev. RNA **4**, 651C–664 (2013)
2. Stewart, J.M., Franco, E.: Learning from DNA nanotechnology. DNA & RNA Nanotechnol. **2**, 23–25 (2016)
3. Wang, C., Schröder, M.S., Hammel, S., Butler, G.: Using RNA-seq for analysis of differential gene expression in fungal species. In: Devaux, F. (ed.) Yeast Functional Genomics. MMB, vol. 1361, pp. 1–40. Springer, Heidelberg (2016). doi:10.1007/978-1-4939-3079-1_1
4. Marioni, J.C., Mason, C.E., Mane, S.M.: RNA-seq: an assessment of technical reproducibility and comparison with gene expression arrays. J. Genome Res. **18**, 1509–1517 (2008)
5. Andronescu, M., Bereg, V., Hoos, H.H., et al.: RNA STRAND: the RNA secondary structure and statistical analysis database. BMC Bioinform. **9**, 1–10 (2008)
6. Zhang, X., Tian, Y., Cheng, R., Jin, Y.: An efficient approach to non-dominated sorting for evolutionary multi-objective optimiza-tion. IEEE Trans. Evol. Comput. **19**, 201–213 (2015)
7. Anderson-Lee, J., Fisker, E., Kosaraju, V.: Principles for predicting RNA secondary structure design difficulty. J. Mol. Biol. **428**, 748–757 (2016)
8. Wang, X., Song, T., Gong, F., Zheng, P.: On the computational power of spiking neural P systems with self-organization. Sci. Rep. doi:10.1038/srep27624
9. Leonard, C.W., Weeks, K.M.: RNA secondary structure modeling at consistent high accuracy using differential SHAPE. RNA Publ. RNA Soc. **20**, 846–854 (2014)
10. Waterman, M.S., Smith, T.F.: Rapid dynamic programming algorithms for RNA secondary structure. Adv. Appl. Math. **7**, 455–464 (1986)
11. Can, D., Narayanan, S.: A dynamic programming algorithm for computing N-gram posteriors from lattices. In: Conference on Empirical Methods in Natural Language Processing (2015)
12. Song, T., Zeng, X., Liu, X.: Asynchronous spiking neural P systems with rules on synapses. Neurocomputing **151**, 1439–1445 (2015)
13. Xingyi, Z., Linqiang, P., Andrei, P.: On universality of axon P systems. IEEE Trans. Neural Netw. Learn. Syst. **26**, 2816–2829 (2015)
14. Pan, L., Wang, J., Hoogeboom, H.J.: Spiking neural P systems with astrocytes. Neural Comput. **24**, 805–825 (2012)
15. Song, T., Zheng, P., Wong, M.D., Wang, X.: Design of logic gates using spiking neural P systems with homogeneous neurons and astrocytes-like control. Inf. Sci. **372**, 380–391 (2016)

16. Zeng, X., Zhang, X., Song, T., Pan, L.: Spiking neural P systems with thresholds. Neural Comput. **26**, 1340–1361 (2014)
17. Xu, J.: Probe machine. IEEE Trans. Neural Netw. Learn. Syst. **27**, 1405–1416 (2016)
18. Nawrocki, E.P., Burge, S.W., Bateman, A., et al.: Rfam 12.0: updates to the RNA families database. J. Nucleic Acids Res. **43**, 130–137 (2015)
19. Shi, X., Wu, X., Song, T., Li, X.: Construction of DNA nanotubeswith controllable diameters and patterns by using hierarchical DNA sub-tiles. Nanoscale. doi:10.1039/C6NR02695H
20. Shi, X., Wang, Z., Deng, C., Song, T., Pan, L., Chen, Z.: A novel bio-sensor based on DNA strand displacement, PloS ONE **9**(10), e108856
21. Shi, X., Chen, C., Li, X., Song, T., Chen, Z., Zhang, Z., Wang, Y.: Size controllable DNA nanoribbons assembled from three types of reusable brick single-strand DNA tiles. **11**(43), 8484–8492 (2015)

The Short-Term Traffic Flow Prediction Based on MapReduce

Suping Liu[✉] and Dongbo Zhang

Department of Computer Science,
Guangdong University of Science and Technology, Dongguan, China
457789090@qq.com

Abstract. Short-term traffic volume forecasting represents a critical
need for Intelligent Transportation Systems. In this paper, we propose
an improved K-Nearest Neighbor model, named I-KNN, in a general
MapReduce framework of distributed modeling on a Hadoop platform,
to enhance the accuracy and efficiency of short-term traffic flow forecasting. More specifically, I-KNN considers the spatial–temporal correlation
and weight of traffic flow with trend adjustment features, to optimize
the search mechanisms containing state vector, proximity measure, prediction function, and K selection. The results of the performance testing
conducted in this paper demonstrates the superior predictive accuracy
and drastically lower computational requirements of the I-KNN compared to either the neural network or the nearest neighbor approach.
And also significantly improves the efficiency and scalability of short-
term traffic flow forecasting over existing approaches.

Keywords: Artificial intelligence · Traffic forecasting · MapReduce ·
Short-term traffic prediction

1 Introduction

Real-time, accurate traffic flow prediction is the key to traffic control, traffic
induction, and providing real-time traffic information. Effectiveness of traffic
information and the accuracy of the detection of abnormal events and so intelligent transportation systems, traffic signal control of real-time traffic information
released traffic predict studies are based on the short-term traffic flow predict
(less than 5 min). The short-term traffic flow predict uses the existing traffic flow
data at time t to estimate traffic flow at the next time $+\Delta t$ [1].

It has witnessed the big data era [2] for transportation coming in recent years,
and the prediction of traffic condition (e.g., traffic flow, travel time) has attracted
great research interest for various D2ITS [3] applications such as advanced traffic management systems (ATMS), advanced traveler information systems (ATIS)
and advanced public transportation systems (APTS). Timely and accurate traffic
flow prediction plays an increasingly essential role in regional traffic management
and control, which can provide design infrastructures, schedule interventions for

© Springer Nature Singapore Pte Ltd. 2016
M. Gong et al. (Eds.): BIC-TA 2016, Part II, CCIS 682, pp. 448–453, 2016.
DOI: 10.1007/978-981-10-3614-9_55

government agencies, inform traffic conditions for travelers, and offer mobility services for passengers in real time. Moreover, it also assists road users to antici-pate traffic congestion, save energy consumption, reduce environment pollution, and improve traffic operation efficiency [4,5]. Owing to the heterogeneous and dynamic nature of traffic with nonlinear interactions between drivers and envi-ronments [6], traffic flow conditions are extremely uncertain in a transportation network. Furthermore, the traffic state of a specific location is highly affected by its upstream and downstream traffic conditions [7,8], thus making it difficult to be accurately predicted, particularly for short-term traffic flow forecasting (STFF) [9]. However, improving predictive accuracy of short-term traffic flow would be vitally important in this context.

The above-mentioned approach is applied to forecast short-term traffic flow of nancheng district dongjun road in the city of Dongguan.

2 Related Work

2.1 Characteristics of Traffic Flow

Urban expressway is the highest level of road in the city, which ensures that drivers can travel quickly and continuously. Characteristics of traffic flow are as follows:

(1) Periodicity. Traffic flow shows cyclical changes.
(2) Randomness. Traffic system is a uncertain system affected by multiple fac-tors, such as travel behavior, weather, accidents, etc.

2.2 K-Nearest Neighbor Nonparametric Regression Algorithm

K-nearest neighbor nonparametric regression method is a broad applied algo-rithm, which has nonparametric, small error ratio and good error distribution.

The basic process of k-nearest neighbor prediction modal is shown in Fig. 1. First, build a representative historical database with large capacity; second, set the model elements, including the state vector value of k and prediction algo-rithm. The state vector and value of k *constitute a model's* search mechanism. Finally, according to the observed values of the input and search mechanism, a close neighbor matching the current real-time observation data from the history database are picked up to predict the traffic flow at the next time.

2.3 k-Nearest Neighbor (k-NN)

k-NN is a prediction method which decides the predicted volume X_{t+1} by finding the k nearest neighbor (i.e. most similar) of the input data item P_{t+1} in a histori-cal dataset, and using their observed outputs. The Euclidean distance is typically used to assess similarity. When k nearest neighbor are found, and assuming their

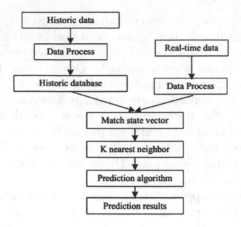

Fig. 1. Process of k-nearest neighbor algorithm.

corresponding output values are $v_i, i = 1, 2, \ldots, k$ the predicted value X_{t+1} can be determined by calculated the weighted average of the neighbors as follows:

$$X_{t+1} = \frac{1}{k} \sum_{i=1}^{k} v_i \qquad (1)$$

Local Linear Wavelet Neural Network (LLWNN). For the simplicity, we use $P = [x_1, \ldots, x_i, \ldots, x_p]$ and y to represent the previously mentioned $P_i = [X_{i-p}, X_{i+1}, X_{i-1}]$ and X_i, $p + 1 \leq i \leq t$, As seen in the Fig. 2, the output of the model will be:

$$y = \sum_{1 \leq j \leq l} W_j * \phi_j \qquad (2)$$

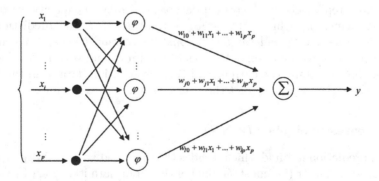

Fig. 2. Structure of LLWNN model.

2.4   MapReduce Framework

The open-source Apache Hadoop[2] provides a distributed computing framework for reliable, scalable and distributed computing, including Hadoop Common, Hadoop Distributed File System (HDFS), Hadoop YARN, Hadoop MapReduce, etc. HDFS and MapReduce are the key components of Hadoop. MapReduce is a parallel processing paradigm that allows for massive scalability across hundreds or thousands of servers on a Hadoop cluster. The processing of MapReduce jobs contains the Map phase and the Reduce phase. Each phase has key-value pairs as an input and output, the types of which may be selected by the programmer which specifies the Map function and the Reduce function. More details about MapReduce can be found in the Apache Hadoop website.

3   Problem Definition

In this work, the historical traffic flow data captured by GPS-equipped taxis are utilized as input patterns of prediction models to predict future traffic flow conditions.

Based on the aforementioned motivation, in this work, we focus on the development of accurate short-term traffic flow prediction model and the effectiveness of forecasting for big traffic data, concerned with producing real-time predictions for 5 min ahead.

It is well known that applying KNN nonparametric regression model to the traffic flow prediction faces four fundamental challenges.

Selecting a forecast generation approach (through prediction function) given a collection of nearest neighbors.

Management of the potential neighbors database with a large number of desired cases for improving the accuracy of prediction.

4   Proposed I-KNN Model

In this section, we propose a spatial–temporal weighted K-nearest neighbor (I-KNN) model to enhance the accuracy of short-term traffic flow forecasting based on the MF-TFF framework.

In the I-KNN model, to find the best nearest neighbors, we aim to optimize the search mechanisms of the traditional KNN model, including the state vector, proximity measure, prediction function and the choice of k which are crucial to the accuracy of forecasting. On the one hand, according to the spatial–temporal correlation of traffic flow, we consider the correlations of both time and space domains in terms of defining state vector. Furthermore, we employ a trend adjustment exponent weighted measure method to compute the neighborhood similarity, and then give the corresponding distance function for the similarity measure of four types of state vectors. On the other hand, we adopt the combined weights between the weighted average of the nearest neighbors and the trend adjustments of each nearest neighbor in building prediction function. Moreover, the Distance Weighted Voting scheme is used to determine the class label for reducing the impact of k selection which is sensitive to the algorithm.

4.1   Performance Evaluation

In this section, we validate the accuracy of the proposed mathematical model (I-KNN) in comparison with several well-known prediction models including basic K-nearest neighbor (KNN), Artificial Neural Networks (ANNs), Naïve Bayes (NB), Random Forest (RF) and C4.5, and then evaluate the efficiency and scalability of the implemented parallel prediction algorithm (MBSTW-KNN) by a case study.

Experimental Setup. In this work, we predict short-term traffic flow of the dongjun road in the city of Dongguan based on real-world trajectory data set, which contains a large number of GPS trajectories recorded by 12,000 taxis in a period of two weeks in September 2015 The total distance of the data set is more than 26 million kilometers and the total size is 26 GB. Specifically, the total number of GPS points reaches 484 million.

Considering the fact that the available data are finite in this effectiveness validation, the test is performed using the leave-one-out cross validation method to offer a consistent validation test. This method is a classic model validation technique to quantify the accuracy of forecasting on this limited data, which has been widely utilized for many application fields containing traffic prediction problems. During testing, different models are performed on each day and the remaining days (14 days) serve as a historical data set. In other words, the 14 days of data are available for model training (training sets), and the remaining 1 day's data are used for model testing (testing sets). Finally, the average performance across the 15 test days is utilized to compare the accuracy of different prediction models.

To evaluate the performance of the proposed distance and prediction functions, with the time domain (TD) state vector and the comparison of their average MAPEs is illustrated in Table 1.

Table 1. Accuracy comparison of KNN, KNN-CCW, KNN-EW, KNN-TAEW, and I-KNN with TD for all days.

Days September 2015	Existing methods			Proposed methods	
	KNN	KNN-CCW	KNN-EW	KNN-TAEW	I-KNN
Avg. of MAPEs improvement (%)	53.765	53.325	51.920	50.412	47.512
	-	0.379	3.343	6.290	11.569
		-	2.912	6.034	11.245
			-	3.123	8.560
				-	5.663

5   Conclusions and Future Work

This paper aims to develop a improved model and implement it in a MapReduce framework on a Hadoop platform, for solving accurate and timely traffic flow forecasting problem. Specifically, to enhance the accuracy of traffic flow prediction, based on the developed MF-TFF framework, the spatial–temporal correlation and weight of traffic flow with trend adjustment features are incorporated into the optimal KNN model, I-KNN. It employs the correlations of both time and space domains on state vector, the trend adjustment with the exponent weighted Euclidean distance on proximity measure, the combined weights between the weighted average of the nearest neighbors and the trend adjustments of each nearest neighbor on prediction function, and the distance weighted voting scheme on the choice of k. Moreover, STW-KNN is parallelized in "Big Data" environment, named MBSTW-KNN, which adopts the Mapper, Combiner and Reducer functions to improve the efficiency and scalability of traffic flow prediction in three phases, respectively. As a conclusion, all the performance evaluations demonstrate that the proposed model and its MapReduce implementation significantly improve the accuracy, efficiency and scalability of KNN over existing approaches, and has the potential to accurately and efficiently predict short-term traffic flow in real time.

Acknowledgements. The work is supported in part by Department of Education of Guangdong Province under Grant 2015KQNCX193.

References

1. Zhang, L., Wei, H., et al.: An improved k-nearest neighbor model for short-term traffic flow prediction. In: Intelligent and Integrated Sustainable Multimodal Transportation Systems Proceedings from the 13th COTA International Conference of Transportation Professionals (CICTP 2013), Procedia - Social and Behavioral Sciences, vol. 96, pp. 653–662 (2013)
2. Marx, V.: The big challenges of big data. Nature **498**(7453), 255–260 (2013)
3. Zhang, J., Wang, F., Wang, K., Lin, W., Xu, X., Chen, C.: Data-driven intelligent transportation systems: a survey. IEEE Trans. Intell. Transp. Syst. **12**(4), 1624–1639 (2011)
4. Wang, Y., Papageorgiou, M., Messmer, A.: A real-time freeway network traffic surveillance tool. IEEE Trans. Control Syst. Technol. **14**(1), 18–32 (2006)
5. Lv, Y., Duan, Y., Kang, W., Li, Z., Wang, F.-Y.: Traffic flow prediction with big data: a deep learning approach. IEEE Trans. Intell. Transp. Syst. **16**(2), 865–873 (2015)
6. Zhang, Y.: Special issue on short-term traffic flow forecasting. Transp. Res. Part C: Emerg. Technol. **43**, 1–2 (2014)
7. Chandra, S., Al-Deek, H.: Predictions of freeway traffic speeds and volumes using vector autoregressive models. J. Intell. Transp. Syst. **13**(2), 53–72 (2009)
8. Schof, M., Helbing, D.: Empirical features of congested traffic states and their implications for traffic modeling. Transp. Sci. **41**(2), 135–166 (2007)
9. Jeong, Y.S., Byon, Y.J., Castro-Neto, M.M., Easa, S.M.: Supervised weighting-online learning algorithm for short-term traffic flow prediction. IEEE Trans. Intell. Transp. Syst. **14**(4), 1700–1707 (2013)

Saliency Detection Model for Low Contrast Images Based on Amplitude Spectrum Analysis and Superpixel Segmentation

Hua Yang[1], Xin Xu[1,2(✉)], and Nan Mu[1]

[1] School of Computer Science and Technology,
Wuhan University of Science and Technology, Wuhan, China
xuxin0336@163.com
[2] Hubei Province Key Laboratory of Intelligent Information Processing and
Real-Time Industrial System, Wuhan University of Science and Technology,
Wuhan, China

Abstract. Traditional saliency detection models face great challenges towards low contrast images with low signal-to-noise ratio property. In this circumstance, it is difficult to extract effective visual features to describe salient information in image. This paper proposes a saliency detection model for low contrast images utilizing efficient features both from frequency domain and spatial domain. The input image is firstly transformed into frequency domain to calculate the amplitude spectrum by a median filter, aiming to suppress the information from non-salient regions. Then, a superpixel based feature extraction method is utilized to generate saliency map via both local and global spatial information. Experiments are carried on the low contrast image dataset to demonstrate the effectiveness of the proposed saliency detection model over other eight state-of-the-art saliency models.

Keywords: Frequency · Spatial · Saliency · Superpixel · Low contrast

1 Introduction

With the development of sensor and imaging technology, the scale and complexity of image data are consistently increasing. How to efficiently process the image such as image segmentation, object recognition, image retrieval, image self-adaption compression, and so on, gradually becomes the focus of the recent research. Because of the visual system mechanism, human can quickly pick out the most interesting areas from a complex environment. The salient object detection methods represented by visual attention system become the vital approach to improve the real-time screening technology and accuracy analysis technology for mass image data.

In general, the saliency detection algorithms can be generally divided into two different aspects, which based on frequency domain processing and spatial domain processing, respectively. The spatial domain algorithm usually applies

© Springer Nature Singapore Pte Ltd. 2016
M. Gong et al. (Eds.): BIC-TA 2016, Part II, CCIS 682, pp. 454–460, 2016.
DOI: 10.1007/978-981-10-3614-9_56

to the images which have low computational complexity; it greatly limits the application in the real-time detection system. By transforming the image into frequency domain and analyzing the parameters of spectrum, the description of image features can be well obtained. The frequency approach is not sensitive to the complicated background, which is quite suitable for low contrast images. Whereas the frequency domain methods tend to highlight the edge of the object, while neglect the inner information. The spatial methods can compensate these drawbacks to some extent. Therefore, the proposed model combines the frequency domain and the spatial domain algorithms to detect the salient object.

In the frequency domain algorithm, we first transform the input image into HSV color space, after executing the Fast Fourier Transform to each color channel; we then keep the phase spectrum and restrain high frequency of amplitude spectrum to suppress redundancy background information. And then, through the Fourier inversion, we combine the original phase spectrum and the new amplitude spectrum to obtain the saliency map into spatial domain. In spatial domain algorithm, the image is first segmented into superpixels. We then utilize the local and global contrast method to process the maps which obtained by the frequency domain algorithm to generate the final saliency map. Experimental results on the nighttime image dataset show that the proposed saliency model can well detect the salient object in low contrast images.

2   Related Work

Recently, the research of salient object detection has received increasingly attention. As a pioneer work, Itti et al. [1] proposed a well-known saliency model based on the feature integration theory, which utilized the center-surround differences of luminance, color and orientation features. For visual attention is driven by the stimulation of low level image features, most existing saliency computational models are based on the bottom-up method in spatial domain. Harel et al. [2] proposed a graph-based algorithm and a measure of dissimilarity to integrate the local uniqueness maps to generate the saliency map. Chen et al. [3] computed the saliency map by estimating the background maps and analyzing the spatial distribution. Wang et al. [4] proposed a saliency model by combining the spatial cues, which based on the mutual consistency-guided. These spatial domain algorithms can detect the salient object with a higher computing complexity.

The frequency domain based model can calculate the saliency map efficiently. Hou and Zhang [5] proposed a spectral residual approach. The redundant information of the image is suppressed through the local average amplitude spectrum filtering. Achanta et al. [6] computed the saliency map based on a frequency tuned method, which can generate the full resolution map fast. Guo et al. [7] proposed a saliency model by using the *phase spectrum of quaternion Fourier transform* (PQFT), which explains why the magnitude spectra can reflect the salient region in a scene. Chen et al. [8] proposed a motion saliency detection method based on the temporal Fourier transform. Through the analysis of frequency domain algorithms, we find that the amplitude spectrum can reflect the background information and highlight the edge information, while the phase spectrum reflects the structure information that contains most of the details information of the image.

The combination of the frequency domain and spatial domain algorithm can take full advantage of both two methods. Sun *et al.* [9] detected the salient gradient changes in the frequency domain and then segmented the regions in spatial domain. Chen *et al.* [10] proposed a frequency based saliency model, which also utilized the multiple spatial Gabor filters. These integration models can generate saliency map in real time, and highlight the salient region uniformly.

We previously proposed a spatial-spectral-domain contrast based method to evaluate the image saliency [11]. The frequency domain saliency map is achieved by adjusting the amplitude spectrum of grayscale image, and the spatial domain saliency map is obtained by calculating the maximum total variation of rectangular blocks. In this paper, we aim to detect the salient object in low contrast images; we convert the image into HSV color space to acquire the effective visual features and utilize the superpixel segmentation to divide the image into irregular blocks to compute the local-global contrast. The proposed model is more efficient and can accurately detect the salient object in low contrast images. The comparisons of this model and our previous model [11] are shown in Fig. 1.

(a) Input image   (b) Frequency [11]   (c) Spatial [11]   (d) Final map[11]   (e) Ground-Truth   (f) Our frequency   (g) Our spatial   (h) Our final map

Fig. 1. Comparisons of the proposed model with our earlier saliency model [11].

3   Proposed Saliency Model

This paper proposes a simple saliency model by combining the frequency domain and spatial domain algorithm to detect the salient objects in low contrast images.

3.1   Frequency Domain Algorithm

For an input image, the amplitude spectrum of the background region is much sharper than the object, which can be illustrated in Fig. 2. Thus the salient region can be highlighted obviously by restraining the redundant backgrounds information from the amplitude spectrum. This operation can be realized by removing the peaks in the amplitude spectrum.

In the proposed model, we first convert the input image into HSV color space, which has a good effect on the specific color segmentation. For the night images, color regions are divided into two major areas: black regions and white regions. The H, S, and V channel of HSV color space can represent the type, degree, and luminance information, respectively. Thus the utilize of HSV color space

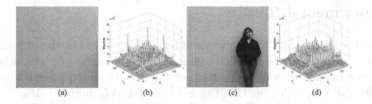

Fig. 2. Magnitude comparisons (b, d) of images without object (a) or with salient object (c), which show that the amplitude of background is higher than foreground.

can well represent characteristics of the night images, which have drab color, low luminance, and low contrast.

Then we calculate the amplitude spectrum of H, S, and V channel respectively by executing the *Fast Fourier Transform* (FFT). Next, we remove the peaks of each amplitude spectrum by utilizing the median filter. By conducting the *Inverse Fast Fourier Transform* (IFFT), the filtered amplitude spectrum and the original phase spectrum can be combined to constitute the spatial saliency maps (denoted as H_{map}, S_{map}, and V_{map}).

3.2 Spatial Domain Algorithm

After computing the saliency maps of H, S, and V color channel by the above frequency domain algorithm. We then process these saliency maps by the spatial domain algorithm.

Firstly, the input low contrast image is divided into superpixels (denoted as $SP(i)$, $i = 1, \cdots, N$, $N = 300$) by the *simple linear iterative clustering* (SLIC) algorithm [12]. This pre-processing operation can reduce the computational complexity and can also play an important role in retaining the boundary and texture information of the salient object.

Then, we regard the obtained three saliency maps (H_{map}, S_{map}, and V_{map}) as saliency features and compute the local-global saliency (denoted as $S_{Hmap}(i)$, $S_{Smap}(i)$, and $S_{Vmap}(i)$) of each superpixel in the three maps, respectively.

$$S_{Hmap}(i) = 1 - exp\left[-\frac{1}{N-1}\sum_{j=1}^{N(j \neq i)}\frac{d_{Hmap}(SP(i), SP(j))}{1 + E(SP(i), SP(j))}\right] \quad (1)$$

The $d_{Hmap}(SP(i), SP(j))$ denotes the difference between the average value of $SP(i)$ and $SP(j)$ in the H_{map}, $E(SP(i), SP(j))$ denotes the Euclidean distance between $SP(i)$ and $SP(j)$. The local-global saliency $S_{Smap}(i)$, and $S_{Vmap}(i)$ of superpixels $SP(i)$ in S_{map} and V_{map} can be generated according to (1).

At last, the saliency value (denoted as $S_{value}(i)$) of each superpixel $SP(i)$ is computed by fusing $S_{Hmap}(i)$, $S_{Smap}(i)$, and $S_{Vmap}(i)$ via:

$$S_{value}(i) = w_1 \times S_{Hmap}(i) + w_2 \times S_{Smap}(i) + w_3 \times S_{Vmap}(i), w_1 + w_1 + w_1 = 1. \quad (2)$$

The final saliency map S_{value} is smoothed by Gaussian filter.

4   Experimental Results

To verify the performance of the proposed model, we carry out the experiment on our nighttime image dataset, which contain 200 night images by a stand camera. We compare our model with eight state-of-the-art saliency models including SR [5], FT [6], NP [13], CA [14], PD [15], SO [16], BL [17], and SC [18].

The true positive rates (TPRs) and the false positive rates (FPRs) performance comparisons are shown in Fig. 3(a). The precision, recall, and F-measure performances comparison are shown in Fig. 3(b). The two methods are executed by thresholding the saliency map into binary map and comparing the difference of each pixel with ground truth. Figure 3 demonstrate that the proposed saliency model outperforms the other saliency models, which acquires the best performance in the nighttime image dataset.

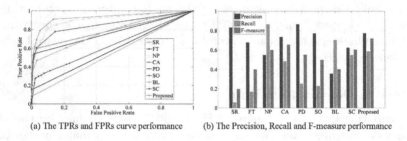

(a) The TPRs and FPRs curve performance   (b) The Precision, Recall and F-measure performance

Fig. 3. Quantitative comparison of the various saliency models in low contrast images.

The AUC (area under the curve) score and the MAE (mean absolute error) score performance comparisons are shown in Table 1, the two metrics can demonstrate how well the generated saliency map predicts the real attention region of human visual system, which show that the proposed model has the state-of-the-art performance.

Table 1. The performance comparisons of various models in low contrast images.

Models	SR	FT	NP	CA	PD	SO	BL	SC	Ours
AUC	0.5415	0.5771	0.9034	0.7895	0.7642	0.6316	0.7695	0.8532	0.9288
MAE	0.1561	0.1558	0.1607	0.1350	0.1375	0.1486	0.3216	0.1641	0.1257
TIME (s)	0.9786	0.7112	4.9095	126.2892	22.5500	2.0938	74.6387	42.0445	5.0883

The average computation time performance comparisons are also shown in Table 1. The experiments are carried out on a PC machine with an Intel(R) Core(TM) i5-5250U 1.60 GHz CPU and 8 GB RAM. The frequency domain methods SR and FT are time-saving, which only contain a few lines of codes.

The proposed model is much faster than the spatial algorithm CA, PD, BL, and SC.

The saliency maps comparisons of various saliency models are shown in Fig. 4, which show that the saliency maps of the proposed model are much similar with the ground truths.

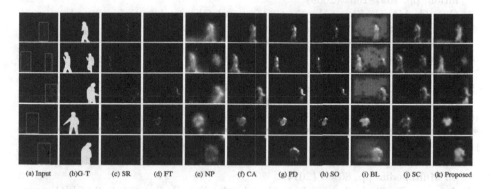

(a) Input   (b)G-T   (c) SR   (d) FT   (e) NP   (f) CA   (g) PD   (h) SO   (i) BL   (j) SC   (k) Proposed

Fig. 4. The comparisons of saliency maps of various saliency model in low contrast images. (a) Input low contrast images, (b) Ground-truths, (c–j) Saliency maps of eight state-of-the-art saliency models, (k) Saliency maps of the proposed model.

5   Conclusions

This paper proposes an effective salient object detection model to deal with the low contrast images. The proposed model combines frequency domain algorithm and the spatial domain algorithm to estimate the salient objects. We eliminate the peaks in the amplitude spectrum of different color channels to suppress the background information, and compute the superpixel based local-global contrast to obtain the salient region. Experimental results show that the proposed salient object detection model has superior performance in the low contrast images.

Acknowledgments. This work was supported by the Natural Science Foundation of China (61602349, 61373109, 61403287, 61602350 and 61273225) and the China Scholarship Council (201508420248).

References

1. Itti, L., Koch, C., Niebur, E.: A model of saliency-based visual attention for rapid scene analysis. IEEE Trans. Pattern Anal. Mach. Intell. **20**(11), 1254–1259 (1998)
2. Harel, J., Koch, C., Perona, P.: Graph-based visual saliency. In: Advances in Neural Information Processing Systems, pp. 545–552 (2006)
3. Chen, S., Shi, W., Zhang, W.: Visual saliency detection via multiple background estimation and spatial distribution. Optik-Int. J. Light Electron Opt. **125**(1), 569–574 (2014)

4. Wang, X., Ning, C., Xu, L.: Saliency detection using mutual consistency-guided spatial cues combination. Infrared Phys. Technol. **72**, 106–116 (2015)
5. Hou, X., Zhang, L.: Saliency detection: a spectral residual approach. In: IEEE Conference on Computer Vision and Pattern Recognition, pp. 1–8 (2007)
6. Achanta, R., Hemami, S., Estrada, F., Susstrunk, S.: Frequency-tuned salient region detection. In: IEEE Conference on Computer Vision and Pattern Recognition, pp. 1597–1604 (2009)
7. Guo, C., Ma, Q., Zhang, L.: Spatio-temporal saliency detection using phase spectrum of quaternion fourier transform. In: IEEE Conference on Computer Vision and Pattern Recognition, pp. 1–8 (2008)
8. Chen, Z., Wang, X., Sun, Z., Wang, Z.: Motion saliency detection using a temporal fourier transform. Opt. Laser Technol. **80**, 1–15 (2016)
9. Sun, X., Zhu, Z., Liu, X., Shang, Y., Yu, Q.: Frequency-spatial domain based salient region detection. Optik-Int. J. Light Electron Opt. **126**(9–10), 942–949 (2015)
10. Chen, D., Jia, T., Wu, C.: Visual saliency detection: from space to frequency. Signal Process. Image Commun. **44**, 57–68 (2016)
11. Mu, N., Xu, X., Chen, L., Tian, J.: Block-based salient region detection using a new spatial-spectral-domain contrast measure. In: IEEE International Symposium on Multimedia, pp. 86–89 (2014)
12. Achanta, R., Shaji, A., Smith, K., Lucchi, A., Fua, P., Susstrunk, S.: SLIC superpixels compared to state-of-the-art superpixel methods. IEEE Trans. Pattern Anal. Mach. Intell. **34**(11), 2274–2282 (2012)
13. Murray, N., Vanrell, M., Otazu, X., Parraga, C.A.: Saliency estimation using a non-parametric low-level vision model. In: IEEE Conference on Computer Vision and Pattern Recognition, pp. 433–440 (2011)
14. Goferman, S., Zelnik-Manor, L., Tal, A.: Context-aware saliency detection. IEEE Trans. Pattern Anal. Mach. Intell. **34**(10), 1915–1926 (2012)
15. Margolin, R., Tal, A., Zelnik-Manor, L.: What makes a patch distinct? In: IEEE Conference on Computer Vision and Pattern Recognition, pp. 1139–1146 (2013)
16. Zhu, W., Liang, S., Wei, Y., Sun, J.: Saliency optimization from robust background detection. In: IEEE Conference on Computer Vision and Pattern Recognition, pp. 2814–2821 (2014)
17. Tong, N., Lu, H., Yang, M.: Salient object detection via bootstrap learning. In: IEEE Conference on Computer Vision and Pattern Recognition, pp. 1884–1892 (2015)
18. Zhang, J., Wang, M., Zhang, S., Li, X., Wu, X.: Spatiochromatic context modeling for color saliency analysis. IEEE Trans. Neural Netw. Learn. Syst. **27**(6), 1177–1189 (2016)

Memetic Image Segmentation Method Based on Digraph Coding

Tao Wu, Jiao Shi, and Yu Lei[✉]

School of Electronics and Information, Northwest Polytechnical University,
ADD:127 West Youyi Road, Xi'an 710072, Shaanxi, China
tao_woe@mail.nwpu.edu.cn, {jiaoshi,leiy}@nwpu.edu.cn

Abstract. In this paper, we propose a method of digraph coding for memetic image segmentation, which adopts an individual coding based on digraph. Moreover, for image segmentation problems, we design two individual learning strategies which classify the similar vertexes into a class by cutting off the individual from the vertex with the largest weight in the digraph code. In order to evaluate the performance of the new algorithm, we take the segmentation experiment on texture images and remote sensing images and comparing with K-means and FCM. It is proved that our method achieve the image segmentation perfectly by the experiments.

Keywords: Memetic algorithm · Image segmentation · Digraph coding

1 Introduction

Image segmentation is a hard task in computer vision. It segments the image into several areas, then extracts the features from these areas and carries on classification and identification based on these features and structure information, and provides the description of the image analysis result finally [8,10,12]. After image segmentation, target feature extraction, target recognition and etc. can be executed further. The features can be used for segmentation are gray scale, color, texture, spectral characteristics, local statistical characteristics and etc. [6], whose differences can distinguish multiple targets in the image.

In the recent year, for the segmentation problems, some methods based on computational intelligence are proposed, such as method based on fuzzy relations [9], method using neural networks (NN) [7], and method based on EC [1]. We can transform the image segmentation problems to optimization problems. K-means is one of the most popular and simplest algorithms. However K-means cant always find the optimal solution, and depends on the selection of initial clustering centers. For global optimization problems, Evolutionary Algorithms (EAs) is a good tool for image segmentation. Memetic Algorithms (MAs) are growing in the field of EC. MAs has been widely applied to many fields, and a lot of research has proved that MAs are more effective than the EAs.

© Springer Nature Singapore Pte Ltd. 2016
M. Gong et al. (Eds.): BIC-TA 2016, Part II, CCIS 682, pp. 461–466, 2016.
DOI: 10.1007/978-981-10-3614-9_57

This paper applies MAs to image segmentation problems, through designing two individual learning strategies, proposes memetic image segmentation method based on digraph coding. This paper is organized as follow, the details of our method are shown in the second section, the third section is the experiment results and analysis, the last section is the conclusion.

2   The Proposed Method

Before applying image segmentation, some preprocesses are taken for the original image, just as feature extraction and watershed segmentation [5,11]. The features include GLCM features and wavelet features [2,4]. This paper adopts the individual coding strategy based on digraph [3]. Our method applies MST theory to generate the initial population, then through learning and evolution to obtain the best individual as the optimal segmentation result, and the flow is shown below.

Step 1: Preprocess, feature extraction and watershed segmentation for the original image.
Step 2: Initialization, stopping criteria and initial parameters are given, and generate the initial population.
Step 3: Learning strategy 1.
Step 4: Crossover and mutation.
Step 5: Learning strategy 2.
Step 6: Selection, adopt the elitism and tournament mechanism.
Step 7: Stopping criteria termination, if the individuals fitness achieves a maximum steadily, then stop to output the results, or go to Step 3.

2.1   Fitness Assignment

In EA, one of key point is fitness assignment. For image segmentation, how to as-sign fitness is another difficulty. Through the analysis and experiment, we design Eq. (1) as fitness assignment method.

In order to ensure the precision of image segmentation, the fitness assignment is carried out not on areas but pixels, and the equality is shown in Eq. (1).

$$fitness = \frac{1}{\sum\limits_{i=1}^{CN} \sum\limits_{j=1}^{RN_i} \sum\limits_{k=1}^{PN_j} dis(p_{ijk}, m_i)} \tag{1}$$

where RN_i represents the i-th category, PN_j represents the j-th area in the i-th category, P_{ijk} represents the k-th pixels feature vector the j-th area in the i-th category, m_i is the mean of all the pixels feature vectors.

$$dis(p_{ijk}, m_i) = \sqrt{\sum\limits_{g=1}^{FN} \left(p_{ijk_g} - m_{i_g}\right)^2} \tag{2}$$

where FN is the dimension of feature. p_{ijk_g} and m_{i_g} represent the feature vector and its mean respectively.

2.2 Learning Strategies

Two learning strategies are designed in this paper, which are executed respectively before and after the crossover. Learning strategies aim to improve the precision and speed of classifying the data to a category. Strategy 1 and Strategy 2 are introduced in detail below.

Strategy 1 replaces the range restriction on the search area by exchanging the genes on the code according to the probability. The number of data in the area is set by experience. And the data is from the several minimal data in the weight matrix.

The high-light in this paper is Strategy 2, the flow is shown below:

Step 1: Set $a = 1$.
Step 2: If $a \leq PS$, go to Step 3, otherwise stop.
Step 3: For individual a, r is a rand value, ranging from 0 to 1, if $r > 0.5$, go to
 Step 4, otherwise $a = a + 1$, go to Step 3.
Step 4: Set $c = 1$.
Step 5: $1 \leq i \leq CN$, find the area $m_i^* = \arg \max \|AG_i - AG_{im_i}\|_2$.
Step 6: $1 \leq i \leq CN$, move m_i^* areas to the area $j^* = \arg \max \|AG_i - AG_{im_i}\|_2$,
 if $i = j^*$, then m_i^* don't need to move.
Step 7: $c = c + 1$, if $c \leq \lfloor LI \times CL \rfloor$, go to Step 5, otherwise go to Step 2. where
 AG_i is the mean of feature of i-th category, and AG_{ij} the mean of feature of
 j-th area in i-th category, PS is the population scale, CN is the class number
 of image segmentation, LI is learning strengthen, CL is the length of code.
 AG_i is shown in Eq. (3).

$$AG_i = \frac{\sum_{j=1}^{RN_i} \sum_{k=1}^{PN_j} p_{ijk}}{\sum_{j=1}^{RN_i} PN_j} \tag{3}$$

where RN_i is areas number of i-th category, PN_j is the pixels numbers in j-th area, P_{ijk} is the k-th pixels feature vector the j-th area in the i-th category, as Eq. (4).

$$p_{ijk} = (p_{ijk_1}, p_{ijk_2}, ..., p_{ijk_{FN}}) \tag{4}$$

Our method learns on the whole population, the learning strength of every individual is related to the length of code. If the strength is too little, then the learning cant achieve the effect, if it is too much, it is easy to be tripped in the local optimal.

3 Experiment Results and Analysis

3.1 Experiment Setting

In order to evaluate the performance of our method, we take the experiment on texture images, remote sensing images and natural images. As Fig. 1 shows, image (a), (b) and (c) are artificial texture image, their size is 256×256. Image (d) to (f) are remote sensing images, their size is 256×256. The comparative algorithm is FCM and K-means.

From the above analysis, the experiment parameters are set as below. The max iteration is 200. Population scale is 30. MST coding individuals radio is 0.7. Crossover probability is 0.9. Mutation probability is 0.005. The strength of strategy 1 is 0.2. The strength of strategy 2 is 0.5.

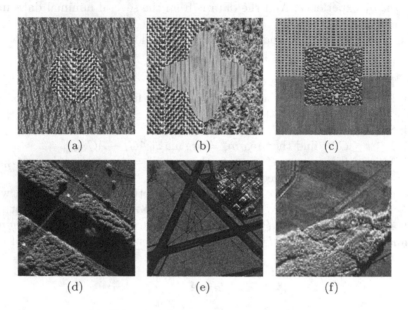

(a)   (b)   (c)

(d)   (e)   (f)

Fig. 1. Test images: (a), (b) and (c) are artificial texture images; (d), (e) and (f) are remote sensing images

3.2   Experiment Results and Analysis

In the experiment, GLCM features and wavelet features are used for texture images, wavelet features and gray features are used for remote sensing images, and wavelet features and gray features are used for nature image. As Fig. 2 shows, from left to right are the results of our method, FCM, and K-means.

For texture images, the results are the best one in visual view absolutely. The results of K-means and FCM have some classification spots and fuzzy boundary. Table 1 is the correct radio of the 30 independent experiment results for our method, FCM, and K-means under same conditions.

From Table 1, the correct radio of our method is higher than K-means and FCM. From the variance of correct radio, we find he correct radio of K-means decrease faster with the number of categories increases, on the contrary, our method is steady, which means our method has better performance and robustness on complex problems.

From the results of remote sensing images and natural images, our method has accuracy on the details, for example, the bridge and bird in image (d) are segmented, but K-means and FCM fail to segment them, even cant distinguish them. Moreover, the segmentation results of image (e) and image (f) can declare that our method maintains consistency in category well.

Image (a)   Image (b)   Image (c)   Image(d)   Image (e)   Image (f)

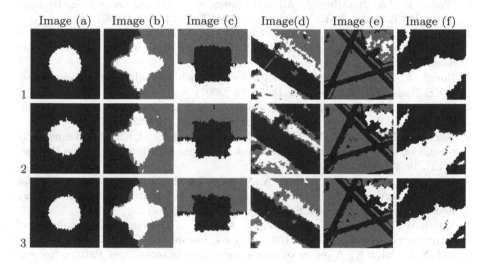

Fig. 2. Experiment results of six test image with three methods: 1 by our method, 2 by FCM and 3 by KM

Table 1. The correct ration of the results

Dataset	Correct ratio(%)		
	Our method	FCM	KM
Image (a)	**98.73**	98.71	98.71
Image (b)	94.57	**94.97**	84.96
Image (c)	**94.32**	93.21	83.56

4 Conclusion

Memetic image segmentation method based on digraph coding is proposed in this paper, the convergence speed is improved through setting initial population by digraph coding and 2 learning strategies. For segmentation problems, the original image watershed segmentation is adopted to transform the operation on pixel to area, which decreases the complexity. In order to evaluate performance of our method, we take the comparative experiments with FCM and K-means on texture images, remote sensing images and natural images, which prove that our method achieves the segmentation for the three images with the best stability and efficiency.

Acknowledgments. This work was supported by the National Natural Science Foundation of China (Grant Nos. 61602385, 61603299).

References

1. Bhanu, B., Lee, S., Ming, J.: Adaptive image segmentation using a genetic algorithm. IEEE Trans. Syst., Man, Cybern. **25**(12), 1543–1567 (1995)
2. Fukuda, S., Hirosawa, H.: A wavelet-based texture feature set applied to classification of multifrequency polarimetric SAR images. IEEE Trans. Geosci. Remote Sens. **37**(5), 2282–2286 (1999)
3. Handl, J., Knowles, J.: An evolutionary approach to multiobjective clustering. IEEE Trans. Evol. Comput. **11**(1), 56–76 (2007)
4. Haralick, R.M., Shanmugam, K., Dinstein, I.: Textural features for image classification. IEEE Trans. Syst., Man, Cybern. SMC-**3**(6), 610–621 (1973)
5. Haris, K., Efstratiadis, S.N., Maglaveras, N., Katsaggelos, A.K.: Hybrid image segmentation using watersheds and fast region merging. IEEE Trans. Image Process. **7**(12), 1684–1699 (1998)
6. Iqbal, K., Odetayo, M.O., James, A.: Content-based image retrieval approach for biometric security using colour, texture and shape features controlled by fuzzy heuristics. J. Comput. Syst. Sci. **78**(4), 1258–1277 (2012)
7. Ku, K.W.C., Mak, M.W., Siu, W.-C.: A study of the lamarckian evolution of recurrent neural networks. IEEE Trans. Evol. Comput. **4**(1), 31–42 (2000)
8. Pal, N.R., Pal, S.K.: A review on image segmentation techniques. Pattern Recogn. **26**(9), 1277–1294 (1993)
9. Patino, L.: Fuzzy relations applied to minimize over segmentation in watershed algorithms. Pattern Recogn. Lett. **26**(6), 819–828 (2005)
10. Peng, B., Zhang, L., Zhang, D.: A survey of graph theoretical approaches to image segmentation. Pattern Recogn. **46**(3), 1020–1038 (2013)
11. Wang, D.: A multiscale gradient algorithm for image segmentation using watersheds. Pattern Recogn. **30**(12), 2043–2052 (1997)
12. Zhang, H., Fritts, J.E., Goldman, S.A.: Image segmentation evaluation: a survey of unsupervised methods. Comput. Vis. Image Underst. **110**(2), 260–280 (2008)

Change Detection in Remote Sensing Images Based on Clonal Selection Algorithm

Tao Wu[1(✉)], Yu Lei[1], and Maoguo Gong[2]

[1] School of Electronics and Information, Northwest Polytechnical University,
ADD: 127 West Youyi Road, Xi'an 710072, Shaanxi, China
tao_woe@mail.nwpu.edu.cn, leiy@nwpu.edu.cn
[2] Key Laboratory of Intelligent Perception and Image Understanding
of Ministry of Education of China, Xidian University,
ADD: 2 South TaiBai Road, Xi'an 710071, Shaanxi, China
gong@ieee.org

Abstract. In this paper we propose a novel change detection method based on clonal selection and optimal entropy threshold. We apply the log-ratio operator to construct the difference image of two temporal images firstly. Then the optimal threshold of the difference image is generated automatically by clonal selection and optimal entropy method. In order to reduce the noise impact of remote sensing images, the results of initial segmentation are morphological processed. Experimental results show that the proposed method is effective and stable.

Keywords: Change detection · Clonal selection · Optimal entropy threshold · Remote sensing image

1 Introduction

The problem of change detection has been treated as a significant issue for decades due to its wide applications in remote sensing [1,4,6,7,9]. In the literatures, it is usually viewed as a process to detect the changes from multi-temporal images, which reflecting the same area but taken at different times. Change detection has been widely used in urban development studies [10,11], land use/cover monitoring [13], damage assessment [12] and environmental investigation. There are two key steps in change detection of remote sensing. The first one is the method of constructing the difference image (DI) of two temporal remote sensing image. The other one is classification of DI included changed and unchanged classes.

Clonal selection algorithm is a new kind of optimization search algorithm that has the function of learning and memory for providing a new approach to information processing. It introduces the affinity function, cloning and memory mechanism based on traditional evolutionary algorithm, and uses the corresponding operator to ensure converging to the global optimal solution quickly [2,3,5,8].

© Springer Nature Singapore Pte Ltd. 2016
M. Gong et al. (Eds.): BIC-TA 2016, Part II, CCIS 682, pp. 467–472, 2016.
DOI: 10.1007/978-981-10-3614-9_58

In this paper, the framework of proposed method is clonal selection algorithm. The difference image denerated by log-ratio operator and using morphologic method to reduce the noise. The remainder of this paper is organized as follow. Section 2 describes the proposed method. Dataset used and experiment results and analysis are presented in Sect. 3. Finally, concluding remarks are presented in Sect. 4.

2   The Proposed Method

The proposed novel change detection method is mainly used in the classification of difference image. The DI consists of unchanged and changed classes in this paper, thus we can transform the classification of the DI into a single image segmentation based on clonal selection optimal entropy threshold.

2.1   Main Steps of the Proposed Algorithm

We defined the antigen as the threshold which maximized the total entropy of image, and the antibody as binary code of the threshold in the processing of image segmentation. The maximum entropy of image is considered as the affinity. Therefore, the optimal threshold of DI is the mature antibody which maximizes the affinity. The main steps of the clonal selection algorithm are as follow:

(1) Generate initial population: Generated a certain number of binary code of threshold randomly. We used 8-bit binary encoding in this algorithm.
(2) Compute the affinity: Compute the value of affinity degree of each antibody in the population and sort them.
(3) Clonal operation: Generate new antibody population by selection, clone, and mutation operators.
(4) Repeat the step 2, 3 until it satisfies the stop criterion.

2.2   Detils of the Proposed Method

Affinity Function. We define the entropy of image based on the concept of Shannon entropy as follow:

$$H(t) = H_o(t) + H_B(t) = \ln p_t(1 - p_t) + \frac{h_t}{p_t} + \frac{H - h_t}{1 - p_t} \tag{1}$$

where t is the threshold to divide target and background, $H_o(t)$ and $H_B(t)$ are the entropy of target and background. Therefore, the optimal threshold t^* of the image equals to the maximize the $H(t)$:

$$t^* = \arg \max_{0 \leq t \leq l-1} H(t) \tag{2}$$

The affinity of antigen and antibody is shown as Eq. (1) in the proposed method. The bigger the entropy, the more accurate the threshold, and the better the segmentation of the DI.

Immune Clonal Operator. We define the clone operation as follow:

$$T_c^C(\bar{A}(l)) = [T_c^C(A_1(l))T_c^C(A_2(l)) \cdots T_c^C(A_k(l))] \tag{3}$$

where $T_c^C(A_i) = A_1 \otimes I_i$, $i = 1, ..., k$, I_i is the q_i-th dimension vector, called q_i clone of antibody A_i. After cloning, the population changed as follow:

$$\bar{A}'(l) = [\bar{A}(l)A_1'(l)A_2'(l) \cdots A_k'(l)] \tag{4}$$

where $A_i'(l) = [A_{i1}(l)A_{i2}(l)...A_{iq_i-1}(l)]$, $A_{ij} = A_i$, $j = 1, ..., q_i - 1$.

The operation that clonal mutation on the antibody population based on the probability of p_m^i aims at keeping the information of original population. To the same purpose, clonal reorganization operation on the new antibody population based on the probability of p_c^i followed by the mutation operation.

For $\forall i = 1, ..., k$, it exist new antibody $B = \{A_{ij}'(l) | \max f(A_{ij}'(l))\}$, where $j = 1, .., q_i - 1$, then the probability of $\bar{A}_l(l) \in \bar{A}(l)$ replaced by B is:

$$f(x) = \begin{cases} 1, & f(A_i) < f(B) \\ \exp\{[-f(A_i) - f(B)/\beta]\}, & f(A_i) \geq f(B), and A_i \neq optimal \\ 0, & f(A_i) \geq f(B), and A_i = optimal \end{cases} \tag{5}$$

where $\beta(\beta > 0)$ is a parameter related to the diversity of antibody population. As usually, β is bigger, the diversity of population is better.

The Selection of Threshold of DI. The difference image generated by log-ratio operator in the proposed method, shown as follow:

$$DI = \log(I_1/I_2) \tag{6}$$

where I_1 and I_2 denote two remote sensing images in different dates, respectively. DI is the difference image.

Because the data distribution of DI generated by log-ratio is different from the normal gray level image which its gray level is between 0 and 255, but the data of DI was not belong to this gray level range and is not an integer but a double number. So we define the transformation formula as follow:

$$DI_{th} = \frac{C_{th} * (DI_{max} - DI_{min})}{256} + DI_{min} \tag{7}$$

where $C_{th}(0 \leq C_{th} \leq 255)$ is the threshold of the primal gray level image automatically produced by clonal selection combined with optimal entropy. DI_{max} and DI_{min} denote the maximum and minimum of the data in DI, respectively. DI_{th} is the final optimal threshold which by transformed.

Morphological Processing of Initial CDI. To further optimize the results of change detection, the morphological processing of dilation and erosion operations with the initial results has been used here. The principle of morphological image processing will be briefly described in the following.

We assume that A is a binary image and B is a structuring element, shown as Fig. 1(a) and (c). The morphological processing of initial CDI is closing of binary image A by the structuring element B, followed by the processing of opening. The initial CDI can be optimized after that. Figure 1(a) and (b) are denoted the CDI which haven't and have been morphological processed, respectively.

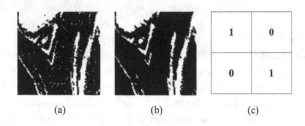

(a)   (b)   (c)

Fig. 1. An illustration of morphological image processing

3   Experiment Results and Analysis

3.1   Criterions in the Analysis of Change Detection Results

In this paper we choose three criterions to evaluate the change detection results in the experiments. Firstly, we calculate the false negatives (FN). The number of pixels that are detected as changed area in reference but detected as unchanged area in the result is defined as FN. Secondly, we calculate the false positives (FP). The number of pixels that detected as unchanged area in reference image but detected as changed area in result is defined as FP. Finally, the overall error (OE) equals to the sum of FN and FP. In addition, we can usually judge the result of them depend on experience, observation and field survey.

3.2   The Experiments Results and Analysis

As described above, there are two datasets used in our experiments. The change detection results of Bern and Ottawa datasets showed in Fig. 2(a) and (b) and respectively. From left to right represent the CDI of K-means clustering (KM), fuzzy C-means clustering (FCM), KI threshold selection method (KI), Ostu threshold (Ostu) and the proposed method in the same experiment conditions in turn.

From Fig. 2, we can see that, the CDI generated by our proposed method is better than that of the other contrast algorithms, shown as having less speckles and being most similar to the reference images. Observed these CDI carefully we can see that the CDI got by Ostu is worst, it means that the threshold spanned by the proposed method is more correctly than that of Ostu. And compared with the reference we can find that loss of areas of CDI got by Ostu haven't been detected yet. In all the contrast methods, the most of detected results got by KM and

FCM are closest to that of the proposed method but the false positives of CDI got by them is much more high than that of proposed method when detected the Bern dataset. The reason may be the Bern dataset are more seriously affected by noise than the other datasets. It proved that the proposed method can produce good results when the SAR images are badly affected by noise. In general, most of changed areas of the datasets can be more exactly detected by the proposed method than that of KM, FCM, KI and Ostu. Although the unchanged class is sometimes detected as changed class by proposed method, the overall error is always can keep lowest. The detailed data as shown in Table 1.

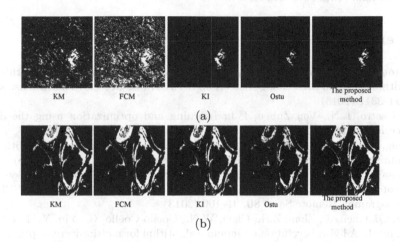

Fig. 2. Change detection images (CDI) of the four datasets

Table 1. Analysis of change detection results

Dataset	Criterion	The algorithm				
		KM	FCM	KI	Ostu	Our method
Bern	FN	34	14	170	622	325
	FP	7543	23902	236	16	74
	OE	7577	23916	406	638	399
Ottawa	FN	1806	1753	2977	7143	1547
	FP	1097	1157	470	38	1322
	OE	2903	2910	3447	7181	2869

4   Conclusion

In this paper, we convert change detection of remote sensing image into an image segmentation problem, and then split the problem into an optimization problem. It is a major innovation. The difference image (DI) of two temporal images is constructed by the ordinary and simple log-ratio operator firstly. Then we focus on how to effectively and accurately dividing DI into the changed and unchanged classes. The optimal threshold of the DI is generated automatically by clonal selection and optimal entropy method. In order to reduce the noise impact of remote sensing images, the results of initial segmentation are morphological processed. The experiments we design shows that transformed the change detection problem into an optimization is effective.

Acknowledgments. This work was supported by the National Natural Science Foundation of China (Grant No. 61603299).

References

1. Carotenuto, V., De Maio, A., Clemente, C., Soraghan, J.J.: Invariant rules for multipolarization SAR change detection. IEEE Trans. Geosci. Remote Sens. **53**(6), 3294–3311 (2015)
2. de Castro, L.N., Von Zuben, F.J.: Learning and optimization using the clonal selection principle. IEEE Trans. Evol. Comput. **6**(3), 239–251 (2002)
3. Gong, M., Jiao, L., Du, H., Bo, L.: Multiobjective immune algorithm with non-dominated neighbor-based selection. Evol. Comput. **16**(2), 225–255 (2008)
4. Hussain, M., Chen, D., Cheng, A., Wei, H., Stanley, D.: Change detection from remotely sensed images: from pixel-based to object-based approaches. ISPRS J. Photogramm. Remote Sens. **80**, 91–106 (2013)
5. Lin, Q., Chen, J., Zhan, Z.H., Chen, W.N., Coello Coello, C., Yin, Y., Lin, C.M., Zhang, J.: A hybrid evolutionary immune algorithm for multiobjective optimization problems. IEEE Trans. Evol. Comput. **PP**(99), 1 (2016)
6. Paglieroni, D.W., Pechard, C.T., Beer, N.R.: Change detection in constellations of buried objects extracted from ground-penetrating radar data. IEEE Trans. Geosci. Remote Sens. **53**(5), 2426–2439 (2015)
7. St-Charles, P.L., Bilodeau, G.A., Bergevin, R.: Subsense: a universal change detection method with local adaptive sensitivity. IEEE Trans. Image Process. **24**(1), 359–373 (2015)
8. Tan, Y.: Artificial Immune System. Wiley-IEEE Press, Hoboken (2016). 208 p
9. Tewkesbury, A.P., Comber, A.J., Tate, N.J., Lamb, A., Fisher, P.F.: A critical synthesis of remotely sensed optical image change detection techniques. Remote Sens. Environ. **160**, 1–14 (2015)
10. Ye, S., Chen, D.: An unsupervised urban change detection procedure by using luminance and saturation for multispectral remotely sensed images. Photogramm. Eng. Remote Sens. **81**(8), 637–645 (2015)
11. Yousif, O., Ban, Y.: Improving SAR-based urban change detection by combining MAP-MRF classifier and nonlocal means similarity weights. IEEE J. Sel. Top. Appl. Earth Obs. Remote Sens. **7**(10), 4288–4300 (2014)
12. Zhang, Q., Antoniou, M., Chang, W., Cherniakov, M.: Spatial decorrelation in GNSS-based SAR coherent change detection. IEEE Trans. Geosci. Remote Sens. **53**(1), 219–228 (2015)
13. Zhu, Z., Woodcock, C.E.: Continuous change detection and classification of land cover using all available landsat data. Remote Sens. Environ. **144**, 152–171 (2014)

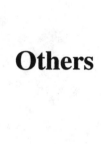

Others

An Improved Algorithm for Constructing Binary Trees Using the Traversal Sequences

Fangxiu Wang[1], Kang Zhou[1(✉)], Huaqing Qi[2], and Bosheng Song[3]

[1] School of Math and Computer, Wuhan Polytechnic University,
Wuhan 430023, China
wfx323@126.com, zhoukang_wh@163.com
[2] Department of Economics and Management, Wuhan Polytechnic University,
Wuhan 430023, China
qihuaqing@sohu.com
[3] School of Automation, Huazhong University of Science and Technology,
Wuhan 430074, Hubei, China
boshengsong@hust.edu.cn

Abstract. The present algorithm can not be applied to construct a binary tree by using the traversal sequences in which there are same elements. That is to say, the previous algorithms require there are not same elements in the binary tree. This paper designs an improved recursive algorithm to solve the problem. Based on the existing recursive algorithm, this algorithm introduces flag sequences for the traversal sequences. According to the relationship among the elements in the flag sequences, it is theoretically proved that there are three recursive algorithms that can construct binary trees from the traversal sequences. Simulation results show that the algorithm designed in this paper can construct binary trees through the traversal sequences in which there are same elements.

Keywords: Preorder traversal · Inorder traversal · Postorder traversal · Flag sequence · Recursive algorithm

1 Introduction

As a typical hierarchical structure, binary trees [1] play a very important role in solving some practical problems in real life. Therefore, it has been a hot issue [2–6] for people to use the traversal sequences to construct a binary tree. Through the research on the properties of the traversal sequences of the binary tree, the researchers have designed a lot of recursive [7,8] and nonrecursive [9–12] [13-16] algorithms for constructing a binary tree from the traversal sequences. However, no matter recursive or non recursive algorithms, they all require there is not any same element in the traversal sequences. Otherwise, this algorithm can not use them to construct a binary tree in which there is even a same element. Obviously, this requirement will greatly limit the application range of the existing algorithms. However, there are same elements in the sequences in

© Springer Nature Singapore Pte Ltd. 2016
M. Gong et al. (Eds.): BIC-TA 2016, Part II, CCIS 682, pp. 475–488, 2016.
DOI: 10.1007/978-981-10-3614-9_59

many cases. For example, as a typical traversal sequence of the binary tree, general arithmetic expression has usually the same operation symbols and operation objects. Therefore, this paper improves the existing recursive algorithm by introducing the flag sequence for the traversal sequence. Algorithm tests show that the improved algorithm does not have any restrictions on the traversal sequence. That is to say, no matter whether the sequences have same elements or not, they can be used to construct the corresponding binary tree by using this algorithm.

2   The Mathematical Model

2.1   The Principle of Using the Preorder Traversal Sequence and in Order Traversal Sequence to Construct a Binary Tree

Theorem 1. If there exist the preorder and inorder traversal sequence of a binary tree, then the binary tree can be constructed uniquely by a recursive algorithm.

Proof. Assume that $X = x_i x_{i+1} \cdots x_j$ and $Y = y_k y_{k+1} \cdots y_l$ are respectively the preorder and inorder traversal sequence of the binary tree T, where T denotes the root node of the binary tree. Taking into account that there may be the same elements in the sequence, we need give a different flag to every element in the sequence so that these flags can be used to distinguish the elements from each other. Therefore, we might as well let $A = a_i a_{i+1} \cdots a_j$ and $B = b_k b_{k+1} \cdots b_l$ be respectively flag sequences of X and Y. Because of the equal length of X and Y, it is easy to find there exists $j - i + 1 = l - k + 1$, namely $j - i = l - k$.

By the properties of the traversal sequence of the binary tree, we have $\{x_i, x_{i+1}, \cdots, x_j\} = \{y_k, y_{k+1}, \cdots, y_l\}$ and $\{a_i, a_{i+1}, \cdots, a_j\} = \{b_k, b_{k+1}, \cdots, b_l\}$. In other words, X and Y are different permutations of the collection of the same elements while as A and B are also different permutations of the collection of the same elements. According to the characteristics of the traversal sequences of the binary tree, the element x_i is the root node of the binary tree T. Because in the inorder traversal sequence B there corresponds a unique positive integer m such that $b_m = a_i$. So y_m is also the root node of the binary tree if we study T from the point of view of the indorder traversal sequence. Therefore, the inorder traversal sequence Y and its flag sequence B can be decomposed in the following forms.

$$\{ Y = (y_k \cdots y_{m-1}) y_m (y_{m+1} \cdots y_l) B = (b_k \cdots b_{m-1}) b_m (b_{m+1} \cdots b_l) \quad (1)$$

By the properties of the inorder traversal sequence, since y_m is the root node of the binary tree, the subsequence $y_k \cdots y_{m-1}$ and the flag sequence $b_k \cdots b_{m-1}$ are respectively the inorder traversal sequence and inorder flag sequence of the left subtree of T. Also, $y_{m+1} \cdots y_l$ and $b_{m+1} \cdots b_l$ are respectively the inorder traversal sequence and inorder flag sequence of the right subtree of the binary tree of T. By the properties of the preorder traversal sequence of a binary tree, there must be a position p in the preorder traversal sequence such that the preorder traversal sequence X and its inorder flag sequence can be decomposed in the following forms.

$$\begin{cases} X = x_i(x_{i+1}\cdots x_p)(x_{p+1}\cdots x_j) \\ A = a_i(a_{i+1}\cdots a_p)(a_{p+1}\cdots a_j) \end{cases} \tag{2}$$

where $x_{i+1}\cdots x_p$ and $a_{i+1}\cdots a_p$ denote respectively the preorder traversal sequence and preorder flag sequence of the left subtree of T, whileas $x_{p+1}\cdots x_j$ and $a_{p+1}\cdots a_j$ denote respectively the preorder traversal sequence and preorder flag sequence of the right subtree of T. To get the two preorder traversal sequences and their preorder flag sequences, we must find the position p under the known condition. Because there is equal length between the preorder traversal subsequence and the inorder traversal subsequence, so we have the following two equations.

$$\{x_{i+1},\cdots,x_p\} = \{y_k,\cdots,y_{m-1}\} \tag{3}$$
$$\{x_{p+1},\cdots,x_j\} = \{y_{m+1},\cdots,y_l\} \tag{4}$$

Knowing that the length of the subsequence is equal according to formulas (3) and (4), so we have

$$p - (i = 1) + 1 = m - 1 - k + 1 \tag{5}$$
$$j - (p + 1) + 1 = l - (m + 1) + 1 \tag{6}$$

On the one hand, the following position p can be obtained from formula (5).

$$p = m + i - k \tag{7}$$

On the other hand, the following position p can be obtained from formula (6).

$$p = m + j - l \tag{8}$$

Because of $j - i = l - k$, we can know that the value of the two positions are equal. That is to say, the position p is unique in the preorder traversal sequence X. According to the position p, subsequences $x_{i+1}\cdots x_p$ and $x_{p+1}\cdots x_j$ can be separated from the preorder traversal. Therefore, we can obtain several different preorder traversal subsequences. On the one hand, $x_{i+1}\cdots x_p$ represents the preorder traversal subsequence of the left subtree of the binary tree T and $y_k\cdots y_{m-1}$ represents the inorder traversal subsequence of the left subtree of the binary tree T. On the other hand, $x_{p+1}\cdots x_j$ represents the preorder traversal subsequence of the left subtree of the binary tree T and $y_{m+1}\cdots y_l$ represents the inorder traversal subsequence of the right subtree of the binary tree T. Similarly, we can not only find the left subtree of T by $x_{i+1}\cdots x_p$, $a_{i+1}\cdots a_p$, $y_k\cdots y_{m-1}$, and $b_k\cdots b_{m-1}$ but also find the right subtree of T by $x_{p+1}\cdots x_j$, $a_{p+1}\cdots a_j$, $y_{m+1}\cdots y_l$, and $b_{m+1}\cdots b_l$. Therefore, it is a recursive process to use the preorder traversal and inorder traversal to construct a binary tree.

On the one hand, its recursive sub structure is as follows.

a. If $m > k$, then we can construct recursively the left subtree of T by $x_{i+1} \cdots x_p$, $a_{i+1} \cdots a_p$, $y_k \cdots y_{m-1}$, and $b_k \cdots b_{m-1}$.

b. If $m < l$, then we can construct recursively the right subtree of T by $x_{p+1} \cdots x_j, a_{p+1} \cdots a_j$, $y_{m+1} \cdots y_l$, and $b_{m+1} \cdots b_l$.

On the other hand, we have the following Recursive termination condition.

a. If $m = k$, then T has not the left subtree.

b. If $m = l$, then T has not the right subtree.

Therefore, the theorem is proved.

In short, we can use the preorder traversal sequence and inorder traversal sequence to construct recursively a binary tree.

2.2 The Principle of Using the Inorder and Postorder Traversal Sequence to Construct a Binary Tree

Theorem 2. If knowing the inorder and postorder traversal sequence of a binary tree, then we can use a recursive algorithm to construct the binary tree.

Proof. Assume that $Y = y_i y_{i+1} \cdots y_j$ and $Z = z_k z_{k+1} \cdots z_l$ respectively are the inorder and postorder traversal sequence of the binary tree T. Assume that furthermore $B = b_i b_{i+1} \cdots b_j$ denotes the inorder flag sequence of Y and $C = c_k c_{k+1} \cdots c_l$ denotes the postorder flag sequence of Z. Because the length of Y and Z is equal, we have $j - i = l - k$. By the relationship between the inorder traversal and the postorder traversal, we have

$$\{y_i, y_{i+1}, \cdots, y_j\} = \{z_k, z_{k+1}, \cdots, z_l\} \tag{9}$$

That is to say, Y and Z are different permutations of the same set of elements. By the properties of the postorder traversal sequence, the element z_l is the root node of the binary tree T. In the inorder flag sequence B there corresponds a unique positive integer m such that $b_m = c_l$, so y_m is the root node of the binary tree T from the perspective of the inorder traversal sequence. Therefore, the inorder traversal sequence and its flag sequence can be divided into the following forms.

$$\begin{cases} Y = (y_i \cdots y_{m-1}) y_m (y_{m+1} \cdots y_j) \\ B = (b_i \cdots b_{m-1}) b_m (b_{m+1} \cdots b_j) \end{cases} \tag{10}$$

By the properties of the inorder traversal sequence, we can know that the sub sequence $y_i \cdots y_{m-1}$ and $b_i \cdots b_{m-1}$ are respectively the inorder traversal sequence and flag sequence of the left subtree of the binary tree T. Similarly, $y_{m+1} \cdots y_j$ and $b_{m+1} \cdots b_j$ are respectively the inorder traversal sequence and inorder flag sequence of the right sub tree of the left subtree of the binary tree T. According to the properties of the postorder traversal sequence of the binary tree, we can know that the postorder traversal sequence Z and its flag sequence C can be divided into the following:

$$\begin{cases} Z = (z_k \cdots z_p)(z_{p+1} \cdots z_{l-1})z_l \\ C = (c_k \cdots c_p)(c_{p+1} \cdots c_{l-1})c_l \end{cases} \tag{11}$$

Where $z_k \cdots z_p$ and $c_k \cdots c_p$ are respectively the postorder traversal sequence and postorder flag sequence of the left subtree of T, whileas $z_{p+1} \cdots z_{l-1}$ and $c_{p+1} \cdots c_{l-1}$ are respectively the postorder traversal sequence and postorder flag sequence of the right subtree of T. According to the relationship between the inorder traversal sequence and the postorder traversal sequence, we have

$$\{z_k, \cdots, z_p\} = \{y_i, \cdots, y_{m-l}\} \tag{12}$$

and

$$\{z_{p+1}, \cdots, z_{l-1}\} = \{y_{m+1}, \cdots, y_j\} \tag{13}$$

Since the subsequences have equal length, we have

$$p - k + 1 = m - 1 - i + 1 \tag{14}$$

and

$$(l - 1) - (p + 1) + 1 = j - (m + 1) + 1 \tag{15}$$

By formulas (14) and (15), we obtain respectively formulas (16) and (17) as follows.

$$p = k + m - i - 1 \tag{16}$$

and

$$p = l + m - j - 1 \tag{17}$$

Because $j - i = l - k$, the p calculated by the two different methods are same. In the same way, we can obtain the left subtree of the binary tree from the inorder traversal subsequence $y_i \cdots y_{m-l}$, the inorder flag subsequence $b_i \cdots b_{m-l}$, the postorder traversal subsequence $z_k \cdots z_p$, and postorder flag subsequence $c_k \cdots c_p$. Similarly, we can obtain the right subtree of the binary tree from the inorder traversal subsequence $y_{m+1} \cdots y_j$, the inorder falg subsequence $b_{m+1} \cdots b_j$, the postorder traversal subsequence $z_{p+1} \cdots z_{l-1}$ and the postorder flag subsequence $c_{p+1} \cdots c_{l-1}$. Therefore, it is a recursive process which uses the inorder traversal sequence and the postorder traversal sequence to construct a binary tree.

According to the recursive principle of the process, it is not difficult to find that the recursive sub structure is as follows.

a. If $m > i$, then we can use $y_i \cdots y_{m-l}$, $b_i \cdots b_{m-l}, z_k \cdots z_p$, and $c_k \cdots c_p$ to construct recursively the left subtree of T.

b. If $m < j$, then we can use $y_{m+1} \cdots y_j$, $b_{m+1} \cdots b_j$, $z_{p+1} \cdots z_{l-1}$, and $c_{p+1} \cdots c_{l-1}$ to construct recursively the right subtree of T.

c. If $m = i$, then T has not left subtree. If $m = j$, then T has not the right subtree. All this are the recursive termination conditions of the establishment of the binary tree.

2.3 The Principle of Using the Preorder and Postorder Traversal Sequence to Construct a Binary Tree

Theorem 3. If knowing the preorder and postorder traversal sequence of a binary tree and there isn't any node whose outdegree is one in the binary tree, then we can use a recursive algorithm to construct the binary tree.

Proof. Let $X = x_i x_{i+1} \cdots x_j$ and $Z = z_k z_{k+1} \cdots z_l$ respectively be the preorder and postorder traversal sequence of the binary tree T. Let $A = a_i a_{i+1} \cdots a_j$ be the preorder flag sequence of T and $C = c_k c_{k+1} \cdots c_l$ be the postorder flag sequence of Z. Similarly, because the length of X and Z is equal, we have $j - i = l - k$. By the relationship between the preorder traversal sequence and the postorder traversal sequence, there exists $x_i = z_l$, they are both the root node of the binsry tree T. In the postorder flag sequence C there corresponds a unique positive integer m such that $c_m = a_{i+1}$, so the postorder traversal sequence Z and its flag sequence C can be divided into the following forms.

$$\begin{cases} Z = (z_k \cdots z_m)(z_{m+1} \cdots z_{l-1}) z_l \\ C = (c_k \cdots c_m)(c_{m+1} \cdots c_{l-1}) c_l \end{cases} \tag{18}$$

By the properties of the postorder traversal sequence, the subsequences $z_k \cdots z_m$ and $c_k \cdots c_m$ are respectively the postorder traversal sequence and postorder flag sequence of the left subtree of T. Likewise, the subsequences $z_{m+1} \cdots z_{l-1}$ and $c_{m+1} \cdots c_{l-1}$ are respectively the postorder traversal sequence and postorder flag sequence of the right subtree of T. According to the properties of the preorder traversal sequence of the binary tree, the preorder traversal sequence X and its flag sequence A can be divided into the following cases:

$$\begin{cases} X = x_i(x_{i+1} \cdots x_p)(x_{p+1} \cdots x_j) \\ A = a_i(a_{i+1} \cdots a_p)(a_{p+1} \cdots a_j) \end{cases} \tag{19}$$

Where $x_{i+1} \cdots x_p$ and $a_{i+1} \cdots a_p$ are respectively the preorder traversal sequence and preorder flag sequence of the left subtree, whileas $x_{p+1} \cdots x_j$ and $a_{p+1} \cdots a_j$ are respectively the preorder traversal sequence and preorder flag sequence of the right subtree. Obviously, we have

$$\{z_k, \cdots, z_m\} = \{x_{i+1}, \cdots, x_p\} \tag{20}$$

and

$$\{z_{m+1}, \cdots, z_{l-1}\} = \{x_{p+1}, \cdots, x_j\} \tag{21}$$

Since the subsequences have same length, we have

$$p - i - 1 = m - k \tag{22}$$

and

$$(l-1) - (m+1) = j - (p+1) \tag{23}$$

By formulas (22) and (23), we have respectively the following two representations.

$$p = i + m - k + 1 \tag{24}$$

and

$$p = j + m - l + 1 \tag{25}$$

By $j-i = l-k$, it is very easy to find the formulas (24) and (25) are equivalent. Therefore, by the preorder traversal sub sequence $x_{i+1} \cdots x_p$, $a_{i+1} \cdots a_p$ and the postorder traversal subsequences $z_k \cdots z_m$, we can obtain the left subtree of the binary tree T. In the same way, by the preorder traversal subsequences $x_{p+1} \cdots x_j$, $a_{p+1} \cdots a_j$ and the postorder traversal subsequences $z_{m+1} \cdots z_{l-1}$, $c_{m+1} \cdots c_{l-1}$, we can obtain the right subtree of the binary tree T. Therefore, it is a recursive process which can construct a binary tree by using the preorder traversal sequence and the postorder traversal sequence.

The recursive sub structures and recursive termination conditions of the recursive construction of the binary tree are expressed as follows:

a. If $m > i$, then we can use $x_{i+1} \cdots x_p$, $a_{p+1} \cdots a_j$, $z_k \cdots z_m$ and $c_k \cdots c_m$ to construct recursively the left subtree of T.

b. If $m < j$, then we can use $x_{p+1} \cdots x_j$, $a_{p+1} \cdots a_j$, $z_{m+1} \cdots z_{l-1}$, and $c_{m+1} \cdots c_{l-1}$ to construct recursively the right subtree of T.

c. If $m = i$, then T is the leaf node of the binary tree, namely T has neither the left child nor the right child. This is the recursive termination condition.

3   The Algorithm Design of Using the Traversal Sequences to Construct a Binary Tree

3.1   Use the Preorder Traversal Sequence and Inorder Traversal Sequence to Construct a Binary Tree

For the convenience of the algorithm design, let $T = f(X, A, Y, B, i, j, k, l)$ be the recursive function of constructing the binary tree, then the recursive process can be described as follows:

a. From the preorder traversal sequence $X = x_i x_{i+1} \cdots x_j$, we know the first element x_i in T is the root node of the binary tree T.

b. We find the location m in the inorder flag sequence B such that $b_m = a_i$.

c. If $m = k$, then the root node of T has not the left child. Otherwise, the left child of the root node of the binary tree T is the root node of the left subtree. Let T_l be the left child, then there are

$$T_l = f(X, A, Y, B, i+1, m+i-k, k, m-1) \tag{26}$$

or

$$T_l = f(X, A, Y, B, i+1, m+j-l, k, m-1) \tag{27}$$

d. If $m = l$, then the root node of T has not the right child. Otherwise, the right child of the root node of the binary tree T is the root node of the right subtree. Let T_r be the right child, then there are

$$T_r = f(X, A, Y, B, m + i - k + 1, j, m + 1, l) \tag{28}$$

or

$$T_r = f(X, A, Y, m + j - l + 1, j, m + 1, l) \tag{29}$$

e. When the recursive process is over, we can obtain a binary tree whose root node is T.

3.2 Use the Inorder and Postorder Traversal Sequence to Construct a Binary Tree

In order to facilitate the algorithm description, let $T = g(Y, B, Z, C, i, j, k, l)$ be a recursive function which is used to construct a binary tree. The recursive process is described as follows:

a. The element z_l in the postorder traversal sequence $Z = z_k z_{k+1} \cdots z_l$ is the root node of the binary tree.
b. The position m needs to be found in the inorder flag sequence B such that $b_m = c_l$.
c. If $m = i$, then the binary tree T has not the left subtree. Otherwise, the root node of the left subtree of the binary tree T is as follows:

$$g(Y, B, Z, C, i, m - 1, k, m + k - i - 1) \tag{30}$$

or

$$g(Y, B, Z, C, i, m - 1, k, l + n - j - 1) \tag{31}$$

d. If $m = j$, then the binary tree T has not the right subtree. Otherwise, the root node of the right subtree of the binary tree T is as follows:

$$g(Y, B, Z, C, m + 1, j, k + m - i, l - 1) \tag{32}$$

or

$$g(Y, B, Z, C, m + 1, j, l + m - j, l - 1) \tag{33}$$

3.3 Use the Preorder and Postorder Traversal Sequence to Construct a Binary Tree

In order to facilitate the algorithm description, let $T = h(X, A, Z, C, i, j, k, l)$ be a recursive function which is used to construct a binary tree, the recursive process is described as follows:

a. The element x_i in the preorder traversal sequence $X = x_i x_{i+1} \cdots x_j$ is the root node of the binary tree T.

b. The position m needs to be found in the postorder flag sequence C such that $c_m = a_{i+1}$.

c. If $j = i$ or $l = k$, then the binary tree has neither the left subtree nor the right subtree. Otherwise, the root node of the left subtree of the binary tree is as follows:

$$h(X, A, Z, C, i+1, i+m-k+1, k, m) \tag{34}$$

or

$$h(X, A, Z, C, i+1, j+m-l+1, k, m) \tag{35}$$

and the root node of the right subtree of the binary tree is as follows:

$$h(X, A, Z, C, i+m-k+2, j, m+1, l-1) \tag{36}$$

or

$$h(X, A, Z, C, j+m-l+2, j, m+1, l-1) \tag{37}$$

4   Algorithm Simulation

Example. Use respectively the above three algorithms to construct the binary tree which is a arithmetic expression shown in Fig. 1.

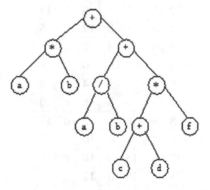

Fig. 1. a*b+(a/b+(c+d)*f)

Solution. From the binary tree as shown in Fig. 1, we can see both the same computing objects and the same operaters appear in the binary tree. Where the computing objects a and b both appear two times in the binary tree, and the operater + appears three times, and operater * appears two times in the

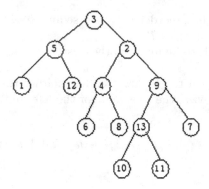

Fig. 2. The corresponding integer flag of the elements in the binary tree

binary tree. Therefore, the binary tree can not be constructed by the traditional algorithm. In order to distinguish the same elements from each other in the binary tree, every element in the tree needs be given a different integer flag. Figure 2 shows the corresponding integer flag assigned to each element in the binary tree.

Thus, the traversal sequence and flag sequences shown in Table 1 can be obtained from the Figs. 1 and 2.

Table 1. The traversal sequences and flag sequences of the binary tree

i	x_i	a_i	y_i	b_i	z_i	c_i
1	+	3	a	1	a	1
2	*	5	*	5	b	12
3	a	1	b	12	*	5
4	b	12	+	3	a	6
5	+	2	a	6	b	8
6	/	4	/	4	/	4
7	a	6	b	8	c	10
8	b	8	+	2	d	11
9	*	9	c	10	+	13
10	+	13	+	13	f	7
11	e	10	d	11	*	9
12	d	11	*	9	+	2
13	f	7	f	7	+	3

In Table 1, $X = x_1 x_2 \cdots x_{13}$ and $A = a_1 a_2 \cdots a_{13}$ respectively represent the preorder traversal sequence and preorder flag sequence of the binary tree, $Y = y_1 y_2 \cdots y_{13}$ and $B = b_1 b_2 \cdots b_{13}$ respectively represent the inorder traversal sequence and inorder flag sequence of the binary tree, whileas $Z = z_1 z_2 \cdots z_{13}$

and $C = c_1 c_2 \cdots c_{13}$ respectively represent the postorder traversal sequence and postorder flag sequence of the binary tree.

Method 1. According to the algorithm 3.1 and the preorder traversal sequence and its preorder flag sequence, and the inorder traversal sequence and its inorder flag sequence, the construction of the bianry tree process is as follows:

a. The root node $x_1(+)$ of the binary tree and $m = 4$ are obtained from $f(X, A, Y, B, 1, 13, 1, 13)$. On the one hand, the left child $x_2(*)$ of $x_1(+)$ and $m = 2$ are obtained from $f(X, A, Y, B, 2, 4, 1, 3)$. On the other hand, the right child $x_5(*)$ of $x_1(+)$ and $m = 8$ are obtained from $f(X, A, Y, B, 5, 13, 5, 13)$.

b. On the one hand, the left child $x_3(a)$ of $x_2(*)$ and $m = 1$ are obtained from $f(X, A, Y, B, 3, 3, 1, 1)$. On the other hand, the right child $x_4(b)$ of $x_2(*)$ and $m = 3$ are obtained from $f(X, A, Y, B, 4, 4, 3, 3)$. Obviously, $x_3(a)$ and $x_4(b)$ have neither the lfet child nor the right child.

c. $x_3(a)$ has neither the left child nor the right child from $f(X, A, Y, B, 3, 3, 1, 1)$ and $m = 1$.

d. $x_4(b)$ has neither the left child nor the right child from $f(X, A, Y, B, 4, 4, 3, 3)$ and $m = 3$.

e. On the one hand, the left child $x_6(/)$ of $x_5(+)$ and $m = 6$ are obtained from $f(X, A, Y, B, 5, 7, 6, 8)$. On the other hand, the right child $x_9(*)$ of $x_5(+)$ and $m = 12$ are obtained from $f(X, A, Y, B, 9, 13, 9, 13)$.

f. On the one hand, the left child $x_7(a)$ of $x_6(/)$ and $m = 5$ are obtained from $f(X, A, Y, B, 7, 7, 5, 5)$. On the other hand, the right child $x_8(b)$ of $x_6(/)$ and $m = 5$ are obtained from $f(X, A, Y, B, 8, 8, 7, 7)$.

g. $x_7(a)$ has neither the left child nor the right child from $f(X, A, Y, B, 7, 7, 5, 5)$ and $m = 5$.

h. $x_7(a)$ has neither the lfet child nor the right child from $f(X, A, Y, B, 8, 8, 7, 7)$ and $m = 7$.

i. On the one hand, the left child $x_{10}(+)$ of $x_9(*)$ and $m = 10$ are obtained from $f(X, A, Y, B, 10, 12, 9, 11)$. On the other hand, the right child $x_{13}(f)$ of $x_9(*)$ and $m = 13$ are obtained from $f(X, A, Y, B, 13, 13, 13, 13)$.

j. On the one hand, the left child $x_{11}(c)$ of $x_{10}(+)$ and $m = 9$ are obtained from $f(X, A, Y, B, 11, 11, 9, 9)$. On the other hand, the right child $x_{12}(d)$ of $x_{10}(+)$ and $m = 11$ are obtained from $f(X, A, Y, B, 12, 12, 11, 11)$.

k. $x_{11}(c)$ has neither the lfet child nor the right child from $f(X, A, Y, B, 11, 11, 9, 9)$ and $m = 9$.

l. $x_{12}(d)$ has neither the lfet child nor the right child from $f(X, A, Y, B, 12, 12, 11, 11)$ and $m = 11$.

m. $x_{13}(f)$ has neither the lfet child nor the right child from $f(X, A, Y, B, 13, 13, 13, 13)$ and $m = 13$.

Through the above process, it is easy to get the relationship between the all elements in the binary tree. We have made the following Table 2.

In Table 2, m denotes the position of the root node in the inorder traversal sequence, m_1 denotes the position of the left child in the inorder traversal sequence, and m_2 denotes the position of the right child in the inorder traversal sequence.

Table 2. The relationship between the elements in the binary tree

i	$root$	$lchild$	$rchild$	m	m_1	m_2
1	$x_1(+)$	$x_2(*)$	$x_5(+)$	4	2	8
2	$x_2(*)$	$x_3(a')$	$x_4(b)$	2	1	3
3	$x_3(a)$	$NULL$	$NULL$	1	0	0
4	$x_4(b)$	$NULL$	$NULL$	3	0	0
5	$x_5(+)$	$x_6(/)$	$x_9(*)$	8	6	12
6	$x_6(/)$	$x_7(a)$	$x_8(b)$	6	5	7
7	$x_7(a)$	$NULL$	$NULL$	5	0	0
8	$x_8(b)$	$NULL$	$NULL$	7	0	0
9	$x_9(*)$	$x_{10}(+)$	$x_{13}(f)$	12	10	13
10	$x_{10}(f)$	$x_{11}(c)$	$x_{12}(d)$	10	9	11
11	$x_{11}(c)$	$NULL$	$NULL$	9	0	0
12	$x_{12}(d)$	$NULL$	$NULL$	11	0	0
13	$x_{13}(f)$	$NULL$	$NULL$	13	0	0

Method 2. According to algorithm 2.2 and the inorder traversal sequence and its flag sequence, and the postorder traversal sequence and its flag sequence, the construction process of the binary tree is as follows:

a. We can obtain the root node $z_{13}(+)$ of the binary tree and $m = 4$ from $g(Y, B, Z, C, 1, 13, 1, 13)$.

b. When $m = 4$, we can obtain $z_3(*)$ which is the left child of $z_{13}(+)$ and $m = 4$ from $g(Y, B, Z, C, 1, 3, 1, 3)$. Likewise, we can obtain $z_{12}(+)$ which is the right child of $z_{13}(+)$ and $m = 8$ from $g(Y, B, Z, C, 5, 13, 4, 12)$.

c. When $m = 2$, we can obtain $z_1(a)$ which is the left child of $z_3(*)$ from $g(Y, B, Z, C, 1, 1, 1, 1)$ and obtain $z_2(b)$ which is the right child of $z_3(*)$ from $g(Y, B, Z, C, 3, 3, 2, 2)$.

d. On the one hand, we can obtain $z_6(/)$ which is the left child of $z_{12}(+)$ and $m = 6$ from $m = 8$ and $g(Y, B, Z, C, 5, 7, 4, 6)$. On the other hand, we can obtain $z_{11}(*)$ which is the right child of $z_{12}(+)$ and $m = 12$ from $g(Y, B, Z, C, 9, 13, 7, 1)$ and $m = 8$.

e. On the one hand, we can obtain $z_4(a)$ which is the left child of $z_6(/)$ from $m = 6$ and $g(Y, B, Z, C, 5, 5, 4, 4)$. On the other hand, we can obtain $z_5(b)$ which is the right child of $z_6(/)$ from $g(Y, B, Z, C, 7, 7, 5, 5)$ and $m = 6$.

f. On the one hand, we can obtain $z_9(+)$ which is the left child of $z_{11}(*)$ and $m = 10$ from $m = 12$ and $g(Y, B, Z, C, 9, 11, 7, 9)$. On the other hand, we can obtain $z_{10}(f)$ which is the right child of $z_{11}(*)$ from $g(Y, B, Z, C, 13, 10, 13, 10)$ and $m = 10$.

g. On the one hand, we can obtain $z_7(c)$ which is the left child of $z_9(+)$ from $g(Y, B, Z, C, 9, 9, 7, 7)$ and $m = 10$. On the other hand, we can obtain $z_8(d)$ which is the right child of $z_9(+)$ from $g(Y, B, Z, C, 11, 11, 8, 8)$ and $m = 10$.

Method 3. According to algorithm 2.3 and the preorder traversal sequence and its flag sequence, and the postorder traversal sequence and its flag sequence, the construction process of the binary tree is as follows:

a. We can obtain the root node $x_1(+)$ of the binary tree and $m = 3$ from $h(X, A, Z, C, 1, 13, 1, 13)$.

b. On the one hand, we can obtain $x_2(*)$ which is the left child of $x_1(+)$ and $m = 1$ from $m = 3$ and $h(X, A, Z, C, 2, 4, 1, 3)$. On the other hand, we can obtain $x_5(+)$ which is the right child of $x_1(+)$ and $m = 6$ from $h(X, A, Z, C, 5, 13, 4, 12)$ and $m = 3$.

c. On the one hand, we can obtain $x_3(a)$ which is the left child of $x_2(*)$ from $m = 1$ and $h(X, A, Z, C, 3, 3, 1, 1)$. On the other hand, we can obtain $x_4(b)$ which is the right child of $x_2(*)$ from $h(X, A, Z, C, 4, 4, 2, 2)$ and $m = 1$.

d. On the one hand, we can obtain $x_6(/)$ which is the left child of $x_5(+)$ and $m = 4$ from $m = 6$ and $h(X, A, Z, C, 6, 8, 4, 6)$. On the other hand, we can obtain $x_9(*)$ which is the right child of $x_5(+)$ and $m = 9$ from $h(X, A, Z, C, 9, 13, 7, 11)$ and $m = 6$.

e. On the one hand, we can obtain $x_7(a)$ which is the left child of $x_6(/)$ from $m = 4$ and $h(X, A, Z, C, 7, 7, 4, 4)$. On the other hand, we can obtain $x_8(b)$ which is the right child of $x_6(/)$ from $h(X, A, Z, C, 8, 8, 5, 5)$ and $m = 4$.

f. On the one hand, we can obtain $x_{11}(c)$ which is the left child of $x_{10}(+)$ from $m = 7$ and $h(X, A, Z, C, 11, 11, 9, 9)$. On the other hand, we can obtain $x_{12}(d)$ which is the right child of $x_{10}(+)$ from $h(X, A, Z, C, 12, 12, 8, 8)$ and $m = 7$.

5 Conclusions

If there exist the same elements in the traversal sequence, the existing algorithms can not construct the binary tree according to the traversal sequences. In this paper, the existing recursive algorithm is improved by introducing the flag sequence such that the improved algorithm is suitable for any traversal sequences. Namely, no matter the sequence has the same elements in the traversal sequences or not, the improved algorithm is effective. Algorithm simulation shows that the proposed algorithm is effective for the construction of any binary tree whose traversal sequences have the same elements in the traversal sequences. Because the algorithm has not any restriction requirement to the traversal sequence, the application scope of the algorithm is greatly extended.

Although the recursive algorithm has not only a clear structure but also convenient design of the algorithm, the recursive algorithm has lower operating efficiency and the computation time and the storage space occupied by the recursive algorithm are much more than that of the nonrecursive algorithm. Therefore, the nonrecursive algorithm is the next research direction. In addition, the algorithm has not yet been studied by using the level traversal sequence and other traversal sequences to construct a binary tree, so it is also the direction of future research.

Acknowledgments. This project was supported by National Natural Science Foundation of China (Grant No. 61179032), the Special Scientific Research Fund of Food Public Welfare Profession of China(Grant No. 201513004-3) and the Research and Practice Project of Graduate Education Teaching Reform of Wuhan Polytechnic University (YZ2015002).

References

1. Yan, Y.M., Wu, W.M.: Data Structure. Tsinghua University Press, Beijing (1992)
2. Xiang, L.M., Lawi, A., Ushijima, K.: On constructing a binary tree from its traversals. Res. Rep. Inf. Sci. Electr. Eng. Kyushu Univ. **5**(1), 13–18 (2000)
3. Mikinen, E.: Constructing a binary tree efficiently from its traversals. Int. J. Comput. Math. **75**, 143–147 (2000)
4. Tang, Z.L.: Algorithm of constructing tree based on ergodic sequence. J. Suzhou Univ. Nat. Sci. Ed. **27**, 26–29 (2011)
5. Tang, Z.L.: An efficient algorithm for constructing a strict binary tree based on the preorder traversal sequence and the left child of the node. J. Nantong Univ. Nat. Sci. Ed. **3**, 9–13 (2013)
6. Tang, Z.L.: A non recursive algorithm for constructing a strict binary tree by the parents of the nodes and the postorder traversal sequence. J. Nantong Vocat. Coll. **12**, 93–98 (2014)
7. Lu, L.: A non recursive algorithm for constructing a binary tree by the traversal sequences. J. Hengshui Univ. **8**, 37–40 (2009)
8. Wang, F.X., Zhou, K.: Establishment of the binary tree based on the sort binary tree. J. Wuhan Polytechnic Univ. **9**, 53–57 (2013)
9. Li, L.S.: An algorithm using the traversal sequences to construct a binary tree. J. Radio TV Univ. **3**, 53–54 (2010)
10. Zhao, G., Li, K.: Using the traversal sequences to determine the binary tree. J. Nanchang Univ. Aeronaut. Astronaut. **24**, 55–59 (2013)
11. Zhu, T.: Reconstruction analysis of the binary tree based on the traversal sequences. J. Honghe Univ. **4**, 27–30 (2013)
12. Hua, Z.Z.: A new method and proof for recovery of the binary tree based on the traversal sequences. J. Jiangxi Normal Univ. **5**, 268–272 (2013)

Improved Multi-step Iterative Algorithms for the Fixed Points of Strongly Pseudo-Contractive Mappings

Jiangrong Liu[1,2], Kang Zhou[1,2(⊠)], Shan Zeng[1,2], Huaqing Qi[1,2],
Bosheng Song[2,3], and Tingfang Wu[2,3]

[1] Department of Math and Computer, Wuhan Polytechnic University,
Wuhan 430023, Hubei, China
liujrjj@163.com, zhoukang_wh@163.com, zengshan1981@whpu.edu.cn,
qihuaqing@sohu.com
[2] Department of Economics and Management, Wuhan Polytechnic University,
Wuhan 430023, Hubei, China
[3] Key Laboratory of Image Information Processing and Intelligent Control School
of Automation, Huazhong University of Science and Technology,
Wuhan 430074, Hubei, China
tfwu@hust.edu.cn

Abstract. In Banach Spaces, we introduce a new improved multi-step
iterative algorithm for the fixed points of strongly pseudo-contractive
mappings, by proving the convergence for modified Mann iterative
sequence, and that the multi-step iterative sequence and Mann iterative
scheme are equivalent. We prove the convergence of iterative sequences
generalized by the improved multi-step iterative algorithms. The results
extend and improve the corresponding related results.

Keywords: Strongly pseudo-contractive mappings · Improved multi-
step iterative algorithms · Fixed point · Convergence · L-Lipschitz
continuous

1 Introduction

The variational inequality theory is a very powerful tool of current mathematical technology. They have been extended and generalized to study a wide class
of problems arising in mechanics, physics, optimization and control, operation
research, economics and transportation equilibrium etc. One of the most important questions is the development of iterative algorithms. There have been a
number of recent results [1–5] on fixed point and convergence of Mann and
Ishikawa iteration for all kinds of nonlinear mapping. Chidume [6], in 2001, gave
an example to us that Mann iteration converges, but Ishikawa iteration doesn't
converge. In 2002, Noor [7] introduced Multi-step iteration, and Glowinski [8]
used Multi-step iterative algorithm solve liquid crystal theory and eigenvalue
calculate. These algorithms have been widely applied to all kinds of variational

© Springer Nature Singapore Pte Ltd. 2016
M. Gong et al. (Eds.): BIC-TA 2016, Part II, CCIS 682, pp. 489–496, 2016.
DOI: 10.1007/978-981-10-3614-9_60

inequalities and variational inclusions. In 2007, Huang [2] proved Equivalence theorems of the convergence between Ishikawa and Mann iterations.

In this paper, we introduce a new improved multi-step iterative algorithm. By proving the convergence for modified Mann iterative sequence and the equivalence of the multi-step iterative sequence and Mann iterative scheme, we prove the convergence of iterative sequences generalized by the proved multi-step iterative algorithms. And illustrate the improved multi-step iterative algorithms is feasible. The results extend and improve the corresponding related results.

2   Preliminaries

Throughout this article, we always assume that E is a Banach space, and K is a convex subset of E. And E^* is the duality space of E.

We denote by the normalized duality mapping $J : E \to 2^{E^*}$ defined by

$$J(x) = \{f \in E^* : <x, f> = ||x||^2 = ||f||^2\}, x \in E.$$

Where $<\cdot, \cdot>$ denotes the generalized duality pairing.

Definition 2.1. Let $T : K \to K$ be a mapping, T is said to be uniformly L-Lipschitz continuous. If for every $x, y \in K$, there exists $L > 0$, such that

$$||Tx - Ty|| \leq L||x - y||, n \geq 1.$$

Definition 2.2. Let $T : D(T) \to E$ be a mapping, T is said to generalized φ-strongly pseudo-contractive. If $\{\lambda_n\} \subset [1, +\infty)$, $\lim_{n\to\infty} \lambda_n = 1$, $j(x-y) \in J(x-y)$, There exists a non-decreasing function $\varphi : [0, +\infty) \to [0, +\infty)$, satisfying $\varphi(0) = 0$, such that

$$||T_i^n x - T_i^n y|| \leq \lambda_n ||x - y||^2 - \varphi(||x - y||), n \geq 1.$$

Lemma 2.1. [9] Let E be a Banach space, then for any $x, y \in E$,

$$||x + y||^2 \leq ||x||^2 + 2\cdot < y, j(x + y) >, j(x + y) \in J(x + y)).$$

Lemma 2.2. [10] Let $\varphi : [0, +\infty) \to [0, +\infty)$ be non-decreasing function, $\varphi(0) = 0$. And let $\{h_n\}, \{\mu_n\}, \{\sigma_n\}$ be three non-negative real sequences satisfying the following conditions

$$h_{n+1}^2 \leq h_n^2 - \mu_n \varphi(h_{n+1}) + \sigma_n, \sum_{n=1}^{\infty} \mu_n = \infty, \sigma_n = o(\mu_n).$$

Then

$$\lim_{n\to\infty} h_n = 0.$$

3   Algorithms

Let E be a Banach Space, and K be a convex subset of E. Let R_i^n, S_j^n, T_k^n be l, m and n mappings.

Algorithm 3.1. Given $x_0 \in K$, we can get an algorithm for (3.1) as follows:

$$
\begin{cases}
x_{n+1} = (1 - \alpha_n)x_n + \alpha_n \sum_{i=1}^{l} r_i R_i^n z_n \\
z_n = (1 - \beta_n)x_n + \beta_n \sum_{j=1}^{m} s_j S_j^n y_n \\
y_n = (1 - \gamma_n)x_n + \gamma_n \sum_{k=1}^{r} t_k T_k^n x_n
\end{cases}
\tag{1}
$$

Where

$$
n = 1, 2, \cdots.r_i, s_j, t_k \in [0, 1], \sum_{i=1}^{l} r_i = \sum_{j=1}^{m} s_j = \sum_{k=1}^{r} t_k = 1.
$$

which is called modified multi-step iterative algorithms.

Algorithm 3.2. If $\gamma_n = \beta_n = 0$, then the algorithm is

$$
u_{n+1} = (1 - \alpha_n)u_n + \alpha_n \sum_{i=1}^{l} r_i R_i^n u_n
\tag{2}
$$

Where

$$
n = 1, 2, \cdots.r_i \in [0, 1], \sum_{i=1}^{l} r_i = 1.
$$

which is called modified Mann iterative algorithm.

4   Convergence and Equivalence

Theorem 4.1. [11] Let E be a Banach Space, and K be a convex subset of E. Let $R_i^n : K \to K$ be l uniformly L-Lipschitz continuous and generalized φ-strongly pseudo-contractive mappings. $\{\lambda_n\} \subset [1, +\infty]$, and $\lim_{n\to\infty} \lambda_n = 1$ Let $\{\alpha_n\}$ be a real sequence satisfying the following conditions

$$
\sum_{n=0}^{\infty} \alpha_n = 0, \sum_{n=0}^{\infty} \alpha_n(\lambda_n - 1) < \infty.
$$

If the fixed point sets $F = \cap_{i=1}^{l} F(R_i) \neq \Phi$ of R_i in K, then the Mann iterative sequence $\{x_n\}$ defined by (3.2) convergences strongly to the unique fixed point of T in K.

Theorem 4.2. Let E be a Banach Space, and K be a convex subset of E. Let $R_i^n, S_j^n, T_k^n : K \to K$ be m, l and r uniformly L-Lipschitz continuous and generalized φ–strongly pseudo-contractive mappings. $\{\lambda_n\} \subset [1, +\infty)$, and $\lim_{n\to\infty} \lambda_n = 1$. Let $\{\alpha_n\}, \{\beta_n\}, \{\gamma_n\}$ be three real sequences satisfying following conditions:

$$\sum_{n=0}^{\infty} \alpha_n = 0, \sum_{n=0}^{\infty} \beta_n = 0, \sum_{n=0}^{\infty} \alpha_n \beta_n < \infty, \sum_{n=0}^{\infty} \alpha_n \beta_n \gamma_n < \infty$$

If the fixed point sets $F = (\cap_{i=1}^{l} F(R_i)) \bigcap (\cap_{j=1}^{m} F(S_j)) \bigcap (\cap_{k=1}^{r} F(T_k)) \neq \Phi$ and $x^* \in F$, then the two results are equivalent:

(1) The improved multi-step iterative sequence defined by (1) convergences strongly to the unique fixed point x^*.
(2) The Mann iterative sequence defined by (2) convergences strongly to the unique fixed point x^*.

Proof. (1) $\Rightarrow$ (2) Let $\gamma_n = \beta_n = 0$, we have

$$x_{n+1} = (1 - \alpha_n)x_n + \alpha_n \sum_{i=1}^{l} r_i R_i^n x_n$$

So (1) $\Rightarrow$ (2) is proved.

(2) $\Rightarrow$ (1) From Algorithm 3.1 and Lemma 2.1, Let $x_{n+1} - u_{n+1} = h_{n+1}$, Then $x_n - u_n = h_n$. Using uniformly L-Lipschitz continuous, we have

$$\begin{aligned}
||h_{n+1}||^2 &= ||x_{n+1} - u_{n+1}||^2 \\
&= ||(1 - \alpha_n)(x_n - u_n) + \alpha_n \sum_{i=1}^{l} r_i(R_i^n z_n - R_i^n u_n)||^2 \\
&\leq (1 - \alpha_n)^2 ||h_n||^2 + 2\alpha_n \cdot < \sum_{i=1}^{l} r_i(R_i^n z_n - R_i^n u_n)||^2, j(h_{n+1}) > \\
&\leq (1 - \alpha_n)^2 ||h_n||^2 + 2\alpha_n \cdot < \sum_{i=1}^{l} r_i(R_i^n z_n - R_i^n x_{n+1})||^2, j(h_{n+1}) > \\
&+ 2\alpha_n \cdot < \sum_{i=1}^{l} r_i(R_i^n x_{n+1} - R_i^n u_{n+1})||^2, j(h_{n+1}) > \\
&+ 2\alpha_n \cdot < \sum_{i=1}^{l} r_i(R_i^n u_{n+1} - R_i^n x^*)||^2, j(h_{n+1}) > \\
&+ 2\alpha_n \cdot < \sum_{i=1}^{l} r_i(R_i^n x^* - R_i^n u_n)||^2, j(h_{n+1}) > \\
&\leq (1 - \alpha_n)^2 ||h_n||^2 + 2\alpha_n \sum_{i=1}^{l} r_i L ||z_n - x_{n+1}|| \cdot ||h_{n+1}|| \\
&+ 2\alpha_n(\sum_{i=1}^{l} r_i \lambda_n ||h_{n+1}||^2 - \varphi(||h_{n+1}||)) \\
&+ 2\alpha_n(\sum_{i=1}^{l} r_i L ||u_{n+1} - x^*|| \cdot ||h_{n+1}||) \\
&+ 2\alpha_n(\sum_{i=1}^{l} r_i L ||x^* - u_n|| \cdot ||h_{n+1}||) \\
&\leq (1 - \alpha_n)^2 ||h_n||^2 + 2\alpha_n L ||z_n - x_{n+1}|| \cdot ||h_{n+1}|| \\
&+ 2\alpha_n \lambda_n ||h_{n+1}||^2 - 2\alpha_n \varphi(||h_{n+1}||) \\
&+ 2\alpha_n L ||u_{n+1} - x^*|| \cdot ||h_{n+1}|| + 2\alpha_n L ||u_n - x^*|| \cdot ||h_{n+1}||
\end{aligned}$$

(3)

And from Algorithm 3.1, using triangular inequality, we have

$$||z_n - x_{n+1}|| = ||x_{n+1} - z_n||$$
$$= ||(1 - \alpha_n)(x_n - z_n) + \alpha_n \sum_{i=1}^{l} r_i(R_i^n z_n - z_n)||$$
$$\leq (1 - \alpha_n)||x_n - z_n|| + \alpha_n(L||z_n - x^*|| + ||x^* - z_n||)$$
$$\leq (1 - \alpha_n)||x_n - z_n|| + \alpha_n(L + 1)||z_n - x_n|| + ||x_n - x^*||)$$
$$= (1 + \alpha_n L)\beta_n ||x_n - x^* + x^* - \sum_{j=1}^{m} s_j S_j^n y_n|| + \alpha_n(L + 1)||x_n - x^*||)$$
$$\leq (1 + \alpha_n L)\beta_n(||x_n - x^*|| + L||x^* - y_n||) + \alpha_n(L + 1)||x_n - x^*||$$
$$= (1 + \alpha_n L)\beta_n + \alpha_n(L + 1)||x_n - x^*|| + (1 + \alpha_n L)L\beta_n||y_n - x_n + x_n - x^*||$$
$$= (1 + \alpha_n L)\beta_n(1 + L) + \alpha_n(L + 1)||x_n - x^*|| + (1 + \alpha_n L)L\beta_n||y_n - x_n|| \quad (4)$$

Where

$$||y_n - x_n|| = ||\gamma_n(\sum_{k=1}^{r} t_k T_k^n x_n - x_n)||$$
$$\leq \gamma_n(\sum_{k=1}^{r} t_k||T_k^n x_n - x^*|| + ||x_n - x^*||) \leq \gamma_n(1 + L)||x_n - x^*|| \quad (5)$$

Substituting (5) into (4), it can be obtained that

$$||z_n - x_{n+1}||$$
$$\leq ((1 + \alpha_n L)\beta_n(1 + L) + \alpha_n(L + 1))||x_n - x^*||$$
$$+ (1 + \alpha_n L)L\beta_n\gamma_n(1 + L)||x_n - x^*||$$
$$= (1 + L)((1 + \alpha_n L)\beta_n(1 + L\gamma_n) + \alpha_n)||x_n - x^*||$$
$$= \theta_n||x_n - x^*|| \quad (6)$$

Where $\theta_n = (1 + L)((1 + \alpha_n L)\beta_n(1 + L\gamma_n) + \alpha_n)$
By conditions:

$$\sum_{n=0}^{\infty} \alpha_n = 0, \sum_{n=0}^{\infty} \beta_n = 0, \sum_{n=0}^{\infty} \alpha_n\beta_n < \infty, \sum_{n=0}^{\infty} \alpha_n\beta_n\gamma_n < \infty$$

We obtain $\lim_{n \to \infty} \theta_n = 0, \sum_{n=0}^{\infty} \alpha_n\theta_n < \infty$.
Substituting (6) into (3), it can be obtained that

$$||h_{n+1}||^2$$
$$\leq (1 - \alpha_n)^2||h_n||^2 + 2\alpha_n L\theta_n||x_n - x^*|| \cdot ||h_{n+1}||$$
$$+ 2\alpha_n\lambda_n||h_{n+1}||^2 - 2\alpha_n\varphi(||h_{n+1}||)$$
$$+ 2\alpha_n L||u_{n+1} - x^*|| \cdot ||h_{n+1}|| + 2\alpha_n L||u_n - x^*|| \cdot ||h_{n+1}||$$
$$\leq (1 - \alpha_n)^2||h_n||^2 + 2\alpha_n L\theta_n(||h_n|| + ||u_n - x^*||) \cdot ||h_{n+1}||$$
$$+ 2\alpha_n\lambda_n||h_{n+1}||^2 - 2\alpha_n\varphi(||h_{n+1}||)$$
$$+ 2\alpha_n L||u_{n+1} - x^*|| \cdot ||h_{n+1}|| + 2\alpha_n L||u_n - x^*|| \cdot ||h_{n+1}||$$

Using average inequality, we obtain

$$||h_{n+1}||^2$$
$$\leq (1-\alpha_n)^2||h_n||^2 + \alpha_n L\theta_n(||h_n||^2 + ||h_{n+1}||^2)$$
$$+ \alpha_n L\theta_n(||h_{n+1}||^2 + 1)||u_n - x^*|| + 2\alpha_n\lambda_n||h_{n+1}||^2 - 2\alpha_n\varphi(||h_{n+1}||)$$
$$+ \alpha_n L||u_{n+1} - x^*|| \cdot (1 + ||h_{n+1}||^2) + \alpha_n L||u_n - x^*|| \cdot (||h_{n+1}||^2 + 1)$$
$$= ((1-\alpha_n)^2 + \alpha_n L\theta_n)||h_n||^2 + (\alpha_n L\theta_n + \alpha_n L)||u_n - x^*||$$
$$+ \alpha_n L||u_{n+1} - x^*|| - 2\alpha_n\varphi(||h_{n+1}||)$$
$$+ (\alpha_n L(||u_n - x^*|| + ||u_{n+1} - x^*||) + 2\alpha_n\lambda_n + \alpha_n L\theta_n + \alpha_n L\theta_n||u_n - x^*||)||h_{n+1}||^2$$

From

$$u_n \to x^* (n \to \infty) \Rightarrow ||u_n - x^*|| \to 0(n \to \infty), \alpha_n \to 0(n \to \infty),$$

We have

$$1 - (\alpha_n L(||u_n - x^*|| + ||u_{n+1} - x^*||) + 2\alpha_n\lambda_n + \alpha_n L\theta_n$$
$$+ \alpha_n L\theta_n||u_n - x^*||) \to 1(n \to \infty)$$

Let

$$A_n = 1 - (\alpha_n L(||u_n - x^*|| + ||u_{n+1} - x^*||) + 2\alpha_n\lambda_n + \alpha_n L\theta_n + \alpha_n L\theta_n||u_n - x^*||)$$

Thus there exists an $N \in N^+$, such that when $n > N, A_n > 0$. Therefore

$$||h_{n+1}||^2$$
$$\leq \frac{(1-\alpha_n)^2 + \alpha_n L\theta_n}{A_n}||h_n||^2 - \frac{2\alpha_n\varphi(||h_{n+1}||)}{A_n}$$
$$+ \frac{(\alpha_n L\theta_n + \alpha_n L)||u_n - x^*|| + \alpha_n L||u_{n+1} - x^*||}{A_n}$$
$$\leq (1 + C_n)||h_n||^2 - 2\alpha_n\varphi(||h_{n+1}||) + \sigma_n$$

Where

$$C_n = \frac{(1-\alpha_n)^2 + \alpha_n L\theta_n - A_n}{A_n}$$
$$\sigma_n = \frac{(\alpha_n L\theta_n + \alpha_n L)||u_n - x^*|| + \alpha_n L||u_{n+1} - x^*||}{A_n}$$

Next we will prove

$$\sigma_n = o(\alpha_n), C_n = o(\alpha_n)$$

In fact,

$$\lim_{n\to\infty} \frac{\sigma_n}{\alpha_n} = \lim_{n\to\infty} \frac{(\alpha_n L\theta_n + \alpha_n L)||u_n - x^*|| + \alpha_n L||u_{n+1} - x^*||}{A_n\alpha_n}$$

$$= \lim_{n\to\infty} \frac{(L\theta_n + L)||u_n - x^*|| + L||u_{n+1} - x^*||}{A_n} = 0 \Rightarrow \sigma_n = o(\alpha_n)$$

For $\{\lambda_n\} \subset [1, +\infty)$, and $\lim_{n\to\infty} \lambda_n = 1$, then

$$\lim_{n\to\infty} \frac{C_n}{\alpha_n} = \lim_{n\to\infty} \frac{(1-\alpha_n)^2 + \alpha_n L\theta_n - A_n}{A_n\alpha_n}$$

$$= \lim_{n\to\infty} \frac{\alpha_n + 2L\theta_n + (L(||u_n - x^*|| + ||u_{n+1} - x^*||) + 2(\lambda_n - 1) + L\theta_n||u_n - x^*||)}{A_n} = 0.$$

$$\Rightarrow C_n = o(\alpha_n)$$

Thus

$$||h_{n+1}||^2 \le (1 + o(\alpha_n))||h_n||^2 - 2\alpha_n\varphi(||h_{n+1}||) + o(\alpha_n)$$

That is to say

$$||x_{n+1} - u_{n+1}||^2 \le (1 + o(\alpha_n))||x_n - u_n||^2 - 2\alpha_n\varphi(||x_{n+1} - u_{n+1}||) + o(\alpha_n)$$

From Lemma 2.2,

$$||x_n - u_n|| \to 0(n \to \infty)$$

So

$$||x_n - x^*|| \le ||x_n - u_n|| + ||u_n - x^*|| \to 0(n \to \infty) \Rightarrow x_n \to x^*(n \to \infty).$$

$(2) \Rightarrow (1)$ is proved.
Therefore, $(1) \Leftrightarrow (2)$. This proof is complete.

Remark 4.1. Combining Theorem 4.1, this theorem indicates that the iterative sequences generalized by the improved multi-step iterative algorithms are convergence strongly to the unique fixed point x^* of pseudo-contractive mappings. And illustrates the improved multi-step iterative algorithms is feasible.

Remark 4.2. From article [2], we have known that Ishikawa and Mann iterations are equivalent in some conditions. Thus, by this theorem we can obtain the result the multi-step iterative sequence and Ishikawa iterative scheme are equivalent. This shows the wide applications of the improved multi-step iterative algorithm.

5   Conclusions

The paper introduces and discusses a new improved multi-step iterative algorithm. By proving the convergence for modified Mann iterative sequence and the equivalence of the multi-step iterative sequence and Mann iterative scheme, we prove the convergence of iterative sequences generalized by the improved multi-step iterative algorithms. The results extend and improve the corresponding related results. For a suitable choice of the parameter, we obtain some known iterative algorithms. For example, let $\gamma_n = 0$, we can get Ishikawa iterative algorithm; Let $\gamma_n = \beta_n = 0$, we can get Mann iterative algorithm. These clearly show the efficiency of the improved multi-step iterative algorithm.

Acknowledgments. This project was supported by National Natural Science Foundation of China (Grant No. 61179032 and 61303116), the Special Scientific Research Fund of Food Public Welfare Profession of China (Grant No. 201513004-3) and the Research and Practice Project of Graduate Education Teaching Reform of Wuhan Polytechnic University (YZ2015002).

References

1. Rhoades, B.E., Soltuz, S.M.: Equivalence between Mann-Ishikawa iterations and multi-step iteration. Nonlinear Anal. **58**, 219–228 (2004)
2. Huang, Z.Y.: Equivalence theorems of the convergence between Ishikawa and Mann iterations with errors for generalized strongly successively pseudo-contractive mappings without Lipschitzian assumptions. J. Math. Anal. Appl. **329**, 935–947 (2007)
3. Zhang, S.S.: Iterative approximation problem of fixed points for asymptotically non-expansive mappings in Banach spaces. Acta Math. Appl. Sinica **24**(2), 236–241 (2001)
4. Zeng, L.C.: On the strong convergence of iterative method for non-Lipschitzian asymptotically pseudo-contractive mappings. Acta Math. Appl. Sinica **27**(3), 230–239 (2004)
5. Schu, J.: Iterative construction of fixed point of asymptotically non-expansive mappings. J. Math. Anal. Appl. **158**, 407–423 (1991)
6. Chidume, C.E., Mutangadura, S.A.: An example on the Mann iteration method for Lipschitz pseudo-contractions. Proc. Am. Math. Soc. **129**, 2359–2363 (2001)
7. Noor, M.A.: Fixed-point iterations f or asymptotically non-expansive mappings in Banach spaces. J. Math. Anal. Appl. **267**, 444–453 (2002)
8. Glowinski, R.P., Tallec, L.: Augmented Lagrangian and Operator-Splitting Methods in Nonlinear Mechanics. SIAM, Philadelphia (1989)
9. Huang, N.J., Cho, Y.J., Lee, B.S., Jung, J.S.: Convergence of iterative processes with error for set-valued pseudo-contractive and accretive type mappings in Banach spaces. Comput. Math. Appl. **40**, 1127–1139 (2000)
10. Liu, L.S.: Ishikawa and Mann iterative processes with errors for nonlinear strongly accretive mappings in Banach space. J. Math. Anal. Appl. **194**, 114–125 (1995)
11. Gu, F.: Strong convergence theorems of a parallel iterative algorithm for two families of uniformly L-Lipschitzian mapping. AcTa Math. Sinica **53**(6), 1209–1216 (2010). Chinese Series

Grammar Automatic Checking System for English Abstract of Master's Thesis

Yueting Xu[2], Ziheng Wu[1]([⊠]), Han Huang[1], Tianxiong Yang[1], Pan Yu[1], and Erang Lu[1]

[1] School of Software Engineering, South China University of Technology, Guangzhou 510006, China
372665764@qq.com
[2] Guangdong University of Foreign Studies, Guangzhou 510006, China

Abstract. Although the technology of natural language processing was proposed several years ago, there are few Internet-based systems of English automatic grammar checking which is of help for beginner academic writers. This paper introduces our research results of an automatic grammar checking system for English article abstracts. We proposed four improved basic methods of natural language processing like sentence segmentation, multi-level indexes of words, Penn treebank and increment artificial rules for the system. Experimental results indicate that the proposed system is able to detect more grammar mistakes than other popular similar systems such as 1Checkerm Microsoft word and Non-Plus. Furthermore, our system provides free service for Internet users.

Keywords: Article abstracts in English · Automatic grammar checking · Web-based system · Internet studies

1 Introduction

English is the most popular language in the world. There are about 400 million people using English as first language, but more than one billion people use it as a second language. Non-native speaker easily make English grammar mistakes when writing. Therefore, the requirement of English grammar automatic checking is necessary.

Recently, the number of theses at different degree levels has surged due to the massification of higher education. English abstracts in theses as part of the Masters degree requirement are oftentimes ignored by both authors and thesis examiners because English is used as a foreign language. As a result, these English abstracts cannot meet the requirement of academic English as most of them suffer from grammatical errors. Therefore, an automatic system for grammar checking is needed and would be helpful for graduate students who are at the same time English as a foreign language (EFL) learners.

There are several existent automatic systems for English grammar checking. Automatic essay scoring (AES) is an automatic computer system to review and

© Springer Nature Singapore Pte Ltd. 2016
M. Gong et al. (Eds.): BIC-TA 2016, Part II, CCIS 682, pp. 497–506, 2016.
DOI: 10.1007/978-981-10-3614-9_61

evaluate English articles. AES has been used for 40 years since it was proposed in the 1960s. Project Essay Grader (PEG) [1] is the earliest automatic essay scoring system for English articles. In addition to grammar check, many systems for scoring English essays have been put into use, such as Intelligent Essay Assessor (IEA) [2], Electronic Essay Rater (E-Rater) [3], and Bayesian Essay Test Scoring system (BETSY) [4]. Notwithstanding their automatic scoring function, manual work is still required for grammar detection in these systems. Recent development can be seen in Stanford POS Tagger [5,6] which has achieved various functions such as grammar check, essay scoring, and topical relevance detection, simultaneously. However, its grammar correction model, which is the core of the system, performs far from satisfaction. Its problems include low accuracy rate, low intelligence and rare scalability. In addition, it is unable to change the detection rules depending on various users.

This paper implements an intelligent automatic system which takes account of writing features among theses written by Chinese graduate students. This system automatically rates theses by using the technology of natural language processing, including spelling check and grammar mistakes detection. In the long term, our Web-based checking system based on accumulation of numerous English abstracts would be able to display a wide range of features of master theses, such as their overall quality, research trends and methodologies used, etc.

2   Key Techniques

Based upon grammatical rules and negative instances, we implemented grammar checking model (process flow chart indicated by Fig. 1), including sentence segmentation, word segmentation, spelling check, part-of-speech tagging correction, and grammar filter, etc.

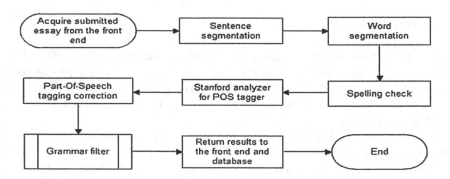

Fig. 1. Flow chart of intelligent algorithm used in grammar checking system for English abstracts.

Grammar filter integrates and manages all matching rules of the system. We will introduce the implementation of critical processes of the whole system sequentially, including algorithm of sentence segmentation, establishment of lexicon used by spelling check, correction of Part-of-speech Tagger, design of grammar check and excogitation of rules scalability.

2.1 Sentence Segmentation

Grammatical error checking is based on a single sentence. Thus how to segment sentences correctly, which we call sentence segmentation [7], is the premise of grammar checking. Dot (.) is the most frequent sign of sentence completion in English writing. Up to 90% of sentence end is dot. But in reality, particularly in abstracts of graduate dissertations, dot has various usages: 1. end of acronym; 2. part of expression; 3. part of special characters in website; 4. part of apostrophe. Due to numerous usages of dot, it seems insufficient to segment sentence with dot only. We adopt the method called English sentence segmentation based on pre-regular expression and rules [8]. Tagging all the period in an English abstract, including . , ? , !:
[left word][prefix][period][suffix][right word]
Prefix is the character string front coterminous with period and Suffix is the character string back coterminous with period. Right word is the next word after period.

2.2 Multi-level Index Structure

To check the spelling error, we need to establish a lexicon of standard English words and then match words in the text with lexicon. Once matching successfully, spelling is correct; otherwise means error in spelling.

Despite our task mainly focuses on grammar check, in a long term we are supposed to build a lexicon containing terminologies for analyzing abstracts of postgraduate theses [9]. So we establish a lexicon presented in Fig. 2. For the moment, our lexicon is still in infancy and it takes to develop and enrich. Another problem is when size of lexicon reaches a certain amount, there is a negative correlation between system matching efficiency and lexicon size [10].

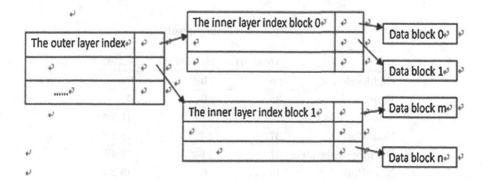

Fig. 2. Multi-level index structure.

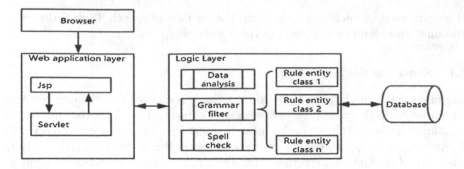

Fig. 3. Extensible design based on grammar filter rules.

To settle this, we should build the lexicon scientifically. In Fig. 3, we show how to optimize words database with Multi-level index structure. By setting index table with the first three letters of words, the number of matching could be controlled within 2 to 4 times.

2.3   Penn Treebank Tag Set

Penn Treebank Tag Set [11] is the most widespread and most scientifically tagged tag set, including thirty-six tags of word classes and twelve special tags of punctuation. Tags of word classes are presented in Table 1. In this paper we adopt Penn Treebank Tag Set.

With Penn Treebank tags set, sentence, He went to school with a dog yesterday could be tagged as:
/He/PRP went/VBD to/TO school/NN with/IN a/DT dog/NN yesterday/NN ./././
In this example, He is tagged with personal pronoun, went is tagged with verbpast tense, to is tagged with infinitive, school, dog, yesterday are tagged with singular or uncountable noun, with is tagged with preposition, a is tagged with determiner.

Table 1. System checking results

	Total error	System check	Rate
Highlevelerror	46	0	0
Word	33	0	0
JuKu	65	27	41.5%
NounPlus	37	13	35.1%
Ourproposedsystem	21	11	52.4%
NounPlus	13	6	46.2%
Ourproposedsystem	16	4	25%

In actual English texts, a number of words are both verbs and adjectives [12]. For example, word close, on one hand, when treated as a verb it may mean to shut something in order to cover an opening; on the other hand, it could serve as an adjective having multiple layers of meaning, such as being not far from something, near something in time, very likely to do something, intimate in relationship, or very similar, to name just a few. Thus the goal of part-of-speech tagger is to allocate right tags for polysemic words in different sentences based on statistics from large amount of data.

Stanford POS Tagger is a part-of-speech tagger based on maximum entropy model [13]. It has high accuracy rate due to the long-term practice and mature technology in the field of natural language processing along the years.

The part-of-speech tagger proposed in this paper bases on Stanford POS Tagger [14] and it is implemented and extended with Java. For a polysemic word, which means a word having several tags in tag set, POS tagger will calculate the most probable tag according to Formula (1).

$$P(tag_n|word_n) * P(tag_n|tag_n - 1, tag_n - 2) \tag{1}$$

Although accuracy rate of tagging and running efficiency are well, part-of-speech tagger still encounter some exceptions and errors. So far artificial correction is indispensable to handling these faults. As the result of this, we spent considerable time collecting and analyzing errors of tagger, based on which we corrected them.

2.4   Increment Artificial Rules

There are two methods to build the base for rules. The first is to artificially establish the base with right rules only. The other is to artificially establish the base which includes wrong rules. However the structure of English grammar is so complex and various that a simple sentence can derive countless combinations. With the first method it is hard to build a base containing right rules only or to match and analyze text with the rule base. It is not only because it is impossible to build the absolutely-right base, but also because there is no answer concerning how we should figure out a nearly infinitely-great base, even if the ideal base exists with well-matching efficiency simultaneously. Hence, in this paper we take the second approach, which discovers the grammar mistakes by matching with wrong grammar rules.

On the basis of rules-based grammar checking algorithm, we combine part-of-speech tagging technology to organize the rule base of our grammar checking system. This is because if we choose only rule-based grammar checking algorithm, there would be too many rules required, which make the process hard to achieve and ineffective. Whats more, a base with tremendous number of rules will lead to running inefficiency. Therefore, in this paper we establish rules based on part-of-speech tagging.

First, according to syntax, we analyzed every word in each sentence of the text through part-of-speech tagger. Then we collected common grammar mistakes by statistics and classification of numbers of English sentences with different grammatical rules. Then, we analyzed errors in logic and modeled grammar mistakes logically. Finally, on the basis of part-of-speech tags of tagger, we designed a series of basic logical processes concluded by error rule of grammar.

During the grammar modeling, we interviewed five university English teachers several times and collected a large number of common grammatical mistakes of English learners in China, which generated error rules processing flow chart based on part-of-speech tagging. Another three English teachers with high proficiency were also invited to evaluate this system in professional ways.

3   The Framework of the Proposed System

3.1   Structure of Grammar Filter Rules

After the system is released, it is harmful to future development of the system if too many modifications or adjustments are required when maintaining rules or updating.

Treating each single word as a basic checking unit, grammar check model adopts different ways according to tags given by part-of-speech tagger and word classes, based on which a unified result will be returned. To realize loose coupling of coding structure, diverse checking rules are highly unified as implementation classes with the same input and output interfaces and separated from main body of codes. Thus, when modifying grammar check rules, we need to do nothing but to correct corresponding implementation classes. The process to add rules is presented by Fig. 3.

3.2   System Structure Diagram

Our target is to design and implement an English abstract smart analyzing system to be used by Chinese postgraduates. As indicated earlier, the whole system includes basic data management, abstract upload, rules feedback, rules setting, rules extension, spell check, grammar check, and back-end management, etc.

Considering requirements for frequent maintaining and extension of rule base, we chose B/S structure, which is also beneficial for English learners in China to use this system with convenience.

It is a long-term process for accumulation and perfection in grammar checking model of English abstract automatic analyzing system. So grammar filter is crucial when building the whole system, which requires highly-separated and highly-decoupling MVC structure. In addition, this system is based on Stanford POS Tagger, whose POS tagger is coded by JAVA. To sum up, we choose Java Web frame to realize the system. Data layers mainly interact with users and do maintaining and managing with back-end data. Logic layer is formed by spelling check model and grammar filter. Combining diverse grammar checking rules, grammar filter opens a close interface to system application layer. Then application layer runs the abstract detection by calling logic layer. Figure 4 is the diagram of the system structure.

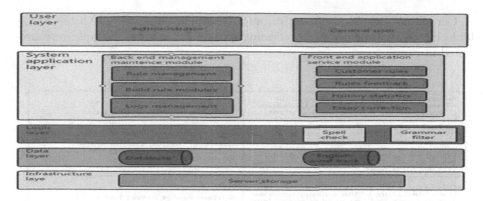

Fig. 4. Intelligent English abstract checking web systems systematic frame.

4   Experimental Results

To evaluate our grammar checking model, unedited corpus is essential. But to date, there is no published authoritative corpus appropriate for grammar error checking. Since our target users are graduate students in Chinese universities, collecting samples of English abstracts from authentic master theses is the only way in which we can evaluate the grammar checking results. To achieve this goal, our testing corpus came from authentic English abstracts in graduate students submitted theses. After testing of the system, we inputted 1008 sentences as presented in Fig. 4. We also invited English researchers in universities to do manual corrections for these texts. All grammar errors had been marked, summing to 231 errors after correction. Subject-verb agreement errors take up the largest proportion.

Among the errors, high level error was mentioned in Sect. 1.2. So far AES system cannot handle the writing errors including semantic error, structure error and pragmatic errors. Testing examples are presented in Fig. 5.

False: At the same time,you will gain fame and fortune and even money.	System can't detect faults.
Correct: At the same time,you will gain fame and fortune.	fortune and even money: 〔Semantic repeat〕 Two similar words express the same thing repeatedly and unnecessarily.
False: But do you know what the success mean?	System can't detect faults.
False: But do you know what success means?	success: 〔grammatical mistake〕 Success means abstract things here,not specific reference.The word 'the' is redundant.

Fig. 5. High-level writing errors.

Complicated errors represent errors in complex sentences which are formidable for computer language processing to handle. Testing examples are presented in Fig. 6.

False : The film tells us never give up whatever matter you have met, because toward your life is the most important, brave to face, you will never know what you take next.	System can' t detect faults.
Correct : The film tells us never to give up whatever you have met, because facing your life is the most important.Be brave to face it, you will never know what you will meet next.	whatever matter: [grammatical mistake] whatever guide the noun attributive clause.
False : By reading a travel book, you can learn the culture of this country when we stay at home and just need to spend few hours.	System can' t detect faults.
Correct : By reading a travel book, we can learn the culture of this country when we stay at home and just need to spend a few hours.	you : [grammatical mistake] The subject should keep consistent in the full text.

Fig. 6. Complicated errors.

By testing, not only our system failed to detect these two errors, but also other four systems under comparison failed.

Meanwhile, we compared our system with other four grammar checking machines, including 1Checker, Microsoft word, Juku automated essay assessment website and NounPlus. Result are indicated in Table 2.

Table 2. A comparison of grammar checking results among different systems

	Total text error	Right check	Recall ratio
1Checker	231	48	20.8%
Word	231	4	1.7%
JuKu	231	33	14.3%
NounPlus	231	28	12.1%
Ourproposedsystem	231	61	26.4%

From the testing results, our systems recall ratio reached 26.4%, higher than the other systems. In general, all detectors had low correctness-checking rate. For the main reason that all the testing corpora are non-preprocessing, which could assure fairness to each grammar detector. But during manual grammar checking in pedagogy in universities, English teachers will need more time to consider global errors, mistakes in complicated sentences, or even other higher-level writing mistakes, all of which cannot be recognized by machines.

5   Conclusion

This paper implemented a web-based system which is not only easy to manage but also compatible with extended grammatical rules. While it has open access to all English learners in China, the system is of value as it would gather more grammatical evidence from various corpora. In addition, the interactive interface of this system is friendlyas we can collect the service condition of rules and feedback from users. Details and detecting accuracy rates are open to all users. To enable text checking to meet personal writing characteristics, users are able to define and choose the rule templates to suit their own needs.

Acknowledgments. This work is supported by National Natural Science Foundation of China (613701 02), Guangdong Natural Science Funds for Distinguished Young Scholar (2014A0 30306050), the Fundamental Research Funds for the Central Universities, SCUT (2015PT022), and Guangdong Degree and Graduate Education Reform Project (2015JGXM-MS02).

References

1. Dikli, S.: Automated essay scoring. Turk. Online J. Distance Educ. **7**(1), 735–738 (2006)
2. Foltz, P.W., Laham, D., Landauer, T.K.: The intelligent essay assessor: applications to educational technology. Interact. Multimedia Electron. J. Comput. Enhanc. Learn. (2005)
3. Powers, D.E., Burstein, J.C., Martin, C., et al.: Stumping e-rater: challenging the validity of automated essay scoring. Comput. Hum. Behav. **18**(1), 103–134 (2002)
4. Dikli, S.: An overview of automated scoring of essays. J. Technol. Learn. Assess. **5**(1), 36 (2006)
5. Stanford Log-linear Part-Of-Speech Tagger. http://www-nlp.stanford.edu/softwa re/taggers.html
6. Toutanova, K., Manning, C.: Enriching the Knowledge Sources Used in a Maximum Entropy Part-of-Speech Tagger (2000)
7. Huang, C.Z., Zhang, X.G.: Auto detection for English sentence boundaries. Micro-processors **01**, 30–34 (2003)
8. Yan, R., Cheng, C.H., Chai, Y.: Formal consistency checking over specifications in natural languages. In: Design, Automation & Test in Europe Conference & Exhibition (DATE), pp. 1677–1682. IEEE (2015)
9. Kifetew, F.M., Tiella, R., Tonella, P.: Generating valid grammar-based test inputs by means of genetic programming and annotated grammars. Empir. Softw. Eng., 1–34 (2016)
10. Diaconescu, S.S., Dumitrascu, I.M., Ingineru, C.I., et al.: Systems and methods for natural language processing including morphological analysis, lemmatizing, spell checking and grammar checking: US Patent 8,762,130, 24 June 2014
11. Hoover, B., Lytvyn, M., Shevchenko, O.: Systems and methods for advanced grammar checking. US Patent Application 14/617, 338, 9 Feb 2015
12. Zhirui, W., Hui, H., Zhengtao, L.: Design and realization of semi-automatic English composition correction component base on B/S structure. Comput. Era **9**, 012 (2015)

13. Ying, J., Jie, Z., Qihong, L., et al.: XML rule customization method of language tool Chinese grammar proof-reading. Libr. Inf. Serv. **5**, 021 (2014)
14. Huang, C.R., Hong, J.F., Ma, W.Y., et al.: From corpus to grammar: automatic extraction of grammatical relations from annotated corpus. Tsou, B., Kwong, O. (eds.) Linguistic Corpus and Corpus Linguistics in the Chinese Context. Journal of Chinese Linguistics Monograph (2014)

Verified Error Bounds for Symmetric Solutions of Operator Matrix Equations

Qingchun Li[1], Ziyu Li[2], Haifeng Sang[1(✉)], and Panpan Liu[1]

[1] College of Mathematics and Statistics, Beihua University, Jilin 132013, Jilin, China
sanghaifeng2008@163.com
[2] College of Economics and Management, Shanghai Maritime University, Shanghai 201306, China

Abstract. Based on the interval theory, the verification for symmetric solutions of operator matrix equations $AX - XB - C = 0, A \in \mathbb{R}^{m \times m}, B \in \mathbb{R}^{n \times n}, C \in \mathbb{R}^{m \times n}$ is studied. We propose the algorithm which outputs an approximate symmetric solution and its error bound with the property that an exact solution exists within this computed bound. The proposed algorithm requires only $O(m^3 + n^3)$ operations if A and B are diagonalizable.

Keywords: Verified computation · Operator matrix equation · Symmetric solution · INTLAB

1 Introduction

The goal of verification methods is ambitious. For a given problem it is proved, with the aid of a computer, that there exists a (unique) solution of a problem within computed bounds [1]. In this paper, we investigate the method for computing enclosing intervals for all entries of the $m \times n$ symmetric solution X of the matrix equation

$$AX - XB - C = 0, \tag{1}$$

where A, B and C are real matrices of size $m \times m, n \times n$ and $m \times n$, respectively. Matrix equation (1) plays an important role in biomathematics, mechanics, physics and control theory [2–4]. Therefore, the verification for symmetric solution of matrix equation is widely used.

The matrix equation (1) can be written as a system of linear equations as follow

$$Px = c, \tag{2}$$

where $P = I_n \otimes A - B^T \otimes I_m, x = \text{vec}(X)$ and $c = \text{vec}(C)$. Here, $\otimes$ represent the Kronecker product [5], so P is the matrix of size $mn \times mn$. And vec is the operation of stacking the columns of a matrix in order to obtain one long vector, so $\text{vec}(X)$ and $\text{vec}(C)$ are mn vectors. Rohn verifies the solution of Eq. (2) by function **verifylss** of INTLAB [6,7]. Furthermore the solution of Eq. (1) is verified. This algorithm requires $O(m^3 n^3)$ operations.

© Springer Nature Singapore Pte Ltd. 2016
M. Gong et al. (Eds.): BIC-TA 2016, Part II, CCIS 682, pp. 507–512, 2016.
DOI: 10.1007/978-981-10-3614-9_62

In 1980, Rump [8] come up with the normal methods for verification to compute the verified error bounds of solution by standard interval algorithms. Based on the interval theory, we study the verification for symmetric solutions of operator matrix equations. We propose the algorithm which outputs an approximate symmetric solution and its error bound with the property that an exact solution exists within this computed bound. The proposed algorithm requires only $O(m^3 + n^3)$ operations if A and B are diagonalizable.

This paper is organized as follows: In Sect. 2 we introduce some basic notation and facts from interval arithmetic. Section 3 contains our main results, including our algorithm. In Sect. 4, numerical results are reported to show the property of the proposed algorithms.

2 Notation and Preliminaries

We introduce the following notation $\mathbb{IR}$, $\mathbb{IR}^n$, $\mathbb{IR}^{n \times n}$ denote the set of all real interval, the set of all n real interval vectors and the set of all $m \times n$ real interval matrices, respectively, and interval quantities will always by typeset in boldface.

Lemma 1. [5] *For any real matrices A, B, C and D with compatible sizes we have*

(a) $(A \otimes B)(C \otimes D) = (AC \otimes BD)$
(b) $\text{vec}(ABC) = (C^T \otimes A)\text{vec}(B)$

Lemma 2. [9] *Let A, B, C be interval matrices of compatible sizes. Then*

$$(C^T \otimes A)\text{vec}(B) : A \in A, B \in B, C \in C \subseteq \begin{cases} \text{vec}((AB)C) \\ \text{vec}(A(BC)) \end{cases}$$

Lemma 3. [10] *Let $A, B, R \in \mathbb{R}^{n \times n}$, $X \in \mathbb{IR}^{n \times n}$, $\widetilde{X}$ is an approximate solution of matrix equation $AX = B$. If hold the decision condition for interval*

$$R(B - A\widetilde{X}) + (I - RA)X \subseteq \text{int}(X),$$

then, there exists a matrix $\widehat{X} \in \widetilde{X} + X$ with $A\widehat{X} = B$, and A, T are non-singular, where $\text{int}(X)$ denotes interior of X.

Remark 1. Generally speaking, matrix R in Lemma 3 is not limited. However, to better satisfy formula (3), we usually define R is an approximation to the inverse of A.

Function for achieving the verification of the solution of the linear system of equation is verifyless in INTLAB. For linear system of equations whose coefficient matrix is interval matrix, verifyless put out interval vector this interval vector contain all solutions of interval linear equations. For matrix equation, the function is applied similarly.

Lemma 4. [11] *Let interval matrix A, $B \in \mathbb{IR}^{n \times n}$, if function verifylss(A,B) operated successfully, then the interval matrix $X \subset \mathbb{IR}^{n \times n}$ by computing stasfied*

$$\Sigma(A, B) = \{X \in \mathbb{R}^{n \times n} : AX = B, A \in A, B \in B\} \subseteq X.$$

3   Main Results

Let us assume that A and B are both diagonalizable, i.e., we have the spectral decompositions

$$A = V_A D_A W_A, \text{ with } V_A, D_A, W_A \in \mathbb{C}^{m \times m}, \quad D_A = \text{diag}(\lambda_1, \ldots, \lambda_m),$$

$$B = V_B D_B W_B, \text{ with } V_B, D_B, W_B \in \mathbb{C}^{n \times n}, \quad D_B = \text{diag}(\mu_1, \ldots, \mu_n),$$

where columns i of V_A and V_B are eigenvectors of A and B with eigenvalue λ_i and μ_i. Then we have

$$P = (V_B^{-T} \otimes W_A^{-1})[I_n \otimes (W_A A W_A^{-1}) - (V_B^{-1} B V_B)^T \otimes I_m](V_B^T \otimes W_A).$$

Define

$$Q = I_n \otimes (W_A A W_A^{-1}) - (V_B^{-1} B V_B)^T \otimes I_m,$$
$$y = (V_B^T \otimes W_A)x,$$
$$f = (V_B^T \otimes W_A)c.$$

Further, we can reformulate the linear system (2) as

$$Qy = f. \tag{3}$$

Note
$$\mathbf{S}_A = (W_A A)\mathbf{I}_{W_A}, \quad \mathbf{S}_B = \mathbf{I}_{V_B}(BV_B),$$

where $W_A^{-1} \in \mathbf{W}_A^{-1}$ and $V_B^{-1} \in \mathbf{V}_B^{-1}$.

Define
$$\Delta = I_n \otimes D_A - D_B^T \otimes I_m,$$

where Δ is a good approximation for Q, and Δ^{-1} is a good approximate inverse for Q.

Theorem 1. *Let* $\widetilde{X} \in \mathbb{K}^{m \times n}$ *be a symmetric solution of the matrix equation* $AX - XB - C = 0$, *and let* $\mathbf{Z} \in \mathbb{IK}^{m \times n}$ *with* $\mathbf{z} = \text{vec}(\mathbf{Z})$. *Define*

$$R = W_A \cdot (A\widetilde{X} - \widetilde{X}B - C) \cdot V_B,$$
$$\mathbf{M} = (D_A - \mathbf{S}_A)\mathbf{Z},$$
$$\mathbf{N} = \mathbf{Z}(D_B - \mathbf{S}_B),$$
$$\mathbf{U} = (-R + \mathbf{M} + \mathbf{N})./D,$$

where $D \in \mathbb{K}^{m \times n}$, $\text{vec}(D) = \boldsymbol{diag}(\Delta)$. *Then, with* $\widetilde{y} = (V_B^T \otimes W_A)\widetilde{x}$, *we have*
(a) $\{-\Delta^{-1}(Q\widetilde{y} - f) + (I_{mn} - \Delta^{-1}Q)\mathbf{Z}, \mathbf{Z} \in \mathbf{Z}\} \subset \text{vec}(\mathbf{U})$,
(b) if $\mathbf{U} \subset \boldsymbol{int}\mathbf{Z}$, *then exist a unique vector* $\widehat{y} \in \widetilde{y} + \text{vec}(\mathbf{U})$ *such that* $Q\widehat{y} = f$, *and matrix* Q *is non-singular.*

Remark 2. Define $V = I_{W_A}UI_{V_B}$, then we can conclude if $U \subset \text{int} Z$, base on Theorem 1, there is a unique matrix $\widehat{X} \in \widetilde{X} + \text{vec}(V)$, which satisfies $A\widehat{X} - \widehat{X}B - C = 0$.

Based on the above theory, design the algorithm as follow.

Algorithm 1
Input: 1. $AX - XB - C = 0$: A, B are both diagonalizable.
       2. X_1: The initial symmetric solution for operator equation.
       3. ε_1: Numerical iterative tolerance.
       4. N: Maximum number of iterations.
       5. ε_2: The numerical tolerance.
Output: 1. The approximate symmetric solution $\widetilde{X}$ and the error bounds $\widetilde{V}$ of matrix operator equation $AX - XB - C = 0$.
        2. Or "failure".

(1) Matrix $A \in R^{m \times m}$, $B \in R^{n \times n}$, $C \in R^{m \times n}$, $X_1 \in SR^{m \times n}$.
(2) Compute

$$R_1 = C - AX_1 + X_1B;$$
$$P_1 = G - M(X_1);$$
$$Q_1 = M(P_1); k = 1.$$

(3) If $R_k = 0$ or $P_k = 0$, so stop, otherwise $k = k + 1$.
(4) Compute

$$X_{k+1} = X_k + \frac{\|P_k\|^2}{\langle Q_k, M(P_k)\rangle}Q_k;$$
$$R_{k+1} = C - AX_{k+1} + X_{k+1}B;$$
$$P_{k+1} = P_k - \frac{\|P_k\|^2}{\langle Q_k, M(P_k)\rangle}M(Q_k);$$
$$Q_{k+1} = P_{k+1} - \frac{\langle P_{k+1}, M(Q_k)\rangle}{\langle Q_k, M(Q_k)\rangle}Q_k.$$

Obtain approximate symmetric solution $\widetilde{X}$ of operator equation, if $\|A\widetilde{X} - \widetilde{X}B - C\| > \varepsilon_2$, turn to (3).
(5) If A and B are diagonalizable, then compute spectral decompositions:

$$A = V_A D_A W_A, \quad B = V_B D_B W_B.$$

Otherwise, turn to "failure", algorithm will be terminated.
(6) Denote

$$D = \begin{pmatrix} \lambda_1 - \mu_1 & \lambda_1 - \mu_2 & \cdots & \lambda_1 - \mu_n \\ \lambda_2 - \mu_1 & \lambda_2 - \mu_2 & \cdots & \lambda_2 - \mu_n \\ & & \cdots\cdots & \\ \lambda_m - \mu_1 & \lambda_m - \mu_2 & \cdots & \lambda_m - \mu_n \end{pmatrix}.$$

(7) Compute interval matrices $\boldsymbol{W_A}$, $\boldsymbol{W_B}$ by verifyless, such that $W_A \in \boldsymbol{W_A}$, $W_B \in \boldsymbol{W_B}$.

(8) Compute interval matrices $\boldsymbol{T} = W_A \cdot (A\widetilde{X} - \widetilde{X}B - C) \cdot V_B$, $\boldsymbol{S_A} = (W_A A)\boldsymbol{W_A}$, $\boldsymbol{S_B} = \boldsymbol{W_B}(BV_B)$, $\boldsymbol{U} = -\boldsymbol{T}./D$.

(9) Let iter=0.

(9.1) If iter ≤ 15, we perform the following steps, otherwise turn to "failure".

(9.2) Let iter = iter + 1, set

$$\boldsymbol{Z} = \texttt{hull}(U \cdot \texttt{infsup}(0.9, 1.1) + e^{-20} \cdot \texttt{infsup}(-1, 1), 0).$$

(9.3) Compute

$$\boldsymbol{M} = (D_A - \boldsymbol{S_A}) \cdot \boldsymbol{Z}, \quad \boldsymbol{N} = \boldsymbol{Z} \cdot (D_B - \boldsymbol{S_B}), \quad \boldsymbol{U} = (-\boldsymbol{T} + \boldsymbol{M} + \boldsymbol{N})./D.$$

(9.4) If $\boldsymbol{U} \subseteq \texttt{int}(\boldsymbol{Z})$, let $\boldsymbol{V} = \boldsymbol{W_A}\boldsymbol{U}\boldsymbol{W_B}$, and return to $\boldsymbol{V}$. Algorithm will be terminated.

We can obtain the proposition as follow by Theorem 1.

Proposition 1. *If Algorithm 1 return to the verified interval* $\boldsymbol{V} = \widetilde{X} + \widetilde{\boldsymbol{V}}$ *successfully, then there is the unique matrix* $\widehat{X} \in \boldsymbol{V}$ *such that* $\widehat{X}$ *is the exact solution of* $AX - XB - C = 0$.

4 Numerical Experiments

The following experiments are done in Matlab R2011a(INTLAB V6) under Windows 7.

Example 1. Consider verified error bounds for symmetric solutions of operator matrix equations $AX - XB - C = 0$, where

$$A = \begin{pmatrix} 5.2269 & 9.9403 & 9.7107 & 0.3091 & 8.1553 \\ 1.2915 & 9.3996 & 9.5767 & 3.6588 & 0.2501 \\ 0.0378 & 4.3414 & 7.2073 & 0.9382 & 4.2420 \\ 3.2582 & 9.3551 & 6.4796 & 3.3465 & 0.3380 \\ 3.6076 & 4.9683 & 8.6260 & 0.0733 & 6.7670 \end{pmatrix}, \; B = \begin{pmatrix} 3.2796 & 6.1644 & 4.2979 & 8.8560 & 1.0890 \\ 5.6007 & 6.2901 & 2.1093 & 9.6291 & 9.3682 \\ 4.2481 & 1.7664 & 5.9099 & 7.6963 & 5.1106 \\ 1.5010 & 4.0792 & 8.3720 & 3.6794 & 2.1128 \\ 0.6436 & 7.0614 & 8.8829 & 0.6814 & 4.2111 \end{pmatrix}$$

$$C = \begin{pmatrix} 97.3989 & -5.5486 & -8.4167 & 85.6895 & 5.5340 \\ 68.1693 & 7.4505 & -21.4787 & 96.0249 & 7.4496 \\ 5.2758 & -61.2142 & -84.5267 & -42.3270 & -49.1131 \\ -1.5447 & -100.3136 & -101.4872 & -27.2384 & -91.1591 \\ 87.7922 & -29.5100 & -45.2041 & 68.2107 & -19.4402 \end{pmatrix}.$$

It can be verified that the operator matrix equation $AX - XB - C = 0$ is consistent and has a unique exact symmetric solution

$$X = \begin{pmatrix} 8.2954 & 0.7995 & 9.2831 & 1.6677 & 3.8677 \\ 0.7995 & 1.4247 & 4.8601 & 8.1087 & 4.0571 \\ 9.2831 & 4.8601 & 3.2163 & 7.9503 & 0.1938 \\ 1.6677 & 8.1087 & 7.9503 & 8.1791 & 9.5666 \\ 3.8677 & 4.0571 & 0.1938 & 9.5666 & 2.9338 \end{pmatrix}.$$

512   Q. Li et al.

We apply Algorithm 1 to compute the error bounds $\widetilde{V}$ and the verified symmetric solution $V = \widetilde{X} + \widetilde{V}$ of operator matrix equations $AX - XB - C = 0$.

Input: $X_1 = \begin{pmatrix} 0\ 0\ 0\ 0\ 0 \\ 0\ 0\ 0\ 0\ 0 \\ 0\ 0\ 0\ 0\ 0 \\ 0\ 0\ 0\ 0\ 0 \end{pmatrix}, \varepsilon_1 = 10^{-9}, N = 100, \varepsilon_2 = 10^{-5}.$

Output : $\widetilde{V} = 1.0e - 009 *$

$$\begin{pmatrix} [0.1679, 0.1680] & [-0.1177, -0.1176] & [0.0866, 0.0867] & [-0.0146, -0.0145] & [-0.0381, -0.0380] \\ [-0.1169, -0.1168] & [0.1255, 0.1256] & [-0.0827, -0.0826] & [0.0654, 0.0655] & [0.0151, 0.0152] \\ [0.0872, 0.0873] & [-0.0825, -0.0824] & [0.0666, 0.0667] & [-0.0650, -0.0649] & [0.0353, 0.0354] \\ [-0.0150, -0.0149] & [0.0637, 0.0638] & [-0.0662, -0.0661] & [-0.1417, -0.1416] & [0.1426, 0.1427] \\ [-0.0386, -0.0385] & [0.0138, 0.0139] & [0.0343, 0.0344] & [0.1424, 0.1425] & [-0.1040, -0.1039] \end{pmatrix},$$

$$V = \begin{pmatrix} [8.2953, 8.2954] & [0.7995, 0.7996] & [9.2830, 9.2831] & [1.6677, 1.6678] & [3.8677, 3.8678] \\ [0.7995, 0.7996] & [1.4246, 1.4247] & [4.8601, 4.8602] & [8.1087, 8.1088] & [4.0570, 4.0571] \\ [9.2830, 9.2831] & [4.8601, 4.8602] & [3.2163, 3.2164] & [7.9502, 7.9503] & [0.1937, 0.1938] \\ [1.6677, 1.6678] & [8.1087, 8.1088] & [7.9502, 7.9503] & [8.1790, 8.1791] & [9.5665, 9.5666] \\ [3.8677, 3.8678] & [4.0570, 4.0571] & [0.1937, 0.1938] & [9.5665, 9.5666] & [2.9338, 2.9339] \end{pmatrix}.$$

Acknowledgments. This work is supported by Jilin Province Department of Education Science and Technology Research Project under Grants 2014213, 2015131 and 2015156.

References

1. Rump, S.M.: Verification methods: rigorous results using floating-point arithmetic. Acta Numerica **19**, 287–449 (2010)
2. Datta, B.N.: Numerical Methods for Linear Control Systems: Design and Analysis. Academic Press, Cambridge (2004)
3. Antoulas, A.C.: Approximation of Large-scale Dynamical Systems, Advances in Design and Control. SIAM, Philadelphia (2005)
4. Sorensen, D.C., Antoulas, A.C.: The Sylvester equation and approximate balanced reduction. Linear Algebra Appl. **351**, 671–700 (2002)
5. Horn, R.A., Johnson, C.R.: Topics in Matrix Analysis. Cambridge University Press, Cambridge (1994)
6. Rohn, J.: VERSOFT: verification software in MATLAB/INTLAB. http://uivtx.cs.cas.cz/rohn/matlab
7. Rump, S.M.: INTLABinterval Laboratory/Developments in Reliable Computing, pp. 77–104. Kluwer Academic Publishers, Dordrecht (1999)
8. Rump, S.M.: Kleine Fehlerschranken bei Matrixproblemen. Universitat Karlsruhe, Karlsruhe (1980)
9. Frommer, A., Hashemi, B.: Verified computation of square roots of a matrix. SIAM. Matrix Anal. Appl. **31**, 1279–1302 (2010)
10. Kearfott, R.B., Nakao, M., Neumaier, A., Rump, S., Shary, S., van Hentenryck, P.: Standardized notation in interval analysis. Comput. Technol. **15**, 7–13 (2010)
11. Moore, R.E., Kearfott, R.B., Cloud, M.J.: Introduction to Interval Analysis. SIAM, Philadelphia (2009)

Immune Multipath Reliable Transmission with Fault Tolerance in Wireless Sensor Networks

Hongbing Li[1(✉)], Dong Zeng[2], Liwan Chen[3], Qiang Chen[3], Mingwei Wang[3], and Chunjiong Zhang[3]

[1] School of Computer Science and Engineering,
Chongqing Three Gorges University, Wanzhou, China
sxxylhb@163.com
[2] Wanzhou Branch of Chongqing Unicom Corperation of China, Wanzhou, China
[3] School of Electronic and Information Engineering,
Chongqing Three Gorges University, Wanzhou, China

Abstract. Transmission reliability is one of the most important metrics to evaluate the performance of wireless sensor networks. For the fault of nodes or links affecting the stability and reliability of network, Immune based multipath transmission algorithm is proposed. For giving the consideration to the factors of transmission delay and energy consumption beside the hops/distance, immune based multiple paths can be quickly established from the source node to the destination node. Metrics of data receiving rate are adopted to evaluate the performance of multipath transmission. The result shows good performance of fault tolerance, stability and reliability of data transmission.

Keywords: Wireless sensor networks · Reliable transmission · Fault tolerance · Multipath routing · Immune algorithm

1 Introduction

Reliability of data transmission is an important metrics to evaluate the performance of wireless sensor networks (WSNs) [1]. High reliability and stability are still difficult issues in the study of the wireless sensor network at present [2]. Fault tolerance and routing strategy is adopted to realize the effective and reliable data transmission which also gives the consideration to the balance of energy consumption and low transmission delay, etc. [3]. Immune system is adopted to multipath routing strategy to deal with faults in wireless sensor network [4]. Various multipath routing protocols such as energy-aware routing, QoS based routing and geographical routing methods are proposed and analyzed: REFER [5], WC-BMR [6], GPSR [7], RDICMR [8], ISRRA [9]. This paper mainly studies the issues that the node failure or link quality affects the stability and reliability of data transmission in the network layer.

© Springer Nature Singapore Pte Ltd. 2016
M. Gong et al. (Eds.): BIC-TA 2016, Part II, CCIS 682, pp. 513–517, 2016.
DOI: 10.1007/978-981-10-3614-9_63

2　Immune Multipath Transmission Algorithm

2.1　Definition of Immune Related Issues

Antibody: defined as the established optimal paths from the source node to the destination node.

Antigen: defined as the cluster heads in the static clustering topology.

Node coding: transmission path is established among the cluster heads from the source node to the destination node. So all the cluster heads need to be encoded in binary code according to the quantity of cluster heads in the network. For example, the quantity of nodes is less than 16. So each cluster head can be encoded in 4 binary code digits, such as 1011. The source node and destination node are supposed to be encode as 0000 and 1111.

Path coding: Path coding is determined as the ordered combination of each nodes' coding. Source node and destination node are respectively encoded in 0000 and 1111. Suppose nodes N21, N22 and N23 are encoded as 001, 0100, 0101. One transmission path can be encoded as 0000 0011 0100 0101 1111 if node set S, N21, N22, N23, D constitute the path.

Fitness calculation: Path fitness is closely related to and decided by hops to the destination node, residual energy and transmission delay. It is defined and calculated by:

$$\sum_{i=1}^{n} C_{P_i} \tag{1}$$

where C_{P_i} represents comprehensive measurement of path P_i.

　　Definition 1 Comprehensive measurement (C) is defined as the weighting sum of normalized values of factors of hops, residual energy and transmission delay. It is adopted to evaluate the quality of established paths. Path's comprehensive measurement function is defined by (2).

$$C_{P_i} = w_1 \frac{E(p_i)}{E_{ini}(p_i)} + w_2 \frac{H(p_i)}{\max\{H(p_i)\}} + w_3 \frac{D(p_i)}{\max\{D(p_i)\}} \tag{2}$$

where $w_1 + w_2 + w_3 = 1$, $E_{ini}(p_i) = \sum_{i=1}^{n} e = ne$, it represents sum of initial energy of each node on path p_i. $\max\{H(p_i)\}$ represents maximum hops of all established paths. $\max\{D(p_i)\}$ represents transmission delay of all established paths.

Memory: Among all multiple transmission paths $\{p_1, p_2, p_3, \cdots\}$ established from source node to destination node, antibodies $\{p_1, p_2, p_3, \cdots p_n\}$ meeting the condition $C_{P_i} \geq \Theta$ are selected as the excellent ones into memory of antibody population which is used for the next iteration variation, where Θ represents the set threshold and is determined by $\sum_{i=1}^{n}(C_{P_i}/n)$ and n is quantity of established paths.

　　Antibody variationVariation rules of antibody are as follows. (1) Variation nodes including all the nodes on one path excluding the source node and the destination node. (2) Direction of nodes' variation is from the source node to the destination node. Variation node should be within the frequency coverage of transmission power of previous hop. (3) Variation nodes excludes ones on the established variation paths. (4) Variation rule is as follow: 0 randomly mutates into 0 or 1, 1 randomly mutates into 0 or 1.

2.2   Details of the Algorithm

Step 1. Initialization the parameters.

Step 2. To calculate paths' C_{P_i} by Eq. (2).

Step 3. To code the nodes and paths according to the coding rules and antibody variation algorithm of transmission paths.

Step 4. To randomly determine the initial multiple transmission paths which constitute the initial antibody population. Quantity n transmission disjoint paths from the source node to the destination node are established.

Step 5. To calculate the fitness of the transmission paths according to Eq. (2).

Step 6. To generate the memory population. According to the established transmission paths $\{p_1, p_2, p_3, \cdots\}$ which are antibodies population. Antibodies with $C_{P_i} \geq \Theta$ are selected into the memory as the excellent antibody population for the next variation.

Step 7. Antibodies mutation. Excellent antibodies in the memory are mutated according the variation rules. New antibody population is generated which is constituted with the original antibodies and new mutated antibodies. Then it calculates C_{P_i} and $\sum_{i=1}^{n} C_{P_i}$ according to the fitness function. If $\sum_{i=1}^{n} C_{p_i}^{new} < \sum_{i=1}^{n} C_{p_i}$ turn to step 6; otherwise turn to step 8, where $\sum_{i=1}^{n} C_{p_i}^{new}$ is the new values after variation.

Step 8. Terminate the iteration and output the optimal solution. The optimal K antibodies with $\min \sum_{i=1}^{n} C_{p_i}^{new}$ and no longer changes are selected and outputted as solutions to the issues so as to establish multiple transmission paths, otherwise turn to step 5.

Step 9. Source node sends the confirmation packets to the destination node along all the established paths and receives the replies from the destination node to confirm the establishment of optimal transmission paths. Simulation and analysis.

3   Simulation and Analysis

3.1   Reliability of Packets Transmission

Figure 1 shows the packets receiving rate of the network when the algorithm runs at 20, 40, 60, 80 and 100 iteration times. Comparison is done among three algorithm: Immune based multipath algorithm, RDICMR [8] and ISRRA [9]. From Fig. 1, Immune based multipath algorithm has higher packets receiving rate than other two algorithms. Two has higher packets receiving rate at the beginning and during the whole process. From 80 iteration times, the proposed algorithm has firstly reached the maximum packets receiving rate. This show the good performance of the reliable transmission.

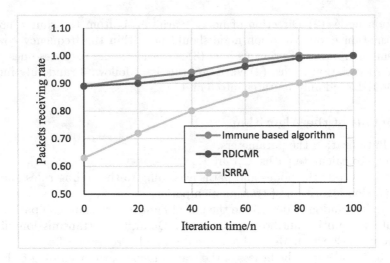

Fig. 1. Packets receiving rate at different iteration times

3.2 Performance of Fault Tolerant

Figure 2 shows the packets receiving rate when fault nodes generate in the network when the algorithm runs. We also adopt the packets receiving rate to testify the quality of established paths and transmission reliability. Iteration times [200, 400, 600, 800, 1000] are selected to testified and compared among these three algorithm: Immune based multipath algorithm, RDICMR and ISRRA. From Fig. 2, Immune based multipath algorithm shows higher packets receiving rate along a certain quantity of fault nodes are generated. This reflects good performance of fault tolerance to the fault nodes.

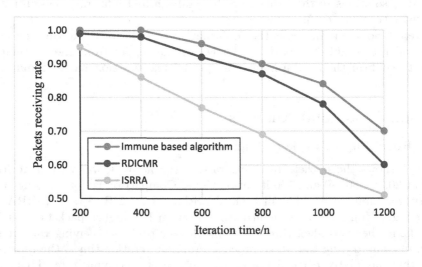

Fig. 2. Packets receiving rate when fault nodes generates

4   Conclusion

For the issues that the node failure or link quality affecting the stability and reliability of data transmission in the network layer, immune algorithm is adopted into multipath fault-tolerant transmission and packets redundancy transmission. Multiple paths can be quickly established from the source node to the destination node. Data receiving rate and fault tolerance are analyzed and simulated. The result shows good performance of fault tolerance and reliability of data transmission.

Acknowledgement. The work was supported by the National Project (61402063), National Science Foundation for Post-doctoral Scientists of China (2015M582616), Chongqing Basic and Advanced Technology Research Project (cstc2014jcyjA1316, cstc2016jcyjA0063, cstc2013kjrc-qnrc40013), Scientific and Technological Research Program of Chongqing Municipal Education Commission (KJ1601003, KJ1401002, KJ1401008, KJ1401010, KJ1603303, KJ1501014), Joint Funds of Natural Science Foundation Project of Guizhou (J-LKG[2013]46), Key Laboratory Open Projects of Chongqing Three Gorges University (063120202), Youth Scientific Project of Chongqing Three Gorges University (15QN09). Doctoral Fund Project of Chongqing Three Gorges University (14ZZ03), Innovation and Entrepreneurship Project of College Students (201610643004).

References

1. Mahmood, M.A., Seah, W.K.G., Welch, I.: Reliability in wireless sensor networks: a survey and challenges ahead. Comput. Netw. **79**, 166–187 (2015)
2. Wu, Z., Xiong, N., Huang, Y., Xu, D., Hu, C.: Optimizing the reliability and performance of service composition applications with fault tolerance in wireless sensor networks. Sensors **15**, 28193–28223 (2015)
3. Bagci, H., Korpeoglu, I., Yazıcı, A.: A distributed fault-tolerant topology control algorithm for heterogeneous wireless sensor networks. IEEE Trans. Parallel Distrib. Syst. **26**, 914–923 (2015)
4. Abo-Zahhad, M., Sabor, N., Sasaki, S., Ahmed, S.M.: A centralized immune-Voronoi deployment algorithm for coverage maximization and energy conservation in mobile wireless sensor network. Inf. Fusion **30**, 36–51 (2016)
5. Shen, H., Li, Z.: A Kautz-based wireless sensor and actuator network for real-time, fault-tolerant and energy-efficient transmission. IEEE Trans. Mob. Comput. **15**, 1–16 (2016)
6. Sun, X., Chen, H., Wu, X., Yin, X., Song, W.: Opportunistic communications based on distributed width-controllable braided multipath routing in wireless sensor networks. Ad Hoc Netw. **36**, 349–367 (2016)
7. Al-Ariki, H.D., Esmail, S., Shanmukha, M.N.: A survey and analysis of multipath routing protocols in wireless multimedia sensor networks, Wirel. Netw. 1–13 (2016). doi:10.1007/s11276-016-1256-5
8. Ding, Y., Chen, R., Hao, K.: A rule-driven multi-path routing algorithm with dynamic immune clustering for event-driven wireless sensor networks. Neurocomputing **203**, 139–149 (2016)
9. Zhang, X., Yao, G., Ding, Y., Hao, K.: An improved immune system-inspired routing recovery scheme for energy harvesting wireless sensor networks. Soft Comput. 1–12 (2016). doi:10.1007/s00500-016-2222-y

The Research of Solving Inverse Problems of Complex Differential Equations

Kangshun Li[1(✉)], Yan Chen[1], and Jun He[2]

[1] College of Mathematics and Informatics,
South China Agricultural University, Guangzhou 510642, China
{likangshun,cheny}@scau.edu.cn
[2] Department of Computer Science, Aberystwyth University,
Aberystwyth, Ceredigion SY23 3DB, UK

Abstract. There are various complicated or non-linear system varying with the time (dynamic system) in the reality and scientific aspects, and such dynamic system is usually expressed by the differential equations. In this paper, a new GEP-based algorithm is put forward to solve the inverse problems of ordinary differential equation (ODE) and complex high-order differential equations by taking advantage of the self-adaptability, self-organization and self-study of Gene Expression Programming (GEP), which is difficult to solve by use traditional methods. Experiments show that this improved GEP algorithm can be used to solve the optimization problems of ordinary differential equations and complex differential equations in shorter time and with higher precision comparing with the traditional ones.

Keywords: Gene expression programming · System of ordinary differential equations · Inverse problem · Runge-Kutta algorithm

1 Introduction

There are various complicated systems or non-linear phenomena varying with the time in the reality, which, called as dynamic systems, include the weather change, population increase and disease diffusion, etc. To study the development trend of such dynamic systems, it is required to establish the model of such dynamic systems, that is, to establish the functional relationship or changing trend among variables of the systems. However, it is difficult to find the functional relations among variables in the complicated changing processes, but it is possible to find out the change rate or differential coefficient of some variables, and thus achieving the differential equation (DE) or differential equations (DEs). Those problems are known as the inverse problems of differential equations [1–4]. For instance, if we have the previous data of a stock market, it is possible for us to create a model for the stock market or forecast its development trend based on those data, which is very important to us in guiding us to accomplish the scientific experiments or actual projects. To this end, a improved

© Springer Nature Singapore Pte Ltd. 2016
M. Gong et al. (Eds.): BIC-TA 2016, Part II, CCIS 682, pp. 518–523, 2016.
DOI: 10.1007/978-981-10-3614-9_64

Gene Expression Programming (GEP) [5,6] is put forward in this paper to solve the inverse problems of ordinary differential equations and complex differential equations. First as the GEP algorithm is in the multi-gene structure, each gene stands for an ordinary differential equation or complex DE and each chromosome for a group of differential equations, in which the individual cannot be used to stand for the group of ordinary differential equations directly by using the traditional algorithms. Experiments show that the GEP algorithm has a better forecasting effect in the shorter time and its time cost is so stable that it cannot be influenced by the complexity of the system. Further experiments indicate that such improvement can quicken the spread of population diversification and increase the GEP rate of convergence as well as solve the inverse problems of ordinary differential equation with higher speed.

2   Inverse Problems of Ordinary Differential Equations

On the assumption that a dynamic system is expressed with n correlative functions: $x_1(t), x_2(t), \ldots, x_n(t)$ As known to us, the system has a series of data as follows at the time of

$$t_i = t_0 + i \times \Delta t (i = 0, 1, 2, \cdots m - 1)$$

$$X = \begin{pmatrix} x_1(t_0), & x_2(t_0), & \ldots, & x_n(t_0) \\ x_1(t_1), & x_2(t_1), & \ldots, & x_n(t_1) \\ \vdots & \vdots & \vdots & \vdots \\ x_1(t_{m-1}), & x_2(t_{m-1}), & \ldots, & x_n(t_{m-1}) \end{pmatrix} \tag{1}$$

where, t_0 is the starting time Δt is the time increment $x_j(t_j)$ $(1, 2, \cdots n)$ Stands for the observed value of x_j at the time of t_i.

It is known that $X(t) = [x_1(t), x_2(t), \cdots x_n(t)]$, $F(X, t) = [f_1(X, t), f_2(X, t), \cdots, f_n(X, t)]$.

Where, $f_j(X, t) = f_j(x_1(t), x_2(t), \cdots x_n(t), t)$ $(j = 1, 2, \cdots, n)$ is expressed by the compound functions, which form a space of F. Suppose that the dynamic system is more suitable to the trends of ordinary differential equation group, and it requires to solve the inverse problems of ODE group via the following formula:

$$dX^*/dt = F(X^*, t) \tag{2}$$

When $\|X^* - X\|$ approaches the minimal value, the difference between the observed values and the data deriving from the model is at minimum level, i.e., the Formula (3) has the minimum value.

$$\|X^* - X\| = \sqrt{\sum_{i=0}^{m-1} \sum_{j=1}^{n} \left(x_j^*(t_i) - x_j(t_i) \right)^2} \tag{3}$$

And then the coming trends of the system can be forecaster, which are the ODE group inverse problems of the dynamic system.

3   Improved GEP and Its Modeling for ODE Group Inverse Problems

3.1   GEP Algorithm

GEP is a new evolutionary algorithm invented by the Portuguese scientist Candida Ferreira, which, based on genome and phenomena and referring to the gene expression rule of the Biogenetics, combines the advantages of both GP and GA although the individual expression is in the tree form, but the specific genetic codes are still the Isometric linear symbols. Therefore, GEP has produced good results in optimizing, evolving and modeling the functional parameters, neural network, classification and TSP problems [7,8].

Suppose the head length of Gene is h (it is selected as per the demand), and the tail length is t, n is the number of the most arguments of the function in the function set, therefore, the relationship between head length (h) and tail length (t) can be expressed as follows:

$$t = h(n-1) + 1 \tag{4}$$

The above formula is to ensure that the gene has the enough length.

3.2   Modeling Process for Inverse Problems of GEP-Based Ordinary Differential Equation Group

Initialize Population. It is known to us that the inverse problems of ordinary differential equation are solved by creating the ordinary differential equation model in compliant with the data set, based on a set of measured values, and thus forecasting the future data in accordance with the ordinary differential equation group model. Take the Formula 5 as an example, which demonstrates that the process of solving inverse problems of linear ordinary differential equation.

$$\begin{cases} \dfrac{dx_1}{dt} = -x_2 x_3 \\[2mm] \dfrac{dx_2}{dt} = x_1 x_3 \\[2mm] \dfrac{dx_3}{dt} = x_3 \\[2mm] \dfrac{dx_4}{dt} = x_4 - x_3 - x_5 \\[2mm] \dfrac{dx_5}{dt} = x_4 + x_5 \end{cases} \tag{5}$$

It can achieve a series of data in accordance Formula 6 on the assumption that the starting time $t = 0$ and the time increment $\Delta t = 0.01$, those data (see Table 1) can be used as the observed data to describe the algorithm process. Model the ordinary differential equation group via the improved GEP based on the data in Table 1, obtain the estimates according the model, and finally calculate the estimated error and forecasting error to verify the efficiency of the model. First, calculate the values according to the solution of the ordinary differential equation when $t = 0$ (starting time) and $\Delta t = 0.01, 0.02, 0.03, 0.04$ (time increment), those values (see Table 1) are used as the observed values to further forecast the values of (x_1, x_2, x_3) when $t = 0.05$, 0.06 and 0.07.

Table 1. Observed data calculated as per Formula 6

t	x_1	x_2	x_3	x_4	x_5
0.00	0.5403	0.8415	1.0000	1.0000	−1.0000
0.01	0.5318	0.8469	1.0101	1.0100	−1.0000
0.02	0.5232	0.8522	1.0202	1.0200	−0.9998
0.03	0.5144	0.8575	1.0305	1.0300	−0.9995
0.04	0.5055	0.8628	1.0408	1.0400	−0.9992

3.3 Improvement of GEP Algorithm

It is known from the GEP codes that a GEP gene has coding regions and non-coding regions. For example: $Q \times + \times a \times Q\underline{aababbbaababaab}$ is a legal gene, and the part without underline is its Head while the underlined segment is the Tail.

Compare the gene with its expression tree in the above example, one can find that the last 10 characters of the gene are noncoding regions. This is the reason why GEP is a non-linear segment and its phenotype form and genotype form of the genes may be different Obviously, only the mutation, transposition and restructuring operators are at the dominant segment of the gene, can they increase the diversity of the population remarkably; if they are at the recessive segment, they can only increase the probability for population diversity before performing the mutation operator. Especially for the four standard evolvement operations of mutation, IS transposition, single-point restructuring and double-point restructuring, all characters have the equal probability to become the position of the operator, therefore, the selection of their position can greatly determine the validity of the evolvement operation. To prove the above statement is true, statistics have been conducted in this paper for the average valid length of GEP genes used in the published papers.

4 Code Generation

4.1 The Set of Experimental Parameters

Experimental parameters are set in Table 2.

4.2 Parameter Configuration for Experiments

Experiment 1. In this experiment, the training data is from the reference. Using the different t_0 and Δ_t from four different date depending on the solution

Table 2. GEP Experimental parameters

Parameters	Value	Parameters	Value
Set of termination symbols	$\{1,2,3,0\}$(experimental data I, II, III, IV) $\{1,0\}$(experimental data V) $\{1,2,0\}$(experimental data VI)	Probability of mutation	0.044
Set of functional symbols	$\{+,-,*,/,s,c,q,e,l\}$	Probability of IS transposition	0.1
Number of iterations	10000	Length of IS transposition	5
Size of populations	50	Probability of RIStransposition	0.1
Number of gene	3	Length of RIS transposition	5
Head length of gene	8	Length of Gene Transposition	0.1

(formula 7) solved from formula 6. Each date consists of 3 columns (x_1, x_2, x_3) and 11 rows $(t = t_0, t_0 + \Delta t, \cdots, t_0 + 10\Delta t)$ of which the first 7 rows of data X_m as the actual observation data, and last 4 rows of data as the forecast data for evaluate the quality of the model.

$$\begin{cases} \dfrac{dx_1}{dt} = x_1 \\ \dfrac{dx_2}{dt} = x_1 + x_2 + x_3 \\ \dfrac{dx_3}{dt} = 2x_1 - x_2 + 3x_3 \end{cases} \tag{6}$$

$$\begin{cases} x_1 = e^t \\ x_2 = e^{2t}(t+1) \\ x_3 = e^{2t}(t+2) - e^t \end{cases} \tag{7}$$

5   Summary

In this study, we proposed a GEP based algorithm to solve the inverse problem of ordinary differential equations, and GEP algorithm's shortcoming, evolution operation in the recessive segment contributes little is overcome. Through experiments, we verified that the algorithm, in terms of solving the inverse problem of ordinary differential equations, was very effective with respect to estimate standard error, prediction standard error and running time. And improvement strategies can further enhance the efficiency of the algorithm convergence. Our study on algorithms provides a powerful tool to automate the process of knowledge discovery for dynamic data, and we expect the approach to be promoted and applied in actual problems related to time series and time fields, such as weather forecasting, market prediction and ecological prediction.

Acknowledgements. This work is supported by the National Natural Science Foundation of China with the Grant No. 61573157, the Fund of Natural Science Foundation of Guangdong Province of China with the Grant No. 2014A030313454, Guangdong Province Science and Technology Research Project with the Grant No. yue ke gui hua zi 2013-137.

References

1. Romanov, V.G.: Inverse Problems of Mathematical Physis. VNU Science Press BV, Utrecht (1987)
2. Charles, W.G.: Inverse Problems in the Mathematical Science. Vieweg, Braunschweig (1993)
3. Isakov, V.: Inverse Problems for Partial Differentiale Equations. Springer, New York (1998)
4. Guofeng, F., Bo, H., Jiaqi, L.: Widely convergent generalized pulse-spectrum methods for 2-D wvae equation inversion. Chin. J. Geophys. **46**(2), 265–270 (2003)
5. Ferreira, C.: Gene expression programming: a new adaptive algorithm for solving problems. Complex Syst. **13**(2), 87–129 (2001)
6. Ferreira, C.: Gene expression programming in problem solving. In: Roy, R., Diplom-Phys, M.K., Ovaska, S., Furuhashi, T., Hoffmann, F. (eds.) Soft Computing and Industry: Recent Applications, pp. 635–653. Springer, Heidelberg (2002)
7. Ghodrati Amiri, G., Amiri, M.S., Tabrizian, Z.: Ground motion prediction equations (GMPEs) for elastic response spectra in the Iranian plateau using gene expression programming (GEP). J. Intell. Fuzzy Syst. **26**(6), 2825–2839 (2014)
8. Ali, N., Shadi, R.: Predicting the effects of nanoparticles on compressive strength of ash-based geopolymers by gene expression programming. Neural Comput. Appl. **23**(6), 1677–1685 (2013)

Fast Algorithms for Verifying Centrosymmetric Solutions of Sylvester Matrix Equations

Ziyu Li[1], Haifeng Sang[2(✉)], and Ying Zhao[2]

[1] College of Economics and Management, Shanghai Maritime University,
Shanghai 201306, China
[2] College of Mathematics and Statistics, Beihua University, Jilin 132013, China
sanghaifeng2008@163.com

Abstract. Based on floating point operations, we study the accuracy of numerically computed centrosymmetric solutions in Sylvester matrix equations. Propose a fast algorithm which outputs the lower bound and upper bound of the exact centrosymmetric solution. Numerical experiments show the properties of the proposed algorithm.

Keywords: Fast algorithm · Sylvester matrix equation · Centrosymmetric solution · INTLAB

1 Introduction

The numerical computation plays a crucial role in scientific calculation. It has the characteristics of fast and it is used widely in our practical work. However, due to the raw data error, calculation error accumulation and the limited precision said real numbers, the numerical calculation cannot guarantee the accuracy of results, which could lead to a major accident in the high risk field [1]. Therefore, reliable computing is widely applied across thees high risk areas such as rocket design, nuclear magnetic resonance (NMR) machine and digital machine theory.

And in many important fields such as biomathematics, mechanics, physics and control theory [2–4], some problems can be come down to compute a centrosymmetric solution of the Sylvester matrix equation

$$AX + XB = C. \tag{1}$$

In this paper, the accuracy of numerically computed centrosymmetric solutions in the Sylvester equation (1) is concerned. We investigate the methods for computing the lower bound and upper bound of the exact centrosymmetric solution $\widehat{X}$, where $A \in \mathbb{C}^{m \times m}$, $B \in \mathbb{C}^{m \times m}$, $X, C \in \mathbb{C}^{m \times n}$.

While there are well-established methods for enclosing solutions of Sylvester matrix equations [5–8], less attention has been paid to centrosymmetric solutions. It is well known Eq. (1) can be written as a system of linear equations as follow

$$P\mathrm{vec}(X) = \mathrm{vec}(C), \tag{2}$$

© Springer Nature Singapore Pte Ltd. 2016
M. Gong et al. (Eds.): BIC-TA 2016, Part II, CCIS 682, pp. 524–529, 2016.
DOI: 10.1007/978-981-10-3614-9_65

where $P = I_n \otimes A + B^T \otimes I_m$, $\otimes$ represent the Kronecker product [9] and vec is the operation of stacking the columns of a matrix in order to obtain one long vector.

The purpose of this paper is to obtain the error bounds $X^\varepsilon \in \mathbb{R}^{m \times n}$ satisfying $|\widetilde{X} - \widehat{X}| \leq X^\varepsilon$, where $\widetilde{X}$ and $\widehat{X}$ denote the numerical solution and exact solution in (1), $|\widetilde{X} - \widehat{X}|$ denotes the matrix with elements $|(\widetilde{X} - \widehat{X})_{ij}|$ and inequalities between matrices hold componentwise. This method requires only $O(m^3 + n^3)$ operations if A and B are diagonalizable.

This paper is organized as follows. In Sect. 2 we introduce the preliminary definitions and notation we shall use. The main result, the algorithm for verifying the centrosymmetric solution of Sylvester matrix equations, is presented in Sect. 3. In Sect. 4 we provide some examples for demonstrating the performance of our algorithm.

2 Notation and Preliminaries

We denote by $M_{ij}, M_{i,:}, M_{:,j}$ the (i, j) element, the i−th row and the j−th column of M, respectively. For matrices M, N, $\min(M, N) = \{\min(M_{ij}, N_{ij})\}$ and $\|M\|_M = \max_{i,j} |M_{ij}|$. For $d_1, \ldots, d_n \in \mathbb{C}$, $\mathrm{diag}(d_1, \ldots, d_n)$ denotes a diagonal matrix whose diagonal elements are $d_1, \ldots, d_n$. Denote $s^{(p)} = (1, \ldots, 1)^T \in \mathbb{R}^p$ and $E = (s^{(m)}, \ldots, s^{(m)}) \in \mathbb{R}^{m \times n}$.

Definition 1. [9] *The matrix* $A \in \mathbb{R}^{n \times n}$ *is centrosymmetric if*

$$a_{ij} = a_{n+1-i, n+1-j}, \; i, j = 1, 2, \ldots, n.$$

Lemma 1. [9] *For any complex matrices* K, L, M *and* N *with compatible sizes, it holds that*

$$(K \otimes L)(M \otimes N) = (KM \otimes LN);$$
$$\mathrm{vec}(LMN) = (N^T \otimes L)\mathrm{vec}(M).$$

Lemma 2. [10] *For* $S \in \mathbb{C}^{m \times n}$ *and* $1 \leq p \leq \infty$, *if* $\|S\|_p < 1$, $I_m - S$ *is nonsingular.*

Lemma 3 is a modification of Theorem 3 in [11] which suites for estimating upper bounds for matrices rather than vectors.

Lemma 3. [6] *Let* $S, G \in \mathbb{C}^{m \times m}, F \in \mathbb{C}^{m \times n}$ *and* $D_F = \mathrm{diag}(\|F_{:,1}\|_\infty, \ldots, \|F_{:,n}\|_\infty)$. *If* $\|S\|_\infty < 1$, *it holds that*

$$|(I_m - S)^{-1} F| \leq |F| + \frac{1}{1 - \|S_\infty\|} |S| E D_F,$$

$$|(I_m - S)^{-1} G| E \leq \left(|G| + \frac{\|G\|_\infty}{1 - \|S_\infty\|} |S| \right) E.$$

Remark 1. $I_m - S$ *is nonsingular if* $\|S\|_\infty < 1$ *by* Lemma 2.

3   Main Results

Throughout this paper we assume that A and B are both diagonalizable. Then there are the spectral decompositions

$$A = V_A D_A V_A^{-1}, \text{ with } V_A, D_A \in \mathbb{C}^{m \times m}, \; D_A = \text{diag}(\lambda_1, \ldots, \lambda_m),$$
$$B = V_B D_B V_B^{-1}, \text{ with } V_B, D_B \in \mathbb{C}^{n \times n}, \; D_B = \text{diag}(\mu_1, \ldots, \mu_n).$$

Proposition 1. [6] Let $\widetilde{X} \in \mathbb{C}^{m \times n}, \widetilde{D}_A, \widetilde{V}_A, W_A \in \mathbb{C}^{m \times n}, \widetilde{D}_B, \widetilde{V}_B, W_B \in \mathbb{C}^{n \times n}$, $\widetilde{D}_A$ and $\widetilde{D}_B$ be diagonal, $\widetilde{D}_A - \widetilde{D}_B$ have no diagonal elements in common, and

$$S_A = I_m - W_A \widetilde{V}_A; S_B = I_n - W_B \widetilde{V}_B;$$
$$R_A = W_A(\widetilde{V}_A \widetilde{D}_A - A\widetilde{V}_A); R_B = W_B(\widetilde{V}_B \widetilde{D}_B - B^T \widetilde{V}_B);$$
$$T_A = |R_A| + \frac{\|R_A\|_\infty}{1 - \|S_A\|_\infty}; T_B = |R_B| + \frac{\|R_B\|_\infty}{1 - \|S_B\|_\infty};$$
$$T = T_A * E + E * T_B^T; \widetilde{D} = \widetilde{D}_A * E + E * \widetilde{D}_B; T_D = T./|\widetilde{D}|. \tag{3}$$

If $\|S_A\|_\infty < 1$ and $\|S_B\|_\infty < 1$, then $\widetilde{V}_A$ and W_A, and $\widetilde{V}_B$ and W_B are nonsingular, respectively. Additionally if $\|T_D\|_M < 1$, (1) has a unique solution $\widehat{X}$.

Proposition 2. [6] Let $\widetilde{X}, W_A, W_B, S_A, S_B, \widetilde{D}$ and T_D be as in Proposition 1, and $\widetilde{D}_A$ and $\widetilde{D}_B$ be diagonal, $\widetilde{D}_A - \widetilde{D}_B$ have no diagonal elements in common, and

$$R = A * \widetilde{X} + \widetilde{X} * B - C; R_W = W_A * R * W_B^T;$$
$$D_W^r = diag(\|R_{W_{1,:}}\|_1, \ldots, \|R_{W_{m,:}}\|_1); R_W^{(1)} = |R_W| + \frac{1}{1 - \|S_B\|_\infty} D_W^r E|S_B|^T;$$
$$D_W^{(1)} = diag(\|R_{W_{:,1}^{(1)}}\|_1, \ldots, \|R_{W_{:,n}^{(1)}}\|_1); R_V^{(1)} = |R_W^{(1)}| + \frac{1}{1 - \|S_A\|_\infty} |S_A| E D_W^{(1)};$$
$$D_W^c = diag(\|R_{W_{:,1}}\|_1, \ldots, \|R_{W_{:,n}}\|_1); R_W^{(2)} = |R_W| + \frac{1}{1 - \|S_A\|_\infty} |S_A| E D_W^c;$$
$$D_W^{(2)} = diag(\|R_{W_{1,:}^{(2)}}\|_1, \ldots, \|R_{W_{m,:}^{(2)}}\|_1); R_V^{(2)} = |R_W^{(2)}| + \frac{1}{1 - \|S_B\|_\infty} D_W^{(2)} E|S_B|^T;$$
$$R_V = \min(R_V^{(1)}, R_V^{(2)}), R_D = R_V./|\widetilde{D}|, U = R_D + \frac{\|R_D\|_M}{1 - \|T_D\|_M} T_D. \tag{4}$$

If all the assumptions in Proposition 1 are satisfied, it holds that

$$|\widetilde{X} - \widehat{X}| \leq X^\varepsilon, \; X^\varepsilon = |\widetilde{V}_A| U |\widetilde{V}_B|^T.$$

To compute the numerical centrosymmetric solution of Sylvester matrix Eq. (1), denote

$$I_n = (e_1, e_2, \cdots, e_n), S_n = (e_n, e_{n-1}, \cdots, e_1),$$
$$M(X) = A^T A X + A^T X B + A X B^T + X B B^T + S_n(A^T A X + A^T X B + A X B^T + X B B^T)S_n,$$
$$G = A^T C + C B^T + S_n(A^T C + C B^T)S_n,$$
$$P(X) = G - M(X), P_k = P(X_k).$$

Based on the above theory, we design the algorithm as follow.

Algorithm 1
Input: 1. $AX + XB = C$: the Sylvester matrix equation.
       2. X_1: the initial centrosymmetric matrix.
       3. N: the maximum number of iterations.
       4. ε: the numerical tolerance.
Output: 1. The approximate centrosymmetric solution $\tilde{X}$ and its verified error
       bounds X^ε.
       2. Or "Failure".

(1) Compute $R_1 = C - AX_1 - X_1 B$; $P_1 = G - M(X_1)$; $Q_1 = M(P_1)$; $k = 1$.
(2) If $R_k = 0$ or $k > N$, return "Failure" and stop. Otherwise $k := k + 1$.
(3) Compute

$$X_{k+1} = X_k + \frac{\|P_k\|^2}{\langle Q_k, M(P_k) \rangle} Q_k;$$

$$R_{k+1} = C - AX_{k+1} - X_{k+1} B;$$

$$P_{k+1} = P_k - \frac{\|P_k\|^2}{\langle Q_k, M(P_k) \rangle} M(Q_k);$$

$$Q_{k+1} = P_{k+1} - \frac{\langle P_{k+1}, M(Q_k) \rangle}{\langle Q_k, M(Q_k) \rangle} Q_k.$$

If $\|R_{k+1}\| \leq \varepsilon$, then return $\tilde{X} = X_{k+1}$ and go to Step 4. Otherwise go to
Step 2.
(4) If A and B are diagonalizable, then compute spectral decompositions:

$$A = \tilde{V}_A \tilde{D}_A W_A, \quad B = \tilde{V}_B \tilde{D}_B W_B.$$

Otherwise, return "Failure" and stop.
(5) Compute matrices S_A, S_B and T_D in Eq. (3).
(6) Compute the matrix $U = R_D + \frac{\|R_D\|_M}{1 - \|T_D\|_M} T_D$ in Eq. (4).
(7) If $\|S_A\|_\infty < 1$, $\|S_B\|_\infty < 1$ and $\|T_D\|_M < 1$, then return

$$X^\varepsilon = |\tilde{V}_A| U |\tilde{V}_B|^T$$

and stop. Otherwise, return "Failure" and stop.

Algorithm 1 stops after finitely many steps and computes verified error
bounds for the approximate centrosymmetric solution, since the strategy to con-
struct $X^\varepsilon = |\tilde{V}_A| U |\tilde{V}_B|^T$ is the same as in the algorithm of [6].
We can obtain the proposition as follow by Proposition 2.

Proposition 3. *Given the Sylvester matrix equation* $AX + XB = C$ *and a
approximate centrosymmetric solution* $\tilde{X}$*, if Algorithm 1 successfully returns the
verified error bounds* $\tilde{V}$*, then there is the unique matrix* $\hat{X}$ *in the interval matrix*
$[\tilde{X} - X^\varepsilon, \tilde{X} + X^\varepsilon]$*, such that* $\hat{X}$ *is the exact solution of* $AX + XB = C$*.*

4   Numerical Experiments

The following experiments are done in Matlab R2011a (INTLAB V6) under Windows 7.

In the following examples, we apply Algorithm 1 to compute the approximately centrosymmetric solution $\widetilde{X}$, the error bounds X^ε and the verified centrosymmetric solution $[\widetilde{X} - X^\varepsilon, \widetilde{X} + X^\varepsilon]$ of the Sylvester matrix equation $AX + XB = C$.

Example 1. [12] Given 3 matrices

$$A = \begin{pmatrix} 9.3424 & 8.7286 & 9.6689 \\ 2.6445 & 2.3788 & 6.6493 \\ 1.6030 & 6.4583 & 8.7038 \end{pmatrix}, \ B = \begin{pmatrix} 0.0993 & 4.3017 & 6.8732 \\ 1.3701 & 8.9032 & 3.4611 \\ 8.1876 & 7.3491 & 1.6603 \end{pmatrix},$$

$$C = \begin{pmatrix} 118.5369 & 319.4746 & 118.5305 \\ 59.3063 & 157.1301 & 59.3423 \\ 76.4947 & 225.7040 & 93.9047 \end{pmatrix},$$

consider the verified centrosymmetric solution of Sylvester matrix equations $AX + XB = C$.

It can be verified that the matrix equation $AX + XB = C$ is consistent and has a unique exact centrosymmetric solution

$$X = \begin{pmatrix} 1.5561 & 8.5598 & 4.2245 \\ 1.9112 & 4.9025 & 1.9112 \\ 4.2245 & 8.5598 & 1.5561 \end{pmatrix}.$$

Input: $\overline{X} = \begin{pmatrix} 0 & 0 & 0 \\ 0 & 0 & 0 \\ 0 & 0 & 0 \end{pmatrix}$, $N = 200$, $\varepsilon = 10^{-4}$.

Output: $\widetilde{X} = \begin{pmatrix} [1.556098, 8.559799, 4.224499] \\ [1.911203, 4.902499, 1.911203] \\ [4.224499, 8.559799, 1.556098] \end{pmatrix}$,

$$X^\varepsilon = 10^{-5} * \begin{pmatrix} 0.699597 & 0.591165 & 0.586469 \\ 0.227413 & 0.114102 & 0.195666 \\ 0.364034 & 0.275506 & 0.307197 \end{pmatrix},$$

$$[\widetilde{X} - X^\varepsilon, \widetilde{X} + X^\varepsilon] = \begin{pmatrix} [1.556091, 1.556105] & [8.559793, 8.559805] & [4.224494, 4.224506] \\ [1.911200, 1.911205] & [4.902498, 4.902500] & [1.911201, 1.911205] \\ [4.224496, 4.224503] & [8.559796, 8.559802] & [1.556095, 1.556101] \end{pmatrix}.$$

Acknowledgments. This work is supported by Jilin Province Department of Education Science and Technology Research Project under Grants 2014213, 2015131 and 2015156.

References

1. Essex, C., Davison, M., Schulzky, C.: Numerical monsters. ACM SIGSAM Bull. **34**(4), 16–32 (2000)
2. Datta, B.: Numerical Methods for Linear Control Systems. Elsevier Academic Press, Amsterdam (2004)
3. Antoulas, A.: Approximation of Large-Scale Dynamical Systems. Advances in Design and Control. SIAM, Philadelphia (2005)
4. Sorensen, D.C., Antoulas, A.C.: The Sylvester equation and approximate balanced reduction. Linear Algebra Appl. **351**, 671–700 (2002)
5. Frommer, A., Hashemi, B.: Verified error bounds for solutions of Sylvester matrix equations. Linear Algebra Appl. **436**(2), 405–420 (2012)
6. Miyajima, S.: Fast enclosure for solutions of Sylvester equations. Linear Algebra Appl. **439**(4), 856–878 (2013)
7. Seif, N.P., Hussein, S.A., Deif, A.S.: The interval Sylvester equation. Comput. **52**(3), 233–244 (1994)
8. Shashikhin, V.N.: Robust stabilization of linear interval systems. J. Appl. Math. Mech. **66**(3), 393–400 (2002)
9. Horn, R.A., Johnson, C.R.: Topics in Matrix Analysis. Cambridge University Press, Cambridge (1994)
10. Meyer, C.D.: Matrix analysis and applied linear algebra. SIAM, Philadelphia (2000)
11. Yamamoto, T.: Error bounds for approximate solutions of systems of equations. Jpn. J. Appl. Math. **1**(1), 157–171 (1984)
12. Sang, H., Li, Z., Cui, Y., Li, Q.: A verified algorithm for the centrosymmetric solution of Sylvester matrix equations. In: Gong, M., Pan, L., Song, T., Tang, K., Zhang, X. (eds.) BIC-TA 2015. CCIS, vol. 562, pp. 342–349. Springer, Heidelberg (2015). doi:10.1007/978-3-662-49014-3_31

Research on Distributed Anomaly Traffic Detection Technology Based on Hadoop Platform

Qiang Chen[✉]

Department of Computer Science, Guangdong University of Science and Technology,
Dongguan 523083, Guangdong, China
cqjxnc@qq.com

Abstract. Cloud security is one of the issues that cloud platform needs to focus on. Cloud platform has powerful computing ability and storage resources, which makes it become the target of hackers. Therefore, in addition to the traditional network security configuration, it is necessary to adopt a more complete security defense measure to protect the data processing platform. In this paper, it proposes a distributed anomaly traffic detection technology based on classifier combination according to the characteristics of massive network data processing in Hadoop platform, which can improve the security of massive network data processing platform.

Keywords: Cloud computing · Hadoop platform · Distributed · Detection technology · Naive bayes classifier

1 Introduction

With the benefits of cloud computing technology, cloud security issues should not be ignored. The current cloud computing industry becomes maturer and security issues have become increasingly significant. It has become one of the most important issues hindering the development of the cloud computing industry [1]. Powerful computing resources and massive storage capacity is the advantage of cloud computing, which develops great appeal to the hackers and makes the platform easily become the target. In recent years, many infrastructures of cloud technology have suffered different attacks. For example, the database of Anthem, the second major Health Insurance Company in the United States, was hacked in February 2015, which affects nearly 8000 users personal information. Therefore, how to strengthen the security of cloud computing and information, effectively monitor and response to network intrusion and other security threats.

IDS (Intrusion Detection System) uses active defense technology to defend various kinds of network intrusion [2]. However, due to the complex network architecture of cloud computing cluster, massive high-speed network traffic and other features, the traditional intrusion detection system is often inadequate to deal with security protection work under the cloud computing environment [3].

© Springer Nature Singapore Pte Ltd. 2016
M. Gong et al. (Eds.): BIC-TA 2016, Part II, CCIS 682, pp. 530–535, 2016.
DOI: 10.1007/978-981-10-3614-9_66

Therefore, it is necessary to carry out the research work facing cloud computing, virtualization intrusion detection technology, and strengthen the information security capabilities under cloud computing environment.

In view of the above-mentioned problems, we proposed a distributed anomaly traffic detection technology based on classifier combination.

2 Related Work

2.1 Network Attack Technology on Cloud Computing

Cloud computing uses a network based service model and according to user needs to provide users with all kinds of hardware and software resources and data information [4]. Massive network data processing platform based on Hadoop also has the network interface for platform management and data stream receiving and storage, which is similar to most of the existing cloud services. They both need to provide services to users on the Internet. Also in recent years, the attack against the network cloud computing cluster have been increased rapidly [5]. Attacks against cloud computing can be divided into the following categories.

(1) Illegal Access
(2) Attacks of Processing
(3) Attacks of Abusing of Authority
(4) Attacks Based on Host or Network
(5) Attacks on Cloud Platform's Loophole

2.2 Anomaly Traffic Detection Technology on Cloud Computing Platform

Aiming at the safety problem of cloud computing, researchers have been carried out a lot of research work. A lot of cloud security technology have been effectively applied to a variety of cloud computing application scenarios, including cloud network firewall, the design and deployment of intrusion detection system.

(1) Intrusion detection technology. The intrusion detection technology is originally designed to mainly aimed at the physical network defense, and generally only aimed at the detection of a single network or object.
(2) Cooperative IDS. Cooperative IDS is a kind of intrusion detection technology based on behavior signature.
(3) Flexible intrusion detection and management system in Cloud Computing. This system with a good augmentability can extend and adjust the detection system as the cloud computing cluster environment changes, and also realize the efficient management and good compatibility.
(4) DDoS attack and defense technology in Cloud Computing. It is a kind of technology that transforms the traditional intrusion detection system and proposes a multi-level intrusion prevention and log management technology.

(5) IDS based on virtual machine. Aiming at the characteristic of virtualization, the system could achieve the overall defense of the cloud computing environment, by classifying the cloud computing environment and deploying the corresponding virtual intrusion detection system as various level.

The above research results show that there is an urgent need for the network intrusion detection method which has the advantages of both feature based detection system and abnormal behavior based detection system in the cloud platform at present. Therefore, we should design a more efficient and quick-responding network security detection system of cloud security. In this paper, a distributed anomaly traffic detection technology based on classifier is implemented.

3 Maths Fuzzy Theory—Fuzzy Assessment Method

3.1 Classificatier Algorithm

Classifier combination based distributed anomaly detection technology is based on Hadoop MapReduce operation mechanism, and as a module of massive network data processing platform, realizes the detection to the network traffic in cloud platform and the judgement of abnormal traffic. The basic idea of the classification algorithm is to construct a training model based on historical data, to match the new measurement data with the model, and to determine whether the new measurement data is abnormal data by a series of multi-level discriminant algorithm.

3.2 Naive Bayes Classifier

Bayes classifier is a statistical classifier based on Bayes theorem which can be used to predict the probability that a certain data sample belongs to a certain class. Naive Bayes Classifier has the computational speed and accuracy better than other classification algorithms.

Naive Bayes classification algorithm is a classification algorithm based on probability operation, it can be found to make the posteriori probability $P(C_i|X)$ maximum of the class, but also become the maximum Posteriori hypothesis.

According to Bayes theorem formula (1), in which $P(X)$ for each class is constant, so in the calculation process, we need to let $P(X|C_i)$ $P(C_i)$ to get the maximum. In the training phase, we can calculate the $P(C_i|X)$ to maximize the classification of traffic data. In which a prior probability $P(C_i)$ can be obtained through the training of the sample traffic data, and based on the formula (2) to get a posteriori probability $P(C_i|X)$. The individual attribute values of conditional probabilities are uncorrelated, as shown in the formula (3). When there are m data in our traffic data, the posteriori probability calculation is as formula (4).

$$P(C_i|X) > P(C_k|X), \quad 1 \le k \le n, k \ne i \tag{1}$$

$$P(C_i|X) = \frac{P(X|C_i)P(C_i)}{P(X)} \tag{2}$$

$$P(X|C_i = c) = \prod_{i=1}^{n} P(X_i|C_i = c) \tag{3}$$

$$P(C|X) = \frac{(\prod_{i=1}^{m} P(X_i|C))P(C)}{P(X)} \tag{4}$$

Naive Bayes Classifier algorithm has the advantage of fast, efficient and low memory requirements. Therefore, we can effectively control the correlation between flow characteristic index through the method based on subsequent flow statistical feature extraction and improve the classification accuracy of Naive Bayes Classifier.

3.3 Combined Classifier Decision Algorithm

The basic idea of the algorithm: first, get the statistical characteristics of flow index, then according to the algorithm, generate the feature index subset. After that, determine the index of a subset with the judging preparation. If the determined results meet the criteria in this set, stop creating index feature subset. At last, verify the selected feature index subset, and complete a selection process of the characteristic index.

During the selection of the statistical characteristics of the flow. The index is a valuable indicator if an index can reflect the attributes of the classifier. However, in the actual feature selection, the characteristic index of data often exists many redundant, even valueless index. Therefore, when selecting the value characteristic indices, we need to choose the index that has a larger correlation with the data classification, and to ensure that there is no correlation between the selected feature index, namely not predictive of one another between the index. In this paper, we use CFS algorithm to select the feature subset.

CFS is a kind of commonly used selection algorithm that uses filter mechanism and based on feature correlation. CFS based on idea that is to weed out the characteristic indices that barely associated with a class, and those are redundant to ensure each selected feature index can effectively reflect a property of a class and the property only relates to one of the selected feature indices. Feature index selection is shown as formula (5). CFS algorithm is used to calculate the value of the feature subset S, n is the number of indicators included in the subset, C indicates the average value of the correlation between the selected indicators and the class. F indicates the average value of the correlation between the selected indicators.

$$M_s = \frac{nC}{\sqrt{n + n(n-1)F}} \quad C = \bar{r}_{cf}, F = \bar{r}_{ff} \tag{5}$$

From the formula, we can see that the values of n and C were positively correlated with MS, and MS and F is negative correlation, namely the more the selected index number, the higher correlation between indices and the classes, the lower relevance among selected indicators, and the greater the calculation result value.

For the correlation of characteristic index, we can use symmetrical Uncertainty method to calculate. Assuming that X and Y are the characteristic indices, then the entropy of Y is as shown in the formula (6), and the entropy of Y in the condition of X is shown in the formula (7). From the formula, we can see that index X and Y correlated with the amount of information that X provided Y, particularly meaning the information gain from X to Y, which is defined as shown in the formula (8). From this formula it can be seen the influence between index X and Y is equal, namely the information gain X on Y and the information gain Y to X is the same.

$$H(Y) = -\sum_{y \in Y} p(y) \log_2(p(y)) \tag{6}$$

$$H(Y|X) = -\sum_{x \in X} p(x) \sum_{y \in Y} p(y/x) \log_2(p(y/x)) \tag{7}$$

$$gain = H(Y) - H(Y/X) = H(X) - H(X/Y) = H(Y) + H(X) - H(X,Y) \tag{8}$$

Combined the CFS algorithm with the correlation to calculate, we can extract appropriate feature index set from the statistical characteristics of flow index, to ensure that there is strong correlation between the selected feature index and the class attribute, and there is no correlation between each index, namely the selected feature index sets are not redundant, and can properly reflect the categorical attributes.

4   Experimental Results and Analysis

In this paper, we compared and analyzed the results of the combined classifiers and the classification results of the individual classifiers to verify the detection effect on the distributed anomaly traffic detection of that combined classifiers.

In the experiment, the flow test data is tested by repeatedly 10-fold cross-validation method. The collected traffic data is divided into 100 parts. Each experiment uses 90 copies as a training sample, the remaining as a test sample, and circulates ten times to get the mean value. We conducted training test on the sample data flow using three classification algorithms. On the basis that we should ensure lower false positive rate and false negative rate, we hope to be able to obtain the highest possible accuracy of detection. The contrast among the experiment results are shown in Fig. 1.

According to the experiment results from data A4, we can see that as the amount of data grows, the accuracy of the distributed anomaly traffic detection algorithm based on classifier combination is slightly decreased. In the experiment, the accuracy of the fuzzy K-means algorithm is higher than that of the Bayes algorithm, but the false positive rate is also higher than the Bayes algorithm's.

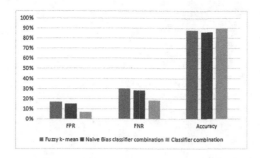

Fig. 1. Comparison of the effects of data A4 in three algorithms.

5 Conclusion

Therefore, the anomaly traffic detection algorithm based on the classifier combination that this paper brings up, can overcome the defects of the single detection algorithm. In the future, we will continue to research the security of cloud platform. The security of cloud platform involves system, server, network, user and other aspects. Thus, when it comes to protect the cloud platform, in addition to deploying the traditional security defense equipment, it needs an overall consideration and in terms of different cloud platform application scenarios, to build perfect network security protection system.

References

1. Hubbard, D., Sutton, M.: Top threats to cloud computing V1.0. Cloud Security Alliance (2010)
2. Dede, E., Govindaraju, M., Gunter, D., Canon, R.S., Ramakrishnan, L.: Performance evaluation of a MongoDB and hadoop platform for scientific data analysis. In: Science Cloud 2013 Proceedings of the 4th ACM Workshop on Scientific Cloud Computing, pp. 13–20 (2013)
3. Scheidell, M.: Intrusion Detection System. Google Patents (2009)
4. Yu, D., Frincke, D.: A novel framework for alert correlation and understanding. In: Jakobsson, M., Yung, M., Zhou, J. (eds.) ACNS 2004. LNCS, vol. 3089, pp. 452–466. Springer, Heidelberg (2004). doi:10.1007/978-3-540-24852-1_33
5. Hao, C., Ying, Q.: Research of cloud computing based on the hadoop platform. In: 2011 International Conference on Computational and Information Sciences (ICCIS) (2013)
6. Armbrust, M., Fox, A., Griffith, R., et al.: A view of cloud computing. Commun. ACM **53**(2), 50–58 (2010)
7. Wang, Y., Wang, S.: Research and implementation on spatial data storage and operation based on Hadoop platform. In: International Conference on Geoscience and Remote Sensing (IITA-GRS), Second IITA (2010)
8. Zissis, D., Lekkas, D.: Addressing cloud computing security issues. Future Gener. Comput. Sys. **28**(1), 583–592 (2012)
9. Agarwal, D., Gonzdlez, J.M., Jin, G., et al.: An Infrastructure for Passive Network Monitoring of Application Data Streams (2003)
10. Owen, S., Anil, R., Dunning, T., et al.: Mahout in Action. Manning, Shelter Island (2011)

Author Index